Mastering IBM i

Jim Buck
Jerry Fottral

MC Press Online, LLC

MC Press Online, LLC
Boise, ID 83703 USA

Mastering IBM i
Jim Buck and Jerry Fottral

First Edition

© 2011 by Jim Buck and Jerry Fottral. All rights reserved.

MC Press Online, LLC, offers excellent discounts on this book when ordered in quantity for bulk purchases or special sales, which may include custom covers and content particular to your business, training goals, marketing focus, and branding interest.

MC Press Online, LLC
Corporate Offices: 3695 W. Quail Heights Court, Boise, ID 83703-3861 USA
Sales and Customer Service: (208) 629-7275 ext. 500; service@mcpressonline.com
Permissions and Bulk/Special Orders: mcbooks@mcpressonline.com
www.mcpressonline.com • www.mc-store.com

ISBN: 978-1-58347-356-6   EB201410

To my Mom, for teaching me persistence

and

To my wife Kathea, whose love and support is irreplaceable

Acknowledgments

Thanks to Jerry Fottral for writing the original text upon which this book is based. His book, *Mastering the AS/400*, provided a great starting point for this expanded volume.

Thanks also to two students at Gateway Technical College, Adam Korbas and Kay Imig, who worked tirelessly through the chapter text and, more important, the end-of-chapter labs, catching most of my mistakes.

Thanks to Saad Yousuf, IBM i programming instructor at Gateway Technical College, who was kind enough to use many of the chapters in his classes as the book was developed. His input was invaluable.

IBM employees Rob Bestgen, Gene Cobb, Jason Hansen, and Don Yantzi answered questions and in some cases giving me a heads up regarding changes in IBM's software. A big thank you to all of you.

And thanks to Sharon Hamm for her editing efforts and to Katie Tipton for believing in this project and working to publish our textbooks.

— *Jim Buck*

Contents

Introduction

The IBM i operating system running on IBM Power Systems is a platform in transition. Many think the system is obsolete, largely due to its infamous green screen. Nothing, though, could be further from the truth. When IBM embraced open-source software such as Linux, MySQL, and Zend PHP, the system cemented a formidable position in today's business environment.

This text starts with the traditional concepts and tools (you need to understand these concepts before improving on them) and then describes IBM's new tools and additional concepts, such as SQL. Those of you familiar with the previous version of this book, *Mastering the AS/400*, will notice that the chapters on DFU and SDA have been removed. The use of Query for i5/OS has been reduced, and emphasis has been placed on the new DB2 Web Query product.

The goal of this book is twofold. First, it aims to introduce new IBM i programmers to system concepts and expose those who have used the platform for years to new concepts such as SQL. Second, the book provides a handbook for many of IBM's new tools, including Rational Developer for Power, IBM i Access for Windows, IBM i Access for Web, and DB2 Web Query for i—providing comprehensive information that will be useful regardless of the programmer's level of IBM i expertise.

Having worked on the platform since 1990, and in teaching new IBM i programmers for more than eight years, I have struggled to find a text that encompassed the general concepts of the system, covered new concepts such as SQL, and presented new graphical tools in a format that the reader can work through. When Bryan Meyers and I updated our CL and RPG textbooks, we decided to provide a complete package for today's IBM i student or programmer. Jerry Fottral's *Mastering the AS/400* provided the perfect foundation for a handbook of IBM i concepts and tools.

With the completion of this text, instructors now have the tools to introduce students to the system and continue the course work through CL and RPG programming classes. Veteran programmers have the resources they need to gain the expertise required to update their current skills.

The student, or programmer, should start at the beginning of the text to gain an understanding of the traditional concepts of the IBM i operating system. When using the book in a classroom, some instructors may choose to present just the newer topics and tools. However, students should be made aware of the traditional tools and concepts as well, for they will find many systems still running software that uses physical and logical files created with DDS or queries developed with Query for i5/OS. If students understand the traditional concepts and tools, they are in a better position to help companies convert their systems to the new technologies. Readers familiar with the traditional concepts may pick and choose the chapters/topics presented in the text.

When I started this project, I had no idea of the time and effort it would take to complete. The goal was to develop a text that would present the essential concepts needed by today's programmer and take a snapshot of the current IBM tools at the time of its printing. Often, I found myself updating the IBM i server with newer software before starting (or during) work on a chapter. A new version of Rational Developer for Power was released shortly after Chapters 11 and 12 were complete, causing me to go back and review those chapters. DB2 Web Query for i had a beta version available that included the new InfoAssist tool. Luckily, Gene Cobb at IBM gave me a heads up, and I scrapped the completed chapter and revised it to include this significant update. Thanks, Gene!

Due to the scope of the topics covered, I have included references to specific books that provide additional information, letting readers quickly find the resources to delve deeper into those topics. I encourage those using this book to investigate these additional resources.

I hope you enjoy the result of my efforts. . . . For the most part, I enjoyed writing it! ☺

Jim Buck
Kenosha, Wisconsin
March 2011

Communicating with the System

Overview

The IBM i operating system (OS) is one of the most sophisticated on the market today. To a new user, the apparent complexity may seem like a huge jigsaw puzzle waiting to be solved. What we hope to provide with this first chapter is simply a place to start collecting critical pieces of the puzzle.

This chapter provides initial exposure to several topics necessary for a basic understanding of how to communicate with the IBM i OS using the different types of screens and menus. The chapter also introduces concepts related to system organization and a few basic **work management** ideas (e.g., how jobs enter, run in, and leave the system).

As in any other technical field, you will need to master a number of terms and concepts to be successful using the OS. Although the IBM i OS will provide comprehensive help as you learn, you are strongly encouraged to ask questions of your instructor or mentor.

Objectives

Students will be able to

- Sign on to the IBM i OS system, properly entering a user profile and password
- Explain the difference between system and subsystem
- Describe the two most common types of jobs
- List several attributes of a user profile
- List several features of the IBM i OS
- Explain the function of IBM i Control Language (CL) and enter a CL command on a command line using proper syntax

Continued

- Explain the purpose of system values and how to check them
- Describe four types of displays, their use, and their components
- Explain the relationship between CL commands and IBM i OS menu paths

The System

The **IBM i OS** is a complex and rich set of programs that not only controls traditional functions such as data access, storage, and task management but also incorporates features that normally would require separate software components on other systems—features such as communications support, database management, security, and interactive support.

A new system running IBM i OS comes with a standard basic configuration, which includes predefined system settings for work management functions that allow interactive and batch jobs to run without need for a customized installation. Later, subsystems can be created and system resources allocated to optimize workload distribution and throughput according to the special needs of a particular business.

IBM i is a **multiuser**, **multitasking** OS (a system on which two or more people can perform two or more tasks concurrently) optimized for the efficient execution of business applications. The basic unit of work is a **job**. The term *job* refers generally to a unit of work that includes all programs, files, and instructions necessary to perform that work. Examples of a job would be an interactive user session for updating a customer master file, or a program compilation running unobtrusively in the background.

The older IBM AS/400 systems used terminals and hardwired (twinaxial, or "twinax") connections to access the system. Today, most users connect to the system using 5250 emulators or Web interfaces. In this book, we present a number of ways to connect to the system, including 5250 emulators, Remote System Explorer (RSE)/Rational Developer for Power (RDP)-based, and IBM i Access for Web and Access for Windows. The IBM i OS has evolved to become one of the most advanced OSs available today.

IBM i Objects

The IBM i OS is an object-based OS. An **object** is anything on the system that has a name and takes up space in storage. IBM supplies a large number of objects through the IBM i OS and licensed program products. These objects typically have names beginning with *Q*. Programmers and operators create other objects and name them according to their organizations' naming conventions.

The system can locate an object by its name; once located, the object can further identify itself to the system by functional attributes that are a part of the object. Objects are grouped into types. An **object type** determines how the object is used on the system (i.e., the actions that one can take when using the object). Common object types include programs, files, and commands. Object types also include user-profile objects, which contain information about users, and subsystem-description objects, which contain the characteristics of subsystems. Object type is always assigned by the system and is determined by the command used to create the object. We continue to explore this concept of objects throughout this book.

Subsystems

All jobs in the IBM i OS are run in **subsystems**. A subsystem is a predefined operating environment the system uses to coordinate workflow and system resources. The system uses a **subsystem description** to define the required resources to process work. The components of a subsystem description determine how the system uses resources to process jobs within the subsystem. When the base IBM i OS is installed, several different subsystems are already defined and active, and each one has a separate subsystem description.

Attributes of subsystems are defined in the subsystem description; these include the subsystem name (e.g., **QCTL** for the controlling subsystem, **QINTER** for the interactive subsystem, **QBATCH** for the batch subsystem), how many jobs can run in the subsystem at one time, which storage pools the subsystem will use (IBM i main storage is divided into a number of different storage pools), and which job queues the subsystem will use.

Different subsystems are necessary because there are many different types of jobs with different characteristics and often-conflicting needs. If we treated all of these various jobs equally, the overall performance of the system would suffer. As system administrators, we can change the existing subsystem descriptions and create new subsystems when necessary. In this way, we can tailor subsystems to efficiently handle the needs of different jobs—for example, to ensure that long-running jobs that require no user interaction but significant CPU time do not interfere with high-priority interactive jobs that need fast response time. Within subsystems, we can prioritize individual jobs to begin execution sooner or later; and, after they begin execution, we can give them a higher or lower runtime priority.

Types of Jobs

IBM i OS jobs can originate from several sources and are classified by how they originate on the system. In this course, and in general, you will deal mostly with two types of jobs: *interactive* and *batch*.

An **interactive job** begins when a user signs on to the system, and it terminates when the user signs off the system or the job is ended. Interactive jobs run in conversational mode, which means there is a dialogue of sorts between the user and the program, utility, or OS function. Because of this conversational, back-and-forth nature of interactive jobs, any CPU- or I/O-intensive request a user makes could lock up the workstation keyboard until the request is completed. Therefore, it is often advisable to direct such requests to a subsystem designed to handle them—that is, to submit them as batch jobs.

Batch jobs can execute without user intervention; they do not require data or controlling values to be input through the workstation once they have started. Batch jobs are sent to a job queue until they can begin execution. A **job queue** is a staging area, managed by the subsystem in which the job will run, where batch jobs wait in line for their turn at processing. Each batch subsystem can execute only a limited number of batch jobs concurrently. If no other higher-priority jobs are waiting, a batch job can start right away; otherwise, it must wait its turn.

Typically, you would submit as a batch job a report program that reads many records from a database file and performs standard calculations written into the logic of the program. Once the program is submitted, it requires no input from the operator or requester of the report. If the program were run interactively, the direct-access storage device (**DASD**, or **hard disk**), access time required for the large file would be substantial and could cause the program to run for an extended period, tying up the workstation until program execution was completed.

In addition, to minimize disruption of workflow, programmers can pack up and send off as batch jobs certain tasks they encounter during a normal interactive session. Consider a programmer in the midst of an interactive session who needs to compile a large program for testing. If she runs the compile as part of an interactive job, she will be locked out of the system during the several minutes it may take to complete the compilation. If other tasks on the computer need attention, she could submit the compilation as a batch job from within the interactive job. Then, while the compilation runs in a batch subsystem, she could go on to other tasks.

Control Language (CL)

For all its complexity, one of the more remarkable things about the IBM i OS is that it provides a single, consistent user interface to its various functions through Control Language (**CL**) commands.

IBM i OS CL is flexible and powerful and allows direct access to IBM i OS functions. More than 2,000 individual CL commands are available. Each individual command is an OS object. Most CL commands consist of a command name and one or more **command parameters**. A command parameter is a value, specified along with a command, that controls and limits the operation of the command and names the files, programs, or other objects the command will work on. Individual commands can be entered on a **command line** (a line beginning with the symbol ===> that appears near the bottom of certain types of display screens), or they can be grouped together into a **CL program** to perform a specific task. Such a program can then be compiled and run from a command line or from within a high-level language (**HLL**) program (e.g., RPG, COBOL, C, or C++).

If you are a new user, you don't need to memorize a large number of CL commands because most IBM i OS functions are available to interactive jobs through the **menu interface** of IBM i. As you choose a series of menu selections, the system determines the CL commands to be run to satisfy your request.

System Values

System values are control and configuration attributes that let you customize certain OS functions. System values define critical aspects of the environment and the general rules that all jobs on the system must follow. System values are not objects, but they describe characteristics of the system that can be displayed, or in many cases changed, with CL commands. Many system values come preset with the OS; others need to be set when the system is installed. The categories of system values include the following:

- *Allocation values* (Type=*ALC)—These values let you control the number of active jobs and how much main storage will be used for different functions necessary to run jobs.
- *Date and time values* (Type=*DATTIM)—These values let you set and change the date and time the system keeps and makes available to application programs and utilities.
- *Editing values* (Type=*EDT)—These values control how dates, decimal values, and numbers involving currency symbols are formatted.
- *Library-list values* (Type=*LIBL)—These values define the system library list and initial user library list. A **library list** is an ordered group of libraries a job uses to search for objects it needs for processing. A **library** is a directory of related objects.
- *Message and logging values* (Type=*MSG)—These values control how the system handles and records certain types of messages.

- *Security values* (Type=*SEC)—These values control certain aspects of security, such as the maximum number of invalid sign-on attempts allowed.
- *Storage system values* (Type=*STG)—These values define the minimum size and activity level (number of active jobs) of the base storage pool.
- *System control values* (Type=*SYSCTL)—These values let you define or obtain certain controlling values of the OS, such as operator console name, user assistance level, and date and time to automatically **IPL** the system. (An IPL, or initial program load, is the IBM i version of a "boot" process, which loads the OS when the power is turned on.)

Most users can display current system values, and, when necessary, authorized users can change these values. This capability to customize system values for a particular job environment can lead to a more efficiently running system. In the lab for this chapter, you learn how to examine system values.

Licensed Programs

Besides the IBM i OS, several software components available from IBM extend the functions and capabilities of the system and let installations tailor the system to the type of work and the communications environment they need. These software components are **licensed program products**. A few licensed program products are shipped with all IBM i systems at no additional cost. But for the most part, licensed program products are chargeable; the actual cost usually is determined by the size of the system and the number of users who have access to the product. Most of the licensed program products fall into one of several categories:

- *Application development tools*—This group of programmer utilities greatly expedites the application development process. Recently, IBM has brought its software tools under the Rational brand. Rational Developer for Power (**RDP**) is a set of GUI-based tools designed to replace traditional 5250 tools such as Source Entry Utility (**SEU**), Screen Design Aid (**SDA**), an interactive file-update utility called Data File Utility (**DFU**), and a programmer's workbench suite called Programming Development Manager (**PDM**). The Rational Business Developer product includes support for Web development. These two toolsets can be used together to give the developer a rich set of tools. In Chapter 11, we will cover Rational Developer tools for IBM i.
- *Communications support*—This category consists of the many System i Access for Windows (formerly known as Client Access or PC Support) programs that let IBM i connect programmable workstations (PCs) through various PC OSs, including

Microsoft Windows. In Chapter 10, we cover System i Access for Windows in depth and in Chapter 13, IBM i Access for Web.

- *Programming languages*—Traditionally, IBM i systems have supported a number of programming languages by making compilers available as licensed programs. In the past, Basic, FORTRAN, Pascal, and PL/I were supported, but current and future compiler support will be targeted at ILE RPG (RPG IV), C, C++, COBOL, and Java. In addition, Structured Query Language (SQL) is available through the DB2 Query Manager and SQL Development Kit.
- *Web products*—These include IBM i Access for Web, IBM HTTP Server for IBM i OS, and WebSphere Application Server products; and as of V6R1, IBM is shipping Zend PHP and MySQL with the IBM i OS.

Some other licensed program products that do not fall clearly into any of the above categories provide services such as automatic routing, IBM Backup Recovery and Media Services for IBM i OS (BRMS), Performance Tools, and double-byte character support for ideographic languages such as Chinese, Japanese, and Korean. In fact, there are many more such products designed to extend the versatility and usefulness of the IBM i OS.

You can see which licensed programs are installed on your system by going through the Work with Licensed Programs (GO LICPGM) menu.

User Profile

When we refer to a **user**, we mean any person who is signed on to the system. This may include students, programmers, data-entry personnel, operators, and administrators. To perform work, a user needs to be defined on the system. A user is defined to the system when a security officer or administrator creates a user profile object for that user. A **user profile** not only identifies a user but also describes the user's authority and is the source of several operational characteristics of that user's job.

Later, we examine user profiles in more detail and see that they contain defining information; for example, a user's profile contains the following:

- *User class*, such as casual user, programmer, operator, or security officer.
- *Special authorities*, such as job control, the capability to save system software, or the capability to create or change user profiles.
- *Initial program*, or the program to be run when sign-on is completed.
- *Initial menu*, the first menu the user sees after sign-on.

- *Current library*, the first user library searched for objects the user has requested.
- *Job description*, which contains a specific set of job-related attributes, such as the job queue to use, scheduling priority, routing data, message queue severity, library list, and output information. The attributes determine how a job will run on the system.
- *Group profile*, which assigns a user to a group of users with similar authorities and restrictions.
- *Status*, which indicates whether the user profile is enabled or disabled.
- *Output queue*, or the queue where the user's printer output is stored.

At this time, you need be aware only of the two user-profile values necessary to sign on: *user name* (profile or user ID) and *password*.

Sign-On

Figure 1.1 shows a normal IBM i **sign-on screen**.

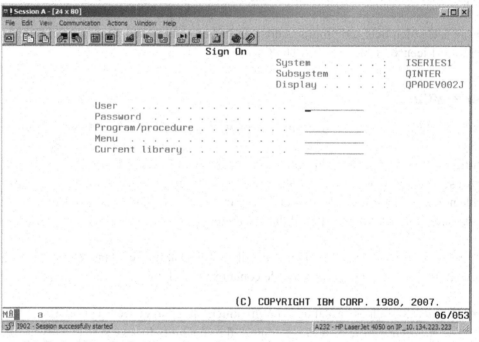

Figure 1.1: Typical Sign-On Screen

The upper-right corner of the sign-on screen displays information that identifies the system, the subsystem the workstation is assigned to, and the display device (or display station). A **display device** is the workstation hardware (monitor and keyboard) that you use to communicate with the system.

Note

As will be the case with many of the figures in this text, certain values in Figure 1.1, such as the System value and the Display device name, will differ for your IBM i system. Although more than half a million IBM i systems are now installed worldwide, it is a safe bet that no two are exactly the same; so screens that deal with configuration values or individual users can certainly vary widely from place to place.

To sign on and start an interactive job, a user must type his user profile and password (these values are not case sensitive). A user profile is up to 10 characters long; the security administrator determines its value according to the standards of the installation. The user profile may be a simple first initial and last name combination, such as JSMITH. Or it may be a more symbolic code, perhaps indicating the user's location or department; for example, JMS05KEN could mean a user with the initials JMS of department 05 in Kenosha.

For a sign-on attempt to succeed, the user profile entered must match the name of the user-profile object created by the system security officer or administrator. If a nonexistent user-profile name is input, the system displays an appropriate error message. An error also occurs if the user profile is valid but the password entered at the sign-on screen does not match the current password stored in the corresponding user profile. In either case, the sign-on attempt fails.

When a user enters proper values on the sign-on screen for User and Password, the system proceeds to collect attributes to define the interactive job. Most attributes are taken from a special or default **job description**, but some attributes come from the user profile or from system values.

When sign-on is completed, the interactive job is directed to the subsystem you see on the display (e.g., QINTER in Figure 1.1). Jobs from all physical display devices may run in the same subsystem, or different display devices may direct their jobs to different subsystems. A system administrator knowledgeable in work management and performance tuning makes these decisions.

User Interface

Unless system defaults are changed, most IBM i interactive jobs begin by displaying the IBM i Main menu, which you see in Figure 1.2.

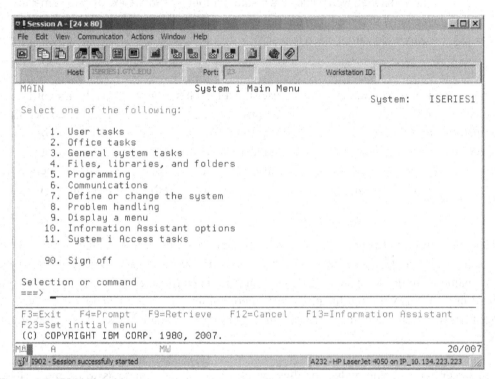

Figure 1.2: IBM i Main Menu

In a hierarchy of menus, the Main menu is the highest-level task-oriented menu, and it can be the starting point to define a menu path to accomplish a specific request. Menus are connected in such a way that a menu choice at a higher level can take you to a lower-level menu. You move through the menu hierarchy until the task is defined to the system. For example, if you wanted to create a library, you would follow the menu path you see in Figure 1.3, starting with the Main menu. We step through this process in the next section.

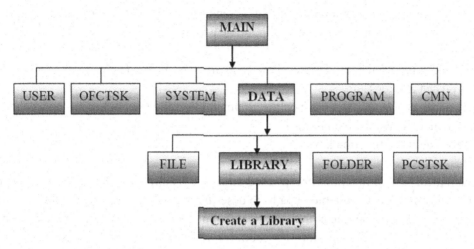

Figure 1.3: IBM i Menu Path for Creating a Library

Menu Screens

We begin our discussion of IBM i display screens by examining the menu screen format. A **menu screen** has four primary sections, which you can observe if you look again at Figure 1.2:

- The **screen header**, including
  - The menu ID, in the upper-left corner
  - The menu description, centered on the first line
  - The system name, in the upper-right corner
- The numbered list of **menu options**
- The Selection or command line, indicated by ===> (here, you can type the number of a menu selection or enter a CL command to be executed)
- The list of active **function keys**

Below the two-line list of active function keys is a message line (in the figure, this is the line showing the IBM copyright notice) and a status line that shows cursor coordinates, whether a message is waiting to be displayed, and the status of the keyboard.

All menu screens have this general appearance. The header information and list of menu options, of course, change, depending on the menu. The menu ID in the upper-left corner is the menu object name, the formal name by which the menu is known to the OS. The list of enabled function keys also changes slightly from menu to menu.

Now that you're familiar with the format of a menu screen, let's look again at the Main menu in Figure 1.2. You can take several possible actions from a menu display:

- You can type and enter a menu choice and go on to the next screen.
- You can ask for Help.
- You can type a CL command on the command line and then either prompt for parameters or run the command.
- You can use a function key.

Although most system functions are invoked directly by using CL commands, it is generally easier for novice users to take menu paths to describe the task to perform and then let the system choose the appropriate command. For example, let us use the menu path to create a library—a task you will be performing soon. If you entered a 4 (for Files, libraries, and folders) on the command line of the Main menu and pressed Enter, you would see the DATA menu in Figure 1.4. (Although the description of this menu is Files, Libraries, and Folders, to the OS its proper object name is DATA. You could go directly to this menu by typing GO DATA on the command line.)

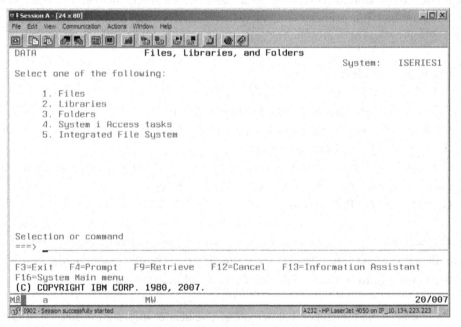

Figure 1.4: Files, Libraries, and Folders (DATA) Menu

Notice the similarity in format between the Main menu and the DATA menu. From the DATA menu, you can select choice 2 (Libraries) by typing a 2 on the command line and then pressing Enter. Doing so takes you to the LIBRARY menu you see in Figure 1.5.

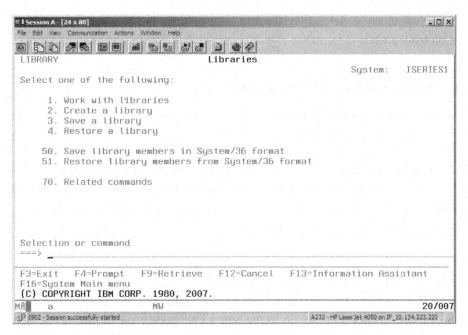

Figure 1.5: Libraries (LIBRARY) Menu

The description of option 2 on the LIBRARY menu, Create a library, suggests that, after three menus, you have just about pinned down what it is you want to do. When you select option 2 from the LIBRARY menu, the system displays the screen in Figure 1.6. The system

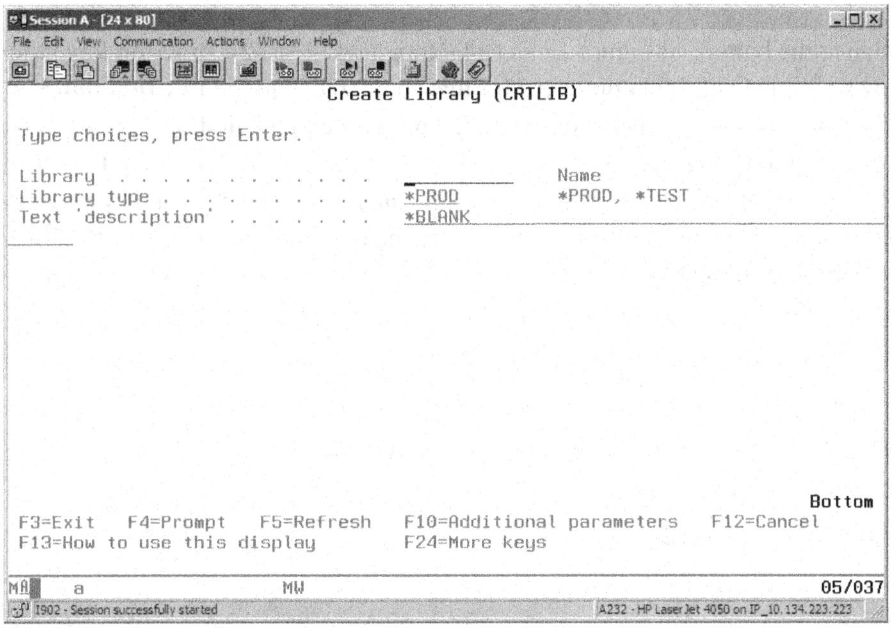

Figure 1.6: Create Library (CRTLIB) Command Prompt Screen

uses this type of screen, generically referred to as a **prompt entry screen**, to request information from a user.

Prompt Entry/Command Prompt Screens

Let us take a moment to study the screen in Figure 1.6. You can see clearly that it differs from a menu screen. First, notice that the heading is different. Rather than the name of a menu, the heading, "Create Library (CRTLIB)," is the description of the CL command in English followed by its IBM i CL command in parentheses. Also in contrast to a menu screen, this screen does not identify the system; and instead of a numbered list of menu choices, you see a list of command parameters. The screen does display a list of active function keys, but no Selection or command line.

This type of screen is considered a prompt entry screen because the system is waiting for you to enter the value or values it needs to process your request. In this case, you enter parameter values for the **CRTLIB** (Create Library) CL command, which the system must execute to create a library. The cursor, as the figure indicates, is positioned at the first character of the entry field for the Library parameter. Because the system is prompting you for a parameter value that it needs to run a command, we refer to such a screen as a **command prompt screen**. A command prompt screen is one kind of entry screen. We reached this particular CRTLIB command prompt screen via a menu path; but if you already know the command name, you could reach the same screen by typing CRTLIB on any command line and pressing the Prompt key, F4.

One option at the bottom of Figure 1.6 is F24=More keys. The **F24 function key** [Shift+F12] will show additional valid function keys for this command, and the **F11 function key** toggles between the display that shows choices and the screen that displays parameter keywords. If you press F24 and then F11, you see that the screen changes to the screen in Figure 1.7. Note that you can request to see all parameters for a command by pressing the **F9 function key**; do so and the screen changes to the one in Figure 1.8, which shows all parameters for the command.

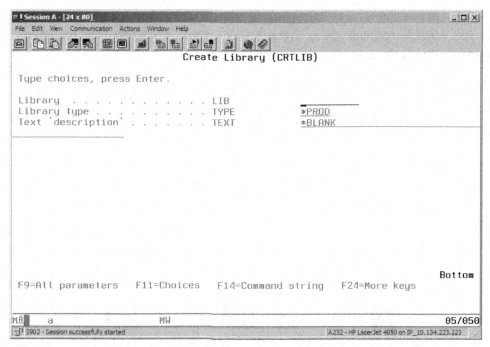

Figure 1.7: Create Library (CRTLIB) Command Prompt Screen, Continued

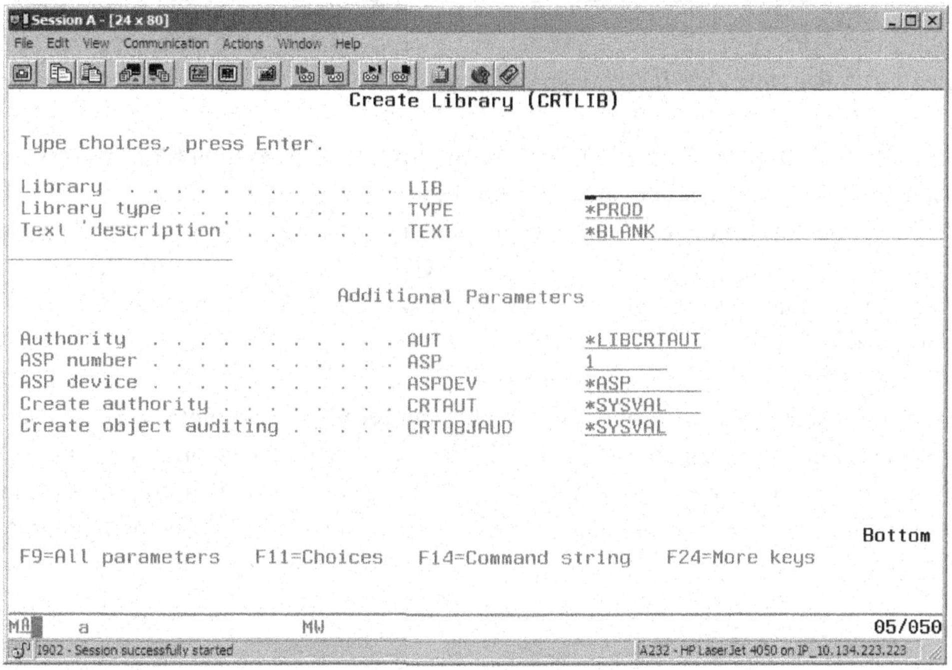

Figure 1.8: Create Library (CRTLIB) Command Prompt Screen with Additional Parameters

If you press F11 to toggle back to the possible-choices screen, you can see the elements that make up a command prompt screen. Figure 1.9 shows the CRTLIB command prompt screen divided into three columns.

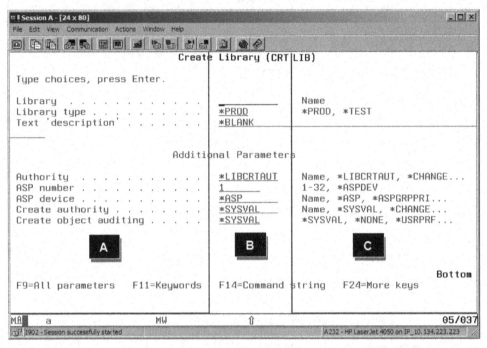

Figure 1.9: Create Library (CRTLIB) Command Prompt Screen Divided into Three Columns

Notice that for each parameter the prompt screen provides a description (A); an entry field showing the parameter's current value, if any (B); and, for most parameters, a list of valid values (C). If the full list of valid values cannot be displayed, an ellipsis (...) indicates additional choices. You can view the entire list of valid values by positioning the cursor anywhere on the line that contains the parameter in question and then pressing **F4**, the Prompt function key.

To run a command, you must provide a value for any **required parameters** (i.e., those whose values must be specified for the IBM i OS to execute the command). Required parameters always appear as empty input fields at the top of the command-prompt parameter list. In the case of the CRTLIB command, the Library parameter is a required parameter. An attempt to run the command without a value for the Library parameter would result in an error. For other parameters in this example, you can use the **default values** provided, or you can type over any default value you need to change. In later chapters we cover command prompting in more detail; for now, it is important only that you can identify a command prompt screen, that you know how to access such a screen, and that you know the reason for using it.

Note

The F9 (All parameters) and **F10** (Additional parameters) **function keys** may seem very similar. You can see the difference between the two function keys by keying in **DSPFD** (Display File Description) on the command line and then pressing F4. If you press F10, one additional parameter is displayed. If you press F9, you will see all the parameters for the DSPFD command. Ask your instructor for a file name and library to see the output of this command. We recommend that you use the F9 function key.

Using Help

The third type of screen is an **information screen**. Information screens do not give you menu choices to select from or prompt fields to fill in. They simply provide information that you request and give you a way back to where you were when you asked for the information.

A common type of information screen is the Help screen. You can get Help information from almost any kind of display. Suppose you were creating a library and were not sure what the parameter Library type meant. You could place the cursor anywhere on the line for that parameter (the cursor does not have to be on the input field), and then press the **F1** (Help) **function key.**

Field or Context-Sensitive Help

When you request information about a particular area on a screen, such as the Library type parameter, you are requesting what is referred to as **field Help** or **context-sensitive Help**. To continue with our example, if you placed the cursor on the Library type field of the CRTLIB command prompt screen and pressed the F1 **Help key**, a window would appear on the screen (Figure 1.10) that contains information about that parameter.

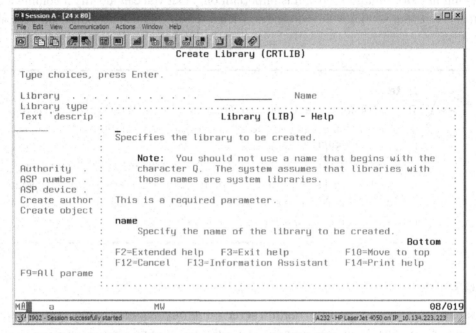

Figure 1.10: Field Help Text for Library Type Parameter of CRTLIB Command

Notice that the window appears just below (or sometimes just above) the field for which you requested Help, and that it has its own list of active function keys. You can enlarge the window, so that it fills up the entire screen, by pressing the **F20 function key**. To cancel the Help request and return to the previous screen, press the **F12 function key**.

Extended Help

If you were looking at a field Help window and wanted more information about the screen in general, you would press the **F2 function key** for **extended Help**. In our continuing example, pressing F2 from the Library type Help would give you general information about the CRTLIB command. This extended Help would then list and describe all the command's parameters, as well as their possible values. For a screen other than a command prompt screen, extended Help describes the parts of the screen and any entry fields or options available on the screen.

If you press function key F2 (for extended Help) from the field Help screen in Figure 1.10, the system displays the screen you see in Figure 1.11.

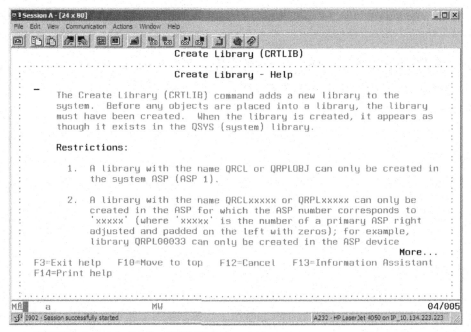

Figure 1.11: Extended Help for the CRTLIB Command

Notice that extended Help begins by explaining what the command (CRTLIB in this case) does. Then it lists and explains any restrictions to the use of the command. Next, it lists the error messages for the command, and, finally, More... in the lower-right corner of the screen tells you that more screens of information are available. To see these additional screens, you would press the Page down (Shift+Roll up) key.

You can get extended Help by pressing F2 from a field Help screen, as we did just now, or you can get it directly by pressing the Help key when the cursor is not in a context-sensitive area of a screen. On a command prompt screen, if the cursor is anywhere on the several lines above the first parameter line—including the screen header —or on a blank line below, pressing F1 should take you directly to extended Help.

The IBM i OS has thousands of Help screens, and you should not hesitate to use them when you have a question about how you can use a certain screen or about the possibilities for responding to a prompt. We rely heavily on Help screens in the lab for this chapter and in subsequent labs.

Information Assistant

Another function key option you will find on Help screens is **F13=Information Assistant.** Pressing F13 takes you to a menu named INFO whose description is Information Assistant Options. (Because this is a menu, you can also access it from any command line by using the CL GO command—i.e., GO INFO.) The menu has two options, as you can see in Figure 1.12.

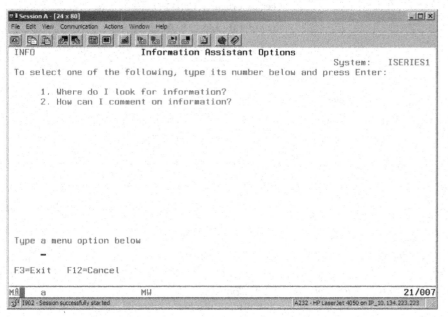

Figure 1.12: Information Assistant Options—F13 from the IBM i Help Screen

Choices 1 and 2 provide a little insight about finding information and providing feedback about the quality of information to IBM. Option 1 displays the screen in Figure 1.13.

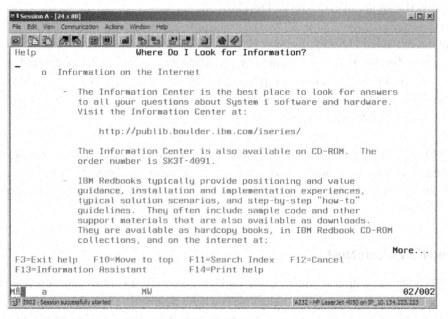

Figure 1.13: Where Do I Look for Information? Screen

In the past few years, IBM has created a Web site called the IBM Information Center. This Web site (*http://publib.boulder.ibm.com/iseries*) covers every area of information concerning the OS. Notice that in the lower right-hand corner of the screen is More. . . . Pressing the PgDn (Page down) key on your PC will display the screen in Figure 1.14.

Figure 1.14: Where Do I Look for Information? Screen, Continued

On some Help screens, you see certain words or phrases highlighted with yellow and underlined. Using these **hypertext links**, you may access additional information about these words or phrases by pressing Tab to move the cursor next to the highlighted word or phrase and then pressing Enter.

As you can see from Figure 1.15, the IBM Information Center includes the capability to search for specific topics or keywords. It also allows you to place bookmarks as you search these topic areas and/or keywords. This Web site gives IBM users a centralized location to find the latest information.

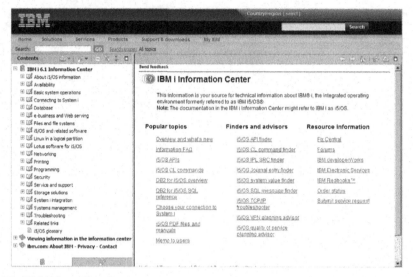

Figure 1.15: IBM Information Center

List or Work-With Screens

The fourth type of screen that we will discuss is the **list screen**. To demonstrate a list screen, press F12 until you return to the LIBRARY menu represented in Figure 1.16.

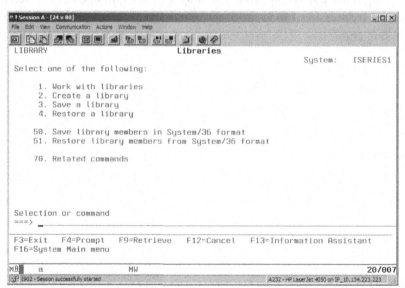

Figure 1.16: Libraries Screen

Select option 1, Work with libraries, and press Enter. Doing this will display the screen in Figure 1.17.

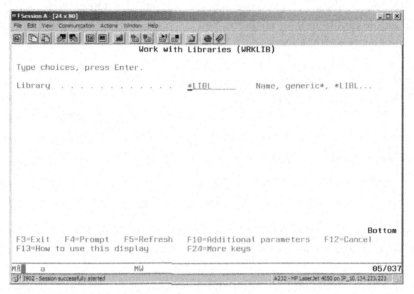

Figure 1.17: Work with Libraries (WRKLIB) Screen

This screen allows you to key in a parameter to control what libraries will be displayed. The default is *LIBL, which means that the libraries in your library list will be displayed. Notice that the screen name includes both the Work with Libraries menu name and the related CL command (WRKLIB). After you press Enter, the system will display Figure 1.18.

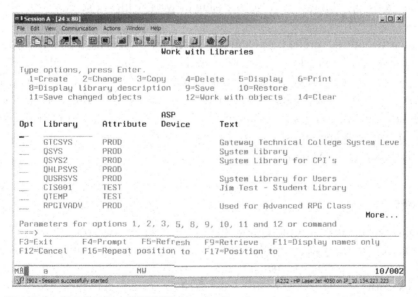

Figure 1.18: Work with Libraries (WRKLIB) Screen, Continued

The type of screen you see in Figure 1.18 is called a list screen, a list-processing screen, or, often, a "work-with" list screen because it so commonly results from running a "work with" CL command. We use these list screens extensively in our labs and explain more about their power and flexibility in later chapters. You also could have typed this command in the command line to access this screen.

Note that the first line of text under the screen heading in Figure 1.18 says Type options, press Enter. Some of the options provided are

- 1=Create
- 2=Change
- 3=Copy
- 4=Delete

The number of options on a list screen is determined by the command that produced the screen. You should always understand the ramifications of using these options.

We now have briefly discussed four different types of screens that IBM i systems use to communicate with interactive users. They are

- Menu screens.
- Entry screens—Command prompt screens are a common type of entry screen.
- Information screens—Help screens are frequently used types of information screens. Help screens include extended Help and field or context-sensitive Help.
- List screens, also known as list-processing or work-with list screens.

Being familiar with these screen types and knowing how each is used can help you overcome that sense of being lost in a foreign environment that users so often have as they learn about a new system. As you work through the lab exercises, try to identify each screen you encounter—doing so will help you maintain your orientation. Think about how you got to each new screen; and if you do get lost, remember that pressing F12 backs you out one screen at a time. When you successfully complete a task, use F3 to return to a common starting point, such as the Main menu.

In Summary

In this chapter, we examined some important IBM i OS characteristics. We discussed the interactive nature of the system and the idea of how jobs are run in subsystems. We know that an interactive job is started when a user signs on to the system, and that, at normal operational security levels, a user profile must exist for a sign-on to be successful.

Once on the system, most of us rely on several different types of screens to accomplish our tasks. As novice users, we do most of our work on the system by traversing a series of menus. As we progress down the menu path, we are clarifying to the system what task we want to accomplish until an appropriate command can be executed. The command may take us to another screen, such as an information screen, or it may run a program; or, if the command has no required parameters, it may invoke a system function.

We also examined the IBM i's Help facility. We determined that for most system displays, Help is available both at the extended and at the field or "context" level.

As you work through subsequent lab exercises, you should always try to maintain your orientation—what kind of display you are at, what the purpose of that display is, and how you got there. Use Help freely when you have questions about a display or are uncertain about the meaning of an input field or the use of a function key.

One of the outstanding features of the OS is its comprehensive Help system. If you need Help, remember F1, and then F2.

Key Terms

batch jobs
CL
CL program
command line
command parameters
command prompt screen
context-sensitive Help
CRTLIB
DASD (or hard disk)
default values
DFU
display device
DSPFD
extended Help
field Help
F1 function key
F2 function key
F4 function key
F9 function key
F10 function key
F11 function key

F12 function key
F13 function key
F20 function key
F24 function key
function keys
Help key
HLL
hypertext links
IBM i OS
Information Assistant
information screen
IPL
interactive job
job
job description
job queue
keyboard mapping
library
library list
licensed program products
list screen

menu interface	SDA
menu options	sign-on screen
menu screen	SEU
multitasking	subsystem description
multiuser	subsystems
object	system values
object type	QCTL
PDM	QINTER
prompt entry screen	QBATCH
RDP	user
required parameters	user profile
screen header	work management

Review Questions

1. What are the two types of jobs discussed in this chapter?
2. Explain the function of the two job types from question 1.
3. List and define the different categories of licensed programs.
4. Explain the term "object" in the IBM i OS.
5. What is the purpose of Control Language (CL)?
6. List and describe the categories of system values.
7. Using the online IBM Information Center, list and define three licensed programs not discussed in this chapter.
8. What is the maximum character length of a user profile?
9. Are the user profile and password case sensitive?
10. What is a user profile?
11. List and define the categories of a user profile discussed in the text.
12. List and define the four primary sections of a menu screen.
13. What does pressing F20 accomplish in a Help screen?
14. How do you prompt a command?
15. When prompting a command, how would you display all the parameters for the command?

Lab 1

Introduction

This lab is intended to provide experience with the main topics we covered in the Chapter 1 text: system values, licensed program products, and basic CL command use. We examine these topics through the use of the four types of screen displays: menus, information screens, entry screens, and lists. Rather than building objects or generating output, the goal of this lab is for you to become accustomed to recognizing and using the four types of screens by having you use them to explore some important system components.

Part 1

Goals   Recognize the IBM i OS sign-on screen.

Sign on successfully.

Start at   IBM i sign-on screen.

Procedure Enter a valid user ID and password.

1.1.   You should see the IBM i sign-on screen, similar to Figure 1.1 (page 8). There are many different possibilities for connecting workstations to a server running the IBM i OS; your instructor/mentor should provide you with specific instructions. If you need additional help, ask your instructor/mentor for assistance.

1.2.   The sign-on screen is a special type of entry screen. You are expected to key in and enter certain information to identify yourself to the system, but function keys and Help information are not available.

Look at the identification information in the upper-right corner of the screen.

1.2.a.   What values are shown for the System, Subsystem, and Display attributes of your workstation?

The Display name is the name by which your workstation is known to the system. It will also be the name of your interactive job.

Note

Before you sign on, let us warn you about **keyboard mapping**. Keyboard mapping is another area in which differences exist from one installation to another (or even among different types of keyboards or connections within installations). In general, the Tab key on a PC keyboard equates to the 5250 (older, nonprogrammable workstation) keyboard's Field advance key. The 5250 Field exit key, which erases everything in the current field from the cursor location and then jumps to the next input field, may be mapped on PC keyboards to either the Enter key or the right Ctrl (Control) key, depending on which 5250 emulation product was used (or whether remapping was done). Other products, such as the popular MochaSoft TN5250 (which sells versions for Windows and Mac), map the Field exit key to the large "+" key on the numeric keypad.

There are too many mapping variations to try to list all of them here; but if you're working through a Windows client, you should see a toolbar with a keyboard button at the top of your screen (or you can try clicking Windows Help for "Keyboard Mapping" information). Clicking the keyboard button lets you find out how various system functions are mapped on your keyboard.

Begin the sign-on procedure by typing the user profile that you were assigned by your instructor. For example FLastname, CIS001D, or JMS05KEN.

Your user profile will appear in capital letters, even if your keyboard is not shifted to upper case. (Don't worry about case.) Remember, a space character is not a valid character within a name. A user profile has a maximum length of 10 characters. If you have problems, ask your instructor/mentor for help.

Don't press Enter yet. If your user ID is 10 characters long, the cursor will already be in the Password input field; otherwise, use the Tab, New line, or Field exit key to move there:

Tab (or New line or Field exit)

Next, type the password that your instructor gave you. The password is not case sensitive, and for security purposes the characters are not displayed on the screen; so type carefully.

If you think you made a mistake and you haven't pressed Enter yet, backspace and type over what you've entered. If you typed too many characters the first time, press Field exit (after you've typed your password) to erase the rest of the input field above and to the right of the cursor.

Once you've keyed in your password, press Enter. (Remember that the Enter function may be mapped to the right Ctrl key on your PC keyboard.)

Enter

If an error code and the message *"Password not correct for user profile"* appear near the bottom of the screen, try rekeying your password and then pressing Field exit and Enter. If the message persists, ask your instructor/mentor for assistance.

If you see a different message —*"CPF1120 - User (user profile) does not exist"*— your user profile cannot be found, and you need to have your instructor/mentor check it out before you can go any further.

Part 2

Goals Recognize the menu screen.

Follow the menu path to licensed programs.

Find out which licensed programs are installed on your system.

Start at Main menu (GO MAIN).

Procedure Enter choice 7 from MAIN.

Enter choice 2 from DEFINE.

Enter choice 10 from LICPGM.

1.3. Once you have successfully signed on, you should be looking at the Main menu, similar to Figure 1.2 (page 10). Notice the cursor located on the Selection or command line. You may either select a menu choice by typing its number here or enter a command on this line.

Let's follow a menu path to examine the installed IBM licensed programs on your system. The submenu descriptions aren't always very clear, and sometimes you may guess wrong; but licensed programs are part of the definition of the system, so choice 7, Define or change the system, might be a good guess. Type 7 on the command line, and then press Enter.

7

Enter

1.3.a. What is the "proper" name (as it is known to the system) of the Define or Change the System menu?

1.4. From here, option 2 is the obvious candidate for our purpose. Type 2 on the command line and press Enter.

2

Enter

1.4.a. Which of the four screen types discussed in the text are you looking at now? (Be careful: Despite its name, it has neither an options list nor input fields to select options.)

1.5.   Let's take choice 10 to display installed licensed programs. Type 10, and press Enter.

10

Enter

The screen you are looking at now should be similar to the one in Figure 1.19, but the actual list of programs will differ depending on what software is installed on your system.

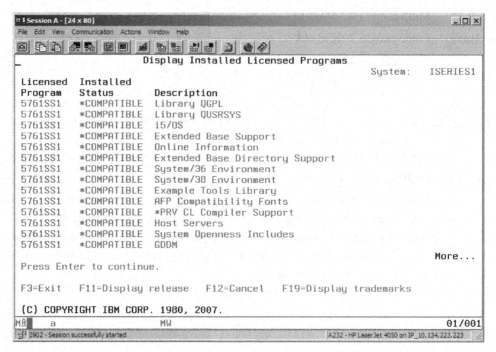

Figure 1.19: Display Installed Licensed Programs Screen

Like many system displays, this screen has more than one format. F11 lets you change the display from one format to another.

1.5.a.   Press F11 to cycle through the screens. How many formats does this display have?

Display the screen that shows *Installed Release*.

All program components have a Licensed Program number, a Description, and an Installed Release, which gives the Version, Release, and Modification for each component. Because IBM upgrades the OS and most of the licensed programs approximately yearly, the Installed Release values tell you which "edition" of the software you have.

1.5.b. Of the four types of screens we discussed in the text, which type is this?

1.5.c. Which "edition" of operating-system software is your system using?

1.5.d. What is the licensed program number of the Application Development ToolSet? We use the Application Development ToolSet and Query extensively in later labs.

1.5.e. What is the licensed program number of IBM Query for i5/OS?

1.5.f. What is the licensed program number of IBM Toolbox for Java?

1.5.g. List the languages installed on your system.

The programming languages most commonly used include RPG, COBOL, C, C++, and Java. SQL, the relational database language, is another powerful tool available for accessing and manipulating database files.

Part 3

Goals Use Help to get more information about displays.

Start at Command line: GO LICPGM.

Enter choice 10 from LICPGM.

Procedure Press the Help key/F1 from the Display Installed Licensed Programs screen and then press F2 to display the extended Help screen.

1.6. Place the cursor on the column heading Licensed Program. If your display does not show the Installed Release column, press F11 to change formats until that column appears. Notice again the layout of the screen—a title, a system identifier, three columns of information, and Enter/function key information toward the bottom. Extended Help explains the purpose of the screen as well as the type of information provided. Press the Help key (F1) now to get more information about this display.

F1

You should now be looking at the Help screen for Display Installed Licensed Programs, Figure 1.20.

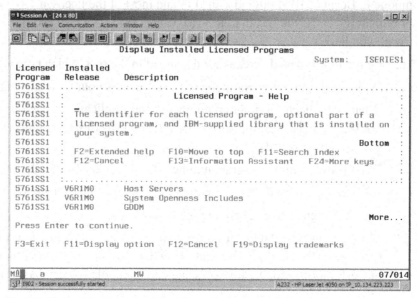

Figure 1.20: Display Installed Licensed Programs Help Screen

Take a few minutes to look over the Help screen; then Press F2 to display the extended Help screen you see in Figure 1.21.

F2

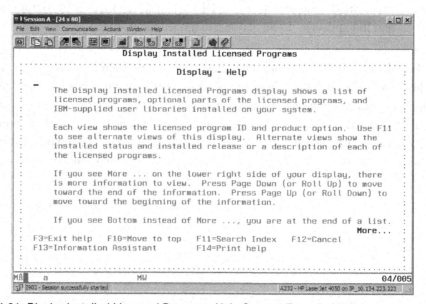

Figure 1.21: Display Installed Licensed Programs Help Screen–Extended Help

Extended Help explains the display in general and then gives information about specific parts of the display—in this case, the columns of information. Whenever More . . . appears at the bottom-right corner of the screen, you can use the Page down key or press Shift+Roll up to see the next screen of information.

Page Down now and read the explanation of Installed Release.

Page Down (PgDn on a PC keyboard)

1.6.a.   How can you tell when a licensed program has not been installed successfully?

Now press F12 twice to exit extended Help. Then press F11 to change to the screen format showing *Product Option*.

F12

F12

F11

Context-sensitive Help provides information about the field or column upon which the cursor is positioned. Move the cursor to the column header itself or anywhere below it within the Product Option column of data; then press F1 for Help.

F1

A window should appear describing the meaning of *Product Option*. Instead of More . . . , the word Bottom should be displayed in the lower-right corner of the screen, indicating that no additional information about this topic exists. Context-sensitive Help gives you information only about the cursor-selected field, but you can learn about other areas of the screen by asking for extended Help (F2) from a context-sensitive Help screen.

1.6.b.   According to the Product Option Help display, what do all licensed programs have in common?

Part 4

Goals	Use the Position field to change the displayed part of a list.
	Locate and display information about specified system values.
Start at	Main menu—use F3 to back up, or GO MAIN.
Procedure	Enter choice 7 from MAIN.
	Enter choice 8 from DEFINE.

Use Page up/down and the Position to field to locate specified system values.

If you have just finished Part 3, press F3 from the Licensed Programs list until you have returned to the Main menu. You should always try to use F3 to back out to a starting screen when you have finished the current task.

1.7. We have mentioned system values as being control and configuration values critical to system operation. Let us use the menu path to examine some system values.

We will start with the same second-level menu because system values would seem to have something to do with the Main menu's Define or change the system selection. Type 7, and then press Enter.

7

Enter

1.8. From the DEFINE menu, select choice 8, Work with system values.

8

Enter

You should now be looking at the screen in Figure 1.22.

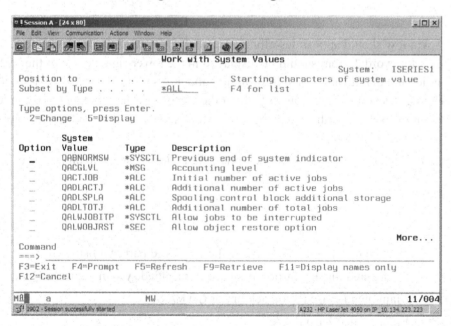

Figure 1.22: Work with System Values Screen

Note
If you receive the message *"Not authorized to command WRKSYSVAL in library *LIBL,"* this means that your user profile does not have authority to use this command. Ask your instructor to give you temporary access to the command WRKUSRPRF.

This is a list screen, also called a list-processing screen or a work-with list screen. The list consists of a number of similar items on which the user can perform processing options. In this case, the items are all system values, and the only option provided with a user's or programmer's authority is Display. The system security officer or another user with sufficient authority would also have a Change option. Notice that all system values begin with *Q*.

1.9. With the cursor on the first Option field, Press Help (F1).

F1

Because Option is a designated area of the screen, you get field (or context-sensitive) Help, which tells you only how to use that field. Now press F2 to display extended Help.

F2

Read the general description of the Work with System Values display.

1.9.a. Where can you find a listing of the shipped (as they come from IBM) system values?

Read the Help information about using the Position to field.

1.9.b. What predefined value positions you to the bottom of the list?

For most list screens, it is possible to show just a subset of the list (i.e., a part of the entire list) by specifying some subset selection criterion. In the case of the Work with System Values list, the criterion would be the type of system value.

1.9.c. How many different system-value types does the Help text show? Note that *ALL is not a system-value type but a keyword or special value that means "include all values."

1.10. Press F3 to return to the Work with System Values list.

F3

1.10.a. What is the current value of Subset by Type?

1.10.b. Can you find, among the list items, all the different types mentioned in the Help text in this list? (You may need to page down.)

1.10.c. Which system value would you display to find out the level of user assistance set for your system?

Move the cursor to the Option field next to that system value name. Type 5 to display the value, and press Enter.

5

Enter

1.10.d. To what level is your system user assistance set?

Notice that this time choosing an option (5) from a list screen has brought you to an information screen. Other options from other list screens may take you to an entry screen, a command prompt, or another list screen. Still other options may run a command, leaving you at the same screen.

Also notice that there are three ways to leave this screen: Enter, F3, and F12. Each alternative takes you to the same place—back to the list screen. Press one of these keys now to return to the work screen.

Enter (or F3 or F12)

1.11. You know from the previous Help information that on list screens with a Position to field, typing *TOP or *BOT positions the list to the very first or the very last item in the list.

Back-tab (Shift+Tab) the cursor to the beginning of the Position to field. Type *BOT, and then press Enter.

Shift+Tab

*BOT

Enter

1.11.a. What is the last system-value name in the list?

1.12. Move the cursor back to the beginning of the Position to field.

To find out how many times you can make a mistake while trying to sign on, locate the Maximum sign-on attempts value. Perhaps you are fairly sure that the system-value name starts with the characters QMAX. If you key the beginning characters of a list item that you're searching for, the system displays that part of the list starting with the first item that matches the characters you entered. Now try it! Type QM on the Position to field, and then press Enter.

QM
Enter

Move the cursor to the option for Maximum sign-on attempts allowed, choose the Display option, and then press Enter.

(Display option)
Enter

1.12.a. How many sign-on attempts are allowed on your system?

Now return to the list screen. The cursor should still be on the Option field for QMAXSIGN.

Next, we will see what happens if you type in the Position to field a value that is less than the lowest (first) value in the list. (Relative values are determined by the computer's collating sequence; as in a telephone directory, any name beginning with *A* through *P* would be less than a name beginning with *Q*.)

Move the cursor to the Position to field (use back-tab), and type a single letter lower than *Q*. Then press Enter.

(a letter character less than *Q*)

Enter

1.12.b. Where in the list has the cursor been repositioned?

1.12.c. What predefined value could you have used to accomplish the same thing?

1.13. Using the information displayed for the appropriate system value, answer the following questions:

1.13.a. Is your system set to AUTOmatically configure newly installed local (not virtual) devices?

Use Help for the system value you discovered in step 1.13a to answer the next two questions.

1.13.b. Auto configuration names each device according to a naming convention. (Hint: Read the Help information for QAUTOCFG.) What other system value controls which naming convention will be used?

1.13.c. Does a change to the system value found in step 1.13.a take effect when the system is re-IPLed or right away?

1.13.d. Display the system value you discovered in step 1.13.b that controls the naming convention. Which naming convention does your system use?

1.13.e. According to the naming convention, what kind of device would the device name PRT01 be used for? (Hint: Use Help.)

1.13.f. From the system-value list, find the device name your system identifies as the system console.

1.13.g. How many system values are there having to do with passwords? (Hint: IBM i OS spells password PWD.)

You examine other system values in later labs, but now you need to look at another frequently used type of entry screen to complete your tour of common user displays.

First, return to the IBM i Main menu by pressing F3 two or three times.

F3

F3

(F3)

Part 5

Goals   Become familiar with the command prompt screen.

Recognize required parameters of the command prompt.

Use Help to get information about specific parameters.

Start at   Any command line (press F3 to back out to a command line if necessary).

Procedure Enter CPYF on the command line.

Request Help from the CPYF command prompt screen.

1.14. In the text of Chapter 1, we briefly discussed CL and examined the syntax of CL commands. We said that most commands have parameters, but the system does not expect us to remember all the parameters and their order for each command. Of course, when you type a command, you may include the required parameters if you know them. If you do not know how to enter them, or if you do not know which ones you need, you can use the command prompting facility simply by pressing F4 after you type the command. Then the system displays a command-prompt entry screen for you. If you type only a command name and press Enter, the OS displays a prompt screen if the command requires parameter values (most commands do).

We will now demonstrate how command prompting works.

Type CPYF, for the CL Copy File command, on the command line, and then press Enter.

CPYF

Enter

You should now see an entry or command prompt display with a message appearing at the bottom of the screen.

1.14.a. What does the message say?

Notice the plus sign (+) at the right side of the message line. If an action causes more than one message, or if a message will not fit on the single line provided, the + appears to let you know that more of the message exists. To get to the additional message text, move the cursor down to the message line and press Page down.

1.14.b. What does the next message say?

The input fields for missing required parameter values are highlighted in reverse-image blocks on the screen. This happens whenever you run a command (by pressing Enter) without providing necessary parameter values. Normally, if you realize that parameter values are required, you would use the prompt function (F4) instead of pressing Enter.

1.15. The command prompt screen shows you information that the system needs to execute the command. For many parameters, the system provides default values. Those values are already entered on the line when the command is initially prompted. The default value for the From member parameter, for example, is *FIRST, which means the first member (subset of records) in the file. Default parameter values are most often predefined "special values" that begin with an asterisk (*).

Notice the indentation of Library under From file and To file. All objects are logically part of a library; the Library value qualifies the file object name, telling the system which library to search for the file object. So Library is not a separate parameter but is part of the From file or To file object name. The default library value is *LIBL, another special value that tells the system to search the list of libraries currently assigned to this job. We explore the important concept of a library list in more detail in Chapter 2.

Also notice that the only valid choice listed for From file is Name (in other words, no special values are allowed for this parameter). This means that you must identify the From file, specifying the user-defined name given to the object when it was created. This is a reasonable request—after all, even an intelligent OS such as IBM i can't read your mind to find out which file you want to copy!

1.15.a. What is the default for Print format?

Even if a command has several screens of parameters, as the CPYF command does, the parameters that require a value are shown on the first screen. The entry fields of these required parameters will be blank, with the underlines in high intensity (on color displays, the underlines will be white or a contrasting color). If you tried to run a command without supplying the required values, the entry fields of the required parameters would be displayed in reverse image, along with an error message. For other parameters, you can simply type over any defaults that need to be changed.

1.16. You can use the online Help facility when you need to know what a certain display is for, what a particular command does, or what value a certain parameter requires. On many displays, you can obtain specific information about a given entry from context-sensitive Help by moving the cursor to that area or line and then pressing Help.

For example, let's see what Help tells you about the From file parameter. Position the cursor anywhere on the From file line of the CPYF command prompt screen. Now press Help (F1) to get information from the system about the meaning of the From file parameter.

F1

1.16.a. The file you name must be one of four types of files—what are they?

General Help that explains the purpose of the screen, the command, entry fields, and perhaps function keys is called extended Help. You can get extended Help in one of two ways.

The first way is to press F2 from a field Help screen like the one you are looking at now.

F2

The second way is to press F1 or Help from a non–field-sensitive area of the screen.

F1

From the extended Help for the CPYF command that you should be looking at now, press F3 to return to the CPYF command prompt screen.

F3

Place the cursor in a part of the screen that is not sensitive to an entry or zone. For example, move the cursor up so it is on a line anywhere above the first input field line. Now press F1 or Help.

F1

You should see the same Copy File Help screen that you saw when you pressed F2 for extended Help previously.

We should review the organization of extended Help. First, there is an explanation of the general topic—in this case, the CPYF command. Now page down and you see restrictions to the use of the command, followed by error messages that could result. Following the error messages, you begin to see field Help—in this case, an explanation of the parameters of the CPYF command and their possible values.

Page Down (several times)

Many screens of Help information are available for the CPYF command because it has a large number of parameters and therefore many fields.

Now press F3 to exit Help and then press F3 again to return to the IBM i Main menu.

F3

F3

1.17. From the Main menu, you can select choice 90 to sign off. Doing so will return you to the IBM i sign-on screen.

Whenever you are finished using the workstation, remember to follow your installation's lab procedures to protect the equipment and leave the workstation ready for the next user.

2

Using CL

Overview

To help you gain confidence when communicating with the IBM i operating system (OS), in this chapter we examine some additional Help and prompting features of the four screen types we discussed in Chapter 1. We also investigate CL commands in more detail and see how the IBM i OS facilitates the preparation of commands for execution. Armed with that knowledge, you will create a user library and then change your user profile so it will recognize your newly created library as the current library. Along the way, you gain knowledge about libraries and library lists and about how they are used in IBM i.

Objectives

Students will be able to

- Correctly enter a CL command from a command line
- Distinguish between keyword and positional notation
- Use command prompt screens to provide parameter values
- Use the GO command to display menus of related commands
- Identify the four parts of the library list
- Create a user library
- Change their user profile so that the library they create is the current library
- Use Help to obtain information about libraries
- Display system values
- Change their password

CL Commands

As we mentioned in Chapter 1, IBM i Control Language (CL) is the primary interface to operating-system functions. You use CL to interact with and get work done on the system. Using IBM i, you have a choice: You can key in CL commands and execute them directly from a command line, or you can follow a menu path to a command prompt screen, a work-with list screen, or an information screen. Unlike some OSs, IBM i does not make you select one mode or the other—the system is not exclusively menu driven or command driven. For example, within an interactive job, you can use a command when it is convenient, or you can use a menu path if you cannot determine the appropriate command. In addition, because most screens have a command line, it is usually not necessary to switch to a different environment to run a CL command.

Control Language Syntax

As you begin working with CL commands, you need to understand the **syntax** of the language. In general, *syntax* refers to the proper arrangement of words to form phrases, clauses, and sentences. A somewhat more rigorous definition of syntax would be the selection and ordering of language elements to form meaningful expressions.

Luckily, the syntax of CL is simple and straightforward. All CL commands consist of a command name, and most CL commands require one or more parameters. You use spaces to separate a command name from its parameters and to separate multiple parameters when a command requires them. A simplified syntax notation for a CL command entered on a command line would look like this:

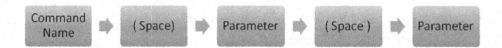

For example, in the command

CRTLIB PAYROLL *TEST

The command name is **CRTLIB** (Create Library), and the specified parameters are PAYROLL and *TEST.

Command Names

Let us examine the structure of command names in more detail. Most command names consist of a verb, or action, part and a noun, or receiver of the action (an object, in the grammatical sense). The CRTLIB command used above—in which CRT stands for *Create* and LIB stands for *Library*—is an example of this command-name form. In addition, some command names use a third segment, which functions as an adjective modifier to the noun. For example, the CL command **CRTBNDRPG** tells the system to Create a Bound RPG program—not a Bound COBOL program (**CRTBNDCBL**) or a Bound CL program (**CRTBNDCL**).

A general rule for CL command naming is most verb, noun, and modifier abbreviations in CL commands are three characters long, and many skip the vowels and use the first consonants of the English word. As you can see, however, the use of LIB to represent *Library* is an obvious exception to this rule.

Table 2.1 lists some commonly used verb abbreviations, the words they represent, and examples of their use.

Table 2.1: Commonly Used CL Verbs			
CL Verb	English	Example	Description
CALL	Call	CALL	Execute program
CLR	Clear	CLROUTQ	Clear output queue
CPY	Copy	CPYF	Copy file
CRT	Create	CRTRPGPGM	Create RPG/400 program
DLT	Delete	DLTUSRPRF	Delete user profile
DSP	Display	DSPMSG	Display messages
EDT	Edit	EDTOBJAUT	Edit object authority
GRT	Grant	GRTUSRAUT	Grant user authority
INZ	Initialize	INZTAP	Initialize tape
OPN	Open	OPNQRYF	Open query file
RCL	Reclaim	RCLSPLSTG	Reclaim spool storage
RCV	Receive	RCVNETF	Receive network file
RLS	Release	RLSSPLF	Release spooled file
RMV	Remove	RMVLIBLE	Remove library list entry
RST	Restore	RSTLICPGM	Restore licensed program
RTV	Retrieve	RTVSYSVAL	Retrieve system value
SAV	Save	SAVCHGOBJ	Save changed object
SBM	Submit	SBMJOB	Submit job
SND	Send	SNDMSG	Send message
STR	Start	STRSEU	Start Source Entry Utility
WRK	Work with	WRKSYSSTS	Work with system status

Most of the verbs listed in the table are consistent in that they consist of three letters, and, unless the English words begin with a vowel (e.g., Edit, Initialize, Open) or do not contain three consonants (e.g., Save), they use only consonants in the abbreviation.

However, two commonly used command verbs are exceptions to this rule:

- CALL—Used to execute a program
- GO—Used to display a menu

Neither of these verbs is used in combination with a noun or modifier abbreviation. We discuss these two CL commands in more detail later. For now, as we look at the command names in the Example column of the table, we can make some observations about the use of the noun and modifier parts of a command name:

a. Not all nouns and modifiers use three letters. For example,
    - D stands for *description*
    - E stands for *entry*
    - F stands for *file* or *field*
    - L stands for *list*
    - Q stands for *queue*

b. Some nouns always need a modifier. For example, you can Copy a File (**CPYF**) but you cannot Work with a Queue; you must Work with a Message Queue (**WRKMSGQ**), an Output Queue (**WRKOUTQ**), or a Job Queue (**WRKJOBQ**). Neither can you Display a Description; you must Display a File Description (**DSPFD**), an Object Description (**DSPOBJD**), a File Field Description (**DSPFFD**), and so on. The List commands (L as a noun) are usually attached to a modifier: Library List (**DSPLIBL**), Authorization List (**DSPAUTL**), Distribution List (**DSPDSTL**), and so on.

c. Some nouns and modifiers are the names of utilities or language compilers:
    - C—C (a programming language)
    - CBL—COBOL (a programming language)
    - CL—Control Language
    - DFU—Data File Utility
    - RPG—Report Program Generator (a programming language)
    - SDA—Screen Design Aid utility
    - SEU—Source Entry Utility

d. The two CL verb forms used most commonly with these noun forms are
    - STR—Used to start (begin execution of) a utility (e.g., STRSEU)

° CRT—Used to create (compile from source code) a program using the named language product (e.g., CRTBNDRPG)

Keyword Notation

An important part of CL command syntax is the use of a **parameter keyword**, a significant word that names a command parameter. CL commands use **keyword notation** to explicitly identify a command's parameters. When you use parameter keywords, the parameter value must immediately follow the keyword, and the value must be enclosed in parentheses, as the following syntax statement illustrates:

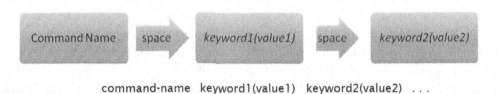

command-name keyword1(value1) keyword2(value2) . . .

Each keyword-value set is a single parameter. One or more spaces must separate the command name from the first parameter and separate each parameter from the next parameter. When you use keyword notation, the order of parameters is not essential. Consider again the CRTLIB command. When you type CRTLIB on a command line and prompt for the command (by pressing F4), the CRTLIB command prompt screen (Figure 2.1) appears.

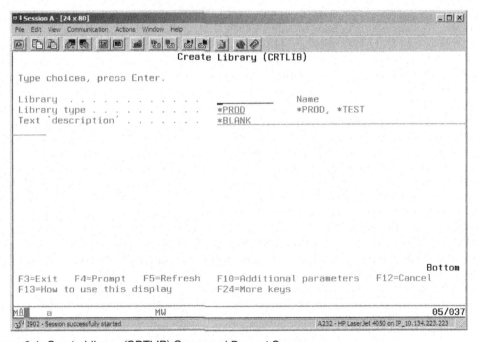

Figure 2.1: Create Library (CRTLIB) Command Prompt Screen

From this screen, you can see that the normal order of parameters is Library, Library type, and Text. Yet if you use keyword notation, either of the following commands, or any of the several other possible permutations, entered on a command line or in a CL program, would work:

CRTLIB LIB(PAYROLL) TYPE(*TEST) TEXT('Payroll Development')

CRTLIB TYPE(*TEST) TEXT('Payroll Development') LIB(PAYROLL)

Both commands work because the system properly interprets a specified parameter value as belonging to the named keyword that immediately precedes the value.

You can determine the parameter keywords for any CL command by observing the command's prompt screen in an alternate, or keyword, format. For example, to get to the CRTLIB command prompt keyword display from the initial command prompt screen you see in Figure 2.1, you might first want to press the F24 function key to view additional function keys. After you press F24, the screen in Figure 2.2 appears.

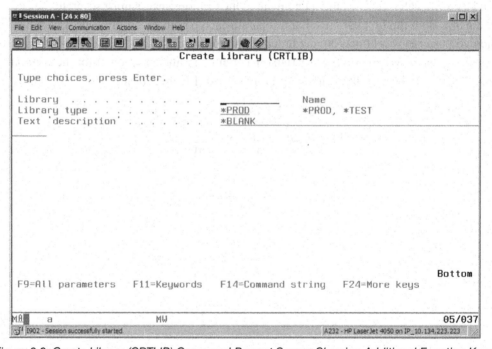

Figure 2.2: Create Library (CRTLIB) Command Prompt Screen Showing Additional Function Keys

The function-key list at the bottom of the screen now includes F11=Keywords. Recall how we used F11 to change the screen format of the Display Installed Licensed Programs display in Chapter 1, Lab 1. In the command prompt context, F11 acts as a toggle between the initial (Choices) command prompt screen (Figures 2.1 and 2.2) and the prompt screen's keyword format you see in Figure 2.3.

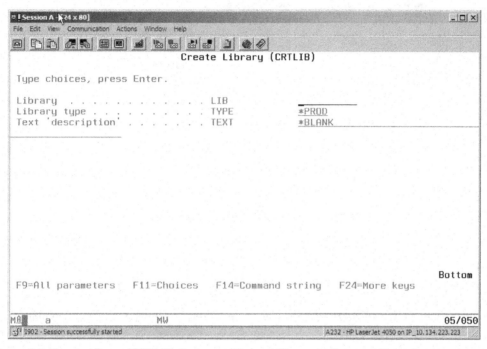

Figure 2.3: Create Library (CRTLIB) Command Prompt Screen in Keyword Format

Tip

All screens have a certain number of active function keys, depending on the type of screen. When many function keys are active and they cannot all be displayed on the two lines allowed, F24=More keys is displayed. But if you know that a function key is active for a certain screen, you can use the key even if it does not appear in the two-line function-key list. For example, F11 works from any command prompt screen; knowing this, you don't have to press F24 first just to see that F11 is active.

By looking at Figure 2.3, you can see that the keywords (LIB, TYPE, and TEXT) we used earlier for the CRTLIB command were correct. If you enter values for the parameters, the command prompt screen looks like the one in Figure 2.4.

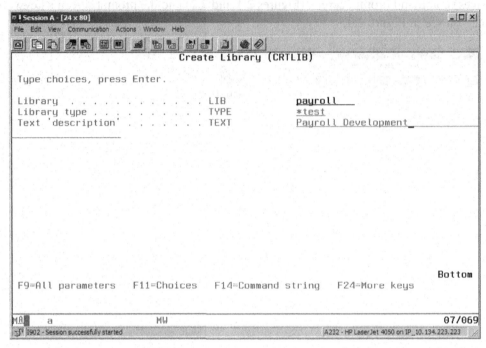

Figure 2.4: Create Library (CRTLIB) Command Prompt Screen with Parameter Values Entered

Notice that even though the value for TEXT is a character-string constant, and as such must be enclosed in apostrophes ('); you do not need to enter the apostrophes here—the command prompter's syntax checker inserts them for you automatically.

After you type in the necessary parameter values, you can press Enter to execute the command. If the values you enter are valid and the command is executed successfully, a message indicating a successful result is displayed, as you see at the bottom of the screen in Figure 2.5.

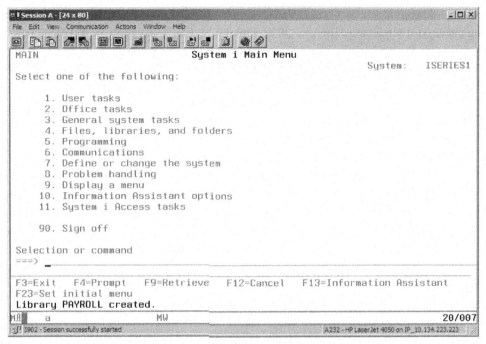

Figure 2.5: Message Indicating the CRTLIB Command Was Executed Successfully

All commands entered or prompted from a command line during an interactive session are maintained in a stack. To recall the most recently executed command, you can press the **F9** (Retrieve command) **function key** on any screen that has a command line. You can recall an earlier command (one lower in the stack) by repeatedly pressing F9.

If you press F9 from the screen you see in Figure 2.5, the previous command (CRTLIB), including as many of its parameters as will fit on the command line, is displayed in keyword notation (depending on the system value). Even if not all the parameters fit, the values are not lost; if you request command prompting (F4) again, you will see the values displayed in the command prompt screen's entry fields. Figure 2.6 shows the result of pressing F9 after having successfully executed the CRTLIB command.

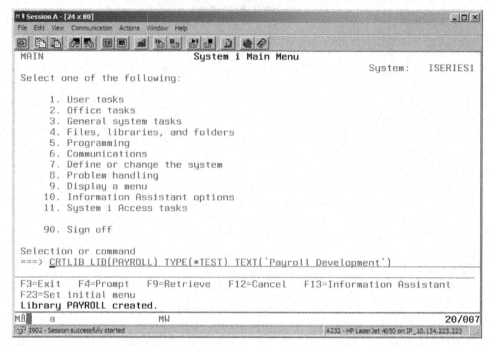

Figure 2.6: Results of Successfully Executed CRTLIB Command Retrieved by F9

Positional Notation

You can execute a command without using keywords; this method is referred to as **positional notation**. When you use positional notation, the order in which you specify parameters is very important. Positional notation works as long as

a. The values you enter for a particular parameter correspond exactly by position to the sequence of parameters as shown on the command prompt screen (or in the documentation at the IBM Information Center Web site, *http://publib.boulder.ibm.com/iseries*).

b. You do not exceed the maximum number of positional parameters allowed for a particular command. (Each command has a maximum positional parameter attribute, which sets the limit for that command.)

To illustrate, if you wanted to create a test library named PAYROLL, you would need to supply the library name and specify the value *TEST for the Type parameter because *PROD is the default value for Type. Using positional notation, you would correctly enter the command as

CRTLIB PAYROLL *TEST

But, if you changed the order of the parameter values without specifying keywords:

CRTLIB *TEST PAYROLL

the system would reject the command and issue the error message *"Value '*TEST' for parameter LIB not a valid name."* In other words, without the keywords, the system assumes that the value *TEST is for the first parameter, which is Library, not Type.

Likewise, if you tried to create a production library named PAYROLL with a text description of "Production Lib" by entering the command

CRTLIB PAYROLL 'Production Lib'

the system would issue the error message *"Production Lib not valid for parameter TYPE."* If you added the default value for the Type parameter, thinking you could then get the values in the correct relative positions, you might enter

CRTLIB PAYROLL *PROD 'Production Lib'

However, the system again would issue an error message, this time saying, *"Number of positional parameters exceeds limit of 2"* (see the second rule above).

As you can see, using positional notation can be tricky. We suggest that, in general, and especially until you get used to the commands and parameters you use frequently, you should rely on command prompting and just enter or change the parameter values in the entry fields of the command prompt screen. As you gain experience, you will find it more convenient to type commands directly on a command line without prompting—particularly for those commands that use the defaults or require you to enter only one parameter.

Do not worry too much about all these abbreviations and commands—there is no need to try to memorize a long list of them. We cover specific commands in more detail when we need to introduce them in the text and labs. The most productive time to study them is when you will be using them. You will be able to recall commands you use often without much effort. Remember, the IBM i OS has menus to help find the commands you are looking for. Once you have found a command, you can easily get to a command prompt screen.

Menus of Commands

IBM i command menus are organized hierarchically. The easiest way to reach the highest level of the command-menu hierarchy is simply to press Prompt (F4) from any empty command line. For example, you just signed on to the system and your cursor is sitting on the Main menu's command line, waiting for action. If you press F4 without typing anything else, the screen in Figure 2.7 will appear.

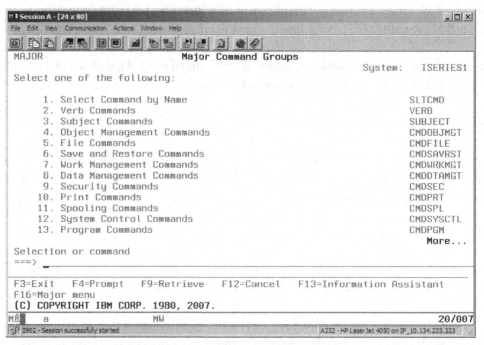

Figure 2.7: Major Command Groups (MAJOR) Menu

This screen is a menu of major command groups whose proper name, as you can see, is MAJOR. The Major Command Groups (**MAJOR**) **menu** arranges its choices in broad categories so that if, for example, you wanted to peruse a list of all the verb or action commands, you could select option 2, Verb Commands. Entering a 2 on the command line of the MAJOR menu causes the first page of the Verb Commands (**VERB**) **menu** (Figure 2.8) to be displayed.

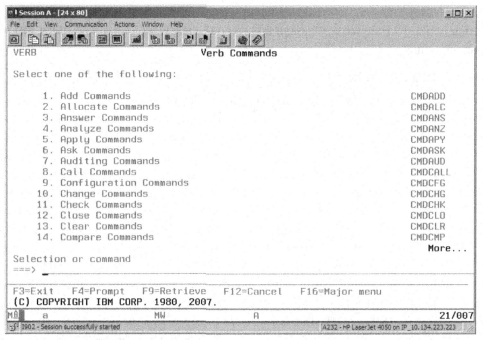

Figure 2.8: Verb Commands (VERB) Menu

All the options displayed on the VERB menu lead to lower-level menus that contain all
the possible commands (i.e., all the valid verb-modifier-noun combinations) for the
selected verb.

As you can see by looking again at the options available from the Major Command Groups
menu (Figure 2.7), there are also menus of commands grouped by Subject (noun), as well
as by functional category (e.g., Work Management, Security, Print). The menu names
of these latter categories, as well as of the lower-level menu choices from the VERB and
SUBJECT menus, all begin with CMD; what follows is the verb, noun, or functional category
abbreviation.

For example, say you want to see the different Clear commands available on the system. Selecting option 13 from the VERB menu takes you to the Clear Commands (**CMDCLR**) **menu** you see in Figure 2.9.

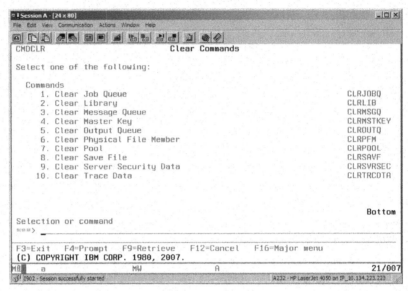

Figure 2.9: Clear Commands (CMDCLR) Menu

From this menu, selecting the option for a specific command (e.g., 5 for Clear Output Queue) takes you to the command prompt screen for that command. For example, if you type 5 on the command line of the CMDCLR menu and press Enter, the **CLROUTQ** (Clear Output Queue) command prompt screen (Figure 2.10) appears.

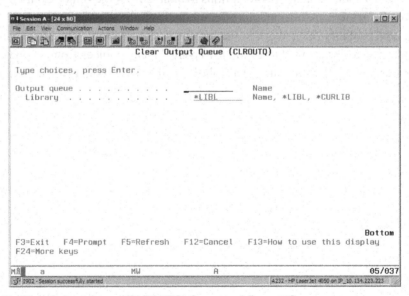

Figure 2.10: Clear Output Queue (CLROUTQ) Command Prompt Screen

This is a typical command-prompt entry screen. It shows the actual command name, CLROUTQ, at the top and has entry fields for parameter values. As you can see, the Output queue parameter requires you to name a value for the output-queue object, and the Library parameter defaults to the predefined value *LIBL, which means the library list of that job. Both contextual and extended Help are available from this screen. Table 2.2 contains a few more examples that show how a named menu can display all commands related to a specified verb or noun (subject).

Table 2.2: Command Group Menu Examples	
Command Group	**Menu Name**
Copy commands	CMDCPY
Display commands	CMDDSP
Library commands	CMDLIB
Message commands	CMDMSG
Output-queue commands	CMDOUTQ
User-profile commands	CMDUSRPRF
Work-with commands	CMDWRK

Menus of command groups are especially useful when you know an action (verb) you need but are not sure how to specify the noun. The menus are also helpful if you know the noun but are not sure how to specify the verb or whether the intended verb is permitted for that noun.

The GO Command

You can get directly to any IBM i menu, including menus of command groups, by using the **GO command**. This CL command always has one required parameter: a menu name. For example, as the diagram in Figure 2.11 illustrates, if you want to go directly to the menu of Clear commands without having to go through the MAJOR and VERB menus, you can enter the command GO CMDCLR on any command line, and the CMDCLR menu will be displayed.

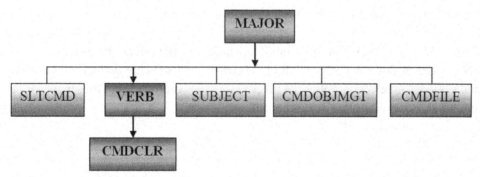

Figure 2.11: Reaching the Clear Commands Menu

Instead of having to traverse the entire path, you can take a shortcut to a known point along the path with the GO command.

To see how this process works, suppose you want to check the current values of your user profile, but you are not sure which command to use. You can deduce from what we have already covered that the abbreviation for *profile* is likely to be PRF. In this case, the shortest route is to use the GO command to have the system list all commands related to profiles. On any command line, you can simply type

GO CMDPRF

and press Enter. This action results in the display of the Profile Commands (**CMDPRF**) **menu** in Figure 2.12.

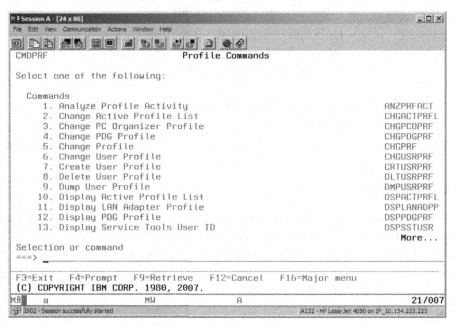

Figure 2.12 : Profile Commands (CMDPRF) Menu

Notice the *"More . . ."* in the bottom right-hand corner of the screen. Press PgDn, and on the second page of this menu you will find the command you need: Display User Profile, which is option 14. Selecting option 14 takes you to the command prompt screen for the **DSPUSRPRF** (Display User Profile) command, as Figure 2.13 shows.

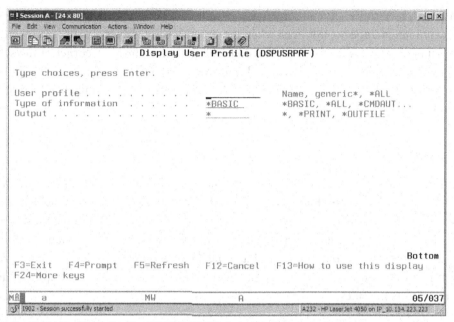

Figure 2.13: Display User Profile (DSPUSRPRF) Command Prompt Screen

This screen requires you to enter a user-profile name and shows default values for two parameters, Type (*BASIC) and Output (*). For this example, use the defaults for these parameters. If user CIS001D were to type her user ID in the entry field and press Enter, the Display User Profile – Basic screen (Figure 2.14) would appear.

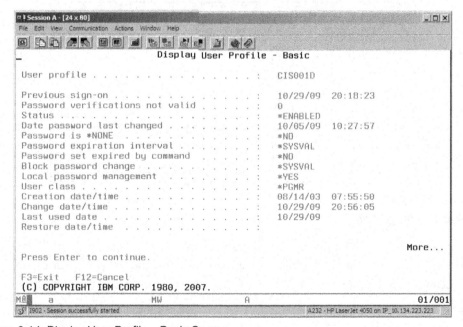

Figure 2.14: Display User Profile – Basic Screen

The Display User Profile – Basic screen shows users the current values of their user profiles; the password never appears, not even when the security officer executes the command. Notice that once again More . . . is displayed in the bottom right-hand corner of the screen. If you press PgDn, you can view additional information about this user. Even though this is an information display, you can get field Help for parameters and extended Help about the command or display.

Library Lists

When using any system object or an object you have created (e.g., to read data from a data file), the system searches for the object in your **library list**. A library list is the definition of the path of libraries a job searches when trying to find commands, programs, files, or other IBM i objects. You have seen a reference to the library list in several commands we have already examined. In the common case of an object name being required as a parameter (e.g., for the CPYF command's FROMFILE parameter), the library part of the object name typically defaults to *LIBL.

A library list is created for each job, usually from system values, a job description, and the user profile's Current library value when the user profile is activated at sign-on. An interactive job's library list contains the names of a limited number of libraries to which a user needs access, and various CL commands can change the library list while the job is running. A library list consists of four parts, which Table 2.3 describes.

Table 2.3: The Library List	
Part of Library List	Examples of Content
System (up to 15)	QSYS QHLPSYS QUSRSYS
Product (none, 1, or 2)	QPDA QRPG
Current (1 only)	CIS001 (personal library created for a student user)
User (up to 250)	QGPL QTEMP PAYLIB (a user library for payroll programs)

System Library List

The **system library list** contains up to 15 libraries that the system needs to operate; you usually will not change the system library list. You can determine which libraries are automatically placed in the system portion of your library list by displaying the system value QSYSLIBL.

In Lab 1, you used menus to get to a Work with System Values screen; but let's try a shortcut. Because you know the name of the system value you're looking for, you can use the **DSPSYSVAL** (Display System Value) command.

If you prompt for DSPSYSVAL command parameters, you see that the only two are System value and Output. System value is required, and Output has a default value of '*'. To check the possibilities for the Output parameter, you would move the cursor to the Output field line and press Help (F1). The screen in Figure 2.15 would appear.

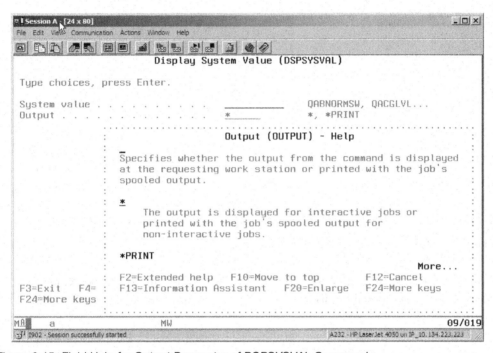

Figure 2.15: Field Help for Output Parameter of DSPSYSVAL Command

As the Help text indicates, the value * means that the output of the display command goes to your workstation screen.

Now, if you enter the system value QSYSLIBL on the DSPSYSVAL command prompt screen, an information screen like the one in Figure 2.16 appears.

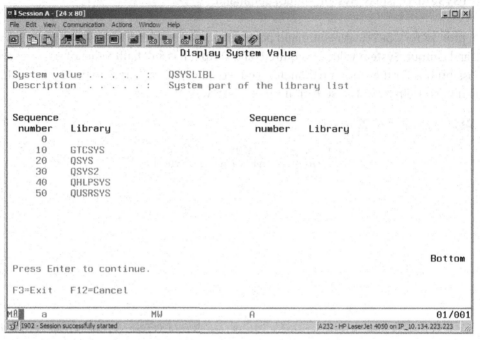

Figure 2.16: Display System Value Information Screen

If your computer's system value for QSYSLIBL was changed from the shipped values, the display might list additional libraries. The shipped system libraries should include the following:

- **QSYS**—Contains essential system objects, such as system programs and commands, as well as pointers to all other libraries
- **QSYS2**—Contains additional system programs and files
- **QHLPSYS**—Contains all the Help information for different screens, including the Search Index information
- **QUSRSYS**—Contains other IBM-supplied objects needed for various system functions, as well as user message queues for holding messages

Note: GTCSYS is an additional library added to the author's system, not a shipped entry.

Product Library

The OS inserts a **product library** when the library is needed for some task a user has requested. For example, if a user requests compilation of an RPG ILE program, the library

QRPGLE is inserted as a product library during the compile process and then removed when the process is finished. The OS handles this adding and removing of the appropriate product libraries automatically with no user intervention.

Current Library

The **current library** is a specially designated user library into which, by default, newly created objects are placed. When a current library is specified, it follows the product library in the library list. The current library is significant because it is searched before other user libraries when an object is requested.

It is helpful for each user to have his own library to keep track of test files, programs, screen layouts, query reports, and so on. Having individual libraries prevents conflicts with other users about object names because all objects of the same type must have unique names within a single library. In the lab for this chapter, you create a library and then designate that library as your current library by changing the value of the user profile's Current library parameter. Once you have done this, all objects you create will go into your library automatically unless you specify otherwise.

User Library List

The **user library list** names the libraries that organize the programs, screens, data files, and applications that users need to do business on the system; the user portion of the library list can contain up to 250 library names. Because different users perform different types of work and have different requirements, the user library list can be customized for each user or for groups of users that have similar needs. The user library list is customized in a number of ways: by using a special job description, by running an initial start-up program at sign-on, or by executing CL commands when needed as the job (either batch or interactive) is run. Normally, many different users need to share objects in user libraries; objects in the current library tend to belong to, and are used by, an individual. For most jobs, several IBM-supplied libraries, which begin with the letter *Q*, also are included in the user list. These libraries are specified in the **QUSRLIBL system value** and normally include at least QTEMP and QGPL.

Objects Within Libraries

You should now understand the following points about the relationship among objects, libraries, and library lists:

a. When objects are created, they are "placed in" (associated with) a library. This association is logical—object storage locations are assigned by the system; objects are not physically stored within a library area on disk.

b. Unless you specify otherwise, most new objects are placed in the current library, if one is designated for the job. (A few object types are always created in QSYS.)

c. If no current library is designated, a default IBM-supplied user library is used.

d. Unless you specify otherwise, the system searches the library list for requested objects. This is the meaning of *LIBL as the Library value for an object name in a CL command.

e. The library list is searched in the following order: system library list, product library, current library, and user library list. Individual libraries are searched in the order specified in the library list, from top to bottom.

f. The needs of the individual user determine the libraries included in the user library list.

g. Every individual user on the system may have a unique, personally tailored library list. More commonly, groups of users with similar work requirements have the same or a similar library list with, perhaps, only the current library being unique.

We examine these library-list concepts again, and in more detail in the following chapters, and you apply them in lab exercises from this chapter on.

In Summary

This chapter has covered CL command syntax and the IBM naming conventions for CL. It is important to remember that a command normally consists of a verb (CRT), a noun (LIB), and a receiver (MYLIB), which in this example would result in the command CRTLIB MYLIB. This chapter also has covered keyword and positional notation, along with the important differences and rules used when users are submitting commands in each format.

IBM i menu commands help users find the commands they need. The hierarchical menu design allows even novice users to find and execute the commands they want. For example, if they do not know the noun of a command but know the verb, and they want to display an object (DSP), they can find a menu that contains all of the display commands by typing the command GO CMDDSP. As an alternative, if they know the noun and want to take an action on a library (LIB), they can type GO CMDLIB to see all of the commands related to libraries.

The library list is an important IBM i concept used to efficiently locate requested objects; the list can be changed to accommodate the needs of a job. The user library list is composed of four parts: the System, Product, Current, and User sections. For user applications, the current library is most important, not only because it is searched before other libraries in the user library list, but also because it is the default location for newly created objects unless we specify otherwise. The system library list can contain up to 15 libraries and is shared by all the users on the system unless a user's library list is customized.

In the following lab, you will use both extended Help and field Help to answer questions about menu choices and command parameters. You should not hesitate to use Help in the future whenever a question arises or you need more information than a lab exercise provides. You will also discover how to change your user profile, display additional message information, create a library, display your library list, and change your library list. After you have completed the lab, you will be able identify and describe the following additional commands not covered in the text: GO, CHGPRF, CRTLIB, DSPLIBL, and CHGLIBL.

Key Terms

CLROUTQ

CMDCLR menu

CMDPRF menu

CPYF

CRTBNDCBL

CRTBNDCL

CRTBNDRPG

CRTLIB

current library

DSPAUTL

DSPDSTL

DSPFD

DSPFFD

DSPLIBL

DSPOBJD

DSPSYSVAL

DSPUSRPRF

F9 function key

GO command

keyword notation

*LIBL

library list

MAJOR menu

parameter keyword

positional notation

product library

QHLPSYS (library)

QSYS (library)

QSYS2 (library)

QUSRLIBL system value

QUSRSYS (library)

syntax

system library list

user library list

VERB menu

WRKJOBQ

WRKMSGQ

WRKOUTQ

Review Questions

1. What general rule does IBM use when naming CL commands?

2. What is the first library that is searched when a user requests use of an IBM i object?

3. List the rules for using positional notation.

4. List the parts of a user's library list.

5. What is the significance of the system library list?

6. What is the maximum number of libraries in the system library list?

7. What libraries are usually in the system portion of a library list?

8. How would you display the libraries that make up the system library list?

9. What is the function of a product library in a user's library list?

10. Why is the current library important?

11. When a user creates a new object, what is the default location of the object?

12. When a user requests an object, in what order is the user's library list searched?

13. Explain how a user's library list can be customized.

14. What is stored in the QSYSLIBL system value?

15. List and describe six commands that begin with the STR or CRT verb.

Lab 2

Introduction

This lab concentrates on some basic skills that every programmer, operator, or technical user often needs. As you work through the lab, you become more familiar with using online Help to get information about a display or input field. You use the GO command to get to a command menu and to shortcut a menu path. You create a library and change your user profile using the CHGPRF (Change Profile) command. You display and change your library list. You also change the password of your user profile.

Part 1

Goals   Use Help to get information about a display.

Start at   Main menu.

Procedure Press Help from an empty command line or other nonsensitive area of the Main menu.

2.1. If you are not already signed on, sign on as before, entering the user profile your instructor gave you (up to 10 characters total) as the User value. Remember that pressing Field Exit (on a PC, Tab serves the same function) jumps you down to the beginning of the next entry field when you are finished entering characters on the current line. For Password, enter your user password. Ignore the last three entries and press Enter. At this time, you should see the Main menu display.

When the cursor is not on a particular item in a menu list, you can obtain general (extended) Help about the screen itself just by pressing Help/F1. Because the cursor is now on the command line, press Help from there to get extended Help.

2.2. You should now see the first of the IBM i Main Menu – Help screens, as you see in Figure 2.17.

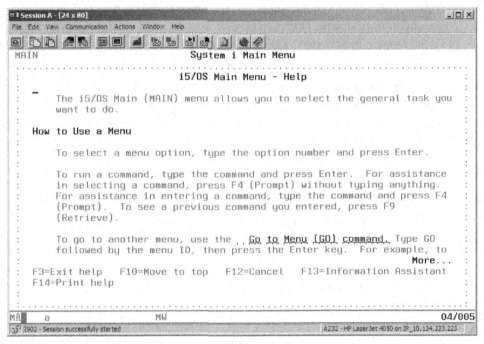

Figure 2.17: IBM i Main Menu – Help

This series of screens contains useful information about function keys and the GO command we discussed in this chapter. It also describes the range of operations available with each Main menu choice. Hypertext links are provided for additional information about the highlighted topics.

Read through the Main menu Help screens, and answer the following questions on the answer sheet:

2.2.a. Which command key (function key) pulls up the last command run from the command line?

2.2.b. Which Main menu option would you use to change your password?

2.2.c. Which menu option (or options) would you use to display the status of a device?

2.2.d. Which option (or options) would you use to display the history log?

2.2.e. Which option lets you work with the hardware resources of the system?

2.2.f. What value would you enter to display a list of menus related to both programming and problem handling? (Read carefully "How to Use a Menu"—see Figure 2.17.)

When you are finished, return to the Main menu.

2.3. If you have questions about a certain menu selection, you can move the cursor to that area of the screen before you press Help, as you did on the entry fields of a command prompt screen. Doing so gives you contextual, or field-sensitive, Help. Now move the cursor up to the line for option 6 (Communications), and press Help to see how this option is used. Then return to the Main menu.

2.4. Use Tab instead of moving the cursor up or down to return the cursor to the command line. You could also use New line on this screen or press F9 to move the cursor there directly, which will recall the previous command (if there was one).

Part 2

Goals   Access a menu using the GO command.

Display your user profile.

Start at   Main menu.

Procedure Enter GO CMDPRF.

Select the option for CHGPRF.

Use context-sensitive Help.

2.5. As you have learned, you can use the GO command to go directly to a menu. To get more information about using this command, type GO on the command line, and then press Help.

Use the GO command's Help to answer the following question.

2.5.a. What is the difference between a "special value" and a "generic name"?

Now return to the Main menu.

2.6. You can also use the GO command to reach a menu of related commands. From this menu, you can select the specific command you need and then prompt for parameters.

The format of this GO command is GO CMD*xxx*, where *xxx* is either the verb part of the command or the noun subject on which the command will perform its action. For example, to see a menu of the various profile commands, you can type GO CMDPRF on the command line and then press Enter. Please do this now.

2.6.a. How many different user-profile commands are there?

2.7. To obtain a description of any of these commands, you can move the cursor to the selection and press Help, or just type the selection number on the command line and then press Help. Using one of these techniques, study the command descriptions of the CHGPRF (Change Profile) and CHGUSRPRF (Change User Profile) commands.

    2.7.a. What are two essential differences between the CHGPRF and CHGUSRPRF commands? (**Hint:** Whose profile is changed? Who can use the command?)

2.8. You can run (execute) any of the commands from the menu either by typing the command itself or by entering its option number on the command line. For example, select the Change Profile (not Change User Profile) command by entering its option number on the command line and pressing Enter.

2.9. You should now be looking at the prompt screen for the CHGPRF command (Figure 2.18).

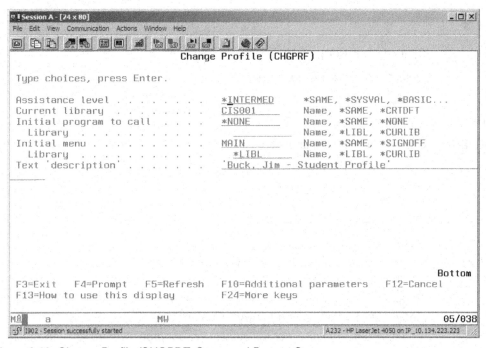

Figure 2.18: Change Profile (CHGPRF) Command Prompt Screen

Note: The profile here is a typical student profile on our system; your profile values will be different.

Although you reached this screen by going to a menu of related commands, you also could have gotten here by entering the command itself, CHGPRF, and then requesting prompting (F4) from any command line.

    2.9.a. What is your "Assistance level?"

2.9.b.   Place your cursor in the "Assistance level" entry field and press F4. What values are allowed in this field? Press F12.

2.9.c.   Now press F1. List the meanings of the values allowed in this field.

2.9.d.   What is listed as your current library?

2.9.e.   With the Current library parameter value as it is, what actual library will be used as your default current library?

2.10.   Exit Help, returning to the Change Profile screen. Study the entries on this screen.

2.10.a.   According to the screen, which menu will you first see after you sign on?

2.10.b.   If you wanted to go directly to the Programming menu (option 5 on the Main menu) after you sign on, what would you change this parameter value to? (Remember how a menu is identified?)

Part 3

Goals   Change your user profile.

Obtain additional message text.

Create a user library.

Start at   CHGPRF command prompt.

Procedure   Change the CURLIB parameter.

Press Help on the message line.

Create your library (CRTLIB).

Caution
Complete Part 3 of this lab entirely before you sign off. If you change your profile and don't create the new library with the same name as the CURLIB parameter value, your normal sign-on procedure will fail. You will need to enter QGPL for the Current library field of the sign-on screen. *Your instructor or the system administrator will need to fix your profile before you can log on.*

2.11.   If you have just signed back on at this time, type CHGPRF on the command line and press F4 to prompt. Doing so should bring you to the Change Profile command prompt screen (Figure 2.18).

We would like each student to have his or her own library in which to store objects created during the course, so try to change the value of the Current library parameter to a library with the same name as your user name (sign-on user ID). You normally would create the library before you change the user profile, but we have chosen this sequence so you can examine the system's response and practice getting the additional text of a system message.

With the cursor on the Current library entry field, type your user name (first initial and last name) over the default value. Remember that the asterisk (*) in *CRTDFT is part of the default special value and you must type over it when you change the value. Press Field Exit if your name is shorter. Notice that if your first initial plus last name exceeds 10 characters, the cursor jumps down to the next entry field; if this happens, be careful not to erase anything by typing over it. Now press Enter.

2.11.a. What does the message at the bottom of the screen say?

2.12. When a message is not clear, or when you aren't sure how to respond, the IBM i Help feature will once again prove useful. Move the cursor down to the message line, and press Help. The Additional Message Information display (Figure 2.19) should appear on your screen.

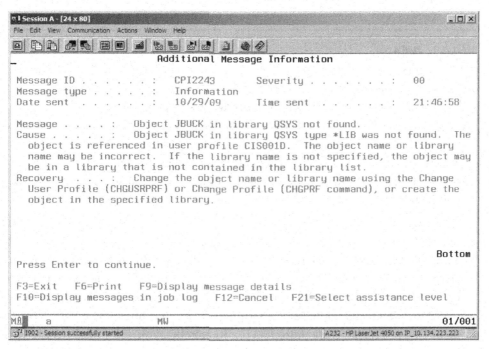

Figure 2.19: Additional Message Information for Message CPI2243

This type of information screen identifies a message by an ID, a type, a date and time sent, and a severity code. Severity level 00 is the lowest level, an informational or warning message. This message type means the message does not require a response. In addition, the information screen gives some explanation about the cause of the message and provides steps to take for recovery.

In this case, the system is trying to tell you that your change-profile request, although granted, does not really make sense because the library you would like to make current cannot be found (i.e., the library name is misspelled or the library does not exist as an object in QSYS, the system library).

The Recovery information indicates that you should check the spelling of the library name you used for the Current library value. But in this case, the problem isn't that the library name was misspelled; the library simply hasn't been created yet. So you need to take the second piece of advice from Recovery and create the library.

2.13. Exit Help and then press F3 if necessary to return to the Main menu. Select option 4 and press Enter. This will take you to the Files, Libraries, and Folders (DATA) menu.

From the DATA menu, select option 2, Libraries, and press Enter. Then, from the LIBRARY menu, select the option to create a library and press Enter.

You have just used the menu-selection path to arrive at a command prompt screen.

2.13.a. What is the actual command name?

Note
It is important to realize that instead of reaching this screen through the menu path, you could have typed the command itself (assuming you knew it) on any command line and then pressed F4 for prompting.

2.14. When you are keying the following parameter values, remember not to press Enter until you have completed the command prompt screen and are ready to run the command.

Type your user name (as for sign-on) as the value for the Library parameter. Case does not matter. Even if you type in lower case, the OS converts all CL parameter values, except quoted character strings, to upper case. When you enter a parameter shorter than the maximum length of the input field, pressing Field Exit moves the cursor ahead to the next field. Then change Library type to *TEST (or *test) by typing over the default value. For Text description, enter your full name and the course name (e.g., "Jane M. Smith, Intro IBM i"). Remember, you don't need to type the quotation marks. Now press Enter.

2.14.a. To which screen have you returned?

2.14.b. What is displayed on the message line at the bottom?

Part 4

Goals   Display your library list.

            Change your library list's current library.

Start at   LIBRARY menu.

Procedure   Execute the DSPLIBL command.

            Execute the CHGLIBL command.

2.15. Now you have changed your user profile and created a library. Let's see whether that library has been activated yet. You should be looking at the LIBRARY menu now (Figure 2.20).

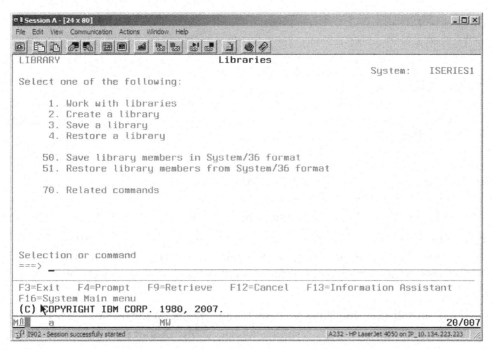

Figure 2.20: Libraries (LIBRARY) Menu

2.15.a. If you were not at the screen you see in Figure 2.20, what action would you take from any command line to get there?

2.16. The LIBRARY menu doesn't really include library-list commands, although you could get to them by selecting option 70, Related commands. Instead, go directly to a menu of library-list commands by entering GO CMDLIBL on the command line. You should now be looking at a screen similar to the one in Figure 2.21.

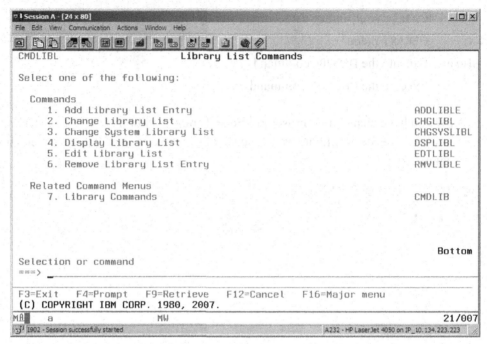

Figure 2.21: Library List Commands (CMDLIBL) Menu

2.17. The library list (*LIBL) contains the names of a limited subset of libraries that the system will check one after another to find an object you want to work with. This feature saves you from having to specify the particular library in which the object is stored whenever you need to reference it, letting you use only the object's simple name.

First, let's display your library list by taking the option to Display Library List from the CMDLIBL menu. On the resulting screen, set the Output parameter default to display (*), and run the command (press Enter).

2.17.a. How many libraries are currently in your library list?

2.17.b. Is the library you just created on the list?

Unless you have signed off and back on again since you completed Part 3 of this lab, you will not find your new library in the library list. When you change the Current library parameter of your user profile, the library list of the current job is not immediately changed; the change takes effect the next time you sign on.

To get your newly created test library into the library list, you can use one of several commands to change the library list during your interactive job.

2.18. Return to the CMDLIBL menu. Find the command to change your library list, enter its option number on the command line, and press Enter.

You should now be looking at a CHGLIBL (Change Library List) command prompt screen similar to the one in Figure 2.22.

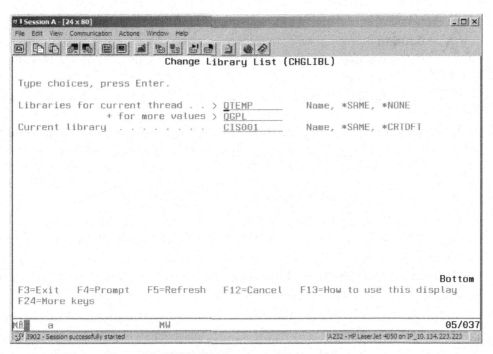

Figure 2.22: Change Library List (CHGLIBL) Command Prompt Screen

Note: The library list here is a typical student library on our system; your library list values will be different.

2.19. From this screen, you can add or remove libraries from the Libraries for current thread parameter.

2.19.a. Use Help to find out which part of the library list is affected by changes to this parameter value.

2.19.b. An additional parameter lets you change the current library. What is the keyword for this parameter? (Can you remember the function key that toggles between choices and keywords?)

Tab or cursor down (don't use Field exit) to the Current library parameter and type your new library name, erasing the default value. Then press Enter.

Unless you misspelled your library name, you should be back at the CMDLIBL menu with the message "Current library changed to (. . .)" displayed on the message line.

2.20. Now press F9 twice to retrieve the DSPLIBL (Display Library List) command you previously executed, and then run the command (press Enter). You should now see your library designated as the current library (list type is CUR). If this is not so, review Part 3 to create your library and/or step 1.19 to change your library list.

 Caution

Before you go on, you must be sure that your test library has been added to your library list.

2.21. Recall from the text that a library list can comprise four list types: system, product, current, and user. But not all library-list types are always present in a particular library list.

    2.21.a. Record on your answer sheet all libraries in your library list that belong to each library list type.

    2.21.b. Which type is not represented in your list, and why do you suppose that is so?

When you have finished recording your library-list information, press F3 until you have returned to the Main menu.

Part 5

Goals   Change your user profile's password.

Start at   USER menu.

Procedure   Select the option to Change Password from the USER menu.

                 Type your old password.

                 Type your new password twice; press Enter.

2.22. Now that you have created a library and made it your current library, it may be time to establish a little security over your work environment. Because most installations standardize on some form of a user's name as the user-profile identification, the *User* part of the sign-on requirement (the user-profile name) would not be hard to figure out, so you don't want to leave your password at the same value as your user ID for long.

The password, like other IBM i names, can be from one to 10 alpha characters—including the special characters @, #, and $—or numbers (but it cannot begin with a number). For security purposes, it is better to use a moderately long password—not just one or two characters—and to avoid using easily discovered personal names, such as those of your spouse, children, or pets.

Because the security of a user profile is in many cases extremely important, IBM i has several security system values that limit password format and use. For example, individual passwords may be required to be changed every certain number of days, may be limited to a certain minimum or maximum length, may not use repeating characters, and may not be able to be used twice within a set number of changes.

A good candidate for a password would be some personal or technical term, perhaps in a foreign language. A potter who studied in Japan, for example, might use the Japanese names of some of his favorite stoneware and porcelain glazes. These are not passwords the average hacker would be likely to hit upon.

It is easy to change your password, and some installations require you to do so regularly. In fact, this policy can be enforced by setting the system value QPWDEXPITV, or password expiration interval, to the number of days for which a password is valid.

Caution

One thing you should remember about IBM i passwords is that if you change yours and then forget it, nobody can find it for you. Passwords are not made available to anyone on the system, regardless of special authority. Not even the system security officer can find out your password should you forget it. But if you do get in a jam, the security officer can change your user profile to recognize a different password so you can get back on the system.

A good way to select a secure but easy-to-remember password is to start with a sentence. For example, start with "Sailing on Lake Michigan is fun." Then select the first letter of each word in the sentence, SOLMIF, and insert at least two numbers and a special character between the letters to develop a password similar to SO5L$M1IF. The system you are using will probably have a list of password rules.

Here are some additional rules for user-generated passwords:

a. The password must be at least 8 characters long.

b. The password must contain at least
   - one alpha character (a–z, A–Z);
   - one numeric character (0–9);
   - and one special character from this set:
     ` ! @ $ % ^ & * ( ) - _ = + [ ] ; : ' " , < . > / ?

c. The password must *not*

- be words in any language—SEGELN;
- be dates—12/10/1951;
- contain spaces;
- contain your system ID;
- or be consecutive numbers—1234.

d. The sequence of the first 3 characters cannot be in your login ID.

2.23. To change your password, first select User tasks from the Main menu. Then, from the USER menu, select option 8 to change your password. Doing so takes you to the Change Password screen (Figure 2.23).

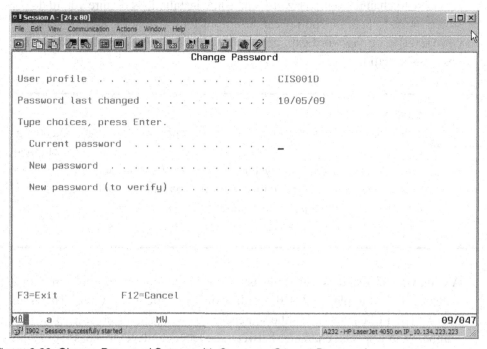

Figure 2.23: Change Password Screen with Cursor on Current Password

The cursor will be positioned on the Current password entry field, but you cannot see the field entry area, and nothing you key on this screen will be displayed. Do not press Enter until you are finished supplying all values.

The system asks for your current password so that someone else can't change your password if you happen to leave your workstation for a short time without signing off. Type in your current password, and press Field exit.

The cursor should now be on the entry field for New password. Carefully type your new password, and then press Field exit. Now repeat your new password on the New password (to verify) line, and press Enter.

If all goes well, you should be back at the USER menu, and the message "Password changed successfully" is displayed at the bottom of your screen. If this is not the case, you may get a message on the Change Password screen saying "New password and verify password not the same." If this happens, try again, and be sure to key in the new password accurately on both lines.

When you have changed your password, return to the Main menu and sign off.

CHAPTER 3

Objects

Overview

One of the IBM i operating system's (OS's) most important architectural concepts is that of objects. **Objects** are the internal structures on which the instruction set of the OS operates. Almost every named entity in the OS is an object, including libraries, source files, commands, programs, database files, user profiles, authorization lists, device descriptions, and many others. Hardware devices are not objects, but all hardware devices that the applications and the OS use, such as display devices, printers, tape drives, and diskette units, are described to the system by device-description objects that define the objects' operational characteristics.

In this chapter, we see how objects are identified to the OS (i.e., by library, name, and type), and we examine where objects are stored when they are created and how they are located when they are requested. We also introduce a few library-list commands that can help ensure that the system can find an object. Finally, we introduce the concept of work management and examine job scheduling, batch processing, and how spooled output is managed and eventually printed.

Objectives

Students will be able to

- List several advantages of an object-based OS.
- Explain the purpose of object types and list several common ones.
- Describe how the system uses a library list to locate a requested object.
- Demonstrate the use of a qualified name to reference an object.
- Use the CHGLIBL (Change Library List) and EDTLIBL (Edit Library List) commands to change the order of user libraries in a library list.
- Explain the importance of spooling.
- Describe the function of an output queue.

Continued

- Determine where spooled output goes by examining user-profile, device-description, and job-description entries.

The IBM i Object-Based Architecture

In the IBM i OS, every object is encapsulated; in this state, an outer layer, or interface, identifies the object and specifies the operations that can be performed on the object. This interface protects each object. Applications and the OS relate to the object through this interface and never deal with hardware-specific details. Figure 3.1 shows some examples of different OS objects and the interfaces allowed for a specific object type. You can "run" a program object or "vary on" a device object, but you cannot run or vary on a database object.

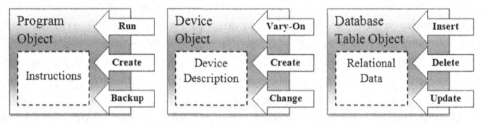

Figure 3.1: IBM i Object Encapsulation

The details of object interfaces are handled by low-level System Licensed Internal Code (**SLIC**) instructions, which are translated across the Technology Independent Machine Interface (**TIMI**) from the application programs and operating-system instructions we discussed above. The diagram in Figure 3.2 depicts this layered IBM i architecture.

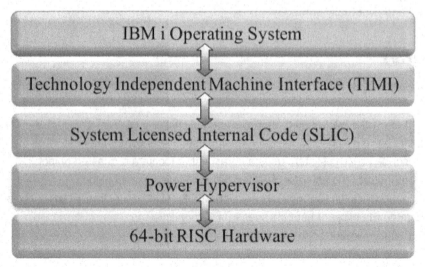

Figure 3.2: IBM i OS Layered Machine Architecture

IBM creates the **licensed internal code**, which is specific to the IBM i OS. The internal code translates the object-based instructions of the **logical machine** (i.e., the application programs and OS) into low-level machine instructions that drive the system processor and other hardware of the **physical machine**.

As you can see from Figure 3.2, an action requested on an object (e.g., by a CL command) is passed through the machine interface (TIMI) and converted into system licensed internal code before it is effected in the hardware. The TIMI layer serves the very useful purpose of insulating the logical machine from the physical machine so that programs are not dependent on the hardware. This translation of the high-level machine instruction set by SLIC to carry out hardware operations is called **layered machine architecture**.

The lower levels of microcode "know" the details of the hardware, and the microcode must be updated whenever new hardware is added to the system. OS upgrades from one version and release to another accomplish this task. However, existing applications and OSs deal with hardware only through the TIMI and so are not directly affected by changes in the hardware. The TIMI makes the IBM i OS hardware independent, and thus able to take advantage of new technology without causing problems for existing applications. This independence also protects the knowledge investment of programmers and users because the screens they use to do their work at the level of the logical machine may change only slightly, even though massively significant changes may occur at the hardware level.

The change to 64-bit Power System RISC processors from older 48-bit CISC processors is a case in point. Software written for the older machines is quickly converted without recompilation (in most cases) and runs as true 64-bit software on the newer RISC boxes—with no need for slowed-down emulation or costly rewrites—even though at the processor hardware level (as well as in many other hardware components), the new Power System is an entirely different machine!

The vertical and horizontal microcode layers of the CISC processors have been rewritten as System Licensed Internal Code with an object-based kernel on the newer RISC-powered systems. New code (more than 1 million lines of the total, which exceeds 2.5 million lines of code below the TIMI) was written in C++, providing all the benefits of object-oriented programming, including code reuse, error reduction, and efficiency. The old high-level machine interface, or HLMI, has been renamed TIMI.

Between the SLIC and the Power technology–based hardware is a software layer called the **POWER Hypervisor**. This code is firmware that is shipped with the hardware; it resides in the flash memory on the service processor. The hypervisor software performs configuration, initialization, and virtualization support for the Power System hardware. This POWER

Hypervisor software layer allows power systems to run different OSs (e.g., IBM i, AIX, and Linux) in partitions on a single server.

With each new release of the OS, IBM makes available expanded communications, networking, and language support (e.g., Java, MySQL, and PHP support). Today's IBM i OS, while continuing to run RPG, CL, and COBOL applications written for earliest-generation machines, functions as a highly cost-effective Internet server—something never imagined just a few years ago.

The Power System hardware of tomorrow will be a very different machine from that of today; and the ability of the OS to adapt so quickly, taking advantage of new hardware technology, makes the IBM i OS virtually obsolescence-proof! What a great return on software development costs, not to mention the programmers' investment to master their skills.

In addition to program–hardware independence, this OS's object-based design has other advantages over conventional architecture. It provides a consistent approach to object management and security (hacking and viruses), protection against inadvertent misuse of an object, and the capability to reference an object by its simple name.

Because programs do not deal directly with hardware and are therefore not concerned with physical storage addresses, the OS treats all storage, both main and secondary, as a single homogenous mass called **single-level storage**. When objects are created, they are written to this single-level storage and are assigned a permanent virtual address. This address is placed in a pointer managed by the library in which the object "resides." This virtual storage address will not be reused during the life of the system, even after the object itself has been deleted. An address-translation algorithm at the microcode level provides efficient, direct addressing of the object in real memory. Real memory management (both main and secondary) becomes a function of the internal code and not of the applications. Among other advantages, this design lets different jobs share the same object concurrently.

The Power Systems of today are certainly a far cry from the first AS/400s, with modern hardware components dramatically smaller, faster, denser, less expensive, and more power-efficient electrically than their predecessors.

Types of IBM i Objects

All OS objects are categorized by **object type**. An object's type defines the object's purpose and how it is used on the system (e.g., the operations that can be performed on the object). The OS provides more than 75 object types that encompass all applications and system resources, including programs, data, and hardware; IBM adds new object types as required.

Table 3.1 lists a few common types of objects and the object-type special values (beginning with *) that identify them.

Table 3.1: Common IBM i Object Types		
Object Type	Object Description	Attribute (Subtype)
*AUTL	Authorization list	—
*CMD	Command	—
*DEVD	Device description	—
*FILE	File	PF (physical file) LF (logical file) DSPF (display file) PRTF (printer file)
*JOBD	Job description	—
*JOBQ	Job queue	—
*LIB	Library	—
*MENU	Menu description	—
*MODULE	Compiler unit	Non-executable program object
*MSGQ	Message queue	Queue for storing messages
*OUTQ	Output queue	—
*PGM	Program (executable)	Source language (e.g., CBL, CLP, RPG)
*QRYDFN	Query definition	—
*USRPRF	User profile	—

When you create an object, you give it a name, but the OS assigns the object type. The command you use to create the object determines the object's type. For example, the command **CRTUSRPRF** (Create User Profile) indicates the object type *USRPRF; the command **CRTLIB** (Create Library) indicates the object type *LIB.

Some CL commands work with any type of object, but each object type has certain CL commands that are used only for that type. For example, the **DSPOBJD** (Display Object Description) command works for objects of any type, but the **DSPUSRPRF** (Display User Profile) command works only for *USRPRF objects.

When you create an object, it "goes into" a **library**. It is important to realize that a library is not a physical collection of objects but a single-level directory to a group of related objects. You can use libraries to organize objects by owner, by application category (e.g., all human resources files and programs), or for security purposes. A library provides a logical reference to objects by using address pointers. In addition to address pointers, the type and authorization of each object is associated with the library entry for that object. In this way, when you request an object by name, the OS—when it finds a matching object name in a library—can determine whether the object type is appropriate for the request and whether you are authorized to use the object.

Requesting an Object

When you request an object, either by selecting a menu option or by entering a command, often it is not necessary to specify the name of the library in which the object resides. When you specify a **simple object name** (i.e., up to a 10-character name without a library reference), the system searches the job's current library list from top to bottom to locate an object matching the specified name and with a type appropriate for the request.

For example, say you want to use the CALL command to execute a program. The CALL command's only required parameter is the name of the program; so if you want to run a program named ACTCUS (to list all active accounts in a customer file), you would enter the command

CALL ACTCUS

on a command line.

If your library list looks like the one in Figure 3.3, the system will find program ACTCUS in library ARLIB and execute it (assuming you have the appropriate authority).

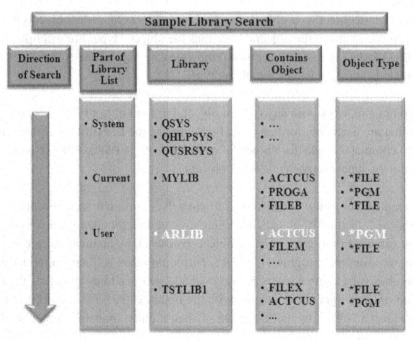

Figure 3.3: Sample Library Search

Notice that although an object named ACTCUS exists in library MYLIB, which is higher in the library list than library ARLIB, the system ignores that object because its object type is *FILE, the wrong type for the command. The only valid object type for a CALL command is *PGM. By including the object type in the library entry, the system can determine immediately, without ever having to locate and load the actual object, whether its type is appropriate for the requested operation (in this case, a program CALL).

Notice also that another program of the same name, ACTCUS, exists in library TSTLIB1. However, because the system searches library ARLIB first because of its higher position in the list, the search ends when the system finds program ACTCUS in library ARLIB. The program in library ARLIB is the one executed, not the program of the same name in library TSTLIB1. When you add new libraries to the library list, it is very important to keep this top-to-bottom search order in mind.

Qualified Names

If you want to run program ACTCUS in library TSTLIB1, you can proceed in two ways. You can use a **qualified name** for the object, or you can change the library list. The most direct approach is to use a qualified name to explicitly identify the object. A qualified name includes a reference to a library as well as the 10-character object name. It takes the form

libref/objname

where libref is either an explicit library-object name (e.g., TSTLIB1) or a reference to part of a library list (e.g., *CURLIB or *USRLIBL).

Thus, to execute program ACTCUS in library TSTLIB1, you would specify the following CALL command:

CALL TSTLIB1/ACTCUS

In this case, because you have specified a library name, the system searches only library TSTLIB1 for program ACTCUS. The system does not search any part of the library list, whether or not it successfully locates a suitable object in the named library.

You should remember the following three points about the use of qualified names:

- The library specified in an explicit qualified name does *not* need to be in your library list, but you (the requester) must be authorized not only to use that library but also to use the object within the library. The first thing the system does is determine whether you have proper authority to the library you named.

- If you are authorized to the library specified in an explicit qualified name, but the system cannot find a matching object name of the appropriate type, or if you are not authorized to use the object, the system does not search beyond the specified library. Instead, the system returns a message such as *"Object* OBJNAME *in library* LIBNAME *not found"* or *"Not authorized to object* OBJNAME *in library* LIBNAME.*"*
- When you use a simple unqualified name, the search for an object is limited to your library list. The system determined that you were authorized to use the library-list libraries when your job began. (Attempting to add to your library list a library to which you are not authorized will cause an error.) Processing your user profile, among other things, validates your authorization to the libraries in your library list.

In summary, most object references use a simple name, which is always syntactically correct in a CL command. It may be necessary to use a qualified name if

- Objects with the same name and type exist in more than one library in your library list
- You need an object that is not in any library in your library list

In any case, to use a qualified name, you need authority adequate for the intended use, both to the object and to the library.

Library-List Commands

Often during an interactive job it may be necessary to add or remove libraries from the library list, or change the order of libraries already in the list. A library that has been removed from the library list still exists on the system, but simple name references cannot be used by that job to access its objects.

The OS has several CL commands that let you work with a library list. We introduce several of these commands in this section.

The DSPLIBL Command

Remember that every job uses a library list to locate objects. An initial library list is created for each job from the job-description/user-profile attributes and from system values. In the lab for this chapter, you explore those attributes to understand the source of your own initial library list. However, any time you need to check the current contents of the library list, the DSPLIBL (Display Library List) command is most useful.

This command requires no parameters; it simply displays your job's current library list on the workstation screen. Figure 3.4 shows the output of the **DSPLIBL** command entered (with no parameters) on the command line.

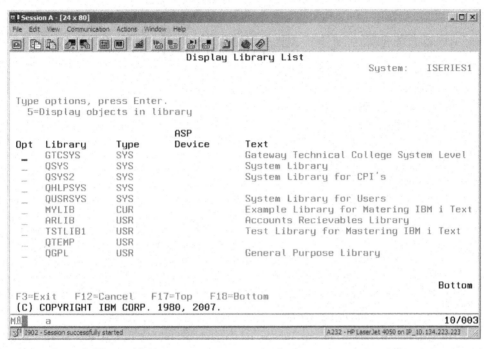

Figure 3.4: Sample Library List

The library list in Figure 3.4 is similar to the one in Figure 3.3 but with a few more libraries added to make it more realistic. Keep in mind that the contents of a library list may differ quite a bit from one user's job to another's.

The CHGCURLIB Command

A library list is not a static, unchanging entity, and often you may need to add new libraries or change the order of libraries currently in the list. You can use several different commands to change the current library or the user part of your library list.

One of these commands, the **CHGCURLIB** (Change Current Library) command, lets you specify a different library to occupy the spot of the current library in your library list. As you can see from the CHGCURLIB command prompt screen in Figure 3.5, the only required parameter value for this command is the name of the library that will become the new current library. The prompt screen shows the library ALLUSER already typed in as the new current library.

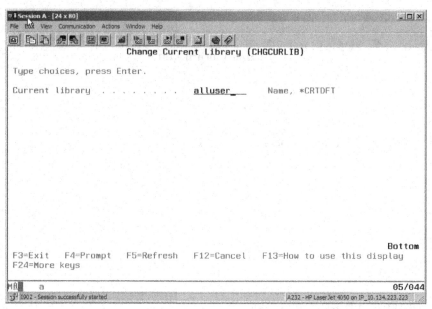

Figure 3.5: Change Current Library (CHGCURLIB) Command Prompt Screen

If you run the CHGCURLIB command with library ALLUSER specified, the library list will look like the one in Figure 3.6 (to display the library list, you use the DSPLIBL command).

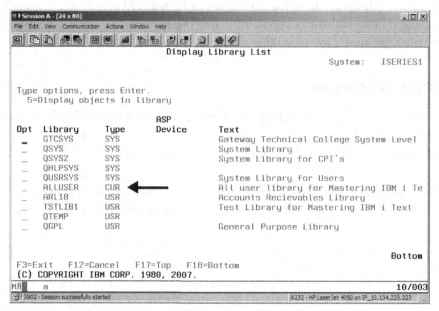

Figure 3.6: Changed Library List Showing a New Current Library

Notice that library ALLUSER is now the current (CUR) library and that the previous current library, MYLIB, has vanished from the list. This is an important point to keep in mind when you are using the CHGCURLIB command: The old current library is not added to the user part of the list; it is removed from the list altogether. For this reason, the CHGCURLIB command would not be the best choice if you wanted only to change the relative order of libraries already in the user part of the library list.

The ADDLIBLE Command

The **ADDLIBLE** (Add Library List Entry) command lets you add a new library to the user-library portion of the library list. The ADDLIBLE command prompt (Figure 3.7) shows library MYLIB being added to the library list.

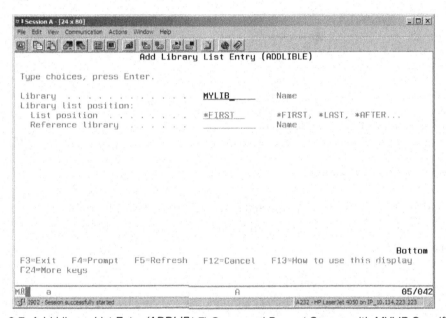

Figure 3.7: Add Library List Entry (ADDLIBLE) Command Prompt Screen with MYLIB Specified

Remember that this command affects only the user part of the library list. The default value of *FIRST for the List position field causes the added library to be placed at the top of the user library list (excluding the current library).

The DSPLIBL command output (Figure 3.8) shows the results of executing our sample ADDLIBLE command.

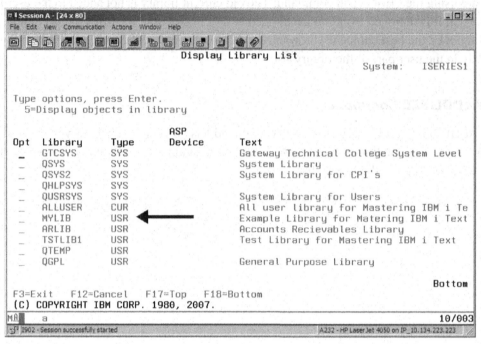

Figure 3.8: Changed Library List with MYLIB Added

Notice that library MYLIB has been inserted at the top of the user library list, just under the current library. The default position of the added library is *FIRST, the top of the user library list.

If you wanted to remove a single library from the user library list, you would use the **RMVLIBLE** (Remove Library List Entry) command, specifying by name the library to be removed.

The CHGCURLIB, ADDLIBLE, and RMVLIBLE commands each work on a single library. Sometimes you need to change the relative order of libraries already on the list or add (or remove) several libraries at a time. Two commands—CHGLIBL and EDTLIBL—let you perform these functions.

The CHGLIBL Command

The **CHGLIBL** (Change Library List) command lets you add, remove, or change the order of libraries in your user library list. You can also use the CHGLIBL command to change the current library. Let us look at how you can use this command to change the library list to run program ACTCUS in library TSTLIB1, as you see in Figure 3.3. Because the system searches the library list from top to bottom, you can accomplish this goal by moving library TSTLIB1 higher than library ARLIB in the library list.

Figure 3.9 shows a command prompt screen for the CHGLIBL command, using a library list similar to the one in Figure 3.3.

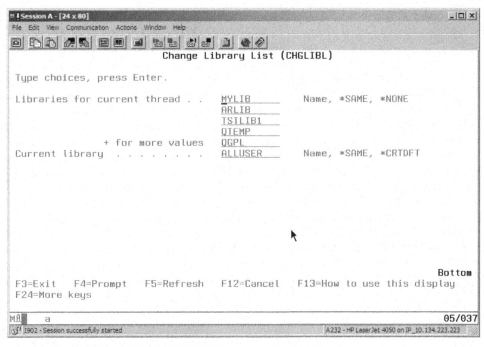

Figure 3.9: Change Library List (CHGLIBL) Command Prompt Screen

Each library name is an entry field. You can type over an existing name (to replace it with a different library name), or add new libraries by entering a plus sign (+) in the + for more values field. Without retyping, you can insert a new user library into the list just before an existing library by typing a greater-than symbol (>) over the first letter of the existing library name, and then pressing Field exit followed by Enter.

Also, you can change the current library by typing over the Current library value displayed on the screen and replacing it with the desired library name. The CHGLIBL command requires you to retype names to change the order of libraries, but you can use the command from within a CL program as well as interactively.

In Figure 3.10, the positions of libraries ARLIB and TSTLIB1 have been reversed, and MYLIB has been moved to the current library position.

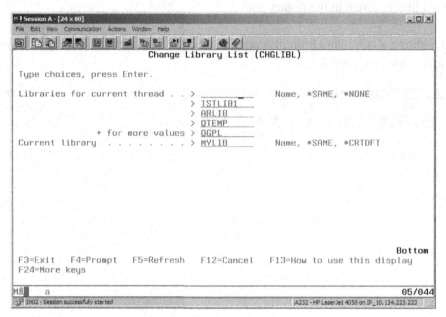

Figure 3.10: Change Library List, Placing TSTLIB1 Before ARLIB

Now, after you execute the CHGLIBL command, the original CALL command,

CALL ACTCUS

runs the program from library TSTLIB1 because TSTLIB1 is higher in the list and will be searched before library ARLIB.

The EDTLIBL Command

Another command that lets you work on multiple libraries is the EDTLIBL (Edit Library List) command. This command lets you add libraries to your library list and/or change the relative order of the libraries simply by renumbering the list. For the purpose of changing the order of user libraries in an interactive job, the EDTLIBL command is the easiest library-list command to use. When using EDTLIBL, you do not need to retype library names—to reorder them in the list, all you need to do is change their sequence numbers.

To see how the EDTLIBL command works, assume that your library list is similar to the one the DSPLIBL command shows in Figure 3.4. Figure 3.11 shows the **EDTLIBL** command prompt screen before you make any changes.

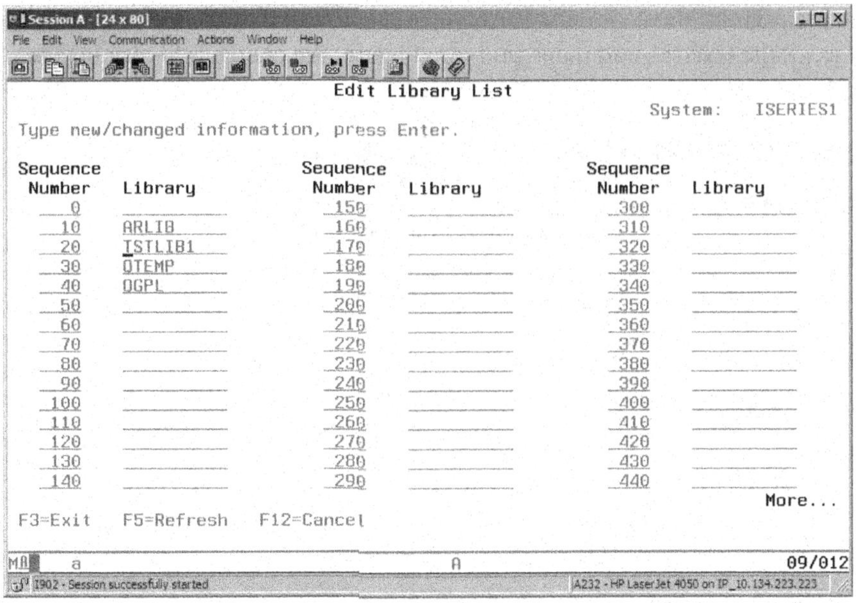

Figure 3.11: Edit Library List Prompt Screen

As you can see, the screen reflects the user-library portion of the library list you see with the DSPLIBL command in Figure 3.4.

To change the relative positions of libraries ARLIB and TSTLIB1, you would type over the sequence numbers, as Figure 3.12 shows.

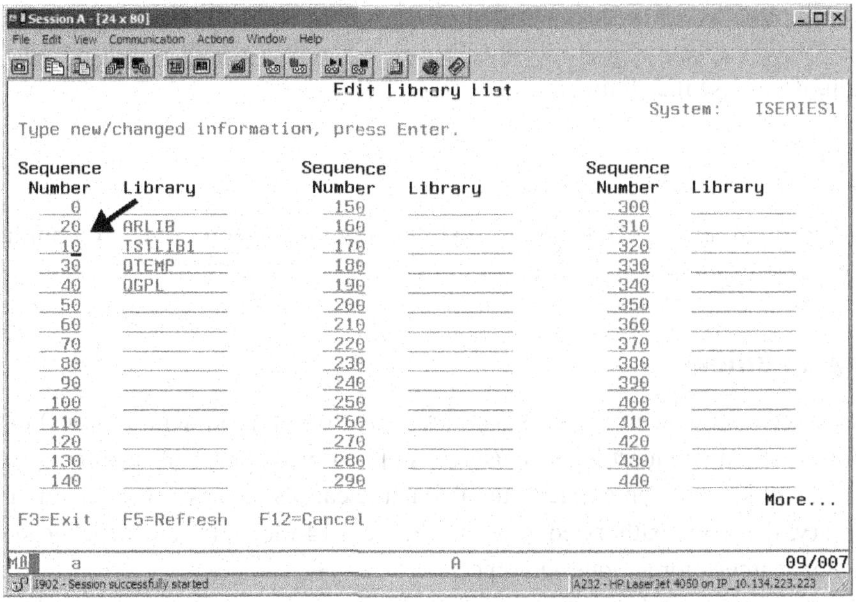

Figure 3.12: Edit Library List (Changed)

When you press Enter, the command is executed, changing the order of the libraries. If you use F9 to recall the DSPLIBL command and run it again, the changed library list appears as in Figure 3.13.

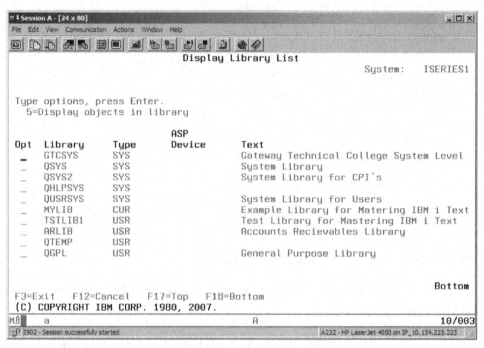

Figure 3.13: Sample Library List After Editing

Notice that library TSTLIB1 is now ahead of library ARLIB in the library list.

Once again, if you use the command

CALL ACTCUS

the version of program ACTCUS in library TSTLIB1, not the version of the program in library ARLIB, is executed.

Locating an Object

As you have seen, the system searches the library list from top (system libraries) to bottom (user libraries) when a request is made using a simple object name. As an alternative, referencing an object with an explicit qualified name causes the system to search only the named library, if you are authorized to use it. Figure 3.14 illustrates the steps the system takes when it searches for a requested object.

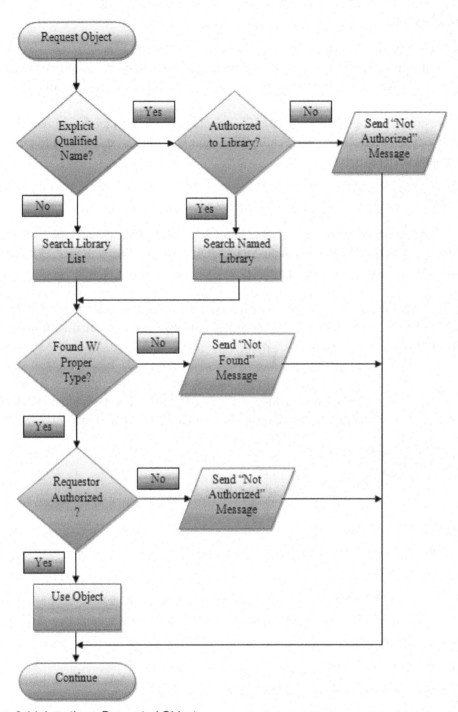

Figure 3.14: Locating a Requested Object

Storing Objects

You have learned how the system finds an object. Now let us examine how the system determines in which library an object should be stored. Where an object is stored depends on its type, and whether you specify a particular library in which to store the object.

Objects are created using a create—CRT*xxx*—command. For most create commands, the *xxx* specifies the type of object you are creating. For example, when you created a library in Lab 2, a command such as

CRTLIB CIS001LAB

told the system you were creating a library, so the system assigned object type *LIB to the new object. Likewise, if you were creating a COBOL program, the command CRTCBLPGM, if successful, would result in a new object of type *PGM, not *FILE or *USRPRF.

Some object types are associated only with the system library QSYS, and you cannot put them anywhere else. Libraries (*LIB), user profiles (*USRPRF), and device descriptions (*DEVD) are examples of these object types.

Most types of objects, however, can go in any library, including user libraries; for these objects, the CRT*xxx* command will include a Library entry field. For example, look at the command prompt for the **CRTOUTQ** (Create Output Queue) command in Figure 3.15.

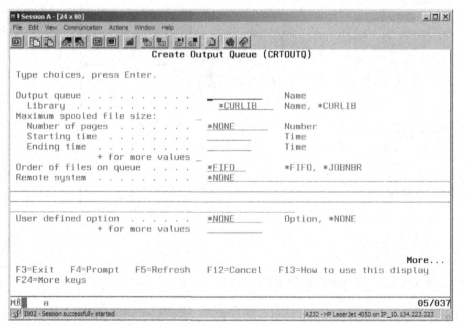

Figure 3.15: Create Output Queue (CRTOUTQ) Command Prompt Screen

(An **output queue** is an object that contains a list of spooled files you can display on a workstation or write to a **printer device**. We talk more about output queues later in this chapter.)

Notice that the Output queue parameter includes an entry field for Library (the default Library value is *CURLIB). The Library field is important because it determines which library the output queue will be placed in. If you remember our earlier discussion, you will notice that the Library field value is the libref part of a qualified name (libref/objname). If you have designated a current library in your library list—for example, by having previously changed your user profile's Current library value to your own library, or by running a CHGCURLIB command within your interactive job—the create command using the default of *CURLIB will send the new output queue to your current library. If, however, you have not created or designated a current library, the new object will go to the library acting as the "create default" (*CRTDFT) in your user profile. And we all know which library that is, right? (If you need to refresh your memory, please refer to step 2.5 in Lab 2.)

Of course, you could specify the receiving library by keying in a library name for the parameter value of the create command. This would be similar to using an explicit qualified name to locate an object, and the same warning would apply: If you name a library on a create command, you must have the proper authority to add new objects to the named library; otherwise, the create command fails.

Figure 3.16 shows the sequence the system follows when it stores an object. Exceptions to Figure 3.16 are those object types that are always placed in library QSYS (e.g., *DEVD, *LIB, *USRPRF).

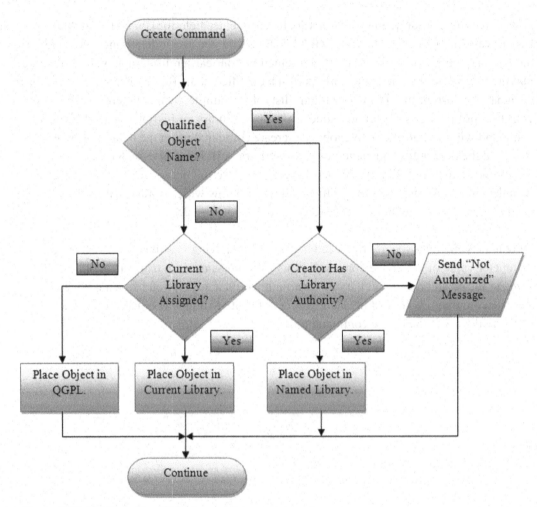

Figure 3.16: Storing a New Object

Simplified Batch Work Management

A detailed discussion of IBM i work management is beyond the scope of this text. It is important, however, for you to have a general understanding of the processes involved in scheduling, dispatching, and processing a batch job; we will discuss this process in this section.

You can think of the OS's work management as the air-traffic-control facility at a major airport. Air traffic controllers avoid potentially dangerous competition for limited resources (e.g., air space, runways) by instructing planes to remain on the runway or in a holding pattern until they are cleared to take off or land.

As the diagram in Figure 3.17 illustrates, the work scheduler controls incoming batch jobs. placing them in a job queue until they can begin execution (land). Similarly, it controls printed output, placing it in output queues (like planes lined up at a runway), until the writer (runway) is available and can print (take off).

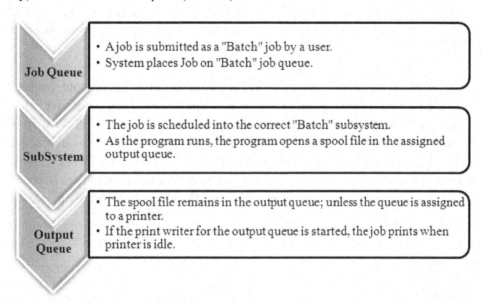

Job Queue
- A job is submitted as a "Batch" job by a user.
- System places Job on "Batch" job queue.

SubSystem
- The job is scheduled into the correct "Batch" subsystem.
- As the program runs, the program opens a spool file in the assigned output queue.

Output Queue
- The spool file remains in the output queue; unless the queue is assigned to a printer.
- If the print writer for the output queue is started, the job prints when printer is idle.

Figure 3.17: Simplified Batch Work Management

Without **work scheduling**, the processor and main storage would be overwhelmed by too many unruly batch jobs, all demanding to be run at once. Likewise, without print spooling, printer buffers would constantly be overflowing and the processor would slow to a crawl, waiting for printers to catch up. Operators would have no option to place huge print jobs on hold until later, or to give important jobs a higher priority to make them print sooner.

You should understand that job scheduling pertains to batch jobs; interactive jobs do not go into a job queue but instead start at a workstation. In this chapter's lab, you examine output queues; so for now we concentrate on the output side of spooling.

Printer Spooling

A specialized part of the OS with its own dedicated subsystem named QSPL handles the process of **print spooling**. This subsystem stages, controls, and manages each printed report (called a **spooled**, or **spool**, **file**) created by a job before the report goes to an actual printer device.

To create printed output, a program, OS utility, or print-key function must write the output data to a **printer file**. A printer file is a type of device file that determines the attributes the printed output will have. It defines the formatting, page size, and special printing features; it also may specify an output queue. Numerous IBM-supplied printer files are available for use by general-purpose printing and system utilities. In addition, users can use the **CRTPRTF** (Create Printer File) command to create new print files for special reports or printing conditions.

A number of factors (the printing elements in Figure 3.18) control what output queue a spool file will eventually be assigned to. The user profile has a PRTDEV parameter, which can have a value of *WRKSTN (refers to the workstation device description) or *SYSVAL (refers to the system value QPRTDEV). The job's **JOBD** (Job Description) contains an output queue for the job. The number of factors might seem confusing, but this variety gives the system administrator and programmers the ability to route spool files to output queues based on the user, the job, and/or type of report. Figure 3.18 shows the sequence of spooling operations and the printing elements.

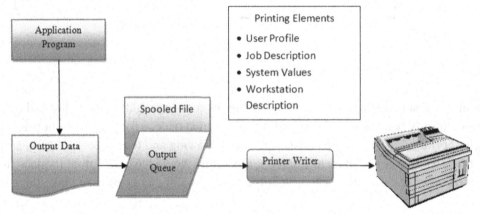

Figure 3.18: Spooling Sequence

The OS uses output queues to temporarily hold printed output from various programs. Each item of printed output in an output queue represents a single report, program compile, print-screen operation, and so on, and each of these is called a spooled file. Spooled files are "printed output" in the sense that they are formatted and ready to be printed; but until they are written to a physical printer device, they exist only as a collection of bits on magnetic storage media. You can think of output queues as areas of secondary storage managed by the OS that can grow or shrink in size as more spooled files pile up in the queue or are sent off to a physical printer device, deleted, or switched to a different output queue.

If an output queue is assigned to a printer, an OS job called a **print writer** monitors the output queue for spool files. If the print writer is started, it checks the spool file to see whether it has the correct form type for the printer, the status is RDY, and it is available to print (spool files can be available to print when they are first created, or they can be available after the job that created them has completed). If the spool file is ready to print, the print writer handles the communication between the system and the printer.

Output queues are created automatically when you describe a new printer device to the system using the **CRTDEVPRT** (Create Device Description [Printer]) command. Likewise, if the device description is deleted, the output queue is also deleted. Every printer on the system should have an output queue created in this way; the output queue takes the same name as the printer device. For example, if there is a physical printer device PRT01, there should also be an output queue PRT01.

Problems can occur when many different users' printed output is directed to the same queue. If the output queue is attached to a printer that is working, inevitably a lot of wasted printed output will be generated unless all spooled files are held (kept in the queue) from the outset. But then the number of spooled files held in the queue may become quite high; and determining what belongs to whom and managing its disposition (i.e., whether a spooled file should be printed, kept on hold, sent to a different queue/printer, or deleted) becomes difficult.

If users had no option to look at screen displays of print output (still in electronic form in an output queue) before they decided whether to go ahead and print, just think of all the paper that would be wasted from printing unnecessary output, such as nonessential program compile and error listings, useless job logs, and reports run with bad data.

Figure 3.19 shows a **WRKOUTQ** (Work with Output Queue) screen that lists one page of the spooled files from several users.

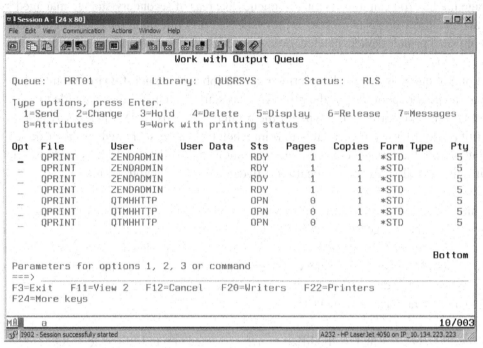

Figure 3.19: Work with Output Queue Screen

The output-queue status (shown near the top of the display) for the output queue PRT01 is currently in RLS (release) status, which means that if the queue is assigned to a printer, the printer is started and set to the correct form type; the files will print as they go to RDY (ready) status. Output queues can also have a status of HLD (held) to prevent the indiscriminate printing of files.

Notice that some of the files in the preceding screen are in RDY (Ready) status, and some are in OPN (Open) status. OPN status tells us that the program that is creating the print files is still running and has the file open.

Luckily, the existence of an output queue does not depend on a printer because you can use the CRTOUTQ command to create a new output queue in any user library to which you have authority. CRTOUTQ is not normally a restricted command, and it is generally a good idea for users (at least trained users) to create and manage their own output queues and dispose properly of their own spooled files.

In the lab for this chapter, after investigating where your printed output currently goes, you create your own output queue to hold future printed output. In the next lab (Chapter 4), you deal with handling spooled files once they have arrived in a designated output queue.

In Summary

In this chapter, we examined some of the important attributes of objects. You learned that objects are identified by library, name, and type. You saw that an object name is usually determined by the creator of the object, but that the system assigns the object type, depending on the command used to create the object. An object is usually placed in a job's current library; but if an explicit library name is used when the object is created, the object goes in that library if the user has the appropriate authority. We know that a few types of objects always go into the QSYS system library.

We also examined some useful library-list commands that let us change our current library or change and resequence our user library list. These commands include DSPLIBL, which we use to display our current library list; CHGLIBL, which allows us to change a job's library list interactively or from a CL program; CHGCURLIB, which allows us to change our current library; and EDTLIBL, which allows us to edit and resequence our library list.

We discussed basic work management. You learned that a user submits a batch job; the OS places the job in a job queue; and when system resources are available, the correct subsystem processes the job.

And we explored the mysteries of printing—from print files, to output queues, to printer writers, to physical printer devices—and how those components work with the QSPL subsystem to manage printed reports. Spool files are created in a number of ways, and a number of print elements decide in which output queue the spool file is placed. All printers should have output queues, but not all output queues have to be associated with a printer.

In the following lab, we explore job attributes and see how they can be assigned by different sources, such as the workstation device, user profile, job description, and system values. Most interactive jobs will include values from each of these sources.

Key Terms

ADDLIBLE	CRTLIB
attributes	CRTOUTQ
CHGCURLIB	CRTPRTF
CHGLIBL	CRTUSRPRF
CRTDEVPRT	DSPLIBL

DSPOBJD	print spooling
DSPUSRPRF	print writer
EDTLIBL	printer device
JOBD	printer file
layered machine architecture	qualified name
library	RMVLIBLE
licensed internal code	simple object name
logical machine	single-level storage
object	SLIC
object type	spooled (or spool) file
output queue	TIMI
physical machine	work scheduling
POWER Hypervisor	WRKOUTQ

Review Questions

1. List the advantages of an object-based OS.
2. Explain object encapsulation in the IBM i OS.
3. List the "layers" of IBM i architecture, and explain how they interact with each other.
4. What function does the POWER Hypervisor provide?
5. What does the term *single-level storage* mean?
6. When you request an object, explain how the system handles the request if you specify a *simple* object name versus a *qualified* name.
7. List and explain three points of using qualified names.
8. Under what circumstances should you always use qualified names when requesting use of an object?
9. What is an initial library list created from?
10. Explain the differences between the ADDLIBLE, CHGCURLIB, and EDTLIBL commands.
11. List the three objects and their object types that can be created only in the QSYS library.
12. What is the name of the subsystem that handles print spooling?
13. List the print elements that decide what output queue a spool file is assigned to.
14. Describe how the OS processes a batch job.
15. What does a print writer do?

Lab 3

Introduction

Every OS job has a set of **attributes** that describes the job's environment, resources, and capabilities. These attributes come from several sources, including the job description, the user profile, system values, and—for interactive jobs—the workstation device description.

In this lab, you examine some attributes of your interactive job. You also look at information about the job description, user profile, and workstation device description. All of these items are objects and, as such, have commands for each object type, including commands to display the values they contain. You use these commands to answer such questions as "What happens to the output of a print operation?" and "Why does the print output go to a certain output queue and not somewhere else?"

By learning the answers to these questions, you will find out what is necessary to control your own printed output. To gain control, you create a new object and an output queue, and change your user profile so that your future interactive jobs will use the output queue you created.

Note

In this and subsequent labs, the instruction to "print screen" refers to the OS print-screen function and *not* to a workstation printer's screen-print function. System print screen always creates a spooled file and displays the message *"Print operation complete to the default printer device file."* You must then press Reset (left Ctrl on a PC) to go on.

   We recommend that students use the IBM System i Access for Windows product for this course. The Print Screen function is not set up as a default keyboard function, and the key must be programmed. A configuration sidebar at the end of this chapter (page 120) shows how to program this function.

Part 1

Goals   Use the system print-screen function of the IBM i system printer.

           Use the Work with User Jobs screen to find your own active job.

           Examine your job status attributes.

           Locate spooled files created by your job.

Start at Sign-on screen.

Procedure   Sign on.

Start Programming Development Manager (PDM).

Change your current library to TSTLIB1.

Follow menu path to the Work with User Jobs screen.

Work with your job's status attributes.

Work with spooled files.

3.1.   Sign on as usual.

Printed output can originate from several different sources. For example, when programs or data-file specifications are compiled (created), a compile listing showing source code and error messages is generated. In addition, many user applications produce various printed reports. What all types of printed output on the system have in common is that they go into an output queue as spooled files before they are printed. To find out where your printed output goes, you will use another convenient way to create printed output: the system Print Screen function. To send a screen image to the default output queue, you can press Print Screen. We describe how to configure this key on your PC in the sidebar at the end of this chapter.

3.2.   After you have configured the Print Screen function on your PC, use Print Screen to print the Main menu. Do not expect to see anything printing right away—remember that printed output is first spooled to an output queue, where it may remain indefinitely.

3.2.a.   What message is returned?

When the keyboard locks because of the returned system message, press Reset (left Ctrl) to clear the message and unlock the keyboard.

3.3.   From the Main menu, select the General system tasks option. When the System menu appears, print the screen.

3.4.   Next, from the System menu, select the Jobs option. Print the screen from the Job menu. Then, from that menu, select the Work with jobs option.

3.4.a.   Which of the four basic screen types is this?

3.4.b.   To reach this screen directly, without taking the menu path, what would you do?

3.5.   Use extended Help to read about working with user jobs.

3.5.a.   What does the value * mean for the USER parameter?

Change the USER parameter to * for this example.

3.5.b.   Every job has a particular status at any time, depending on whether it's waiting to run, in process, or finished. Use contextual Help to examine the

STATUS parameter. As a job runs, what are the different statuses it could pass through? (*ALL means all possible statuses; it is not a type of status.)

Change the STATUS parameter value to *ACTIVE, but do not run the command yet!

3.6. Press F10 to see additional parameters. Use Help to find an explanation of the valid values for the ASTLVL parameter. (It may be useful to enlarge the Help window.) Select the value for the system user interface, and type that value over the current ASTLVL parameter value. Using the default values for the other parameters, run the command.

You should now see a Work with User Jobs screen similar to the one in Figure 3.20.

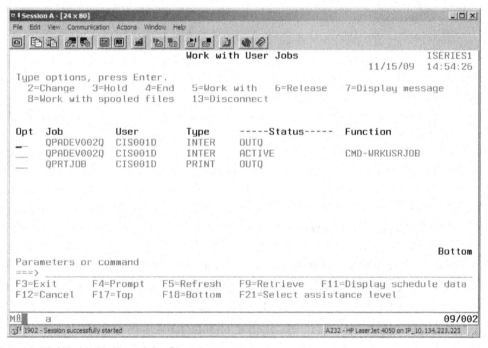

Figure 3.20: Work with User Jobs Screen

The screen layout should be the same, but the listed items will be different, and there may be several pages. (If you have arrived at a screen with quite a different appearance, back up and review the Help information and check your ASTLVL value from the WRKUSRJOB command prompt. Make sure you have chosen the system user interface value.)

3.7. From the Work with User Jobs list-processing screen, find your own active job. (Look under the User column for your user ID.) Select the option that lets you work with your job.

3.8. From the Work with Job screen, select the option to display the job status attributes of your job.

You should now see a screen similar to the one in Figure 3.21, but with different values for the parameters Job, User, and Number. These three variables identify interactive and batch jobs on the system.

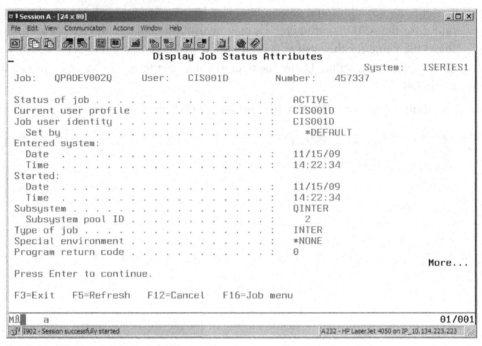

Figure 3.21: Display Job Status Attributes Screen

3.8.a.   Generally speaking, what are job status attributes? (Use Help.)

3.8.b.   The system assigns a unique serial number to every job as it starts. What number has been assigned to your job?

3.8.c.   How is the job name assigned to an interactive job? (Use Help.)

Note your job name here for future reference: _____.

Remember that the values for job name, the system-assigned job number, and the user-profile name that started the job are the three pieces of information that identify every job to the system.

3.8.d.   At what date and time did your job start?

3.8.e.   In which subsystem is your job running?

Press Enter or F12 when you have finished examining your job-status attributes.

3.9.   From the Work with Jobs screen, select the Work with spooled files option. This selection takes you to a list screen that shows spooled files created during your current job. Other spooled files you created during other jobs, and that still exist on the system, are not displayed here. So if you sign off and then sign back in and take the same menu path back to this screen, you will not see the spooled files created in the earlier session. There is, of course, a command to work with all spooled files by user. We use that command soon.

If the printer writer of the default output queue was not started, or if there was no writer attached to the output queue when you did the print screen, there should be a number of spooled files showing with status RDY.

3.9.a.   What file name does this spooled file have? _____

Now use the Display option to verify that the spooled file is actually your program that you printed in section 3.2.

The Display Spooled File display uses the first several lines of each screen for ID information. The actual spooled file starts under the ruler line. If the job requests it, four lines of user and system information are also prefixed to each spooled file. These lines appear directly under the ruler line.

Press F12 to return to the Work with Job Spooled Files display. Notice that the display tells you to which device or queue each spooled file is currently assigned. If your print files are in an output queue, their status should be RDY or HLD, and you should leave them there and not attempt to print them at this time. If a writer was attached and started and the spooled files were printed, they should show status FIN. In that case, retrieve your output from the printer, and clip it to your answer sheet (but not right now).

Part 2

Goals   Find a command from a menu of related commands.

            Examine a printer file's description to find out parameter values.

Start at   Any command line.

Procedure   Go to the CMDDSP menu.

            Display the file description for the system print-screen printer file.

To answer the question "Why did your print output go to this output queue?" you must remember that OUTQ is a parameter of both the printer file, which specifies the format of the printed output, and the job. If the printer file specifies a certain output queue, that is where any printed output using that printer file goes.

In answer to question 3.9.a, you should have written down the name of the printer file that was used to create your spooled output. Remember that the printer file is an object, and if we examine it we can see where it sent its output. Now let us find a command to display that printer file's description.

3.10. On a command line, enter the command to take you to a menu of Display (DSP) commands. You should end up at a screen like the one in Figure 3.22.

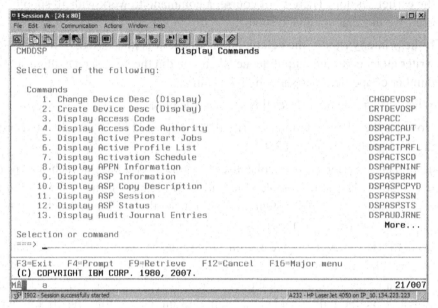

Figure 3.22: Display Commands (CMDDSP) Menu

3.11. Find the command to display a file description, and enter its number on the command line. At this point, you should see a command prompt screen like the one in Figure 3.23.

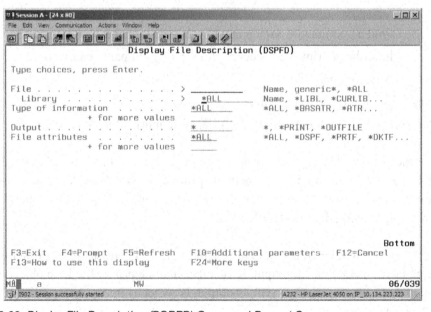

Figure 3.23: Display File Description (DSPFD) Command Prompt Screen

3.12. Enter the name of the printer file you discovered in question 3.9.a for File name. Change the Library parameter to *LIBL, and then run the command.

You should now see a display of the file description like that in Figure 3.24.

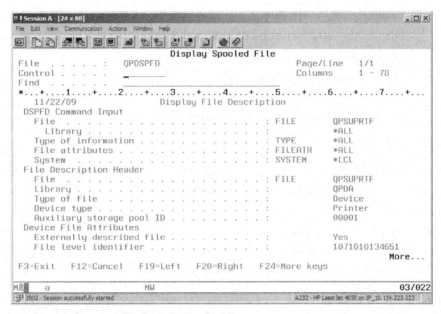

Figure 3.24 Display Spooled File Description Screen

3.12.a. What value is assigned to the Device parameter under Printer Attributes? (You'll need to Page Down.)

3.12.b. What value is assigned to the Spooled output queue under Spooling Description?

You should have found that for both parameters, this printer file defers to the job description. You could create a printer file with specific values for these and other parameters, and in most installations, there will indeed be customized printer files for special print jobs. However, QPSUPRTF is a general-purpose print file, so it points back to the controlling job for any changes to the device or output queue.

Part 3

Goals   Find the job definition attributes of your job.

Find the job description used by your job and specified by your user profile.

Examine the job description for certain parameter values.

Examine the device description of your workstation.

Find and display the system values defining the system printer.

Start at   Work with Job screen for your active job.

Procedure   Display job definition attributes.

Display your user profile.

Display the job description of your active job.

Display the device description of your workstation.

Display system value QPRTDEV.

Now, let us examine the job attributes of your current interactive job.

3.13. Press F12 until you return to the Work with Job screen for your job. If you are unable to find the screen, or you have just signed back on, enter WRKUSRJOB on the command line, and then take option 5 on the active job, which will be on the Work with User Jobs list.

3.14. From the Work with Job screen, select the Display job definition attributes option. You should now be looking at a screen like the one in Figure 3.25. Many of the attributes you see will probably be different for your job.

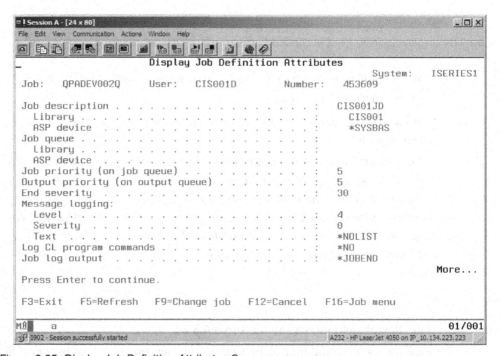

Figure 3.25: Display Job Definition Attributes Screen

These are the attributes of the job that came from the job description (and other sources) when the job was started.

3.14.a. Which job description was used to define your interactive job?

3.14.b. Which printer device was assigned?

3.14.c. What is the value for the Default output queue parameter?

3.15. Return to the Work with Job screen, and on the command line, key in the command to DiSPlay your USeR PRoFile. Remember to name the profile you want to display.

Page Down to find the Job description value. The value shown should agree with the value you discovered in question 3.14.a. Normally, if it is not overruled by a workstation entry, the user profile determines the job description to use for an interactive job.

Note the job description used by your user profile: _____.

3.16. A job description is an object and, like most objects, can be displayed. Return to the Work with Job command line. Using the GO command to reach a menu of commands related to DSP, find the command to display a job description.

3.16.a. What is the menu option of this command?

3.17. Request the command by entering its menu option. For the Job description name, use the name you found in your user profile, noted in step 3.15 above, and then run the command.

You should now be looking at a screen similar to the one in Figure 3.26.

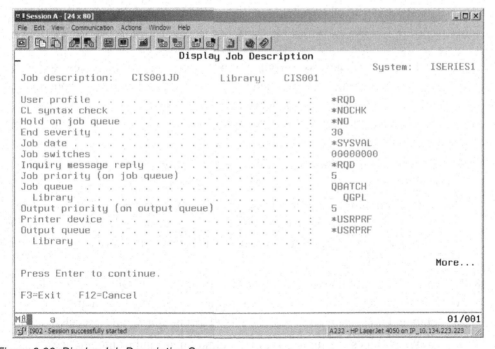

Figure 3.26: Display Job Description Screen

3.17.a. What value is given for Printer device?

3.17.b. What value is given for Output queue?

Wow! Are you starting to feel a little dizzy? Let's see if you have this right:

- Your user profile tells which job description to use when you sign on (start the interactive job).

- If the job description you noted in step 3.15 is not QDFTJOBD, your school/ installation has set up a special job description for student profiles. In that case, it is also likely that installation-specific values have replaced the defaults QDFTJOBD uses for certain parameters, such as Printer device and Output queue.

- If your user profile specifies QDFTJOBD, that job description points right back to the user profile for certain values, such as those for the printer and output queue.

Note

Remember, some of the displays you see will be a little different from the ones illustrated; this is because most organizations customize their systems. Have your instructor/mentor interpret the differences for you, but understand that although specific values can be assigned for different job attributes at different levels, the process of collecting these attributes and defining a job is the same on all systems.

This makes sense because you would not want to tie a generic job description (QDFTJOBD) used as a default by many jobs to a specific printer or output queue. This job description is generalized even further by pointing to system values (*SYSVAL) for other attributes. For example, Page Down to the last page of the job-description display.

3.17.c. What is the last attribute of the job description listed, and what value is used?

3.17.d. How might it be possible to have a tailored library list for any user that would take effect as soon as that user signs on? (Hint: The answer requires at least two steps. Keep in mind that all user profiles do not necessarily use QDFTJOBD.)

3.18. If your job description uses *USRPRF for Printer device and Output queue, let us see what values it picks up as it points back to the user profile. Press Enter to return to the command line. Then retrieve the DSPUSRPRF command, and execute it again.

3.18.a. What values are supplied for the output queue and printer device?

If your user profile has not been tailored, the default values for Output queue and Printer device point in turn to the workstation. A workstation, being a device, has an ID, or name, and also has a description associated with it. This description is an object of type *DEVD (device description) and has a display command you can use on it.

3.19. Press Enter and F12 as needed to return to the Work with Job screen. Remember where the interactive job name comes from? If you're not sure, move the cursor to the area on the screen where the job is identified, and ask for Help.

Now let us use a command to examine the device-description values. Type DSPDEVD on the command line, and prompt for the command. Enter your workstation device name on the input field. (If you are not sure about your device name, review question 3.8.c of this lab.)

You should be looking at a screen like the one in Figure 3.27, except the Device description value should be your workstation name.

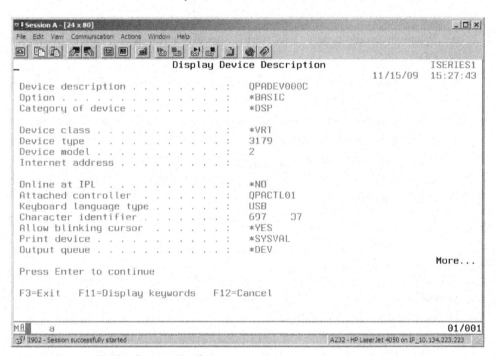

Figure 3.27: Display Device Description Screen

Notice that the value for Print device is *SYSVAL, and that the value for Output queue is *DEV. You should also see the IP address of your PC. **Note:** The IP address of the PC used for this graphic has been removed from the display.

3.19.a. Use field Help to learn what *DEV means for Output queue. What does it indicate?

3.19.b. Use field Help again to find out about the Print device value. Which system value specifies the default system printer?

3.20. Return to the command line, and run the command to display the system value you discovered in question 3.19.b. If you are not sure which command to use, execute the GO command to get to the menu of DSP commands.

3.20.a. Which printer device is currently assigned to the system value?

Because the Help information told you about value *DEV for the Output queue parameter, you realize that the value used for Output queue will be the same as the name of the printer device. Every printer device has an output queue of the same name, so by default printed output is sent to the output queue of the printer device designated as the system printer (QPRTDEV). Now you understand why your print-screen files ended up where they did, right?

Let's review (for students whose user profiles have not been tailored and are therefore still using job description QDFTJOBD):

a. When you sign on, your user profile specifies a job description to be used: QDFTJOBD.

b. In the process of assembling job attributes, QDFTJOBD points back to the user profile for Printer and Output queue attributes.

c. The user-profile default values for Printer and Output queue point to the workstation where the job starts.

d. If the Print device and Output queue values for the workstation device description have not been changed, they both, in effect, point to the system value QPRTDEV.

e. Finally, the value assigned to system value QPRTDEV is what is used to define the Printer and Output queue attributes for the job.

Suppose we decided that every user should have his own output queue. Then, if you wanted to have all your printed output sent to your own output queue, where would be the best place to effect this change?

You could set up a separate job description for each individual user, with the user's own output queue specified in the job description. This technique would interrupt the chain of pointers at point b in the review list above. But that would require a potentially large number of job descriptions, which would result in considerable system overhead and system maintenance.

As an alternative, you could change the workstation device description at point d, if you knew that every user used only a single workstation and, conversely, that each workstation was used by no other user. But that's an unlikely scenario, and you would prefer to have a user's output go to her own output queue, regardless of which device she may be working at.

Therefore, point c looks like the best bet. If you change the user profile's Output queue value to the name of an output queue created just for that user, the current reference to the workstation will no longer apply. The job description will look at the user profile, the user profile will name a specific output queue, and that will be the output queue used by the job. Wherever that user signs on, his printed output will go to the same output queue—unless, of course, the printer file used for a certain print operation (e.g., QSYSPRT) names a specific output queue instead of the default, *JOB.

We will use this method to manage output created in this class. Before you make the change to your user profile, however, you need to create your new output queue.

Part 4

Goals	Verify your current library.
	Create an output queue.
	Change your user profile to use the new output queue.
Start at	Any system command line.
Procedure	Display your library list.
	Create an output queue.
	Change the user profile.

We would like to use the default current library when we create an output queue, but it would be prudent to check first to make sure our library is indeed the current library for our job.

3.21. First, run the DSPLIBL (Display Library List) command to make sure your own library is the current library in your library list. If it is not, stop right now and go back to Lab 2. Repeat the steps to create your own library (the system will tell you if it already exists), and to change the Current library parameter of your user profile. Then use the CHGCURLIB (Change Current Library) command to assign your library as the current library.

3.22. Now type the command to CReaTe an OUTput Queue on the command line, and prompt for parameters. Use your user name, the same name as the library you created in Lab 2, as the name of the output queue. (For example, a student output queue might be CIS001Q in library CIS001.)

3.22.a. What value is supplied for the Library parameter? With the exception of the few object types that always go into library QSYS, the system defaults to the current library when you create an object. You want to put this new output queue in the library you created earlier.

Press F10 for additional parameters, and then Page Down; locate the Text 'description' parameter.

Type your full name and the class name in the Text field. Then press Enter.

3.22.b. What message is displayed on the screen?

If the message does *not* indicate successful creation of the output queue, you need to ask your instructor/mentor for help.

3.23. Now change the user-profile value by prompting for the CHGPRF (Change Profile) command. You need to display additional parameters and Page Down to the Output queue parameter. Be sure to change only the Output queue, not the Print device.

Type in your output-queue name, and then press Enter.

Note

Remember, many user-profile changes, including this one, do not take effect until the next sign-on; so even if you printed more screens now without signing off, they would still end up in the same place as before.

In the Chapter 4 lab, you will make sure your new output queue is functioning properly, and you will take care of those print-screen spooled files still hanging out in the default output queue. But for now, you may return to a menu with a sign-off selection, or just enter the SIGNOFF command from any command line.

Programming the Keyboard Print Screen Function

We recommend that students use the IBM System i Access for Windows product for this course. The Print Screen function is not set up as a default keyboard function, and the key must be programmed. The following steps show you how to set up your 5250 session to accomplish this.

Start keyboard remapping:

Start a 5250 session, and click on the Map Keyboard icon (Figure 3.28).

Figure 3.28: Remap Keyboard Functions

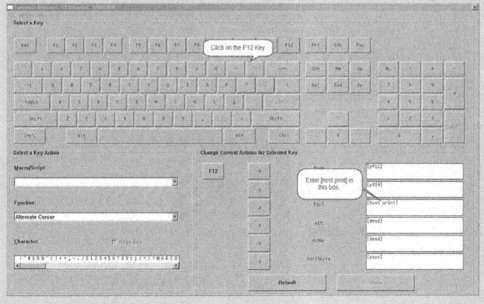

Figure 3.29: Remapping the F12 Key

Keyboard mapping screen:

Figure 3.29 shows the screen that allows you to remap the 5250 emulators screen. The first step is to select the key you want to remap; in this case, you are remapping the F12 key. Notice that we have selected the Ctrl section and we have entered [host print] in the field. It is not necessary to use the Ctrl + F12 function key. Any key combination that you rarely use or that is difficult to accidentally press is acceptable.

When the keyboard is mapped in this way, pressing Ctrl + F12 causes the emulator to send the [host print] string to the server, in turn causing the contents of the 5250 screen to be sent to your printer output queue.

Saving keyboard mapping:

Click File in the top left-hand corner of the screen, and then click Save, as Figure 3.30 shows. You will then be presented with the screen you see in Figure 3.31.

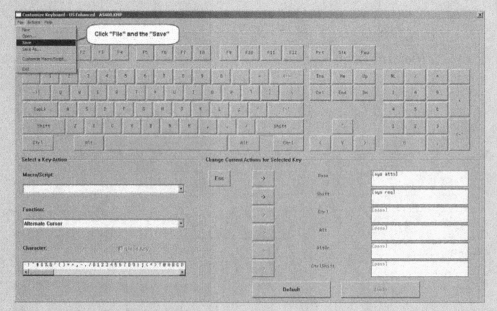

Figure 3.30: Save F12 Remapping

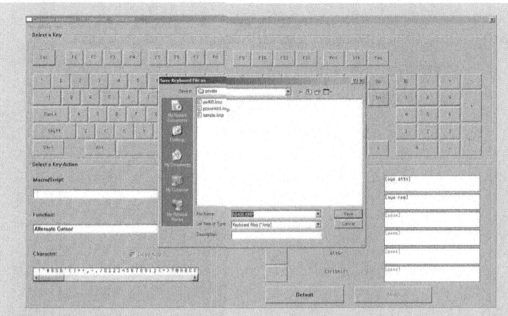

Remap Figure 3.31: Save F12 Remapping, Continued

Saving keyboard mapping, continued:

You will save the changes using the default keyboard file; you could rename this file with a different file name.

Remember, any changes to this file will affect anyone who uses the emulator on the computer.

The screen in Figure 3.32 shows the result of pressing Ctrl + F12. Notice the Input inhibited icon in the lower left-hand corner of the screen. Pressing Ctrl will clear this icon.

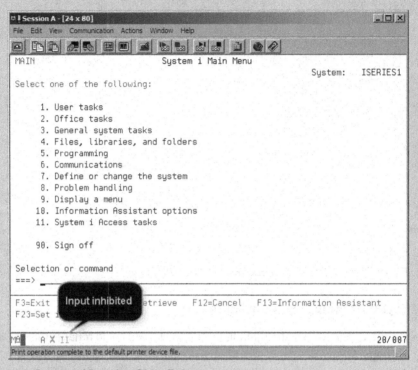

Figure 3.32: Results of Pressing Ctrl + F12

Displaying the Print Screen results:

At the command line, type WRKOUTQ and your output queue name. You will see your output queue, as the screen print in Figure 3.33 shows.

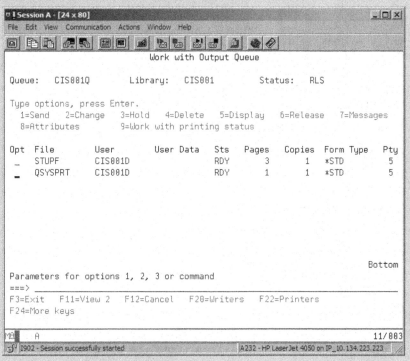

Figure 3.33: Contents of Output Queue

Displaying contents of the print file:

If you put a 5 on the second print file (QSYSPRT), you will then see the contents of the print file, as in Figure 3.34.

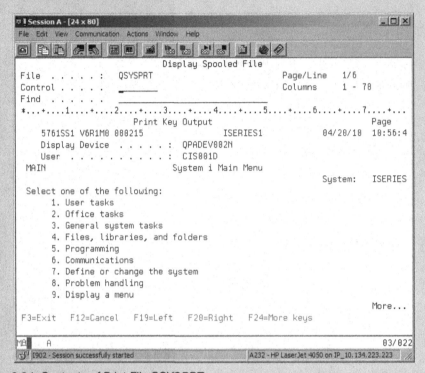

Figure 3.34: Contents of Print File QSYSPRT

You can see that the screen showing the contents of the print file (Figure 3.34) is the screen that was displayed when you pressed Ctrl + F12 in Figure 3.32.

CHAPTER 4

Handling Spooled Files

Overview

In this chapter, we discuss how to handle spooled files once they reach output queues. We look at how you can use the WRKOUTQ (Work with Output Queue) and WRKSPLF (Work with Spooled Files) commands to manage spooled files. We explain how to use several options frequently taken from WRKOUTQ and WRKSPLF list screens, and we examine how your choice of assistance level affects the appearance of these screens. We also discuss printer functions and look at options available for controlling printers and responding to messages.

Objectives

Students will be able to

- Explain the components of printer spooling
- Describe the differences between the WRKOUTQ and WRKSPLF commands
- Examine the contents of an output queue and release, hold, and reroute spooled files to output queues with attached writers
- Work with a list of printers
- Display printer messages and print selected files
- Explain the use of the CLROUTQ command
- Recognize the difference between screen formats when Basic or Intermediate assistance level is selected for certain display screens

Printer Files

In Chapter 3, we discussed printer device files and output queues. A short review of these IBM i objects might be useful here.

A *printer device file* is an object that specifies format and other print attributes of printed output produced by an application program, utility, or system operation. You can create and change printer device files by using the **CRTPRTF** (Create Printer File) and **CHGPRTF** (Change Printer File) commands, respectively.

For example, look at what you can do with the CHGPRTF command. In the previous lab, you learned that printer file QSYSPRT is used to control the format of output generated by the Print key. Figure 4.1 shows the first screen of the CHGPRTF display for QSYSPRT.

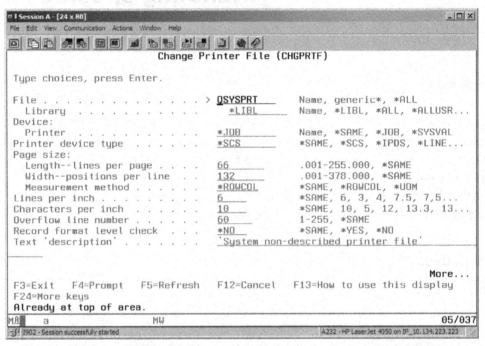

Figure 4.1: Change Printer File (CHGPRTF) Command Display for Printer File QSYSPRT

On this first screen, you can see some of the formatting parameters common to printer files: lines per page (66), print positions per line (132), lines per inch (6), and characters per inch (10). Subsequent screens show parameters that control attributes such as print quality, font, duplexing, overlay, output queue, form type, and number of copies.

The physical layout of lines and pages of printed output is determined when data from an application or utility is sent to a particular printer file. (The application itself determines the data sent and how individual fields will be formatted on each printed line.) The formatted output—a **spooled file** still in electronic form (i.e., not yet printed)—is then sent to an output queue. The diagram in Figure 4.2 illustrates this process.

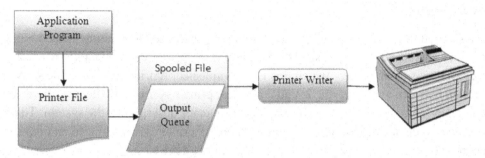

Figure 4.2: Overview of IBM i Printing Process

The print writer is a part of the operating system dedicated to the control and management of printed output. From the time printed output is formatted by a printer file and placed on an output queue, and until it leaves the system, the print writer monitors it. The print writer runs in its own subsystem, called **QSPL**, and functions independently within control parameters established at the system and job levels. Users and operators can interact with the spooler via several CL commands. Figure 4.3 shows the subsystem QSPL with three active writers.

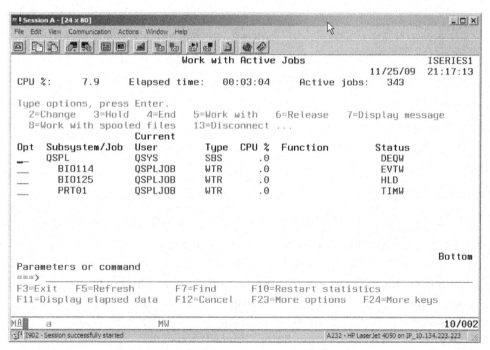

Figure 4.3: Active Writers in QSPL Subsystem

Printer Writer

After a spooled file has arrived at an output queue, the next step in creating printed output deals with transferring it to a physical printer device. A spooler component known as a **printer writer** is the means by which this is accomplished. A printer writer is the software connection between an output queue and a physical printer. A printer writer is generated automatically when a printer device (a physical printer) is described to the system. The creation of this device description generates not only a printer writer but also an output queue, both of which have the same name as the printer device.

We can look at the device description by using the **DSPDEVD** (Display Device Description) command. Figure 4.4 shows the device description for a printer named PRT01.

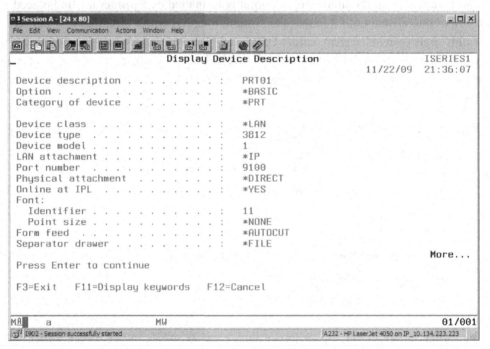

Figure 4.4: Display Device Description Screen for Printer PRT01

This description in the figure shows only the first screen of the Display Device Description command's output for printer PRT01. Notice that this is a LAN-attached printer. Most printers on today's system are LAN or network attached. This description was created using the **CRTDEVPRT** (Create Device Description [Printer]) command.

At the time the device was created via the CRTDEVPRT command, both a printer writer and an output queue with the same name came into existence. The printer writer will always be "connected" to the physical printer device that generated it. Normally, on the output side, the writer will be "attached" to the output queue created along with the printer device description (i.e., the output queue with the same name as the printer).

Changing Writers

As you know, you can create output queues that have no relationship to a physical printer and, therefore, have no printer writer attached to them. You created such an output queue in your previous lab (Chapter 3).

Using the **CHGWTR** (Change Writer) command, you can attach the printer writer for printer PRT01 to output queue CIS001Q or any other output queue. If you attach printer writer PRT01 to output queue CIS001Q, for instance, the writer begins sending spooled files that are ready to be printed from the newly attached queue (CIS001Q) to printer PRT01. As the illustration in Figure 4.5 indicates, you can use the CHGWTR command to attach a printer writer to a different output queue.

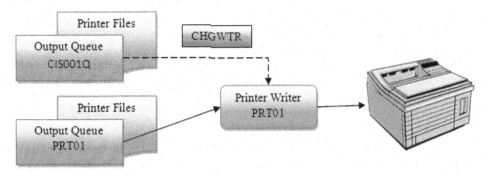

Figure 4.5: Overview of CHGWTR Command

This technique can be useful in certain cases. In another example, suppose the writer for printer device PRT01 is currently attached to printer output queue PRT01. Now suppose that several spooled files that need a nonstandard paper stock are in output queue NITEQ. Perhaps a night batch process created them. When the operator is ready to print these spooled files, she can simply turn off the printer, change forms, and then change the writer to the output queue that is holding the reports (NITEQ). Because the writer is now attached to output queue NITEQ, the printer will print only the reports in the NITEQ output queue—those needing the special forms—when it is started. In this way, the operator avoids having to hold or change the priority of other spooled files in printer output queue PRT01. Another advantage is that no new spooled files will enter the printer output queue and start printing on the special forms. When the NITEQ reports have been printed, the operator can return to the standard stock and once again use the CHGWTR command to change the writer from NITEQ back to printer output queue PRT01.

As you can see from this example, changing writers involves some responsibility. Once spooled files have been printed, the writer must be changed, typically back to the printer output queue to which it was attached originally. This process could lead to problems of priority control and authorization. If, for example, someone changed the writer to his own output queue before it had finished printing, the spooled files in the originally attached printer output queue would not print, and users waiting for their printed reports would be upset. To prevent such problems from occurring, many installations let only a system operator start, stop, or change printer writers.

So if you (or other individual users) are not authorized to change writers, how do you print a spooled file when your own output queue has no writer attached to it? Instead of changing the writer, you change the spooled file's output queue. Using the **CHGSPLFA** (Change Spooled File Attributes) command, you can cause a spooled file to be sent to an output queue that has an attached, active writer. This normally would be the output queue of a printer device, as the illustration in Figure 4.6 indicates.

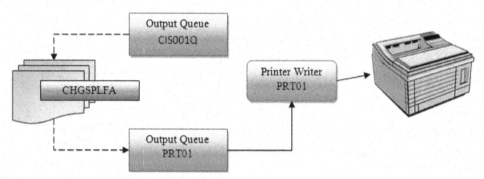

Figure 4.6: Overview of CHGSPLFA Command

In this illustration, spooled files in output queue CIS001Q can be changed (sent) to output queue PRT01. This printer output queue has an active writer, and the spooled files will be printed on printer PRT01 when their turn comes.

Changing Spooled Files

The IBM i operating system supports several important commands that let you change or invoke spooler operations and make changes to spooled print files. The work-with commands let you perform most of these operations from list-processing screens; this capability offers a convenient and fast way to redirect spooled files; change the attributes of spooled files; or hold, release, or display spooled files.

Two commands similar in function but different in the way they select spooled files to include in their lists are

- **WRKOUTQ** (Work with Output Queue)—This command lists all spooled files in a named output queue, regardless of which user's job created them.
- **WRKSPLF** (Work with Spooled Files)—This command lists all spooled files created by a user, regardless of which output queues they are in.

Working with Output Queues

Figure 4.7 shows the WRKOUTQ command prompt screen.

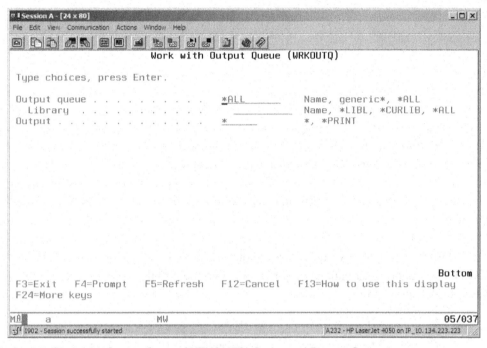

Figure 4.7: Work with Output Queue (WRKOUTQ) Command Prompt Screen

If you type WRKOUTQ and press F4, you will notice that the Output queue parameter defaults to *ALL. If you ran the command as is, it would gather information about all the output queues on the system and list them in alphabetical order by queue. Depending on the number of queues on your system, this command could take a little while to process. In addition, you may not be authorized to use any output queue other than your own anyway.

Therefore, when you are using the WRKOUTQ command, always be sure to specify which output queue you want to work with by providing an Output queue parameter value rather than taking the default (*ALL). For example, if you want to list all print files in output queue PRT01, you can enter the command in positional notation on the command line as

WRKOUTQ PRT01

The output would first be displayed in a format similar to that in Figure 4.8.

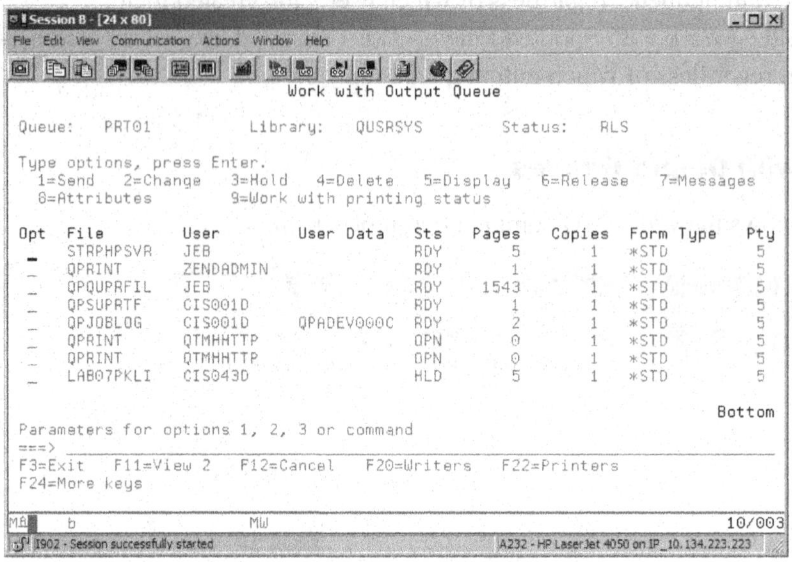

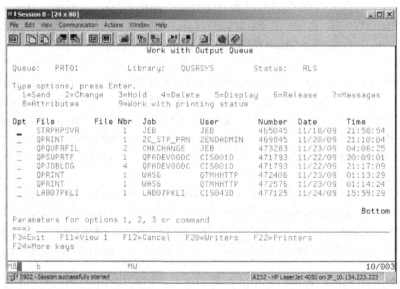

Figure 4.8: Work with Output Queue List Screen for Output Queue PRT01

You can see that several different file names from several different users are in the PRT01 output queue.

Figure 4.9 shows another view of the list; we obtained this view by pressing F11, which displays the job name, user name, and job number (in the middle three columns) of the job that created the spooled file.

Figure 4.9: Work with Output Queue Screen, View 2 of Output Queue PRT01

You should recall that we use these three values to identify a job on the system. You can see that when a job creates several different spooled files—each with the same job name, user name, and job number—they can be identified within the job by the spooled file number, which is assigned to each spooled file consecutively as it is placed in a queue. The spooled file number appears in the File Nbr column in Figure 4.9. Regardless of which output queue a spooled file is written to—and a job can write spooled files to several different output queues—each spooled file is assigned a unique file number within the job. This file number, along with the job name, user name, and job number, distinguishes any spooled file from all other spooled files on the system.

For example, QPSUPRTF and QPJOBLOG, with file numbers 1 and 4 in Figure 4.9, identify the different print files user CIS001D created during job number 471793. These spooled files are both in output queue PRT01, but CIS001D may have other spooled files (numbered 2, 3, 5, and so on) in other output queues.

The options available from the screen in Figure 4.9 let you perform several useful operations on individual or groups of spooled files. A brief description of the options follows in Table 4.1. (You can use Help to get more detailed information.)

Table 4.1: Options Available When Using the WRKOUTQ Command	
Option	Function
1=Send	Used to route a copy of a file across a network.
2=Change	Used to change attributes of a spooled file, such as number of copies, whether the file should be kept on the queue after printing, which queue to move it to, and so on.
3=Hold	Used to prevent printing of a file—for example, to wait until special forms can be mounted on a printer.
4=Delete	Used to get rid of unnecessary spooled files. You will be asked to confirm; if you do, specified spooled files will be erased from the system.
5=Display	Used to view a spooled file. With this option, you can make sure that the file you are planning to hold, delete, or send is the right one.
6=Release	Used to let a held file (option 3) go ahead and be printed.
7=Messages	Used to view messages that may be generated if a problem arises in the printing of a file.
8=Attributes	Used to check details of formatting and printer requirements for a spooled file.
9=Work with printing status	Used to find out where a file is in the printing process. For example, a file may be waiting for a message reply or waiting for files ahead of it to be printed.

Although the WRKOUTQ command lists spooled files in the specified queue that belong to other users, you may not be authorized to take options on these files. For example, if user CIS001D, having no special authority, tried to display user JEB's spooled file STRPHPSVR (listed in Figure 4.10), the message *"Not authorized to spooled file"* would appear.

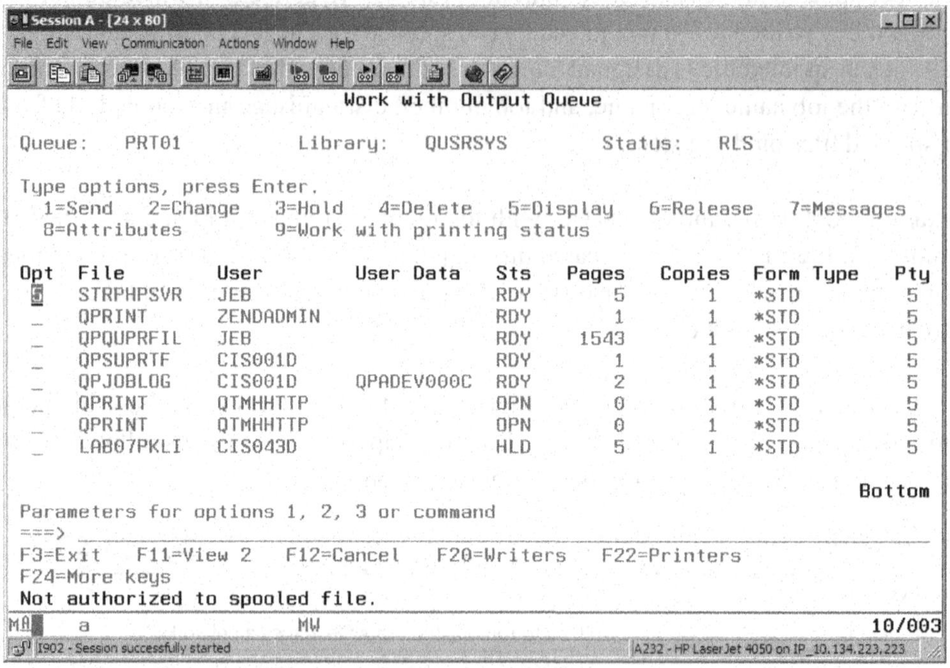

```
I Session A - [24 x 80]                                                    _ □ ×
File  Edit  View  Communication  Actions  Window  Help

                       Work with Output Queue

Queue:    PRT01          Library:    QUSRSYS        Status:    RLS

Type options, press Enter.
  1=Send   2=Change    3=Hold    4=Delete   5=Display   6=Release   7=Messages
  8=Attributes         9=Work with printing status

Opt  File       User       User Data   Sts   Pages   Copies   Form Type   Pty
 5   STRPHPSVR  JEB                     RDY       5      1     *STD          5
 _   QPRINT     ZENDADMIN               RDY       1      1     *STD          5
 _   QPQUPRFIL  JEB                     RDY    1543      1     *STD          5
 _   QPSUPRTF   CIS001D                 RDY       1      1     *STD          5
 _   QPJOBLOG   CIS001D    QPADEV000C   RDY       2      1     *STD          5
 _   QPRINT     QTMHHTTP                OPN       0      1     *STD          5
 _   QPRINT     QTMHHTTP                OPN       0      1     *STD          5
 _   LAB07PKLI  CIS043D                 HLD       5      1     *STD          5

                                                                       Bottom
Parameters for options 1, 2, 3 or command
===> _____
F3=Exit    F11=View 2    F12=Cancel    F20=Writers    F22=Printers
F24=More keys
Not authorized to spooled file.
MA  a                    MW                                            10/003
I902 - Session successfully started        A232 - HP LaserJet 4050 on IP_10.134.223.223
```

Figure 4.10: Work with Output Queue Screen with "Not Authorized" Message

Normally, this limitation would not cause a problem because users would work only with their own spooled files and wouldn't need to perform list options on other users' spooled files. The system operator, however, may need to hold or change the priorities of spooled files to schedule printing efficiently. The operator would therefore have **spool-control special authority** over files spooled to a printer output queue. This special authority, granted through the user profile, lets the operator take necessary actions (e.g., hold, change, release, delete) on spooled files in the output queue.

When you use the WRKOUTQ command, it is important to be familiar with the available function keys. You have already seen that F11 provides an alternate view of the list, and you can see that F3=Exit and F12=Cancel work as usual. You can use F20 to examine the status of all printer writers on the system—whether they are active or on a job queue. If you need to check the status of printers on the system, F22 takes you to such a list screen, which appears either as Figure 4.11 for Basic assistance level or Figure 4.12 for Intermediate assistance level. (We talk more about assistance levels later in this chapter.)

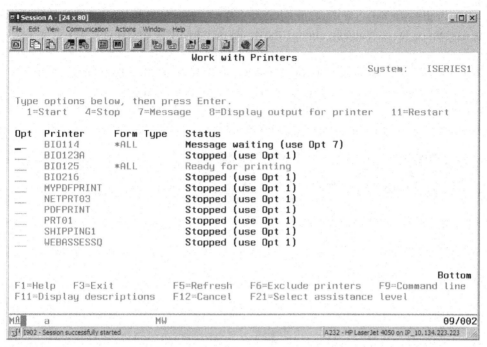

Figure 4.11: Work with Printers Screen, Basic Assistance Level

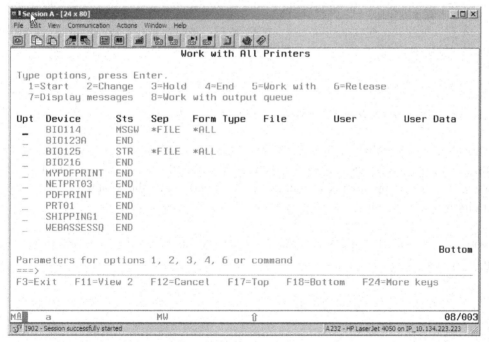

Figure 4.12: Work with All Printers Screen, Intermediate Assistance Level

The items in the two lists are the same, but both the format and the options vary, depending on the assistance level. You can change the assistance level by pressing F21.

When a printer has a status of MSGW or Message waiting, as printer BIO114 does, choosing option 7 from either screen lets you view the message—and respond to it if you are authorized. Selecting option 7—in this case, for printer BIO114—results in the Additional Message Information screen you see in Figure 4.13.

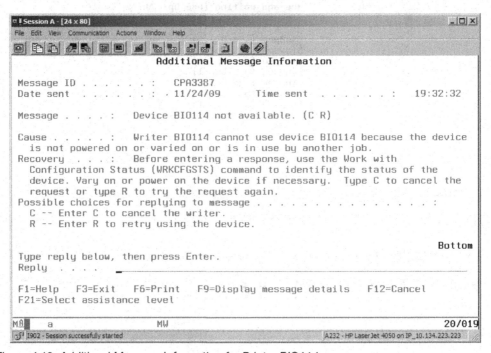

Figure 4.13: Additional Message Information for Printer BIO114

The message tells you that the printer "*device is not powered on,*" and it gives you two options for reply: C for *cancel* and R for *retry*. If you were the person responsible for this printer or the system operator, you could respond by turning on the printer and then typing R for Retry on the reply line.

As you can see, using F22 gives you an easy way to check the status of printers from your own output queue.

Working with Spooled Files

The other work-with command, WRKSPLF (Work with Spooled Files), has a format similar to WRKOUTQ, but with one major difference: WRKSPLF lists all spooled files belonging to a single user, regardless of which output queues they are in. The command prompt for the WRKSPLF command looks like the one in Figure 4.14.

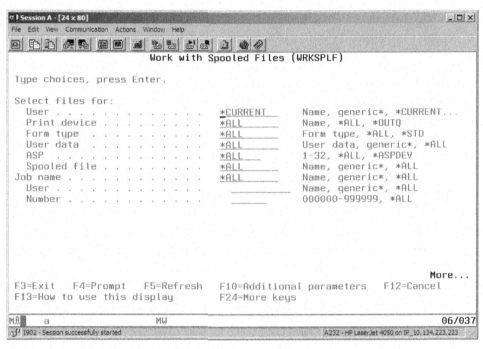

Figure 4.14: Work with Spooled Files (WRKSPLF) Command Prompt Screen

Notice that the value of the first parameter, User, defaults to *CURRENT. The OS Help text will tell you that *CURRENT means *"Only files created by the user running this command are selected."* The default values of *ALL for the other parameters mean that the list will not be restricted by printer device, form type, or user data. So when you enter the WRKSPLF command on a command line with no parameters (i.e., you take the defaults), you get a list of all your own spooled files. Such a display would be similar to the one in Figure 4.15.

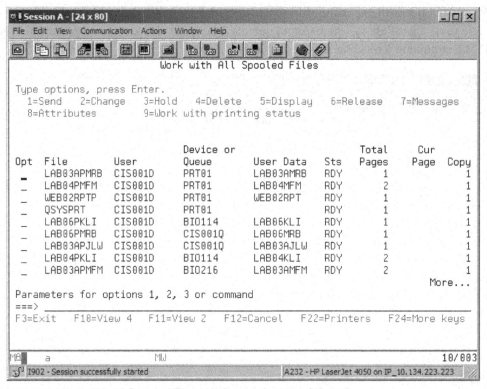

Figure 4.15: Work with All Spooled Files List Screen for User CIS001D

As you can see in this partial list, spooled files belonging to user CIS001D are on four different output queues. The spooled files are listed in the order created: older files at the top of the list, within priority, within status. The WRKSPLF command, therefore, is especially useful when you need to locate print files that you may have created under different jobs, using different output queues.

The available options for the WRKSPLF command are the same as for the WRKOUTQ command, and they work the same way.

Changing Spooled File Attributes

Earlier, we talked about changing a spooled file to an output queue with an active writer. For example, if you wanted to print spooled file LAB04PKLI, which (according to the Work with All Spooled Files screen in Figure 4.15) is in output queue BIO114, you would select option 2 (Change) on the Work with All Spooled Files screen. This action would bring you to the Change Spooled File Attributes screen in Figure 4.16.

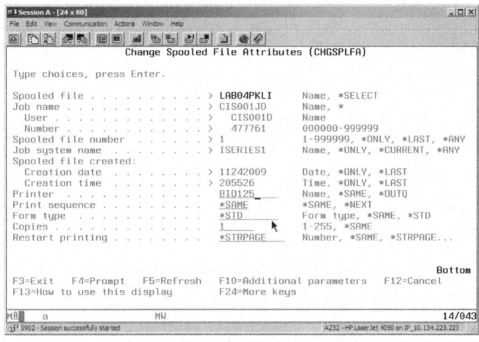

Figure 4.16: Change Spooled File Attributes (CHGSPLFA) Screen for Spooled File LAB04PKLI

The cursor in Figure 4.16 is positioned on the first input-allowed field, the Printer parameter value, which is now set to BIO125. Because we want to print this file, we have typed over the default setting of BIO114 and specified the name of BIO125, which has an active writer. When you press Enter, the command is executed, and you are returned to the Work with

All Spooled Files list screen. This screen, which you see in Figure 4.17, indicates that file LAB04PKLI has a status of *CHG (changed) and that the Device or Queue is now BIO125.

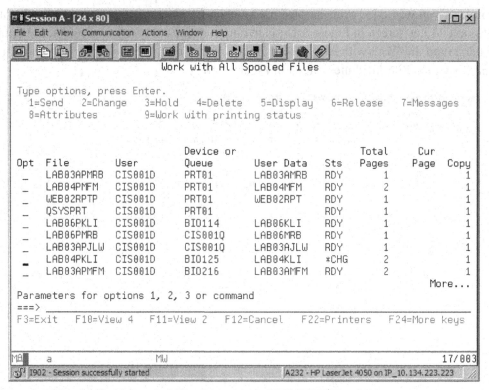

Figure 4.17: Work with All Spooled Files Screen with QPSUPRTF Changed

You should understand that although we changed the Printer parameter value, the file LAB06PMRB is actually sent to the output queue of the originally specified printer. If other large print jobs of an equal or higher priority are already on the queue, if the queue itself is on hold, or if the printer device is out of paper or not turned on, your spooled file—although ready—might not be printed right away.

If you refresh your screen by pressing F5, and the printer is ready to go, with no backlog of print files, your spooled file will probably show a status of PRT for printing.

Note that spooled files initially sent to nonprinter output queues—such as CIS001Q or QEZJOBLOG, as you see in Figures 4.15 and 4.17—will display value *OUTQ for the Printer

parameter on the Change Spooled File Attributes screen. Also, the additional parameter
Output queue (and Library) will be displayed without a request for additional parameters.
This just means that the spooled file is not assigned to a specific printer and is currently in
the queue indicated by the Output queue parameter value.

You can perform several other useful functions using the Change option. This time, we
will look at the attributes for spooled file LAB06PKLI. Figure 4.18 shows the resulting screen.

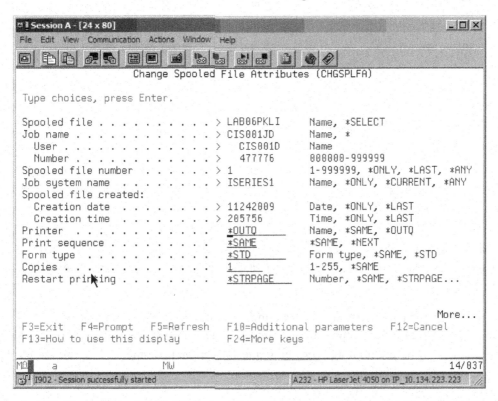

Figure 4.18: Change Spooled File Attributes (CHGSPLFA) Screen for Spooled File LAB06PKLI

From this screen, you can specify a different type of form on which to print, change the
number of copies, or specify where to restart in case printing was interrupted. The Printer
parameter allows you to move the spool file to a printer.

Notice that More... is displayed at the bottom right-hand corner of the screen; pressing PgDn (or Page Down) will display Figure 4.19.

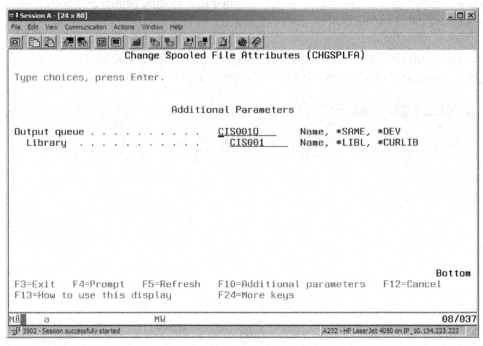

Figure 4.19: Change Spooled File Attributes (CHGSPLFA) Screen for Spooled File LAB06PKLI, Continued

The Output queue parameter lets you send this print file to another output queue not attached to a writer; for example, if you want to send a report to a co-worker's output queue for her to review before printing. You can request additional parameters by pressing F9. The next screen (Figure 4.20) provides even more parameters.

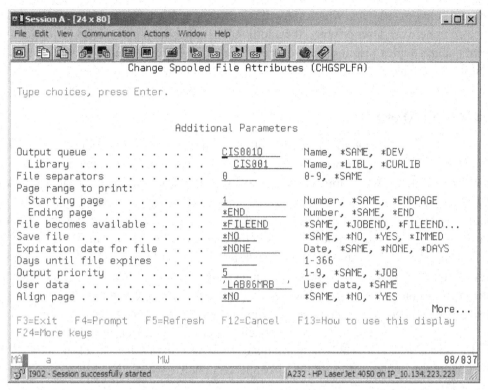

Figure 4.20: Change Spooled File Attributes (CHGSPLFA) Screen for Spooled File LAB06PKLI, Continued

Two of the more useful parameters here let you specify a range of pages to be printed (Page range to print) and retain a spooled file in an output queue after printing (Save file). If the Save file parameter is set to *NO (the normal default), the spooled file will no longer be available after printing.

As the operator, you can use the Output priority parameter to schedule when certain files should be printed in relation to other files. For example, if several files are waiting to be printed, you can give an important file a higher priority, moving it ahead of others in the queue. The highest priority is 1, and the lowest priority is 9.

Another useful parameter is User data. This parameter lets you add up to 10 characters of identifying information to a spooled file. You can then use this identifying information to organize spooled files by function or application, and to select specific spooled files to be listed by specifying a value for the User data parameter on the WRKSPLF command.

There are additional screens, which we will not discuss at this time. Today's systems are connected to network laser printers; the additional pages contain parameters for options such as print quality, duplex printing, and source drawers. Take a few minutes and look at the additional parameters.

Clear Output Queue

We first mentioned the **CLROUTQ** (Clear Output Queue) command in Chapter 2; it is useful to clear all of the print files from an output queue with one command. When we were discussing the WRKOUTQ command, we noted that you need the proper authority to work with output files. There is also security on the output queue. When you create an output queue, one of the parameters is **AUTCHK** (Authority to check). This parameter specifies the authority required to control all of the files in the queue. When the system is creating an output queue, the default value for the AUTCHK parameter is *OWNER. This means that to issue the CLROUTQ command on an output queue, the user issuing the command must also be the owner of the output queue. The other value for the AUTCHK command is *DTAAUT. When this parameter value is specified, any user with add, read, and delete authority can issue the CRLOUTQ command. As we discussed earlier in the chapter, we do not want users to indiscriminately be able to manipulate spool files or, in this case, clear output queues. However, a user with spool-control special authority would be able to issue this command.

Assistance Levels

As we noted earlier, two of the three operating system assistance levels—**Basic assistance level** and **Intermediate assistance level**—work with the spool commands. The assistance level determines the amount of information displayed, and how the information is formatted. The **QASTLVL system value** sets the default assistance level, but the default can be changed for individual users through a user-profile parameter. You can also change the assistance level as you view screens that have alternate assistance levels by pressing F21.

Let us look again at the Work with All Spooled Files display in Figure 4.17. Like the Work with All Printers screen, the WRKSPLF command display can appear in two different formats, depending on the assistance level. The difference in formats for the WRKSPLF command is quite pronounced. If you press F21 and select Basic, you see a screen like the one in Figure 4.21.

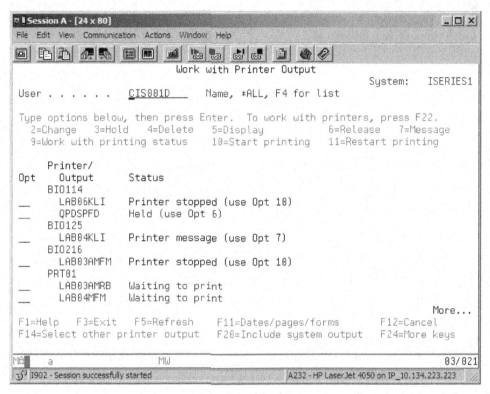

Figure 4.21: Work with Printer Output Screen, Basic Assistance Level

This screen, titled Work with Printer Output, organizes its list by printer. If a spooled file is not in a printer output queue, you are told only that it is *"Not assigned."* You cannot tell which output queue it is in. The alternate display (F11) shows date and time but still does not specify the output queue.

Also, if you select the Change option for a file listed on the Work with Printer Output screen in Basic assistance level, you can change only a limited number of attributes.

Figure 4.22 shows the screen that results when you specify the Change option for file
LAB03AMRB.

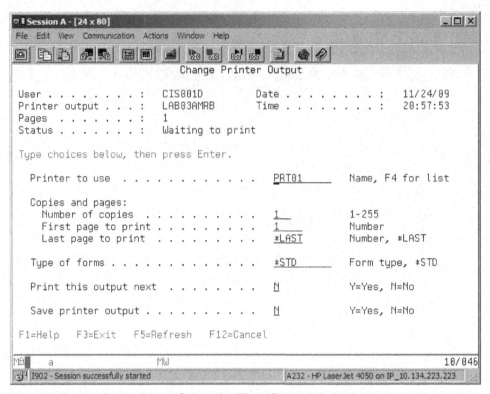

```
 ⌐ I Session A - [24 x 80]                                          _ □ x
  File  Edit  View  Communication  Actions  Window  Help
 ┌──┐ ┌──┐┌──┐ ┌──┐┌──┐ ┌──┐┌──┐ ┌──┐ ┌──┐┌──┐ ┌──┐┌──┐ ┌──┐ ┌──┐┌──┐
 │  │ │  ││  │ │  ││  │ │  ││  │ │  │ │  ││  │ │  ││  │ │  │ │  ││  │
 └──┘ └──┘└──┘ └──┘└──┘ └──┘└──┘ └──┘ └──┘└──┘ └──┘└──┘ └──┘ └──┘└──┘
                          Change Printer Output

   User . . . . . . . . . :   CIS001D       Date . . . . . . . . :   11/24/09
   Printer output . . . :     LAB03AMRB     Time . . . . . . . . :   20:57:53
   Pages  . . . . . . . :     1
   Status . . . . . . . :     Waiting to print

   Type choices below, then press Enter.

     Printer to use  . . . . . . . . . . .    PRT01        Name, F4 for list

     Copies and pages:
       Number of copies  . . . . . . . . .    1            1-255
       First page to print . . . . . . . .    1            Number
       Last page to print  . . . . . . . .    *LAST        Number, *LAST

     Type of forms . . . . . . . . . . . .    *STD         Form type, *STD

     Print this output next  . . . . . . .    N            Y=Yes, N=No

     Save printer output . . . . . . . . .    N            Y=Yes, N=No

   F1=Help    F3=Exit    F5=Refresh    F12=Cancel

 MA▌    a              MW                                           18/046
 ┌♪│ I902 - Session successfully started        A232 - HP LaserJet 4050 on IP_10.134.223.223
```

Figure 4.22: Change Printer Output Screen for File LAB03AMRB, Basic Assistance Level

Notice the differences between this screen and the screens for LAB06PKLI in Figures 4.18
and 4.20. The name of the screen is Change Printer Output, rather than Change Spooled
File Attributes, as you saw at the Intermediate assistance level, and this screen displays
fewer parameters. For example, no option is available to send this spooled file to another
nonprinter output queue, nor can you change priority or add identifying user data as you can
on the CHGSPLFA prompt screen.

For users new to the OS, the Basic assistance level's Work with Printer Output interface will
be adequate. More advanced users set their assistance level to Intermediate when they are
working with spooled files.

There is a third level, called the **Advanced assistance level**, which allows more list entries per screen. This "expert" interface does not display option numbers and function keys on certain screens. If a screen does not have an advanced display, the settings for the intermediate level are used.

An example of the different information displayed for different assistance levels is the **DSPSYSSTS** (Display System Status) command, which displays the status of the system. The information displayed includes the current CPU usage, current ASP (disk) usage, and number of jobs in the system. You can set the assistance level when the command is run by including the ASTLVL*(xxxxx)* parameter, where *xxxxx* can be *BASIC, *INTERMED, or *ADVANCED. Figure 4.23 shows the results of keying DSPSYSSTS ASTLVL(*BASIC). Each value in Figure 4.23 is descriptive and helps users understand what the value means.

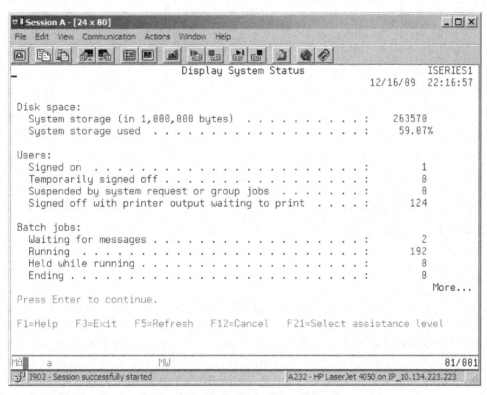

Figure 4.23: Display System Status Screen, Basic Assistance Level

Figure 4.24 shows the results when the command is run using the form DSPSYSSTS ASTLVL(*ADVANCED). Notice that the only function key displayed is F21, which allows the user to switch between assistance levels.

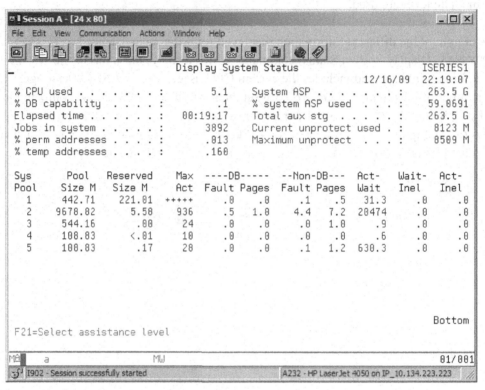

Figure 4.24: Display System Status Screen, Advanced Assistance Level

In Summary

In this chapter, you extended your knowledge of printer spooling. You saw how the spooler component called the *printer writer,* which sends spooled files to a printer device, can be "attached" to different output queues. You also saw how a spooled file can be changed, to send it to an output queue with a writer already functioning. You learned about two important work-with commands: WRKOUTQ, which lists all spooled files in a specified output queue, and WRKSPLF, which lists all spooled files on the system that belong to a user. You examined options common to both commands, and you saw the difference in display format and functions available depending on user assistance level, *BASIC, *INTERMED, or *ADVANCED.

In the following lab, you will use options to delete or change the status of spooled files, and you will move spooled files to a queue with a printer attached. You will look at the printer's output queue, hold print files, and release a print file to be printed.

It is important that you understand these tasks. For all future occasions when you must generate printed output, you will need to manage the spooled files in your own output queue. For example, you will need to dispose of unnecessary files and direct good files to a printer queue so that you can print them when required.

Key Terms

Advanced assistance level

AUTCHK

Basic assistance level

CHGPRTF

CHGSPLFA

CHGWTR

CLROUTQ

CRTDEVPRT

CRTPRTF

DSPDEVD

DSPSYSSTS

Intermediate assistance level

printer writer

QASTLVL system value

QSPL

spool-control special authority

spooled file

WRKOUTQ

WRKSPLF

Review Questions

1. What is a printer device file?

2. What is a printer writer?

3. Why would a system operator need to use the CHGWTR command?

4. If you were a user who had reports in an output queue that is not connected to a printer, what would be the procedure to print these spool files? What commands would you use?

5. List and describe the options available to you when you use the WRKOUTQ command.

6. What is spool-control special authority? Why should this authority be granted only to a limited number of users on the system?

7. If a user checks the status of a printer and sees the status set to MSGW, how would she resolve the problem?

8. Explain why there needs to be security on spool files. Give an example.

9. List the three values that uniquely identify a job on the system. What additional value is used to differentiate between spool files a job produces?

10. List three changes you can make to a spool file using CHGSPLFA.

11. One of the parameters of the CHGSPLFA command is User data; explain the purpose of this parameter.

12. What is the significance of the AUTCHK parameter?

13. How can a user's assistance level be changed?

14. Explain the differences between the three system assistance levels.

15. Explain why you might not be able to clear an output queue using the CRLOUTQ command.

Lab 4

Introduction

In this lab, you should become familiar with finding spooled files and taking appropriate actions to display, print, or send those files to other output queues. In the lab, instructions to print a screen refer to the system print-screen facility, not to a network or workstation Print Screen. If you are not sure of the difference, be sure to ask your instructor/mentor.

Before starting this lab, you should be sure you have successfully completed Lab 3. That is, you should have created an output queue in your own user library and changed your user profile to use that output queue.

Note

In this and subsequent labs, the instruction to Print Screen refers to the operating system Print Screen function and not to a workstation printer's screen-print function. System Print Screen always creates a spooled file and displays the message *"Print operation complete to the default printer device file."* You must then press Reset (left Ctrl on the micros) to go on.

We recommend that students use the IBM System i Access for Windows product for this course. The Print Screen function is not set up as a default keyboard function, and the key must be programmed. If the workstation you are using has not been programmed, ask your mentor/instructor for assistance in completing this task. (For details on this procedure, see the sidebar following Lab 3 in Chapter 3.)

Part 1

Goals   Display your spooled files using the Work with Printer Output screen.

Use the information displayed on this screen to identify spooled files.

Use the Change Printer Output display to send a spooled file to a printer.

Start at   Any command line.

Procedure   Go to USER menu.

Select the option to Work with . . . your spooled output files.

4.1. Sign on as usual. You want to work with the spooled files you created in the previous lab, so select option 1, User tasks, from the Main menu. (We are following a menu path in this lab to increase your familiarity with the commands.) From the USER menu, read through the initial list of tasks that can be performed, and choose the appropriate one. This choice should take you to the Work with Printer Output screen (Figure 4.25).

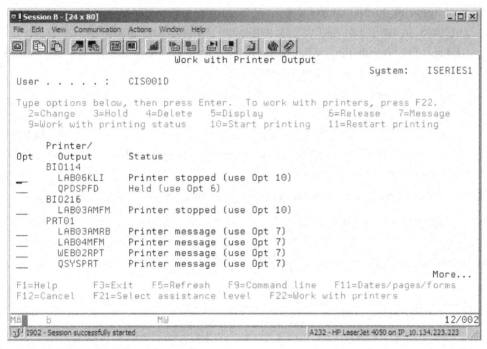

Figure 4.25: Work with Printer Output Screen

If the screen you see at this time doesn't look like Figure 4.25, and instead is titled Work with All Spooled Files, press F21 to change the assistance level to Basic.

4.2. On this screen (Figure 4.25), printer files are listed under the printer device whose output queue currently contains them.

4.2.a. Move the cursor to the Printer/Output column, and use Help to find out the value that would be displayed for the printer if the spooled file were in an output queue that does not belong to a printer.

4.3. Return to the Work with Printer Output screen. A different view of this display is available by pressing F11. Please do that now.

With this alternate view, the date and time of creation, number of pages, number of copies, and form type are displayed for each spooled file. Pressing F11 typically presents an alternate view of a list or command prompt screen. Now switch back to the Status display by pressing F11 again. Move the cursor over to the Status column, and press Help. Use the appropriate function key to enlarge the Help window.

    4.3.a.   What status will be displayed if a spooled file is currently being printed?

4.4.   Exit Help, and look again at the Work with Printer Output screen. Notice how the list items are formatted in the Printer/Output column. The output file names are grouped beneath a printer device name and indented two positions.

    4.4.a.   On your display, what name is used for the Output file? If you see more than one name, list all the different names.

    4.4.b.   How are the Output file names assigned? (Where do they come from?)

4.5.   From this screen, you can take various options for spooled files. One of them is the Change option, which lets you change certain attributes of a spooled file. Select that option now for the first file in your list by typing 2 in the option input field and pressing Enter.

4.6.   You should now be looking at the Change Printer Output screen (Figure 4.26).

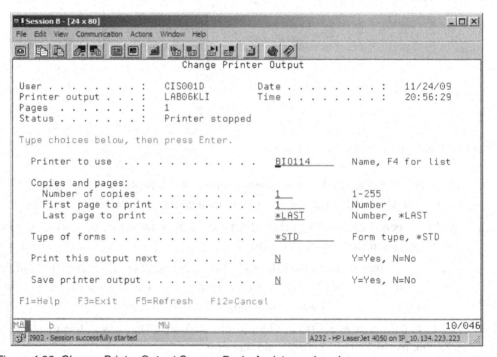

Figure 4.26: Change Printer Output Screen, Basic Assistance Level

Use extended Help to read about the meaning of the displayed attributes and the possible values they can take.

4.6.a.   Can any user change any printed output to print next?

Exit Help, and look again at the Change Printer Output screen.

4.7.   Notice that although you can redirect a spooled file to a defined printer, no option is available to send a spooled file to another (nonprinter) output queue.

On some entry screens, a list of valid parameter values can be generated by pressing F4 on an input field. When this is true, the values themselves, such as printer names, which depend on the naming convention and the number of printers in a particular installation, often vary from one system to another. This prompting capability is identified for a particular parameter by showing F4 for list as a choice.

For the spooled file we are currently changing, let us use this feature to select a different printer to use by pressing Prompt with the cursor on the entry field.

4.7.a.   List all printers whose status is not Stopped that can be selected at this time.

Now change the parameter value by selecting PRT01 from the prompt list. Press Enter to place the selected printer name in the entry field. Press Enter again to execute the command and return to the Work with Printer Output screen.

4.7.b.   What message is displayed on the message line?

Notice the changed status of your spooled file (see Figure 4.27).

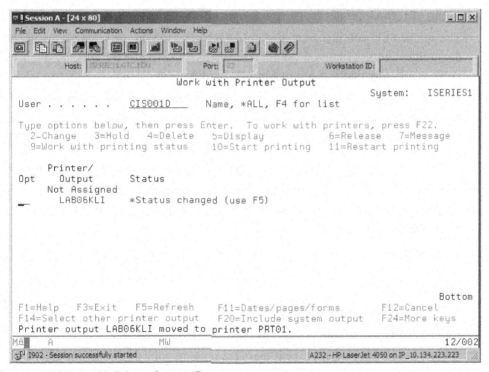

Figure 4.27: Work with Printer Output, Basic Assistance Level

Part 2

Goals   Change the assistance level for Work with Spooled Files.

Test system Print Screen to ensure that output is going to your output queue.

Change your existing system printer spooled files to your own output queue.

Start at   Work with Printer Output (WRKSPLF, Basic assistance level).

Procedure   Press F21 to change the assistance level.

Print the screen; then press F5 to find the new spooled file.

Select option 2 on the PRT01 spooled files to change to your own output queue.

4.8.   Now print the Work with Printer Output screen itself. You should be using the IBM i system Print Screen function; the message *"Print operation complete to the default printer device file"* will appear at the bottom of your screen. Remember to press Reset after the message appears.

4.8.a.   Does the new print file appear on the screen?

This type of screen is not automatically updated when, for example, a new spooled file enters an output queue. To update the screen, press F5.

4.8.b.   To which printer is the new spooled file assigned?

The spooled file you just created should have gone to your own output queue, but the problem here is that you cannot tell which output queue the spooled file is in; you can tell only that it is not in a printer output queue.

The current Work with Printer Output screen appears as it does because Basic assistance level is in effect. Although this display is useful in showing which spooled files are in a given printer's output queue, it does not show which output queue a spooled file is in if that queue is not a printer queue. In addition, some spooled files of different status do not show up at all. The Change option that you just looked at also lacks certain functions when taken from a Basic assistance level. However, you can see a different display of spooled files by using a different assistance level.

4.9.   Find the function key to select the assistance level, and press it. Select Intermediate for the assistance level, and then press Enter. Notice the different title and format of the resulting screen.

4.9.a.   How many spooled files are there?

4.9.b.   Which output queues are they in?

4.10.   If you have no spooled files, or if there are none in your own (user-name) queue, create one by printing the current screen. Reset to clear the message, and then press F5 to refresh. At this point, all system print screens should be going to your own output queue, and you should now have at least one spooled file in your user-name output queue.

Note

If the file you just created went to PRT01 (the default output queue) instead of to your user-name output queue, you need to review Lab 3, making sure that

- Your user-name output queue actually exists in your library
- Your user-profile Output queue parameter was changed to the user-name output queue that you created (CHGPRF, prompt, check OUTQ parameter)

If both of these conditions are true but your output is still going to the default output queue, you may just need to sign off and back on again. *If that does not work, you need to seek help from your instructor/mentor before you go on.*

4.11. Under the Device or Queue column, you might also see one or more files listed and not shown when the Basic level was in effect, as Figure 4.28 shows. In this case, these files are two job logs.

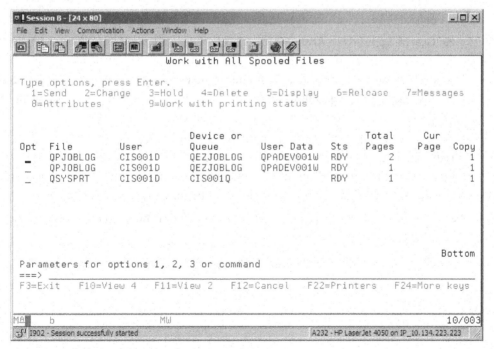

Figure 4.28: Work with All Spooled Files Screen, Intermediate Assistance Level

4.12. If these files exist, select option 2 for each so that you can change them to your own queue. When you press Enter (after you type 2 in the Opt field for each file to be changed), you should see the Change Spooled File Attributes command prompt screen (Figure 4.29). The cursor will be on the Printer parameter.

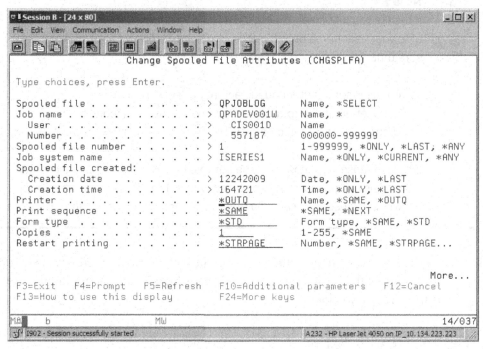

Figure 4.29: Change Spooled File Attributes (CHGSPLFA) Screen, Intermediate Assistance Level

You could send the spooled file to another printer from this screen, just as you could from the Change Printer Output screen of Basic assistance. But you really want to send these files to a different output queue (your own), not a printer.

4.13. First, you need to find the Output queue parameter. (If it doesn't appear on the initial screen, try looking at Additional parameters.) Use Field advance (Tab) or New line to move down to the Output queue parameter. Type in your output queue name. Remember, your output queue name does not begin with an asterisk (*).

4.13.a. Is it necessary to specify your library name for the Output queue Library field?

Now press Enter. Do the same for any other files that were sent to PRT01.

Caution

At this point, the Work with All Spooled Files screen should show that all other spooled files are in your own user-name output queue. *Do not proceed until you are certain of this.*

Part 3

Goals   Use the Work with Output Queue command to find and hold a spooled file.

Send a spooled file to a printer; delete other spooled files.

Check the printer output queue and release a spooled file.

Check for messages pending for a printer.

Start at   WRKSPLF at the Intermediate assistance level.

Procedure   Run the command to work with your output queue.

Select option 2 to change to a printer output queue.

Select option 4 to delete.

Use F22 to work with printers.

Select option 8 to work with printer output queue.

Select option 6 to release a spooled file.

Note

You may need your instructor's help with this portion of the lab. The printers described in the following lab are the ones configured on our college's system. The names of the printers will be different on your system.

4.14. Without leaving the Work with All Spooled Files screen, print the screen, and then reset. From the command line, type the command to work with output queues, and request parameter prompting. (Not sure of the command? Try GO CMDOUTQ.)

Specify your own output queue (do not use *ALL) and library, and run the command.

The Work with Output Queue command is concerned only with the files in the specified queue. This differs from the Work with Spooled Files command, which lists all output files for a given user, regardless of queue.

4.14.a. How many files are in your output queue now?

To find a particular spooled file in a list, you could use option 5 to display each one until you find the one you are looking for. Keep in mind that more recently created spooled files appear at the bottom of the list; within priorities, you could press F11 on the Work with Output Queue screen to display an alternate view that shows date and time of creation; that information should help you locate the spooled file more quickly.

4.15. Find the print-screen file created in step 4.14, and select the appropriate option to hold it. You should notice the change in its status. (Press F11 again to see status, if necessary.) Delete the other files.

4.15.a. What happens when you select Delete?

Go ahead and confirm to delete your other spooled files.

4.16. Use F9 to retrieve the previous WRKOUTQ command, and change the OUTQ parameter value to PRT01. (Be sure to delete excess characters within the parentheses.) Run the command, and then page through the files in the queue. Do you find any files with your user name? If so, delete them. At this point, there should be no files in the PRT01 output queue with your name. *Be sure this is true before you go on.*

4.17. To print the file you held in step 4.15, you need to send it to a printer with an active writer, such as BIO125 (*or an active printer on your system; if you are not sure what printer to use, ask you instructor*). First, return to your own output queue by pressing F3 from the WRKOUTQ PRT01 display screen. (If this doesn't take you to the Work with Output Queue display for your own queue, either recall or enter the WRKOUTQ command that names your output queue.) Now you should see only the single held spooled file in your output queue. Use the Change option to change the printer parameter value to BIO125. Press Enter to make the changes.

4.18. Back at the Work with Output Queue screen, find the function key for Printers and press it. You should now see a list of printers similar to that in Figure 4.30.

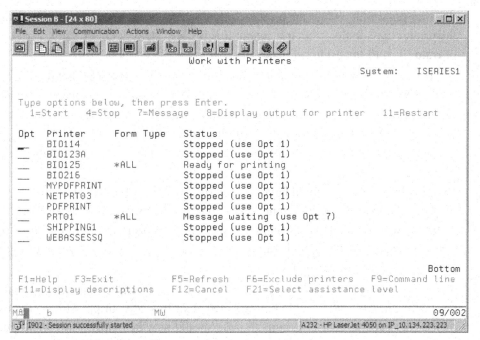

Figure 4.30: Work with Printers Screen, Basic Assistance Level

If your display is titled Work with All Printers and formatted differently from Figure 4.30, you are probably using Intermediate assistance level. To make your display appear similar to the figure, change to Basic assistance level.

4.18.a. What is the current status of BIO125? Of PRT01? Of BIO216?

From the list of printers, choose BIO125, and select the option to display output for the printer.

4.18.b. Is your spooled file in the list?

Return to the Work with Printers display, and change the assistance level to Intermediate. Select option 8 on device BIO125, but notice that this time the option is defined as Work with Output Queue.

4.18.c. How many files are now displayed? Is your file (the print screen of Work with All Spooled Files) there?

Select the option to display your file to make sure it is the one you redirected. What is its status? If its status is HLD, as it should be, release it.

4.19. Once you've released your print file, the change in status should register, and the file should be printed. If you refresh the screen at this point, the file should be gone or the status should show that the file is being printed. If it has not been printed, check the status of the queue itself to make sure the queue is not on hold. (The output queue status is displayed in the upper-right corner of the screen.) If the queue is on hold, notify the system operator.

Another possibility is that the printer could be "ended" (status END). If so, starting the printer may do the trick; but, again, this is the system operator's job, so ask the operator to start the printer if necessary.

If the printer is not on hold and not ended, there may be messages that require a reply. From the Work with All Printers screen, select option 7, Display messages. If messages such as *"Verify alignment on device BIO125"* are pending, they need to be replied to before printing can continue. Such replies are also the operator's responsibility; please alert the system operator to the need for a reply to the message.

4.20. By this time, your file should have been printed. Be sure to collect the printed output and clip or staple it to your answer sheet. When you return to the Work with Output Queue screen for the printer and refresh, your print file should be gone. If you have carefully followed the above instructions and still cannot get your file to print, see your instructor/mentor.

4.21. You should now have hardcopy printouts of display screens to hand in with your answer sheet. Also, you should have deleted any other of your print files on output queue BIO125, and your own output queue should now be empty. Files on output queues take up disk space. Disk space costs money and is limited. To keep clutter to a minimum, all users should perform necessary housekeeping on the spooled files they create. Whenever you are about to end a session, use the WRKSPLF command to clean up any spooled files you have. Print out those that need printing, and delete anything else not required for future reference.

Part 4

Goals   Change the Assistance level parameter of your user profile.

Use the CLROUTQ command to clear any print files left in your output queue.

Start at   Any command line.

Procedure   Type CHGPRF and prompt; find and change the Assistance level parameter value.

4.22. To avoid confusion caused by different assistance levels, it would be beneficial for everyone to be using the same assistance level from this point on. From a command line, prompt for the CHGPRF (Change Profile) command.

The default value of the Assistance level parameter is *SYSVAL, but each user can specify her own assistance level, regardless of the level to which the system is set. Change the value to *INTERMED, for Intermediate level, and then press Enter. (Of course, if system value QASTLVL on your system is already set to *INTERMED, this change will have no effect.)

The change causes commands whose display output varies depending on assistance level to use the Intermediate display the first time the command is executed. It does not automatically change levels for commands run previously and whose assistance level has been selected (using F21). So if you just selected *BASIC for the WRKSPLF command, this change to your user profile does not cause the WRKSPLF display to come up as *INTERMED the next time you use it. And, of course, you can still select a different assistance level for any command that has a variable display (e.g., WRKSPLF, WRKOUTQ, WRKWTR, DSPMSG). If you do so, that display will remain at the level you selected until you change it back, even if you sign off and back on again. So the user-profile change affects only command displays that have not been selected yet. You will find that the Intermediate assistance level is more useful to work with than the Basic assistance level because the Intermediate level provides more complete information and allows greater flexibility.

4.23. There are two ways to access the CLROUTQ command. You could type CRLOUTQ from the command line, or use the GO CMDOUTQ command to go to the Output Queue Commands menu and select the appropriate menu item.

Using one of the methods described above, you will see the screen in Figure 4.31. Enter your output queue and library, and then press Enter.

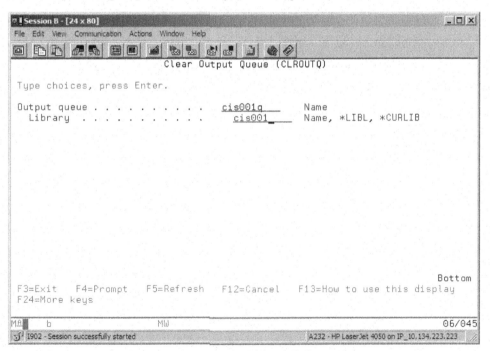

Figure 4.31: Clear Output Queue (CLROUTQ)

4.23.a. What happens if you run the command WRKOUTQ using your output queue name and library?

CHAPTER 5

Describing a Database File

Overview

SQL (**Structured Query Language**) is an integrated part of DB2 for IBM i and is replacing the use of the **Data Description Specifications** (DDS) language to describe data on the system. This chapter discusses DDS because many systems still use it to describe data. We feel that people new to the system should understand the traditional tools but also appreciate the move to SQL. In Chapter 11, we describe Remote System Explorer, which is part of the Rational Developer Toolset for Power (RDP). In Chapter 13, we describe and learn about SQL. These tools will eventually replace the PDM toolset and describing files with DDS.

We also discuss the concept of externally described files and explain how to use the traditional DDS language to describe a physical database file. In this chapter you also use **Programming Development Manager** (PDM) and **Source Entry Utility** (SEU), two traditional development tools for creating database files and developing programs.

Specifically, in this chapter's lab, you create a source physical file and then use PDM to create a source member. Finally, you use SEU to enter DDS source code for a database physical file into the source member.

Objectives

Students will be able to

- Tell the difference between externally described files and program-described files
- Demonstrate the basic operations of SEU
- Use PDM to move from a list of libraries to a list of objects and to a list of members
- Use DDS to describe a simple physical file
- Create a source physical file and enter specifications for a data-file member using SEU

File Varieties

All files in the IBM i operating system (OS) are classified as object type *FILE. Within that classification, the system recognizes more than 90 types of objects. A particular *FILE type is identified by a subtype, or attribute. When a file is created, the system assigns the attribute, which describes how the file is to be used within the system. The attribute assigned is determined by the CL command used to create the file.

It is beyond the scope of this text to explain all file attributes, but programmers and operators commonly use several of them, and those bear mentioning here. These common file attributes include the following:

- PRTF—*Printer files*, which we discussed in Chapters 3 and 4, format output from programs or utilities to create spooled print files in output queues.
- DSPF—*Display files* are similar to printer files in function, but they format data going to or coming from display screens rather than printers. Display files let you position data fields on screen displays and control color, high intensity, reverse image, and other display attributes. You also can control placement of constants, such as screen-identification information and field identifiers. Application programs and utilities can write data to and read data from display files. You will create your own display files in a later chapter.
- PF—*Physical files* have two distinct functions: to hold and organize user data, such as a customer master file or sales transaction file; and to organize source programs and source-data file descriptions written by programmers in languages such as COBOL, DDS, and RPG. In the latter capacity, physical files are similar to source-program libraries or source-file subdirectories other OSs use. The IBM i OS uses an attribute identifier to distinguish between these two functions: PF-DTA for data physical files and PF-SRC for source physical files.
- LF—*Logical files* are created over physical database files and cannot be created before the physical file or files with which they are associated. A logical file is always based on one or more physical files. Logical files do not contain data; rather, they store access paths, or pointers, to records in physical files. You can think of logical files as "filters" or limiting "views" of data stored in physical files. You can use logical files to secure data (for example, to restrict the type or amount of data presented to an application), or for efficiency (for example, to present data records in an order different from the order in which the records are stored in the physical file).

Now let us look at how to describe physical files to the system. (You will learn about logical files and display files and how to create them in later chapters.) You can describe physical files to the OS in two ways: as program-described files or as externally described files.

Program-Described Files

Physical files described at the record level contain only a record name and a record length. Any program that uses a file described in this manner must supply field-level attributes (e.g., field name, data type, field length) for every field in the record. Because files described at the record level require the programs that use them to provide additional specifications, they are referred to as **program-described files**.

Program-described files are useful when you need to convert older, nonrelational files to the DB2 relational database format, or when you need to move files from another system (AIX or Windows) to IBM i DB2. The permanent use of program-described files is discouraged because having to describe a record's fields in every program that uses the file is tedious and prone to errors.

Externally Described Files

Physical files that contain detailed field-level descriptions of their record formats, as well as information about how the files are to be accessed, are referred to as **externally described files**. That is, the detailed description of the file exists outside of, or external to, the programs that use the file.

Because an externally described file contains field-level descriptions within the file object itself, the file carries its own record "blueprint" with it wherever it goes. Therefore, any user program or system utility that accesses the file can determine the details of its record layout and all field-level attributes just by knowing the object's name (assuming the program is authorized to use the file).

Externally described files offer several major advantages:

- *Standardized record formats.* Because field attributes (including field names) are stored in the file object itself, the use of externally described files eliminates the confusion caused when programmers use different names for the same field. Also, with externally described files, it is almost impossible to incorrectly specify field length, data type, or number of **decimal positions** when using the file because the file object itself contains these critical attributes. You can easily check or compare an externally described file's record format by executing a **DSPFFD** (Display File Field Description) command on the file object.
- *Utilities that are easier to use.* Because externally described file objects describe themselves and name all their fields and attributes, system utilities—such as **Data File Utility** (DFU), DB2 Query Manager, or **Screen Design Aid** (SDA)—can obtain this critical information directly from the file. Less work is therefore required on the

part of programmers when they use these utilities to update data files, create queries and reports, and code display files.

- *Less-tedious programming.* When programmers use externally described files in programs written in high-level languages (HLLs) such as COBOL and RPG, they no longer need to code the record structures and field-level specifications in each program that uses the file. Instead, they simply name the file and indicate to the compiler that it is externally described; when the program is compiled, the information in the file is pulled into the program and converted into the proper syntax for the HLL. Because the source of the record-format information is the file object itself, not a source-library member or a copybook (a source-code description separate from the physical data structure), you eliminate the possibility of pulling in a wrong version of the record format when the program is compiled.

Externally described files contain information at three levels of data hierarchy: the file level, the record-format level, and the field level. We can best illustrate this hierarchy by looking at a file field-description display for an existing database physical file. You can access such a display through a menu path, but getting there that way is somewhat indirect. A more direct approach is to use the DSPFFD command; the command's only required parameter is the file name.

If you ran the DSPFFD command on a database physical file named STUPF in library CIS001, the display in Figure 5.1 would appear.

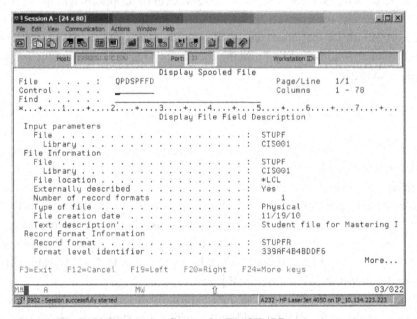

Figure 5.1: Display File Field-Description Screen for File STUPF

The file information tells you the file name (STUPF); the library name (CIS001); the file location (*LCL, which means the file is on the local system—it is not a distributed database file and not located on a remote system); that the file is externally described; the number of record formats (one); and the file type (physical).

The record-format information lists the name of the record format (a physical file contains a single record format, which must be named); in this case, the record-format name is STUPFR. The system also uses a format-level identifier to ensure that programs and files agree on version.

On the second screen of the display (Figure 5.2), you can see two additional record-format attributes: Number of fields (6) and Record length (103).

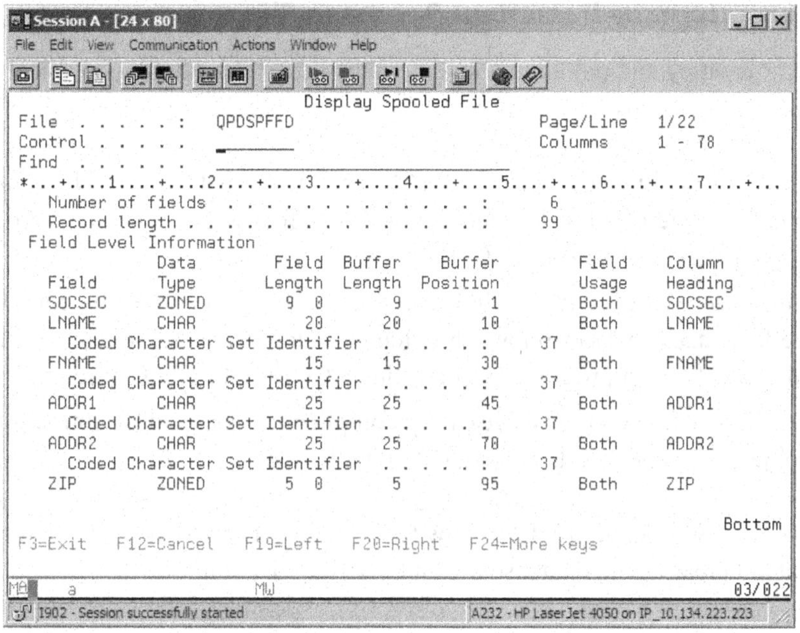

```
Session A - [24 x 80]                                               _ □ X
File  Edit  View  Communication  Actions  Window  Help

                          Display Spooled File
 File . . . . . :   QPDSPFFD                     Page/Line   1/22
 Control . . . . .      _____                  Columns     1 - 78
 Find . . . . . .
 *...+....1....+....2....+....3....+....4....+....5....+....6....+....7....+...
     Number of fields . . . . . . . . . . . . :       6
     Record length . . . . . . . . . . . . . . :      99
 Field Level Information
                 Data      Field  Buffer   Buffer        Field    Column
     Field       Type     Length  Length  Position       Usage    Heading
     SOCSEC      ZONED       9  0      9         1        Both     SOCSEC
     LNAME       CHAR       20        20        10        Both     LNAME
       Coded Character Set Identifier  . . . . . :    37
     FNAME       CHAR       15        15        30        Both     FNAME
       Coded Character Set Identifier  . . . . . :    37
     ADDR1       CHAR       25        25        45        Both     ADDR1
       Coded Character Set Identifier  . . . . . :    37
     ADDR2       CHAR       25        25        70        Both     ADDR2
       Coded Character Set Identifier  . . . . . :    37
     ZIP         ZONED       5  0      5        95        Both     ZIP

                                                             Bottom
 F3=Exit   F12=Cancel   F19=Left   F20=Right   F24=More keys

MA      a              MW                                        03/022
  I902 - Session successfully started        A232 - HP LaserJet 4050 on IP_10.134.223.223
```

Figure 5.2: Display File Field-Description Screen, Page 2

The essence of an externally described file is in the field-level information. All the critical information is already there in the file object. For each field, the system records a name, data type, length (characters or **digits**), position in the record buffer, length in bytes, field usage (input, output, or both), and a column heading for use by utilities. Character-type fields also have a coded character set identifier (**CCSID**), which identifies both a character set and an encoding method; the CCSID lets many different types of character data, including many national languages, be stored on the system.

This may seem like a lot of information for each file to carry around with it. In addition, creating and maintaining this information involves some overhead, which is offset by several benefits. Once recorded, this information never needs to be repeated, and it is always available for programs and utilities to use. It is also available to you, should questions about a file's record format arise.

Record format is an important concept for externally described files. The OS examines record formats to determine whether two files share the same record structure (e.g., when you are executing a CPYF, or Copy File, command). Figure 5.2 shows all the defining characteristics of record format, including the number of fields and total record length; the relative order of fields; and each field's name, data type, and length.

Creating an Externally Described Database File

The process of creating and populating an externally described database physical file involves three distinct steps:

1. *Describe*—You must first describe the file's record format and field-level attributes at the source-language level, much as you would first write a computer program in a source language (e.g., Basic, C, COBOL, RPG).
2. *Create*—After you describe the file, you can create the file object by compiling the source-language file description. This step is analogous to creating an executable machine-level object program by compiling a COBOL or RPG source program.
3. *Insert data*—When you've successfully compiled the source description into a *FILE type object, you can insert, or load, data into the file.

In this chapter, you learn in more detail how to describe a database file. In Chapter 6, you learn more about creating the database file and inserting data into it.

Methods of Describing Database Files at the Field Level

There are two approaches to describing files at the field level. You can use SQL, or you can use DDS.

SQL

SQL is a powerful relational database language that lets you describe and create physical or logical files. You can also use SQL to limit access to, maintain, and retrieve information from files, regardless of whether they were created with SQL.

SQL is a standardized database language used extensively not only in IBM OSs but all viable platforms. SQL's wide support means SQL-based applications are highly portable, which provides a significant incentive for learning SQL.

You should understand that using SQL to exclusively define, control, and manipulate database files does have certain challenges:

- First, to develop SQL applications, you need IBM DB2 Query Manager and SQL Development Kit for iSeries products, which are not part of the IBM i base OS support. You must purchase these products separately, just as you would a C, COBOL, or RPG compiler.
- Second, SQL is a powerful tool capable of using huge numbers of DASD input/output (I/O) operations and CPU machine cycles if misused, and mastering it requires a fair amount of time and practice.
- Third, the object overhead created by SQL schemas, catalogs, indexes, data dictionaries, views, journals, and journal receivers is substantial compared to DDS-described physical and logical files.
- Last, you cannot use SQL alone to describe and create a display file with any degree of sophistication for screen interactive I/O. Regardless of your proficiency with SQL, you need another tool for display files.

DDS

As mentioned, we focus on DDS in this chapter because it is a commonly used method to code source descriptions for several types of files, including physical and logical database files, display files, and printer files on the system. Although the complexity of DDS precludes anything more than a brief introduction here, you will get at least some initial exposure to the language and an indication of its capabilities.

SDA, a generator of display-file screens for interactive jobs, converts user-supplied screen layout specifications into DDS source. For physical and logical files, SEU, a general-purpose editor, lets you enter and syntax-check DDS source statements. The availability of these utilities, along with the convenience and flexibility they provide for describing physical and logical files, makes learning DDS worthwhile.

Before we discuss DDS further, however, we need to introduce two important software tools, both of which are part of **Application Development ToolSet** (ADTS). Although not included in the base OS, ADTS is such a valuable aid for creating and maintaining programs and files of all kinds that it would be inconceivable to attempt such work without it.

- The first tool is PDM, which provides a convenient way to create source members and access SEU and includes many other useful tools for programmers.
- The second tool, SEU, is used to enter all kinds of source code on the system. SEU is a "smart editor" that not only knows the line formats of different languages' source statements but also can check for syntax errors in the source code of various languages, including CL, COBOL, DDS, and RPG. Although SEU has been indispensable for programming as well as for describing physical and logical database files using DDS for many years, IBM's new Rational Development tools are quickly replacing it.

Note

There were no enhancements to the ADTS toolset for i6.1. IBM recommends that you use the Eclipse-based workstation tool Rational Developer for Power (**RDP**) for development of traditional IBM i applications. We introduce these traditional tools to the new user because of the widely continued use of these products. We have an in-depth introduction to RDP in Chapter 11.

Introduction to PDM

Programming Development Manager is a workbench environment that allows programmers and system operators to navigate the three levels of the OS's object-based architecture: the library level, the object level, and the member level. PDM, which provides access to system functions through a standard list interface, lets you move easily from one level to the next. For instance, you can start at the library level and then drop down to the object level. From the object level, you can either go back up to the library level or drop down to the member level.

Through PDM you can work with libraries, objects, or members by selecting from predefined options; or you can define your own options, similar to creating macros in other software products. You can start PDM by following a menu path: From the system Main menu, select option 5 to reach the PROGRAM menu and then option 2 to reach the PDM menu. As an alternative, to go directly to the PDM menu, you can simply type the STRPDM (Start PDM) command on any command line. You can also use the appropriate "work with" command (e.g., the WRKOBJPDM, or Work with Objects Using PDM, command) to go immediately to PDM lists of libraries, objects, or members.

The STRPDM Command

The PDM menu you reach when you follow the menu path or execute the STRPDM command is similar to the one in Figure 5.3.

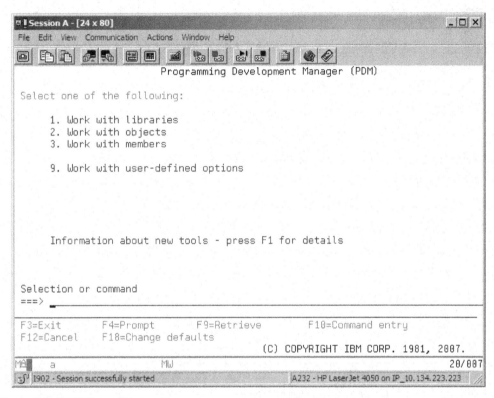

Figure 5.3: PDM Menu Screen

As you can see, the three levels of the IBM i object hierarchy (libraries, objects, and members) are listed as menu choices. A fourth choice, Work with user-defined options, lets you define or change your own PDM options. We examine user-defined PDM options later; for now, we will describe how the PDM library, object, and member levels are connected.

Selecting choice 1, Work with libraries, results in an entry screen that asks for the name of the library or libraries with which you want to work. At this screen, you can request a list of user libraries—a list of libraries whose names all begin with, end with, or contain certain characters (for example, you could enter JAF* to list all libraries beginning with *JAF*). If you leave the first-time default *LIBL, the system will list all libraries in your library list.

When you take the default, the system displays a Work with Libraries Using PDM screen similar to the one in Figure 5.4 (the composition of the library list will vary from user to user).

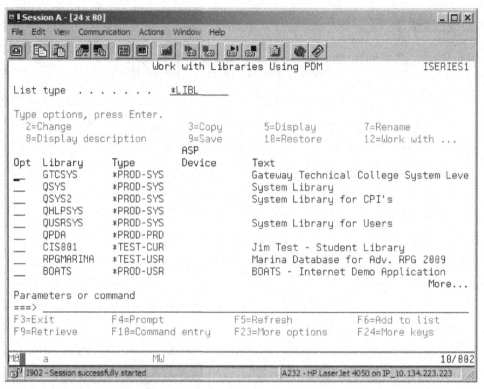

Figure 5.4: Work with Libraries Using PDM Screen

Work with Libraries Using PDM

The Work with Libraries Using PDM screen displays a library name, type, and text (if any) for each library. Each list item occupies an entire line of the display. Because of this, the entire library list for some users' jobs will not fit on a single screen (that is why you see More . . . near the bottom of the screen in Figure 5.4). If you press F11 (which does not appear on the initial function key list—to see it, press F24), the list is formatted to show library names and types only. When the Text field is not displayed, as many as three

columns of listed items can appear at once, as in Figure 5.5. (Although the display has room
for three columns, the library list shown here needs only two columns.)

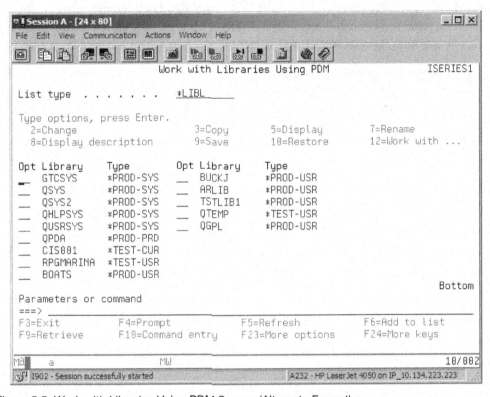

Figure 5.5: Work with Libraries Using PDM Screen (Alternate Format)

Notice that you can take various actions on the listed libraries by entering the appropriate
option number on the input field for a particular list item. More options are available than
those displayed above the list; to view the additional options, press F23. You can also
display IBM-supplied user-defined PDM options (which use letters instead of numbers) by
pressing **F16**. When you select an option, PDM invokes the appropriate CL command. PDM
supplies the required command parameters based on a list item's name and type, and on the
name of the library or file from which the PDM list item came.

Because PDM draws from information contained in its list, you are spared considerable keying effort. In addition, you can select the same option for multiple objects in the list, and PDM will repeat the necessary command automatically. For example, you can specify option 7—to rename an object—for several different libraries, as Figure 5.6 illustrates for libraries RPGMARINA, BOATS, BUCKJ, and TSTLIB1.

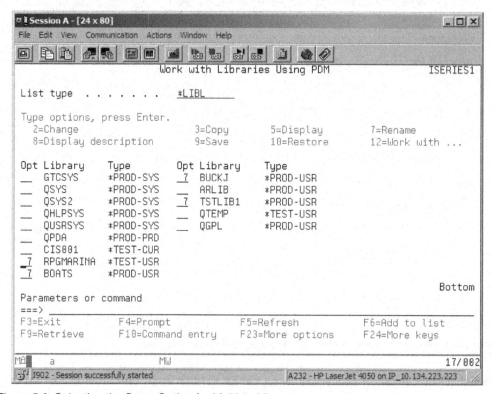

Figure 5.6: Selecting the Same Option for Multiple Libraries

Before you pres Enter, you might want to see the actual command that the specified option invokes. You can do so by pressing F4 after you type the option number in the option field. You will then see the command prompt screen—in this case, for the Rename Object (**RNMOBJ**) CL command, as you see in Figure 5.7.

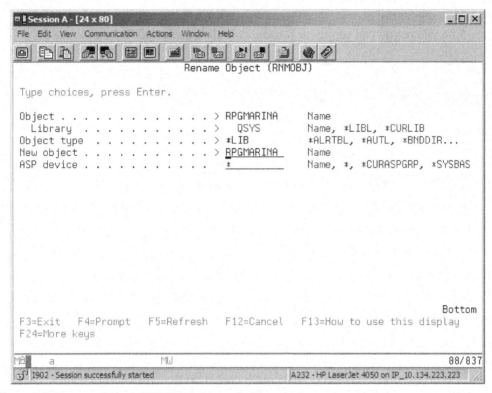

Figure 5.7: Rename Object (RNMOBJ) Command Prompt Screen

You can see that all parameters have been given values. The Object (name) and Object type values came from the PDM list item for which the option was taken. The New object value is the same as the current object name. Executing the command would make no sense in this example and would result in an error (you cannot rename an object to the same name), but PDM still assigns the value to facilitate the change. The point is that all PDM options invoke commands; and when you type an option and request prompting, you see the prompt screen for the command that PDM is prepared to execute. You can also see how list-item values have been substituted for the command as parameter values.

If you press Enter at this screen, the system displays the Rename Libraries input screen (Figure 5.8), where you can supply new names for all the selected libraries at once.

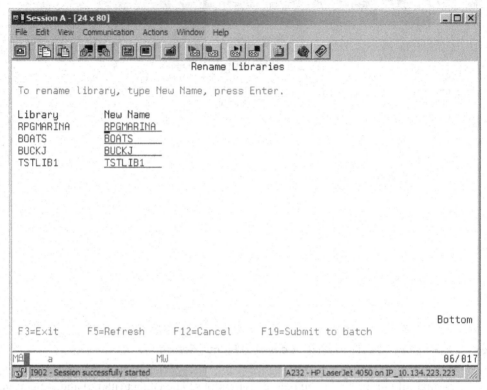

Figure 5.8: Rename Libraries Input Screen

For example, in the list above you could change all of the names by simply keying over the displayed library names. Changing library names or typing in new ones is the closest you would come in this case to entering parameter values.

As you have seen, when using PDM, you can select an option on several list items at the same time, and the options will either be grouped together, as for renaming, or be processed one after another. You can also select different options on different list items, in which case the options will be processed from top to bottom and grouped (e.g., all the Rename options together) where applicable.

Now that you have seen how PDM handles options selected on list items, let us see how the Work with Libraries Using PDM function connects to the next level (objects) in the OS object-based hierarchy. Now let us cancel the prompt (F12) and return to the PDM screen in Figure 5.6.

Work with Objects Using PDM

If you simply execute the command WRKOBJPDM with default parameter values, a list of all objects in a specified library is displayed. When no library is specified, PDM uses the library name from the preceding PDM session. You can reach the Work with Objects Using PDM screen from the PDM menu (Figure 5.3) by selecting choice 2, Work with objects. If you are already at a Work with Libraries Using PDM screen, you can get to the Work with Objects Using PDM screen by selecting option 12, Work with, on one of the libraries in the list. For example, for the Work with Libraries Using PDM screen in Figure 5.6, selecting option 12 on library CIS001 takes you to the Work with Objects Using PDM screen you see in Figure 5.9.

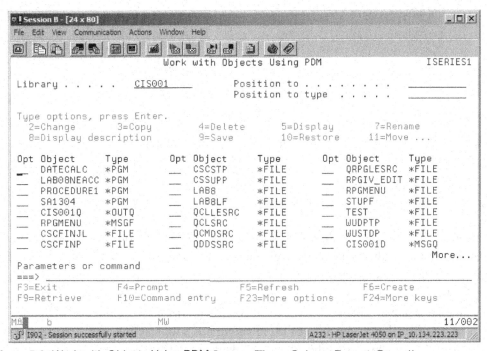

Figure 5.9: Work with Objects Using PDM Screen (Three-Column Format, Page 1)

Tip

In PDM, you can return to the library list from the Work with Objects Using PDM screen by pressing F12 when you are finished with the object list.

The Work with Objects Using PDM screen, in a format similar to the Work with Libraries Using PDM screen, lists all objects in a single library and—in the three-column format you see in Figure 5.9—displays the object type. If you press F11 to change the screen's format, only a single column of objects is displayed, but attribute and text are shown for each (Figure 5.10).

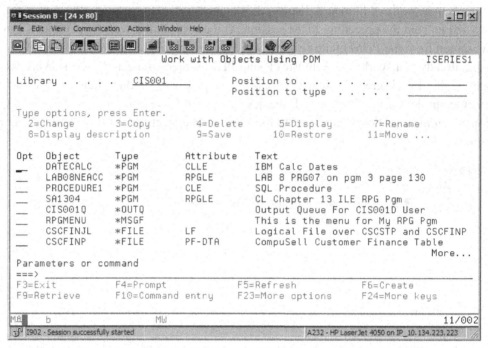

Figure 5.10: Work with Objects Using PDM Screen (Single-Column Format, Page 1)

The attribute information that PDM lists for *FILE- and *PGM-type objects can be useful if you are trying to find the source code used to create the object. For *PGM-type objects, the attribute indicates the language in which the program was written. For example, starting at the top of the list in Figure 5.10 and Table 5.1: The *PGM-type objects show attributes that display the language in which the program was written. The last two objects listed are of type *FILE. CSCFINJL has an attribute of LF, meaning it is a logical file, and CSCFINP has the attribute PF-DTA, indicating that this object is a database physical file.

Table 5.1: Examples of Object Type and Attributes			
Name	Type	Attribute	Description
DATECALC	*PGM	CLLE	ILE Control Language (CL) program
LAB08NEACC	*PGM	RPGLE	ILE RPG program
PROCEDURE1	*PGM	CLE	ILE C program
CIS001Q	*OUTQ		Printer output queue
RPGMENU	*MSGF		Message file for a menu
CSCFINJL	*FILE	LF	Logical file
CSCFINP	*FILE	PF-DTA	Database physical file

Another example of the Work with Objects Using PDM display, Figure 5.11, shows several files with the attribute PF-SRC, indicating that these files are **source physical files**, which hold source programs, file descriptions, and so on.

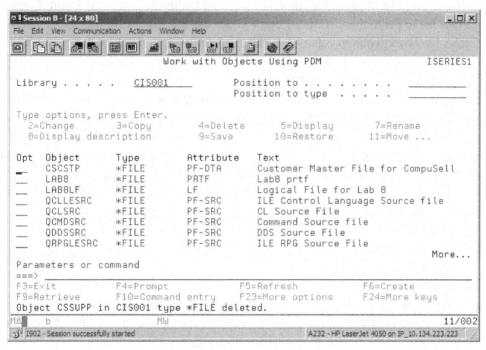

Figure 5.11: Work with Objects Using PDM Screen (Single-Column Format, Page 3)

The file named QDDSSRC is a source physical file intended to hold source code for database and display files described using DDS. The name itself is symbolic. Although a name beginning with *Q* is usually an IBM-supplied name, a user created this particular file. Programmers commonly use IBM's naming convention as an aid in recognizing source physical files. The names of IBM's default source physical files begin with a *Q* and include the type of source the file is intended to store. For example, default source physical files in IBM-supplied library QGPL are named QCLSRC (if they contain CL source programs), QRPGSRC (if they hold RPG source programs), and so on. The *DDS* part of the name QDDSSRC indicates that the source physical file holds members coded in DDS; the *SRC* part of the name stands for *source*.

As IBM i developers continue to the Integrated Language Environment (ILE), they name source files containing these programs by adding *LE* to the traditional names. For example, a source file containing RPG ILE programs would be stored in a file named RPGLESRC.

Notice that most of the options displayed on the Work with Objects Using PDM screen are similar to those on the Work with Libraries Using PDM screen, and additional options are available for working with objects, including 4=Delete and 11=Move. Option 12=Work with has been bumped to a second display of options, which you can view by pressing F23.

Just as you can use the Work with option on a selected library from the Work with Libraries Using PDM list to get to this list of objects, you can use the Work with option on a specified object from the Work with Objects Using PDM screen to get to some kind of a "work-with" list. The nature of the list screen you see depends on the type and attribute of the list item upon which you take the option. A *FILE object whose attribute is PF, whether a source or a database physical file, usually contains one or more data components called **members**. Members are the lowest level of a physical file object. All physical files have a lower level that is referred to as a member. A source physical file has members that contain source code, and physical data files have members that contain the actual data. On older systems, you might have a physical file named ORDERS and the members in the physical file might be named JAN1990, FEB1990, and so on. These members would contain the orders for the respective month (JAN) and year (1990). Taking the Work with option on such an object brings you to the lowest level of PDM, Work with Members Using PDM.

Work with Members Using PDM

Selecting option 12 on source physical file QDDSSRC results in a Work with Members Using PDM screen like the one in Figure 5.12. (The list of members will be different for different users.)

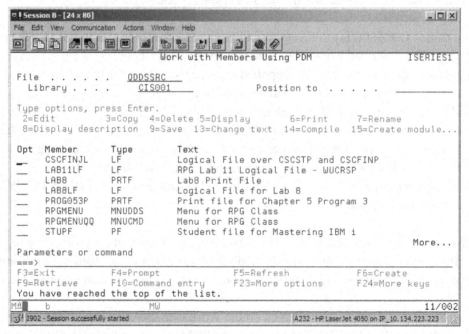

Figure 5.12: Work with Members Using PDM Screen for File QDDSSRC

When you want to create or change a source member in a source physical file, the Work with Members Using PDM screen provides an efficient work environment.

The File and Library fields in the screen's upper-left corner remind you which member list you are viewing. Because these fields are both input enabled, you can change to the member list of another file and/or library by keying over the displayed value (or values) and pressing Enter.

The options list for working with members is different from the options list for working with objects. Although no save/restore capability is available for individual members, you can use option 9 to save the file of which the member is a part. In addition, for source physical files, an edit option (2) lets you change existing source-file members, and a print option (6) lets you create hard copy of the source code.

Creating a Member via SEU

To create a new member from the Work with Members Using PDM screen, you use F6. Pressing F6 invokes the STRSEU (Start Source Entry Utility) command and takes you to the command prompt screen for that command (Figure 5.13).

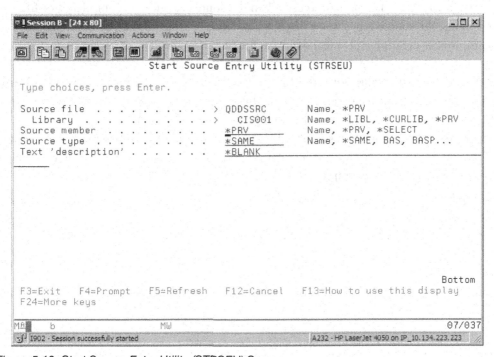

Figure 5.13: Start Source Entry Utility (STRSEU) Screen

As the figure shows, PDM supplies the first two parameter values (source-file name and library name) based on the file and library information on the preceding Work with Members Using PDM screen. For the Source member parameter, you enter the name of the source program or file description you plan to create. Usually, you use the same name that you intend to use for the compiled program or file; it is less confusing to use the same name for both the source member and the object created from it. The batch compile option on the Work with Members Using PDM screen assigns the member name to the newly created object by default.

As an example, we will name the new member EMPPF (for EMPloyee Physical File).

Note
For most parameters, SEU changes the values to upper case except for quoted strings, which are case sensitive.

The value supplied for the Source type parameter is important. In addition to determining which source-language syntax checker and prompter are used, this value tells PDM which Create (CRT*xxx*) command to use when the source member is compiled. For file descriptions, the source type can be PF (physical file), LF (logical file), or DSPF (display file). Because we are creating a physical database file, we use type PF.

The system stores the value you enter for the Text 'description' parameter as a quoted string; it is the only case-sensitive parameter value. In our example, we will describe the file as Employee Master PF Source. Remember that you do not need to enclose the text within apostrophes ('); the command prompter does that for you. This field is important to describe the function of the member for documentation purposes. Figure 5.14 shows the completed Start SEU screen for our example.

Figure 5.14: Filled-Out STRSEU Screen

When you press Enter from this screen, the SEU Edit work screen (Figure 5.15) appears.

Figure 5.15: SEU Edit Work Screen

A message at the bottom of the screen tells you that the new member has been added to file QDDSSRC.

The column of apostrophes at the left on the Edit work screen indicates that a screen full of lines has been inserted and that full-screen entry of DDS source code can begin. For fixed-format languages such as DDS, however, it is usually more productive to use prompting to insert one line at a time into the source member workspace. When you use prompting, SEU provides a prompt area that identifies each entry field and indicates its length. When you fill out the prompt and press Enter, the values you entered are correctly formatted in the work area.

Because different programming languages use different formats, you can tell SEU which prompt format to use via a line command (which we discuss shortly), or you can let SEU choose an appropriate format based on the Source type value entered on the Start SEU screen. In our example, we used source type PF, and, as you can see in the upper-left corner of the Edit screen, the format selected is for a physical file (FMT PF). You also can change the prompt format at any time during an edit session; doing so may be necessary when you are using a language such as RPG, which has several format types.

To use prompting to enter lines of source, first clear the work space by pressing Enter at the Edit work screen. The new Edit work screen looks like the one in Figure 5.16.

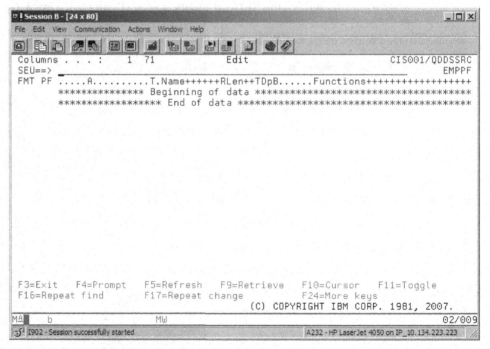

Figure 5.16: Cleared SEU Edit Work Screen

On the screen's first line, Columns identifies the range of columns currently displayed in the work area. F19 and F20 let you shift the work-area window left or right, respectively. The screen title identifies the SEU mode (e.g., Edit, Browse), and CIS001/QDDSSRC identifies the name of the library and source physical file.

On the second line is the SEU command line; the source member is identified at the far right. On the third line, you find the current member format (in this case, PF for physical file) and a format ruler that indicates the field positions for the format. Because the Beginning of data and End of data markers are on consecutive lines, you can tell that nothing has been entered yet.

SEU Help

A lot of useful Help information is available from SEU. If you press Help with the cursor on the SEU command line, for example, the context-sensitive Help you see in Figure 5.17 appears.

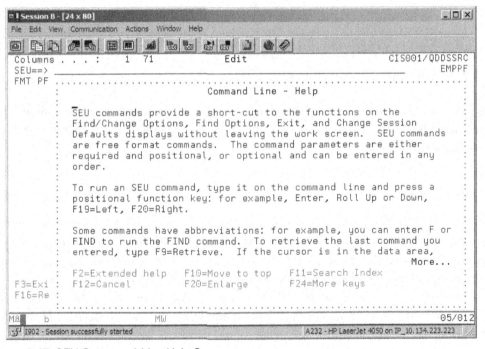

Figure 5.17: SEU Command-Line Help Screen

This Help text tells you how to use the command line to perform tasks such as saving the source member and finding a certain value in an existing member.

Pressing F2 while displaying context-sensitive Help calls extended Help (Figure 5.18).

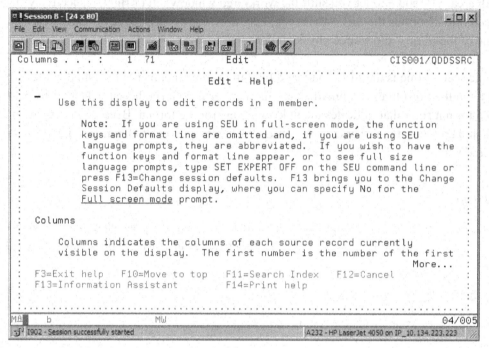

Figure 5.18: SEU Edit Help Screen (Extended Help)

This screen contains several pages of general information about using SEU and about SEU line commands. In the lab exercises, you will access the extended Help screen for SEU and read through it.

SEU Line Commands

From the SEU Edit work screen, you can start insert mode simply by typing a line command in the sequence column of the Beginning of data line. The sequence column, a seven-position field for each line, is at the far left of the work screen. The sequence column has two purposes: to maintain line sequence numbers for all lines of a source member, and to allow entry of SEU line commands. **SEU line commands** let you change the edit work area and manipulate source member lines; for example, you can move, copy, delete, add, or insert lines.

Let us see what happens when you enter an SEU line command. First, ensure that the cursor is one line below and one position to the left of the *F* in FMT in the sequence column of the Beginning of data line. (The cursor should already be in that position as a result of your pressing Enter to clear the Edit work screen). If the cursor is not in that position (the cursor will be on the first tab setting, if tabs are turned on), you can press Tab or New line repeatedly to move it to that position.

If you are editing an existing source member, you can enter a line command over the sequence number of any existing record (line) of the member. In our example, to insert a line with prompting, you would enter the SEU line command IP (I for Insert and P for Prompting) on the Beginning of data line. The line command (before you press Enter) would look like that in Figure 5.19.

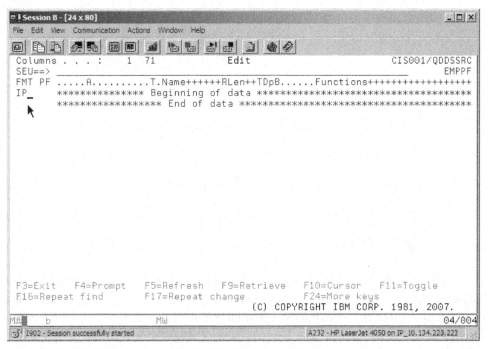

Figure 5.19: IP SEU Line Command to Insert with Prompting

When you press Enter, the screen is split horizontally to show a work area above and prompt lines below, as in Figure 5.20.

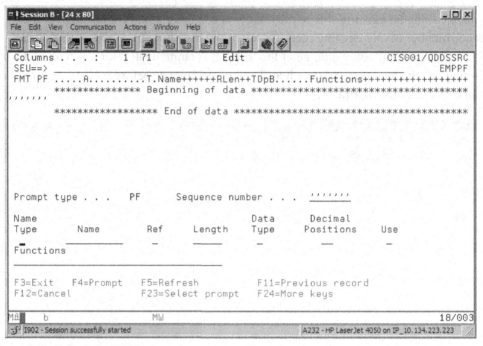

Figure 5.20: Prompt for PF Type

This screen prompts for a DDS source entry for a physical file (PF). Eight entry fields are available, but for now, we discuss only those you need in order to enter a simple physical file description. A more detailed description of DDS will come later.

Tip
All entry fields on the SEU prompt screen respond to the Help key, so when you are working in the lab, you can request context-sensitive Help on any field about which you have a question.

The minimal database physical-file description contains a single record-format entry on the first line. Field-level entries, to describe each field, can follow. For a simple file description, each field-level entry also occupies one line in the editor work space and constitutes one record of the source member when saved.

DDS Record-Format Entry

In a DDS file description, several different types of records may be used. Not all are required for every file description, but when used, they must be entered in a specific order. For a physical file, the record types are

- *File*—Blank name type; optional; when used, must precede record type
- *Record*—R name type; one required for physical file
- *Field*—Blank name type; describes fields; follows record; almost always present
- *Key*—K name type; optional; follows field entries

To describe a simple physical file, minimum requirements would include only a record-format line and a few field entries.

To key a **record-format specification** in the prompter, you need only specify the value R for the Name Type field and a value for the Name field (for this example, we will use EMPPFR as the name of the record). When you press Enter, the record is moved up to the Edit screen's work area, and a new, empty prompt is provided (Figure 5.21).

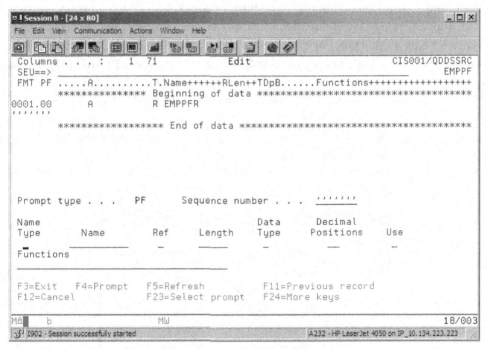

Figure 5.21: New, Empty Prompt Provided after Pressing Enter

You can see that a sequence number (1.00) has been assigned to the inserted record. The decimal portion of the number lets you insert up to 99 new records between two existing records during the edit session without renumbering.

Field-Level Entries

After you insert a record-format line, you can enter **field-level specifications**. For these, you leave the Name Type field blank. However, you must enter values for Name (field name), Length (number of characters or digits), and Data Type (e.g., character, **zoned decimal**, **packed decimal**, **binary**, date, time). For numeric fields, you must also enter the number of Decimal Positions. For a physical file, the four required attributes of a field are Name, Length, Data Type, and Decimal Positions.

Name. For record and field names, use from one to 10 characters, the first of which must be uppercase alphabetic (A–Z) or one of the special characters @, $, or #. Subsequent characters can consist of the numbers 0 through 9, and the underscore character (_). Embedded blanks are not allowed in a name. Within a record format field, names must be unique.

Length. Length is the number of characters or digits in the field. For character, hexadecimal, and zoned-decimal fields, the length defines the field size in bytes. The system uses the Extended Binary-Coded Decimal Interchange Code, or **EBCDIC**, method of encoding characters and zoned-decimal numbers into binary code. For all code points encompassed by EBCDIC (uppercase and lowercase alphabetic characters, numbers, and special characters), one character equals one byte. For example, an address field of length 30 occupies 30 bytes of record-buffer space. Languages whose alphabets do not code to EBCDIC (e.g., Chinese, Japanese) use a two-byte-per-character coding scheme called double-byte character set (**DBCS**). The examples and exercises in this book assume EBCDIC data.

Because length and data type are related, we cannot discuss one without the other. Each data type has a valid maximum length, as Table 5.2 shows.

Abbreviation	Data Type	Maximum Length
P	Packed decimal	31 digits
S	Zoned decimal	31 digits
B	Binary	18 digits
5	Binary character	32,766 characters
F	Floating-point (short)	9 digits
F	Floating-point (long)	17 digits
A	Character	32,766 characters
H	Hexadecimal	32,766 bytes
L	Date	6, 8, or 10 characters
T	Time	8 characters
Z	Timestamp	26 characters

Table 5.2: Data Types and Maximum Lengths

Remember that for numeric data types, the length specification really means the number of digits in the field. For date, time, and timestamp types, you do not specify a value for length; the value is determined by type. The values shown above for date, time, and timestamp data types are the number of characters needed to display the stored values, not the number of bytes required for disk storage. This longer (display) length is used in the record format.

An **internal date field** can have three different lengths, depending on which date format is specified by the DATFMT keyword in DDS. If you do not use keyword DATFMT, the default is *ISO format (International Standards Organization), whose display format is *yyyy-mm-dd* (10 characters). The default time format (also *ISO) is displayed as *hh.mm.ss* (eight characters). You can change this format by using either a different time format, such as TIMFMT(*USA), or a different separator, such as TIMSEP(':'). Timestamp data includes both the date and the time and is formatted as *yyyy-mm-dd-hh.mm.ss.uuuuuu* (26 characters), where *uuuuuu* represents millionths of a second. You can find a more detailed discussion of date and time formats and separators by accessing the IBM Information Center (*http://publib. boulder.ibm.com/iseries*).

The obvious advantage to using date-type fields is that they use four digits to record the year. Programs using files with four-digit years (e.g., a DATFMT value of *ISO or *USA) would have had few year 2000 modification problems. A less obvious advantage is the ability to perform date-duration calculations easily. For example, if the system knows a transaction date (type L) and the current date, it can calculate the difference in number of days without resorting to complex date-table lookups and without concern about the change of millennium.

Data Type. Table 5.2 lists the data types most commonly used by the OS. Fields of type character, zoned decimal, and hexadecimal all occupy a number of bytes of storage equal to the length of the field. However, for other numeric types, the length of the field in bytes is calculated from the number of digits. For example, if a Social Security number is typed S for zoned decimal, the true length of the field is 9 (bytes and digits). If the same field is typed P for packed decimal, then the value 9 specified for length really means nine digits, and the true field length is five bytes. (Length in bytes of a packed-decimal field can be calculated as (Total digits / 2) + 1, throwing away any decimal part.) This difference in length is the result of how numeric data is stored in packed-decimal format: two digits per byte except for the rightmost byte, which codes the least significant digit in the high-order four bits and the sign in the low-order four bits.

The advantages of storing numeric data in packed-decimal format are that the field itself is smaller, requiring fewer bytes of storage space, and arithmetic and logic operations are more efficient, requiring fewer intermediate conversion steps. There may be minor disadvantages to storing numbers as packed decimal. For one thing, only a zoned-decimal numeric field of a physical file can be redefined as a character field through a logical file. For another, you cannot directly observe the packed-decimal field value by using a DSPPFM (Display Physical File Member) command, which does no conversion. (For sensitive data, this may not be a disadvantage at all!) DFU, DB2 Query Manager, and SQL, on the other hand, convert all numeric representations, including packed decimal, to display format.

You can use hexadecimal fields to store data whose code is not to be interpreted by the system. You can store any possible binary code in a hexadecimal field. For the most part, hexadecimal fields are treated like character fields. When the binary code corresponds to a printable character in EBCDIC, you can display or print the character; but the system doesn't translate hexadecimal code into other character sets.

The number of bytes of storage occupied by other numeric data types is determined by the number of digits specified for length, as Table 5.3 shows.

Table 5.3: Other Numeric Data Types and Storage Bytes		
Type	Number of Digits	Bytes of Storage
Binary	1 to 4	2
	5 to 9	4
	10 to 18	8
Floating-Point		
Short (single precision)	Short (single precision)	Short (single precision)
Long (double precision)	Long (double precision)	Long (double precision)

Floating-point short and long formats are both identified by F for data type, but a long (double-precision) number must be specified with the Float Precision keyword FLTPCN(*DOUBLE); the default is FLTPCN(*SINGLE). **Floating-point** formats represent values in scientific notation as mantissa and exponent, and generally are not used for business applications that deal with integers or dollars-and-cents values.

Date, time, and timestamp fields all result in a fixed number of storage bytes regardless of the format or separators used (Table 5.4).

Table 5.4: Date, Time, and Timestamp Fields		
Type	Display Size	Bytes of Storage (Disk)
Date	6, 8, or 10 characters	4
Time	8 characters	3
Timestamp	26 characters	10

The values listed for bytes of storage are the field sizes when they are stored internally on disk. The fields are always expanded to the display size as they are moved to the record format, so both HLL programs and CL commands, such as DSPFFD, deal with these fields according to their display size, with separation characters already inserted. In other words, if you look at a record format that contains a timestamp, you see 26 bytes of storage allocated, not 10.

Decimal Positions. You should use a value in the Decimal Positions field for physical-file fields that represent numeric data, especially for those fields whose type is packed decimal, zoned decimal, or binary. The Decimal Positions value specifies the number of digits to the right of the decimal point—the fractional part of a real number. The value can never be greater than the length. It is important to remember that the Decimal Positions field is a part of the Length field, not an addition to it. For example, for a field defined as

BIGNBR   15P 5

the total number of digits is 15, five of which are to the right of the (implied) decimal point.

When you code 0 for the decimal positions, the field is considered an integer. For example, field SOCSEC, when defined as follows, is an integer:

SOCSEC   9S 0

DDS does not insist that you code a value for the decimal positions, yet the field is compiled as an integer if you do not. For documentation and consistency, it is better to code 0 for the Decimal Positions field. For nonintegers, decimal positions are always implied, never explicitly coded in the field; the system keeps track of the implied decimal point for you.

Note that if you do not explicitly provide a data type, the default is A (character) when no Decimal Positions value is specified. If you provide a Decimal Positions value and do not specify a Data Type, DDS defaults to the numeric packed-decimal (P) data type.

To illustrate how different types of fields defined in DDS are incorporated into the compiled physical-file record format, Figure 5.22 shows a kind of nonsensical DDS record description. Nevertheless, you can gain some understanding of data types and field lengths by studying it.

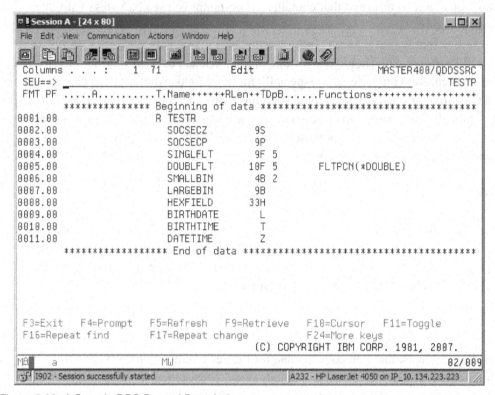

Figure 5.22: A Sample DDS Record Description

The record has numeric fields of all types except DBCS, which supports characters for languages such as Chinese, Japanese, and Korean. The following bullets describe the fields.

- SOCSECZ and SOCSECP are nine-digit integers; because no Decimal Positions value is coded, the default is 0. (We do not recommend this practice but use it only for illustration.)
- SINGLFLT and DOUBLFLT are single-precision and double-precision floating-point numbers, respectively. Note that DOUBLFLT requires the FLTPCN(*DOUBLE) keyword to be coded.
- SMALLBIN is a binary number with two decimal positions.
- LARGEBIN is a binary number and an integer by default.

- HEXFIELD is a hexadecimal field whose length, 33, should be the actual number of bytes the field occupies. Hexadecimal fields cannot have a decimal position's value coded.
- The last three field names are Date, Time, and Timestamp fields, which do not allow coding of either length or decimal positions.

Figure 5.23 shows the compiled file information. The figure itself is the printed output of the DSPFFD command for file TESTP. This command is useful for checking the record-format and field definitions of database files.

```
5761SS1 V6R1M0  080215      Display File Field Description
  1
Input parameters
  File . . . . . . . . . . . . . . . . . . . :   TESTP
    Library . . . . . . . . . . . . . . . . :   *LIBL
File Information
  File . . . . . . . . . . . . . . . . . . . :   TESTP
    Library . . . . . . . . . . . . . . . . :   CIS001
  File location . . . . . . . . . . . . . . :   *LCL
  Externally described . . . . . . . . . . :   Yes
  Number of record formats . . . . . . . . :     1
  Type of file  . . . . . . . . . . . . . . :   Physical
  File creation date . . . . . . . . . . . :   01/13/10
  Text 'description'. . . . . . . . . . . . :   Figure 5.22 Example
Record Format Information
  Record format . . . . . . . . . . . . . . :   TESTR
  Format level identifier . . . . . . . . . :   4E3E0983A340B
  Number of fields  . . . . . . . . . . . . :    10
  Record length . . . . . . . . . . . . . . :    109
Field Level Information
              Data      Field   Buffer   Buffer        Field    Column
  Field       Type      Length  Length   Position      Usage    Heading
  SOCSECZ     ZONED       9 0      9         1          Both     SOCSECZ
  SOCSECP     PACKED      9 0      5        10          Both     SOCSECP
  SINGLFLT    FLTSNG      9 5      4        15          Both     SINGLFLT
  DOUBLFLT    FLTDBL     10 5      8        19          Both     DOUBLFLT
  SMALLBIN    BINARY      4 2      2        27          Both     SMALLBIN
  LARGEBIN    BINARY      9 0      4        29          Both     LARGEBIN

                                                           Continued
```

```
HEXFIELD    HEX             33      33       33        Both    HEXFIELD
  Coded Character Set Identifier   . . . . :  65535
BIRTHDATE   DATE            10      10       66        Both    BIRTHDATE
  Date Format . . . . . . . . . . . . . . :  *ISO
  Coded Character Set Identifier   . . . . :     37
BIRTHTIME   TIME             8       8       76        Both    BIRTHTIME
  Time Format  . . . . . . . . . . . . . :  *ISO
  Coded Character Set Identifier . . . . . :     37
DATETIME    TIMESTAMP       26      26       84        Both    DATETIME
  Coded Character Set Identifier   . . . . :     37
```

Figure 5.23: DSPFFD Command Output Showing Compiled File Information for File TESTP

Under the Field Level Information heading, you can see that the field, data-type, and field-length information corresponds to the DDS in Figure 5.22. The Buffer Length column shows the number of bytes each field occupies in the record buffer. Buffer Position shows where in the buffer each field begins, relative to byte 1. Notice that the packed-decimal version of SOCSEC (SOCSECP) takes five bytes of storage. A single-precision floating-point number takes four bytes of storage, whether it is defined as one digit or nine digits. A double-precision number can be from one to 17 digits but always occupies eight bytes of storage.

Notice that there is only one data type for the binary numbers; the system determines from the number of digits you specify for length whether to reserve a two- or a four-byte field. You can see that the Date and Time fields default to *ISO format and that their buffer lengths, as well as that for the Timestamp field, are consistent with the information given above. Because BIRTHDATE uses *ISO format (*yyyy-mm-dd*), it occupies 10 bytes in the buffer.

Now let us return to our sample Employee file. If you entered an employee ID field using prompting in SEU, the completed prompt line would look like that in Figure 5.24.

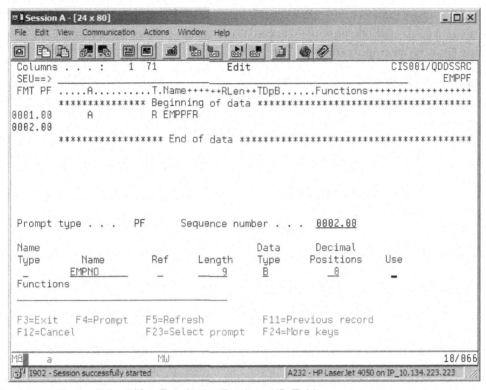

Figure 5.24: Prompt Lines After Entering an Employee ID Field

 Caution
Be careful when you enter digits in one of the numeric prompt fields (Length or Decimal Positions); the numbers you type must be right-aligned in the entry field. If you press the Field exit key after typing the digits, SEU properly aligns them in the field and advances the cursor to the next field.

After you press Enter, the new line is inserted into the work area following the record-format line.

Figure 5.25 shows the work area after several more fields have been inserted and you have pressed F5 to clear the prompt. You can also clear the prompt by pressing F12, or by pressing Enter on an empty prompt.

```
 Session A - [24 x 80]                                                    _ □ ×
File  Edit  View  Communication  Actions  Window  Help

[toolbar icons]

  Columns . . . :     1  71               Edit                   CIS001/QDDSSRC
  SEU==>  _____     EMPPF
  FMT PF .....A..........T.Name++++++RLen++TDpB......Functions+++++++++++++++++
         *************** Beginning of data ****************************************
 0001.00      A          R EMPPFR
 0002.00      A            EMPNO        9B  0
 0003.00      A            LASTNAME    16A
 0004.00      A            FIRSTNAME   12A
 0005.00      A            HOMEPHONE    7S  0
 0006.00      A            ADDR1       40A
 0007.00      A            ADDR2       40A
 0008.00      A            ZIP          5S  0
 0009.00      A            DEPT        12A
 0010.00      A            BIRTHDATE    L
 0011.00      A            HIREDATE     L
 0012.00      A            SALARY       7P  0
         ***************** End of data ****************************************

  F3=Exit    F4=Prompt    F5=Refresh   F9=Retrieve   F10=Cursor   F11=Toggle
  F16=Repeat find        F17=Repeat change          F24=More keys
                                     (C) COPYRIGHT IBM CORP. 1981, 2007.
 MA    a                 MW                                           02/009
  I902 - Session successfully started         A232 - HP LaserJet 4050 on IP_10.134.223.223
```

Figure 5.25: SEU Work Area after Inserting Several More Fields and Pressing F5

Notice on the SEU display in Figure 5.25 that BIRTHDATE and HIREDATE are coded as date fields, type L. Also note that SALARY is declared as a packed-decimal field and EMPNO as a binary field. Normally, the database administrator decides which internal data format to use for different fields. For the example, we chose binary and packed-decimal formats partly for illustration but also because binary is the most efficient format for a nine-digit integer to be used as a key. In addition, the likelihood that calculations will be done with SALARY, as well as the size advantage, make the packed-decimal data type ideal for this field.

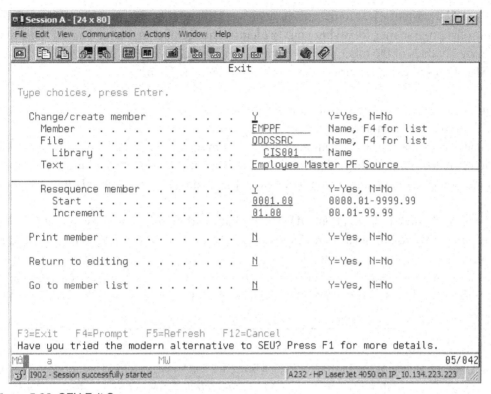

Figure 5.26: SEU Exit Screen

Exiting SEU

When you have finished entering DDS source, press F3 to go to the SEU Exit screen (Figure 5.26). From this screen, you can decide whether to save the work you have done during your SEU session. If you have made changes or added records, the Change/create member prompt will be set to Y automatically. If you choose not to save your work, just type an N here to exit SEU and discard the changes made during this editing session.

From the Exit screen, you also can change the member name or the file and/or library in which the member will be stored. This capability is useful if you have created a new source member by editing an existing member whose name you do not want changed. As you exit, you can simply assign a new name to the edited (changed) member, thus saving your changes under the new name and leaving the original member intact under the original name.

Options are also available to add a text description for the member, resequence the line number, print the member, return to editing, or go to a member list. Initial values are displayed for all these parameters, except the Text parameter. We recommend that you always add descriptive text to describe a member; without this text, it can be difficult for you (or the programmer following you) to identify the member at a later date. In most cases, the current values of the other parameters are sufficient, and you can just press Enter from the SEU Exit screen and return to the Work with Members Using PDM screen.

In this chapter, you have seen how to use the IBM i DB2 DDS to describe a simple physical file. You have also seen how the general-purpose editor SEU facilitates entering DDS language statements through prompting and line commands. And you have seen how PDM, using options or function keys that invoke CL commands, provides a working environment that lets you perform operations on libraries, objects, and members with relative ease.

There is much more to learn about DDS, SEU, and PDM than we can present in this brief introduction; but you now have an idea of how these tools work together to help you create and manage database files, source files, and members. You will add more detail to your understanding of these tools in later chapters; but for now, it is time to work through the lab exercises so you can solidify what you have learned so far.

Note
Notice at the bottom of Figure 5.26 the text *"Have you tried the modern alternative to SEU? Press F1 for more details."* IBM is referring to the new Rational tools you will learn about in Chapter 11.

In Summary

Programmers and operators frequently deal with four kinds of files: physical files, logical files, display files, and printer files. Physical files hold data and may be program described or externally described. Externally described files can be defined at the field level using SQL, or they can be available for DDS members.

To facilitate the definition, creation, and management of files and other objects, PDM provides work-with lists at the library, object, and member levels. When files are defined using DDS, a source physical file, QDDSSRC, is created first. QDDSSRC holds descriptions of individual files coded in the DDS language. Each file description is a separate member of the source physical file.

The DDS file description is entered and maintained using SEU. You can start SEU using a CL command on the command line, or through PDM. You use SEU line commands to manipulate individual records of a source member.

As Figure 5.27 illustrates, the library object CIS001 contains a number of objects, including an output queue, a runable program object (SA1304), a physical file (CSCFINP), and two source physical files.

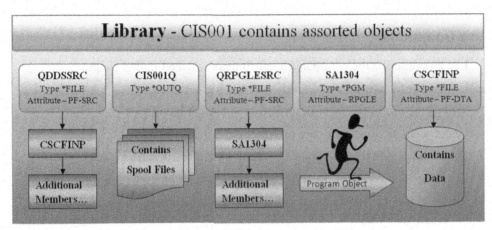

Figure 5.27: Illustration of IBM i Object Hierarchy

The source physical files, QDDSSRC and QRPGLESRC, contain source members. Each member is a description of a file or program. A source physical file can contain virtually an unlimited number of members.

In the next chapter, you learn how to compile a source file-description member, creating a new object of type *FILE in a library.

After completing the Chapter 5 lab, you will have created objects and members at all three levels of the system data-structure hierarchy.

Key Terms

Application Development ToolSet	field-level specifications
binary	floating-point
CCSID	internal date field
Data Description Specifications	*ISO format
Data File Utility	members
DBCS	packed decimal
decimal positions	program-described files
digits	Programming Development Manager
DSPFFD	record format
EBCDIC	record-format specification
externally described files	RDP
F16	RNMOBJ

Screen Design Aid   source physical files
SEU line commands   Structured Query Language
Source Entry Utility   zoned decimal

Review Questions

1. List and describe the common file attributes described in this chapter.
2. How is the file attribute assigned when the file is created?
3. Why is the use of program-described files discouraged?
4. Under what circumstances are program-described files useful?
5. List and describe the advantages of using externally described files.
6. Describe the three steps involved in creating and populating a physical file.
7. Where is the critical information for a physical file stored on the system? List the information stored.
8. List and explain the challenges of describing data using only SQL.
9. What is the purpose of the DDS language?
10. What tools make up ADTS?
11. PDM allows the programmer to work with what types of IBM objects?
12. When you are using PDM, what does the attribute of a *PGM object show?
13. Why do programmers commonly start a source physical file with a Q?
14. How do you create a new member using SEU?
15. Why is the Source type parameter important when using PDM?
16. List and explain the different record types that can be used in a source member.
17. Explain the rules for describing field-level specifications.
18. What is the default format for dates if the DATFMT keyword is omitted?
19. What are the advantages of using internal date fields?
20. What are the advantages of using packed-decimal numeric fields?

Lab 5

Introduction

This lab exercise helps you become familiar with PDM and SEU. You create a source physical file, QDDSSRC, in your library. You then use SEU to enter the DDS source code for a data-file member named STUPF, which will eventually contain data for a STUdent Physical File.

Part 1

Goals   Create a source physical file.

Examine PDM options.

Use a screen option to move from Work with Objects Using PDM to Work with Members Using PDM.

Start at   Any command line.

Procedure   Create source physical file QDDSSRC.

Use Work with Objects Using PDM.

Take option 12 on QDDSSRC to go to Work with Members Using PDM.

5.1.   Sign on to your workstation as usual.

5.2.   First you must create a source physical file. The file will contain file-description members; the first member you create will be the DDS for a physical database file. Go to the menu of source commands and select the command to create a source physical file.

5.2.a.   What is the command name?

5.3.   Name the file QDDSSRC (be sure to spell it correctly), and create it in your own user library (*CURLIB). The default for RCDLEN is 92; change this value to 112. The longer record length is required for ILE source members. Ignore the other options, but key in a description that consists of your full name and the class name. Press Enter.

5.3.a.   What message is returned?

5.4.   Now, to access PDM, use the GO command to display the PDM-related commands menu.

5.5.   On the menu of PDM commands, notice the Start PDM command, which we referred to in the chapter. This command is useful when you need to change defaults or work with PDM options. But when you need to get directly to a list of libraries, objects, or members, the appropriate WRK*xxx*PDM command is more efficient. You want to work with members of the source physical file you just created; but to see how the PDM object and member levels are related, first select the option to work with objects using PDM.

5.6.   Notice that *PRV is a valid value for the Library parameter and is the normal default. PDM remembers which library you worked with the last time you used Work with Objects Using PDM and returns to that library unless you tell it otherwise.

At this time, you are concerned only with objects in your own user (current) library. If the Library parameter value is not your current library name, from the Work with Objects Using PDM command prompt screen, either enter your library name or use the default, *CURLIB. You want to look at *ALL objects and *ALL object types and attributes in your library. When you are ready, press Enter to run the command.

5.7.   The screen you see now should be similar to the one in Figure 5.28.

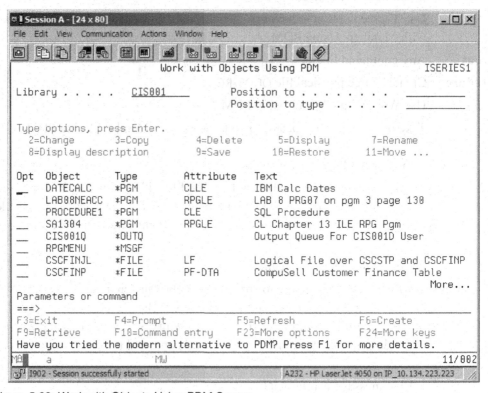

Figure 5.28: Work with Objects Using PDM Screen

5.7.a.   List the names, types, and attributes of the objects in your library.

5.8.   Notice all the object-management options and the function keys.

5.8.a.   How do you display more options?

5.8.b.   What is the option to find a string?

5.8.c.   What is the option to work with the contents of an object?

The Work with Objects level of PDM lets you display objects in a selected library and perform certain management functions on these objects. The Work with option lets you examine and perform management functions on the members of certain types of objects. For example, you should have both an output queue created in a previous lab and the source physical file, QDDSSRC, which you just created in your Work with Objects Using PDM list. Both of these object types allow the Work with option.

5.9.   Take the Work with option on your output queue.

    5.9.a.   What screen have you arrived at?

        This screen should look familiar to you from the preceding lab. If you completed that lab correctly, no spooled files should now be showing, but keep in mind how to get here from PDM. Now press F12 to return to PDM.

5.10.   Next, take the Work with option on your newly created source physical file.

    5.10.a.   What screen is displayed now?

5.11.   Check the File and Library values at the upper left of the screen. They should tell you that you are in file QDDSSRC of your library. Both fields allow input; you can change lists by typing over either or both values and pressing Enter. This sequence gives you a quick way to switch between different source physical files in different libraries.

Part 2

Goals	Create a physical-file source member using F6 from Work with Members Using PDM.
	Use SEU to enter a simple file description.
	Save the DDS source-file description.
Start at	Work with Members Using PDM (WRKMBRPDM your library/QDDSSRC).
Procedure	Press F6 to create a member; provide the member name, and type PF.
	Use the IP line command in SEU to enter the file description.
	Press F3 to save and exit.

5.12.   At this time, no members are listed for your source physical file because you just created the file.

    5.12.a.   What action do you take to create a new member? (Examine the screen carefully.)

5.13. Take the action you discovered in step 5.12. You should see the screen shown in Figure 5.29.

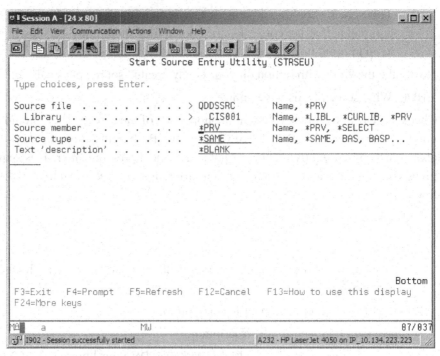

Figure 5.29: Start Source Entry Utility (STRSEU) Screen

5.13.a. What kind of screen is this, and for what command?

Remember that you arrived at this screen by choosing the Create function from Work with Members Using PDM. This should give you some insight into the workings of PDM. In this case, PDM assumes that because you want to create a member in a source file, you need the editor; so PDM takes you to SEU, the traditional all-purpose editor for source files and programs.

Enter STUPF as the source-member name. Move the cursor to the Source type parameter, and press the prompt function key.

5.13.b. What is displayed?

Notice the many source types that SEU can accommodate. Each different type identifies the PDM attribute of a source file or program member that can be entered using SEU. Each type uses a different language syntax checker for verifying the source code, and, upon completion of the source code, tells PDM which specific create command to use to compile the member.

5.14. From the prompted list screen, enter PF as the source type, and press Enter to return to the STRSEU command prompt screen. Key in the description using your full name and class name. Press Enter to continue.

5.14.a. What message appears at the bottom of the screen?

5.15. Displayed now is the SEU Edit work screen with inserted blank lines indicated by apostrophes at the left (sequence-number) margin. You will use SEU's line-prompting facility rather than try to key in the necessary DDS free-form, so press Enter to get rid of the inserted lines and close up the workspace.

The screen should now consist of five lines at the top, a large open area in the middle (the workspace for new lines), and the function keys, message line, and status line at the bottom. The cursor should be at the leftmost sequence-column position of the Beginning of data line. If it is not, you can press Tab or Field exit to move it there.

Before you start the file description, press Help to view help text for the editor. Carefully read through the information about line commands and function keys. Exit Help when you are finished.

5.16. Key IPPF on the sequence column of the first line (Beginning of data). The I means insert a line, the first P means prompt for a line, and PF tells the editor what type of prompting to use (insert and prompt for a physical-file line). Assuming you properly assigned PF to this member type when you created it, the PF in the line command is redundant but harmless. IP by itself uses the specified member type to determine the prompt. Press Enter. You should now see the prompt for a physical-file line in the lower part of the screen, as in Figure 5.30.

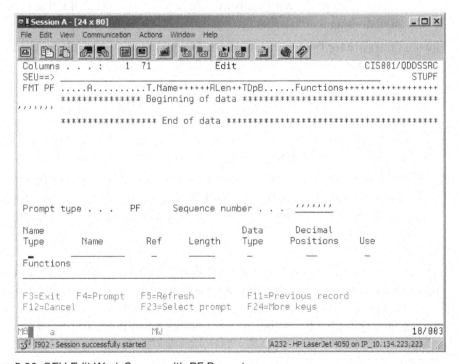

Figure 5.30: SEU Edit Work Screen with PF Prompt

During prompting for DDS, the screen is split between the work-area window above and the prompt-entry fields for each insertion line below.

5.17. The first line of this file description is the record-format line. As we mentioned in the text of this chapter, a database physical file has a single, record-level entry that names the record format, and a number of field-level entries that describe the data fields that make up the file.

Press Help to see the valid values for the Name Type field.

5.17.a. What is the value for a record format?

Press Enter or F12 to exit Help. In the Name Type field, key in the value used for a record format.

Notice that the value you entered is in uppercase. SEU automatically selects uppercase keyboard shift for DDS source members because DDS field values and keywords do not permit lowercase. Only character strings (enclosed within apostrophes) may be typed in mixed case.

5.18. In the Name field, enter STUPFR. Recall that the name of the record format is a programmer-supplied value, but a name related to the file name is commonly used. Only the type and name are required for the record-format line. Press Enter.

5.18.a. What occurs as you enter each inserted line?

Notice that an A is added at column 6. DDS source files all have an A in column 6, so the editor inserts this character for you (but if a line is missing an A, nothing bad happens).

5.19. The next lines are for field descriptions. Before you begin keying, let's review some important points regarding prompting with DDS:

- You can press Enter on an empty prompt line or press Refresh (F5) or Cancel to exit prompting. If you get out by mistake, just type IP (or IPPF) over the sequence number of the line after which you want to continue inserting new lines; then press Enter, and you will be back in prompting.
- Always use the Field exit key to advance to the next prompt field when the characters or numbers entered don't fill the entire field. For numeric values (Length and Decimal Positions), this procedure ensures proper (right) alignment within the field.

Key in the following field descriptions one line at a time. Use Field exit or Tab to skip through prompt-line input fields not listed in Table 5.5. (If no value is listed in the decimal positions column in the table, don't key anything in; 0 is valid only for numeric integer fields.) Press Enter to add each new line to the edit file and clear the prompt.

Table 5.5: Lab Exercise Field Descriptions			
Name	Length	Data Type	Decimal Positions
SOCSEC	9	S	0
LNAME	20	A	—
FNAME	15	A	—
ADDR1	25	A	—
ADDR2	25	A	—
ZIP	9	S	0

5.19.a. What does data type A mean? (Press Help on the Data Type field on the prompt line.)

5.19.b. What does data type S mean?

You should now see the completed entry screen in Figure 5.31.

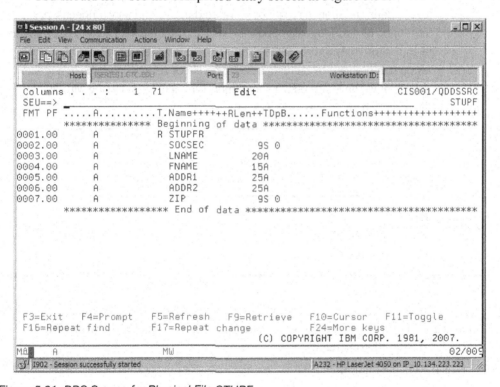

Figure 5.31: DDS Source for Physical File STUPF

Note

You might have noticed that the student physical file in Figure 5.31, as does the employee file described in the text, contains address lines and a zip-code field, but no city or state fields. The reason is that although the files for our lab exercises may be simplified, we would nonetheless like them to conform to important rules for properly designed relational databases. Although an explanation of those rules is beyond the scope of this course, one of them stipulates that the value of a field in a record should not be dependent on the value of another (nonkey) field.

Because the value for zip code dictates the valid values for city and state (i.e., city and state are functions of zip code), including those dependent fields in the same record format with the nonkey field ZIP violates this rule and creates an undesirable dependency relationship within the file. Such dependency relationships not only create data redundancy (unnecessary repetition of data), but also open the way for data inconsistency (e.g., records with different city and/or state values for the same zip code). We choose to avoid this problem by building a separate file of zip-code records in a later lab, after we have discussed some important concepts dealing with the organization and access of file data.

5.20. Press F3 to get to the SEU Exit screen (Figure 5.26) when you are done.

Note

If you reach this screen by mistake, you can use the Return to editing option to return to the editing screen.

Press Enter to save your file description, keeping all the default values.

5.20.a. What message is displayed when you return to the Work with Members Using PDM screen?

5.21. Exit PDM, and sign off.

Creating and Using an Externally Described Database File

Overview

In this chapter, you extend your knowledge of Source Entry Utility (SEU) so that you can use SEU line commands to change existing source members easily. We access SEU through the Programming Development Manager (PDM) Work with Members list, as we did in Chapter 5. You also increase your familiarity with PDM as a convenient way to invoke the appropriate create command when you want to create a file or program from a source member. Last, you learn enough about Data File Utility (DFU) to be able to enter data records into a database file.

Objectives

Students will be able to

- Use SEU line commands to change an existing source member
- Use PDM options to copy and compile source members
- Use CL commands or PDM options to display object, file, and file field descriptions
- Enter data into a database file using DFU

More About SEU

As you learned in Chapter 5, SEU is a general-purpose, full-screen editor that lets you enter or change the source statements that will be used to create an **externally described file**, a CL program, or a program written in a high-level language (HLL), such as C, COBOL, or RPG. In addition to using SEU to create or edit a source member, you can use it to display or print an existing member of a **source physical file**. SEU assumes that a source physical file (e.g., QDDSSRC, QRPGLESRC) exists—that is, the file must have been created in your library using the **CRTSRCPF** (Create Source Physical File) command—and it requires you to identify the file when you start SEU. In Lab 5, you created a source physical file, QDDSSRC, to contain Data Description Specifications (DDS) source members.

Starting SEU

Although it is generally more convenient to invoke SEU by taking a Work with Members Using PDM option on the source physical-file member that you want to edit, display, or print, you also can start an SEU session by entering the **STRSEU** (Start SEU) command on any command line. If you prompt (F4) for the STRSEU command on a command line, a prompt screen similar to the one in Figure 6.1 appears.

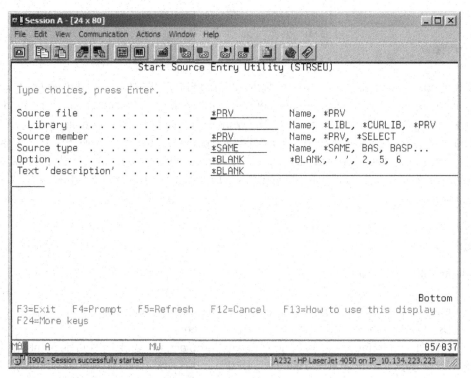

Figure 6.1: STRSEU Command Prompt Screen

The predefined value displayed for the Source file and Source member parameters, *PRV (for *previous*), tells SEU to access the same member from the same source file as the last time you executed the STRSEU command. If you are working with an existing member, the parameter value *SAME for Source type tells SEU to use the source type already specified. If you are creating a new member, *SAME tells SEU to choose a default member type based on the source physical-file name. For example, the default member type for a source physical file named QDDSSRC is PF. If you choose a non–IBM-supplied name for the source physical file, the Source type defaults to TXT. Source type TXT indicates a member whose records contain only 80 characters of text, and the system supplies no syntax checking or prompting.

The value specified for the STRSEU command's Option parameter corresponds to a PDM option—that is, to PDM's 2=Edit, 5=Display (Browse), or 6=Print. In the example, the default value, *BLANK, has been specified. Taking the default is the same as typing 2 or taking PDM option 2; the resulting display is an SEU Edit screen.

If you enter 5 or 6 as the value of the Option parameter, you can browse or print the source member from the STRSEU command. However, just as in starting an Edit session, accessing SEU through the PDM workbench is the more efficient and programmer-friendly way to accomplish either of these tasks. The obvious advantage of using PDM is that the other parameter values (Source file, Library, and Source member) are known to PDM and automatically passed to the STRSEU command. PDM is not an alternative to the STRSEU command—it uses the STRSEU command—but PDM automatically fills in the command-parameter values for you.

If you pressed Enter on the STRSEU command-prompt screen you see in Figure 6.1, and you last used SEU to edit a DDS member named EMPPF, the screen in Figure 6.2 would appear. This is the edit screen for source-file member EMPPF as we left it in Chapter 5 (Figure 5.25).

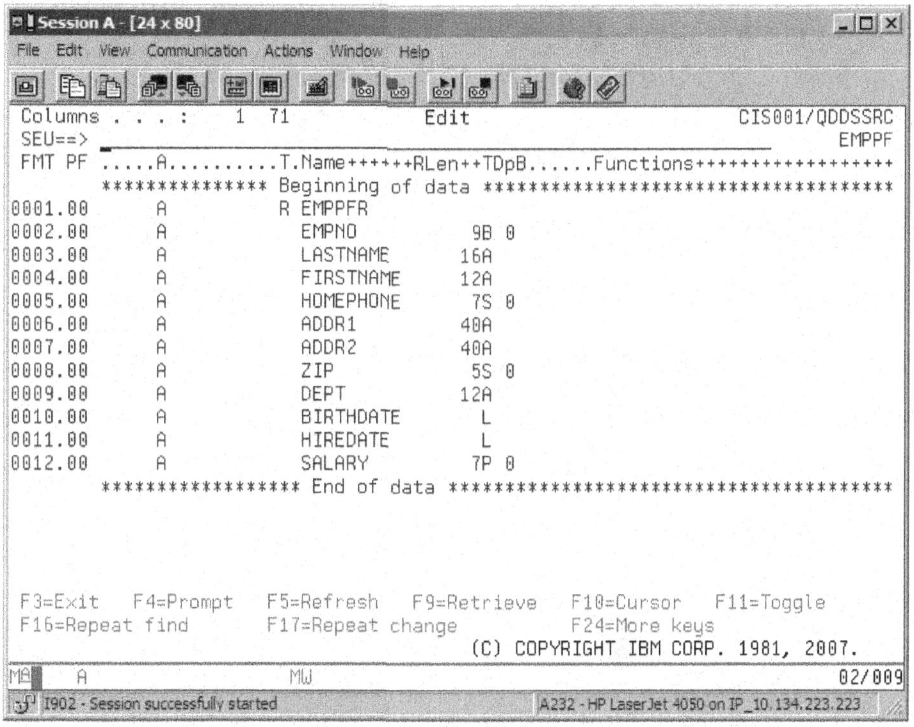

Figure 6.2: SEU Edit Session for Source File EMPPF

Using PDM to Access SEU

Although you can start SEU directly using the STRSEU command, programmers normally access the SEU Edit screen by choosing the Edit option for the source member with which they want to work from the Work with Members Using PDM screen. You can reach this screen in several ways:

- From the PDM menu that appears when you run the **STRPDM** (Start PDM) command, take choice 3, Work with members. Then, if necessary, change the values for File and Library name from the Specify Members to Work With screen (Figure 6.3). (The first time you reach this screen, you will need to fill in the File and Library values; thereafter, PDM remembers where you were the last time.)
- At the Work with Objects Using PDM screen, take the Work with option on the appropriate source physical file (e.g., QDDSSRC).
- From any command line (or from within an initial CL program), execute the **WRKMBRPDM** (Work with Members Using PDM) command, specifying the source physical file whose members you want to work with (e.g., QDDSSRC).

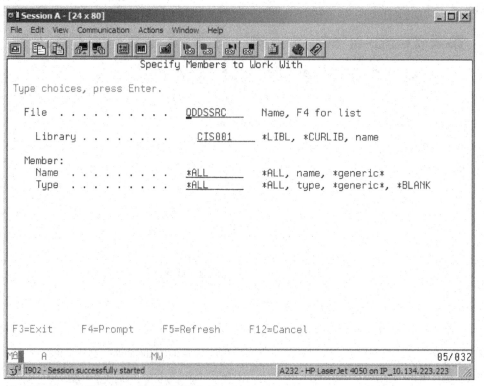

Figure 6.3: Specify Members to Work With Screen

Once you reach the Work with Members Using PDM screen, you can start SEU in edit mode by taking the PDM Edit option (2) for the appropriate member. Figure 6.4 shows the Work with Members Using PDM screen in multicolumn format, with the Edit option entered for file EMPPF.

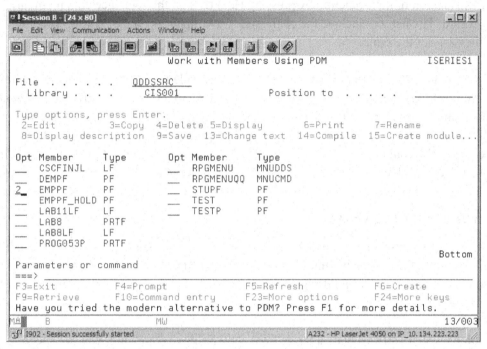

Figure 6.4: Work with Members Using PDM, Edit Option Entered for EMPPF

SEU Line Commands

Recall from Chapter 5 that you enter **SEU line commands** over the sequence numbers of the source-member lines you want to manipulate. In its simplest form, an SEU line command consists of a single letter—for example, you enter a D in the sequence-number area of a line you want to delete. The most commonly used SEU line commands are

- C (Copy), used to copy one or more lines to another place in the source member, retaining the original lines. The copied lines are properly sequenced at the new location.
- D (Delete), used to delete one or more lines.
- I (Insert), used to insert lines of code. We used the insert command in Chapter 5. Because SEU is a full-screen editor, you can Insert a line and then type directly on it if you want to, or you can use the SEU line command IP, a variation that inserts and also provides a prompt line, a feature especially useful for fixed-format or column-oriented languages.

- M (Move), used to move one or more lines to a different place in the source. The moved lines will be properly resequenced at the new location.

You can view a list of the valid line commands for an SEU Edit or Browse session and a brief explanation of their function by pressing Help (F1) on the sequence column of any SEU record. The list will include the commands for whichever type of session you are in—they are not the same.

The line commands that manipulate records of source code let you specify how many lines to copy, delete, or move. For example, the command to delete 10 lines is D10; the command to move three lines is M3. When the number of lines to copy, delete, or move becomes too large to count easily (i.e., if the lines span several pages), you can mark a block of lines by repeating the command letter (e.g., CC, DD, MM) on the first line and the last line of the block. The entire block will then be copied, deleted, or moved.

Target Designator for Copy and Move

SEU's copy and move line commands require you to specify the place in the source code where you want the designated lines of code to be copied or moved. You do this by marking the new location with a "target designator": either an A for *after* or a B for *before* the line on which you enter the target.

In addition, when you designate a target for a copy or move command, you can specify the number of times the copied or moved lines should be repeated. For example, if you are copying or moving several lines and you want them repeated four times, you can type A4 on the target line to tell SEU to repeat the designated lines of code four times right after the target line. To see how this works, observe the SEU line commands entered on source member DEMOPRF in Figure 6.5.

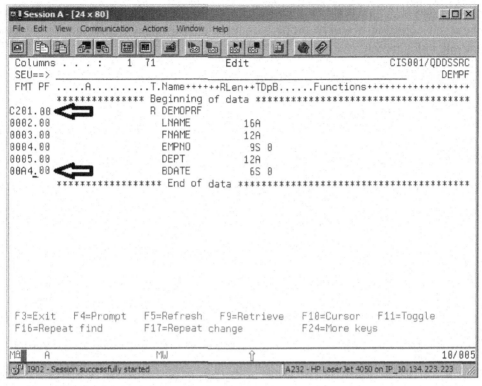

Figure 6.5: Edit Line Commands

Notice that the first line (the record-format line) has a copy command for two lines (C2); A4 has been specified for the target, line 6.

Note

It doesn't matter that the target designation A4 has been typed over the sequence number 6; you can type a command or target anywhere in the seven-character sequence column.

When you press Enter, the first two lines will be copied four times in succession after line 6, and the newly copied lines will be properly sequenced. The resulting member would look like the one in Figure 6.6.

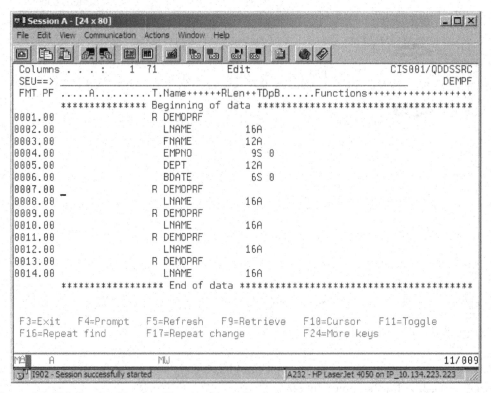

Figure 6.6: Edit Source Member Showing Lines Copied

Compiling the File Description

Now that you know how to use a few SEU line commands necessary to edit a source member, we will look at the second step in the three steps—describe, create, and insert (or load)—of database file construction. In the create step, we use the source member that describes the file to compile a file object that the system can use.

Remember that what we have done so far is *describe* a database file using a DDS source-file member (member STUPF, created in Lab 5). The file description is like the blueprint of a house—the blueprint is not the house itself, but simply a design specification. We have described a database file using DDS, a language designed for the convenience of human programmers. However, the computer cannot use the DDS file description until the description is changed into *object code*, the "native language" of the computer. The same is true of a source program written in a programming language such as BASIC, COBOL, or RPG.

Just as a source program must be translated into executable machine code by a language compiler, so too must a DDS file description be "compiled" into an "executable" file object. As usual, the IBM i operating system provides a number of ways to perform this task. You can enter and run the appropriate create command on a command line, or you can use the PDM Compile option and let PDM select the proper command and fill in the command-parameter values for you.

Create (CRT) Commands

The most direct way to create an object is to use the proper create command and prompt for parameters. For example, to create a database physical-file object, you would use the **CRTPF** (Create Physical File) command. On the command prompt, you must carefully identify the source member, the source physical file, and the library. However, PDM offers an easier alternative: the Work with Members Compile option—option 14.

The PDM Compile Option

Figure 6.7 shows the Work with Members Using PDM screen with the Compile option (14) entered for file EMPPF.

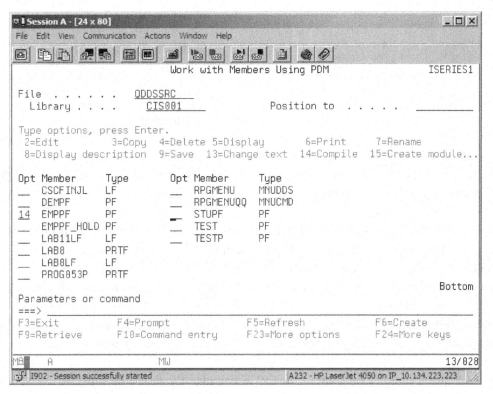

Figure 6.7: Work with Members Using PDM, More Options

You can usually request prompting for PDM options that invoke a CL command, and the Compile option always uses some kind of CRT*xxx* command. In this case, if we used F4 to prompt for the command from the Work with Members Using PDM screen, we would see the CRTPF command prompt screen in Figure 6.8.

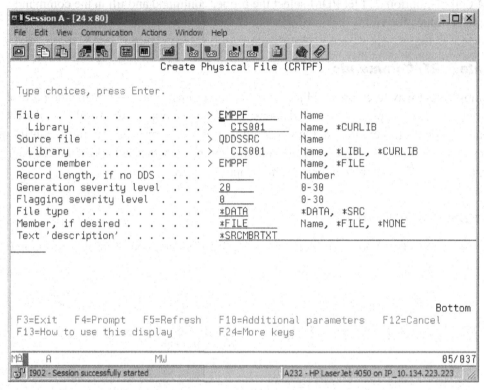

```
  I Session A - [24 x 80]                                                 _ □ ×
 File  Edit  View  Communication  Actions  Window  Help

                          Create Physical File (CRTPF)

 Type choices, press Enter.

 File . . . . . . . . . . . . . . >  EMPPF         Name
   Library . . . . . . . . . . . >    CIS001       Name, *CURLIB
 Source file . . . . . . . . . . >  QDDSSRC        Name
   Library . . . . . . . . . . . >    CIS001       Name, *LIBL, *CURLIB
 Source member . . . . . . . . . >  EMPPF          Name, *FILE
 Record length, if no DDS . . . .   _____         Number
 Generation severity level . . .   20             0-30
 Flagging severity level . . . .   0              0-30
 File type . . . . . . . . . . .   *DATA          *DATA, *SRC
 Member, if desired . . . . . . .  *FILE          Name, *FILE, *NONE
 Text 'description' . . . . . . .  *SRCMBRTXT



                                                                        Bottom
 F3=Exit    F4=Prompt   F5=Refresh   F10=Additional parameters   F12=Cancel
 F13=How to use this display         F24=More keys

 M    A                   MW                                            05/037
    I902 - Session successfully started          A232 - HP LaserJet 4050 on IP_10.134.223.223
```

Figure 6.8: Create Physical File (CRTPF) Command Prompt Screen from Option 14

The command itself, CRTPF, was selected from the large list of create commands. The member type, PF, of the list member for which we took the Compile option (14), told PDM which particular CRT*xxx* command to use.

The parameter values shown for the CRTPF command are the command defaults or have been taken from the PDM list values. The File name will be the compiled object name; by default, it takes the same name as the Source member. The Source member name comes from the PDM list-member value on which the Compile option 14 was selected. The Source file and Library values are from the Work with Members Using PDM screen's File and Library screen headers. Unless you want to give the new file object a name different from the source member or put it in a different library, this command is ready to run.

When you press Enter, PDM submits the CRTPF command to the batch subsystem so that you can continue working while the source member is compiled.

Tip
Compiling in batch is the default PDM option, but you can change the default
by pressing the Change defaults function key, F18, from any PDM screen.

After you press Enter on option 14, a message will appear that tells you the compile has
been submitted to job queue QBATCH in library QGPL. If no other messages are waiting, your
terminal will beep at you when the message indicating the end of the batch job enters your
message queue. (You may need to turn on Message Sound from your emulator's Settings
button to hear the beep.) You can view this message by entering the **DSPMSG** (Display
Messages) command on the command line, or by using the IBM-supplied, user-defined
PDM option DM (Display Message) on any PDM list member. For Basic assistance level,
the messages are grouped by "Messages needing a reply" and "Messages not needing a
reply"; the most recent messages are listed first. Figure 6.9 shows an example of a Basic-
assistance-level Work with Messages screen reached using the DSPMSG command.

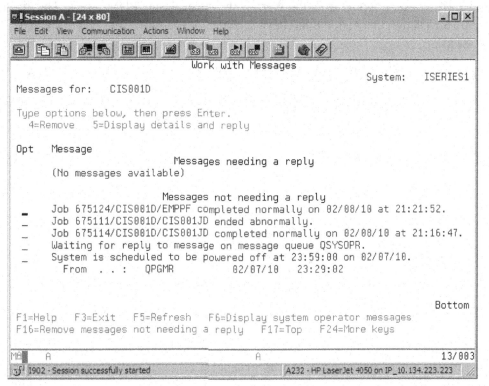

Figure 6.9: Work with Messages—Basic Assistance Level

Notice that a batch compile takes its job name from the file or program being created. The
message for job EMPPF shows that the compile of the source member completed normally.

The message screen lets you change the assistance level, just as you did in Chapter 4 for the Work with Spooled Files (WRKSPLF) screen, using F21.

Because the compile was successful, a new object of type *FILE should have been created in the specified library (usually your current library). To verify that this is the case, you would return to the Work with Objects Using PDM screen by pressing F12 from the Work with Members screen.

If you had not started from the WRKOBJPDM screen, you could type the **WRKOBJPDM** (Work with Objects Using PDM) command on the command line. If you came originally from the Work with Objects Using PDM screen, you would need to refresh the screen (F5) upon returning to it.

Displaying an Object's Description

All objects have descriptions, and you can display the description of an object by choosing option 8, Display description, from the Work with Objects Using PDM screen. The display in Figure 6.10 shows that option 8 has been selected for file EMPPF, our newly created database file.

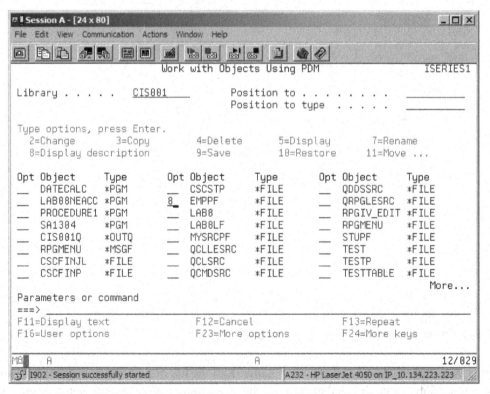

Figure 6.10: Work with Objects Using PDM — Display Description Option Taken on EMPPF

When you press Enter after choosing option 8 from this display, the Display Object Description – Full screen appears. This screen displays information that the system maintains about all objects, including

- Object type
- Attribute (where applicable)
- Owner
- When, where (on what system), and by whom the object was created
- When the object was last modified

The first page of this display, when requested for file EMPPF, would look like the screen in Figure 6.11.

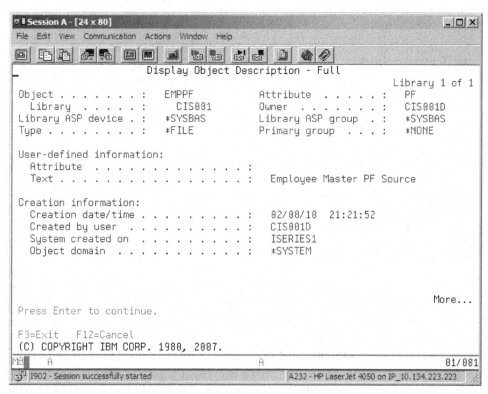

Figure 6.11: Display Object Description – Full, Page 1

Additional pages of this display would show change/usage information, storage information, and save/retrieve information. The system maintains these attributes for all object types, and you can display the attributes by entering the **DSPOBJD** (Display Object Description) command on any command line. DSPOBJD is the command invoked when you select PDM option 8; when you run the command from the PDM option, the object name and type (required parameters) are filled in for you.

Displaying a File Description

Another PDM option, 5=Display, lets you display information about an object; the output depends on the object type. For some object types, option 5 is not valid. For example, for a *PGM object, the option displays information about the program. Selecting option 5 for file EMPPF results in the screen you see in Figure 6.12. The screen heading, Display Spooled File, indicates that the **DSPFD** (Display File Description) command output has been temporarily spooled to an output queue by printer file QPDSPFD.

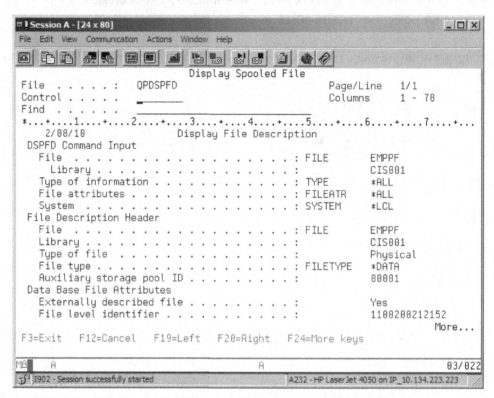

Figure 6.12: Screen Display from PDM Option 5 (DSPFD) for File EMPPF, Page 1

Notice that this output provides more detail than the Display Object Description screen; it tells not only where the file is stored, but also what type it is and whether it is externally described. Additional pages of the display provide information such as number and size of members, record capacity, record length, number of fields, and how the file can be accessed.

Although the Display File Description output tells you that file EMPPF is externally described, it does not provide much information about the record format of the file. The DSPFD command output shows record length and number of fields, but it does not show field-level information.

Displaying Record-Format Information

To see the field-level attributes of file EMPPF, you would need to use the **DSPFFD** (Display File Field Description) command, which we introduced in Chapter 5. You can enter the command on a command line with its sole required parameter, file name; for example,

DSPFFD EMPPF

When you run the DSPFFD command, the first page of the output display looks like that in Figure 6.13.

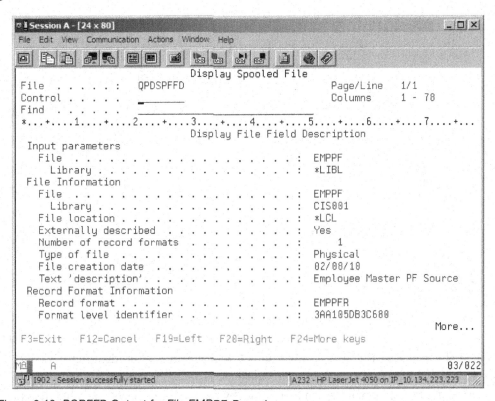

Figure 6.13: DSPFFD Output for File EMPPF, Page 1

Some of the information on this screen is the same as that the DSPFD command makes available, but the second page of the display (Figure 6.14) provides the field-level descriptions of the record, including all field names, data types, sizes, buffer lengths and positions, field usage, and column-heading information.

```
┌──────────────────────────────────────────────────────────────────────────┐
│ ▫ I Session A - [24 x 80]                                         _ □ ×   │
├──────────────────────────────────────────────────────────────────────────┤
│ File  Edit  View  Communication  Actions  Window  Help                     │
│ [toolbar icons]                                                            │
│                       Display Spooled File                                 │
│  File  . . . . . :   QPDSPFFD                      Page/Line   1/22        │
│  Control . . . . .   _____                      Columns     1 - 78      │
│  Find  . . . . . .   _____                                              │
│  *...+....1....+....2....+....3....+....4....+....5....+....6....+....7....+...│
│      Number of fields  . . . . . . . . . . . . :    11                      │
│      Record length . . . . . . . . . . . . . . :   160                      │
│  Field Level Information                                                    │
│              Data      Field  Buffer    Buffer        Field   Column        │
│      Field   Type     Length  Length  Position        Usage   Heading       │
│      EMPNO    BINARY    9  0      4        1           Both    EMPNO         │
│      LASTNAME CHAR       16     16        5           Both    LASTNAME      │
│        Coded Character Set Identifier  . . . . . :    37                     │
│      FIRSTNAME CHAR      12     12       21           Both    FIRSTNAME     │
│        Coded Character Set Identifier  . . . . . :    37                     │
│      HOMEPHONE ZONED     7  0      7       33           Both    HOMEPHONE    │
│      ADDR1    CHAR       40     40       40           Both    ADDR1         │
│        Coded Character Set Identifier  . . . . . :    37                     │
│      ADDR2    CHAR       40     40       80           Both    ADDR2         │
│        Coded Character Set Identifier  . . . . . :    37                     │
│      ZIP      ZONED      5  0      5      120           Both    ZIP          │
│                                                               More...       │
│  F3=Exit   F12=Cancel   F19=Left   F20=Right   F24=More keys                │
│ MA▮    A                                                        03/022       │
│ ⌐▯ I902 - Session successfully started      A232 - HP LaserJet 4050 on IP_10.134.223.223 │
└──────────────────────────────────────────────────────────────────────────┘
```

Figure 6.14: DSPFFD Output for File EMPPF, Page 2

All this information came originally from the DDS entries coded in source member EMPPF in source physical file QDDSSRC. In addition, a Coded Character Set Identifier (CCSID) value is displayed for character fields. This attribute is added by the CRTPF command and is assigned either by a command-parameter value, by the job, or by a system value. Its value identifies the coding scheme used for character data.

Note

It is important to realize that the information about the DSPFFD command comes directly from the compiled file object itself, not from the source member. The object contains this information within it, so it can reveal its complete field-level record layout to any application program or utility requesting it. The system does not maintain record-description synchronization between the file object and the source member; so if the source member were changed, the changes would not be adopted by the file object automatically. Even if the source member were deleted, the capability of the externally described file object to identify its fields would not be compromised.

Data File Utility

We have now covered the first two steps of IBM i database design. In Chapter 5, we described the file (using DDS), and in this chapter we have created the file object. Now let us consider the third step: loading or entering data into the file.

When a file is created, it is like a house under construction. The house has gone from the blueprint to a standing framework of studs, beams, and rafters. The structure is determined, but until the walls and ceilings are finished and the furnishings moved in, it is not a functional home. Likewise, the structure of the compiled file has been decided (we just looked at such a structure using the DSPFFD command), but the file is empty; and until it is populated with data records, it is of little use.

Several possibilities exist for entering data records into a file. If all or most of the data elements already exist in another file, you can use a CL command (for example, CPYF) or a program to copy that data into your new file. If the data has to be entered from source documents, some kind of interactive data-entry program may be required. If there is time and the need warrants, the programming staff may be called on to create a sophisticated interactive data-entry/file-maintenance program written in COBOL, RPG, or another HLL.

However, for quickly and conveniently populating newly created files with test data—for example, to be used in prototyping new applications—**Data File Utility** (DFU) is a better solution. DFU provides a convenient and easy way to change records in and add records to a physical (or logical) database file—without the need to write an HLL data-entry program. Although DFU's limited validation and formatting capabilities prohibit its use for end-user applications, the utility is useful for entering and changing test data for programmers. DFU is another member of the Application Development ToolSet (ADTS).

You access DFU by using the STRDFU (Start DFU) command or by choosing option 18, Change using DFU, on a database *FILE-type object from the Work with Objects Using PDM screen. If you enter the STRDFU command on any command line, the DFU menu in Figure 6.15 appears.

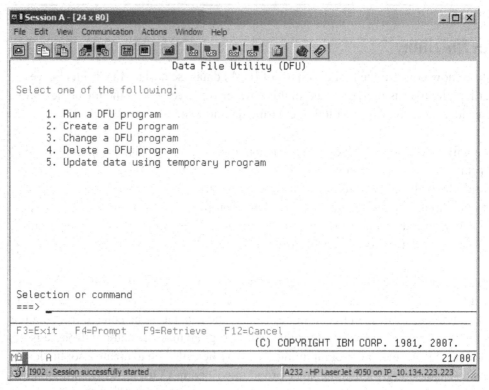

Figure 6.15: Data File Utility (DFU) Menu

DFU works in two ways: It both creates and executes a temporary entry/update program, and/or it builds and stores a "permanent" update program that can be called and used again. To update data using a temporary program, you select option 5 from the DFU menu. Providing a temporary update program is also the approach the system takes when you select option 18 on a file from the Work with Objects Using PDM screen.

The advantage of DFU when working with externally described files is that you do not need to specify a screen layout or field headers, or edit and select fields; DFU generates a default update program using the record-format field-level attributes and file information stored in the data-file object. The disadvantages of DFU are a lack of flexibility and, for a temporary DFU, the machine time required to re-create the program each time you need it. For the purposes of this example, select option 5, to update using a temporary program, from the DFU menu.

Note

Remember, DFU is a programmer's tool and is not used for data entry by the typical user. This tool is restricted on many systems because it is difficult to audit these changes. ProData (*www.prodatacomputer.com*) sells a tool called DBU that many shops now use. This product has both 5250 and GUI interfaces. The new Rational tools and IBM i Access for Windows allow the programmer easier ways to add data to data files; we cover these tools in detail in later chapters of this book.

Using a Temporary DFU Program

Selecting option 5 from the DFU menu takes you to an entry screen (Figure 6.16) that requests the name and member of the file to be updated.

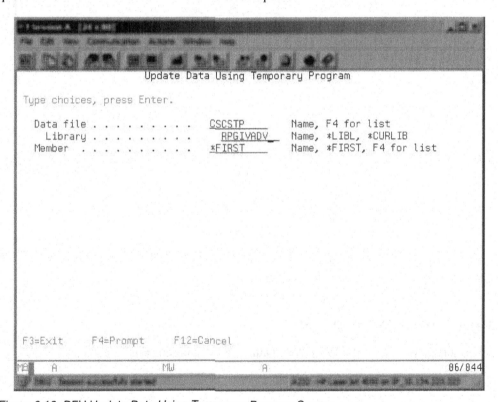

Figure 6.16: DFU Update Data Using Temporary Program Screen

Notice in this case that the current value of the Data file parameter is not the name of the file we have been using in our example (EMPPF). This is because DFU remembers the last time you used a temporary program and provides that data-file name as a default value when you start another temporary DFU program from the menu.

You need to type over the old name, replacing it with the name of the file you want to use—in this case, EMPPF. When you press Enter, DFU creates an update program using the field-level attributes from the file description of EMPPF. While this is going on, the message "*DFU is creating temporary program QDZTD00001 for you to run*" is displayed on the message line. The screen that appears during this rather short time looks like the one in Figure 6.17.

Figure 6.17: DFU Prompt Screen Showing Message

Starting DFU on an Empty File

The next screen you see is the Work with Data in a File screen (Figure 6.18).

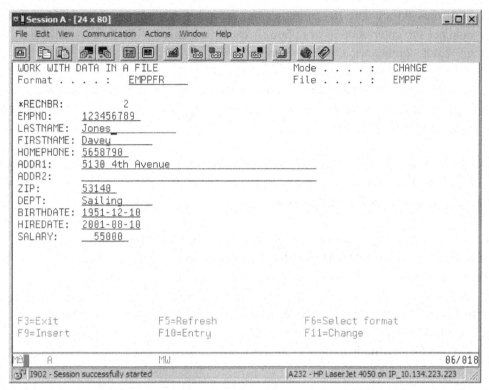

Figure 6.18: Filled-In DFU Entry Screen

When you start DFU using an empty data file, as file EMPPF is right now, DFU's entry mode is active. (The mode is displayed in the update screen's upper-right corner.)

When you are entering data, either the Field advance (Tab) or the Field exit key moves the cursor to the next field. Character data is stored exactly as entered into the field (if you key leading blanks, the data is stored that way). Numeric data is treated as right aligned within the field; for example, 123___ entered in a six-digit integer field would be stored as 000123. The same value entered for a dollars-and-cents field with six digits with two decimal positions would also be stored as 000123, but it would have an implied decimal point between the 1 and the 2 and would be interpreted as 0001.23.

A temporary DFU program does not let you enter any editing characters, such as a decimal point or a comma/thousand's separator, in a numeric field. This restriction also applies to dates and times stored as numbers. For example, you could not enter 6/6/66 or 6666 in a six-digit field used for a date. To properly enter the date June 6, 1966, in *mmddyy* format, you would need to enter 060666 or 60666 (because alignment is on the low-order digit, the leading 0 is not significant), and then press Field exit.

Date and time data (data types L and T) must be entered using the proper format and separator character. For example, you would enter a birth date of August 2, 1956, in an *ISO Date field as 1956-08-02.

The fields in Figure 6.18 have been entered correctly. Note that when the last field you type in is numeric and you do not enter the maximum number of digits, you must press Field exit or Tab to exit the field before you press Enter.

When you have inspected the data and are ready to write the record to the file, you press Enter or F10. Pressing either key saves the record, but Enter is easier to reach. The system stores the record and then displays an empty entry screen for the next record.

In entry mode, you cannot back up to retrieve a previously entered record. If you realize, after you press Enter or F10, that there was an error in the data, you must get out of entry mode and into change mode to correct the error.

DFU Change Mode

F11 takes you to DFU's change mode. For the type of files we have created so far, when you first reach change mode, the only input field on the screen will be one named *RECNBR. All physical-file records are given a **record number** that indicates their order of entry. For example, the fifth record entered would be record number 5, the 100th record number 100, and so on. If you know the record number of the erroneous record, you can enter it in this field, and DFU will search for and retrieve it, if it exists. Otherwise, you can press Page up to retrieve the last record entered. From any record currently displayed in change mode, pressing Page up takes you to the next lower record number; Page down takes you to the next higher record number.

When you have found the bad record and corrected it, you can continue to enter new records by returning to entry mode. To do so, you simply press F10 from change mode.

If you want to delete the bad record instead of correcting it, you must first display the record in change mode, and then press F23. You are then asked to press F23 again to confirm.

Tip

DFU will not allow you to change the list of available keys as you can in SEU. If you want to see the list of available function keys, you should move the cursor to the function key area and press F1 for the full list. Remember, this is a programmer's utility, and at the time it was developed the interfaces were not what they are today.

Exiting DFU

When you are finished entering records, pressing F3 takes you to the End Data Entry screen (Figure 6.19).

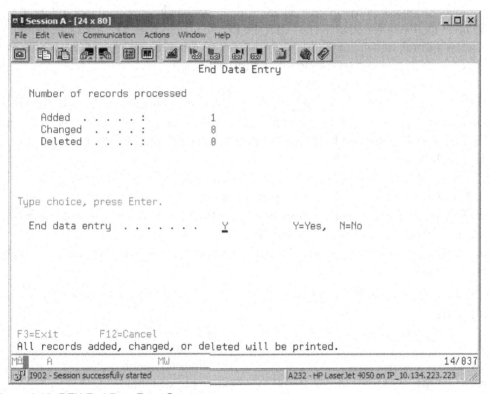

Figure 6.19: DFU End Data Entry Screen

This screen reports the number of record adds, changes, and deletions, and asks whether you really are finished with your data entry. If you arrived at this screen by pressing F3 by mistake, you can return to the DFU data-entry screen by typing N over the default value of Y for the screen's End data entry prompt.

You will learn more about DFU in the next chapter. Meanwhile, when you are using DFU in the lab exercise, do not forget that online Help is available for DFU if you want to explore the topic further or refresh your memory while you are adding or changing records.

In Summary

In this chapter, we covered the creation and data-entry steps of building a database file. Using a slightly modified form of the DDS source-file description we created in Chapter 5, we employed Work with Members Using PDM option 14 to compile the source member into a file object. The compile option invokes a create command; the particular command used is determined by the member type. In our example, the CRTPF (Create Physical File) command was invoked. The PDM compile option usually eliminates the need to type command-parameter values because PDM inserts these values automatically. In addition, the compile option normally submits the compile to the batch subsystem, leaving your workstation available for other work. After the file object has been created successfully, you can display information about the file at the object, file, and record-format levels by using the DSPOBJD, DSPFD, and DSPFFD commands, respectively.

You also learned that the DFU utility provides a quick and convenient way to enter and update data in a file. Entry mode allows interactive data entry; change mode retrieves an existing record by record number or via the Page up/Page down keys, letting you make changes to the record.

In the following lab exercise for this chapter, we will use SEU line commands to edit a source file. We will use the Move, Copy, and Delete SEU line commands to manipulate records in a DDS source member. We will then compile the source file using the PDM compile option, and enter data records into the physical file using the temporary entry/ update-program feature of DFU.

Key Terms

CRTPF	record number
CRTSRCPF	SEU line commands
Data File Utility	source physical file
DSPFD	STRPDM
DSPFFD	STRSEU
DSPMSG	WRKMBRPDM
DSPOBJD	WRKOBJPDM
externally described file	

Review Questions

1. List and explain the "steps" in creating a physical file.
2. Why is it important to properly name source files when using PDM?
3. What is the default member type for a source physical file with a non-IBM-supplied name?
4. Explain how messages are displayed when the user's Help level is set to Basic.
5. List and explain the SEU line commands discussed in this chapter.
6. Explain the term *target designator*.
7. Describe the relationship between PDM and SEU.
8. List the advantages of using PDM to create (Compile) objects.
9. List the information on objects that the system maintains that we discussed in this chapter.
10. What are the advantages of using externally described files?
11. Explain the difference between the DSPFD and the DSPFFD commands.
12. What is the purpose of DFU? Are there other tools that perform the same function?
13. How many modes does DFU have?
14. What are the advantages and disadvantages of DFU?
15. How do you delete a record in DFU?

Lab 6

Introduction

In this lab, you become more familiar with PDM, using its options to copy source members and create a physical database file. You also use PDM to access SEU and DFU. You practice using SEU line commands to edit a source-file member, and you create a temporary DFU program and use it to load data records into a physical-file member.

Part 1

Goals   Clear your output queue.

Copy source physical-file member STUPF to TESTSEU.

Use SEU to alter TESTSEU and then return it to its original state.

Start at   System command line.

Procedure WRKOUTQ your output queue, and print/delete any spooled files.

WRKMBRPDM QDDSSRC.

Copy STUPF to TESTSEU.

Edit copied member TESTSEU using SEU line commands.

6.1. Sign on as usual. From the Main menu command line, use the WRKOUTQ (Work with Output Queue) command to examine your output queue. Remember to provide your output-queue name as a parameter when you run the command. If your output queue contains spooled files, either delete them or print them now so that you begin this lab with an empty output queue.

6.2. Start PDM, selecting the Work with objects option. Specify all objects of all types in your library (these should be the defaults).

6.3. From the objects list in your library, select the option to work with the source physical file you created in Lab 5.

6.4. At the Work with Members Using PDM list screen, you should see member STUPF. You will use this member to practice entering SEU line commands; but to make sure you do not accidentally damage the good member, let us make a copy of it. Take the PDM option to copy member STUPF. You should now see a Copy Members screen similar to the one in Figure 6.20.

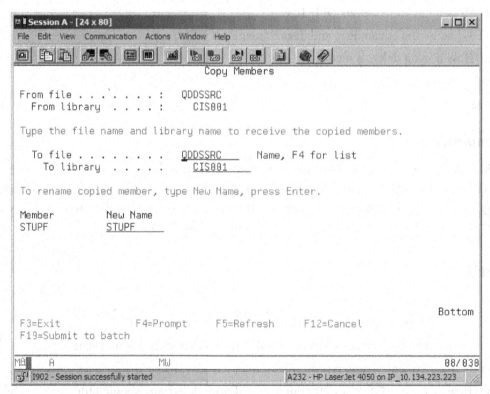

Figure 6.20: Copy Members, from Work with Members Using PDM Option 3

6.5. At the Copy Members screen, the cursor should be on the To file entry field. You can see that PDM has already provided the file and library names of the member you are copying. You will keep the copy in the same file and library, so press Tab or Field advance (not Field exit) to move the cursor down to the New Name entry field. Name the new member TESTSEU, and press Enter.

> 6.5.a. After you return to the Work with Members Using PDM screen, what message is displayed at the bottom of the screen?

6.6. Now, take the option to edit member TESTSEU.

Let us start editing the member by inserting a new field for middle initial just after the first-name field. Remember that you type SEU line commands, such as Insert, right over the sequence numbers. Using the New line key, move the cursor to the sequence number for the first-name field. Type IP to insert a line with prompting, and then press Enter.

Remember that field entries do not use the Name Type field. Name the new field MI, give it a length of 1 (remember to press Field exit after you type the length), and make it alphanumeric. When you press Enter, notice that the line is inserted after the line on which you keyed the Insert command. Also, notice that you remain in insert mode in case you need to insert more than one record.

To get out of insert mode, as you should do now, press F5 or F12 (you can also press Enter on an empty prompt).

6.7. Besides the Insert command, the most useful SEU line commands are Copy, Delete, and Move. The Copy and Move commands require you to specify which lines are to be copied or moved, and to what location in the source file they are to be copied or moved. The location designator is called the "target." You specify the target by moving the cursor where you want the copied or moved line (or lines) to go, and then typing either an A (for *after*) or a B (for *before*) on the sequence number of the target line.

Let's move the last-name field by typing M anywhere on the sequence number of the last-name field line. Then, to move the last-name field after the middle-initial field, type A on the middle-initial line's sequence number. After you press Enter to execute the line command, the name fields should be in the following order: first, middle initial, last.

To move several lines at a time, you can type the number of lines to be moved immediately after the M (e.g., M5), or you can mark a block of contiguous lines by typing MM on the first line's sequence number and another MM on the sequence number of the last line of the block.

To move all three name fields as a block to a location after the zip-code field, type MM on the sequence number for the first-name field and MM on the sequence number for the last-name field. Alternatively, because you can easily see that three lines are to be moved, you could type M3 on the sequence number for the first-name field. In either case, you need to enter the target designator (A) on the sequence number for the zip-code field. If you haven't done so already, please do that now, and remember to press Enter to execute the command.

Note

Target B is allowed on the Edit screen's End of data line, so you could use that approach instead of entering target A on the zip-code line—the result would be the same.

6.8.	SEU's Copy command is similar to the Move command; the difference, of course, is that Copy leaves the copied lines at their original location and "clones" them at the target location. As with the Move command, you can copy a single line or multiple lines. For example, to copy the two address lines and place them before the first-name field, type the Copy command C2 on the ADDR1 line's sequence number, type target B on the FNAME field's sequence number, and then press Enter.

At this point, your SEU work screen should look like the one in Figure 6.21.

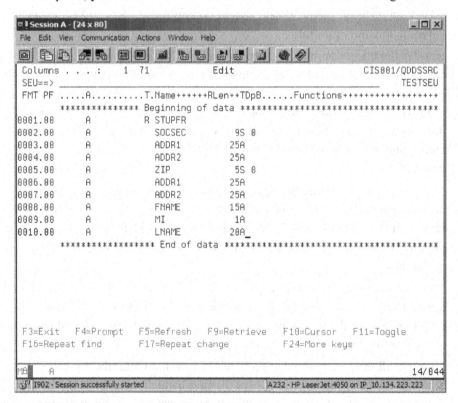

Figure 6.21: SEU Edit Screen Showing Changed Member

Now, print the screen showing your changes. At the end of the lab, change the spooled file in your output queue to printer PRT01 (or another printer designated by your instructor/mentor), and hand in the printed output with your answer sheet.

6.9. SEU's Delete command removes a single line or a block of lines from a source file. To delete a single line, you type D on that line's sequence number. To delete a specific number of lines, you type D*n* on the first line of the block, where *n* is the number of lines to be deleted. If the block is large, use the block Delete command by typing DD on the first line of the block to be deleted and DD on the last line. As always, you type the command itself over the sequence number of the line. Unlike the Copy and Move commands, the Delete command does not need a target; that is, you do not have to specify A or B.

To get more practice using SEU's line commands, try putting your TESTSEU file back the way it was when you started, in the field order SOCSEC, LNAME, FNAME, ADDR1, ADDR2, ZIP. When you are finished, print the screen to hand in with your answer sheet.

6.10. We are done with TESTSEU for now, but we will keep it in your QDDSSRC file for future use. Exit SEU now. The Exit screen values should specify, "Change/create member...Y." Whether or not you successfully returned TESTSEU to its original state, there is no need to save your work, so change this value to N. Doing so will simply keep the original TESTSEU member as it was before editing. Leave the other defaulted values alone, and press Enter to exit.

Note

If you decided to compile the source member TESTSEU, you should understand that it will not compile as Figure 6.21 shows it. The reason for this is that ADDR1 and ADDR2 are duplicate field names and DB2 does not allow duplicate field names in a physical file.

Part 2

Goals Add a field to DDS source member STUPF.

Compile the source member, creating physical file STUPF.

Display a message to find out whether the compile was successful.

Check the record format of the new physical file.

Start at Work with Members Using PDM, your library/QDDSSRC.

Procedure Edit STUPF, adding the PHONE field.

Save and compile STUPF.

> DSPMSG to check compile success.
>
> DSPFFD to observe the record format.

6.11. Make sure you are at Work with Members Using PDM file QDDSSRC, in your library. If you are not, change the file or library entry fields at the top left of the screen and enter correct values.

6.12. Take the option to Edit on member STUPF. Make sure you are looking at an SEU work screen in edit mode for source member STUPF. Insert a field named PHONE right after field FNAME; make it a 10-digit, zoned-decimal (signed) field with no decimal positions. Then reverse the order of the name fields so that field FNAME precedes field LNAME. The source member should now look like the one in Figure 6.22.

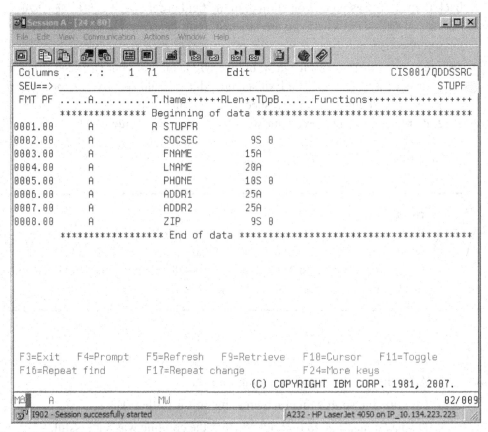

Figure 6.22: SEU Showing Correct STUPF

6.13. Exit SEU, taking the default (Y) for the Change/create member option and the defaults for the rest of the options. Be sure to press Enter from the Exit screen.

6.14. From the Work with Members Using PDM screen, type 14 (for Compile) in the option field of the member you just edited (STUPF). Do not press Enter, but request prompting for the command. You should see a screen like the one in Figure 6.23.

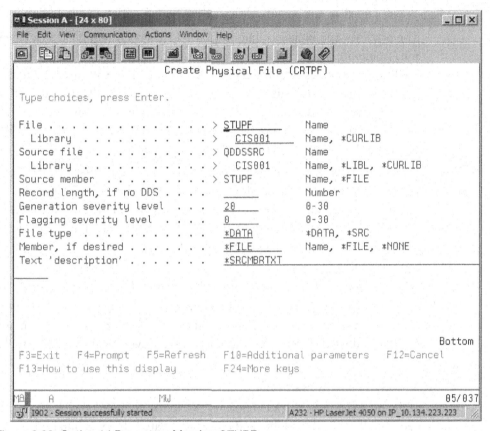

```
⌨ I Session A - [24 x 80]                                          _ □ ×
 File  Edit  View  Communication  Actions  Window  Help

 [toolbar icons]
                    Create Physical File (CRTPF)

 Type choices, press Enter.

 File . . . . . . . . . . . . . > STUPF          Name
   Library . . . . . . . . . . > CIS001          Name, *CURLIB
 Source file . . . . . . . . . > QDDSSRC         Name
   Library . . . . . . . . . . >   CIS001        Name, *LIBL, *CURLIB
 Source member  . . . . . . . . > STUPF          Name, *FILE
 Record length, if no DDS . . . .                Number
 Generation severity level  . . . 20             0-30
 Flagging severity level  . . . . 0              0-30
 File type . . . . . . . . . . . *DATA           *DATA, *SRC
 Member, if desired . . . . . . . *FILE          Name, *FILE, *NONE
 Text 'description' . . . . . . . *SRCMBRTXT


                                                            Bottom
 F3=Exit   F4=Prompt   F5=Refresh   F10=Additional parameters   F12=Cancel
 F13=How to use this display       F24=More keys

 MA▮   A                    MW                                    05/037
 ⌨ I902 - Session successfully started        A232 - HP LaserJet 4050 on IP_10.134.223.223
```

Figure 6.23: Option 14 Prompt on Member STUPF

6.14.a. What CL command does PDM option 14 invoke in this context?

The context in which an option is taken is significant, and it is what makes PDM such a powerful tool. The option you select (in this case, option 14) tells PDM which verb form to use as part of the command; the source-member type (in this case, PF) tells PDM which noun form to use. By analyzing the option and member type, PDM can choose the correct command (in this case, CRTPF).

By default, PDM creates an object of the same name as the source member. But, as you can see, you could change the name of the object about to be created if, for some reason, you wanted it to be different from the member name on the CRTPF command-prompt screen. PDM also places the object in the same library as the source file unless you specify otherwise on the prompt screen.

6.15. Without making any changes to the default values, press Enter to run the command.

6.15.a. What is the first message displayed at the bottom of the screen?

The first message indicates that the compile has been submitted as a batch job (from within your interactive job). Page down on the message line to read the second message. It tells you that your compile job was sent to the job queue of the batch subsystem, QBATCH. By default, PDM sends option 14 compiles to the batch subsystem so you can continue to work while the compile is running. The programmer or operator can change this, as well as other PDM options, for her own PDM environment.

6.16. When the compile is finished, a message is sent to your (user) message queue telling you whether the compile was successful. If no undisplayed message is already waiting in your message queue, the terminal beeps at you and the message-waiting indicator (MW on PCs, a torn-form symbol on dedicated terminals) lights up on the status line, the bottom-most line of your display device.

You can examine the message by entering the DSPMSG (Display Messages) command on the command line or by entering the IBM-supplied, user-defined PDM option DM (Display Message) on any member's option field. If you get to the message queue before the message arrives, you can press F10 to display any new messages. If your display is set at the Basic assistance level, use F5 instead of F10 to refresh.

6.16.a. What does the message say?

If the message indicates an abnormal end to the compile, you need to return to the source member and compare it carefully to the member in Figure 6.22. Correct any discrepancies in your source code before you try the compile again. If the compile is still unsuccessful, seek help from your instructor/mentor.

6.17. At this point, return to the Work with Objects Using PDM screen by pressing F12 twice. After refreshing the screen, you should be able to see the newly created *FILE object in your list (you might need to Page Up).

6.17.a. What is the *FILE object's attribute?

6.18. Because this is an externally described file, detailed information at the file, record, and field levels are kept as part of the object itself. You can examine information at the different levels by using appropriate commands.

Move the cursor to the command line (use F9) and type the DSPFFD (Display File Field Description) command. This command needs a single parameter value, the name of the file (STUPF), which you can enter as a positional value or by prompting. Run the command.

Examine the file and record-format information on the first page of the display, and then page down to the field-level descriptions of the record format. You should be looking at a screen similar to the one in Figure 6.24.

```
Session A - [24 x 80]                                                    _ □ ×
File  Edit  View  Communication  Actions  Window  Help

 [toolbar icons]

                        Display Spooled File
File  . . . . . :    QPDSPFFD                        Page/Line   1/22
Control . . . . .    _____                        Columns     1 - 78
Find  . . . . . .    _____
*...+....1....+....2....+....3....+....4....+....5....+....6....+....7....+...
   Number of fields  . . . . . . . . . . . . . :      7
   Record length . . . . . . . . . . . . . . . :    113
 Field Level Information
              Data      Field  Buffer   Buffer          Field    Column
   Field      Type     Length  Length  Position         Usage    Heading
   SOCSEC     ZONED      9  0      9        1            Both     SOCSEC
   FNAME      CHAR       15      15       10            Both     FNAME
     Coded Character Set Identifier  . . . . . :     37
   LNAME      CHAR       20      20       25            Both     LNAME
     Coded Character Set Identifier  . . . . . :     37
   PHONE      ZONED     10  0     10       45            Both     PHONE
   ADDR1      CHAR       25      25       55            Both     ADDR1
     Coded Character Set Identifier  . . . . . :     37
   ADDR2      CHAR       25      25       80            Both     ADDR2
     Coded Character Set Identifier  . . . . . :     37
   ZIP        ZONED      9  0      9      105            Both     ZIP
                                                                   Bottom
 F3=Exit   F12=Cancel   F19=Left   F20=Right   F24=More keys

MA    A                     MW                                        03/022
  I902 - Session successfully started        A232 - HP LaserJet 4050 on IP_10.134.223.223
```

Figure 6.24: STUPF Record Format from DSPFFD Command

It is important to realize that although this information originally came from the DDS source member, the information now exists independently as part of the file object itself. Because of this fact, any program or utility using the file can immediately identify and use the record format, including all fields and their attributes.

6.18.a. How many fields are there in the record, and what is the total record length?

Now return to the Work with Objects Using PDM screen.

Part 3

Goals   Start DFU and create a temporary update program.

Add data records to your STUPF file.

Observe the data added to the file.

Locate, identify, and print spooled files created during this lab session.

Start at   Work with Objects Using PDM, your library.

Procedure   STRDFU.

Take option 5 from the DFU menu.

Add records using DFU.

WRKMBRPDM STUPF, option 5.

WRKOUTQ your output queue.

6.19. Next, you will use DFU to enter data into your database file member. Key the STRDFU command on the command line. Choose option 5 from the DFU menu to update using a temporary program; press Enter.

Enter your database file name (STUPF), and check the other parameter values for correctness. Press Enter.

6.19.a. What message is displayed? (Look quickly and write down as much as you can.)

6.20. After a moment or two you should see a screen for interactively entering data and updating your file. This is a temporary DFU program created for your file, STUPF. The utility can create a similar update program on demand for any externally described database file.

6.20.a. Which mode are you in?

6.21. Type in the data for the first record. Use your own name, but use Social Security number 111110001. Use fictitious data for the other fields. Do not use any editing characters (e.g., commas, hyphens) in the numeric fields. Use the Field exit key or Field advance (Tab) key to jump to the beginning of each field. After typing the zip code, press Enter.

Tip

If you press Enter on an incomplete numeric field, an error code flashes and the keyboard locks up. If this happens, press Reset (usually the left Ctrl key on PC keyboards), and finish keying the field, or press the Field exit key.

Each time you enter a filled-in screen, the current data is stored as a new record in the file, and a fresh input screen is provided. If you press Enter too soon (before you complete a screen), use F11 to switch to change mode, Page Up or Page Down until you find the incomplete record, finish it, and then press Enter to save the changes. F10 returns you to entry mode.

6.22. Enter the following four data records, pressing Enter after each one.

111110002	111110003	111110004	111110005
Bilbo	Karikool	Matilda	Sammy
Baggins	Clapsaddle	Twiddlebotham	Higgins
3193778466	3074559999	3193668824	8383668824
345 Hawthorne Ln.	Sundown Rd.	1812 River Rd.	3245 Sheridan Rd.
Apt. Z	Bunkhouse #2		
52302	82301	52404	53142

Use your own data to add at least 10 more records. Enter Social Security numbers in the range of 111110005 to 111110020. We are using this sequence to help you remember the numbers in later lab exercises. Avoid using the same Social Security number twice, because this will cause problems later on.

Use local zip codes for at least half the records. After you have entered the last record, press F3 to exit.

6.22.a. What screen do you see now? How many records were added?

6.22.b. What does the message at the bottom of the screen tell you?

Press Enter, leaving the defaults as they are. Exit from the next two screens, or until you have returned to the Work with Objects Using PDM screen.

6.23. From the Work with Objects Using PDM screen, enter option 12 in the option field for file STUPF. When you press Enter, you should be at the Work with Members Using PDM screen. Although you took the Work with option on a database physical file, the file also has a member, and certain limited PDM options are available for that member.

6.23.a. What is one of the options you have used on a source-file member (your DDS file description) that is not available for a database file member?

Take the option to display the member, and press F4 to prompt.

6.23.b. Which CL command does this option invoke?

Run the command. Shift right. Notice where the last digit of the zip code lines up on the ruler line. Compare that value to the second part of your answer to question 6.18.a.

6.24. Return to the Work with Objects Using PDM screen. Work with your output queue.

6.24.a. How many print files has Lab 6 generated?

Two of these files have file names that are not the name of the default printer-device file, QSYSPRT, used by the Print Screen key. Display those files. Use the function key to shift your view to the right. Notice that page headers and other information require more than 80 print positions. As you examine these spooled files, keep in mind that they had to have come from actions taken in this lab.

6.24.b. What do you think these two files are, and where did they come from (what action generated them)?

Reroute your files to printer PRT01 or to the printer designated as your class printer. Print the files created in this session. Clip the printed output to your answer sheet to hand in.

7

Introduction to Query

Overview

This chapter introduces you to Query for i5/OS, the IBM i traditional report generator, and steps you through the process of producing a query report based on a single database file. Then we explore the concept of joined files and create a query to combine data from two files. In the lab, you put into practice what you learn by printing a listing of the database file you created in Lab 6. Chapter 15 discusses DB2 Web Query for i, IBM's replacement for Query for i5/OS. Many companies still use Query, so new programmers should understand this tool.

Objectives

Students will be able to

- Describe several features of Query for i5/OS, such as record selection, column formatting, summary functions, and report breaks
- Create result fields (derived columns) from existing fields
- Use Query for i5/OS to generate a display or printed report based on a single file
- Change query output from display to a printed report
- Determine the need to join files to get the information needed for a report
- Use Query for i5/OS to create a report that joins data from two files

What Query for i5/OS Does

One of the main components of a database management system (DBMS) is a **report generator**, or query utility. In the IBM i OS, **Query for i5/OS**, an IBM licensed program product, provides this function. Other, more powerful, products are available—both from IBM and from third-party vendors—but Query for i5/OS is widely used, easy to learn, and available on most systems.

You can use Query for i5/OS to obtain information from any externally described database file. The file may have been defined using either of the methods we discussed in Chapter 5: Data Description Specifications (DDS) or Structured Query Language (SQL). Query for i5/OS lets you generate printed reports, screen displays, or new database files using data from one file, or by joining data from up to 32 different files. You can select from one to all fields and organize them into a printed report, display them, or write them to another file.

Query for i5/OS is easy to use. It is menu driven, with entry screens that help you select and format data; no programming skill is required. Once you have gained some experience, most query reports take little time to set up. For example, the simplest report requires entering only the name of a database file.

Features that Query for i5/OS supports include the following:

- *Selection and arrangement of records*. You can use simple relational expressions to select specific records from files. You then can order those records in ascending or descending sequence by using any field or combination of fields as sort keys. For example, you could sort all records in an employee file by employee name within department.
- *Selection and placement of fields*. You can choose specific fields to display or print, and you can place the fields in any desired order. You can edit the fields—for example, insert slashes (/) in a date field for readability—or perform arithmetic operations on the fields to create new result fields. In addition, you can easily adjust column widths and change column headings.
- *Specification of report breaks*. You can print or display groups of records sorted by the values of designated sort-control fields. This Query for i5/OS feature, also called *control-break logic,* lets you select control fields to be used on up to six levels of report breaks (e.g., department within section within division). You can also choose column functions for desired fields. These functions let you print automatic calculations, such as total and average, when the value of a sort-control field changes. For example, if the employee file is sorted by department, after you list all employees in the same department you could print a count of department employees and the total salary for the department.
- *Ability to examine a report layout and preview a report*. At any time while specifying a query, you can use the **F13 function key** to display a layout of the query output as it might appear on a printer spacing chart. You also can use the **F5 function key** to test the query to see what the report will look like with actual data. You then can make any necessary changes to your query without having to exit Query for i5/OS.
- *Execution of query programs*. Although a complete, saved query specification is not a program in the sense of object type—a query's object type is *QRYDFN, not *PGM— you can run a query just as you would a program by using option 16 on a *QRYDFN

object from the Work with Objects Using PDM screen, or by entering the RUNQRY (Run Query) command on any command line. When a query is run, it uses the current data from the selected file (or files) in the same way a program written in a high-level language (HLL) (e.g., COBOL, RPG) would when the program is executed.

Starting Query for i5/OS

The STRQRY (Start Query) command takes you to the Query Utilities menu (Figure 7.1), which provides a list of query functions.

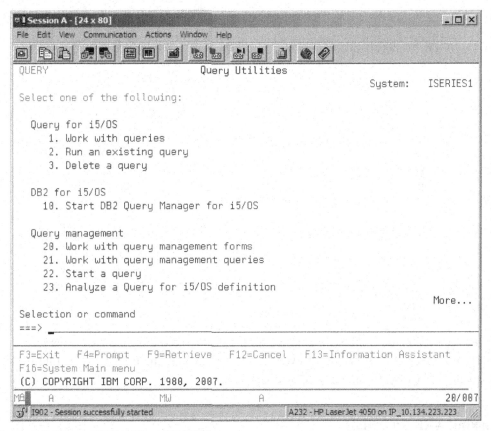

Figure 7.1 : Query Utilities Menu (QUERY)

Because this screen is a menu, you can also reach it by using the GO command (GO QUERY).

For this chapter, you will be concerned only with the options listed under the heading Query for i5/OS on this menu. You can perform two of these options, Run an existing query and Delete a query, more conveniently from the Programming Development Manager (PDM) environment by taking option 16 or 4, respectively, on the appropriate *QRYDFN list item.

The function we are most concerned with in this chapter, Work with queries (option 1), takes you to the Work with Queries screen (Figure 7.2).

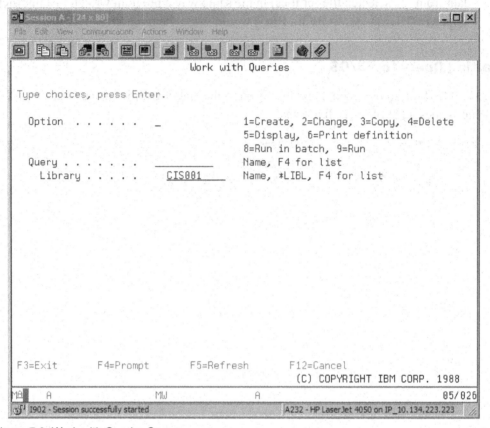

Figure 7.2: Work with Queries Screen

You also can reach the Work with Queries screen—and avoid the Query Utilities screen entirely—by executing the WRKQRY (Work with Queries) command or by selecting PDM's Work with option (12) for any *QRYDFN object.

Working with Queries

From the Work with Queries screen, you can

- Create a query
- Change, copy, delete, or display an existing query
- Print a query definition
- Run a query either as a batch job or interactively

To create a new query, you take option 1, Create; you can name the query at that time or wait until the query definition is completed. The other options listed on the Work with Queries screen (e.g., 2=Change, 3=Copy) work only with existing queries. If you cannot remember the name of an existing query, you can place the cursor on the Query input field and press F4 to view a list of existing query definitions in the selected library. Figure 7.3 shows such a list.

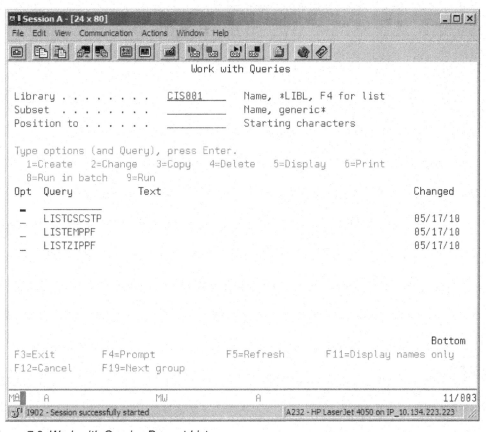

Figure 7.3: Work with Queries Prompt List

The first time you use Query for i5/OS, the library displayed is your current library. After that, the WRKQRY command returns you to the library you were using on the previous occasion.

As with any other work-with list, you can move the cursor down the list you see in Figure 7.3 and type the option you want next to the query to be used. If the query you're looking for is not in the list, you can change the Library value specified at the top of the screen and press Enter to see a new list.

Defining a Query

In the next few pages, we will step through the process of creating a query. When you type a 1 in the Opt (option) field of the Work with Queries screen, and then press Enter, the main query specification screen, Define the Query (Figure 7.4), appears.

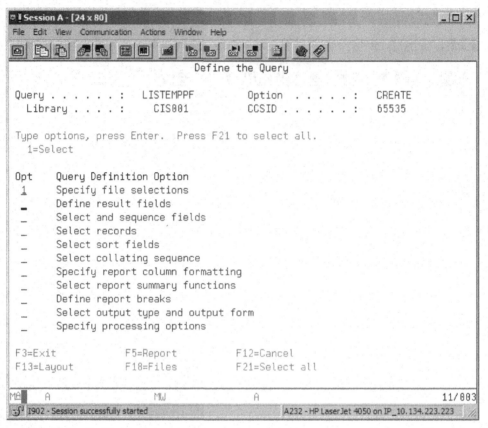

Figure 7.4: Define the Query Screen

This screen presents all the available query features you can use to create a customized query. After you select one of these features, Query for i5/OS prompts you through a series of related lower-level screens to define exactly how you want the feature to work for this report. Most of this process is menu-driven—you simply select option numbers or respond to prompts—but parts of some features require you to reorder list items or enter expressions or functions.

When you finish defining one feature, you return to the Define the Query screen. From there, you can select the next feature or Exit and save your query if you are finished.

Selecting Files

When the Define the Query screen first appears, the Specify file selections option is selected automatically (i.e., a 1 is entered for that option). Query for i5/OS automatically selects this option because, at the very least, you must tell Query for i5/OS which file to use.

When you press Enter from the Define the Query screen, you see the Specify File Selections screen in Figure 7.5.

Figure 7.5: Specify File Selections Screen

From here, you can prompt to see a list of physical and logical database files in your current library (the initial default) or in another library to which you are authorized. Pressing the **F4 function key** on the File name input field takes you to the Select File screen (Figure 7.6).

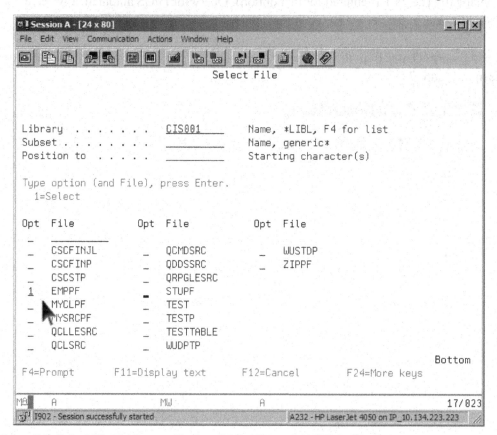

Figure 7.6: Select File List Screen Displayed After Prompting (F4) on File Name

In the figure, file EMPPF has already been selected for use in this query (note arrow).

If you realize, after looking at the list of files, that this is not the library that contains your file, you can simply type over the Library value (CIS001 in the example), replacing it with the name of the library of the file you need. Pressing Enter will then change the display to list files from the new library (assuming, as always, that you're authorized to use that library).

When you press Enter on the Select File screen, Query for i5/OS fills in the File name field
(in this case, using file name EMPPF) and Record name field (EMPPFR), and then asks you
to confirm that the file name and record are correct. You are then returned to the Define
the Query screen. At that point, the Define the Query screen would look like the one in
Figure 7.7.

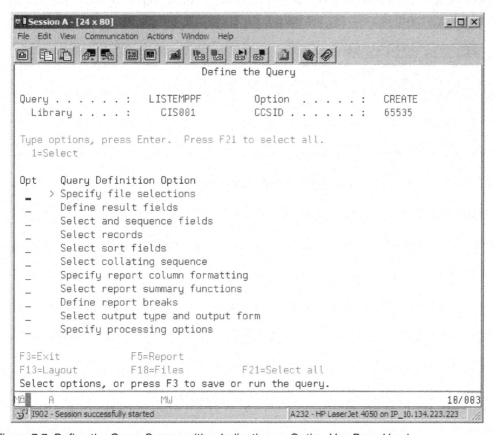

Figure 7.7: Define the Query Screen with > Indicating an Option Has Been Used

Notice that a greater-than symbol (>) displayed to the right of the Opt (option) field has
replaced the 1 on the Specify file selections line; this is to remind you that this feature has
been used. (If you need to, however, you can always go back and change the values you
specified for any feature by again taking option 1 on that feature.)

Previewing a Query Layout

That is all you would need to do to generate a "bare-bones" query of a single database file. To see how the query is formatted at this point, you would press F13 from the Define the Query screen. Figure 7.8 shows the first 72 print/display positions of the query layout for our example. (You could see the additional columns of the report by pressing the **F20 function key** to shift the view to the right.)

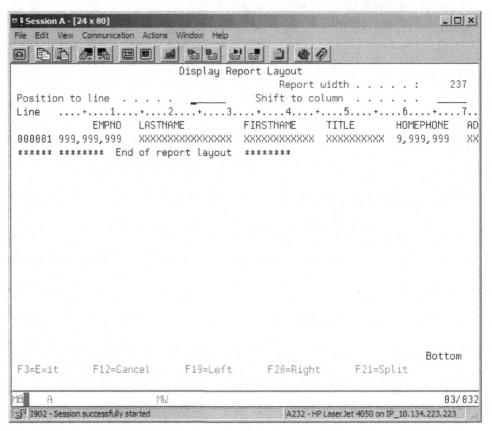

Figure 7.8: Display Report Layout Screen

Notice that field names are used as column headers, spaces are inserted between columns, and numeric fields (EMPNO and HOMEPHONE) are edited with commas to separate thousands.

Let us say that after viewing the report layout, you have decided to change the way the numeric fields EMPNO and HOMEPHONE were edited. Before you can edit these numeric fields, you must first press Enter or F12 to return to the Define the Query screen. There, select the Specify report column formatting option, as Figure 7.9 shows.

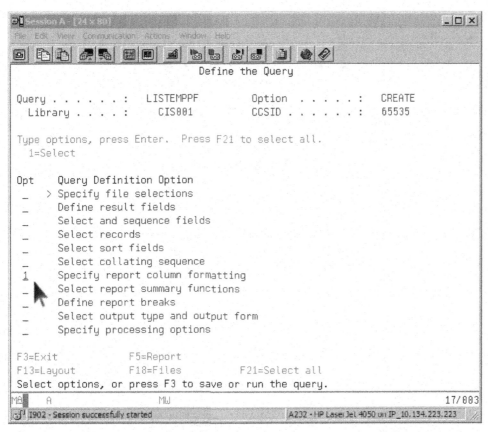

Figure 7.9: Define the Query Screen with Specify Report Column Formatting Selected

Formatting Report Columns

The Specify Report Column Formatting screen (Figure 7.10) displays three fields at a time and lets you change column spacing, column headings (which can be up to three lines long), and field length.

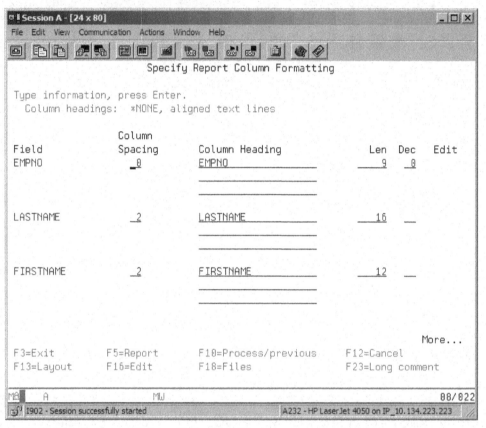

```
□ I Session A - [24 x 80]                                          _ □ ×
File   Edit   View   Communication   Actions   Window   Help
[icons]
                    Specify Report Column Formatting

Type information, press Enter.
  Column headings:  *NONE, aligned text lines


                    Column
Field               Spacing        Column Heading          Len  Dec  Edit
EMPNO                 _0           EMPNO_____        9   _0
                                   _____
                                   _____


LASTNAME              _2           LASTNAME_____       16   __
                                   _____
                                   _____


FIRSTNAME             _2           FIRSTNAME_____       12   __
                                   _____
                                   _____

                                                              More...
F3=Exit          F5=Report     F10=Process/previous    F12=Cancel
F13=Layout       F16=Edit       F18=Files               F23=Long comment

MA   A                  MW                                        08/022
□ I902 - Session successfully started      A232 - HP LaserJet 4050 on IP_10.134.223.223
```

Figure 7.10: Specify Report Column Formatting Screen

Caution

On the Specify Report Column Formatting screen, if you make a field's length shorter than the actual database field, you could lose data in the report. This setting does not change the data in the actual database, only the presentation of the data on the report.

On this screen, you need to edit numeric field EMPNO. You will find the function you need, the **F16=Edit function key**, listed among the function keys at the bottom of the screen.

To edit the field, you would move the cursor to anywhere in the horizontal zone for field EMPNO—that is, the line starting with the field name, EMPNO, and the two lines following it—and press F16. Doing this would take you to the Define Numeric Field Editing screen you see in Figure 7.11.

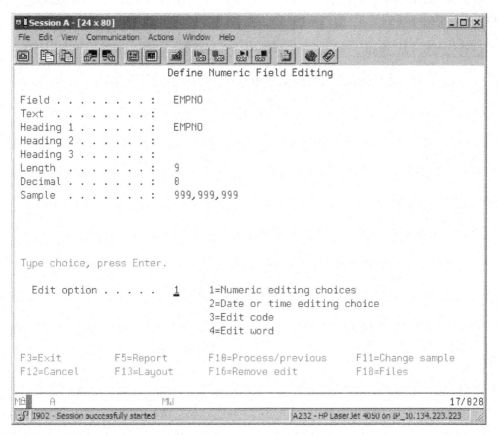

Figure 7.11: Define Numeric Field Editing Screen for EMPNO

This screen identifies field EMPNO and displays its column headings, its length, and a sample of how the field would appear when printed.

Editing Options

As you can see in Figure 7.11, the sample for field EMPNO shows that commas are used
as separators. To eliminate the commas, you would use the default Edit option 1, Numeric
editing choices. Selecting this option takes you to the Describe Numeric Field Editing
screen (Figure 7.12).

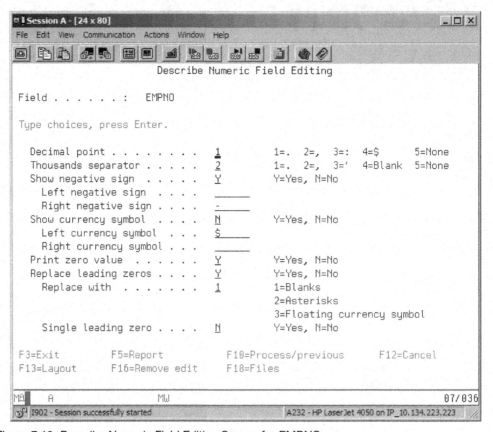

Figure 7.12: Describe Numeric Field Editing Screen for EMPNO

Here, you can change the Thousands separator value from a comma to None by typing a 5
over the 2, which is the default. You can see the other options available on this screen that
have to do with the display of the negative sign, currency symbol, and leading zeros.

When you change a value on an entry screen such as the Describe Numeric Field Editing
screen, it is important to press Enter, rather than F12, to save changes; F12 does not save
your changes. Although pressing F3 saves your changes, it takes you to the query exit
screen; don't use F3, therefore, unless you are finished specifying the query.

Pressing Enter on the Describe Numeric Field Editing screen returns you to the Specify
Report Column Formatting screen (Figure 7.13).

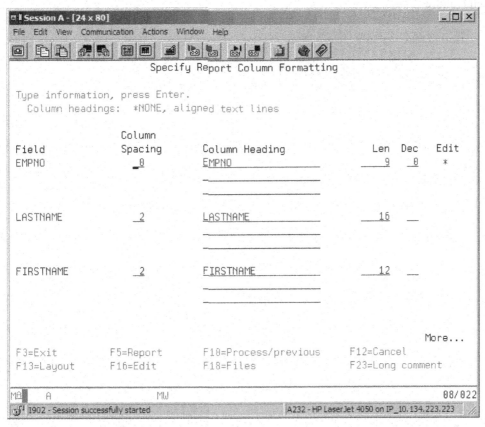

Figure 7.13: Specify Report Column Formatting with * Indicating Field EMPNO Has Been Edited

Notice that an asterisk (*) now appears under the Edit column for field EMPNO; this is to
remind you that the field has been edited.

Now let us say that after viewing the layout of file EMPPF again, you still are not satisfied
with the appearance of field EMPNO. The field contains a Social Security number, and you
would like to separate the parts of the number with blanks (spaces) so that the number

would appear as 999 99 9999. To accomplish this, you would press F16 again, with the cursor in the EMPNO field's horizontal zone, to return to the Define Numeric Field Editing screen (Figure 7.14).

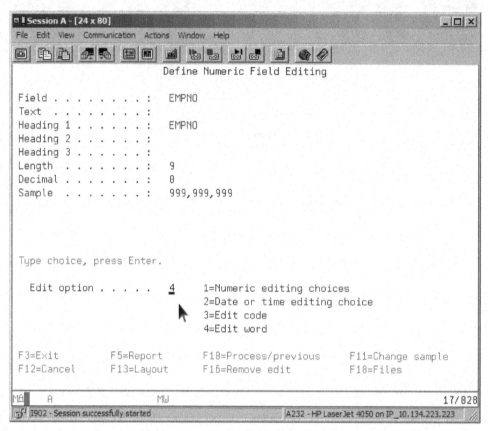

Figure 7.14: Define Numeric Field Editing Screen Revisited

To use blanks as separators, you need to create an **edit word** by using option 4. (This option has already been entered in Figure 7.14.) Only one edit choice, code, or word can be active for a field at any time, so by creating an edit word for field EMPNO, you will override the numeric edit choice (remove comma thousands separator) that you made previously. After you take choice 4, the Specify Edit Word screen (Figure 7.15) appears.

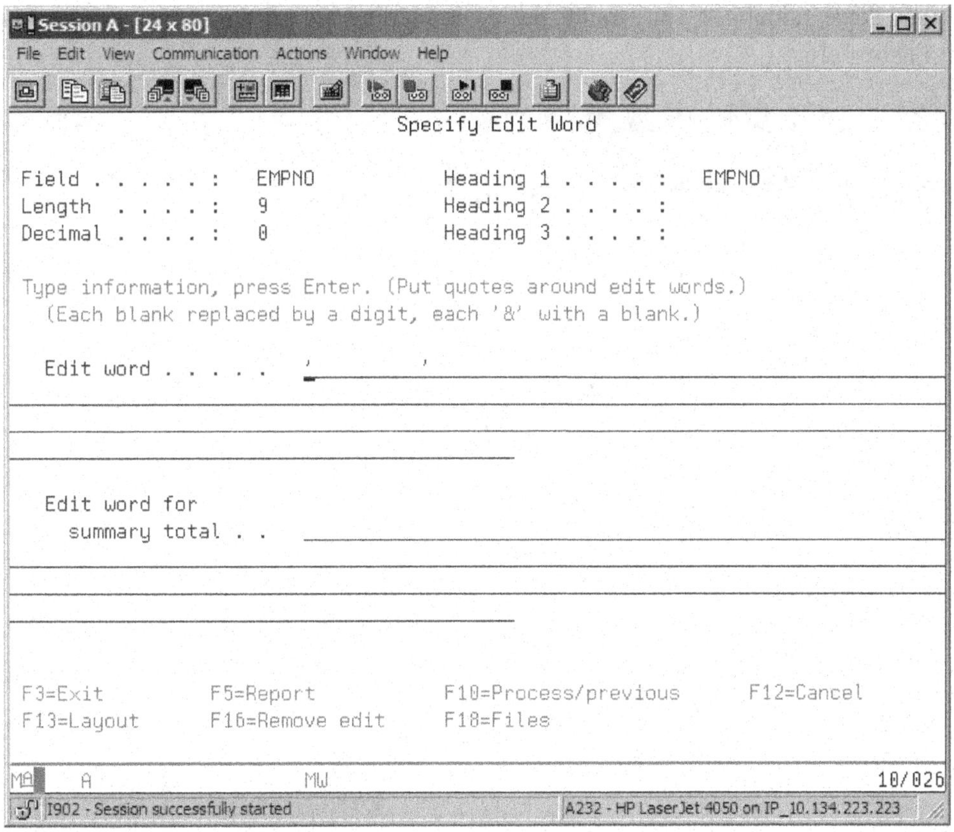

```
 I Session A - [24 x 80]                                          _ □ ×
 File  Edit  View  Communication  Actions  Window  Help
 ▢ ▣ ▣  ▣ ▣  ▣ ▣  ▣  ▣ ▣  ▣ ▣  ▣  ▣ ▢
                        Specify Edit Word

  Field . . . . . :  EMPNO          Heading 1 . . . . :  EMPNO
  Length  . . . . :  9              Heading 2 . . . . :
  Decimal . . . . :  0              Heading 3 . . . . :

  Type information, press Enter. (Put quotes around edit words.)
    (Each blank replaced by a digit, each '&' with a blank.)

     Edit word . . . . .    '_____      '
  _____
  _____
  _____

     Edit word for
       summary total . .   _____
  _____
  _____
  _____

  F3=Exit        F5=Report        F10=Process/previous    F12=Cancel
  F13=Layout     F16=Remove edit   F18=Files

 MA    A              MW                                    10/ 026
    I902 - Session successfully started     A232 - HP LaserJet 4050 on IP_10.134.223.223
```

Figure 7.15: Specify Edit Word Screen

This screen works like this:

- The apostrophes (') delimit the edit word, and initially the number of blanks (spaces) within the apostrophes is equal to the number of digits in the field.
- As the display indicates, each digit is represented by a blank. To insert an actual blank (spacebar) into the edited field, you would use the ampersand character (&).
- If you wanted to use other edit characters, such as hyphens (-) or slashes, you would insert the characters where you needed them to appear within the edit word.

Following these guidelines, you would specify your edit word for the EMPNO field as you see in Figure 7.16.

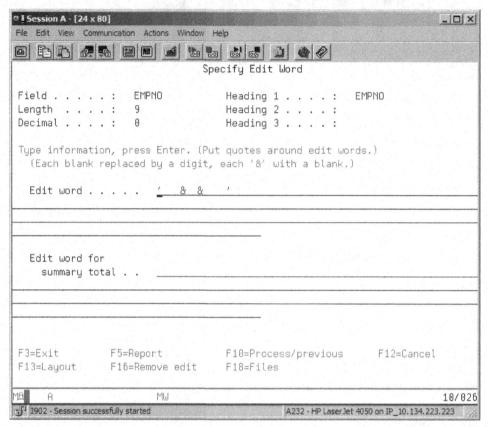

Figure 7.16: Specify Edit Word with Edit Characters Entered

Notice that the two ampersands have been inserted inside the apostrophes so that the number of spaces (digits) is still nine, the same as the length specified at the top of the screen for field EMPNO. If the number of digit placeholders within the apostrophes differs from the length value, Query for i5/OS considers it an error and puts the entire quoted string in reverse image until you fix it. It also displays the error message *"Edit word does not match field length"* at the bottom of the screen.

When you press Enter and return to the Specify Report Column Formatting screen, you can try the Layout function again to see the effect your edit word will have. The Display Report Layout screen for our sample query now looks like the one in Figure 7.17; you can see that the blank insertion was successful.

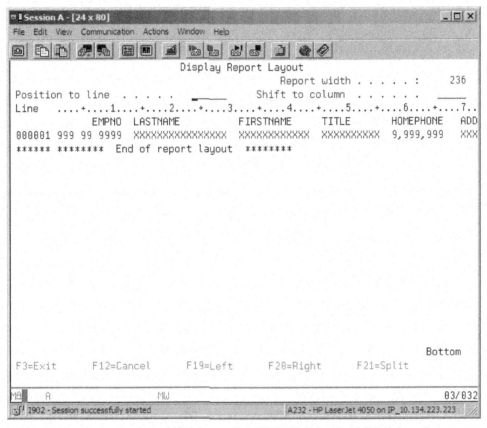

Figure 7.17: Display Report Layout Screen — Field EMPNO Edited with Blank Insertion

Using another edit word, you could easily format the HOMEPHONE field to eliminate the comma thousands separator and insert a hyphen between the exchange and the subscriber code, which is the standard way to display a seven-digit telephone number in the United States. Figure 7.18 shows the edit word to accomplish this formatting.

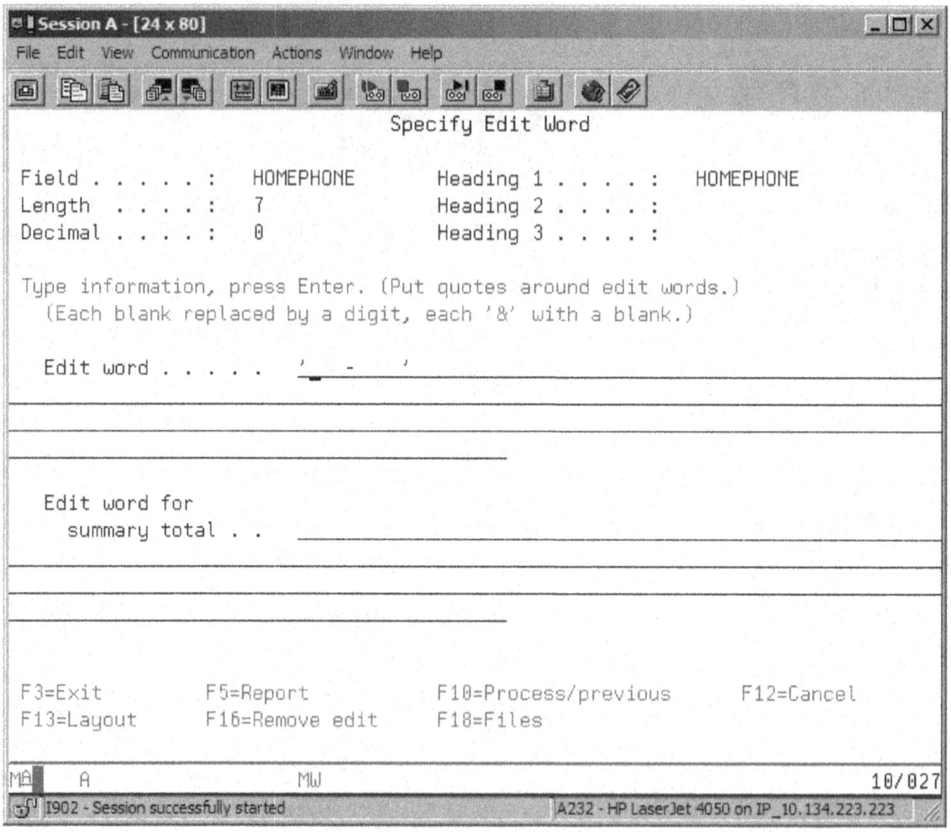

```
 I Session A - [24 x 80]                                          _ □ ×
 File  Edit  View  Communication  Actions  Window  Help

 [toolbar icons]
                           Specify Edit Word

 Field . . . . . :   HOMEPHONE        Heading 1 . . . . :   HOMEPHONE
 Length  . . . . :   7                Heading 2 . . . . :
 Decimal . . . . :   0                Heading 3 . . . . :

 Type information, press Enter. (Put quotes around edit words.)
   (Each blank replaced by a digit, each '&' with a blank.)

    Edit word . . . . .      '   -    '

 _____
 _____
 _____

    Edit word for
       summary total . .    _____

 _____
 _____


 F3=Exit        F5=Report        F10=Process/previous    F12=Cancel
 F13=Layout     F16=Remove edit   F18=Files

 MA   A                     MW                                  10/027
    I902 - Session successfully started       A232 - HP LaserJet 4050 on IP_10.134.223.223
```

Figure 7.18: Specify Edit Word Screen to Edit Field HOMEPHONE

In Figure 7.18, the hyphen is inserted, but the number of spaces (digit placeholders) remains seven. As we indicated above, when you use an edit word, it isn't necessary to first change numeric editing choices (code 5 to eliminate thousands separators) because all default editing options are turned off automatically if you select an edit code or edit word.

Editing Numeric Date and Time Fields

Both the HIREDATE and BIRTHDATE fields in our EMPPF file are defined as date (data type L) fields. When you are using Query, date or time (data type T) fields are automatically edited according to their format and separators.

However, many older database files store date or time data as numeric zoned- or packed-decimal fields, and Query for i5/OS edits such data as numbers by using the comma thousands separator. You could always create an edit word, as we did above, to format such fields; but an easier way to insert slashes, hyphens, or colons (:) in date and time fields is to use another option on the Define Numeric Field Editing screen (Figure 7.11): option 2, Date or time editing choice. Selecting this option takes you to the Describe Date/Time Field Editing screen (Figure 7.19).

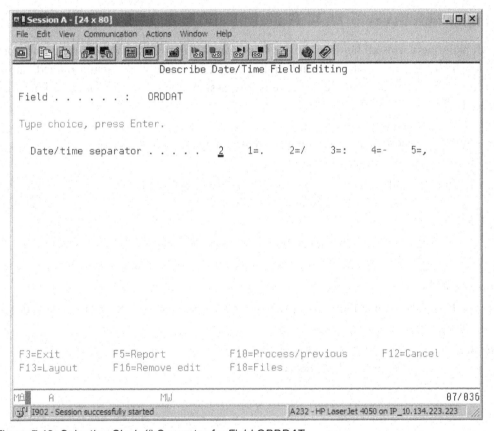

Figure 7.19: Selecting Slash (/) Separator for Field ORDDAT

We have included a numeric field (ORDDAT) from an older database that shows the Date/time capabilities. From this screen, you can choose which separator to use. Choice 2, for example, causes a six-digit birth date in *mmddyy* format to appear as 6/21/73 for a person born on June 21, 1973.

Note

When a date field is defined as data type L, insertion characters determined by the date format (*ISO uses hyphens) are already part of the field; so no further editing is needed. In fact, Query for i5/OS does not permit editing of L-type fields.

Refining Your Query

The default query uses all fields in the database record. To define a usable query, you must decide which fields you want to include in this report, how you want them arranged, and any other report specifications. In the example below, assume the following specifications are required:

1. Select all records, but group them by department. Within department, you want the records sorted in ascending sequence on last name.
2. Include the following fields, in this order: DEPT, LASTNAME, FIRSTNAME, HOMEPHONE, EMPNO, BIRTHDATE, GENDER, and WORKPHONE. You do not want to include fields ADDR1, ADDR2, or ZIP.
3. Display meaningful column headers (e.g., Employee Number instead of EMPNO).
4. Include count of number of employees in each department and a final count of all employees.
5. Include subtotal and the average salary for each department, and a final total salary for the whole company.
6. Calculate the number of years each employee has been employed, and find the average years employed per department.

To accomplish the first specification, you need to sort the records coming into the query by last name within department. Then you can define a report break that lets you print subcounts, subtotals, and averages when the department changes. Figure 7.20 shows the Define the Query screen, with Select sort fields and Define report breaks already selected. As in PDM, multiple options can be selected and then processed in order.

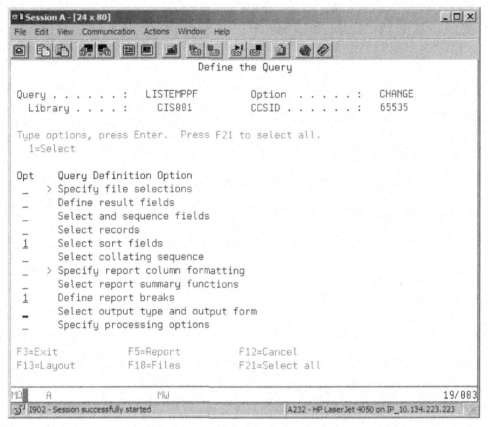

Figure 7.20: Define the Query Screen with Two Options Selected

Selecting Sort Fields

When you press Enter from Figure 7.20, the first screen that appears is the Select Sort Fields screen you see in Figure 7.21.

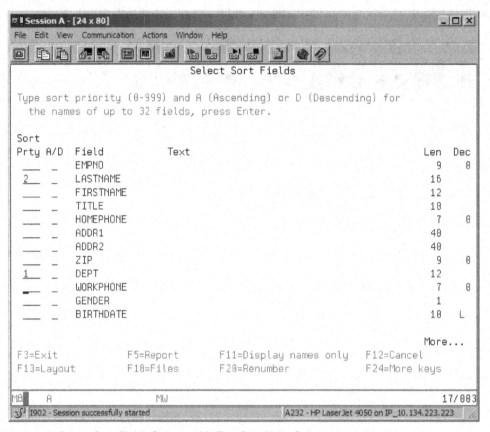

Figure 7.21: Select Sort Fields Screen with Two Sort Keys Selected

Query for i5/OS lets you select up to 32 different sort-key fields, although in practice it is uncommon to use more than three or four key fields. To specify a sort key, you simply assign a number to the field in the Sort Prty (sort priority) column. Lower numbers have a higher priority; so to produce a report sorted like a telephone book, for example, you might give LASTNAME a priority of 1 and FIRSTNAME a priority of 2. Normal sequence is ascending (A, B, C, . . . , Z; 1, 2, 3, . . . , 99), and that is what the A/D (sequence) column defaults to; if you wanted to list all Zachs before Andersons, you would enter a D (for Descending) in the A/D column for the LASTNAME field.

In this case, we have given a sort priority of 1 to field DEPT in default ascending sequence and a sort priority of 2 to field LASTNAME, also in ascending sequence. Remember: The lower the number, the higher the priority. As entered, the values specify to sort the file in ascending sequence by minor sort key LASTNAME within major sort key DEPT, ascending. This specification groups all employees alphabetically by last name within their departments.

When you press Enter, Query for i5/OS asks you to confirm your choices (Figure 7.22).

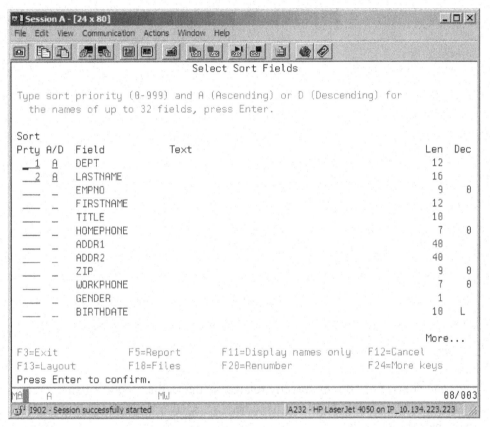

Figure 7.22: Confirm Request for Select Sort Fields

If you make a mistake, or change your mind, you can make adjustments from this screen.

Defining Report Breaks

Because we also selected Define report breaks in Figure 7.20, Query for i5/OS next takes us directly to that screen (Figure 7.23).

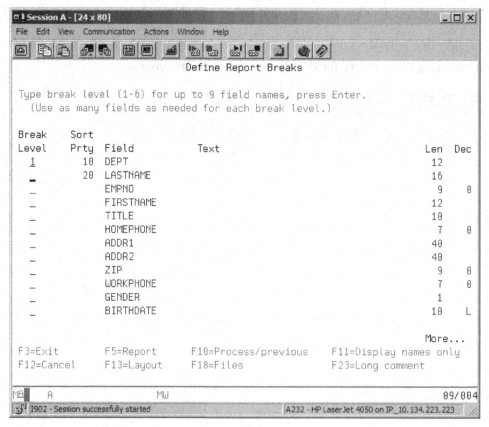

Figure 7.23: Define Report Breaks Screen

Sort fields and **control breaks** are directly related, so the Define Report Breaks screen already shows that DEPT and LASTNAME have been selected as the sort-key fields by displaying their sort priorities.

You now need to assign a Break Level to the DEPT field to provide counts, subtotals, or other functions by department. Query for i5/OS automatically assigns break level 0 to final totals, so you could assign up to six more break levels; the lower the number, the more inclusive the break level. For example, if population records were sorted by city within county within state, you would assign break level 1 to state (most inclusive), 2 to county, and 3 to city (least inclusive) to do counts or subtotals on all levels. In our example, you want a subtotal only on DEPT, so Figure 7.23 shows break level 1 entered for that field. Note that sort priority is provided for your information only—it is not an input-enabled field on the Define Report Breaks screen.

When you press Enter, the Format Report Break screen (Figure 7.24) appears.

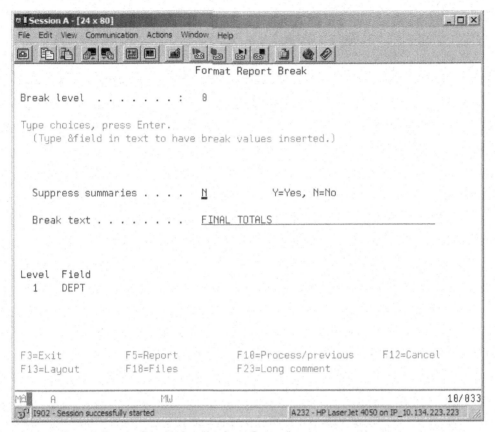

Figure 7.24: Format Report Break—Level 0 (Last Record)

A screen similar to this one will be displayed for each break level requested. The screen in Figure 7.24 is for break level 0; Query for i5/OS automatically generates a level 0 control break that prints final totals after the last record.

As the screen shows, the Break text for this level defaults to FINAL TOTALS. You could change the text by typing over these words, but for our example FINAL TOTALS will do just fine.

The default value shown for the Suppress summaries option, N, tells you that any summary functions you request, such as count or total, will be printed for break level 0 (final totals). (We haven't selected report summary functions yet; but once we do, they will be printed/ displayed with the level 0, or final, control break when the query is run.)

The display-only information above the function keys reminds you of the other break levels you have chosen and the fields on which you selected them.

After pressing Enter, you see the Format Report Break screen for break level 1 on field DEPT (Figure 7.25).

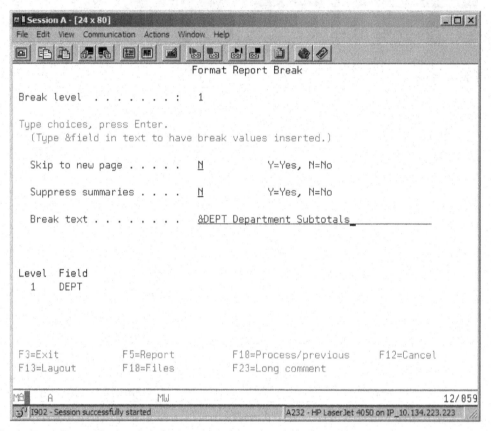

Figure 7.25: Format Report Break—Level 1

You don't want to start on a new page every time the department changes, nor do you want to suppress summaries, so you can leave the first two input fields—Skip to new page and Suppress summaries—at their default values of N.

To include the break control-field value on the subtotal line, you can ask Query for i5/OS to substitute the actual field value by using the field name prefixed with an ampersand as part of the break text. For example, when the accounting-department subtotals are printed, the value Accounting would be substituted for &DEPT on the subtotal line of the printed report. Figure 7.25 shows the break text entered so that the department name will be printed before the constant part of the text.

Pressing Enter now returns you to the Define the Query screen. With that, we have accomplished report specification number 1. You will test it shortly, but first, select and sequence the report fields according to specification 2.

Selecting and Sequencing Fields

From the Define the Query screen, take the option to select and sequence fields. You will see the screen in Figure 7.26.

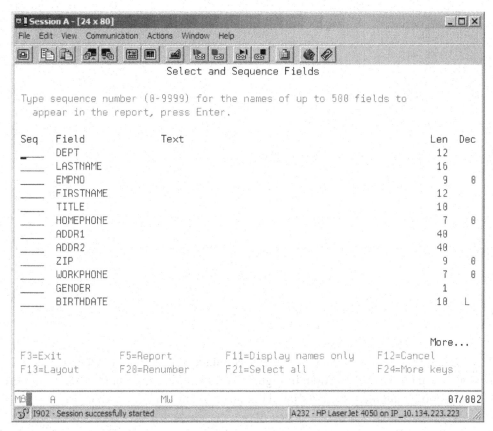

Figure 7.26: Select and Sequence Fields Screen

Notice that even though they did not start out in that order, the department and last-name fields have moved to the top of the list as a result of being selected as the primary and secondary sort-key fields, respectively.

On this screen, you select fields to include in the query by giving them a number. The left-to-right order of the fields across the report depends on the relative magnitude of the number, with the leftmost field having the lowest number. In Figure 7.27, the fields have been assigned numbers to place them in the order requested in specification 2.

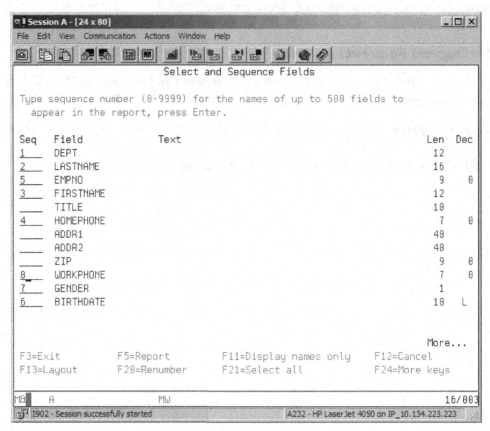

Figure 7.27: Ordering Fields for a Query Report

You can assign the numbers in any increments as long as they are in the relative order that corresponds to their desired position. In Figure 7.27, the fields have simply been numbered 1, 2, 3, and so on, but Query for i5/OS will renumber them in increments of 10.

Notice that the fields not needed in this report are simply left without numbers. If you later decide to include one of those fields, you can return to this screen and give that field a number within an appropriate range to position it before, after, or between any fields currently selected.

When you press Enter, you will be asked to confirm the sequenced list of fields. Pressing Enter again does that and then returns you to the Define the Query screen. However, you may first want to verify the accuracy of the report as it is defined so far.

From the Select and Sequence Fields screen (or the Define the Query screen), you can press F5 to run the query and show how the report will look at this point. Figure 7.28 shows how the report will be displayed.

```
 I Session A - [24 x 80]                                            _ □ x
 File  Edit  View  Communication  Actions  Window  Help

                              Display Report
                                  Report width . . . . . :      100
 Position to line  . . . . .      _____     Shift to column . . . . . .    _____
 Line    ....+....1....+....2....+....3....+....4....+....5....+....6....+....7..
         DEPT         LASTNAME         FIRSTNAME    HOMEPHONE            EMPNO  BI
 000001 Accounting.  Jackson          Ralph         817-0619  244 81 9503   19
 000002 Accounting.  Worthy           Mary          802-1119  312 89 3418   19
 000003
 000004      Accounting. Department Subtotals
 000005
 000006 Engineering. Ari Gur          Meshulam      806-0710  219 84 4605   19
 000007
 000008      Engineering. Department Subtotals
 000009
 000010 Finance.     Brigham          Kent          815-0702  354 19 0278   19
 000011 Finance.     Chow             Huan Lin      807-0102  322 29 3198   19
 000012
 000013      Finance. Department Subtotals
 000014
 000015 Human Res    Hunn             Atilla        857-4211  111 11 0009   19
 000016
                                                              More...
 F3=Exit      F12=Cancel      F19=Left      F20=Right      F21=Split

 MA    A                 MW                                          03/032
  I902 - Session successfully started    A232 - HP LaserJet 4050 on IP_10.134.223.223
```

Figure 7.28: Preview of Query Report Format

You can see that the records are properly grouped and sorted by last name within department, and the home-phone and employee-number fields appear properly edited. A report line is too wide for all fields to be displayed at once, so you can press F20 to shift the view to the right side of the report. You would then see that all the selected fields are present and in the correct order.

We have now satisfied the first and second specifications. We will now move on to the third specification and use the Report column formatting feature to change the column headers.

More Report Column Formatting

You have already used the report column formatting option to edit employee number and home phone, but you can return to any feature as many times as necessary simply by typing 1 on its option field and pressing Enter. After doing so for this option, you will see the Specify Report Column Formatting screen again (Figure 7.29).

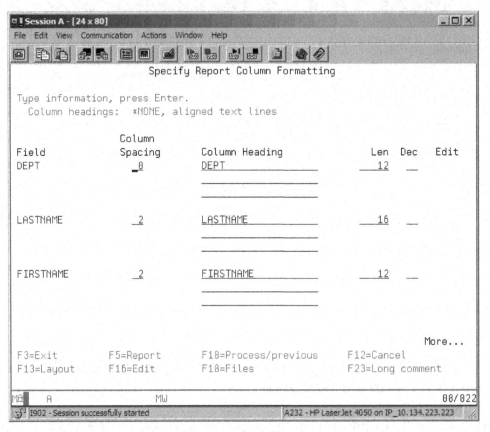

Figure 7.29: Specify Report Column Formatting Screen

Notice that the sequence (and presence) of fields on this screen differs from before (Figure 7.10) and is now determined by our previous Select and sequence fields activity.

We can use this screen now to address specification 3, displaying more meaningful column headers. On this screen, you can change column headings by typing over or blanking out the default field-name column heading that is currently displayed. Also, you can change column spacing (the number of blank spaces to precede each column) from the defaults of 0 for the first field and 2 for each subsequent field. We will rekey the column headings to mixed case and expand them, using two or three lines when necessary.

Tip

If a column heading is wider than the associated data field, Query for i5/OS automatically adjusts the column width to avoid truncating any part of the column heading. Therefore, when you try to scrunch many columns of data into a narrow report or display, you may want to stack headings on the three lines provided on the Specify Report Column Formatting screen rather than use all 20 print positions allowed per column.

Figure 7.30 shows the first display of the modified Specify Report Column Formatting screen.

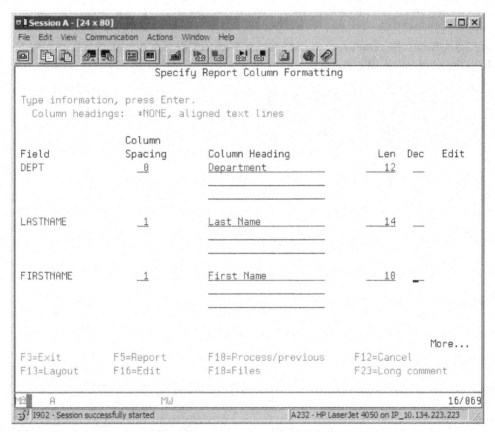

Figure 7.30: Specify Report Column Formatting Screen, with Changes

Because the DEPT field is 12 characters wide, we have spelled out its column heading. The last- and first-name column headings have also been expanded, but the data-field lengths have been reduced to 14 and 10 for last name and first name, respectively. In addition, the column spacing for last name and first name has been changed to 1 in the modified report.

Character fields are often defined to a larger size than is needed to hold all but the most extreme case of data, and Query for i5/OS users commonly reduce such fields to a more reasonable size to fit more columns on a page without having to condense the type beyond readability. If a name has more characters stored in the record than the report column allows, the excess rightmost characters are truncated in the query output; this abridgment does not keep the query from running.

Tip

When you change numeric specifications such as column spacing and field length, it is convenient to Tab or Field advance to the desired field, type in the new value, and then use the Field exit key to erase the old value.

Figure 7.31 shows the second screen of Specify Report Column Formatting with changes made to the next group of column headings to improve readability.

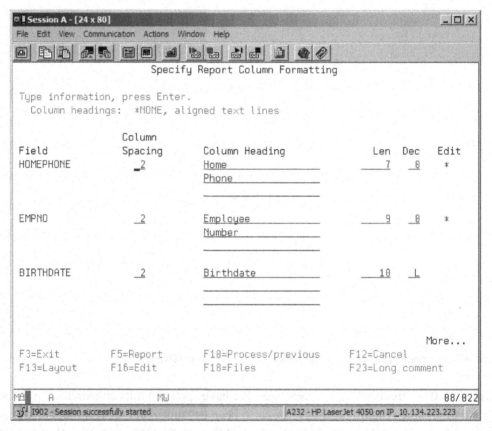

Figure 7.31: Specify Report Column Formatting Screen Showing Changed Column Headings

To see the effect of your changes immediately, you can check the layout or run the report from this screen by pressing F13 or F5, respectively. Remember to press Enter to save the changes once you're finished specifying report column formatting.

Report Summary Functions

Next, to satisfy the fourth and fifth specifications, we need to Select report summary functions for our query. If you select that option from the Define the Query screen, you see a screen like Figure 7.32 (although, of course, without the options entered).

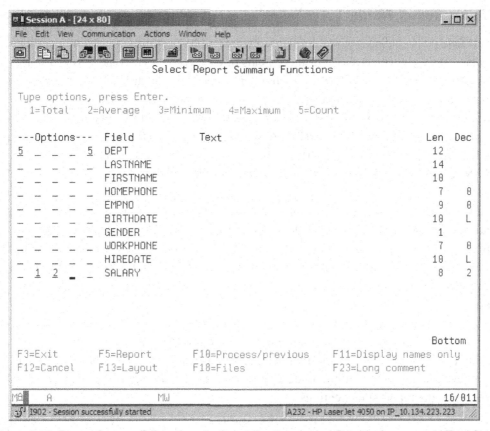

Figure 7.32: Report Summary Functions to Count Employees and Provide Average and Total Salary

You can add summary information to the control-break total lines by selecting up to five different functions per field. You can use options 1 and 2, Total (sum values in the field) and Average (sum values in the field and divide by the number of records in the report), only with numeric fields. You can use option 3, Minimum (the algebraically least-value or lowest-sequence-value alphanumeric item in a control group); option 4, Maximum (the algebraically highest value or highest sequence value); and option 5, Count (used to determine the number of records in a control group) with either numeric or character (alphanumeric) fields.

Figure 7.32 shows the summary functions selected so far for our sample report. Note that it doesn't matter which of the five option-input fields you use for a report field, or in which order you enter multiple options. We are doing a count on last name, and a total and average on the salary field. You can use the Layout and Report function keys from this screen to check the formatting of the report or to see how it will look with data.

We have now met the first five specification requirements for our query and are ready to tackle the sixth.

Defining Result Fields

Result fields, also called *derived columns*, are created by performing certain operations on data already contained in one or more fields of each record. The type of operation allowed depends on the data type of the field or fields to be operated on. String operations (concatenate and substring) can be performed on alphanumeric (character) fields. Concatenate (||) puts two character fields (or subfields) together to form a new field with a new name—for example, FIRSTNAME || LASTNAME becomes FULLNAME. Substring creates a new field from part of an existing field—for example, the first byte of FIRSTNAME becomes FIRSTINIT, or first initial. We return to character result fields later.

For numeric fields, you can use an almost infinite combination of numeric expressions to create new columns. These expressions consist of numeric field names and/or constants combined with the arithmetic operators for addition (+), subtraction (-), multiplication (*), and division (/). For example, to create a new field, RAISE, defined as 6.2 percent of salary, you would code the expression SALARY * .062, assuming SALARY is a field of the record format.

Query for i5/OS also provides several functions for converting between alphanumeric and numeric types, and for performing date- and time-duration calculations on date and time fields. We will use a couple of these functions to calculate the years of employment requested in the report specifications.

When you take the option on the Define the Query screen to Define result fields, you are presented with a screen like that in Figure 7.33.

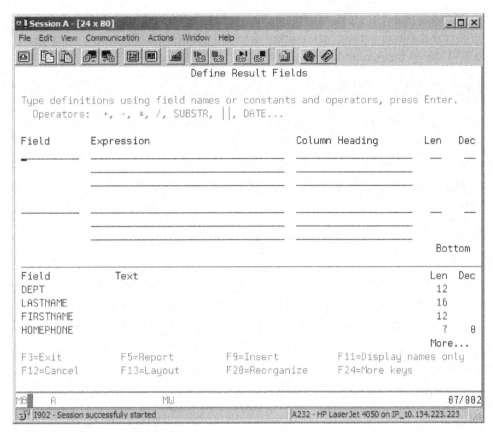

Figure 7.33: Define Result Fields Screen

In the Field column, you name the new field being defined. Then you key the expression used to derive the new field's value. You can provide a column heading if you don't want the field name used as a heading. Length (Len) and decimal-position (Dec) entries are often used to shorten the size of a calculated numeric result, including date and time duration, but Query for i5/OS determines the length of any string (alphanumeric) expression.

For our purposes, we will create a new field named YRSEMPLD (years employed) by converting the duration between the current date and field HIREDATE to an integer year. Figure 7.34 shows the required expression.

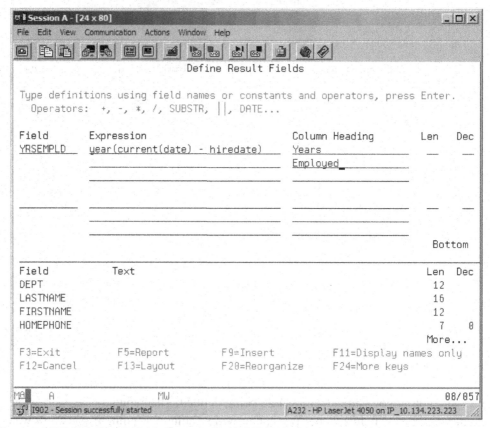

Figure 7.34: Define Result Fields Screen with YRSEMPLD Calculation

The function current with the argument date takes the current date from the system. Other possibilities for the argument include time and time stamp. The date of hire in the date field HIREDATE is then subtracted from the current date, and the result is converted to years.

To understand how the arithmetic works, think of the numeric value of any date field as the number of days since the beginning of the calendar, January 1 of 1 AD, or 0001-01-01 in *ISO format. The current date would be the count of all the days since then—a large number. HIREDATE, being closer to the beginning of the calendar, should be a somewhat smaller number, unless the employee was just hired today. So when we subtract HIREDATE from the current date, we get the duration of employment in days. The year function converts this result to years. No rounding is done in this conversion, and no fraction of a year is calculated. If the current date is August 1, 2000, and the date of hire is August 1, 1999, the year function will return a value of 1; but if the hire date is August 2, 1999, a 0 will be returned.

Tip

For a good overview of the functions available for creating expressions, as well as some examples of their use, request extended Help from the Define Result Fields screen.

Finishing the Report

When you create a result field and you have already selected report fields, you need to return to the Select and Sequence Fields screen to add the new field to the report. Figure 7.35 shows our new field, YRSEMPLD, given a sequence number that positions it between the HIREDATE and SALARY fields.

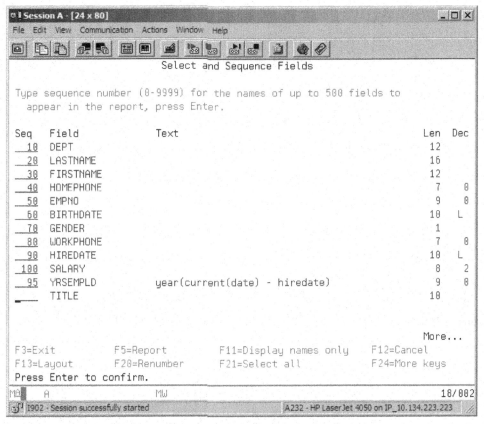

Figure 7.35: Select and Sequence Fields Screen with New Field Sequenced

You might notice that Query for i5/OS calculated the field size as nine digits, which seems a bit much for the extent of a human life by today's standards. Even Methuselah did not last that long, and if he had, he surely would have retired long before reaching a ninth digit. You could change the size of this field to two digits, either on the Define Result Fields screen or from the Specify Report Column Formatting screen.

Last, to calculate the average years of employment for each department, you need to return to the Select Report Summary Functions screen and select the Average function (2) for the new field. Figure 7.36 shows this screen. Notice that the screen displays the date expression; Query for i5/OS automatically shows the expression for a calculated field.

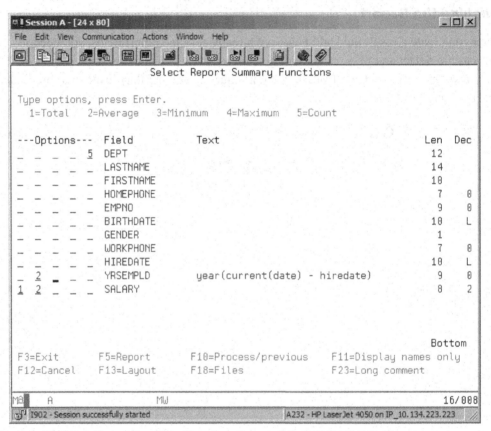

Figure 7.36: Select Report Summary Functions Screen with YRSEMPLD Field

Figure 7.37 shows the output of the completed Query for i5/OS report.

```
04/17/10  20:31:46                                                                         PAGE    2
       Department    Last Name     First Name    Home       Employee   Birthdate   Hire        Years      Salary
                                                 Phone      Number                 Date        Employed
          Manager.   Beckman       Joel          799-0801   311 24 1555 1936-11-19  1981-11-19      28      64,500.00
                     Sanders       Debra         827-0914   316 78 3022 1941-06-19  1986-06-19      23      50,124.00
                     Schramm       Trudy         808-0515   386 50 0129 1950-05-30  1995-05-30      14      24,000.00
                     Warren        Robin         821-1015   289 14 7840 1947-05-28  1992-05-28      17      50,000.00
Manager. Department Subtotals
TOTAL                                                                                                     188,624.00
AVG                                                                                              21       47,156.00
COUNT 4
          Marketing  Disney        Walter        455-2323   111 11 0010 1952-10-10  1982-10-01      27     168,300.00
                     Gootch        Martha        848-9799   111 11 0008 1948-02-21  1993-11-01      16      56,100.00
Marketing Department Subtotals
TOTAL                                                                                                     224,400.00
AVG                                                                                              22      112,200.00
COUNT 2
          Research   Einstein      Albert        363-2550   111 11 0003 1945-04-25  1956-03-28      54     299,950.00
                     Takahashi     Musashi       857-4321   111 11 0004 1954-12-01  1992-03-30      18      75,000.00
Research Department Subtotals
TOTAL                                                                                                     374,950.00
AVG                                                                                              36      187,475.00
COUNT 2
          Research.  Clinton       Rudy          810-0701   329 88 3744 1940-08-21  1978-08-21      31      59,351.00
                     Groh          Jack          804-0530   283 11 9853 1941-07-21  1979-07-21      30      41,500.00
                     Rizzo         Gene          816-0801   288 19 4222 1945-11-30  1983-11-30      26      41,600.00
                     Showers       Lois          827-0812   206 91 0282 1953-08-01  1991-08-01      18      28,000.00
Research. Department Subtotals
TOTAL                                                                                                     170,451.00
AVG                                                                                              26       42,612.75
COUNT 4
          Sales      Badman        Billy         355-6789   111 11 0007 1975-07-18  1997-04-15      13      22,500.00
                     Fendor        Denton        656-9876   111 11 0002 1972-11-19  1997-03-29      13      33,150.00
                     Kartblanch    Emil          377-7040   111 11 0006 1950-05-11  1986-05-15      24      48,250.00
                     Rachanoffski  Natasha       377-7383   111 11 0005 1960-04-16  1994-07-01      15      32,000.00
                     Slick         Sam           765-9876   111 11 0001 1966-06-06  1992-10-01      17      28,000.00
Sales Department Subtotals
TOTAL                                                                                                     163,900.00
AVG                                                                                              16       32,780.00
COUNT 5
Final Totals
TOTAL                                                                                                   2,126,199.00
AVG                                                                                              21       64,430.27
COUNT 33
  * * *  E N D   O F   R E P O R T   * * *
```

Figure 7.37: Output of the Query (Without Line Numbers)

You could see the same information by pressing the Report function key, F5, but you would have to shift right because the report is too wide for one screen. The output you see in Figure 7.37 results from printing the query, a technique we cover a little later.

Exiting Query

When you are finished working with a query, you need to save your work and exit. Normally, when a query sends its output to a display device, it adds line numbers as a leftmost column (see Figure 7.28). These line numbers are not included in printed output or database-file output, and they do not appear in Figure 7.37.

From the Define the Query screen, pressing F3 takes you to the Exit this Query screen (Figure 7.38).

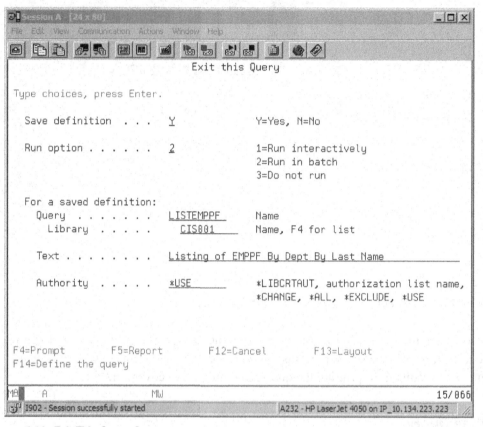

Figure 7.38: Exit This Query Screen

For a new query, the Save definition option is set to Y and the Run option is set to whatever option the user chose the last time query was run, in this case, 2. This will cause the query to be submitted to batch. We will keep these values for this query. When you save a query definition, you must give it a name if it has not been given one already. It is always a good idea to add some descriptive text to help you remember what the query does; I have spent hours looking for queries we had written and subsequently forgotten the names of. When you have completed the screen, pressing Enter saves the definition and runs the query, returning you to the Work with Queries screen. If you want to return to the Query definition screen, you can press the **F14 function key**.

A Conceptual Foundation for Joining Files

In the query example we just worked through, you learned how to create a control-break report that required the selection of sort fields. You also defined a result field, selected and sequenced fields, and used some report summary functions in the report. This is a common type of report created over a single file. Query for i5/OS also lets you combine data from more than one file by specifying a **join** operation. Simply stated, a **join** operation lets data elements (field values) from records of two or more files be included in a single result record.

Suppose, for example, that you needed a listing of all employees in the company sorted by last name and including address, city, state, and zip code. Two of these data elements, city and state, are not included in the record format of employee file EMPPF. At the end of Chapter 5, we talked about the need for a separate zip-code file that could be maintained independently. Figure 7.39 shows the record-format information of the DSPFFD (Display File Field Description) command output for such a file.

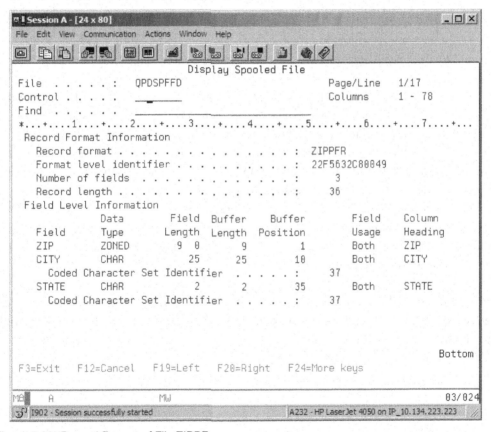

Figure 7.39: Record Format of File ZIPPF

This physical file has been created using DDS, and test data for the zip codes found in the employee file has been added using Data File Utility (DFU). The zip-code file and employee file are related to each other based on what is assumed to be a common value of the ZIP field in each file. We could draw a **Bachman diagram**, a useful tool for documenting the relationships among files in a database, for the employee and zip-code files as follows:

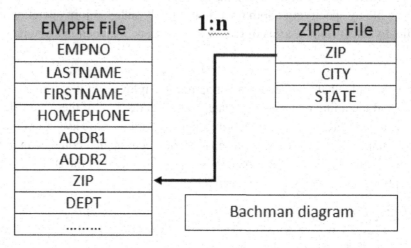

Figure 7.40: Bachman Diagram Showing the Relationship Between the EMPPF and ZIPPF Files

In the diagram, Field ZIP in file ZIPPF is the primary-key field for the ZIPPF file. A **primary key** is a field or set of fields whose value or values when taken together are unique for every record in the file. It is the field or set of fields used to identify the record and, therefore, the field(s) through which individual records will most often be accessed. In our example, no two records in file ZIPPF will have the same zip code. This is a reasonable assumption— the postal service would not want to assign the same zip code to two different physical locations. Of course, large cities might have several different zip codes, but that would not be a problem. For example, if St. Paul, Minnesota, had 10 different zip codes, file ZIPPF would have 10 St. Paul records. Each record would have the same city and state values but a different, unique zip-code value.

Employee-file records, in contrast, might very likely share the same value for zip code (e.g., when two or more employees live in the same zip-code area). However, this is not a problem either, because the ZIP field is not the identifying field or primary key of an employee record, but only an attribute that describes where an employee lives. Because many employees could live in the same area, many records in the employee file could have the same zip code. In other words, one record in the zip-code file with a unique zip-code value could be related to many records in the employee file (i.e., those employees with the same zip code). Nevertheless, any one record of the employee file, which has a single zip code, will always be related to only one zip-code file record.

This common type of relationship, called a **one-to-many relationship** (abbreviated 1:n), is the foundation of relational database systems, including IBM's DB2 Universal Database. Another name for this type of relationship is **parent-child relationship**. A record in a parent file (in our case, ZIPPF) can have many children (i.e., records in file EMPPF), but a record in a child file can have only one parent.

Query for i5/OS lets you easily extract data from two or more files that have a common field such as the ZIP field. The files do not necessarily have to be in a one-to-many relationship, but because this type of relationship is most common, they often are. As we mentioned earlier, up to 32 related files can be joined in a single report, although the number is usually much smaller.

When you join files in a query, it is necessary to specify a **primary file** first. The primary file is not necessarily the parent file of a 1:n relationship (ZIPPF in our example), and you should not confuse the two. Rather, the primary file is the one that contains the critical data we want to report on (i.e., the main topic or focus of the query). In our case, because we want to create a list of employees, the main topic is "employee" and the primary file should be the one containing data primarily describing employees—namely, file EMPPF. For this query, the child file in the 1:n relationship becomes the primary file because it describes the entity (employee) on which we are reporting.

Creating a Join Query

When you create a join query, the first option listed on the Define the Query screen, Specify file selections, is most critical. Figure 7.41 shows the Specify File Selections screen with EMPPF entered as the primary-file name. In addition, Enter has already been pressed on this screen, and a message at the bottom tells you to *"Select file(s) or press Enter to confirm."*

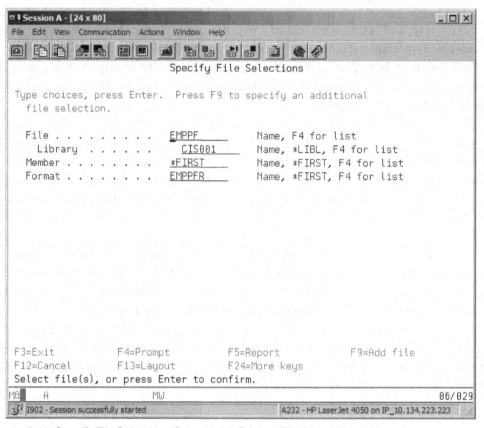

Figure 7.41: Specify File Selections Screen with Primary-File Name Entered

At this point, you need to select another file, the zip-code file; you do so by using F9 (Add file). After you press F9, the Specify File Selections screen displays another set of entry fields for identifying a **secondary file** (Figure 7.42).

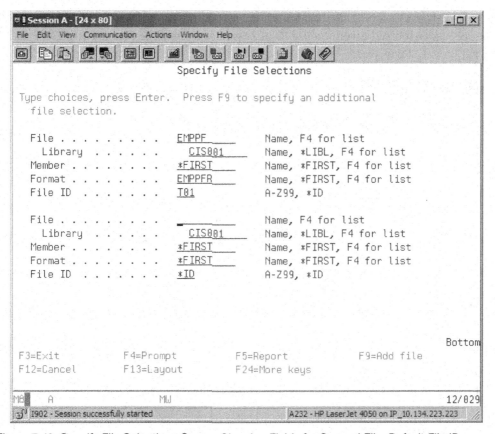

Figure 7.42: Specify File Selections Screen Showing Fields for Second File, Default File ID

Notice the File ID entry field, which did not appear on the select screen for only one file. You use this field to define up to a three-character prefix for field names so that Query for i5/OS can distinguish fields with the same name in different files. In our example, ZIP is the only field name common to both files (ZIPPF and EMPPF). However, once the File ID is decided, Query for i5/OS qualifies all field names on subsequent screens using the File ID prefix. Query for i5/OS supplies the default File ID of T01; it would assign IDs of T02, T03, and so on to any other secondary files we included. You can change the ID names if you like; it is often more desirable to use a one- or two-character abbreviation of the file name.

Figure 7.43 shows the completed Specify File Selections screen. We have named file ZIPPF as the secondary file and given it a File ID of Z; we have given the primary file, EMPPF, a File ID of E.

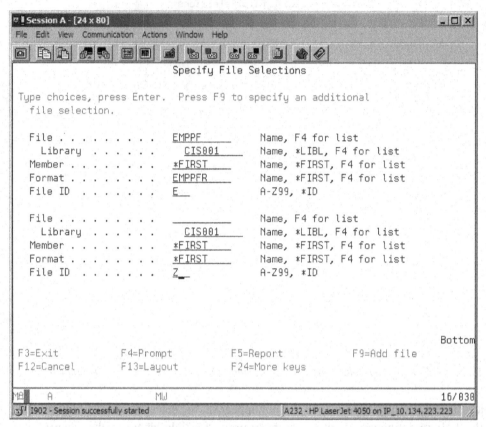

Figure 7.43: Completed Specify File Selections Screen with EMPPF as Primary File and ZIPPF as Secondary File

Now that you have told Query for i5/OS that you are using more than one file, it needs to know which type of join to use. The next display you see will be the Specify Type of Join screen (Figure 7.44). As the screen indicates, Query for i5/OS can select records from the primary and secondary file (or files) in three different ways to create the report.

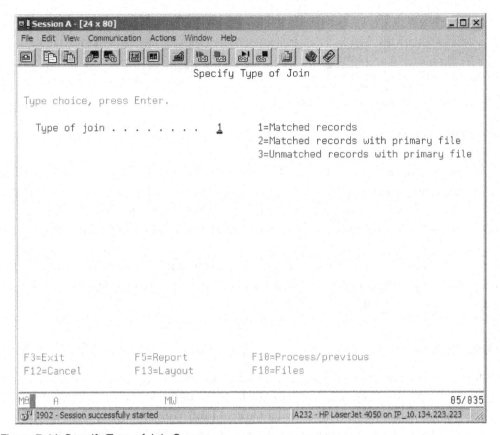

Figure 7.44: Specify Type of Join Screen

Before you decide how you want the records selected, let us step through an example of the joining process. Let us say you are joining matching records and can assume the employee and zip-code files include the records in Figure 7.45.

EMPPF					ZIPPF		
111110006	Kartblanch	Emil	...	523389910	522339910	Swisher	IA
111110007	Badman	Billy	...	524566789	52338	Hiawatha	IA
.					52402	Cedar Rapids	IA
.					.		
.					.		

Figure 7.45: Record Sample from EMPPF and ZIPPF Physical Files

The output you see in Figure 7.46 could then result, depending on the type of join selected:

Kartblanch	Emil	Swisher	IA	523389910
.				
.				
.				

Figure 7.46: Joined Query Records

In this example, which ignores other fields in the employee file, a record has been selected for the query because the join field in the primary-file record with a value of 523389910 matches a join-field value of a record in the secondary file. The desired fields from the matching records of both files can then be included in the joined query record.

Which type of join do we need to specify for our example? To answer that question, let us look at each of the three types of join operations and, using the limited data from the example above, see what the different output is.

1=Matched Records

The Matched Records join type (type 1) uses what is known in relational database terminology as an inner join. An inner join in which one of the matching fields is eliminated from the result record is commonly called a **natural join**. With an **inner join**, a result record is selected when at least one matching record is found in every file. In other words, a primary-file record must have at least one matching record in each of the secondary files in order for it to be selected as part of the query output. However, if a record in the primary file has no match in one or more of the secondary files, that primary-file record is ignored and nothing is added to the query output.

Using the sample data in Figure 7.45, a result record would be added to the query report for Emil Kartblanch because a record with matching zip code would be found in the zip-code file. But Billy Badman would not be included in the query output because no zip-code record matches his ZIP field value of 523456789.

In many cases, you would not want output created for unmatched primary-file records, so this type of join would be okay. Consider, for example, a report that lists students enrolled in summer classes. There may be 5,000 students in the student file, but only 1,000 of them are enrolled for summer classes, and these would have a record matching their student ID in the summer enrollment file. If a student ID field of a student-file record has no match in the file of summer enrollments, you would not want that student listed, so a type 1 inner join would be fine.

2=Matched Records with Primary File

Using our example, suppose you want to list all employees, even those who do not have a valid zip code (i.e., one matching a ZIPPF record). When you need to include all records in the primary file regardless of whether matching records exist in the secondary file (or files), you need to use the type 2 join, Matched records with primary file, also called an **outer join** (or, more correctly, a **left outer join**).

With an outer join, all records in the primary file are selected for the query. If no matching record is found in one or more secondary files, the selected data fields from those unmatched files are set to default values in the query output record (zeros for numeric fields, spaces for alphanumeric fields). This is the type of join to select when it is important to include all primary-file records in the query, even if some of those records may not have matching secondary-file records. If you use an outer join, an employee who has an invalid zip code or a zip code that is correct for his or her domicile but hasn't been entered into file ZIPPF would still be listed in the query—only city and state would have values of blanks (spaces). In this way, you would notice the problem easily and correct it.

Using our illustration, both Emil and Billy would be listed as a result of this join type, but the city and state values for Billy would be set to spaces because they were not retrieved from a matching record of the zip-code file, as Figure 7.47 shows.

Kartblanch	Emil	Swisher	IA	523389910
Badman	Billy			524566789
.				
.				
.				

Figure 7.47: Joined Query Records from Type 2 Join

The reason Billy's zip code appears is that, in selecting fields for the query report, you would have used field E.ZIP, from the primary file, instead of Z.ZIP. For a left outer join, the relationship-supporting field from the primary file is normally selected.

3=Unmatched Records with Primary File

Sometimes it is useful to list or display only the records that do not have matches in all files—for example, students not registered in any class, customers not having any outstanding invoices, or, in our case, employees not having a valid zip code. The type 3 join operation accommodates this need. It writes to the query output only those records whose primary-file record was not matched to at least one secondary file. This operation is called **difference** in relational database terminology; you can understand why if you think of it as "subtracting" from the primary file all records with matches in the secondary file (or files). What is left—the difference—is the unmatched primary-file records. The query record fields from the unmatched secondary file (or files) are set to defaults in the output, as in the type 2 outer join.

When unmatched primary-file records are considered an exception, this join type is a very useful and powerful tool for identifying and isolating them. Using the Figure 7.48 illustration, the output would include only the Billy Badman primary-file record because Emil's EMPPF record will be "taken away" by the matching ZIPPF record in the difference operation.

| Badman | Billy | 524566789 |

Figure 7.48: Joined Query Records from Type 3 Join

The type 3 join is also referred to as an **exception join**, a term that is a little misleading because result rows are created only when no join occurs.

Specifying the Join Relationship

We will examine Query for i5/OS reports created from all three types of join operations to help you understand the different ways they work. If you first wanted a report including all employees, even those with invalid (unmatched) zip codes, you would want to use a type 2 join because this type meets the criteria for listing all employees. To specify such a query, you enter a 2 for the Type of join field shown on the screen in Figure 7.44. Pressing Enter takes you to the Specify How to Join Files screen (Figure 7.49), which shows the proper relational expression, E.ZIP EQ Z.ZIP, already typed in.

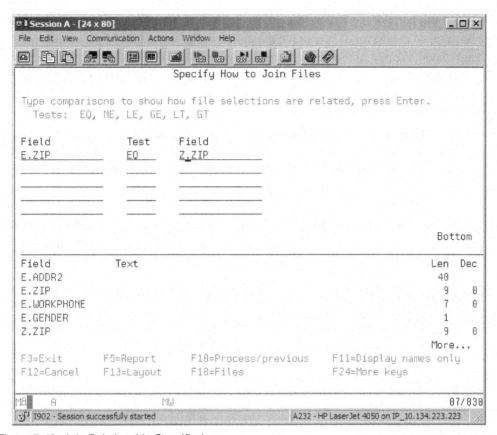

Figure 7.49: Join Relationship Specified

The relational expression tells Query for i5/OS the condition that defines "matched" records. In our case, the zip code of an employee record must equal the zip code of a zip-code file record. As Query reads each record of the primary file, it tries to find a record (or records) in the secondary file that satisfies the join relationship.

When the relationship-supporting fields of two related files are expected to have equal values, the join is generally referred to as an **equijoin**, and the relational operator is either EQ or an equal sign (=). Inner joins and left outer joins are both equijoins, and when the difference operation (Query for i5/OS's type 3 join) is used, an equality relationship is also specified. To use any relational operation other than EQ for a Query for i5/OS join is very unusual.

Notice that the Specify How to Join Files screen is divided horizontally into two parts. You use the upper part to code the relational expression (or expressions) that defines the join. There is usually one expression for each pair of related files. The lower part of the screen lists all fields involved in the primary and secondary files, with their file IDs prefixed to the field name. Both parts of the screen respond to the Page Up and Page Down keys, depending on the position of the cursor. If you move the cursor to the lower half of the screen and press Page Down, the rest of the fields in the employee file will be displayed, followed by the fields in the zip-code file. With all the field names listed for reference, you can avoid incorrectly naming the fields used in a join relational expression.

Pressing the **F11 function key,** with the cursor on the lower half of the screen, toggles from a single-field-per-row display showing text, length, and data type to a multifield-per-row display showing file IDs and field names only. The latter format is useful when you are joining several files with many fields.

When we press Enter at the Specify How to Join Files screen, we are returned to the Define the Query screen. From there, we could choose the Select and Sequence Fields option to display the screen you see in Figure 7.50, to simplify the output for our example.

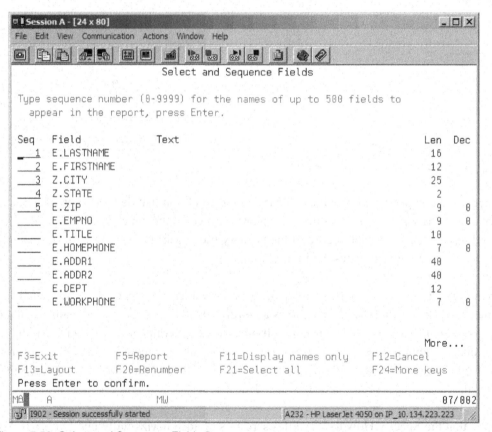

Figure 7.50: Select and Sequence Fields Screen

Note

We could also have selected any other fields from the employee file for output. In addition, although both the employee file and the zip-code file contain a ZIP field, it is important to select the field from the primary (employee) file. That way, if no match occurs, at least we can see what value the ZIP field has in the employee file. If we choose the field from the zip-code file and no match occurs, only zeros will appear in the output.

After selecting and sequencing fields, you can test the query immediately by pressing F5. Figure 7.51 shows the output of this query.

```
 File  Edit  View  Communication  Actions  Window  Help

 [toolbar icons]
                          Display Report
                                    Report width  . . . . . :      72
   Position to line  . . . . .  _____      Shift to column  . . . . . .  _____
   Line     ....+....1....+....2....+....3....+....4....+....5....+....6....+....7..
            Last Name     First Name  City                      State         Zip
   000001   Slick         Sam         Cedar Rapids              IA      52404-3367
   000002   Fendor        Denton      Guthrie Center            IA      50115-3498
   000003   Einstein      Albert      Clarinda                  IA      51632-1200
   000004   Takahashi     Musashi     Cedar Rapids              IA      52406-6523
   000005   Rachanoffski  Natasha     Cedar Rapids              IA      52402-1010
   000006   Kartblanch    Emil        Swisher                   IA      52338-9910
   000007   Badman        Billy                                         52456-6789
   000008   Gootch        Martha      Pleasantville             IA      50225-7810
   000009   Hunn          Atilla      Anamosa                   IA      52205-3421
   000010   Disney        Walter      Amana                     IA      52203-2378
   000011   Zanzibar      Tilly       Kalona                    IA      52247-9012
   000012   Stonehart     Rocky       Amana                     IA      52203-2378
   000013   Deerfield     Cynthia     Amana                     IA      52203-2378
   ****** ******** End of report ********

                                                                      Bottom
   F3=Exit      F12=Cancel      F19=Left      F20=Right      F21=Split

 MA    A              MW                                              03/032
   I902 - Session successfully started       A232 - HP LaserJet 4050 on IP_10.134.223.223
```

Figure 7.51: Output of Type 2 Join of EMPPF and ZIPPF

Besides seeing the need for some formatting, notice that the output displays no city or state for the Billy Badman record on line 7. Although not explicitly flagged as such, this is a good indication of an unmatched-record condition because you know that the city and state values were supposed to come from the secondary file, ZIPPF. If you checked a listing of all the ZIPPF records, you would see that no record exists for zip code 524566789.

For large files, it would be convenient to have Query for i5/OS search for unmatched records. You can do that simply by returning to the Specify Type of Join screen and changing the join type to 3, Unmatched records with primary file. Nothing else needs to be changed. After making that change and running the report again, you would see the display in Figure 7.52.

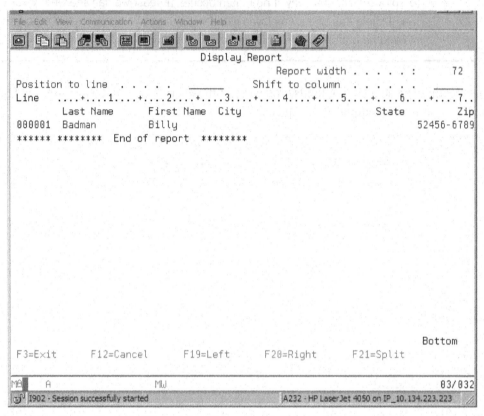

Figure 7.52: Display Report of Unmatched Records with Primary File, Type 3 Join

This time, only the Billy Badman record is listed, verifying that no matching ZIPPF record exists.

If you again change the type of join—this time to 1, Matched records—you would see that the Badman record is missing altogether when the report is run (Figure 7.53).

```
 File  Edit  View  Communication  Actions  Window  Help
 ┌──┐┌──┐┌──┐┌──┬──┐┌──┬──┐┌──┐┌──┬──┬──┬──┐┌──┐┌──┬──┐
 │  ││  ││  ││  │  ││  │  ││  ││  │  │  │  ││  ││  │  │
 └──┘└──┘└──┘└──┴──┘└──┴──┘└──┘└──┴──┴──┴──┘└──┘└──┴──┘
                         Display Report
                                   Report width . . . . . :        72
    Position to line  . . . . .     _____   Shift to column  . . . . . .    _____
    Line     ....+....1....+....2....+....3....+....4....+....5....+....6....+....7..
              Last Name     First Name  City                    State        Zip
    000001   Slick         Sam         Cedar Rapids              IA    52404-3367
    000002   Fendor        Denton      Guthrie Center            IA    50115-3498
    000003   Einstein      Albert      Clarinda                  IA    51632-1200
    000004   Takahashi     Musashi     Cedar Rapids              IA    52406-6523
    000005   Rachanoffski  Natasha     Cedar Rapids              IA    52402-1010
    000006   Kartblanch    Emil        Swisher                   IA    52338-9910
    000007   Gootch        Martha      Pleasantville             IA    50225-7810
    000008   Hunn          Atilla      Anamosa                   IA    52205-3421
    000009   Disney        Walter      Amana                     IA    52203-2378
    000010   Zanzibar      Tilly       Kalona                    IA    52247-9012
    000011   Stonehart     Rocky       Amana                     IA    52203-2378
    000012   Deerfield     Cynthia     Amana                     IA    52203-2378
    ****** ******** End of report  ********

                                                                       Bottom
    F3=Exit       F12=Cancel      F19=Left      F20=Right      F21=Split

 ┌──┐                                                                          
 │MA│  A                   MW                                          03/032
 └──┘
    I1902 - Session successfully started        A232 - HP LaserJet 4050 on IP_10.134.223.223
```

Figure 7.53: Display of Matching Records for Type 1 Join—No Billy Badman

This is how a type 1 inner join works. When a primary-file record does not have a match in every secondary file, it is not included in the output.

Although several important query options remain to be covered, you should be ready now to create some queries of your own. We examine additional query options in Chapter 10. Meanwhile, do not hesitate to explore—Query for i5/OS provides useful Help information about all of its functions.

In Summary

Query for i5/OS creates reports that can be sent to a display device, a printer, or a database file. Using mostly list and entry screens, you can conveniently specify which file or files to use, which records to select, which fields to include, and how to order them all on a report line. You can change column headings and field widths; use editing to control the appearance of data; and select summary functions, such as total, average, and count, on designated fields.

By selecting up to 32 sort fields, you can group records by common field values and specify control-break processing to print subtotals for control groups when needed. Join queries combine data from two or more related files based on matching values of common fields. The one-to-many relationship is the primary relationship between database files, and it usually exists between the primary and secondary files of a join query.

The primary file of a join query is the file whose data best describes the main topic of the report. Query for i5/OS allows three types of operations on the primary and secondary files, often referred to as inner or natural join, outer join, and difference. Completed queries are stored as objects of type *QRYDFN; they can be run using the RUNQRY command or by taking option 16 from the Work with Objects Using PDM screen.

In this chapter's lab, you will use several of the options mentioned above to create a query report based on one file and save it in your user library. In the additional lab exercise, you will use join operations to identify unmatched records, copy and update a physical file, and create a printed report using an outer join of matched records to the primary file. Many other options are available in Query for i5/OS to tailor reports to users' needs. You explore some of these options, along with reports based on logical files, in subsequent lab exercises.

Key Terms

Bachman diagram	inner join
control breaks	join
difference	left outer join
edit word	natural join
equijoin	one-to-many relationship
exception join	outer join
F4 function key	parent-child relationship
F5 function key	primary file
F11 function key	primary key
F13 function key	Query for i5/OS
F14 function key	report generator
F16 function key	result fields
F20 function key	secondary file

Review Questions

1. What is a Bachman diagram?
2. What options does the programmer have when at the Work with Queries screen?
3. List and explain the features of Query for i5/OS we discussed in this chapter.

4. What is the difference between the WRKQRY and STRQRY commands?

5. What function key will allow the programmer to "Preview" the report formatting?

6. What function key allows the programmer to "Preview" the report? When can this function key be used?

7. What function key is used to see columns of a report greater that 72?

8. When you are at the Describe Numeric Field Editing screen, why is it important to press Enter after making changes?

9. When you are on the Specify Report Column Formatting screen, what does an asterisk (*) signify under the edit column?

10. Explain how an edit word works in Query.

11. How are date and time fields formatted in Query?

12. How are numeric date and time fields formatted in Query?

13. How many sort fields are allowed in Query?

14. What is a control break? Give an example of using one.

15. What needs to be done to a field before you can break on it?

16. Why would you "stack" headings on a report?

17. What summary functions are supported in Query?

18. List the expressions that we discussed in this chapter that can be used for result fields.

19. Describe what a parent-child relationship means in a relational database.

20. What is the difference between a primary and secondary database file?

21. Explain the three types of joins that are supported in Query.

Lab 7

Introduction

In this lab exercise, you learn how to use Query for i5/OS to create a simple printed listing of the physical database file you created in the previous lab. An additional lab exercise provides experience in creating join queries.

Part 1

Goals   Examine the data member of your physical file.

                Use STRQRY to create a new query.

                Specify a file for your query.

                Perform report-column formatting, such as changing headers and editing.

Run the query and display the report.

Change the default output to printer.

Save the query in your library.

Start at   Any command line.

Procedure   Clear your output queue.

DSPPFM INTROCLASS/STUPF.

STRQRY; work with queries.

Create a query.

Define query specifications through Define the Query.

7.1.   Sign on as usual. As in Lab 6, use the WRKOUTQ (Work with Output Queue) command to ensure no spooled files are in your output queue. If any are, print or delete them to clear the output queue.

7.2.   Now enter the command to work with objects using PDM on a command line. Be sure to prompt the command so you can enter the library INTROCLASS; from the Work with Objects Using PDM list screen, take the Work with option on your physical file, STUPF.

7.3.   The option should take you to the Work with Members Using PDM screen, showing member STUPF. Take the option to display the member.

The DSPPFM (Display Physical File Member) command, which this option invokes, shows the data as it is stored within records of the file member, unformatted, with no field separators. You could run the command directly from the command line by keying

DSPPFM STUPF

The data displayed by DSPPFM is not easy to read, but the command is useful if you need to check field contents quickly for data you are using to test applications. (However, if the file member contains numeric data fields whose data type is other than S, for zoned decimal, the DSPPFM command will not convert that data to a display format, and you won't be able to read the contents of the field.)

Although DSPPFM gives you a quick way to view physical-file data, its lack of formatting and data conversion makes it unacceptable for end-user use or a permanent report. Luckily, Query for i5/OS is easy to use, and, once you become accustomed to it, you can easily use it to create simple reports.

Exit the DSPPFM command output display and return to the Work with Objects Using PDM screen.

7.4.   As you know from the text of this chapter, Query for i5/OS is a menu-driven report generator that can create screen displays, printed output, or database files. In this lab, you will use the utility to generate a simple report of your database physical file.

To define a query, begin by typing STRQRY on any command line. After keying the command, press Enter.

7.4.a.   What type of screen appears? What is its name?

Select option 1, Work with queries, and then press Enter.

7.5.   You should see the Work with Queries screen. From here, you can create a new query or take various options (e.g., Change, Copy, Display) on existing queries. Because you are creating your first query, take option 1. Name the query STUQRY1. Be sure to enter your library name for the Library part of the Query name parameter. Then press Enter.

7.6.   The Define the Query screen (Figure 7.54) lets you perform various design and selection options to tailor the query to the needs of the application.

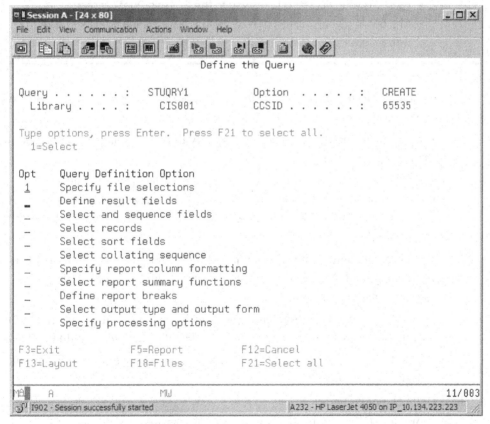

Figure 7.54: Define the Query Screen

Type 1 to select each option you want to use. Notice that a 1 already appears in front of the Specify file selections option because, at the very least, you must tell Query for i5/OS which file to use for the query.

Because this is a list-processing screen, you can type 1 in front of multiple options and Query for i5/OS will process them one after another. Each option on this screen takes you to one or more lower-level screens, where you supply information for that option. When you have finished specifying an option, you press Enter. Query for i5/OS then saves your specifications and returns you to the Define the Query screen.

Tip

Remember, from within a Define the Query selection (e.g., Define result fields or Select records):

- Enter saves your work and returns you to the Define the Query screen.
- F3 saves your work and takes you to the Exit this Query screen.
- F12 backs up one screen or returns you to the Define the Query screen *without* saving your work.

If you get to the Exit this Query screen by mistake, press F14 to return to the Define the Query screen.

At this point, there should be a 1 in front of only the Specify file selections option. Go ahead and press Enter.

7.7. You want to use your physical file, whose name is STUPF. If you could not remember the spelling of the name or you wanted to check a list of files, you could request prompting from the File entry field of the screen you are viewing. Do that now by pressing F4.

You should see the Select File screen with all files of the specified library (your current library) listed. Move the cursor to the option field for your student file, STUPF. Type 1, and then press Enter.

Notice that the prompt operation has copied the file name into the entry field of the Specify File Selections screen. The Library and Member defaults should be okay.

7.7.a. Use Help to find out what the FORMAT parameter specifies. Is the default all right for your file?

Exit Help, and press Enter.

7.7.b. What value is displayed now for the FORMAT parameter?

Read the message at the bottom of the screen and confirm.

7.8. You should now be back at the Define the Query screen. Is the screen any different? The greater-than symbol to the right of an option field indicates that the option has been taken. The symbol is just a reminder; you can go back to that option any time, if necessary, to add information or make changes.

7.9. Notice the function keys below the option list. Move the cursor to the function-key area, and press Help. Read through the descriptions of the function keys.

   7.9.a. What does F5 do?

   7.9.b. What does F13 do?

   7.9.c. What is the main difference between these two function keys?

   When you use F5 or F13, you can press F12 to return to the previous screen after you view the display.

7.10. Exit Help. Display the report layout (F13).

   7.10.a. What is the report width?

   7.10.b. Notice the column headers. Where do they come from?

   7.10.c. How are the column headers aligned over the fields?

   Notice that fields are separated on the format line, unlike the DSPPFM command output.

   7.10.d. How are the numeric fields edited?

   Use the appropriate function key to shift your view to the right so you can see the entire report layout. When you are finished viewing the layout, exit and return to the Define the Query screen.

7.11. You would like to suppress comma-insertion editing of the numeric fields in your report and make the column headings easier to understand. To do so, you need to choose the option to Specify report column formatting. Go ahead and do that now.

   The Specify Report Column Formatting display divides the screen horizontally into zones for each field named on the left side of the display. The first page of the screen should look like the one in Figure 7.55. (Dotted lines have been added between fields in this figure to emphasize the horizontal zones.)

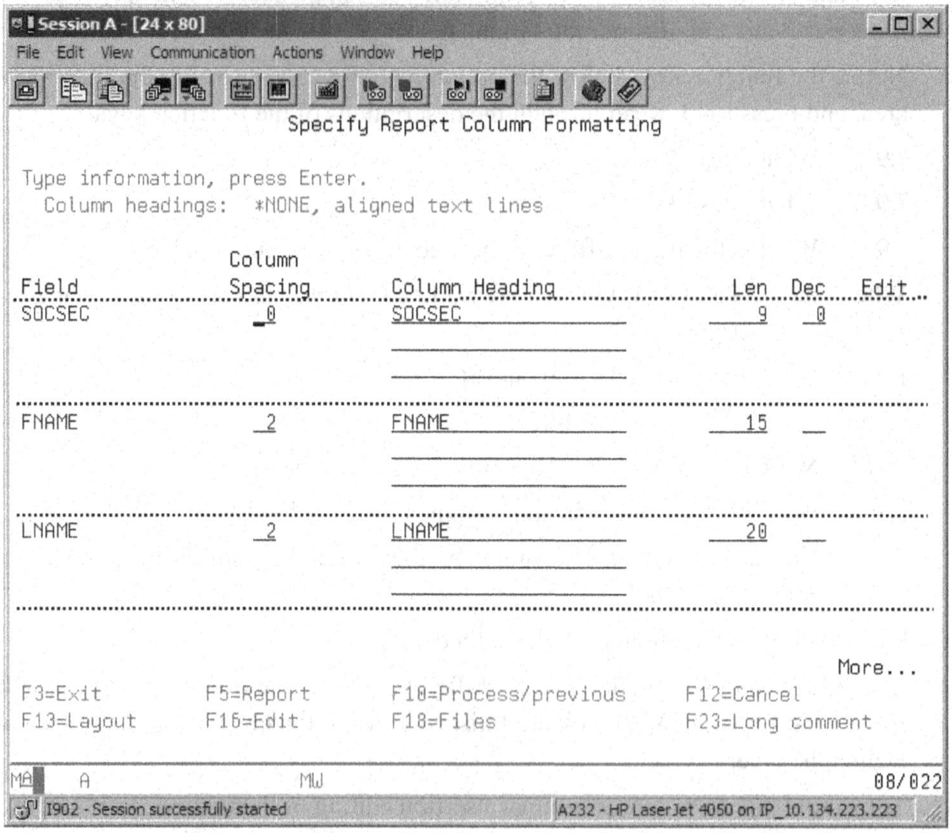

Figure 7.55: Specify Report Column Formatting

The column-heading values usually come from the COLHDG keyword contained in the physical-file object itself. If you do not specify COLHDG values in the source DDS (we did not), the system uses field names as column headings. In the query, if you want to change or clarify the column heading for the report, you can do that simply by typing over the values that have been taken from the file.

Change the column heading for the SOCSEC field to Soc Sec # by typing over the old column heading. Also, change the headings for fields FNAME and LNAME to First Name and Last Name, respectively. You could change any other column headings in the same way—by typing over what is already there. Notice that you can use up to three lines for each column heading; using multiple lines is a good idea when the data field is narrow but the column heading consists of several words.

Caution
Do not press Enter yet.

7.12. For each numeric field, you will select the edit function, F16. This function key
applies to the field in whose horizontal zone the cursor is located when the key
is pressed. The cursor does not have to be on the field name but can be anywhere
within the (three-line) zone.

Move the cursor back up to the SOCSEC field zone, and press F16. You should see a
screen like the Define Numeric Field Editing screen in Figure 7.56.

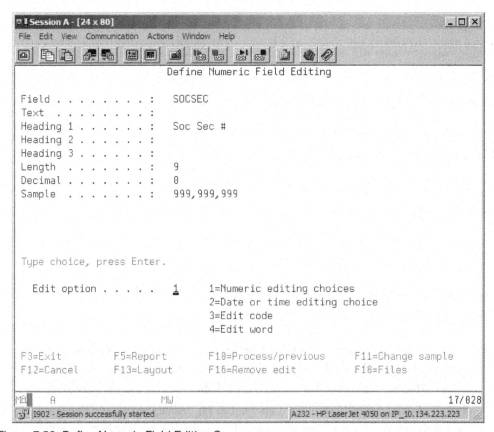

Figure 7.56: Define Numeric Field Editing Screen

Take a minute to look at this screen. Notice that the field's name, heading, length,
and number of decimal positions, as well as a sample showing current formatting,
are displayed in the top part of the screen. As you make editing changes to the field,
the sample changes accordingly.

As you can see, you have four choices for the type of editing you need to perform. For numeric fields that require no special spacing or insertion characters, you can use Edit option 1 to specify options such as thousands separator and leading zeros. Option 1 is the default, so just press Enter at this time.

You should see the Describe Numeric Field Editing screen in Figure 7.57.

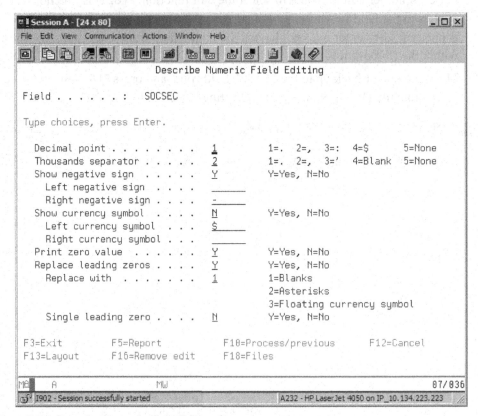

Figure 7.57: Describe Numeric Field Editing Screen

Notice some of the options available on this screen. For example, you can specify how to display a decimal point and thousands separator, whether to show negative signs, whether to display a currency symbol, and how to handle leading zeros.

For the Social Security number, you want to eliminate the comma thousands separator, so move the cursor down one line and enter a 5, for None, for the Thousands separator option. Then press Enter.

7.13. Back at the Specify Report Column Formatting screen, you should notice an asterisk in the Edit column (to the far right) for field SOCSEC. The asterisk tells you that the field has been edited.

Press F16 again. This time, the sample of the field shown on the Define Numeric Field Editing screen should have changed to reflect your request to eliminate the thousands-separator symbol; the sample should display the Social Security number as a nine-digit integer with no comma separators.

Now, press F12 to return to the previous screen, Specify Report Column Formatting. Page Down from this screen, and make a similar change to the other numeric fields, PHONE and ZIP, eliminating the thousands separator as you did for the Social Security number field. After making these changes, remain at the Specify Report Column Formatting screen.

7.14. Display the layout again. Do the numeric fields look better?

    7.14.a. What is the report width now?

When you're finished looking at the layout, press Enter to continue with the Specify report column formatting function.

7.15. As you adjust the various query-definition specifications, it is useful to be able to examine a report with data. Fortunately, without leaving the Specify Report Column Formatting screen, you can run the report as it is currently defined by pressing F5. Press F5 at this time.

The display report should now be visible on your screen. It should look something like Figure 7.58.

```
 Session A - [24 x 80]                                              _ □ ×
File  Edit  View  Communication  Actions  Window  Help

[toolbar icons]
                         Display Report
                              Report width . . . . . :      130
Position to line  . . . . .    _____    Shift to column . . . . . .   _____
Line    ....+....1....+....2....+....3....+....4....+....5....+....6....+....7..
          Soc Sec #   First Name    Last Name           PHONE   ADDR1
000001 154488932   Patricia      Smith             3138473283   647 18th
000002 223084359   Leslie        Rupert            6163892834   514 Pica
000003 269968069   Pamela        Stufflebeam       4148392447   502 Jers
000004 276681868   Yoshie        Suzuki            6162274973   2029 Eck
000005 282361745   Eileen        Zaremba           6166572835   2422 Log
000006 287559012   Brian         Eschenburg        5172930849   3948 Bri
000007 339588603   Yvonne        Armine            6162834993   3300 Mck
000008 349049381   Roger         Newburry          6164881935   1408 Dou
000009 359688909   Matthew       Zimmer            2194835568   2211 92n
000010 362858208   Katherine     Jay               6163293049   45300 Wo
000011 362882033   Richard       Decker            2174533257   27148 Ma
000012 363111879   Heng          Lai               6163895682   1429 Cro
000013 363483930   Amy           Crawford          6163321093   703 Vill
000014 363582156   William       Deaver            6162918492   3811 Wes
000015 364859756   Jorge         Ramon             6163872414   2536 Rid
000016 364905803   Julian        Kaywood           6163441908   7816 Por
                                                            More...
F3=Exit     F12=Cancel      F19=Left      F20=Right     F21=Split

MA    A                      MW                              03/032
   1902 - Session successfully started     A232 - HP LaserJet 4050 on IP_10.134.223.223
```

Figure 7.58: Output of Display Report Function

Notice that lines of the report are numbered serially on the far-left side. These line numbers would not appear if the finished query directed its output to a printed report. Also, remember that the default spacing between columns is two character positions. Knowing this, you can see which fields on this report you could shorten without losing data.

For example, maybe you need to reduce your report to a width of no more than 110 print positions. You can see that you could considerably shorten both the first-name and last-name fields of the sample report without cutting off any name characters. However, if new records with longer names were added to the file later on, the next query report could truncate part of a name; so you might want to shorten a less significant field than those containing the names. Shift right and examine the address fields of your report. You can probably shorten these fields without losing data.

When you have finished examining your report, press F12 to return to the Specify Report Column Formatting screen. Select one or two fields to shorten—perhaps the address fields. For each field you want to shorten, change its length value (Len) accordingly.

Look at the layout again. If necessary, shorten another field until the report lines fit within 110 print positions.

7.16. From the Specify Report Column Formatting screen, use the function key to display the report. Make sure you have not truncated data in the process of shortening fields, and that the report will look all right when it is printed. If some data has been truncated, re-adjust print fields accordingly.

When you are satisfied with your report, press Enter (not F3) from the Specify Report Column Formatting screen. Remember, if you go to the Exit this Query screen by mistake, you can press F14 to return to the Define the Query screen.

7.17. The query would run now without any further changes, but you may want to examine the output type to see where the report would be directed. To do so, on the Define the Query screen, move the cursor down to the Select output type and output form option, and take that option.

7.18. The screen you see now should look like the one in Figure 7.59.

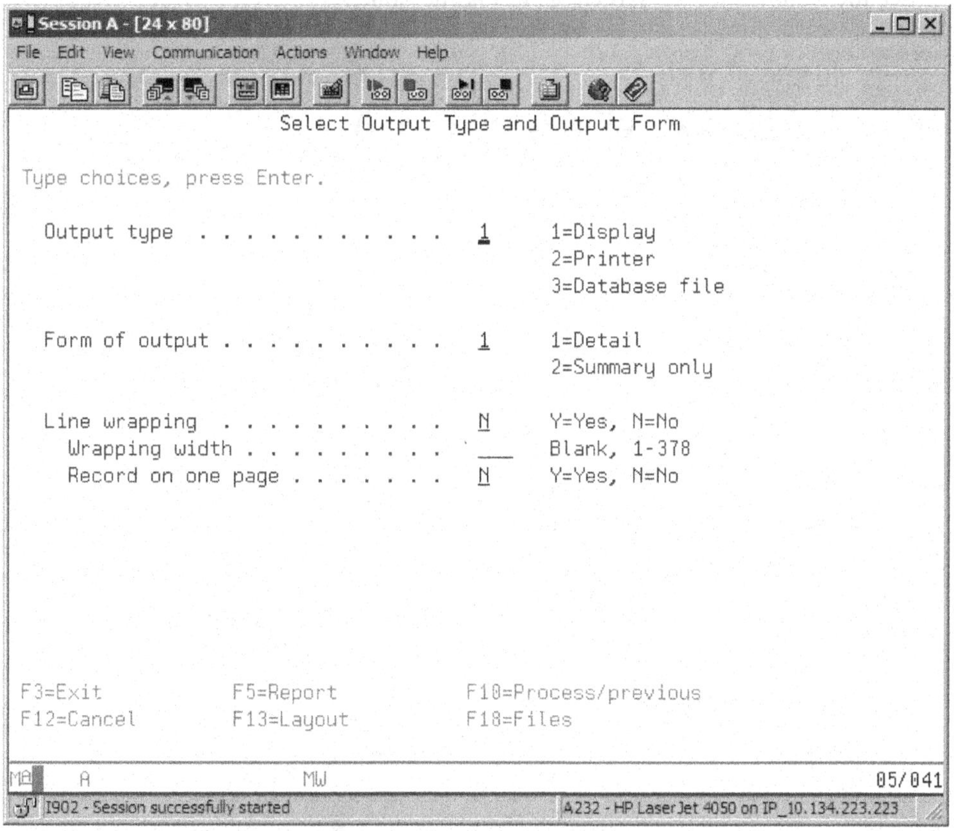

```
Session A - [24 x 80]                                          _ □ ×
File  Edit  View  Communication  Actions  Window  Help

                  Select Output Type and Output Form

 Type choices, press Enter.

   Output type . . . . . . . . . . .   1       1=Display
                                               2=Printer
                                               3=Database file


   Form of output . . . . . . . . . .  1       1=Detail
                                               2=Summary only


   Line wrapping . . . . . . . . . .   N       Y=Yes, N=No
      Wrapping width . . . . . . . . .  ___     Blank, 1-378
      Record on one page . . . . . . .  N       Y=Yes, N=No




 F3=Exit           F5=Report          F10=Process/previous
 F12=Cancel        F13=Layout         F18=Files

 Mᴬ     A                  MW                                    05/041
    I902 - Session successfully started          A232 - HP LaserJet 4050 on IP_10.134.223.223
```

Figure 7.59: Select Output Type and Output Form Screen

Three options are available for Output type. Use Help to find out more about the three output types and to answer the following questions.

7.18.a. If you kept the Display option for Output type, what would the output look like?

7.18.b. If you took the Printer option, what screen would you see next?

7.18.c. If you selected detailed output to a Database file, what would happen to report-break and summary-function output?

For now, let's leave the default values as they are: Display (1) for Output type and Detail (1) for Form of output. Exit Help, and then press Enter to return to the Define the Query screen.

7.19. From the Define the Query screen, press F3 to exit and save the query. You should see the Exit this Query screen, as in Figure 7.60.

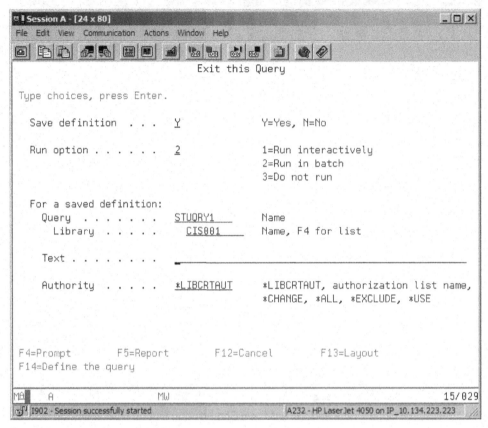

Figure 7.60: Exit this Query Screen

The defaults here are set to save the definition and to run the query in batch. Also, notice that values you provided when you took the option to create a query are used for the Query and Library names.

Because you will save the query definition, use the Field advance key to move the cursor down to the Text field and type in your full name, followed by Query 1 of STUPF. Then press Enter. Because the Run option was set to 1, the query should now be running.

7.20. Use F20 to shift right and examine the whole report. It should look just like it looked from the Display report function in Query.

After you have examined the report, press F3 to exit the display. Doing this should return you to the Work with Queries screen; pressing F3 again returns you to the Query Utilities menu. From the Query Utilities menu, pressing F3 once more should return you to the Work with Objects Using PDM screen.

Part 2

Goals   Find your query definition in the Work with Objects Using PDM list.

Run the query directly from PDM.

Prompt on the PDM Run option and change the Report output type and Record selection parameters of the RUNQRY command.

Find the report and verify record selection.

Change the query definition to send output to a spooled file.

Add standard page headings to the print query.

Start at   Work with Objects Using PDM, your library.

Procedure   Take option 16 on STUQRY1.

Prompt on option 16, and select only records with zip codes in your area; send output to printer.

Find the spooled report in your output queue; display and verify WRKQRY; change STUQRY1.

Select output type and form to print.

Exit and run the query.

Print the report.

7.21. If you are not already looking at your Work with Objects Using PDM list, take the Work with objects option from STRPDM or enter the WRKOBJPDM (Work with Objects Using PDM) command from the command line.

7.21.a. Is there any evidence in your objects list of the query you just created?

If you signed off between parts 1 and 2 of this lab, you should see your query; otherwise, press F5.

The reason you didn't see the query if you are continuing directly from Part 1 is that you entered Query for i5/OS from within Work with Objects Using PDM. Because that screen was not updated while you were in Query for i5/OS, you need to refresh the screen after returning to it to see the new query definition.

7.21.b. What is the object type and attribute of the new object?

7.22. Use F23 to display more PDM options. Notice option 16. You can use this option to execute programs, query definitions, and stored DFU programs. Enter the Run option on your query definition object. A report should be displayed just as it was previously. Press F3 once you have examined the report. PDM options make it easy to run a query definition or a program from the Work with Objects Using PDM screen.

7.23. As with other PDM options, you can request prompting on option 16. Type the option again for STUQRY1, and this time request prompting. You should see a screen similar to Figure 7.61.

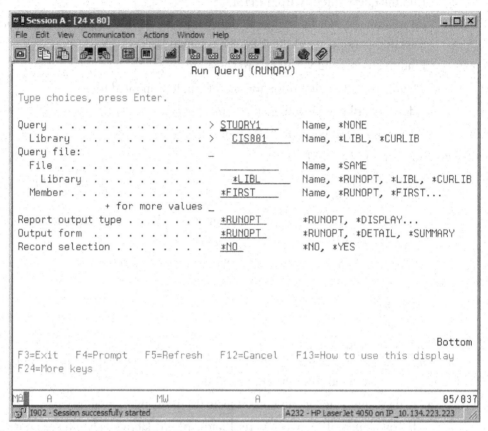

Figure 7.61: Run Query (RUNQRY) Command Prompt Screen

The RUNQRY command will run an existing query definition object (type *QRYDFN) when the object name is supplied for the Query parameter value. On the prompt screen for option 16, PDM has already filled in the object name based on the list-item name on which you took the option. (The command itself, RUNQRY, was selected based on the list item's object type.) You can change certain aspects of the defined query at runtime by supplying overriding parameter values on the RUNQRY command-prompt screen. These changes affect only the current run and do not change the query definition.

7.23.a. What does the *RUNOPT value of the output type and output form do?

7.24. On the RUNQRY command-prompt screen, change the value of the Report output type parameter so that the query output will be sent to a printer (spooled).

In addition, you can cause the query to prompt you for record selection when it begins to run by changing the Record selection parameter value to *YES. Do that now.

Even if you did not use record selection in the query definition, by typing *YES you can add record selection at runtime. If you specified record selection in the query definition, you can change the selection criteria or cancel the predefined selection.

At this point, your Report output type parameter value should be *PRINTER, and the Record selection parameter value should be *YES. Press Enter. When you have changed the output to *PRINTER, additional parameters are provided that let you, for example, widen a report line from the 132-position default. Because that should not be necessary for this report, press Enter again to run the query. After a pause, the Select Records screen should appear. Figure 7.62 shows that screen with a selection expression already entered.

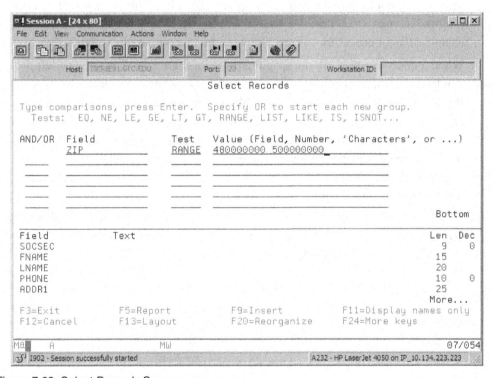

Figure 7.62: Select Records Screen

The expression instructs the query to select only those records having ZIP field values in the range of 480000000 through 500000000 (inclusive). Records in input file STUPF having zip-code values outside this range will not be included in the query report.

Enter a similar selection expression on your prompt screen, but use a range of zip-code values for your own area, so that you can be sure to select at least a few records from your file. Then press Enter to run the query.

7.25. This time, the output should not be displayed on your workstation screen. To find your report, work with your spooled files or output queue. Query for i5/OS uses a printer file named QPQUPRFIL; if you look in the File column, the report should be easy to find.

   7.25.a. How many records were selected for your report?

   7.25.b. Are the zip codes of the report records all within the range you selected?

7.26. Return to the Work with Objects Using PDM screen, and take the Work with option on your query definition object.

   7.26.a. At what screen have you arrived?

   Take the option to Change, and on the Query input field, press F4 for a list. From the prompt list, move the cursor down to the option field for your query, and type 2 to change. It's not necessary to erase the 2 on the line above. Press Enter.

7.27. When a query is saved, all the specifications for it are stored as you last left them. If you take the Change option, you can modify an existing query in any way necessary. If you had decided your query should always be printed, you wouldn't want to prompt on the RUNQRY command (as you did in the previous step) every time you ran the report; it would make more sense to change the output type in the query definition itself. Let us change our query so that it uses a spooled printer file as output instead of the display screen. Move the cursor down to the Select output type and output form option field, and enter 1.

7.28. This time, from the resulting Select Output Type and Output Form screen, specify Output type 2 for Printer. Leave the other options at their defaults, and press Enter. You should see the Define Printer Output screen (Figure 7.63).

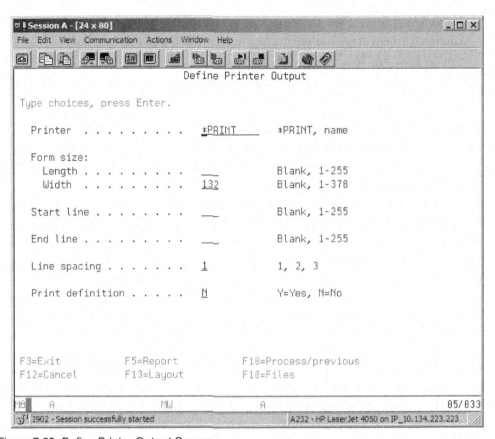

Figure 7.63: Define Printer Output Screen

7.28.a. What does *PRINT mean for the printer device?

The form width defaults to 132 print positions, and even though you made your report lines narrower than this (110 characters), the form size itself can remain at the default of 132.

Tip

If you got to this point and could not remember the exact width of your report, you could use function key F13 to check the width.

If your report were wider than 132 positions, you would need to change the Width value to accommodate the report; otherwise, data beyond the 132nd position would be truncated (unless you had changed the previous screen's Line wrapping value to Y).

7.29. It should not be necessary to change any values on this screen, so press Enter to continue. You next should see the Define Spooled Output screen.

    7.29.a. Based on previous experience, what do you think will happen to your report if you provide no value for the Spool the output field? (Not sure? Try Help.)

    7.29.b. Use Help to find out what happens when you leave the Form type field blank.

    Unless your instructor/mentor tells you otherwise, leave Form type blank to default to the value specified in the printer device file. Leave the other values as they are, and press Enter.

7.30. For now, you will not print a cover page, so type N for the Print cover page option, and then press Enter. You should now see the Specify Page Headings and Footings screen.

7.31. Print the Standard page headings (leave the default at Y), and key in an appropriate page heading, such as

Student File Listing Prepared by: (your name).

When you are finished, press Enter to return to the Define the Query screen.

7.32. You have now changed your query definition to direct its output to a spooled print file. From the Define the Query screen, press F3 to save and run the query.

7.33. This time, no changes should be needed from the Exit this Query screen (Save definition should be Y, and Run option should be 1), so simply press Enter to run the query. You should briefly see a *"Query running . . ."* message, followed by a message from the Work with Queries screen indicating successful completion.

Return to the Work with Objects Using PDM screen. You should still see your query definition listed even though it has been changed. Move the cursor up to the option field for your output queue, and Work with the output queue.

7.34. Find the new file named QPQUPRFIL, and display it. If you aren't sure which spooled file is the more recent, use F11 to display date and time. Is it your query report? (The spacing will look different from when the report is printed because the printer form-control characters are ignored on the display.)

This report should have more records than the earlier version that used record selection. Also, in this report, you declined the cover page when you changed your query definition, but the RUNQRY prompted version shows a standard cover page (which would be printed as the first page). You should also see the page heading with your name, which you added to the new report.

7.35. Change this print file to redirect it to printer PRT01 or to the printer assigned by your instructor/mentor to print class lab projects. When you retrieve your printed report, hand it in along with your answer sheet.

Additional Lab Exercise

To help you acquire more skill in working with Query for i5/OS, this additional lab exercise is recommended. Do not attempt this exercise until you have successfully completed the main lab exercise for this chapter. The instructions tell you what to do, but they are less specific about how to do it. The intent is for you to apply what you have learned to new situations. Think about each step, and use the abundant Help information available on the system. Rely on your instructor/mentor when you are not sure how to proceed.

7.36. From the Work with Objects Using PDM screen, take the Work with option on your current query definition, STUQRY1.

7.37. From the Work with Queries screen, take the option to change STUQRY1.

7.38. From the Define the Query screen, choose Specify file selections. Use the function key to add a file. Change the File ID of the primary file (STUPF) to S. Now specify a secondary file named STUZIPPF in library INTROCLASS. Make its File ID Z.

7.39. For the Type of join parameter, specify 3, Unmatched records with primary file. This join type will produce a listing of all student records in file STUPF that do not have matching zip codes in file STUZIPPF in the INTROCLASS library.

7.40. Enter a join relation equating the zip code of the student file to the zip code of the ZIPPF file. Remember to use file IDs to qualify the field names. From the Specify How to Join Files screen, use the appropriate function key to run the report.

Note
If no records are selected for the report, then all zip codes in your student file must have matched STUZIPPF zip codes, so there are no unmatched records.

Because you did not explicitly select fields in the original query, all fields from both files will be included in the report. If you shift right, you will see the column of zip codes from the student file and, next to it, the column of default zeros from the unmatched secondary file. City and state will also have default values of spaces.

7.41. Use the function key to cancel the report, and then press Enter to save your file specifications and return to the Define the Query screen.

7.42. Select and sequence fields, including last name, first name, address line 1, city, state, and the student file's zip-code field, in that order, for your report.

7.43. After selecting the fields, use the layout function to make sure the width of the report does not exceed the 132 positions of the standard line width allowed by Select Output Type and Output Form for printer output.

7.44. Exit the query. From the Exit screen, save the definition and run the query interactively, but change the query name to STUQRY2; doing so will save the new query as a separate query definition, keeping the original STUQRY1 intact. Give the new query a text description indicating that it lists student records with unmatched zip codes.

7.45. Return to the Work with Objects Using PDM screen, and change the library to INTROCLASS. In the INTROCLASS library PDM list, find the physical file named STUZIPPF, and copy it to your own library.

7.46. Return to the Work with Objects Using PDM list of your own library. Work with your output queue. Find the report your new query just created and display it. On scratch paper, jot down the unmatched zip codes.

7.47. Run a temporary DFU program on the STUZIPPF file you just copied into your library. (Make sure you are running the DFU on your STUZIPPF file and not the one in the INTROCLASS library; you should not be able to add records to the file in the INTROCLASS library.) Add records for the unmatched zip codes you jotted down from your student file, using real or fictitious city and state values.

7.48. Return to the Work with Queries screen, and take the Change option on your join query, STUQRY2.

7.49. Using the Specify file selections option, first change the library value of your secondary file (STUZIPPF) to your own current library. Then run the query to see whether you added STUZIPPF records for all the previously unmatched student zip codes. If you were successful, the report should come up empty.

7.50. Now change the type of join to 2, Matched records with primary file. If you run the report, you should now see all student records listed. Any records still having unmatched zip codes will show city and state values as blanks.

7.51. Saving your changes, return to Define the Query, and then proceed to the exit screen. Name the type 2 join query STUQRY3, and give it a text description indicating an outer join of STUZIPPF on STUPF. Run the query interactively. (Its output is still going to be printed.)

You should now see two query reports in your output queue. Send them to the class printer, and then hand in the hard-copy reports to your instructor.

CHAPTER 8

Using Logical Files

Overview

In previous chapters, you learned about physical files and how to describe them using Data Description Specifications (DDS). In this chapter, we discuss the usefulness of logical files and contrast them with physical files. Specifically, we examine the use of access paths in logical files to retrieve data records in a different order from how they are stored in physical files. We also examine several other powerful relational database operations, such as selection, projection, and join, that can be employed through the use of logical files. You step through the process of describing and creating a logical file using several of these operations.

Because any create command can fail, we want to prepare you for dealing with failed compiles. Thus, in the lab we intentionally cause the initial compile of your logical file to fail. You then learn how to read a job log and a compile listing to determine what caused the compile to fail and how to correct the problem.

Objectives

Students will be able to

- Create a simple logical file over an existing physical file
- Explain record selection and show how it is coded using DDS
- Explain field projection and why it is used
- Identify arrival-sequence and keyed-sequence access paths and show how each is coded in DDS
- Locate and use a job log and a compile listing to find and correct DDS source code errors

Physical Files and Access Paths

As you recall from earlier chapters, externally described **physical files** contain data records whose format is defined according to a specific layout. This record format not only specifies the name and relative order of fields but also identifies each field's data type and length. A physical file has only one record format, which is designated in the Data Description Specifications (DDS) source code by an R in the Name Type field followed by a name for the record format in the Name field.

The record format provides a blueprint of a record's fields, but it does not tell us in what order records of data are available to applications. This information—describing the way in which records can be read or retrieved from files—is called an **access path**.

Arrival-Sequence Access Paths

In DB2 for IBM i, there are two kinds of access paths: **arrival-sequence** and **keyed-sequence**. Every file uses one access path, and, unless otherwise specified, the records in a physical file are both stored and retrieved in arrival sequence—that is, in the order in which they were added to the file. Both the EMPPF sample file we used in previous chapters and the STUPF file you created in a previous lab (Chapter 5) use arrival-sequence access paths. No special action was needed to create those files with arrival-sequence access paths; when no other specific access-path information is provided in the DDS source-file description, the system defaults to arrival sequence. Files using arrival-sequence access paths may have their records read in two ways: sequentially or directly.

Sequential Retrieval

With **sequential record retrieval**, records are presented one after another in the order in which they entered, or "arrived in," the file—first in, first out. You can illustrate this type of retrieval by paging down (or up) from the initial display of a temporary Data File Utility (DFU) program for an arrival-sequence file. If you paged down from the beginning of the file, the 10th record you added to the file would be the 10th record to appear.

In addition, the order in which a **DSPPFM** (Display Physical File Member) command lists records is in arrival sequence. To locate the 1,000th record in a file being read sequentially, you would need to read through the 999 records preceding it.

Note

You should realize that sequential retrieval for a file with an arrival-sequence access path does not imply the sequencing of records by any field value, but only by the order in which records arrived or were entered into the file.

Direct Retrieval

Direct record retrieval (random access) implies that you can access a specific record in a file without having to read all the other records that precede it. Any record in an arrival-sequence file can be retrieved directly if its **relative record number** is known. Relative record numbers are assigned to records as they are added to a file, in a consecutive series of integers, starting from 1. Therefore, the 1,000th record added to a file would have relative record number 1000. (This may not be true if the database is told to reuse deleted record space.) You could randomly read this record without having to page through the preceding 999 records by typing 1000 in the *RECNBR (relative record number) entry field of a DFU program in change mode. In addition, high-level language (HLL) programs can read a file randomly by relative record number.

Keyed-Sequence Access Paths

It is often useful or necessary to be able to read an entire file or access an individual record by the value of a certain field, called the **key field**. For example, it might be useful to retrieve individual records from a large student file by name, regardless of how the records may be physically stored in the file.

By defining one or more fields in the record format as keys, you can specify a keyed-sequence access path for a physical file when it is created. A program can then process the file's records in key-field order instead of in arrival sequence.

For files that contain many records, having the option to process a file in keyed sequence can be useful. For example, if you needed to find the record for a certain employee in an employee master file, retrieving the record according to a key field such as Social Security number would be much quicker than searching through the file in arrival sequence; it would also be more convenient than trying to remember a meaningless relative record number.

If you know that a file will most often be accessed using the value of a certain field, you can specify a keyed-sequence access path when the file is created. The ZIPPF file we introduced in Chapter 7 is a good example. By far, the most common access to that file would be through the zip-code field, as in the join relationship for the query: E.ZIP EQ Z.ZIP. So file ZIPPF could well have been created with a keyed-sequence access path.

Specifying Key Fields

You specify key fields in the DDS source code of the file description. The key itself can be a single field in the file's record format, or it can consist of several fields used together (a **composite key**). If the value of the field must be unique for every record (recall the zip code field in the ZIPPF file), the field is a **primary key**, and you can code a special file-level keyword, **UNIQUE**, in DDS. When you treat a key as a primary key by specifying the UNIQUE keyword, the system does not permit **duplicate keys** (i.e., the insertion of a new record whose key-field value is the same as that of a record that already exists).

When the UNIQUE keyword is not used, the system lets records having the same key-field values be stored in the file. Although records with duplicate keys generally are made available in first-in, first-out order, you can specify the file-level keyword FIFO to ensure that they are. This keyword, used as an alternative to UNIQUE, tells the system to make records with duplicate keys available in first-in, first-out order.

As we mentioned above, you code keyword UNIQUE (or FIFO) in DDS as a file-level entry, before the record-format specification line. The actual declaration of the key follows the field-level DDS specifications. You define keys by coding a K in the Name Type field, followed by the name of the field that will serve as the key in the Name field of the DDS specification.

For example, Figure 8.1 shows the DDS specifications for physical file EMPPF as if the file had originally been created with a keyed-sequence access path.

```
 ▣ ▌Session A - [24 x 80]                                              _ □ ✕
 File  Edit  View  Communication  Actions  Window  Help

 ▣  ▤▤  ▤▤  ▦▦  ▥▥  ▦▦  ▦  ▦▦  ▦▦  ▦▦  ▥  ◈ ◢
   Columns . . . :    1  71              Edit                CIS001/QDDSSRC
   SEU==>  _____         EMPPF
   FMT PF  .....A..........T.Name+++++RLen++TDpB......Functions+++++++++++++++++
         *************** Beginning of data *************************************
 0001.00     A                                        UNIQUE
 0002.00     A           R EMPPFR
 0003.00     A             EMPNO          9B 0
 0004.00     A             LASTNAME      16A
 0005.00     A             FIRSTNAME     12A
 0006.00     A             HOMEPHONE      7S 0
 0007.00     A             ADDR1         40A
 0008.00     A             ADDR2         40A
 0009.00     A             ZIP            5S 0
 0010.00     A             DEPT          12A
 0011.00     A             BIRTHDATE      L
 0012.00     A             HIREDATE       L
 0013.00     A             SALARY         7P 0
 0014.00     A           K EMPNO
         ****************** End of data *******************************************



   F3=Exit   F4=Prompt   F5=Refresh   F9=Retrieve   F10=Cursor   F11=Toggle
   F16=Repeat find       F17=Repeat change          F24=More keys
                                     (C) COPYRIGHT IBM CORP. 1981, 2007.
 MA▮    A               MW                                            02/009
  ⌨ I902 - Session successfully started          A232 - HP LaserJet 4050 on IP_10.134.223.223
```

Figure 8.1: DDS for File EMPPF Keyed on EMPNO (Social Security Number)

The keyword UNIQUE, specified at the file level, tells us that no duplicate keys are permitted. (Remember, when you specify UNIQUE, DB2 does not let you add a record to the file that duplicates an existing key value.) Field EMPNO (Social Security) has been specified as a primary key through the use of the UNIQUE keyword and entering a K in the DDS Name Type field and the name of the field itself, EMPNO, in the DDS Name field.

Specifying a UNIQUE key makes sense in this example because you would not expect to encounter duplicate Social Security numbers; if you did, it would be an error, and the system should alert you. However, if you need to access records in the file by last name/first name instead of by Social Security number, you cannot be sure that no duplicate keys exist. Because there could be a Steven Smith in marketing and a different Steven Smith in sales, using the UNIQUE keyword would be inadvisable. In this case, to ensure that records having duplicate keys are processed in the order entered, you must code the DDS as you see in Figure 8.2.

```
Session A - [24 x 80]                                                    _ □ ×
File  Edit  View  Communication  Actions  Window  Help

 □  ▣▣  ▣▣  ▣▣  ▣▣  ▣▣  ▣▣  ▣▣  ▣▣  □  ▨◈

 Columns . . . :    1  71               Edit                    CIS001/QDDSSRC
 SEU==> _____    EMPPF
 FMT PF .....A..........T.Name++++++RLen++TDpB......Functions++++++++++++++++++
          *************** Beginning of data ***********************************
 0001.00      A                                          FIFO
 0002.00      A            R EMPPFR
 0003.00      A              EMPNO         9B 0
 0004.00      A              LASTNAME     16A
 0005.00      A              FIRSTNAME    12A
 0006.00      A              HOMEPHONE     7S 0
 0007.00      A              ADDR1        40A
 0008.00      A              ADDR2        40A
 0009.00      A              ZIP           5S 0
 0010.00      A              DEPT         12A
 0011.00      A              BIRTHDATE     L
 0012.00      A              HIREDATE      L
 0013.00      A              SALARY        7P 0
 0014.00      A            K LASTNAME
 0015.00      A            K FIRSTNAME
          ****************** End of data ***********************************

 F3=Exit   F4=Prompt   F5=Refresh   F9=Retrieve   F10=Cursor   F11=Toggle
 F16=Repeat find       F17=Repeat change          F24=More keys

 MA    A                MW                                           19/001
   I902 - Session successfully started        A232 - HP LaserJet 4050 on IP_10.134.223.223
```

Figure 8.2: DDS for File EMPPF Keyed on Name

Notice that a composite key is specified for physical file EMPPF—that is, two fields are used as the key. The key fields, LASTNAME and FIRSTNAME, are coded in the DDS in order of most significant to least significant. In this way, the access order will be like that of a telephone book, with "Smith, Arnold" coming before "Smith, Betty."

Although it may be the primary means of retrieving records, this composite key cannot be a primary key in the strict relational database sense because a primary key requires uniqueness. Because in a large company two or more employees with the same first and last names certainly could exist, we cannot use keyword UNIQUE. Instead, we have coded the **FIFO** keyword to guarantee first-in, first-out retrieval of records with duplicate keys.

To summarize, you can create physical files with either an arrival-sequence access path (the default) or a keyed-sequence access path that lets you retrieve records by the value of a key field. However, regardless of whether a physical file uses an arrival-sequence access path or a keyed-sequence access path, you can easily build a different access path over the physical file by using a logical file. This capability of **logical files** lets you provide an alternate keyed-sequence access path over an existing keyed- or arrival-sequence physical file. In fact, multiple alternate access paths can exist over a single physical file. For example, you could have a name-keyed logical file and a Social Security–keyed logical file over an arrival-sequence employee physical file. This use of logical files to build different access paths over an existing physical file is a common and powerful one.

Logical Files

Perhaps the simplest way to think of logical files is that they represent different ways to present all or part of the data of one or more physical files. Logical files function as a set of rules that tell DB2 how to select, limit, combine, and present the data of the underlying physical file (or files). Logical files themselves contain no data records—they get their data from the physical file (or files) on which they are based, but programs and utilities such as DFU can access and manipulate logical files as if they contained data. A physical file must exist before any logical file is created over it, and many different logical files can be based on the same physical file.

Logical files, which for the most part correspond to **views** in a relational database, need to be able to perform several basic functions on physical-file data. These functions include the ability to

- Allow the random access of data by the value of a field other than the primary key, or present the logical file in sequence by an alternate key (logical-file access path or relational database index)
- Select only certain records of the physical file to be included in the logical file and omit the others (selection)
- Include in the logical file only those fields necessary to the user/application from the physical-file record format, thus ensuring that users have access to data strictly on a need-to-know basis (projection)
- Combine data elements (fields) from two or more physical files into a single logical-file record format by matching records from the physical files with the value of a common field (join)

Three distinct types of logical files exist: *simple, join,* and *multiple-format* logical files. We will look at examples of the latter two later in this chapter; but first, we will consider the most commonly used type, the simple logical file. We also will use our example of a simple logical file to demonstrate the concepts of *access path, selection/omission,* and *projection.*

Describing a Simple Logical File

Simple logical files are created over a single physical file that must already exist as a *FILE type object. When describing a simple logical file, you must name the underlying physical file in the DDS record-format statement. To illustrate, we will use the physical file EMPPF (the original nonkeyed version) as the based-on file. In this example, you would use the **PFILE** record-level keyword followed by the physical-file name in parentheses to establish the link between the simple logical file and its single based-on physical file. The record format entry would look like this:

```
R EMPPFR          PFILE(EMPPF)
```

Alternate Access Path

Because physical files can have only one keyed-sequence access path, logical files play an important role by providing the capability to use a different (alternate) key to access the data in physical files. As we mentioned above, logical files can serve as indexes that provide another sort sequence (access path) for physical-file data—that is, a sort sequence different from the one specified when the original physical file was created.

When a logical file's only purpose is to provide a different access path than the physical file does, as is the case in this example, its description is an easy matter. If you wanted to access the data records in the underlying physical file EMPPF in key sequence by last name and first name, the DDS for the simple logical file Figure 8.3 describes would do the job.

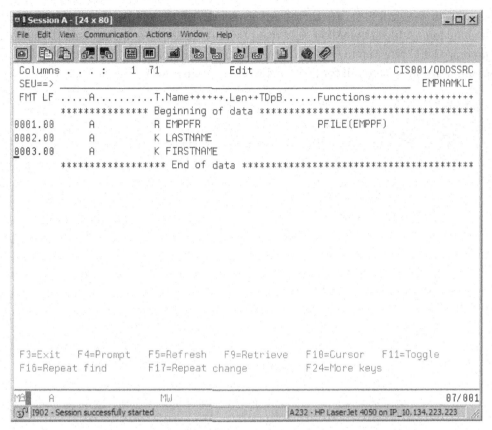

Figure 8.3: DDS for a Simple Logical File to Access EMPPF by Employee Name

As you can see, the record-format name used for the logical file (EMPPFR) is the same as the one used for physical file EMPPF. Regardless of whether the physical file is keyed or in arrival sequence, when you use the physical file's record-format name for the logical file and include no field-level entries, the logical file copies the physical file's record format as it exists at the time the logical file is created. All the fields currently in the physical file are included in the logical file—with the same attributes. The record-format entry must also identify the based-on physical file as the value of the PFILE keyword. The only other required entries are those to identify the key. By specifying fields LASTNAME and FIRSTNAME as key fields (using a K in the DDS Name Type field), we tell the compiler that the new file will have a keyed-sequence access path using the composite key of last name (major) and first name (minor). The compiler expects to find key-field names in the based-on physical file's record format. If you misspell one of the key-field names, a compile error results.

To see how this logical file accesses records in physical file EMPPF, assume that you have created the logical file EMPNAMKLF, and that physical file EMPPF contains data. If you create a temporary DFU program to work with the logical file and then run the temporary DFU program, it displays a prompt for the two key fields (Figure 8.4).

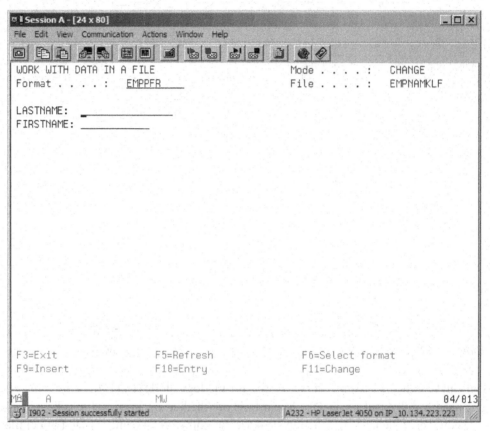

Figure 8.4: DFU for Logical File EMPNAMKLF in Change Mode

When you type the name of a known employee and press Enter, DB2 searches the logical-file access path for matching values. If a match is found, the system retrieves the appropriate record from the physical file and displays it on the screen. Figure 8.5 shows the record that would be displayed if you entered Kartblanch and Emil as the key-field values.

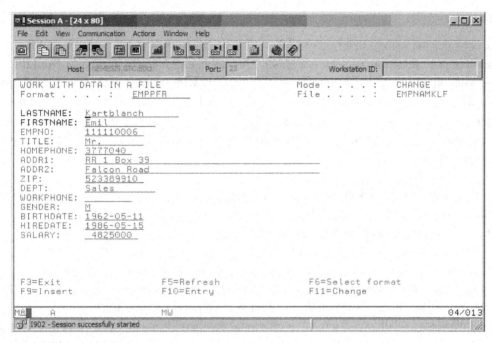

Figure 8.5: DFU Showing Record Retrieved for Key "Kartblanch", "Emil"

If you were to Page Up or Page Down from this record, subsequent records would be
retrieved and displayed in alphabetical sequence by name, relative to the currently displayed
record. This logical file illustrates the technique of using the same record-format name as the
physical file's record format. When you do this and supply no field attributes, the logical file
includes all the fields from the physical file with their same attributes. In general, however,
it is wise to list all fields to be included in the logical file even when the list exactly matches
the current field list of the based-on physical file. This approach lets RPG and COBOL
applications accessing the data through the logical file continue to function without change
if fields are later added to the physical file.

In summary, to build a logical file whose only purpose is to provide an alternate access path
over the physical file, code keyword PFILE in the record-format entry, and list the fields to be
included by name. Following the field list is a key-level entry (or entries), with a K in DDS
column 17, to identify the key field (or fields).

Selection

Now consider the second function of logical files we mentioned above, selection. When a logical file uses selection, its population is limited to a certain group of records from the underlying physical file. Selection lets users work only with the data records needed for an application, and it protects excluded data from users who do not need that data or are not authorized to it. (This operation was originally called *restriction*, which may be a better term because the operation's primary purpose is to restrict access to data that users or applications should not have.)

In DB2, you implement selection in DDS by using Select and Omit entries, and by keywords that define how the select/omit operation is to occur. Unlike key entries that can be used by both physical and logical files, Select/Omit entries are used only with logical files.

To illustrate selection, let us assume you want to provide all department managers with information about employees in their own departments. Creating separate physical files that contain employee records for each department is not a good solution for many reasons, and it is not necessary when you are using a relational database. You can keep all employee data in a single physical file and create a different logical file for each department. Figure 8.6 shows the DDS source code for a simple logical file named EMPSLSLF, whose population consists only of sales department records.

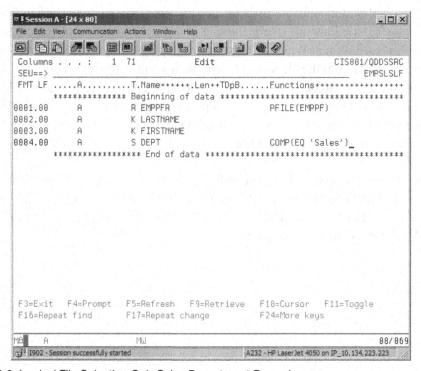

Figure 8.6: Logical File Selecting Only Sales Department Records

Note

For the purpose of focusing on select/omit logic, we are simply using the same record-format name as the physical file, implicitly including all physical-file fields. It would be better, however, to explicitly list the fields when you are creating a working logical file. We have given this file a keyed-sequence access path, but selection does not require keying, and an arrival-sequence access path would have worked as well.

Notice that the file in Figure 8.6 is very similar to logical file EMPNAMKLF in Figure 8.3. The only difference is the Select entry following the key fields (LASTNAME and FIRSTNAME). The letter S coded in the Name Type field designates this entry as a Select entry and is followed by the name of the field (DEPT) that you want to test to determine whether the record should be selected or omitted. Although we are testing the DEPT field in this example, we could test any other field (or fields) in the logical file. Because we have coded the logical file with the same record-format name as the physical file and with no field-level entries, all physical-file fields will be included in the logical file's record format, and we can reference any field name in a Select/Omit entry. You can use three function keywords with Select and its counterpart, Omit: COMP, VALUES, and RANGE.

COMP

You specify the **COMP** keyword using the format

COMP(op comparand)

The COMP keyword selects or omits records in which the value of the named field used as the subject of the relational operator (op) tests true for the specified **comparand** value.

The valid codes for the relational operator are

- EQ (equal)
- NE (not equal)
- LT (less than)
- NL (not less than)
- GT (greater than)
- NG (not greater than)
- LE (less than or equal to)
- GE (greater than or equal to)

Note: If the field is alphanumeric (date or time), the comparand must be a quoted string.

The following COMP function tells DB2 to select physical-file records whose DEPT field value is equal to the quoted string constant 'Sales':

```
S DEPT          COMP(EQ 'Sales')
```

This COMP function selects employees hired since January 1, 1990:

```
S HIREDATE      COMP(GE '1990-01-01')
```

VALUES

You specify the **VALUES** keyword using the format

```
VALUES(value1  value2  value3 . . . )
```

The VALUES keyword selects or omits records in which the value of the named field matches one of the values in the list.

Here are some rules to remember:

- List items are separated by one or more spaces.
- Each value in alphanumeric and date and time fields must be enclosed in apostrophes (').
- Only digits and a decimal point are needed for numeric fields.

The following Select entry selects records for the logical file having a zip code equal to 52247, 52338, or 52404:

```
S ZIP           VALUES(52247 52338 52404)
```

RANGE

You specify the **RANGE** keyword using the format

```
RANGE(lowval  highval)
```

The RANGE keyword selects or omits records in which the named field contains a value in the range of lowval to highval, inclusive. For example, the Select entry

```
S SALARY            RANGE(20000 34500)
```

selects records for the logical file that have a salary of at least $20,000 and not more than $34,500. For alphanumeric and date and time fields, both values must be enclosed in apostrophes.

When coding DDS keywords and the associated parameters, you need to keep a couple of rules in mind:

- DDS uses upper case exclusively, and you must enter all DDS keywords in uppercase format. Only quoted strings can be in mixed case (e.g., 'Sales'). If a quoted string is a constant used to compare an actual database-field value, the string must be entered exactly as the data is stored. For values stored in database records, DB2 is case sensitive (i.e., 'SALES', 'sales', and 'Sales' are not equal). In the example in Figure 8.6, we used 'Sales' because we know that is how the data is stored in the physical file.
- Keyword parameter values must be enclosed in parentheses. The left parenthesis must immediately follow the keyword. If there are multiple values, at least one space must separate values in the list. This is also true if one of the values is an operator, such as EQ in our example; at least one space must separate EQ and the following value 'Sales'.

Following these rules will help you avoid most syntax errors. You can find additional rules and examples of other keywords on the IBM Information Center Web site.

Omit: The Inverse of Select

The Omit operation entry, which is coded with the value O in the Name Type field, functions as the inverse of Select. Sometimes it is easier to state which records we do not want in the logical file than which records we do want. If, for example, the human resources department manager asks for a file of all employees except those in sales, you might find it easiest to code

```
O DEPT            COMP(EQ 'Sales')
```

Of course, you could create the same logical file by using a Select entry with an NE (not equal) operator:

```
S DEPT            COMP(NE 'Sales')
```

You can perform more than one Select or Omit operation with a logical file. When the Name Type S or O is repeated for each entry, the series of Selects or Omits is considered connected by logical OR operators; for example,

```
S  DEPT            COMP(EQ  'Research')
S  SALARY          COMP(GE  45000)
```

Taken together, these entries state that records should be included in the logical file if their department is research *or* if their salary is greater than or equal to $45,000. If either or both conditions are true, the record is selected for the logical file. As soon as one select or omit condition is satisfied, starting with the first entry coded, the record is selected (or omitted) and not considered again. This fact does have some bearing on the ordering of Select/Omit entries, especially if you use both Select and Omit.

For example, consider employee Jack Sprat of the marketing department, who has a salary of $38,500. If you code the DDS in the following order

```
S  DEPT            COMP(EQ  'Marketing')
O  SALARY          COMP(LT  45000)
```

you are telling DB2 to first select any marketing department records; and then, of the records remaining, to omit any records in which salary is less than $45,000. This means that all records in the marketing department, regardless of salary, should be selected. That would include Jack, even though his salary is low. In addition, all remaining records not explicitly omitted (i.e., those having salaries of at least $45,000) will be included in the logical file.

In contrast, the results achieved by reversing the order of the entries may be quite different. If you code the DDS as

```
O  SALARY          COMP(LT  45000)
S  DEPT            COMP(EQ  'Marketing')
```

you are telling DB2 to first omit all records for which salary is less than $45,000 (there goes Jack); and then, of the records remaining, to select only those whose department is marketing. In this case, even though Jack is in marketing, his record will not be in the logical file because he was first eliminated by the Omit. Once omitted, a record will not be selected.

In effect, the code above says, "Select only those records for which salary is greater than or equal to $45,000 *and* that are in the marketing department." This expression using a logical AND may be easier to understand than the Select/Omit combination above; and, in fact, you can code multiple Selects or Omits connected by logical ANDs. When two or more entries are coded and only the first uses the Name Type S or O, the entries are considered logically connected by the AND operator. To code the selection as a logical AND operation, you would simply enter

```
S SALARY          COMP(GE  45000)
  DEPT            COMP(EQ  'Marketing')
```

This code tells DB2 to select records for which salary is at least $45,000 *and* that are part of the marketing department.

It is important to realize the difference in the use of OR and AND with multiple Select/Omit entries. For example, if you code the following entries

```
S DEPT            VALUES('Human Res'  'Sales')
  SALARY          RANGE(35000  55000)
```

you are specifying that both conditions must be true—for a record to be selected, the department must be 'Human Res' or 'Sales' *and* salary must be in the range of $35,000 to $55,000. Requiring both conditions to be true would select a smaller number of records than using an OR relationship. Simply adding an S Name type to the second line of the above code changes its meaning significantly:

```
S DEPT            VALUES('Human Res'  'Sales')
S SALARY          RANGE(35000  55000)
```

This combination connects the two entries using a logical OR. Now we are telling DB2 to select any record in the human resources or sales department and then, of the remaining records, to select all records with a salary in the range of $35,000 to $55,000. This specification would certainly select a much larger number of records for the logical file.

To help you understand this difference, consider the illustration in Figure 8.7.

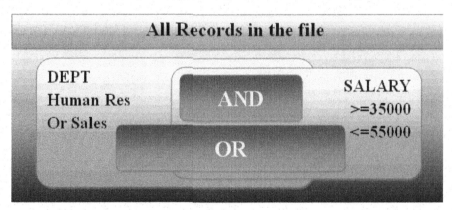

Figure 8.7: Difference in the Use of OR and AND

The selection using AND would include only the intersection of DEPT and SALARY, shown as the shaded center "AND" graphic, while OR would include all records in the two shaded graphics, shown as the shaded "OR" graphic, which includes the records in the "AND" box that have both conditions true.

Each Select or Omit entry adds a new select "rule" to the file description. Each line that names a field and uses a COMP or VALUES keyword adds one rule, regardless of whether that field test was in an AND or an OR relationship with a previous Select/Omit entry. The RANGE keyword is implemented using two limit tests, which results in two rules, although only one field is named. All the examples we have just covered create two or three rules.

In addition, even a single Select or Omit entry adds one more select or omit rule, inserted automatically, to the logical file. That rule will be the opposite operation of the last one coded and will apply to all records not yet selected or omitted. If your logical file includes the following Select/Omit entries,

```
O DEPT              COMP(EQ  'Human Res')
S SALARY            COMP(GT  40000)
```

the last rule that DB2 adds would be

```
O                   ALL
```

Figure 8.8 shows the Select/Omit Description information the DSPFD (Display File Description) command using the Select/Omit entries that the example above provides for a logical file.

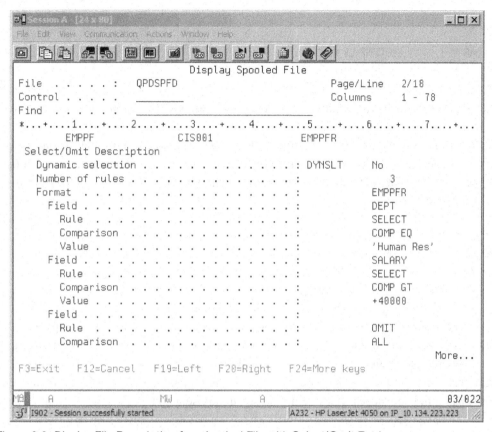

Figure 8.8: Display File Description for a Logical File with Select/Omit Entries

Notice that the number of rules is three; the first two come from the source code, and the third is the inverse of the last Select entry.

The last omit operation is not coded in the DDS but is added by DB2 at compile time. When you code any Select/Omit entries for a logical file, this last rule serves the purpose of clarifying what happens to records of the physical file that are neither explicitly selected nor omitted by the coded rules. The keyword ALL takes the place of any COMP, VALUES, or RANGE entry; and when it is used, no field name is specified.

It is possible for you to code the last ALL rule yourself; but because you would probably never want to change the default rule of opposites, there would be nothing to gain by doing so. For example, neither

```
S  SALARY          COMP(GT 40000)
S                  ALL
```

nor

```
O SALARY            COMP(LE 40000)
O                   ALL
```

makes much sense. The first example selects everything, and the second omits everything.

A last consideration for using select/omit relates to access paths. If a logical file has a keyed-sequence access path, **select/omit operations** are performed on the access path itself. Assume a physical file (EMPPF) has 1,000 records, and you compile a logical file over it with the following description:

```
                    UNIQUE
R EMPPFR            PFILE(EMPPF)
K EMPNO
S DEPT              COMP(EQ 'Sales')
```

A new access path will be created for the logical file even if a unique, keyed-sequence access path on EMPNO already exists for the physical file. If exactly half of all employees are salespeople, the logical file's access path will have 500 entries, one for each sales-department record in the physical file. When a program opens the logical file, it reads records using the new access path—only those already selected.

This is fine from the standpoint of a program needing only sales-employee records, but now an additional access path exists on the system—one more to take up space and be maintained. For example, if you add a new sales-department employee to the physical file, both access paths must be updated, and UNIQUE keys require immediate (*IMMED) access-path maintenance. You can imagine that if you created 20 different select/omit logical files, each having a keyed-sequence access path, the overhead resulting from access-path maintenance when you are performing updates, adds, and deletes to the physical file (or through any of the logical files) could be substantial.

In our example, and in many practical situations, the logical file whose code is shown above and its based-on physical file use the same field (EMPNO in this case) as the key. When this is the case, you can instruct DB2 not to build a new access path, but to share the existing access path and to dynamically select and omit records as they are read through the existing access path. Then, only those records selected by the logical file's select/omit rules are passed on to the application program. There are other factors you must consider before making such a decision; but in many cases, using dynamic select/omit can reduce the total number of access paths on the database without negatively affecting program performance. To use this technique, simply code the **DYNSLT** keyword at the file level for the logical file.

Whenever you create a Select/Omit logical file without a keyed-sequence access path, you must use the DYNSLT keyword (or K   *NONE). In this case, DYNSLT tells DB2 to read the records of the physical file in arrival sequence (even if the physical file itself is keyed), and to apply the select/omit rules to each record in deciding whether to pass the file on to the application program. The term *dynamic*, used in the context of record selection, can be a little misleading. As it is used above, *dynamic select* simply means that the select/omit rules have not been applied to a separate index that contains only entries for selected records; instead, records are selected "dynamically" as they are read from the based-on physical file. In either case, the select/omit rules are hard coded into the logical file and can be changed only by recompiling. Therefore, the word *dynamic* really applies to when the rules are being applied, not to any ability to dynamically alter the rules at runtime.

Although for the sake of illustration the examples above are somewhat frivolous, the select/omit operation is in fact a useful and powerful tool for implementing record-level security. It ensures that users have access only to records of a file that they have a demonstrated need to use, and that other records will not be available to them.

In HLL applications, using select/omit with logical files can significantly reduce the complexity of program logic and make programs easier to understand and maintain.

Projection

As we mentioned earlier, **projection** has to do with limiting access to fields of a physical file that are sensitive and need to be secured, or are simply unnecessary for a given user or application. When you use projection, the logical-file record format includes only those fields needed by the applications that use the logical file. In other words, a projected logical file's record format is a subset of fields of the based-on physical file. Projection works for field security in much the same way that selection works for record security: The restricted fields are excluded from the logical file's record.

As an example, we will use the DDS for our original employee file, EMPPF (Figure 8.9).

```
Session A - [24 x 80]
File  Edit  View  Communication  Actions  Window  Help

 Columns . . . :    1  71              Edit              CIS001/QDDSSRC
 SEU==>                                                           EMPPF
 FMT PF .....A..........T.Name++++++RLen++TDpB......Functions++++++++++++++++++
         *************** Beginning of data **************************************
 0001.00        A         R EMPPFR
 0002.00        A           EMPNO       9B 0
 0003.00        A           LASTNAME    16A
 0004.00        A           FIRSTNAME   12A
 0005.00        A           HOMEPHONE    7S 0
 0006.00        A           ADDR1       40A
 0007.00        A           ADDR2       40A
 0008.00        A           ZIP          5S 0
 0009.00        A           DEPT        12A
 0010.00        A           BIRTHDATE    L
 0011.00        A           HIREDATE     L
 0012.00        A           SALARY       7P 0
         ***************** End of data ******************************************




 F3=Exit    F4=Prompt    F5=Refresh    F9=Retrieve    F10=Cursor    F11=Toggle
 F16=Repeat find         F17=Repeat change            F24=More keys
                                        (C) COPYRIGHT IBM CORP. 1981, 2007.
MA     A                  MW              A                          02/009
  I902 - Session successfully started        A232 - HP LaserJet 4050 on IP_10.134.223.223
```

Figure 8.9: DDS for Physical File EMPPF

Suppose that certain employees in the human resources department need access to records in this file, but you don't want these employees (or the programmers who write applications for them) to have access to the BIRTHDATE and SALARY fields. The best solution would be to create a projected logical file that eliminates these fields from the record format. To do so, you could not simply use the same record-format name as that of the physical file. You also would need to name the fields you wanted to include. Only the named fields would be projected to the logical file; fields not named would be omitted from the logical file. Figure 8.10 shows the DDS for a logical file using projection to screen out the BIRTHDATE and SALARY fields of the underlying physical file.

```
 ⌐I Session A - [24 x 80]                                               _|□| ×|
 File  Edit  View  Communication  Actions  Window  Help
 ▣ | 📋 📋 | 🖥 🖥 | 🔳 🔳 | 📷 | 🔳 🔳 | 🔳 🔳 | 🔳 | 🔶 📎
 Columns . . . :    1   71              Edit                    CIS001/QDDSSRC
 SEU==> _____           EMPPLF1
 FMT LF .....A..........T.Name++++++.Len++TDpB......Functions++++++++++++++++++
        *************** Beginning of data ***************************************
0001.00       A          R EMPPFR                   PFILE(EMPPF)
0002.00       A            EMPNO
0003.00       A            LASTNAME
0004.00       A            FIRSTNAME
0005.00       A            HOMEPHONE
0006.00       A            ADDR1
0007.00       A            ADDR2
0008.00       A            ZIP
0009.00       A            DEPT
0010.00       A            HIREDATE
        ****************** End of data ****************************************

 F3=Exit   F4=Prompt    F5=Refresh   F9=Retrieve   F10=Cursor  F11=Toggle
 F16=Repeat find        F17=Repeat change          F24=More keys
                                    (C) COPYRIGHT IBM CORP. 1981, 2007.
 MⒶ    A                    MW              A                        02/009
 ⌐🖳 I902 - Session successfully started       A232 - HP LaserJet 4050 on IP_10.134.223.223
```

Figure 8.10: DDS for Logical File EMPPLF1 with BIRTHDATE and SALARY Not Projected

In this example, we used the same record-format name as the underlying physical file, but doing so is not a requirement. When you specify field names, as you do with projection, you can use a record-format name different from that of the underlying physical file. When only the field name is coded in the DDS, as in Figure 8.10, the other attributes of data type, length, and decimal position come from the physical file's record format. As with key-field names, projected logical-file field names must be spelled exactly as they are in the based-on physical file.

Figure 8.11 shows the second page of output from the DSPFFD (Display File Field Description) command for the compiled logical file EMPPLF1.

```
┌─────────────────────────────────────────────────────────────────────┐
│ ⊡▯ Session A - [24 x 80]                                    _ □ × │
│ File  Edit  View  Communication  Actions  Window  Help              │
│ ▣ ▣▣ ▣▣ ▣▣ ▣▣ ▣ ▣▣ ▣▣ ▣ ▣ ▣                                        │
│                     Display Spooled File                            │
│ File . . . . . :   QPDSPFFD              Page/Line   1/27           │
│ Control . . . . .  _____              Columns     1 - 78         │
│ Find . . . . . .   _____                          │
│ *...+....1....+....2....+....3....+....4....+....5....+....6....+....7....+...│
│            Data         Field  Buffer   Buffer       Field  Column  │
│   Field    Type         Length Length   Position     Usage  Heading │
│   EMPNO    BINARY        9  0     4         1         Both   EMPNO   │
│   LASTNAME CHAR          16     16         5         Both   LASTNAME │
│     Coded Character Set Identifier . . . . . :   37                  │
│   FIRSTNAME CHAR         12     12        21         Both   FIRSTNAME│
│     Coded Character Set Identifier . . . . . :   37                  │
│   HOMEPHONE ZONED        7  0     7        33         Both   HOMEPHONE│
│   ADDR1    CHAR          40     40        40         Both   ADDR1    │
│     Coded Character Set Identifier . . . . . :   37                  │
│   ADDR2    CHAR          40     40        80         Both   ADDR2    │
│     Coded Character Set Identifier . . . . . :   37                  │
│   ZIP      ZONED         5  0     5       120         Both   ZIP     │
│   DEPT     CHAR          12     12       125         Both   DEPT     │
│     Coded Character Set Identifier . . . . . :   37                  │
│   HIREDATE DATE          10     10       137         Both   HIREDATE │
│                                                            More...   │
│ F3=Exit  F12=Cancel  F19=Left  F20=Right  F24=More keys             │
│ MA▮  A              MW              A                        03/022  │
│ ⌐▯ I902 - Session successfully started   A232 - HP LaserJet 4050 on IP_10.134.223.223 │
└─────────────────────────────────────────────────────────────────────┘
```

Figure 8.11: DSPFFD Command Output for Logical File EMPPLF1, Page 2

It is important to realize that the logical file has a different record format than the underlying physical file (EMPPF). It has a different number of fields and a different record length. A program using this logical file has no access to the BIRTHDATE and SALARY fields—they are not there!

You can also combine projection with selection and the use of an alternate access path within a single logical file. Suppose you needed to create a logical file without BIRTHDATE and SALARY fields for human resources personnel to use, but you did not want them to have access to records of co-workers in the same department. In addition, suppose you wanted them to be able to access the file randomly by typing in an employee's last name and first name. Figure 8.12 shows the DDS for the required logical file to accomplish this (EMPPSKLF1).

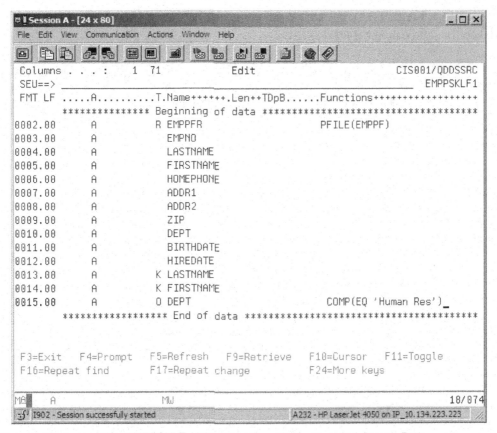

```
Session A - [24 x 80]                                              _|□|X|
File  Edit  View  Communication  Actions  Window  Help

[toolbar icons]

  Columns . . . :    1  71              Edit                 CIS001/QDDSSRC
  SEU==>  _____  EMPPSKLF1
  FMT LF .....A..........T.Name++++++.Len++TDpB......Functions+++++++++++++++++
         *************** Beginning of data ***************************************
0002.00        A         R EMPPFR                    PFILE(EMPPF)
0003.00        A           EMPNO
0004.00        A           LASTNAME
0005.00        A           FIRSTNAME
0006.00        A           HOMEPHONE
0007.00        A           ADDR1
0008.00        A           ADDR2
0009.00        A           ZIP
0010.00        A           DEPT
0011.00        A           BIRTHDATE
0012.00        A           HIREDATE
0013.00        A         K LASTNAME
0014.00        A         K FIRSTNAME
0015.00        A         O DEPT               COMP(EQ 'Human Res')_
         ****************** End of data ****************************************


  F3=Exit    F4=Prompt    F5=Refresh   F9=Retrieve   F10=Cursor   F11=Toggle
  F16=Repeat find       F17=Repeat change          F24=More keys

MA    A                      MW                                        18/074
  I902 - Session successfully started      A232 - HP LaserJet 4050 on IP_10.134.223.223
```

Figure 8.12: Logical File EMPPSKLF, Using Selection, Projection, and Access Path

Note that whenever key specification and Select/Omit entries are used together, the S and O entries must follow all K entries.

Creating a Logical File

When you complete the DDS code for a logical file, you press F3 to go to the Source Entry Utility (SEU) Exit screen, as usual. From there, you can change the new member name if, for example, you created it by changing an existing source member that you did not want changed.

When you return to the Work with Members Using PDM screen, a message tells you that the new member has been added to your source physical file. To create the logical-file object, you compile the logical-file source member by using the same option you use for a physical file: option 14. Figure 8.13 shows the Work with Members Using PDM screen with option 14 taken for source member EMPPSKLF1.

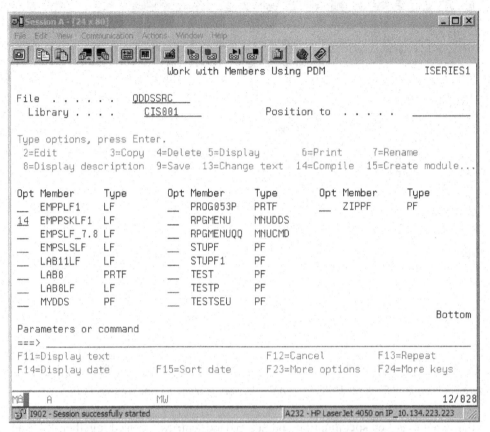

Figure 8.13: Work with Members Using PDM—Compile Option on EMPPSKLF1

If you request prompting on the compile option, you see the CRTLF (Create Logical File) command prompt screen. In this case, Programming Development Manager (PDM) chooses the CRTLF command for the compile option because the source member type is LF. Figure 8.14 shows the first screen of the CRTLF command prompt.

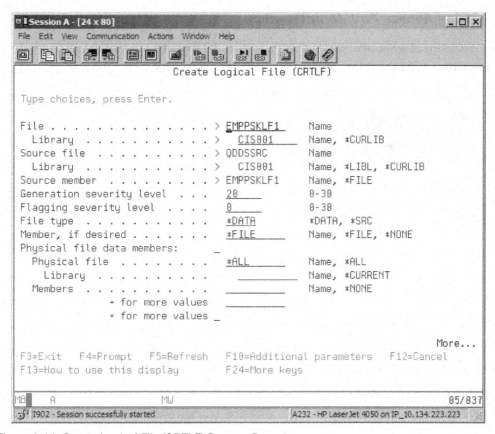

Figure 8.14: Create Logical File (CRTLF) Screen, Page 1

Notice that PDM has filled in the first five parameter values. For the file name, PDM uses the name of the source member; but if you wanted the logical-file object to have a different name, you could change the File parameter value.

Specifying Access Path Maintenance

When you request additional parameters using the F10 function key on the CRTLF command prompt screen and Page Down, you see the second screen of the command prompt (Figure 8.15).

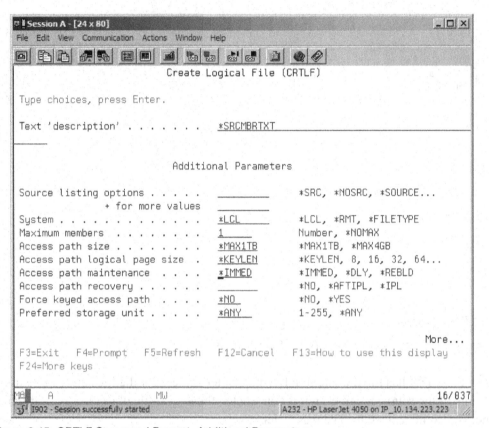

Figure 8.15: CRTLF Command Prompt, Additional Parameters

You can see that a short text description of the logical file has been entered. Notice that the Access path maintenance parameter value defaults to *IMMED. Whether a keyed-sequence access path is being created for the physical file itself or is defined in a logical file built over the physical file, changes to data-record key fields or additions or deletions of data records in the physical file require changes to the access-path index entries. When the maintenance parameter value is *IMMED, such changes to the data records that affect index entries cause an immediate update of the logical file's access path (and of the access path of the physical file, if it is keyed sequence), regardless of whether the changes are made through the logical file or through the physical file.

Immediate maintenance ensures that as soon as a record is added to the physical file it will be available (if selected) to the logical file. This is the desired state of affairs in an environment in which most files are processed interactively. For files whose keyed-sequence access path uses UNIQUE keys, immediate maintenance is not only the default—it is required. But for large physical files with nonunique keys and with high **volatility** (i.e., the population of records changes frequently), as the number of access paths with immediate maintenance increases, the average **response time** of individual transactions also increases. Response time is the time that elapses between a user's request for an action (e.g., pressing a function key to Add a new record to the file) and the system's completion of the action (e.g., the record is written, all *IMMED maintenance access paths are updated, and the system is waiting for the next request). When many access paths require immediate maintenance, the system must take care of those access paths before it can service the next user request. In severe cases, this requirement can contribute to a noticeably slower response time.

To reduce the negative impact on response time, you could limit the number of different access paths built over physical files. For some necessary access paths, you might be able to use either delayed (*DLY) or rebuild (*REBLD) maintenance. When you specify delayed maintenance, the system stores in a temporary file the necessary data to update the access path. When the logical file using the access path is needed (e.g., when a program, query, or DFU uses that logical file), its old access path is updated using changes stored in the temporary file. (But even with *DLY maintenance, the access path is immediately updated while the file is in use.) Although this approach may require more time when the logical file is opened, it saves much of the ongoing overhead of keeping the access path current throughout the day. Using delayed maintenance is especially useful for nonunique, keyed-sequence logical files that are used infrequently and that are not used by time-critical interactive applications, especially if such files are built over large, active physical files.

When you specify rebuild maintenance, the system neither performs ongoing maintenance nor saves changes—the access path is rebuilt when the logical file using it is opened (i.e., when a program or utility uses the file). If the based-on physical file is very large, this method could be quite time consuming, and it isn't suitable for files used frequently by interactive jobs. But if the logical file is used only by report programs that always run during nonbusiness hours in the batch subsystem, this approach might be ideal. If the based-on physical file is highly volatile, *REBLD maintenance completely eliminates the unnecessary overhead that otherwise results from keeping a file's access path immediately current.

Although junior programmers probably will not make decisions about access-path maintenance, it is important to know that options exist and that, over time, the choices made have an impact on interactive response time and **throughput** (the amount of work a system can perform within a certain period of time). The database administrator (DBA) will use dynamic select/omit, access-path maintenance, and other techniques to reduce both the number of access paths and the time required to maintain them.

After you have entered the CRTLF command and the logical file is compiled, the system by default creates a **compile listing**. If a message in your message queue indicates that the compile has not been successful, you can display or print the compile listing to determine what errors caused the problem. When the logical file is compiled successfully, you should delete the compile listing from your output queue. After the logical file is compiled, a new object whose type is *FILE will exist in your library.

Using DFU on Logical Files

How does a temporary DFU program work with our sample logical file? When you run option 18, Change using DFU, on logical file EMPPSKLF1 from the Work with Objects Using PDM screen, the screen for the temporary DFU appears in change mode. This tells you that the logical file contains records; otherwise, the temporary DFU would be in entry mode. (It is possible, through a logical error in your select/omit specification, to create an "empty" logical file even though abundant data exists in the based-on physical file.)

If you typed the name of a human resources employee (e.g., Hunn and Atilla) in the key fields and pressed Enter, the key would be displayed in reverse image, which indicates an error (Figure 8.16). The error message *"Record not found in file EMPPSKLF1 . . . "* would appear at the bottom of the screen.

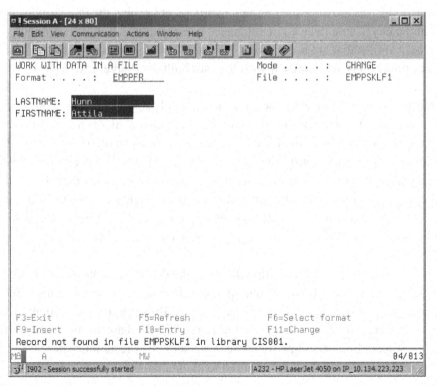

Figure 8.16: Error Message for Hunn, Attila

As you would expect, Mr. Hunn's record is not included in the logical file because he works in the human resources department and those records have been omitted. When you enter the key of another employee (who is not in human resources), the record will be displayed.

Figure 8.17 shows Sam Slick's record. You can see that, as the logical file specified, neither the BIRTHDATE nor the SALARY field is displayed.

Figure 8.17: Record Retrieved for Slick, Sam

If you were to Page Down from here, the next employee record in alphabetical sequence would appear, as determined by the LASTNAME and FIRSTNAME sequence of the access path. You could make changes to any of the fields shown in Mr. Slick's record. It is important to understand that such changes, made through the logical-file record, affect the data stored in the underlying physical file, EMPPF.

Creating Join Logical Files

Now that we have discussed some of the basic operations of logical files, using simple logical files as examples, let us broaden our discussion. We will talk first about join logical files and then about multiple-format logical files.

A **join logical file** lets you include fields from two or more related physical files in a single record format. This technique gives you a convenient way to pull together data from several files under one file (with a single name) that application programs can open and read. You can use join logical files to display information or print reports, but you cannot use join logical files to update the underlying physical files or DFU with join logical files.

Query for i5/OS does support join logical files. When the Join operation has been specified in the logical-file description, Query for i5/OS treats the join logical file like any other physical or simple logical file—only a single file is selected, and no Query for i5/OS join specifications are needed.

As a first example, consider a join logical file that would include data from the EMPPF and ZIPPF physical files that you see in Figure 8.18.

Figure 8.18: Employee (EMPPF) and Zip-Code (ZIPPF) DDS

Figure 8.19 shows the DDS for such a file. The code illustrates several new techniques.

```
■ I Session A - [24 x 80]                                          _ □ ×
File  Edit  View  Communication  Actions  Window  Help
 ▢  ▣▤  ▤▤  ▦▦  ▧▧  ▨▨  ▩▩  ▪▪  ▫▫  ▬▬  ▭▭  ▮  ▯◇
 Columns . . . :    1  71              Edit                 CIS001/QDDSSRC
 SEU==> _____    EMPZIPJLF1
 FMT A* .....A*. 1 ...+... 2 ...+... 3 ...+... 4 ...+... 5 ...+... 6 ....+... 7
       *************** Beginning of data **************************************
0001.00       A**********************************************************************
0002.00       A* Employee and ZipCode Joined Logical File - EMPZIPJLF1
0003.00       A* Compiled - 04-15-2010              Programmer - Jim Buck
0004.00       A**********************************************************************
0005.00       A          R EMPZIPREC              JFILE(EMPPF ZIPPF)
0006.00       A          J                        JOIN(1 2)
0007.00       A                                   JFLD(ZIP ZIP)
0008.00       A            EMPNO
0009.00       A            LASTNAME
0010.00       A            FIRSTNAME
0011.00       A            ADDR1
0012.00       A            ADDR2
0013.00       A            CITY
0014.00       A            STATE
0015.00       A            ZIP                     JREF(1)
       ***************** End of data ****************************************

 F3=Exit   F4=Prompt   F5=Refresh   F9=Retrieve   F10=Cursor   F11=Toggle
 F16=Repeat find       F17=Repeat change          F24=More keys
                                   (C) COPYRIGHT IBM CORP. 1981, 2007.
MA    A                  MW                                            02/009
 ⊡ I902 - Session successfully started       A232 - HP LaserJet 4050 on IP_10.134.223.223
```

Figure 8.19: Employee and Zip-Code Join Logical File

First, some basic identification has been included in the first four lines of code. As the format line indicates, an asterisk (*) in column 7 is a valid character and tells the DDS compiler to treat that line as a comment—and not to syntax check it or try to compile it. It is always a good idea to identify the date compiled, the author, and any special techniques used in the file, and most installations have standards for this type of documentation.

Line 5 names the record format, EMPZIPREC. This record-format name can be unique; you gain nothing by using the same name as one of the based-on physical files because all fields included in the join logical file must be named. Also as part of the record-format entry (line 5), the JFILE keyword must be coded. This keyword takes the place of the PFILE keyword of a simple logical file and names the physical files that will be participating in the join. Although you can name as many as 32 physical files, no more than three or four are commonly used. As with Query for i5/OS, the first file named is the primary file.

When the join type is left outer join (explained in Chapter 7), the primary file is crucial in determining which records will be selected for the Join operation. Because left outer join selects even unmatched primary-file records, this file should contain the data that is the primary topic or focus of the report or display. For an inner join (the default type for logical files), the existence of an access path keyed on the join field of each secondary file is a more important consideration. Our report focuses on employees; but, more important, an access path already exists on the join field (ZIP) of ZIPPF; so the employee file, EMPPF, should be the primary file and the zip-code file, ZIPPF, the secondary file. Because we are using an inner join, the result record set would be identical (although in different order) regardless of which file was primary—the choice is based on performance factors.

Following the record format and JFILE entry are one or more join specifications. These always begin with a J coded in the Name Type field (column 17), followed by the JOIN keyword in the Functions field (starting in column 45). There will be one JOIN specification for each pair of files. If you are joining four files, there will be three join entries, each starting with a J Name Type value followed by the JOIN keyword; if you are joining two files, as in our example, there is only one entry. The JOIN keyword identifies the two related files, either by name or, as we have done here, by relative number in the JFILE list. Following the JOIN keyword, on a line by itself (line 7 in the example), is the JFLD keyword. Any keyword on a line by itself belongs to the previous file, record, join, field, key, or Select/Omit entry.

Keyword JFLD identifies the fields from each file that are common (relationship-supporting fields). In our example, both field names are ZIP, but a positional relationship exists between the fields of the JFLD keyword and the files of the JOIN keyword: The first JFLD field name must belong to the first file identified by the JOIN keyword, and the second JFLD field name must belong to the second JOIN file. The implicit relationship is equality of field values (i.e., records from the two files match and are therefore joined when the first JFLD field value equals the second JFLD field value). In Query for i5/OS, we explicitly stated this relationship, called *equijoin,* as E.ZIP EQ Z.ZIP. For a join logical file, the keyword entry JFLD(ZIP ZIP) has the same meaning, with the files specified in the order they are.

It is important to realize that the relationship-supporting fields of two joined files do not need to have the same name. In our example, both are called ZIP, but one could just as well be EMPZIP and the other ZIPCD. What is important is that what the fields represent be common to both files. In addition, for the join to work correctly, the fields' definitions (type and length) must be similar, and they must share the same **domain** (i.e., the entire list of possible values that are valid for the field in any record).

After all JOIN and JFLD specifications (each set starting with J in the Name Type field) are completed, field-level entries are coded. For the most part, the field names are the same as those defined in the underlying physical files. You must name all fields you want included in the join record format. The fields can be from any of the based-on physical files and can be in any order you want. But if a field name is not unique, as in the case of ZIP in our example, you must code the JREF keyword for that field to identify, by name or number, the file from which the field value is to be taken.

Projection, Selection, and Access Path with Join Logical Files

DDS-defined join files are always an equijoin, which selects only those records from both database tables that have matching values (e.g., EMPPF.ZIP = ZIPPF.ZIP). So you should exclude at least one of the relationship-supporting fields from the join-logical-file record format. For example, in Figure 8.19, the ZIP field from EMPPF was included, while the ZIP field from ZIPPF was not. Because a join logical file is by default an inner join, to include both fields would be redundant—they always have the same value, or a join record is not selected. Typically, only certain fields from each of the participating files are projected to the join logical file. You can use any number of fields (but at least one) from the based-on physical files, depending on the purpose of the new join logical file. In our example, we are collecting mailing-label data, so the fields DEPT, BIRTHDATE, HIREDATE, and SALARY have all been excluded.

You also can use Select/Omit entries for join logical files in much the same way as for simple logical files. The field names used for the select/omit operation must be part of the join logical file's record format—that is, they must be listed in the field entries coded after the JOIN specifications—and they can be from any of the based-on physical files. You can code multiple Select/Omit entries, and you can use both AND and OR relationships.

You can use key fields with join logical files, but the fields must be named in the record format and must come from the primary file only. It is important to emphasize that if you specify no key fields for the join logical file and you use select/omit logic, you must use the DYNSLT file-level keyword. (We discussed this keyword earlier in regard to sharing access paths.) Another rule for join logical files is that, regardless of whether you specify key fields, keyword DYNSLT is required if you use the JDFTVAL file-level keyword (covered in the next section) to create a left outer join (Query for i5/OS type 2 join). Figure 8.20 shows the DDS for a join logical file using select/omit to include only employees who live in Kenosha or whose zip code is in the range of 520000000 to 531440000.

```
┌─────────────────────────────────────────────────────────────────────────────┐
│ ⬛ Session A - [24 x 80]                                            _ □ ×      │
├─────────────────────────────────────────────────────────────────────────────┤
│ File  Edit  View  Communication  Actions  Window  Help                        │
├─────────────────────────────────────────────────────────────────────────────┤
│ [toolbar icons]                                                               │
│  Columns . . . :    1  71              Edit                    CIS001/QDDSSRC │
│  SEU==> _____   EMPZIPGOOD   │
│  FMT A* .....A*. 1 ...+... 2 ...+... 3 ...+... 4 ...+... 5 ...+... 6 ...+... 7 │
│ 0003.00     A* This Also includes and example of Selection                    │
│ 0004.00     A* Compiled - 04-15-2010                   Programmer - Jim Buck  │
│ 0005.00     A*******************************************************************│
│ 0006.00     A                                          DYNSLT                 │
│ 0007.00     A          R EMPZIPREC                      JFILE(EMPPF ZIPPF)     │
│ 0008.00     A            J                              JOIN(1 2)             │
│ 0009.00     A                                           JFLD(ZIP ZIP)         │
│ 0010.00     A            EMPNO                                                │
│ 0011.00     A            LASTNAME                                            │
│ 0012.00     A            FIRSTNAME                                           │
│ 0013.00     A            ADDR1                                               │
│ 0014.00     A            ADDR2                                               │
│ 0015.00     A            CITY                                                │
│ 0016.00     A            STATE                                               │
│ 0017.00     A            ZIP                            JREF(1)              │
│ 0018.00     A          S CITY                           COMP(EQ 'Kenosha')   │
│ 0019.00     A          S ZIP                            RANGE(520000000 531440000)│
│                                                                               │
│  F3=Exit    F4=Prompt    F5=Refresh   F9=Retrieve   F10=Cursor   F11=Toggle  │
│  F16=Repeat find         F17=Repeat change           F24=More keys           │
├─────────────────────────────────────────────────────────────────────────────┤
│ MA    A                    MW                                        02/009   │
│ 🖳  I902 - Session successfully started    A232 - HP LaserJet 4050 on IP_10.134.223.223 │
└─────────────────────────────────────────────────────────────────────────────┘
```

Figure 8.20: Inner Join of Employee and Zip-Code Files with Field Projection and Record Selection

Both CITY and ZIP are included in the record format, so both can be used for select/omit operations. The issue of which ZIP to use is settled by the JREF entry on line 17, so there is no ambiguity about the selection test. Because no key is specified, keyword DYNSLT is required.

Using Query for i5/OS with a Join Logical File

You compile a join logical file like any other file; and when the compilation is complete, you can use Query for i5/OS to easily create a display or printed report. Figure 8.21 shows the Query for i5/OS Specify File Selections screen, filled out for join logical file EMPZIPLF1A.

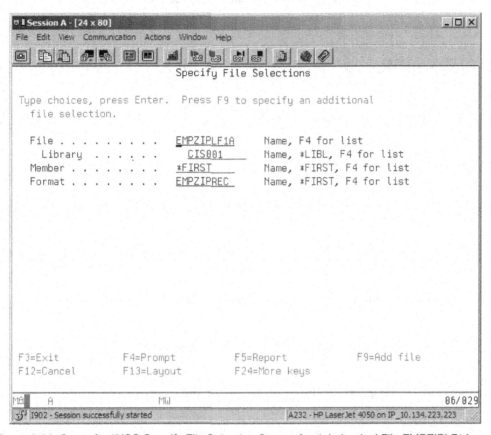

Figure 8.21: Query for i5/OS Specify File Selection Screen for Join Logical File EMPZIPLF1A

Because all the important join specifications are now part of the externally described file itself, nothing more than the file name is required here; Query for i5/OS supplies the library and format names. After we use the Edit feature of the Report Column Formatting screen to edit the employee number and remove commas from the zip code, we can use F5 to examine the output. From the report screen, we have used the vertical split feature (F21) of the query report to show how the join worked. In Figure 8.22, you can see the first two fields, employee number and last name, to the left of the split screen; on the right, you see city and state from the ZIPPF file and the zip code from the employee file.

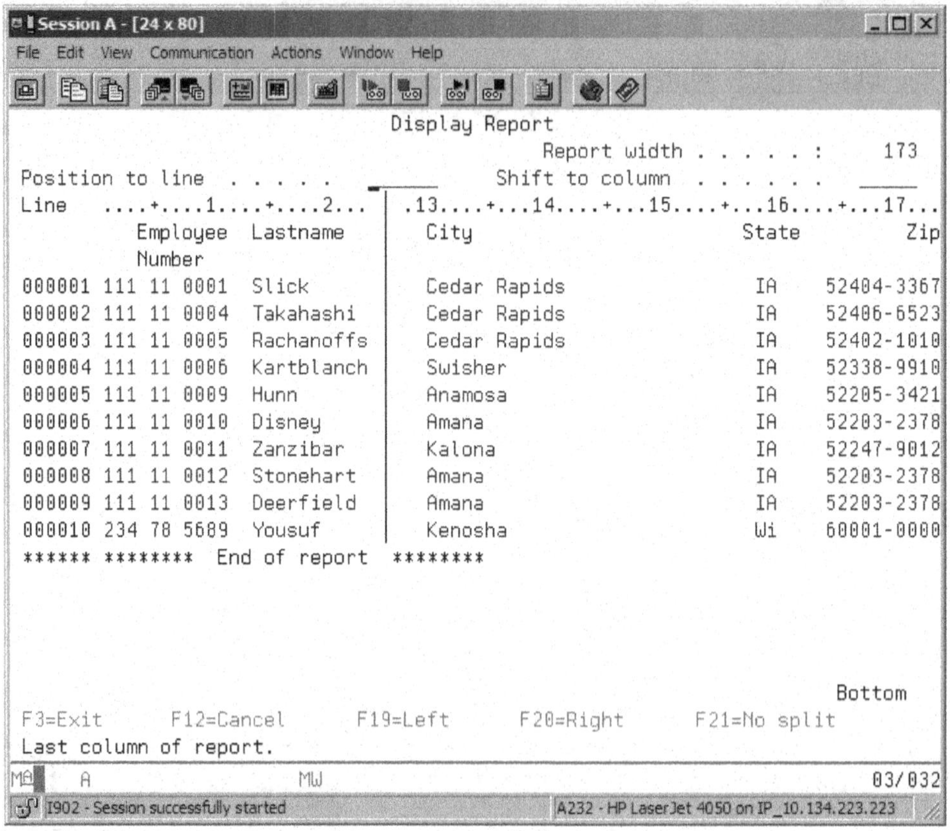

```
□ I Session A - [24 x 80]                                              _ □ x
 File  Edit  View  Communication  Actions  Window  Help
 [toolbar icons]
                              Display Report
                                    Report width . . . . . :       173
 Position to line  . . . .    _____    Shift to column  . . . . . .    ____
 Line      ....+....1....+....2...  .13....+...14....+...15....+...16....+...17...
         Employee  Lastname         City                  State          Zip
         Number
 000001 111 11 0001  Slick          Cedar Rapids          IA        52404-3367
 000002 111 11 0004  Takahashi      Cedar Rapids          IA        52406-6523
 000003 111 11 0005  Rachanoffs     Cedar Rapids          IA        52402-1010
 000004 111 11 0006  Kartblanch     Swisher               IA        52338-9910
 000005 111 11 0009  Hunn           Anamosa               IA        52205-3421
 000006 111 11 0010  Disney         Amana                 IA        52203-2378
 000007 111 11 0011  Zanzibar       Kalona                IA        52247-9012
 000008 111 11 0012  Stonehart      Amana                 IA        52203-2378
 000009 111 11 0013  Deerfield      Amana                 IA        52203-2378
 000010 234 78 5689  Yousuf         Kenosha               Wi        60001-0000
 ****** ********  End of report  ********
                                                                    Bottom
 F3=Exit       F12=Cancel      F19=Left      F20=Right      F21=No split
 Last column of report.
 MA   A                  MW                                          03/032
 I1902 - Session successfully started       A232 - HP LaserJet 4050 on IP_10.134.223.223
```

Figure 8.22: Query Report of EMPZIPJF1A with Split Screen

There are a couple of important things to observe about this report. First, the records of the report are presented in arrival sequence of the join logical file's primary (physical) file. Because neither the primary physical file, EMPPF, nor the logical file itself uses a keyed-sequence access path, this is what you would expect. Second, not all records of the primary physical file are accounted for—Billy Badman is missing. As you may recall, Billy had a zip code that did not match any ZIPPF record, so his record was also excluded from the Query for i5/OS type 1 (inner) join. The conclusion you might draw (and you would be correct to do so) is that a default join logical file uses what we described in Chapter 7 as an inner join; that is, when a primary-file record does not match at least one record of every secondary file, the primary-file record is not included in the join.

You can choose a left outer join operation (Query for i5/OS type 2) for a join logical file instead of an inner join simply by including the file-level keyword JDFTVAL in the file description. Figure 8.23 shows a version of our join logical file that uses keyword JDFTVAL.

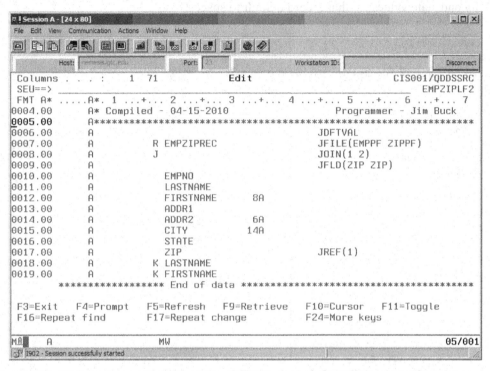

```
 □ I Session A - [24 x 80]                                                    _ □ ×
 File  Edit  View  Communication  Actions  Window  Help
 ▣  ▤▤  ▰▰  ▤▤  ▤  ▰▰  ▰▰  ▤  ▰◈
         Host:  remess.gtc.edu.        Port: 23          Workstation ID:            Disconnect
 Columns . . . :    1  71            Edit                        CIS001/QDDSSRC
 SEU==>  _____  EMPZIPLF2
 FMT A*  ....A*. 1 ...+... 2 ...+... 3 ...+... 4 ...+... 5 ...+... 6 ...+... 7
 0004.00     A* Compiled - 04-15-2010                 Programmer - Jim Buck
 0005.00     A********************************************************************
 0006.00     A                                          JDFTVAL
 0007.00     A          R EMPZIPREC                     JFILE(EMPPF ZIPPF)
 0008.00     A          J                               JOIN(1 2)
 0009.00     A                                          JFLD(ZIP ZIP)
 0010.00     A            EMPNO
 0011.00     A            LASTNAME
 0012.00     A            FIRSTNAME        8A
 0013.00     A            ADDR1
 0014.00     A            ADDR2            6A
 0015.00     A            CITY            14A
 0016.00     A            STATE
 0017.00     A            ZIP                            JREF(1)
 0018.00     A          K LASTNAME
 0019.00     A          K FIRSTNAME
          **************** End of data *********************************************

  F3=Exit    F4=Prompt    F5=Refresh   F9=Retrieve   F10=Cursor   F11=Toggle
  F16=Repeat find       F17=Repeat change          F24=More keys

 MA▮    A              MW                                              05/001
 ⌨ I902 - Session successfully started
```

Figure 8.23: DDS for Join Logical File Using JDFTVAL, for Left Outer Join, Keyed Sequence

In addition to keyword JDFTVAL, some field attributes have been changed—the lengths of the FIRSTNAME, ADDR2, and CITY fields have all been shortened. Because you cannot use join logical files to change underlying physical-file data, changes to field attributes made in the logical file are convenient to use to affect presentation format without causing inadvertent changes of the data. Last, the new file is keyed on the composite key LASTNAME plus FIRSTNAME. Remember that key fields of a join logical file must come only from the primary file.

To create a query for this new logical file, the previous query was copied and only the file specification was changed, telling it to use the new file, EMPZIPLF2. When the query is run, as you can see in Figure 8.24, the previously missing Billy Badman is included on line 7, and city and state values for that record default to spaces.

```
I Session A - [24 x 80]                                               _ □ ×
 File   Edit   View   Communication   Actions   Window   Help
 [toolbar icons]
                            Display Report
                                  Report width . . . . . :        126
 Position to line  . . . . .     _____    Shift to column  . . . . . .     _____
 Line     ....+....1....+....2...  | ....+....9....+...10....+...11....+...12....+.
         Employee  Lastname        |  Address  City            State         Zip
         Number                    |  Two
 000001 111 11 0001  Slick         |  Apt D   Cedar Rapids      IA    52404-3367
 000002 111 11 0002  Fendor        |          Guthrie Center    IA    50115-3498
 000003 111 11 0003  Einstein      |          Clarinda          IA    51632-1200
 000004 111 11 0004  Takahashi     |  # 127A  Cedar Rapids      IA    52406-6523
 000005 111 11 0005  Rachanoffs    |          Cedar Rapids      IA    52402-1010
 000006 111 11 0006  Kartblanch    |  Falcon  Swisher           IA    52338-9910
 000007 111 11 0007  Badman        |                                  52456-6789
 000008 111 11 0008  Gootch        |          Pleasantville     IA    50225-7810
 000009 111 11 0009  Hunn          |  Apt. B  Anamosa           IA    52205-3421
 000010 111 11 0010  Disney        |          Amana             IA    52203-2378
 000011 111 11 0011  Zanzibar      |          Kalona            IA    52247-9012
 000012 111 11 0012  Stonehart     |          Amana             IA    52203-2378
 000013 111 11 0013  Deerfield     |          Amana             IA    52203-2378
 000014 234 78 5689  Yousuf        |          Kenosha           Wi    60001-0000
 ****** ********  End of report  ********
                                                                Bottom
 F3=Exit      F12=Cancel      F19=Left      F20=Right      F21=No split

 MA   A                  MW                                           03/032
 [icon] I902 - Session successfully started     A232 - HP LaserJet 4050 on IP_10.134.223.223
```

Figure 8.24: Query of EMPZIPLF2, Outer Join with Split Display

Billy's zip code is printed because it is taken from the primary file (JREF(1)). Also, notice that a new employee, Tilly Zanzibar, has appeared in the report. Apparently, Tilly's zip code had not been added to the zip-code file, and so with the natural join (no JDFTVAL keyword), her EMPPF record was not included.

Also notice that the report still appears in arrival sequence of the primary file, despite the fact that the logical file was keyed. If a programmer wrote an RPG or COBOL program to randomly read records from the logical file when a user typed a last and first name on a display, the access path would function as we expect, and the proper join-logical-file record would be returned. Also, if the RPG or COBOL program read the entire file sequentially, the keyed-sequence access path would present the records in FIRSTNAME within LASTNAME order. But neither Query for i5/OS nor SQL displays records in order of a keyed-sequence access path unless sorting is selected. So to display the data as it would be presented through the access path, we have changed the new query to select sorting on our key fields. Figure 8.25 shows the output from that modification.

```
Session A - [24 x 80]                                                _ □ ×
 File  Edit  View  Communication  Actions  Window  Help

                            Display Report
                                     Report width . . . . . :       126
  Position to line  . . . . .   _             Shift to column  . . . . . .   ____
  Line      ....+....1....+....2...  |  ....+....9....+...10....+...11....+...12....+.
          Lastname          First     |  Address  City          State        Zip
                                        Two
  000001  Badman            Billy                                         52456-6789
  000002  Deerfield         Cynth                Amana         IA         52203-2378
  000003  Disney            Walte                Amana         IA         52203-2378
  000004  Einstein          Alber                Clarinda      IA         51632-1200
  000005  Fendor            Dento                Guthrie Center IA        50115-3498
  000006  Gootch            Marth                Pleasantville IA         50225-7810
  000007  Hunn              Atill    Apt. B      Anamosa       IA         52205-3421
  000008  Kartblanch        Emil     Falcon      Swisher       IA         52338-9910
  000009  Rachanoffski      Natas                Cedar Rapids  IA         52402-1010
  000010  Slick             Sam      Apt D       Cedar Rapids  IA         52404-3367
  000011  Stonehart         Rocky                Amana         IA         52203-2378
  000012  Takahashi         Musas    # 127A      Cedar Rapids  IA         52406-6523
  000013  Yousuf            Saad                 Kenosha       Wi         60001-0000
  000014  Zanzibar          Tilly                Kalona        IA         52247-9012
  ****** ********  End of report  ********
                                                                         Bottom
  F3=Exit       F12=Cancel       F19=Left       F20=Right      F21=No split
  Last column of report.
 MA    A                MW                                               03/032
   I902 - Session successfully started         A232 - HP LaserJet 4050 on IP_10.134.223.223
```

Figure 8.25: Report of EMPZIPJLF2 (Outer Join) in Same Sort Sequence As Access Path

If an application program sequentially accessed the join logical file using its keyed-sequence access path, this is the order in which the records would be read.

Joining More Than Two Files

A join logical file often needs to include data from more than two files. To accomplish this, you must base the join operation on relationships among the files in a relational database. The relationships themselves are supported by the existence of common fields in the record formats of the different files. A database can consist of only two files, related by a one-to-many relationship (notated 1:n), but typically a larger number of files is involved. To illustrate, let us expand the structure of the employee/zip-code database described in Chapter 7. As we left it, the two related files were diagrammed as you see in Figure 8.26:

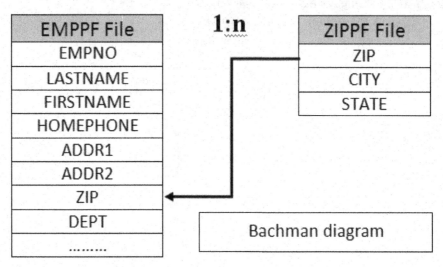

Figure 8.26: Relationship Between EMPPF and ZIPPF

We would now like to add two new files to the database: one that identifies the different projects to which employees might be assigned, and another that keeps track of all current project assignments, or members of a project. We will call the first file PRJPF; Figure 8.27 shows its source DDS.

```
┌──────────────────────────────────────────────────────────────────────────┐
│ ▣ ▌Session A - [24 x 80]                                        _ ☐ ✕      │
├──────────────────────────────────────────────────────────────────────────┤
│  File  Edit  View  Communication  Actions  Window  Help                    │
│ ┌──┐┌──┐┌──┐┌──┐┌──┐┌──┐┌──┐┌──┐┌──┐┌──┐┌──┐┌──┐┌──┐┌──┐                    │
│ └──┘└──┘└──┘└──┘└──┘└──┘└──┘└──┘└──┘└──┘└──┘└──┘└──┘└──┘                    │
│  Columns . . . :    1  71             Edit                 CIS001/QDDSSRC  │
│  SEU==> _____   PRJPF    │
│        *************** Beginning of data ********************************* │
│ 0001.00      A*********************************************************** │
│ 0002.00      A* Projects PF   Identifies a task having specific objectives, *│
│ 0003.00      A*               to which some number of employees will be as-  *│
│ 0004.00      A*               signed for a total (estimated) number of hours.*│
│ 0005.00      A* Primary Key:  Project Code (PRJCD)                        * │
│ 0006.00      A* Compiled: 2010-04-15_                Programmer: J Fottral * │
│ 0007.00      A*********************************************************** │
│ 0008.00      A                              UNIQUE                         │
│ 0009.00      A          R PRJPFR                                           │
│ 0010.00      A            PRJCD        5A        COLHDG('Project' 'Code')   │
│ 0011.00      A            PRJLDR       9S 0      COLHDG('Project' 'Leader') │
│ 0012.00      A            STRDAT        L        COLHDG('Start' 'Date')     │
│ 0013.00      A            ENDDAT        L        TEXT('Need done by')       │
│ 0014.00      A                                  COLHDG('Est' 'Finish' 'Date│
│ 0015.00      A            DESC         40A       COLHDG('Description')      │
│ 0016.00      A            ESTHRS       4S 0      COLHDG('Est' 'Hours')      │
│ 0017.00      A          K PRJCD                                            │
│        ***************** End of data ************************************* │
│                                                                            │
│                                                                            │
│                                                                            │
│                                                                            │
│ MA▌  A              MW             A                           09/037      │
│ ⌨ I902 - Session successfully started    A232 - HP LaserJet 4050 on IP_10.134.223.223 │
└──────────────────────────────────────────────────────────────────────────┘
```

Figure 8.27: DDS of Projects Physical File

This file has a primary key of project code, PRJCD. The fields are all attributes of a project: the project's description, when the project started, when it is expected to finish, its leader, and so on. Using the column heading (COLHDG) keyword lets us use more meaningful names as field identifiers on queries; and placing separate quotes around each word stacks the words of each column heading vertically instead of printing them side by side. Be sure to separate each quoted word by at least one space.

The TEXT keyword allows for some explanation of field meaning or use. This keyword will not be printed on reports; but it is retained with the file object, and you can see it, for example, by viewing the DSPFFD command output.

The second new file is the project-members physical file, PRJMBRPF. Figure 8.28 shows the source code for this file.

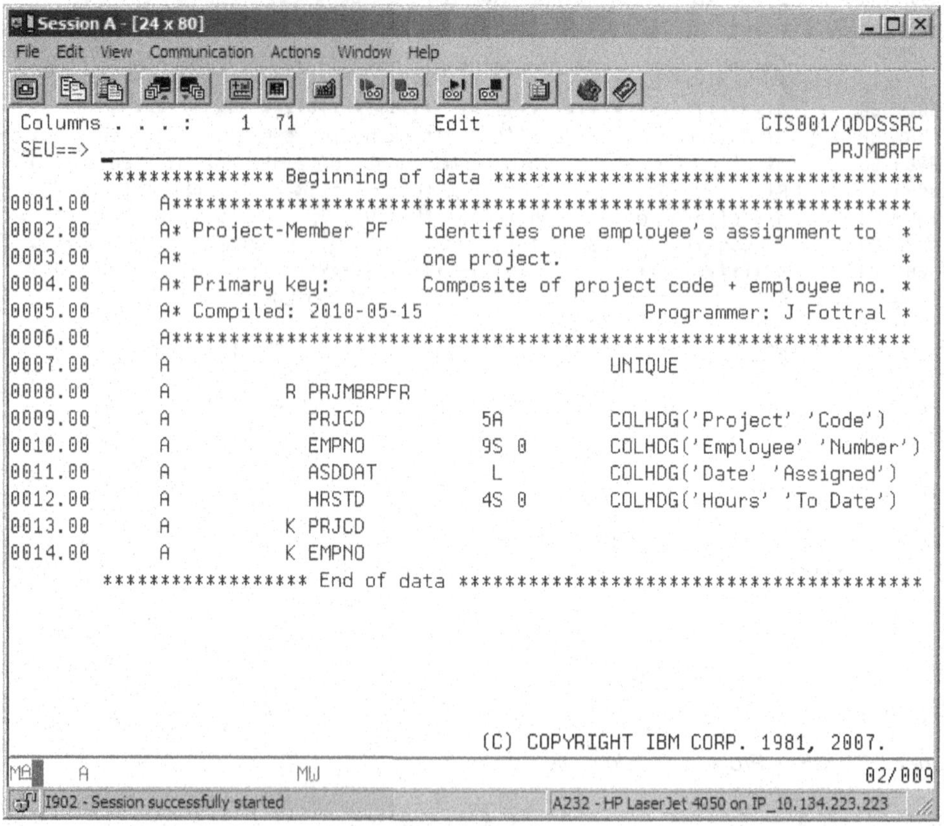

```
┌─────────────────────────────────────────────────────────────────────────┐
│ ▣▐ Session A - [24 x 80]                                         _ □ X    │
├─────────────────────────────────────────────────────────────────────────┤
│  File  Edit  View  Communication  Actions  Window  Help                   │
├─────────────────────────────────────────────────────────────────────────┤
│  ▣  ▣▣ ▣▣  ▣▣▣  ▣▣  ▣▣  ▣▣▣  ▣▣ ▣▣  ▣▣ ▣▣  ▣  ▣ ▣                          │
│   Columns . . . :    1  71              Edit                CIS001/QDDSSRC │
│   SEU==>                                                          PRJMBRPF │
│         *************** Beginning of data ******************************** │
│  0001.00      A********************************************************    │
│  0002.00      A* Project-Member PF    Identifies one employee's assignment to  * │
│  0003.00      A*                       one project.                     *  │
│  0004.00      A* Primary key:         Composite of project code + employee no. * │
│  0005.00      A* Compiled: 2010-05-15                  Programmer: J Fottral * │
│  0006.00      A********************************************************    │
│  0007.00      A                                  UNIQUE                    │
│  0008.00      A          R PRJMBRPFR                                       │
│  0009.00      A            PRJCD        5A        COLHDG('Project' 'Code')  │
│  0010.00      A            EMPNO        9S 0      COLHDG('Employee' 'Number') │
│  0011.00      A            ASDDAT       L         COLHDG('Date' 'Assigned') │
│  0012.00      A            HRSTD        4S 0      COLHDG('Hours' 'To Date') │
│  0013.00      A          K PRJCD                                           │
│  0014.00      A          K EMPNO                                           │
│         ***************** End of data ********************************     │
│                                                                           │
│                                                                           │
│                                                                           │
│                                 (C) COPYRIGHT IBM CORP. 1981, 2007.        │
│  MA▪  A              MW                                          02/009    │
│  ▣▓ I902 - Session successfully started       A232 - HP LaserJet 4050 on IP_10.134.223.223 │
└─────────────────────────────────────────────────────────────────────────┘
```

Figure 8.28: DDS of Project-Member Physical File

The fields in file PRJMBRPF identify the participation of an employee in a project. If an employee were currently involved in five different projects, there would be five records in the file with the same employee number but different project codes. The total number of records in this file should be the product of the number of projects multiplied by the average number of employees per project.

The project-member file is keyed on two fields: Project code is the high-order key, and employee number is the low-order key. Defining this composite key means an access path will be built that will allow quick lookup of employees within projects. By specifying keyword UNIQUE, we are enforcing a primary-key constraint, that only one record with a given project code and employee number can be present in the file. This restriction prevents the error of assigning an employee to the same project twice.

If you add the new files to the diagram of the database you see in Figure 8.29, you can see how the common fields provide the connections for the relationships among files:

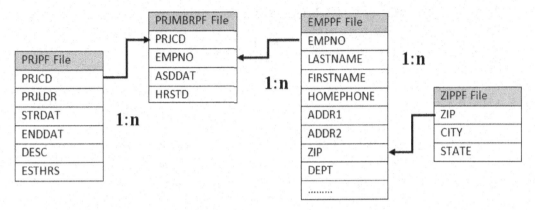

Figure 8.29: File Relationship Using a Bachman Diagram

Both EMPPF and PRJPF have one-to-many relationships to the project-member file PRJMBRPF. When two parent files are both related in one-to-many relationships to the same child file, a many-to-many (n:m) relationship must exist between the two parent files. A many-to-many relationship means that any one record of either file could be logically related to many records of the other file. In our example, one record of EMPPF, as defined by field EMPNO, could be assigned to several projects, each defined by its PRJCD primary key. Likewise, one record of the project file could connect to many different employees, who are all members of that project. Notice that there are no common fields in the EMPPF and PRJPF files that can support this logical many-to-many relationship. This is, in fact, the nature of an n:m relationship; DB2 would be unable to extract project-member information from these two files if it were not for the presence of the PRJMBRPF file, which serves as the link between them. (Incidentally, there is a one-to-many relationship not shown in the Bachman diagram between field EMPNO of file EMPPF and field PRJLDR of file PRJPF, not to be confused with the n:m relationship described above.)

Figure 8.30 shows the DDS for a join logical file, JOINME, that creates the linkage, through PRJMBRPF, between projects and employees.

```
Session A - [24 x 80]
 File  Edit  View  Communication  Actions  Window  Help

 Columns . . . :    1  71              Edit                    CIS001/QDDSSRC
 SEU==>  _____            JOINME
        *************** Beginning of data ******************************************
0001.00  A**********************************************************************
0002.00  A* Join Project, Members and Employees in one Record format
0003.00  A* using inner (Natural) Join
0004.00  A* Compiled - 04-15-2010                   Programmer - Jim Buck
0005.00  A**********************************************************************
0006.00  A            R JOINPMER              JFILE(PRJPF PRJMBRPF EMPPF)
0007.00  A            J                       JOIN(1 2)
0008.00  A                                    JFLD(PRJCD PRJCD)
0009.00  A            J                       JOIN(2 3)
0010.00  A                                    JFLD(EMPNO EMPNO)
0011.00  A              PRJCD                 JREF(1)
0012.00  A              DESC
0013.00  A              PRJLDR
0014.00  A              ESTHRS
0015.00  A              EMPNO        B        JREF(2)
0016.00  A              LASTNAME
0017.00  A              FIRSTNAME
0018.00  A              HRSTD
        ****************** End of data ******************************************

                              (C) COPYRIGHT IBM CORP. 1981, 2007.
MA   A              MW              A                          02/009
 I902 - Session successfully started       A232 - HP LaserJet 4050 on IP_10.134.223.223
```

Figure 8.30: DDS for Join File of PRJPF, PRJMBRPF, and EMPPF

Because the main topic is projects, PRJPF is listed first in the JFILE list and so becomes the primary file. The JFLD keyword for the first join, between PRJPF and PRJMBRPF, establishes the project code fields of both files (PRJCD) as the relationship-supporting fields. Although it is certainly not necessary for these fields to have the same name, they "mean" the same thing in the two files, so using the same name would be appropriate. When two fields with the same name occur in the same context, they can be uniquely identified by qualification, as the JREF keyword does in line 11. The second join operation is specified on lines 9 and 10, between files PRJMBRPF and EMPPF. In this case, EMPNO is the relationship-supporting field. Not coincidentally, both secondary files have access paths keyed on the relationship-supporting (JFLD) fields. This fact should have a positive impact on performance because DB2 can use the existing access paths in executing the join logic and avoid the costly creation of temporary indexes.

The record format for logical file JOINME includes eight fields: four from PRJPF, two from PRJMBRPF, and two from EMPPF. When no field-level attributes are provided in the logical file, all necessary information for the named fields is taken from the based-on physical files.

In the case of our join logical file, however, a slight problem exists. The second join specification uses the EMPNO fields from PRJMBRPF and EMPPF. Although both fields are numeric, nine-digit integers, the usage in EMPPF is binary (B), while in PRJMBRPF it is zoned decimal (S). To compare for equal values, the fields need to have the same usage, so in the logical file, we have redefined the EMPNO from PRJMBRPF as binary. We could have redefined the EMPPF field as zoned decimal if we had been using it; but keyword JREF tells us that the join record format is using the EMPNO from PRJMBRPF, so that is the one whose usage we must redefine.

When no JDFTVAL keyword is used, the system returns a join record only when records exist in each file to satisfy the matching conditions defined by each JOIN and JFLD specification. This is an inner join or Query for i5/OS type 1 join. For an inner join, if matching records must be present in each file, the only real significance of the primary file is that its records are read first and so become the starting point of matching to the other secondary files. In Figure 8.30, the project file, PRJPF, not only is the main topic of information but also has been selected as the primary file because it is likely to contain the fewest records.

In general, for an inner join, the file with the fewest records should be made the primary file for purposes of efficiency, unless a larger secondary file has no access path to support the join operation. In our example, both secondary files have access paths, so the process of returning join records proceeds as described in the following paragraphs.

1. The first record of the primary file is read, using arrival sequence (relative record number order) even if the physical file itself has a keyed-sequence access path. The first record is for project code Y2KCV. Data for file PRJPF, shown in arrival sequence, appears in Figure 8.31.

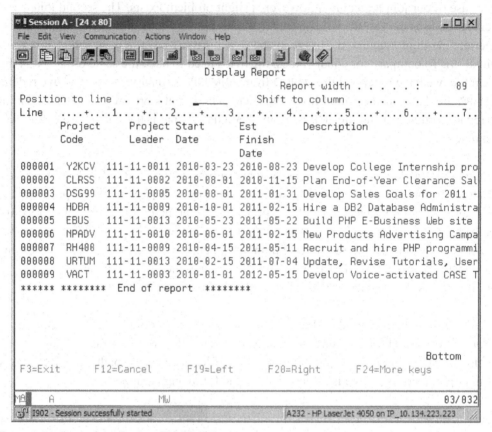

Figure 8.31: Data of the Project File PRJPF

2. Because project code is the join field, DB2 now tries to find a matching project code in the related, secondary file, PRJMBRPF. Because it is searching for a specific matching value, Y2KCV, DB2 needs an index, a keyed-sequence access path on PRJCD. As it turns out, a suitable access path already exists because the file PRJMBRPF had a composite key of PRJCD and EMPNO. Because PRJCD is the high-order key, the existing access path works just fine. Using the access path, the first record is located with a matching project code, and that record is read from the PRJMBRPF file.

Figure 8.32 illustrates part of PRJMBRPF, shown in sequence of its composite key.

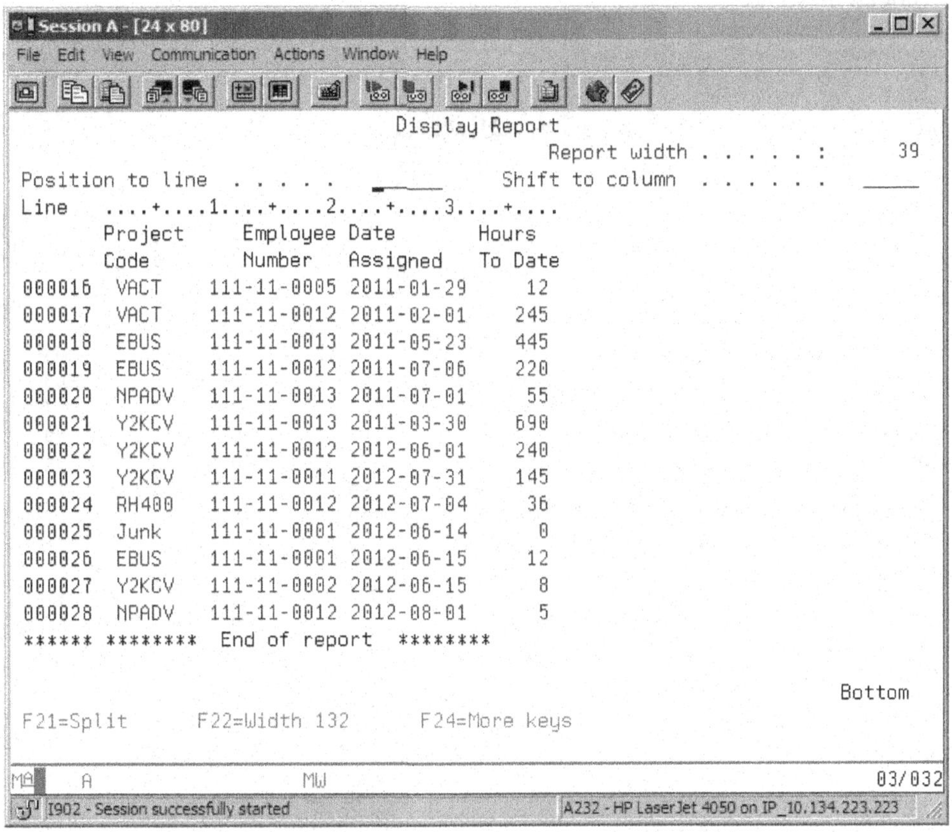

```
┌─ I Session A - [24 x 80]────────────────────────────────────────── _ □ ×─┐
│ File  Edit  View  Communication  Actions  Window  Help                     │
│ ┌──┐┌──┐┌──┐ ┌──┐┌──┐ ┌──┐┌──┐ ┌──┐ ┌──┐┌──┐┌──┐┌──┐ ┌──┐ ┌──┐┌──┐           │
│                          Display Report                                     │
│                                      Report width . . . . . :      39       │
│   Position to line  . . . . .    ____      Shift to column  . . . . . .  ___ │
│   Line     ....+....1....+....2....+....3....+....                           │
│           Project    Employee Date       Hours                              │
│           Code       Number   Assigned   To Date                            │
│   000016  VACT    111-11-0005 2011-01-29    12                              │
│   000017  VACT    111-11-0012 2011-02-01   245                              │
│   000018  EBUS    111-11-0013 2011-05-23   445                              │
│   000019  EBUS    111-11-0012 2011-07-06   220                              │
│   000020  NPADV   111-11-0013 2011-07-01    55                              │
│   000021  Y2KCV   111-11-0013 2011-03-30   690                              │
│   000022  Y2KCV   111-11-0012 2012-06-01   240                              │
│   000023  Y2KCV   111-11-0011 2012-07-31   145                              │
│   000024  RH400   111-11-0012 2012-07-04    36                              │
│   000025  Junk    111-11-0001 2012-06-14     0                              │
│   000026  EBUS    111-11-0001 2012-06-15    12                              │
│   000027  Y2KCV   111-11-0002 2012-06-15     8                              │
│   000028  NPADV   111-11-0012 2012-08-01     5                              │
│   ****** ********  End of report  ********                                  │
│                                                               Bottom        │
│   F21=Split      F22=Width 132      F24=More keys                           │
│ MA    A                    MW                              03/032           │
│ I902 - Session successfully started    A232 - HP LaserJet 4050 on IP_10.134.223.223 │
└────────────────────────────────────────────────────────────────────────────┘
```

Figure 8.32: Data of the Project-Member File PRJMBRPF

3. The employee number of the first matching project number record is 111-11-0011. Using that value, DB2 now tries to satisfy the second join condition—that employee number in the project-member file equal an employee number of the employee file. Again, in matching specific values, an index is needed, and the keyed-sequence access path of EMPPF—keyed on EMPNO—is just what the system is looking for. An index search reveals a record with a key value matching the project-member employee number; that record, for employee Tilly Zanzibar, is read from EMPPF. Assuming a

keyed-sequence access path on employee number, the file would look like Figure 8.33 (not all fields are shown).

```
⌐ I Session A - [24 x 80]                                              _ □ ×
File  Edit  View  Communication  Actions  Window  Help
[toolbar icons]
                          Display Report
                                    Report width . . . . . :        72
 Position to line  . . . .      _____    Shift to column  . . . . .    _____
 Line     ....+....1....+....2....+....3....+....4....+....5....+....6....+....7..
           EMPNO LASTNAME      FIRSTNAME  DEPT        BIRTHDATE  HIREDATE
 000001 111-11-0001 Slick        Sam        Sales       1966-06-06 1992-10-01
 000002 111-11-0002 Fendor       Denton     Sales       1972-11-19 1997-03-29
 000003 111-11-0003 Einstein     Albert     Research    1945-04-25 1956-03-28
 000004 111-11-0004 Takahashi    Musashi    Research    1954-12-01 1992-03-30
 000005 111-11-0005 Rachanoffski Natasha    Sales       1960-04-16 1994-07-01
 000006 111-11-0006 Kartblanch   Emil       Sales       1950-05-11 1986-05-15
 000007 111-11-0007 Badman       Billy      Sales       1975-07-18 1997-04-15
 000008 111-11-0008 Gootch       Martha     Marketing   1948-02-21 1993-11-01
 000009 111-11-0009 Hunn         Atilla     Human Res   1949-04-25 1979-06-01
 000010 111-11-0010 Disney       Walter     Marketing   1952-10-10 1982-10-01
 000011 111-11-0011 Zanzibar     Tilly      MIS         1947-05-11 1997-01-01
 000012 111-11-0012 Stonehart    Rocky      MIS         1947-05-11 1998-06-01
 000013 111-11-0013 Deerfield    Cynthia    MIS         1966-08-02 1998-06-01
 000014 234-78-5689 Yousuf       Saad       IT          1987-10-01 2001-11-10
 ****** ********  End of report   ********

                                                              Bottom
 F3=Exit      F12=Cancel      F19=Left      F20=Right     F24=More keys

MA   A              MW                                            03/032
I902 - Session successfully started         A232 - HP LaserJet 4050 on IP_10.134.223.223
```

Figure 8.33: Select Data Fields of Employee File EMPPF Shown in Employee Number Key Sequence

4. Because both join conditions have been met, the first join record is assembled in the join logical file and made available to the program or utility requesting it. This provides the field values from the three matched records as specified in the record format of Figure 8.30.

5. The system now returns to step 2 to see whether another Y2KCV record exists in the PRJMBRPF index. If so, steps 3 and 4 are repeated, and another join record is assembled for the logical file. This process continues until no more PRJMBRPF records with matching project codes are found. When that occurs, the system returns to step 1 above to read the next record of the primary file.

This loop-within-a-loop processing continues until all records of the primary file are read and all attempts to match the JFLD values are made. If keyed-sequence access paths to meet the system's need for indexes do not already exist, and the number of records in the file is large enough to warrant, the system creates those access paths on the fly. Even if the employee file, EMPPF, had an arrival-sequence access path, any related logical file keyed on EMPNO could supply the needed index as long as it didn't use select or omit (or, if it did, it specified the DYNSLT keyword).

Once the join logical file is compiled, running a query on the file is again a simple matter. Because the join operations have already been described in the file itself and the fields have already been projected, you need only to identify the join logical file to Query for i5/OS. This has been done for join logical file JOINME in Figure 8.34, the Query for i5/OS Specify File Selections screen.

Figure 8.34: Specify File Selections Screen for JOINME Query

After we use the Specify Report Column Formatting feature to narrow column widths and edit employee numbers, the query output looks like the report shown in Figure 8.35.

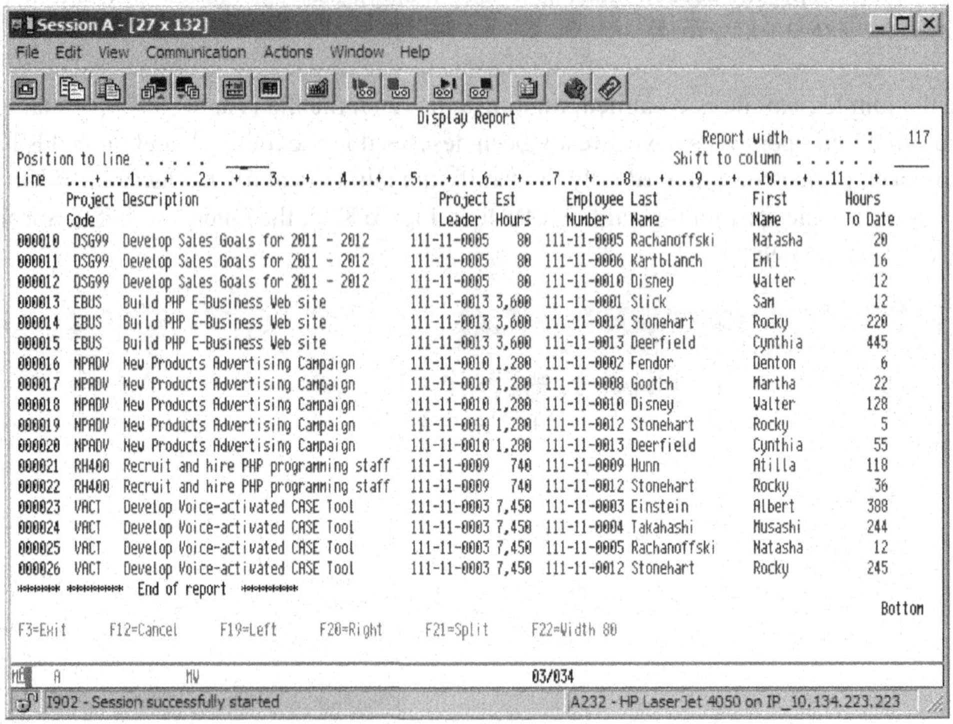

Figure 8.35: Report Output of Query on JOINME

The contents of the report show how the join-logical-file records have been assembled. There are seven different projects (only five of which are shown), each with at least two employees assigned to it. Remember that for a record to be selected for this logical file there must be a successful join of records from all three physical files. Records from the member file PRJMBRPF that have a project number not found in the primary file, or that have an employee number not matched in the EMPPF file, would be omitted from the join logical file. But suppose there was a project with no members assigned. Because this is an inner join, a PRJPF record without a matching PRJMBRPF record would not be included in the join logical file.

Adding the JDFTVAL file-level keyword to the join-logical-file DDS, as shown in Figure 8.36, changes the way records are selected for the logical file.

```
⊡ I Session A - [24 x 80]                                            _ □ ✕
File  Edit  View  Communication  Actions  Window  Help
 ▣  ▤  ▥   ▦  ▧   ▨  ▩   ▤   ▨  ▨   ▨  ▨   ▤   ◈  ✎
 Columns . . . :    1  71            Edit                CIS001/QDDSSRC
 SEU==>  _____        JOINMEO
         *************** Beginning of data *************************************
0001.00       A**************************************************************************
0002.00       A* Join Project, Members and Employees in one Record format
0003.00       A* using Left Outer Join.
0004.00       A* Compiled - 04-15-2010               Programmer - Jim Buck
0005.00       A**************************************************************************
0006.00       A                              JDFTVAL
0007.00       A        R JOINPMER            JFILE(PRJPF PRJMBRPF EMPPF)
0008.00       A        J                     JOIN(1 2)
0009.00       A                              JFLD(PRJCD PRJCD)
0010.00       A        J                     JOIN(2 3)
0011.00       A                              JFLD(EMPNO EMPNO)
0012.00       A          PRJCD               JREF(1)
0013.00       A          DESC
0014.00       A          PRJLDR
0015.00       A          ESTHRS
0016.00       A          EMPNO        B      JREF(2)
0017.00       A          LASTNAME
0018.00       A          FIRSTNAME
0019.00       A          HRSTD
         ***************** End of data *********************************************
                               (C) COPYRIGHT IBM CORP. 1981, 2007.
MA▌    A              MW                                            02/009
🖳 I902 - Session successfully started        A232 - HP LaserJet 4050 on IP_10.134.223.223
```

Figure 8.36: DDS for Outer Join, Using JDFTVAL

By using keyword JDFTVAL, you are specifying a left outer join. In this case, when a primary file record is unmatched in the secondary file, it is still selected, but the missing fields are set to defaults. This lets you see any projects with no members yet assigned. Secondary-file records unmatched in the primary file are still omitted.

When the same query specifications are used with the newly created logical file, the results appear as in Figure 8.37.

```
Session B - [27 x 132]                                                                    _ □ X
File  Edit  View  Communication  Actions  Window  Help

[toolbar icons]
                              Display Report
Query . . . :  CIS001/LSTJOINMEO                           Report width . . . . . :    117
Position to line  . . . . :                                Shift to column  . . . . . :  ____
Line     ....+....1....+....2....+....3....+....4....+....5....+....6....+....7....+....8....+....9....+....10....+....11....+..
         Project  Description                      Project Est      Employee Last         First      Hours
         Code                                       Leader  Hours    Number   Name         Name       To Date
000011   DSG99  Develop Sales Goals for 2011 - 2012  111-11-0005    80  111-11-0006 Kartblanch    Emil         16
000012   DSG99  Develop Sales Goals for 2011 - 2012  111-11-0005    80  111-11-0010 Disney        Walter       12
000013   HDBA   Hire a DB2 Database Administrator    111-11-0009   120                                          0
000014   EBUS   Build PHP E-Business Web site        111-11-0013 3,600  111-11-0001 Slick         Sam          12
000015   EBUS   Build PHP E-Business Web site        111-11-0013 3,600  111-11-0012 Stonehart     Rocky       220
000016   EBUS   Build PHP E-Business Web site        111-11-0013 3,600  111-11-0013 Deerfield     Cynthia     445
000017   NPADV  New Products Advertising Campaign    111-11-0010 1,200  111-11-0002 Fendor        Denton        6
000018   NPADV  New Products Advertising Campaign    111-11-0010 1,200  111-11-0008 Gootch        Martha       22
000019   NPADV  New Products Advertising Campaign    111-11-0010 1,200  111-11-0010 Disney        Walter      128
000020   NPADV  New Products Advertising Campaign    111-11-0010 1,200  111-11-0012 Stonehart     Rocky         5
000021   NPADV  New Products Advertising Campaign    111-11-0010 1,200  111-11-0013 Deerfield     Cynthia      55
000022   RH400  Recruit and hire PHP programming staff 111-11-0009  740  111-11-0009 Hunn         Atilla      118
000023   RH400  Recruit and hire PHP programming staff 111-11-0009  740  111-11-0012 Stonehart    Rocky        36
000024   RH400  Recruit and hire PHP programming staff 111-11-0009  740  111-11-0099                           46
000025   URTUM  Update, Revise Tutorials, User Manuals 111-11-0013 1,250                                        0
000026   VACT   Develop Voice-activated CASE Tool    111-11-0003 7,450  111-11-0003 Einstein      Albert      380
000027   VACT   Develop Voice-activated CASE Tool    111-11-0003 7,450  111-11-0004 Takahashi     Musashi     244
000028   VACT   Develop Voice-activated CASE Tool    111-11-0003 7,450  111-11-0005 Rachanoffski  Natasha      12
                                                                                                           More...
F3=Exit     F12=Cancel     F19=Left     F20=Right     F21=Split     F22=Width 80

MA▌  B                                                          03/035
I902 - Session successfully started                         A232 - HP LaserJet 4050 on IP_10.134.223.223
```

Figure 8.37: Query Report on Left Outer Join Logical File

Notice that the new report shows projects (codes HDBA and URTUM—note the arrows) that did not appear before. Because these project records did not match any project-member records, a join record was not selected using the inner join operation. With the left outer join, the fields from the two unmatched secondary files have been set to default values.

Also, notice that the outer join report shows an additional record in the RH400 project. An employee was supposed to be a member of that project, but the incorrectly entered number (111-11-0099) of the project-member file did not match any employee-file number, so the inner join did not select a join record for the missing employee. This is in accordance with the inner join rule that at least one matching record must be found in *all* secondary files. The outer join, in contrast, selected the record but set the missing EMPPF fields (LASTNAME and FIRSTNAME) to blanks.

Control Breaks and Group Indicators

A more useful query of the join logical file might include a **control break** to separate projects, and perhaps a summary function to total the hours spent so far on each project by its members. Also, if the report break includes all four primary-file fields together as Break Level 1 (Figure 8.38), you can use **group indication** in printing the report.

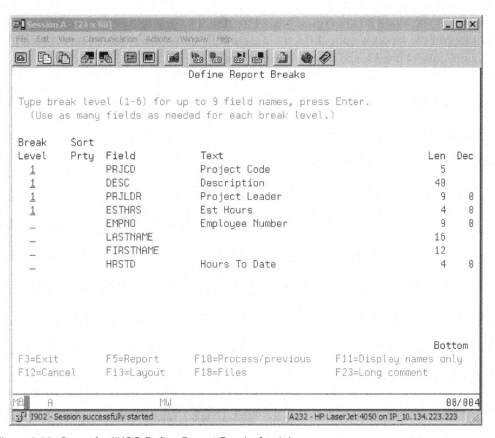

Figure 8.38: Query for i5/OS Define Report Breaks for Join

When you use group indication, the control-field values are printed on only the first line of a new report-control group. On subsequent lines, these values are replaced by spaces. This approach generally makes a report easier to read. Query for i5/OS automatically uses group indication for printed reports when you define report breaks. When one primary-file record is joined with several secondary-file records, you can get all the common primary-file fields to group indicate simply by assigning Break Level 1 to each common field, as Figure 8.38 shows. Note, however, that group indication works only for printed files; if the report described in Figure 8.38 were output to a display device instead of a printer, or if you pressed F5=Report from within the query definition, there would be no sign of group indication.

When we use the modified query to create a report of the outer join logical file, the appearance of the report is quite different. Figure 8.39 shows the modified report with group indication, control breaks, and summary functions.

```
05/22/10  22:33:40              Projects, Members and Hours-to-Date                           PAGE    1
Project Description                 Project Est      Employee Last          First            Hours
Code                                Leader  Hours    Number   Name          Name             To Date

Y2KCV  Develop College Internship program.  111-11-0011 5,000  111-11-0002 Fendor      Denton             8
                                                               111-11-0011 Zanzibar    Tilly            145
                                                               111-11-0012 Stonehart   Rocky            240
                                                               111-11-0013 Deerfield   Cynthia          690
                                                                                       Hours for Y2KCV
                                                                                       TOTAL          1,083

CLRSS  Plan End-of-Year Clearance Sale Strategy 111-11-0002  120  111-11-0001 Slick    Sam               20
                                                               111-11-0002 Fendor      Denton            12
                                                               111-11-0007 Badman      Billy              6
                                                               111-11-0008 Gootch      Martha            24
                                                                                       Hours for CLRSS
                                                                                       TOTAL             62

DSG99  Develop Sales Goals for 2011 - 2012  111-11-0005   80  111-11-0004 Takahashi    Musashi           24
                                                               111-11-0005 Rachanoffski Natasha          20
                                                               111-11-0006 Kartblanch  Emil              16
                                                               111-11-0010 Disney      Walter            12
                                                                                       Hours for DSG99
                                                                                       TOTAL             72

HDBA   Hire a DB2 Database Administrator   111-11-0009  120                                              0
                                                                                       Hours for HDBA
                                                                                       TOTAL             0

EBUS   Build PHP E-Business Web site       111-11-0013 3,600 111-11-0001 Slick         Sam               12
                                                               111-11-0012 Stonehart   Rocky            220
                                                               111-11-0013 Deerfield   Cynthia          445
                                                                                       Hours for EBUS
                                                                                       TOTAL            677

NPADV  New Products Advertising Campaign   111-11-0010 1,280 111-11-0002 Fendor        Denton             6
                                                               111-11-0008 Gootch      Martha            22
                                                               111-11-0010 Disney      Walter           128
                                                               111-11-0012 Stonehart   Rocky              5
                                                               111-11-0013 Deerfield   Cynthia           55
                                                                                       Hours for NPADV
                                                                                       TOTAL            216

RH400  Recruit and hire PHP programming staff 111-11-0009  740  111-11-0009 Hunn       Atilla           118
                                                               111-11-0012 Stonehart   Rocky             36
                                                               111-11-0099                                46

05/22/10  22:33:40              Projects, Members and Hours-to-Date                           PAGE    2
Project Description                 Project Est      Employee Last          First            Hours
Code                                Leader  Hours    Number   Name          Name             To Date
                                                                                       Hours for RH400
                                                                                       TOTAL            200

URTUM  Update, Revise Tutorials, User Manuals 111-11-0013 1,250                                          0
                                                                                       Hours for URTUM
                                                                                       TOTAL             0

VACT   Develop Voice-activated CASE Tool   111-11-0003 7,450 111-11-0003 Einstein      Albert           388
                                                               111-11-0004 Takahashi   Musashi          244
                                                               111-11-0005 Rachanoffski Natasha          12
                                                               111-11-0012 Stonehart   Rocky            245
                                                                                       Hours for VACT
                                                                                       TOTAL            889
                                                                                       Final Totals
                                                                                       TOTAL          3,199

* * *  E N D   O F   R E P O R T  * * *
```

Figure 8.39: Query for i5/OS Report of Left Outer Join Logical File, with Control Breaks

You can see how conveniently join logical files can present data from several related physical files. But, as we mentioned earlier, join logical files do not let you update data records in the based-on physical files. It would be convenient to associate related records, such as projects and project members, when you add new records or update existing records. The third type of logical file, multiple-format logical files, provides this capability.

Multiple-Format Logical Files

Multiple-format logical files let you display or update related records from two or more physical files. These logical files specify a different record format for each of the based-on physical files—unlike join logical files, which combine the fields of related files into a single record format. Multiple-format logical files must specify key fields, and either each record format must have the same key, or at least the higher-order fields of composite keys must be common in each of the different record formats. DB2 merges records from the different physical files according to the values of these common key fields. This merging operation establishes the relationship between records of the different files and determines the access order of records. Records with matching key values are arranged first in the order in which the files are specified within the multiple-format logical file. If duplicate records exist within one record format, you can use a file-level keyword telling how to process duplicate keys, such as FIFO (first in, first out).

Figure 8.40 shows DDS for a multiple-format logical file using the project (PRJPF) and project-members (PRJMBRPF) physical files.

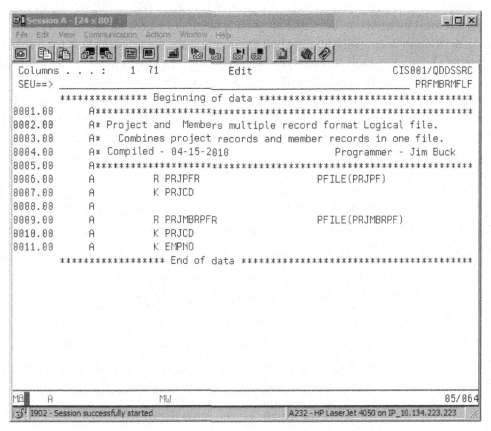

Figure 8.40: Project/Project-Member Multiple-Format Logical File DDS

Notice that both record-level entries (lines 6 and 9) use the same record-format names as the physical files, and that no field-level entries are coded. This combination tells DB2 to include all fields with attributes unchanged. Each record format also names the physical file on which it is based in the PFILE keyword value. Of course, listing the necessary fields from each physical file under its record-format entry would be fine. The key field for the PRJPF record format is Project Code (PRJCD); for the PRJMBRPF record format, the key field is PRJCD and, within PRJCD, Employee Number (EMPNO). The important point here is that the PRJCD key is common to both records and is in the same relative (high-order) position.

When the file is created, the system builds an access path that orders all records by their key-field values. This access path is used to pull records from their based-on physical files as an application or utility reads the multiple-format logical file. The first file serves as a primary file and is usually the parent file in a one-to-many relationship. In Figure 8.40, PRJPF is the primary file, and its key field PRJCD is the primary key in the based-on physical file. The second file, PRJMBRPF, is a child or dependent file of PRJPF; and there may be zero, one, or many project-member records for each PRJCD value of the project file. **Referential integrity** dictates that all project member records have PRJCD values already existing in the parent file. So when the multiple-format logical file is read, the first record should be a project record (primary file) with the lowest key. The next record should be a project-member record with a matching project code. If several employees are assigned to the project, all of their records with the same project code would be read from the project-member file before another record is read from the project file. Because we made EMPNO a low-order key of the project-member format, the group of project-member records with the same project code appears in the logical file in order of employee number.

The following example (Tables 8.1, 8.2, and 8.3) should help illustrate this file-merge operation. Assume records in the project (P) and project-member (PM) files are as shown and in key sequence.

Table 8.1: PRJPF File (P)		
Project Code	**Project Leader**	**Start Date**
CLRSS	111110002	2010-08-01
DSG99	111110005	2010-08-01
EBUS	111110013	2010-05-23

Table 8.2: PRJMBRPF File (PM)			
Project Code	Employee Number	Date Assigned	Hours To Date
CLRSS	111110001	2010-09-05	20
CLRSS	111110002	2010-09-01	12
CLRSS	111110007	2010-08-15	6
CLRSS	111110008	2010-08-05	24
EBUS	111110001	2012-06-15	12
EBUS	111110012	2011-07-06	220

Table 8.3: PRFMBRMFLF Multiple-Format Logical File			
Project Code	Employee Number/ Project Leader	Start Date/ Date Assigned	Hours To Date
CLRSS	111110002	2010-08-01	
CLRSS	111110001	2010-09-05	20
CLRSS	111110002	2010-09-01	12
CLRSS	111110007	2010-08-15	6
CLRSS	111110008	2010-08-05	24
DSG99	111110005	2010-08-01	
EBUS	111110013	2010-05-23	
EBUS	111110001	2012-06-15	12
EBUS	111110012	2011-07-06	220
EBUS	111110013	2011-05-23	445

Notice that the EBUS record from the (P) file immediately follows the DSG99 record, also from the (P) file. This occurs because, in this example, no project members have been assigned to project DSG99. Unlike join logical files, all records from both (or all) files are included in the multiple-format logical file, even if they have unmatched keys in another file.

When this multiple-format logical file is compiled, you can access the data through a temporary DFU program using the logical file. Because data already exists in the underlying physical files, the DFU comes up in change mode, prompting for a project code of the PRJPFR record format. If you page down, the first record of that format is displayed in key sequence. Figure 8.41 shows the appearance of the DFU screen after you press Page Down once. The record format is identified in the upper-left corner of the screen.

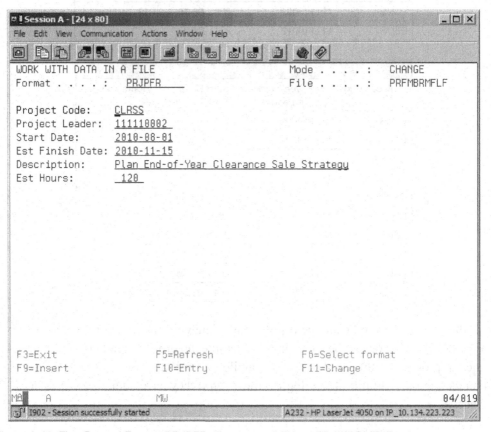

Figure 8.41: First Record Format PRJPFR, Temporary DFU on PRJMBRMFLF

If you Page Down again (Figure 8.42), you see a record from the PRJMBRPFR format, with the same project code and the lowest employee number assigned to that project.

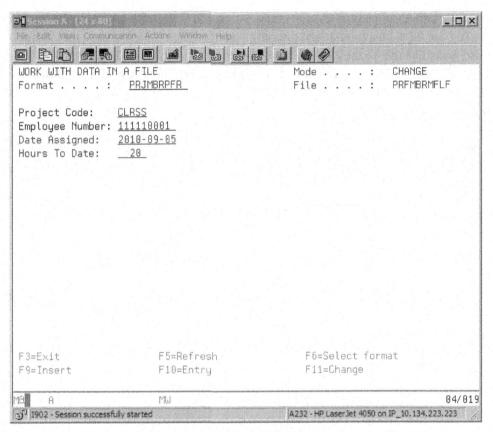

Figure 8.42: First Project-Member Record, Format PRJMBRPFR, for Project CLRSS

Because the DFU is already in change mode, you could update this record by tabbing to the Hours To Date field, changing it, and pressing Enter (or Page Down) to save the change. You can also make changes to the PRJPFR records when they are displayed. And you don't need to rely only on Page Up/Page Down to locate records; you can directly retrieve a project record by entering its key value in the Project Code entry field. Figure 8.43 shows a prompt screen with VACT entered as the project code.

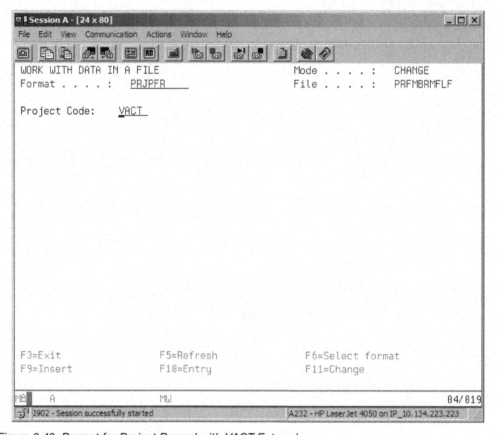

Figure 8.43: Prompt for Project Record with VACT Entered

When you press Enter, the project record of that code is displayed (Figure 8.44).

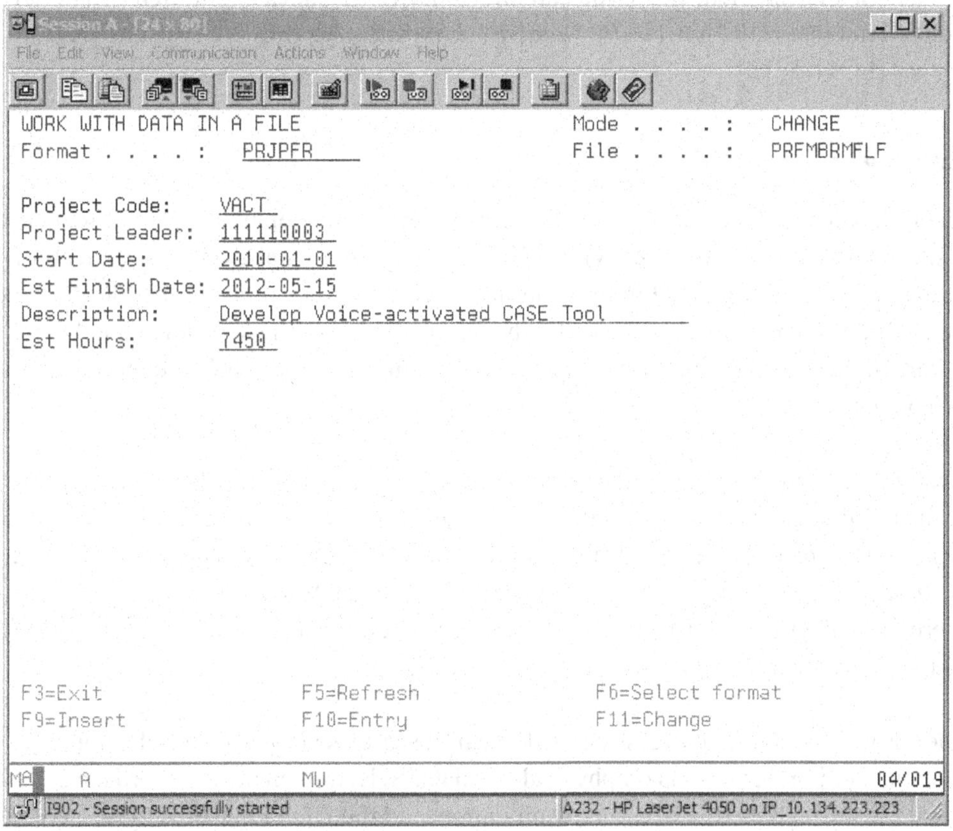

```
Session A - [24 x 80]                                              _ □ ×
File  Edit  View  Communication  Actions  Window  Help
□  □ □  □ □  □ □  □  □ □  □ □  □  □ □

WORK WITH DATA IN A FILE                    Mode . . . . :    CHANGE
Format . . . . :    PRJPFR                   File . . . . :    PRFMBRMFLF

Project Code:     VACT
Project Leader:   111110003
Start Date:       2010-01-01
Est Finish Date:  2012-05-15
Description:      Develop Voice-activated CASE Tool
Est Hours:        7450




F3=Exit                F5=Refresh            F6=Select format
F9=Insert              F10=Entry             F11=Change

MA      A                    MW                                   04/019
I902 - Session successfully started        A232 - HP LaserJet 4050 on IP_10.134.223.223
```

Figure 8.44: Project Record for VACT Displayed

From here, pressing Page Down displays the project-member records of that project in order by employee number, from low to high.

At any time, you can enter a new record of either format by pressing F9 when a current record of the desired format is displayed. The current record format is shown in the upper-left corner of the DFU screen, and you can change it by pressing F6. When you use F10 to enter new records, the entry screen displayed is for the record format currently selected by the F6 function.

Remember that the multiple-format logical file uses a keyed-sequence access path. So newly entered records are presented within the file by key sequence, regardless of whether the insert or the entry function was used to add them to the file.

From this brief introduction, you should have an idea of the power and flexibility of logical files for organizing and accessing data stored in the DB2 database. There is much more to learn about logical files than we can possibly cover here. If you cannot wait for your database management class, you can find about 1,000 pages of additional material in the IBM manuals *DB2 for AS/400 Database Programming* (SC41-5701) and *DDS Reference* (SC41-5712).

In Summary

All database files have an access path. The access path either defaults to arrival sequence or is specified as keyed sequence. When an arrival-sequence database file is sequentially accessed, records are presented in the order in which they were added to the file. A keyed-sequence file presents records in order by the relative value of the key-field data. Direct retrieval or random access requires a relative record number for arrival-sequence files or a key value for keyed-sequence files.

Logical files can provide an alternate keyed-sequence access path over existing physical files. Such access paths require maintenance when the based-on physical file's records are changed or new records are added. Three options available for access path maintenance are immediate (*IMMED), delayed (*DLY), and rebuild (*REBLD). When duplicate key values are not permitted, keyword UNIQUE is coded at the file level. Unique keyed-sequence access paths require immediate maintenance.

Besides providing alternate access paths, logical files are used to provide selection, projection, and join operations on physical-file data. Selection creates a record subset of the physical file through the use of Select/Omit entries and the DDS keywords COMP, VALUES, and RANGE. Projection creates logical-file record formats that consist of a field subset of the physical-file record. We use projection to protect data elements from applications that do not require or are not authorized to them. The join operation lets data from two or more separate but related physical files be retrieved as one record when relationship-supporting fields have matching values. An inner join returns a join record when at least one matching record is found in each of the related files. A left outer join returns a join record for each primary-file record even if a matching record is not found in one or more of the secondary files.

The three types of logical files are simple, join, and multiple-format. Simple logical files are based on one physical file and have one record format. We can use simple logical files to provide selection, projection, and an alternate access path for the based-on physical file.

Join logical files permit the join operation we mentioned above to be specified within an actual file object, kept permanently, and used by queries or HLL applications. Join logical files cannot be updated, but they provide a powerful tool for pulling data together for reports and displays. When Query for i5/OS is used to display or print records from a join logical file, the file selection needs to identify only the single logical file; specification of secondary files or type of join is not necessary. When all primary-file fields are defined as the same (level 1) control field, group indication is used automatically for printer reports.

Multiple-format logical files provide a convenient way to display and update data in two or more physical files. Each record format in a multiple-format file is based on a record format of an underlying physical file and can include all or a subset of the fields of the physical file (projection). Multiple-format logical files must be keyed, and all record formats must specify at least the same high-order key. Records are arranged and presented by this merged key sequence, with the primary file (first record format) records being presented first within a key group.

In the lab, you will create a simple logical file and then expanded your database by creating three new physical files. You create a multiple-format logical file to add records to related files; you create a join logical file using four of the database physical files. You then use your join logical file as input to create a Query for i5/OS report of students enrolled in sections of courses.

Key Terms

access path

arrival sequence

COMP

comparand

compile listing

composite key

control break

direct record retrieval

domain

DSPPFM

duplicate keys

DYNSLT

FIFO

group indication

join logical file

key field

keyed sequence

logical files

PFILE

physical files

primary key

projection

RANGE

referential integrity

relative record number

response time

select/omit operations

sequential record retrieval

simple logical files

throughput

UNIQUE

VALUES

views

volatility

Review Questions

1. Explain the significance of the UNIQUE file-level keyword.
2. How do you describe a key field in a DDS source member?
3. What is the purpose of the FIFO keyword?
4. List and explain the functions provided by logical files in DB2.
5. Summarize the DDS keywords used for logical files we discussed in this chapter.
6. List the types of logical files used in DB2.
7. List and describe the keywords we described in this chapter that are used in a selection logical file.
8. Go to the IBM Information Center Web site and find three DDS keywords not described in this chapter; explain the function of these keywords.
9. When you are describing a keyed file, what is the purpose of the UNIQUE keyword?
10. Why would you not use the UNIQUE keyword on an employee file keyed on last name?
11. What is the purpose of a composite key?
12. What basic functions must a logical file or a view provide to the database?
13. List and explain the types of logical files.
14. Why should a logical file be created with DDS listing all of the fields in a physical file?
15. What security implications can *selection* have on a database file?
16. What are the three selection keywords used in a logical file?
17. Explain the rules for keying DDS keywords and the associated parameters.
18. When coding Selects and/or Omits in a logical file, why can the order sometimes cause unexpected results? How can this problem be resolved?
19. When you create a logical file with a keyed sequence, does the file display in the sequence you would expect? Why or why not?
20. When you create a query with a number of breaks, how is it displayed? Why can this confuse new users to Query?

Lab 8

Introduction

In this lab, you begin by creating a simple logical file over the physical file STUPF, which you created in previous labs. Instead of keying in new DDS for this logical file, you copy the DDS source code of the original physical file and change it for the logical file. The new logical file will use a keyed-sequence access path, projection, and selection. It will also change an attribute of an existing field.

After completing the lab, you will be able to use PDM to copy a source-file member; use SEU to edit the copied member, creating DDS for a new logical file; use PDM to compile the new logical-file description; and use DFU to browse through the file and add new records.

An error in the initial file description will cause the first compile to fail, giving you an opportunity to examine the job log and compile listing to find the error. An additional lab exercise provides more practice in creating physical and logical files, and in setting up a query on a join logical file.

Part 1

Goals   Copy the DDS source code of STUPF.

Change the copied DDS to create a new logical file, STULF1.

Save the changes.

Start at   WRKOBJPDM (Work with Objects Using PDM), your library.

Procedure Work with object QDDSSRC.

Copy member STUPF to STULF1.

Edit STULF1.

Exit and save.

8.1.   Start PDM, and work with all objects in your library. From the Work with Objects Using PDM screen, take option 12 on your DDS source physical file.

8.2.   From the Work with Members Using PDM screen, use the PDM option to copy member STUPF to a new member within QDDSSRC. Call the new member STULF1.

   8.2.a.   After the copy option is executed, what message is displayed?

8.3.   From the Work with Members Using PDM screen, you should now see member STULF1. What is its type? Using Tab or Field advance, move the cursor to the Type entry and change the type of STULF1 to LF. Then press Enter. If the Type field is not an input-permitted field, press F18 from the Work with Members Using PDM screen to change PDM defaults. By typing Y in the Change type and text entry field, you should be able to change the member type of STULF1 from PF to LF. If you are not able to do so, you can make the change from within SEU.

8.4.   Take the option to edit STULF1. From the SEU work screen, place the cursor anywhere on the Record format line, and press F4.

   8.4.a.   What happens?

8.4.b. According to the prompter information above the entry fields, what is the prompt type?

If the prompt type is not LF, you need to press F13 to change session defaults and, from that screen, change the source type to LF; then press Enter before continuing.

8.5. You should now see a screen like the one in Figure 8.45.

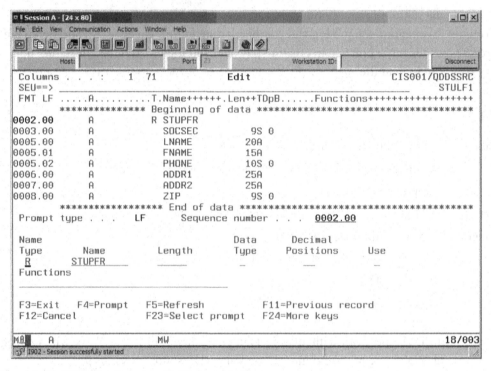

Figure 8.45: SEU Work Screen with Prompted Line

The cursor will be on the Name Type field, and the prompt type should be LF. Use the New line key (Shift+Enter) to move the cursor to the Functions field. Type in PFILE(STUPF), and then press Enter. PFILE is a record-level keyword that identifies the physical file on which the logical file will be built.

8.6. Press the Refresh or Cancel function key to exit prompting. Position the cursor in the sequence-number area of the Beginning of data line, type IP, and press Enter to insert a line with prompting just before line 1.00, the record-format line.

8.7. The new first line will contain only a file-level keyword, UNIQUE. This keyword specifies that the keys for this file must all be unique values; no duplicate keys will be permitted. Key UNIQUE in the Functions field, and then press Enter.

8.7.a.   What sequence number is given to the new line?

The COLHDG function lets you use a more descriptive identifier than the field name for fields that appear on DFU screens and Query for i5/OS reports. If you don't provide a COLHDG value, the DDS compiler uses the field name.

8.8.   Press Refresh again. Move the cursor to the SOCSEC line, and prompt again. Type COLHDG('Social' 'Security') in the Functions field, and then press Enter. Remember that you must enter DDS keywords in upper case. Be sure to leave at least one space between the two quoted words.

If you are unable to enter lowercase letters, find the function key for Change session defaults. Figure 8.46 shows the Change Session Defaults screen.

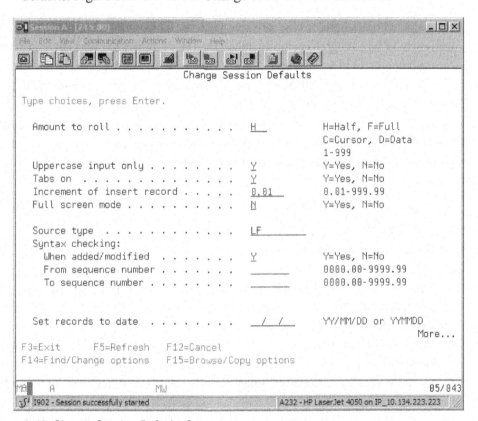

Figure 8.46: Change Session Defaults Screen

On this screen, change the Uppercase input only value to allow lowercase entry. Then press Enter. When you return to the editor, the display will show that the line you were working on is in error. (Errors are displayed in reverse image.) You can correct the error by prompting and finishing the column-heading field. In fact, prompting is not necessary; SEU is a full-screen editor, so you can finish keying the column heading right in the work area. Give appropriate column headings of First

Name, Last Name, Address Line 1, and Address Line 2 to the respective fields; skip the PHONE field.

Change the length of both the ADDR1 and ADDR2 fields to 20. Logical files can change certain field-level attributes of the based-on physical-file fields. If, for example, the applications using the logical file placed tighter length restrictions on fields, you could impose those restrictions once in the logical-file description instead of in each application program. Of course, existing data might appear truncated when viewed through the logical file; but the database administrator would anticipate this, and it should not result in mapping problems or a system-level error. At any rate, shortening a field in the logical file has no effect on the physical-file data.

For fields whose length or type attribute you aren't changing, using only the field name would be enough to compile the DDS. The compiler uses the same attributes for each named field as defined in the physical file. You copied the physical-file DDS to modify for the logical file, so the length and type attributes are already there, and it's not necessary to erase them.

If you misspell a keyword, the SEU editor flags the error and displays the incorrect field in reverse image on the prompt line. If this happens, correct the error and then press Enter. Remember that function keywords (e.g., COLHDG) must be upper case.

8.9. Delete the PHONE field from the source DDS.

8.10. Insert one line with prompting after the ZIP field. At this point, you will intentionally introduce an error into the DDS source code.

On the first inserted line, declare a Select operation (S for the Name Type field) for the ZIP field. (The previously defined field name you are using for the Select goes in the S record's Name field.) In the Functions field, enter an appropriate keyword to select records that have local zip codes (e.g., all zip codes with the same first two digits as those of your school or company). There is more than one way to do this, but for this lab, use the keyword that correctly specifies the Select operation with only one line of DDS code.

8.10.a. How could you code this selection using a different keyword (and two lines of code)?

Insert the select line. Then, on the next prompt, declare a key field (Name Type K) and identify SOCSEC as the key (in the Name field). Press Enter.

8.11. Exit prompting (F5 or F12), and Page Up to the top of the screen. Check your work. The file-level keyword UNIQUE must be first, followed by the record-format line, which now contains the PFILE keyword. The Select and Key fields should be last. Your source file should now look like Figure 8.47, except that your Range values for the ZIP field will differ unless you live in eastern Iowa.

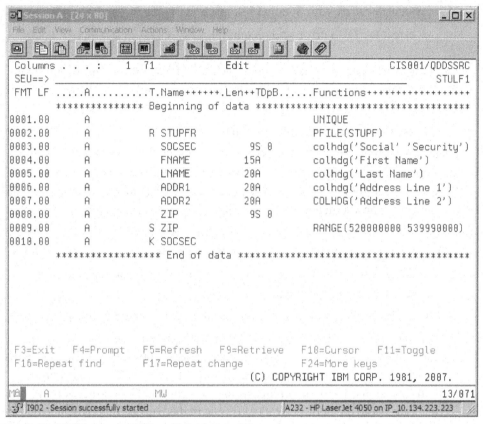

Figure 8.47: DDS for Logical File with Intentional Error

8.12. Exit SEU, and save the updated member as STULF1.

    8.12.a. What message is displayed at the bottom of the PDM screen to which you
          returned?

Part 2

Goals   Invoke the CRTLF command using the PDM option.

             Find the Access path maintenance parameter.

             Find and display the job log.

             Find and display the spooled file of the compile listing.

             Determine the cause of the compile failure.

Start at   WRKMBRPDM, your library/QDDSSRC.

Procedure Prompt with option 14 on STULF1.

             Find the Access path maintenance parameter, and read the context Help.

             Compile STULF1.

WRKSPLF (Work with Spooled File) to find the job log and compile listing. Correct the DDS error, and recompile.

8.13. From the Work with Members Using PDM screen, use option 14 to compile the source member you just created. Type 14 on the option line beside STULF1, and prompt.

8.13.a. What command did option 14 invoke?

Notice the current parameter values for File (the logical file to be created), Source file, and Source member. The values were supplied from the Work with Members Using PDM list screen for the option (14) you took for the particular source type (LF). If you don't want the new logical-file object to have the same name as the source member, you can change the new object name or library—simply type over the file name.

8.13.b. Find the parameter for Access path maintenance. To what value is it set?

8.13.c. What are the other two possible values for this parameter, and what is the difference between them?

8.13.d. Under what condition must you use the default value of this parameter?

8.14. Press Enter from the CRTLF command prompt screen, and observe the message that appears after you run the command. Remember that option 14 normally submits (sends) the CRT*xxx* command to the batch subsystem, QBATCH. This compile method lets you perform other requests and run commands interactively from your workstation while the compile (CRT*xxx*) runs in the background. If you Page Down with the cursor on the first message, you will see a second message that identifies the new job started when you submitted your compile to the batch job queue.

When the compile is completed, a message will be waiting in your message queue. Your terminal will beep at you when a message enters your message queue and no other message is already waiting. (If unattended messages already exist in your message queue, the torn-form symbol, or MW in reverse image, appears on the status line.) Display the message.

8.14.a. What does the message say?

Return to a command line.

8.15. When a submitted job, such as a source program or DDS compile, ends abnormally, two print files are created and sent to output queues. Enter the WRKSPLF command (or PDM option SP) to examine them. They should be the last two files listed: one named STULF1 in your output queue, and the other named QPJOBLOG in output queue QEZJOBLOG. The latter is a specially designated output queue for holding job logs—normally only logs of failed jobs.

If you cannot find a QPJOBLOG file, it may be because you are using *BASIC assistance level. If that is the case, press F21 to change the assistance level to

Intermediate. If you have more than one QPJOBLOG file in your list, press F11 to find the one most recently created by comparing the dates and times shown in view 2 (the file you are looking for should be the last spooled file in the queue).

8.16. Display the job log. On an 80-character display screen, the job log is hard to read because it extends to 132 print positions. Pressing F20 shifts your view one screen to the right, but often that does not make reading the screen any easier. Try F20 now to see how the shifted screen looks. Use F19 to shift left again.

You can display one print line at a time, folded to two display lines: Press F11 and then Page Down to display each next line. Try that now. If you looked far enough, you might find the information you need, but the folded line isn't very easy to read, either. Press F11 again to remove folding.

Another possibility is to shift the view a specified number of display/print positions to the right or left by using a Control command. If the cursor is not already there, move it up to the Control field, and press Help. Read the syntax summary for Control commands. You could use either absolute or relative windowing to shift the view to begin at column 36. When you are finished reading, exit Help and enter the command to window to column 36 on the Control input field. Page Down to the error messages. Your screen should now look like Figure 8.48.

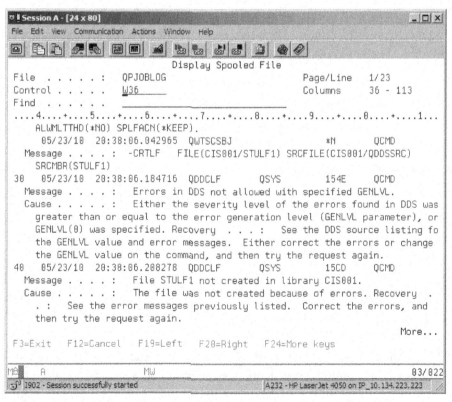

Figure 8.48: Job Log Display Windowed to the Right, Page 2

The error messages should be much easier to read now. If you scan through them, you will see a message to the effect that the file (STULF1) was not created because of severe errors that occurred during the create operation. In effect, the job log tells you that the compile failed. When you are finished reading the messages, return to the WRKSPLF list.

8.17. You are now finished with the QPJOBLOG print file, so delete it. As a general rule, try to keep print files from cluttering up output queues. If your job fails, find the job log, take any information you need from it, and then get rid of it.

8.18. From the WRKSPLF screen, display the compile listing for file STULF1. The first page of identification information is taken from the CRTLF command parameter values and current compiler options. Page Down to the second page that lists the DDS source. You should now see a screen like Figure 8.49.

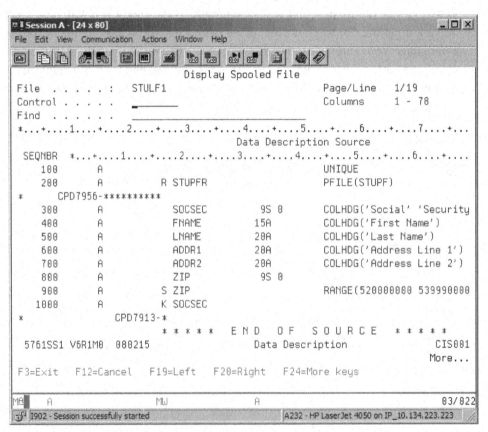

Figure 8.49: Compile Listing of STULF1, Page 2

Notice the asterisks (*) on the far left of the listing; each of these indicates an error. The error code follows. You should see the error codes CPD7956 and CPD7913.

Error codes have messages associated with them, and you need to find these messages.

Page Down until you can see the error messages under END OF EXPANDED SOURCE. Change the window through the Control field to view the complete error-message text. You should be able to read the text as you see it in Figure 8.50.

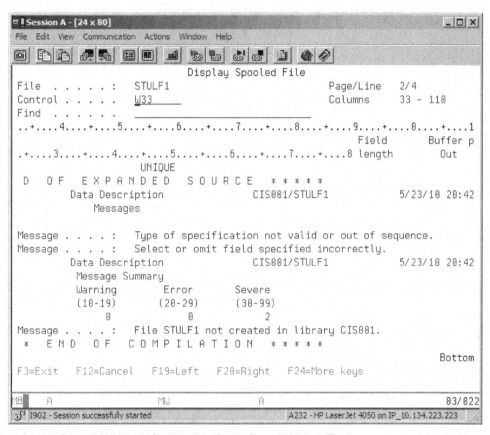

```
Session A - [24 x 80]                                                _ □ ×
File  Edit  View  Communication  Actions  Window  Help

🖵 🗎 🗎 🗎 🗎  🗎 🗎 🗎  🗎 🗎 🗎 🗎  🗎 🗎 🗎
                     Display Spooled File
File  . . . . . . :   STULF1                     Page/Line   2/4
Control . . . . .    W33                         Columns     33 - 110
Find  . . . . . .    _____
..+....4....+....5....+....6....+....7....+....8....+....9....+....0....+....1
                                                 Field        Buffer p
.+....3....+....4....+....5....+....6....+....7....+....8 length    Out
                UNIQUE
  D   O F   E X P A N D E D   S O U R C E   * * * * *
          Data Description          CIS001/STULF1          5/23/10 20:42
             Messages

Message . . . . :   Type of specification not valid or out of sequence.
Message . . . . :   Select or omit field specified incorrectly.
          Data Description          CIS001/STULF1          5/23/10 20:42
             Message Summary
             Warning        Error         Severe
             (10-19)        (20-29)       (30-99)
                  0              0             2
Message . . . . :   File STULF1 not created in library CIS001.
  *   E N D   O F   C O M P I L A T I O N   * * * * *
                                                               Bottom
F3=Exit   F12=Cancel   F19=Left   F20=Right   F24=More keys

MA    A                    MW                A                    03/022
  I902 - Session successfully started        A232 - HP LaserJet 4050 on IP_10.134.223.223
```

Figure 8.50: Compile Listing Windowed to Show Error Message Text

The error message for CPD7913 says, *"Type of specification not valid . . . ,"* and this error was really caused by the second error. The second error message, for CPD7956, tells us that the select or omit field was specified incorrectly. Although this is a little more informative than the job log, this error message still doesn't really tell us what was incorrect about the Select statement.

We will now try a more productive method to find and correct compile errors.

8.19. Return to the Work with Members Using PDM screen, and edit the source member STULF1. From the SEU edit screen, find and press the function key for Browse/Copy Options. The resulting screen should look like the one in Figure 8.51.

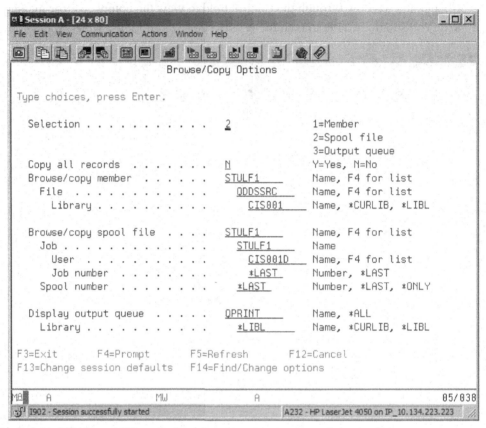

Figure 8.51: SEU Browse/Copy Options Screen

Browse/Copy Options provides a convenient way to find compile errors and correct the offending source code at the same time. It uses a split-screen format that lets you move easily from the source code to the compile listing. The options screen in Figure 8.51 gives you three choices: you can browse/copy another member of a source file, browse a spooled file, or get to a work-with-output-queue screen. We want to examine the spooled file created by the attempted compile of STULF1, so we need option 2. Of course, the compile listing with its error messages must still exist as a spooled file in your output queue.

Notice that the input fields for each option have already been filled in with substitution values provided by SEU. Because you are editing STULF1, SEU assumes you want to examine the spooled file of the same name—the compile listing. A job name is also needed to identify a particular spooled file, and SEU assumes compiles are submitted to QBATCH (the PDM option 14 default), thereby causing the batch job name to be taken from the name of the program or file being compiled. In our example, this is once again STULF1. CIS001D is the user who is signed on, so SEU takes the interactive job's user ID (CIS001D) for this value. Last, the job and spool file number are assumed to be most recent (*LAST).

Whenever you want to browse the spooled listing of a batch-submitted file or program compile, the only thing you should have to change on the Browse/Copy Options screen is the Selection. Change that value to 2 now, and then press Enter.

8.20. You should now see an SEU split screen similar to Figure 8.52.

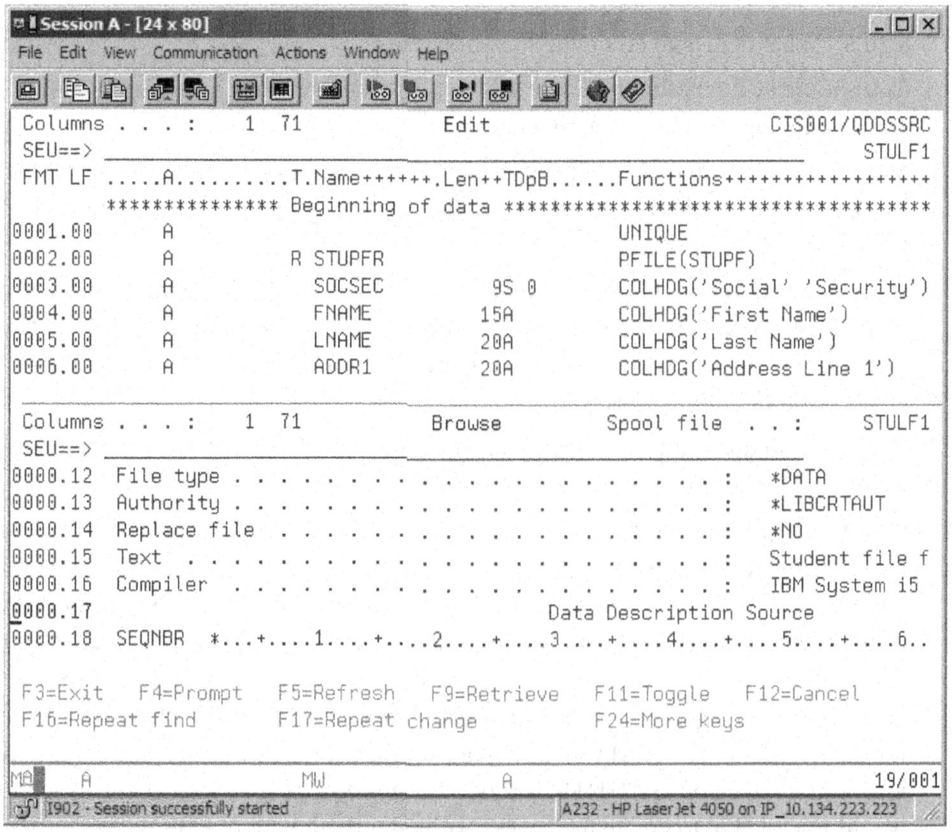

```
□ I Session A - [24 x 80]                                                    _ □ ×
 File  Edit  View  Communication  Actions  Window  Help
 ▣  ▤▤  ▤▣  ▦▥  ▥▦  ▦  ▦▦  ▦▦  ▣  ◈ ◇
  Columns . . . :   1  71              Edit                  CIS001/QDDSSRC
  SEU==>  _____        STULF1
  FMT LF  .....A..........T.Name++++++.Len++TDpB.....Functions+++++++++++++++++++
          *************** Beginning of data ***************************************
 0001.00      A                                     UNIQUE
 0002.00      A         R STUPFR                     PFILE(STUPF)
 0003.00      A           SOCSEC        9S 0         COLHDG('Social' 'Security')
 0004.00      A           FNAME        15A           COLHDG('First Name')
 0005.00      A           LNAME        20A           COLHDG('Last Name')
 0006.00      A           ADDR1        20A           COLHDG('Address Line 1')

  Columns . . . :   1  71              Browse      Spool file . . :     STULF1
  SEU==>  _____
 0000.12  File type . . . . . . . . . . . . . . . . . . . . . :   *DATA
 0000.13  Authority . . . . . . . . . . . . . . . . . . . . . :   *LIBCRTAUT
 0000.14  Replace file  . . . . . . . . . . . . . . . . . . . :   *NO
 0000.15  Text  . . . . . . . . . . . . . . . . . . . . . . . :   Student file f
 0000.16  Compiler  . . . . . . . . . . . . . . . . . . . . . :   IBM System i5
 0000.17                                    Data Description Source
 0000.18  SEQNBR  *...+....1....+....2....+....3....+....4....+....5....+....6..

  F3=Exit   F4=Prompt   F5=Refresh   F9=Retrieve   F11=Toggle   F12=Cancel
  F16=Repeat find       F17=Repeat change          F24=More keys

 MA    A              MW           A                            19/001
 ⌨ I902 - Session successfully started      A232 - HP LaserJet 4050 on IP_10.134.223.223
```

Figure 8.52: SEU Split Screen with Spooled File for Failed Compile

Notice that your source code is still in an Edit session in the upper screen, while the beginning of the compile listing is in a Browse session in the lower screen. You can use SEU Copy or Block Copy line commands to copy single lines or blocks of lines from the Browse session to the Edit session when you are editing/browsing two members. Since we are using the browse operations to find errors, this won't be needed.

You can use the SEU command

F *ERR

to locate compile errors. F is the abbreviated version of FIND, and *ERR means any compile error. The cursor should be on the Browse session's SEU command line. If not, position it there and type

F *ERR

Then press Enter.

8.20.a. What is displayed on the message line?

You should see the same message that you saw before when you displayed the compile listing in your output queue.

8.21. Move the cursor up to the Edit screen, and press Page Down. Then fix the problem by changing the order of the Select and Key entries so that the K entry comes before the S entry.

If you needed to find additional compile errors, you could move the cursor back to the lower screen and repeat the Find error command just by pressing F16. This shortcut will allow you to quickly navigate through your compile listing, fixing errors without exiting SEU.

8.22. Exit, save, and recompile. Check your messages (try DM from the option entry field), and make sure the CRTLF command was completed successfully.

8.23. If your compile was still unsuccessful, review the steps above, make the necessary changes to your source file, and try again! If the compile appears to be successful, but the logical file is not created, check your spooled files for a job log. Job logs are created when a batch job (e.g., running CRTLF from option 14) fails. Such a failure could occur if you tried to create a logical file specifying a UNIQUE keyed-sequence access path over a physical file that already contains data. If the physical-file data for the key field (or fields) was in violation of the UNIQUE key constraint (e.g., a logical file keyed on LASTNAME and two Smith records are present), the system would not be able to create the access path, and the job would fail.

If your job has failed, read the job log and find the cause of the failure. If you are unable to determine the cause of the problem, ask your instructor/mentor for help.

Part 3

Goals   Examine the data member of your logical file.

Insert new records through the logical file.

Determine where the new records are added in the physical file.

Start at   WRKOBJPDM, your library.

Procedure   Take the PDM options to create a temporary DFU on STULF1.

Enter two new records.

Browse the logical file to see whether you can find the new records.

Display the physical-file member to find the inserted records.

8.24. Press F12 to return to the Work with Objects Using PDM screen. Refresh the screen to make sure the logical database file you just created is in the list.

Look at More options, and select Change using DFU for your newly compiled logical file.

8.25. By taking the PDM option on a file object, you can avoid having to type the STRDFU (Start DFU) command or select the file name for DFU.

8.25.a. When the Work with data . . . DFU screen comes up, what does it prompt you for?

8.25.b. What mode are you in? (**Note:** If you are in entry mode, your logical file is empty. This normally would mean that no physical-file records were selected for the logical file. Either you miscoded the Select entry, or there are no records with local zip codes in your physical file. You need to add records to your physical file or fix your logical-file select so that at least three to four records are selected for the logical file.)

Type in a Social Security number of one of your physical-file records, and then press Enter. (If you don't remember a number, just Page Down).

8.26. Page Down and/or Page Up to browse through the file.

8.26.a. In what order are the records in the file presented?

8.26.b. How many records are in this file compared to the based-on physical file STUPF?

8.26.c. What is the reason for this difference? (Note: If you made all STUPF zip codes "local," there won't be a difference.)

8.27. Go into Entry mode and add two records, one with a local zip code (within the RANGE of your Select) and one without.

8.28. Now return to change mode, and browse through the file again.

8.28.a. Are the records you added there?

Exit DFU, and return to the Work with Objects Using PDM screen.

8.29. Select the Work with option for physical file STUPF. From the Work with screen, choose the Display option.

8.29.a. Are the new records there?

8.29.b. Where in the physical file do they appear?

8.29.c. From your observation of questions 8.28.a and 8.29.a, how would you say the selection operation of the logical file works regarding changes versus additions?

Print the display screen showing the records you just added, and hand it in with your answer sheet.

Additional Lab Exercise

You should attempt this exercise only after you have successfully completed the primary lab exercise above. This exercise assumes an understanding of the material presented in the previous lab steps, as well as of the text of this and earlier chapters.

In this exercise, you build three new physical files, populate them with test data, and then create join and multiple-format logical files over them. You use a temporary DFU program to add data through the multiple-format logical file, and then you run a query to display the join-logical-file data.

Note

This is a fairly long exercise, but you don't need to complete it in one sitting. It is well worth the effort if you are trying to understand physical and logical files and Query for i5/OS.

8.30. Create a member in source file QDDSSRC named CATPF to describe a catalog file. This file will be a simplified version of the information contained in a college catalog, which describes the various courses offered. The file's record-format name is CATPFR, and it contains the fields you see in Table 8.4:

Table 8.4: CATPF Field Descriptions			
Field Name	Type	Length, Decimal Positions	Column Heading
CATNO	Char	6	'Catalog' 'Number'
CATNAM	Char	40	'Course' 'Title'
CATDES	Char	400	'Course' 'Description'
LECHRS	Zoned	1,0	'Lecture' 'Hours'
LABHRS	Zoned	1,0	'Lab' 'Hours'
PREREQ	Char	30	'Prerequisites'

Make CATPF a keyed file with unique keys. The key field is CATNO.

Compile the file, and check your message queue for successful completion. Use the DSPFFD command to ensure that the fields of the compiled file exactly match those shown above. The DSPFFD command output should show that there are six fields and a record length of 478 bytes.

8.31. Use the CPYF (Copy File) command to copy the data from INTROCLASS/CATPF to your file. Change the MBROPT parameter to *ADD, and make sure parameter CRTFILE is set to *NO. If any discrepancy exists between the INTROCLASS library's CATPF record format and that of the file you just created, the CPYF command will fail. If it does fail, you will need to compare the two record formats to find out where you went wrong.

8.32. Create another QDDSSRC member to describe a file of section data. Name the file SECTPF. Section records document an occurrence at a certain place and time of one course being taught that is in the catalog file. For example, catalog number PC101T, General Psychology, may have several sections offered in a semester, each meeting in a specified room of a building at a specified time, and each taught by a certain professor. Our simplified version of the file will be keyed on field SECTNO, with unique key values. The record-format name is SECTPFR, and the record layout is as follows in Table 8.5:

Table 8.5: SECTPF Field Descriptions			
Field Name	Type	Length, Decimal Positions	Column Heading
SECTNO	Zoned	5,0	'Section' 'Number'
INSTID	Zoned	9,0	'Instructor'
CATNO	Char	6	'Catalog' 'Number'
DAYS	Char	5	'Days' 'Met'
STIME	Time	—	'Start' 'Time'
ETIME	Time	—	'End' 'Time'
BLDG	Char	2	'Building'
ROOM	Char	4	'Room'

For the fields STIME and ETIME, code the function TIMFMT (*USA) to get an eight-character date with a.m./p.m. format.

8.33. After you enter and save the DDS for this file, compile it and check for successful completion. The physical file should consist of eight fields with a total record length of 47 bytes.

8.34. A third file will describe a student's enrollment in a section. It will relate a record in your student file, STUPF, to a section of a course being taught. The file's name is ENRLPF, and it is also keyed, with a unique composite key of SECTNO (high order) and SOCSEC (low order). The unique key enforces the constraint that an individual student can enroll in a certain section only once. The record-format name is ENRLPFR, and it contains only two fields (see Table 8.6):

Table 8.6: ENRLPF Field Descriptions			
Field Name	Type	Length, Decimal Positions	Column Heading
SECTNO	Zoned	5,0	'Section' 'Number'
SOCSEC	Zoned	9,0	'Student' 'SSN'

Save the DDS for ENRLPF, and compile it from the Work with Members Using PDM screen. Check for successful completion.

8.35. Run a temporary DFU on your SECTPF file, adding several sections. The section numbers should be easy to remember (e.g., 1, 2, 3). For the instructor ID, use all 9s except for the last four digits (e.g., 999990001, 999990002). Have at least one instructor teaching a couple of different sections. Use catalog numbers from the records copied to your CATPF, or add some new CATPF records to your file if you like. It is important that the catalog numbers you use in your SECTPF file match existing catalog numbers in the CATPF file (yes, Alice, they *are* case sensitive) or the join cannot occur.

8.36. Create a multiple-format logical file that will let you conveniently display and update enrollment records through student records. You could call the file STUENRLMLF. The first record format is STUPFR, from the physical file STUPF. The record format should specify SOCSEC as the only key field. Use the same record-format name as that of the physical file, and include all fields. The second record format is ENRLPFR, from the physical file ENRLPF. The high-order key fields of all record formats must agree, so use SOCSEC as the first (high-order) key field, and use SECTNO as the second (low-order) key field.

Note: This is *not* a joined logical but a logical file with two record formats (refer to Figure 8.40).

Compile the file, and use a temporary DFU program on the new logical file to add from one to several sections for several students in your student file. Use section numbers that you have already added to file SECTPF in step 8.35. Notice that keys cannot be changed when you are using DFU in change mode on a multiple-format logical file. Therefore, if you have already created an ENRLPF record for a student and used a wrong section number, you need to delete it and try again; however, nothing bad will happen if you just leave the record there. If you are entering several sections for the same student, try typing the SOCSEC value only the first time and then using the Dupe key (when using the IBM 5250 emulator, use the Shift+Insert keyboard combination). Doing so will copy the previously entered record's value and store it in the current field. (However, the copied value will not be displayed in the field when you first press Dupe.)

8.37. Before you create a join logical file to pull all this data together in a report, it is important that you understand the file structure of your ever-expanding database. Using the examples in the text, create a Bachman diagram in Microsoft Word similar to Figure 8.26 on page 368. The diagram should show the relationships among the files, identifying their primary keys, the relationship-supporting fields (foreign keys) of each child file, and the type of relationship. Be sure to name each file. When you are satisfied with your diagram, hand in a copy of it to your instructor/mentor.

8.38. Now, create a join logical file named SECTJLF1 that you can use to display or print all sections and the students enrolled in them. Include the section and catalog numbers from file SECTPF; the course name, lecture hours, and lab hours from file CATPF; the Social Security number from file ENRLPF; and the first name, last name, and phone number from file STUPF. ENRLPF supplies the Social Security number (SOCSEC) and functions as a link between files SECTPF and STUPF. Because files SECTPF and STUPF have a many-to-many relationship, there are no fields to directly relate records from these files. Therefore, joining records of SECTPF and STUPF requires going through the ENRLPF file.

The SECTLF1 logical file should look like that in Figure 8.53.

```
5761WDS V6R1M0  080215                    SEU SOURCE LISTING
SOURCE FILE . . . . . . .   CIS001/QDDSSRC
MEMBER  . . . . . . . . .   SECTLF1
SEQNBR*...+... 1 ...+... 2 ...+... 3 ...+... 4 ...+... 5 ...+... 6 ...+... 7 ..
   100     A************************************************************************
   200     A* Join Project, Members and Employees in one Record format
   300     A* using Left Outer Join.
   400     A* Compiled - 04-15-2010                      Programmer - Jim Buck
   500     A************************************************************************
   600     A            R JREC1                       JFILE(SECTPF CATPF ENRLPF +
   700                                                    STUPF)
   800     A            J                             JOIN(1 2)
   900     A                                          JFLD(CATNO CATNO)
  1000     A            J                             JOIN(1 3)
  1100     A                                          JFLD(SECTNO SECTNO)
  1200     A            J                             JOIN(3 4)
  1300     A                                          JFLD(SOCSEC SOCSEC)
  1400     A*
  1500     A              SECTNO                      JREF(1)
  1600     A              CATNO                       JREF(1)
  1700     A              CATNAM
  1800     A              LECHRS
  1900     A              LABHRS
  2000     A              SOCSEC                      JREF(3)
  2100     A              FNAME
  2200     A              LNAME
  2300     A              PHONE
                    * * * * E N D   O F   S O U R C E   * * * *
```

Figure 8.53: DDS for Join Logical File Using Four Physical Files

The JFILE parameter list identifies four files. File SECTPF is listed first, making it the primary file. This file is joined to both CATPF (line 800) and ENRLPF (line 1000).

ENRLPF is then joined to STUPF (line 1200) to extract student name and phone number for each enrollment record. The fields to be included in the join record are listed starting on line 1500. Remember that if a field name is not unique, you must qualify it using the JREF keyword.

After you enter the source DDS, compile your file and check to make sure it was a clean compile.

8.39. Last, create a Query for i5/OS report like the one in Figure 8.54.

```
                              Current Student Enrollment by Section Number
                         QUERY NAME . . . . .  SECTJQRY
                         LIBRARY NAME . . . . . CIS001
                         FILE         LIBRARY       MEMBER        FORMAT
                         SECTLF1      CIS001        SECTLF1       JREC1
                         DATE . . . . . . . .  01/06/11
                         TIME . . . . . . . .  15:09:59
                                      Final Lab Chapter 8
01/06/11  15:09:59                        Current Student Enrollment by Section Number                            PAGE   1
          Sect   Catalog  Catalog Name              Lect Lab  CHI    Social      Last       First      Phone
          Nbr    Nbr                                 Hrs  Hrs        Security    Name       Name       Nbr
          14050  DG138U   Introduction to IBM i Con   2   2   3.00  87-55-9012  Eschenburg  Brian      517-293-0849
                                                                    866-42-6400  Lepard     Deborah    616-485-7129
                                                                    349-04-9381  Newburry   Roger      616-488-1935
                                                                    223-08-4359  Rupert     Leslie     616-389-2834
                                                                    154-48-8932  Smith      Patricia   313-847-3283
Section Number Total 14050
COUNT      5
          14051  DG132U   DB2 Database Management     3   2   3.50  269-96-8069  Stufflebeam Pamela    414-839-2447
                                                                    276-68-1868  Suzuki     Yoshie     616-227-4973
                                                                    369-92-0174  Whitte     Andrea     616-498-5925
Section Number Total 14051
COUNT      3
          14052  PC230T   Abnormal Psychology         3   0   1.50  339-58-8603  Armine     Yvonne     616-283-4993
                                                                    365-64-6998  Hunter     James      515-283-9422
                                                                    367-58-7174  Taplin     Malissa    616-224-1654
                                                                    282-36-1745  Zaremba    Eileen     616-657-2835
                                                                    359-68-8909  Zimmer     Matthew    219-483-5568
Section Number Total 14052
COUNT      5
          14053  AR220T   Advanced Wheel-throwing T   0   6   6.00  900-10-8702  Al-sharif  Amhad      616-366-8198
                                                                    368-94-0073  Beebe      Dennis     616-388-2511
Section Number Total 14053
COUNT      2
Total Students Enrolled
COUNT     15
* * * E N D  O F  R E P O R T * * *
```

Figure 8.54: Query for i5/OS Report from SECTJQRY Inner Join Logical File, with Calculated Field and Control Breaks

Name the query SECTJQRY. This report lists all students enrolled in each section. The sort sequence is student last name within section. Because the join logical file to be used by the query is an inner join, sections must have a valid catalog number and at least one valid student enrolled in ENRLPF to be listed. The columns in Figure 8.54 have been narrowed to fit the report on the book page.

CHI is a calculated field (circled in Figure 8.54). Select the Define result fields option on the Define the Query screen, and read the Help information. You must give the new field a name (CHI), and provide an arithmetic expression to define the calculation. CHI is equal to one-half lab hours plus lecture hours.

Don't forget to select the fields for output. Use all the fields from file SECTPF together (SECTNO, CATNO, CATNAM, CHI, LECHRS, and LABHRS) as break-level 1 control fields. When all primary-file fields are defined as the same (level 1) control field, group indication will be used automatically for printed reports.

If you have created the necessary files and added data records but your report comes out empty, it is probably because one or more of the join relationships failed. Remember that for an inner join result record to be written, matching records must exist in *all* files. Check the relationship-supporting field values of each join pair in your logical file, and make sure there are matching records.

When you are satisfied with your report, print a copy of it to hand in to your instructor/mentor.

CHAPTER 9

Additional Database Facilities

Overview

Despite the best planning and design methodology, record formats of existing database files may require modification at some point (i.e., fields may need to be changed or added). In this chapter, we look at ways to accommodate these needs without destroying the data already in the file that needs to be changed. We use Programming Development Manager (PDM) options and CL commands to accomplish these tasks. We also introduce the idea of object authorization and see how library and object authorities are used to limit access to database files. In addition, we briefly discuss group profiles and authorization lists.

Objectives

Students will be able to

- Distinguish between the CRTDUPOBJ (Create Duplicate Object) and CPYF (Copy File) commands and select the appropriate command for a specific situation
- Use the RNMOBJ (Rename Object) command to change the name of an object
- Change and compile Data Description Specifications (DDS) for a database source physical file
- Use the necessary parameters of the CPYF command to accomplish field mapping in a copy operation
- Understand the capability of the CHGPF (Change Physical File) command and use it to change an existing physical file
- Use the EDTOBJAUT (Edit Object Authority) command to observe and change individual and public authority to libraries and objects

Creating a File (Review)

As we begin this chapter, take a moment to review the process of creating a database file. Computer programs and file descriptions are written in a language, called a *source language*, that has its own syntax and vocabulary. Programming languages include C, COBOL, and RPG; data description languages include DDS and Structured Query Language (SQL). DDS is always compiled from source statements, but you can run SQL directly from a command line—in which case it is more similar to an interpreted language such as Basic.

Usually, the programmer creates a separate source physical file to hold and organize source members for each language. A single source member may contain all the source code for a single COBOL or RPG program, or all the DDS source statements to describe a single file.

For example, a programmer's library might contain several different source physical files: one named QCBLSRC for COBOL source members, one named QDDSSRC for DDS source members, and one named QRPGLESRC for RPG ILE source members. These source physical files are created using the **CRTSRCPF** (Create Source Physical File) command, and each source file can hold any number of members. The DDS source physical file, QDDSSRC, might contain the members you see in Figure 9.1.

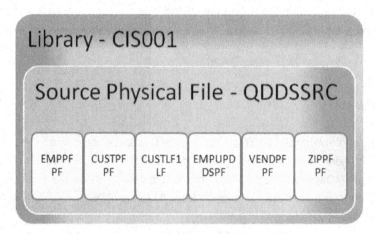

Figure 9.1: Conceptual Content of Source Physical File CIS001/QDDSSRC—Each Member Is a "Recipe" for a Certain File

Each of these members would contain the necessary DDS to externally describe a physical or logical database file, a printer file, or a display file, as indicated.

You could think of a source physical file as a recipe box and each member as one or more recipe cards that contain the list of ingredients and instructions for mixing and baking some delectable delight, such as banana bread, muffins, or rhubarb crumb pie (Figure 9.2).

Figure 9.2: Like a Recipe Box Containing Instructions (Recipe Cards) for Creating Goodies, a Source Physical File Contains Instructions (Members) for Creating File Objects

Like a source physical file, which may contain a few or many members, the recipe box may contain only a few or a large number of recipes. In addition, just as we clearly realize the distinction between the recipe for the rhubarb crumb pie and the pie itself, we understand that the source DDS for the employee master file, EMPPF, is not the actual file but merely the instructions for creating the file.

Just as we keep the recipes in a box, although for slightly different reasons, we keep the source members in their source physical file even after the database or display file is created. The recipe allows us, for instance, to create another pie after the current pie has disappeared. The source-file member, in contrast, undergoes a considerably more mundane transformation into a file object. Nevertheless, it is a transformation we may need to repeat, and keeping the source member in its source physical file makes that possible. The creation of the file object usually occurs via option 14 from the Work with Members Using PDM screen, as Figure 9.3 illustrates.

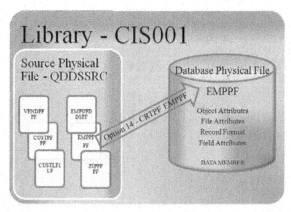

Figure 9.3: Results of Taking the Defaults for Option 14 on Source Member EMPPF from the Work with Members Using PDM Screen

Once the database physical file is created, the system maintains no physical link between it and its DDS source-member description. However, it is useful to keep the source member, whether it is a program or a file description, so that we can correct errors or make changes to and recompile it when necessary.

When we change the source code of a program, we can normally recompile with little concern, but recompiling the source description of a database physical file is a different story. To recompile the changed DDS source for a physical file using the same name (i.e., executing the **CRTPF**, or Create Physical File, command on the source member), we must first delete the previous file object and all its data. If data records have been added to the physical file's data member, we must save the data before we recompile the changed source description.

Changing the Source DDS

For this example we will use the physical file EMPPF, which we created in an earlier chapter, to demonstrate how to modify DDS. Suppose we need to add a work phone-number field (WORKPHONE) to the file. Figure 9.4 shows the SEU Edit screen for the modified EMPPF file—field WORKPHONE has been inserted after field DEPT.

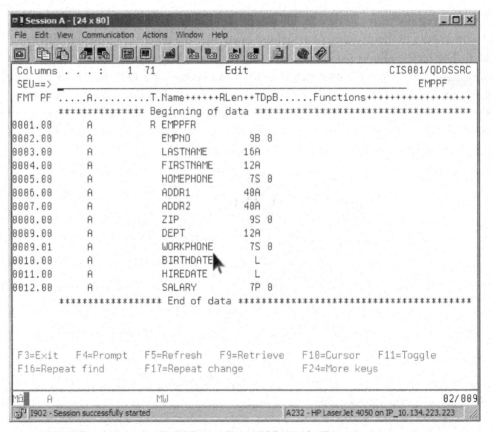

Figure 9.4: SEU Edit Screen for EMPPF with Field WORKPHONE Inserted

However, this change to the source member will have no effect on the existing *FILE object, EMPPF, until we recompile the DDS source.

After we exit SEU and save the changed member, the next step is to review the defaults assigned by PDM when we invoke the CRTPF command via option 14 from the Work with Members Using PDM screen. Figure 9.5 shows the CRTPF command-prompt screen. You reach this screen by typing 14 in the option field for physical file EMPPF, and then prompting (F4).

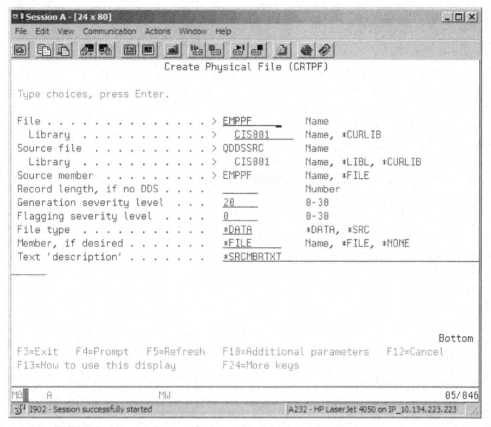

Figure 9.5: CRTPF Command-Prompt Screen with Additional Parameters

Preserving the Existing Data

The File and Library parameters specify the name of the new file and the library in which it will be stored when the CRTPF command is executed. Notice that, initially, the File name is the same as the Source member name. If we were to run the command as is, the Confirm Compile of Member screen (Figure 9.6) would appear, unless the PDM session defaults had been changed from N to Y for the *Replace object* option.

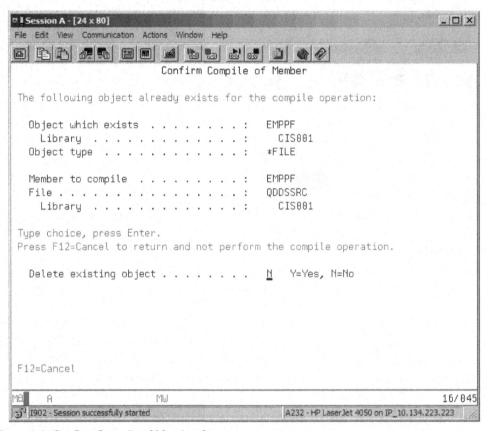

Figure 9.6: Confirm Compile of Member Screen

The Confirm Compile of Member screen should always serve as a warning—the system is telling us that if we override the default response (N) for the Delete existing object parameter, we will lose the existing object. If the object was a program still being tested and we simply needed to recompile the most recent version, we would not hesitate to type Y and press Enter. In this case, the object that would be deleted is a data file, and we should proceed with caution! Because we already have data in physical-file object EMPPF that we do not want to lose, we would cancel the CRTPF command for now by pressing F12.

We might consider returning to the CRTPF command-prompt screen (Figure 9.5) and changing the File name parameter value to a name other than EMPPF so that the existing file object would not be deleted when the CRTPF command is executed. However, existing programs, queries, logical files, and display files expect to find their data in a file named EMPPF. If we changed the name of the modified physical file to something other than EMPPF, we would have to change all references in programs, queries, and logical files, as well. Moreover, after performing significant maintenance on the source members, we would have to recompile all of them. Therefore, creating the file under a different file name is probably not a workable solution.

We should analyze the problem, as is illustrated in Figure 9.7, and consider an alternative.

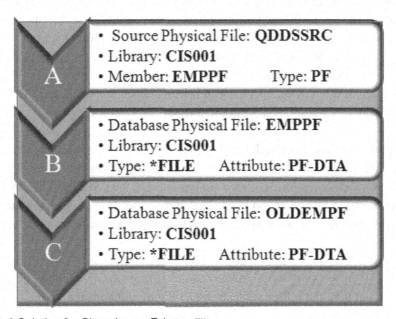

Figure 9.7: A Solution for Changing an Existing File

A. The changed DDS source member for file EMPPF needs to be recompiled (option 14—CRTPF) because the field WORKPHONE has been added.

B. There is already a *FILE object, EMPPF, which contains data that would be destroyed, and the data would be lost.

C. The solution is to *temporarily* rename (option 7—*Rename*) the *FILE object that contains the data to a different, unique name (e.g., OLDEMPPF), and then recompile the modified DDS source for the new file object using the original name.

After recompiling the changed file, we can copy the data from the (old) renamed file back into the changed (new) file's record format.

Renaming the File

Renaming the file object is an efficient, fast way to get rid of the original file name without getting rid of the data. If we were to rename file EMPPF to OLDEMPPF, for example, the data would still be there under the different file name, OLDEMPPF. We could then make the necessary changes to the original file's (EMPPF's) source DDS and recompile the changed source member, creating a new file with the original name. Finally, we could copy the old data from OLDEMPPF into the new recompiled file object.

The rename operation changes pointers—the pointer in the library that contains the old object will be changed to recognize the different name, but it still points to the same object. In addition, any logical files that reference the previous physical-file name as the based-on file would automatically be changed to point to the new name; but programs, queries, Data File Utility (DFU) programs, and so on would not be changed automatically to reference the new file name. Because the file will be renamed only temporarily, it will not be necessary to change the file references in objects such as programs, queries, and DFUs. It will be necessary to perform the rename operation and subsequent steps to change the physical file when the file is not being used by a program, query, or logical file.

In this example, we will step through the process for renaming our file. First, we must look at any logical files built over physical file EMPPF. When you know the physical-file name and want to find out which logical files, if any, are based on it, the **DSPDBR** (Display Database Relations) command is just what you need. The command's only required parameter is the name of the physical file you want to check on. If we run the command

DSPDBR EMPPF

from the command line, the information shown in Figure 9.8 appears.

```
I Session A - [24 x 80]                                                    _ □ X
File   Edit   View   Communication   Actions   Window   Help
┌──┐┌──┐┌──┐┌──┐┌──┐┌──┐┌──┐┌──┐┌──┐┌──┐┌──┐┌──┐┌──┐┌──┐
└──┘└──┘└──┘└──┘└──┘└──┘└──┘└──┘└──┘└──┘└──┘└──┘└──┘└──┘
                        Display Spooled File
File . . . . . . :   QPDSPDBR                       Page/Line   1/7
Control . . . . .    _____                        Columns    1 - 78
Find . . . . . .     _____
*...+....1....+....2....+....3....+....4....+....5....+....6....+....7....+...
   Output . . . . . . . . . . . . . . . . . . . : OUTPUT      *
 Specifications
   Type of file . . . . . . . . . . . . . . . :         Physical
   File . . . . . . . . . . . . . . . . . . . :         EMPPF
     Library . . . . . . . . . . . . . . . . . :        CIS001
     Member . . . . . . . . . . . . . . . . . :         *NONE
     Record format . . . . . . . . . . . . . . :        *NONE
     Number of dependent files . . . . . . . . :            6
 Files Dependent On Specified File
   Dependent File         Library      Dependency    JREF    Constraint
     EMPZIPLF1            CIS001        Data           1
     EMPZIPLF1A           CIS001        Data           1
     EMPZIPLF2            CIS001        Data           1
     JOINME               CIS001        Data           3
     JOINMEO              CIS001        Data           3
     EMPNAMKLF            CIS001        Data
                                                                   Bottom
 F3=Exit    F12=Cancel    F19=Left    F20=Right    F24=More keys

MA    A                      MW                                        03/022
I902 - Session successfully started          A232 - HP LaserJet 4050 on IP_10.134.223.223
```

Figure 9.8: DSPDBR Output for File EMPPF

In addition to displaying the number of dependent files, the command output lists each of them. Before you decide to change a physical-file record format, you should use this information to examine the logical files to determine what effect, if any, such changes might have on the logical files and their applications.

Looking at database relations from the other direction, you might need to determine which physical file a particular logical file is based on. An easy way to find out is to use the *Display* option (5) from the Work with Objects Using PDM screen. Taken on a *FILE object, this option invokes the **DSPFD** (Display File Description) command. If you took option 5 on the simple logical file EMPNAMKLF (the keyed-sequence access path on last name and first name of file EMPPF), you would see the information several screens down in Figure 9.9.

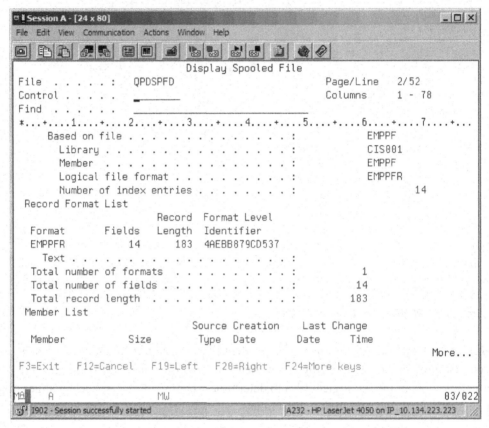

Figure 9.9: Display File Description: Based-On File Information for EMPNAMKLF

Tip
A quick way to locate a key word or phrase is to type it in the Find field at the top of a Display Spooled File screen, and then press F16.

As Figure 9.9 shows, the based-on physical file is identified by the Based on file information. As you will see, this reference to the physical file changes when we rename the based-on physical file.

We can rename the file using option 7 from the Work with Objects Using PDM screen. This option takes us to the Rename Objects screen (Figure 9.10).

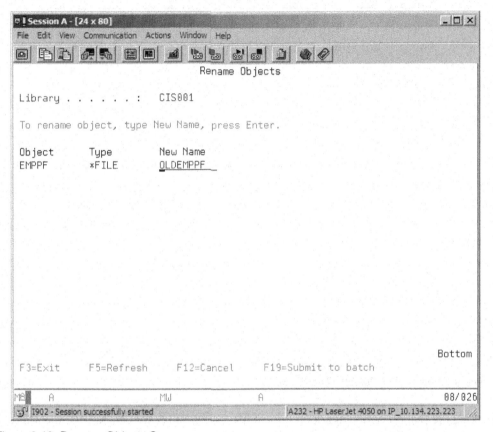

Figure 9.10: Rename Objects Screen

Keep in mind that we are renaming the data-file object itself, not the source member. The New Name for the physical file, OLDEMPPF, has already been entered in our example screen.

After you press Enter, the Work with Objects Using PDM screen will look like the one in Figure 9.11. A message at the bottom of the screen verifies that the rename operation worked.

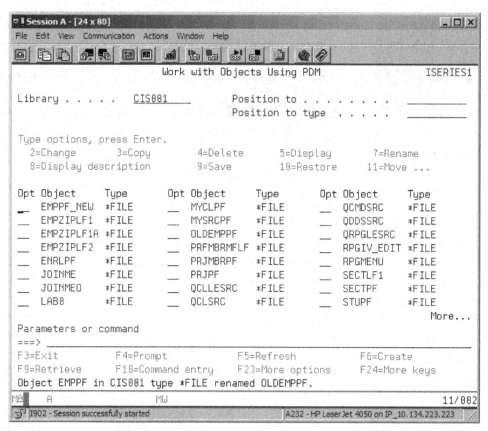

Figure 9.11: Work with Objects Using PDM, CIS001

By taking the Display option again on logical file EMPNAMKLF, we can see that the reference to the physical file has been changed. The logical file now points to the newly renamed file OLDEMPPF, as Figure 9.12 shows (note the arrow).

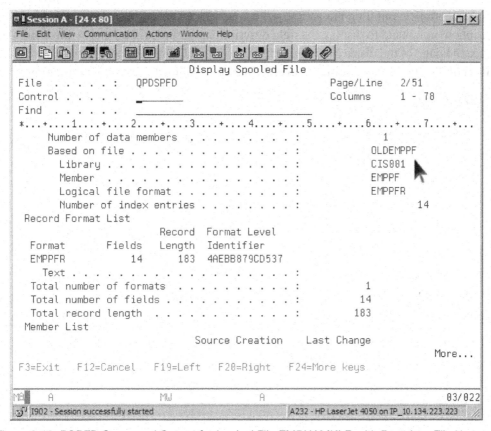

Figure 9.12: DSPFD Command Output for Logical File EMPNAMKLF, with Based-on File Name Changed

If we tried to run a query built for file EMPPF, however, we would receive the error message *"Input file EMPPF in CIS001 not found"* because the query would still point to the original file name. This fact supports our earlier observation: Logical-file references to an underlying physical file are changed automatically when the physical file is renamed; other file references, such as for programs, queries, or DFUs, aren't changed.

Now that we have renamed our physical file, we can return to the Work with Members Using PDM screen and compile the changed DDS source for file EMPPF. When we enter option 14 to create file EMPPF this time, the Confirm Compile of Member warning screen doesn't appear because we no longer have an EMPPF object in our library.

After successfully compiling the source, we can use the **DSPFFD** (Display File Field Description) command to display the field descriptions for the revised EMPPF physical file. The second page of the display (Figure 9.13) shows the changed record format with the addition of the new field, positioned several lines down in the Field-level information.

```
◰▮ Session A - [24 x 80]                                              _ □ ×
 File   Edit   View   Communication   Actions   Window   Help
 ▣ ▣ ▣ ▣ ▣ ▣ ▣ ▣ ▣ ▣ ▣ ▣ ▣ ◈ ◈
                       Display Spooled File
 File . . . . . :   QPDSPFFD                        Page/Line   1/28
 Control . . . . .    +1                            Columns     1 - 78
 Find . . . . . .    _____
 *...+....1....+....2....+....3....+....4....+....5....+....6....+....7....+...
    Field      Type       Length  Length  Position       Usage   Heading
    EMPNO      BINARY       9  0      4        1          Both    EMPNO
    LASTNAME   CHAR        16     16           5          Both    LASTNAME
       Coded Character Set Identifier  . . . . . :    37
    FIRSTNAME  CHAR        12     12          21          Both    FIRSTNAME
       Coded Character Set Identifier  . . . . . :    37
    HOMEPHONE  ZONED        7  0      7       33          Both    HOMEPHONE
    ADDR1      CHAR        40     40          40          Both    ADDR1
       Coded Character Set Identifier  . . . . . :    37
    ADDR2      CHAR        40     40          80          Both    ADDR2
       Coded Character Set Identifier  . . . . . :    37
    ZIP        ZONED        9  0      9      120          Both    ZIP
    DEPT       CHAR        12     12         129          Both    DEPT
       Coded Character Set Identifier  . . . . . :    37
    WORKPHONE  ZONED        7  0      7      141          Both    WORKPHONE
    BIRTHDATE  DATE        10     10         148          Both    BIRTHDATE
                                                                     More...
  F3=Exit   F12=Cancel   F19=Left   F20=Right   F24=More keys

 MA    A              MW                                           03/022
 I902 - Session successfully started        A232 - HP LaserJet 4050 on IP_10.134.223.223
```

Figure 9.13: DSPFFD Command Output Showing New WORKPHONE Field in Record

The file has been created successfully. The next step is to copy the existing data from the old file into the new file.

Comparing the record format of the new file (Figure 9.13) with that of the old file verifies what we already know: The record formats are different, and the field positions after the DEPT field are not the same. Thus, we cannot simply move a whole data record left to right from the old record format into the new file because field boundaries would be violated; we would end up with zoned-decimal data in date-format fields and date data in packed-decimal fields—in other words, our data would be corrupted. (In fact, unless you specifically overrode its warning, the system would prevent you from making such a mistake.)

The Copy File Command

The **CPYF** (Copy File) command, however, provides just what we need to get our existing data into the changed record format of the new file. CPYF is a powerful command that allows several significant variations on the copy process. These variations give the CPYF command flexibility that the **CRTDUPOBJ** (Create Duplicate Object) command, which simply creates a clone of an existing object, does not have. You can invoke the CRTDUPOBJ and CPYF commands by taking Work with Objects Using PDM options on the file to be copied (the From file). Option 3 invokes the CRTDUPOBJ command, and option 15 invokes the CPYF command.

For our example, we will take PDM option 15 on the file that contains the data, OLDEMPPF, and prompt. If you were not using Work with Objects Using PDM, you could simply type CPYF on any command line and prompt.

Figure 9.14 shows the first screen of the CPYF command prompt (with additional parameters).

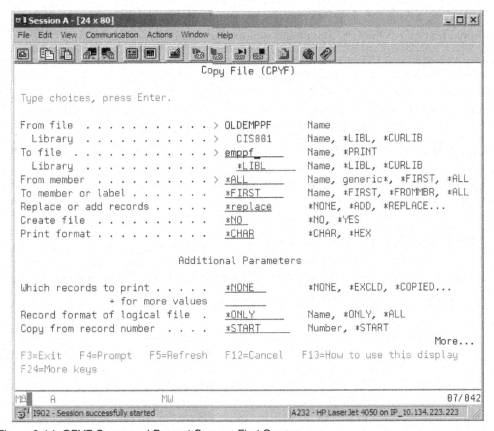

Figure 9.14: CPYF Command Prompt Screen, First Screen

The required parameters are From file and To file. In our example, the From file—which PDM has filled in for us—is OLDEMPPF (the original physical file holding the data). The To file should be EMPPF (the newly compiled file with the added field). If we were simply creating an exact, duplicate of an existing file, instead of copying data into an existing file, that is all we would need. In fact, the new To file file would not even need to exist—the CPYF command would create the file for us if we changed the Create file parameter value to *YES. In such a case, CPYF functions like the CRTDUPOBJ command. Nevertheless, we have already compiled the new file with an additional field, so we do not want CPYF to create a clone of the From file for us. In this case, because the To file already exists, we need to tell the command whether copied records are to replace or be added to the existing file. Because we know that our newly compiled file does not contain data, we can specify a Replace or add records value of *ADD to avoid the unnecessary clearing of the To file member. We would also use *ADD when we want to extend an existing file by adding data from another file. In a situation in which bad data already exists in the To file member, we could specify *REPLACE to clear the data so that the member would be empty before the From file data is copied in.

Additional features of the CPYF command include the capability to

- Print the copied records in character or hexadecimal format
- Specify a range of relative record numbers of the From file to be copied to the To file (or printed)
- Specify which record format of a multiple-format logical file to copy
- Specify, for a file ordered in key sequence, the beginning and ending key values to be included in the new file
- Select records to be copied by specifying a relational test on one or more fields (e.g., DEPT *EQ 'Sales')
- Tell the copy function to move data field-by-field from the From file record to the To file record with fields of the same name

It is this last feature that we really need now, given the different formats of the From file and To file records of our original and modified files.

Record-Format Field Mapping

Figure 9.15 shows the CPYF command-prompt screen that includes the Record format field mapping parameter. (This is the fifth screen of parameters.)

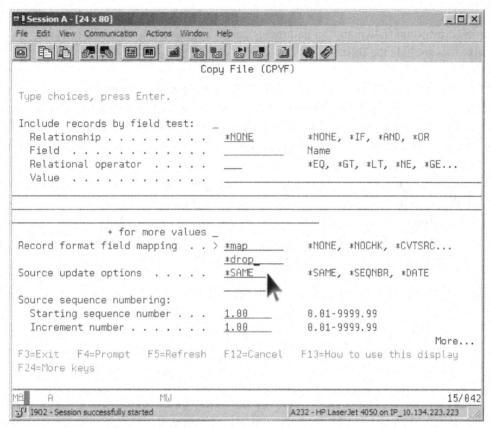

Figure 9.15: CPYF Record Format Field Mapping

The parameter's default value is *NONE, but this value is valid for copying database files only when the From file and the To file have identical record formats. For two record formats to be identical, they both must have

- The same record length and number of fields
- Corresponding fields with the same names and in the same order
- The same field length and data type for each pair of corresponding fields

In our case, the files do not have identical record formats, so we must provide a value: *MAP. The ***MAP** parameter (note the arrow) tells the CPYF command that it should copy data in a From file field to a To file field of the same name—a process called **field mapping**. Any fields in the To file record format—such as our newly added field WORKPHONE—that do not exist in the From file record format will be set to default values (i.e., spaces for alphanumeric fields and zeros for numeric fields). In a separate step, and after the CPYF command is completed, we need to replace these default values with actual data using a temporary DFU data-entry program or some other means.

Other Record format field mapping parameter values commonly used when copying database files include the following:

- ***NOCHK** (no check), for record formats whose field names are different but whose field boundaries align and whose data class is not in conflict. We also use this value when we are copying data from a program-described file with no defined fields to an externally described file whose named fields coincide exactly with the data contained in the From file member.
- ***DROP** (to omit, or drop, certain fields), which must be used with *MAP if not all fields in the From file member will have corresponding named fields in the To file member. For example, you might be copying data from an existing file but need only certain fields in the new file's record format. In such a case, the unnecessary fields in the From file record format would have to be dropped.

Figure 9.16 illustrates the operation of a CPYF command with record-format field mapping.

CPYF FROMFILE(OLDEMPPF) TOFILE(EMPPF) +
MBROPT(*REPLACE) FMTOPT(*MAP *DROP)

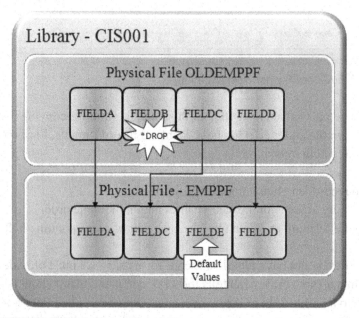

Figure 9.16: CPYF with Record-Format Field Mapping

For each record in OLDEMPPF, the copy operation creates a new record in EMPPF by copying the data in FIELDA to the new FIELDA, in FIELDC to the new FIELDC (in a different location in the record format), and in FIELDD to FIELDD. The EMPPF FIELDE, which does not correspond to any OLDEMPPF field, is set to default values. The OLDEMPPF FIELDB, which is not included in the new record format, is dropped.

For our example, we would run the CPYF command with the parameter values you see in Table 9.1.

Table 9.1: Parameters Used with the CPYF Command	
Parameter	Value
From file	OLDEMPPF
To file	EMPPF
Replace or add records	*REPLACE
Record format field mapping	*MAP *DROP

When the CPYF command is completed successfully, it tells us how many records were copied from the file.

Tip

Online Help information is available to explain these and other CPYF command parameters. And the multivolume IBM manual *CL Reference* (SC41-5722) is the exhaustive reference when you need detailed information about CPYF—or any other CL command, for that matter.

Verifying the Copy Operation

We can see what the data looks like in the new version of physical file EMPPF by entering the **DSPPFM** (Display Physical File Member) command for physical file EMPPF on a command line. Figure 9.17 shows the output of DSPPFM for the new EMPPF, windowed to position 120.

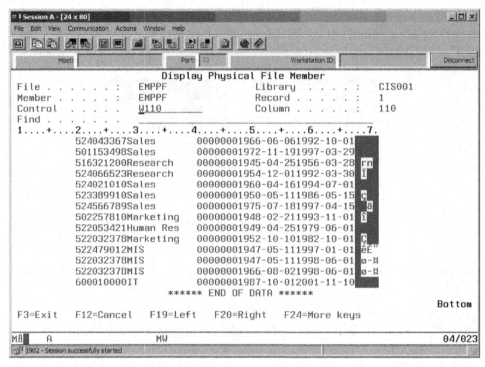

Figure 9.17: Display Physical File Member Screen—New EMPPF, Windowed to Position 120

You can see the zip-code zoned-decimal data in the leftmost column, followed by the alphanumeric department-field data. Starting in position 141 is the new WORKPHONE field, with all records set to default zeros because there was nothing to copy in from the From file.

You can get an easier-to-read version of the new EMPPF data by using the **RUNQRY** (Run Query) command on the file. This command lets you name an existing Query for i5/OS query definition or a file. If you do not have an appropriate query definition and just want a default report to see the file data, you simply name the file and let Query for i5/OS create the report.

To create a default report on any file (we'll use EMPPF), you could enter

RUNQRY QRY(*NONE) QRYFILE((EMPPF))

or positionally,

RUNQRY *N EMPPF

on any command line. The output is formatted and uses column headers. In addition,
packed-decimal and binary numbers are converted to display format, making such data
comprehensible (as opposed to the DSPPFM command, which performs no data conversion).
Figure 9.18 shows the output of the above RUNQRY command, with the screen split to show
the new field.

```
Session A - [24 x 80]                                                    _ □ ×
File  Edit  View  Communication  Actions  Window  Help

                                Display Report
                                      Report width . . . . . :        216
    Position to line  . . . . .  _____     Shift to column  . . . . . .    _____
    Line   ....+....1....+....2...   ....+...18....+...19....+...20....+...21....+.
                    EMPNO    LASTNAME   WORKPHONE    BIRTHDATE   HIREDATE      SALARY
    000001  111,110,001  Slick              0   1966-06-06  1992-10-01    28,000
    000002  111,110,002  Fendor             0   1972-11-19  1997-03-29    33,150
    000003  111,110,003  Einstein           0   1945-04-25  1956-03-28   299,950
    000004  111,110,004  Takahashi          0   1954-12-01  1992-03-30    75,000
    000005  111,110,005  Rachanoff          0   1960-04-16  1994-07-01    32,000
    000006  111,110,006  Kartblanc          0   1950-05-11  1986-05-15    48,250
    000007  111,110,007  Badman             0   1975-07-18  1997-04-15    22,500
    000008  111,110,008  Gootch             0   1948-02-21  1993-11-01    56,100
    000009  111,110,009  Hunn               0   1949-04-25  1979-06-01   135,000
    000010  111,110,010  Disney             0   1952-10-10  1982-10-01   168,300
    000011  111,110,011  Zanzibar           0   1947-05-11  1997-01-01    52,717
    000012  111,110,012  Stonehart          0   1947-05-11  1998-06-01    70,609
    000013  111,110,013  Deerfield          0   1966-08-02  1998-06-01    70,609
    000014  234,785,689  Yousuf             0   1987-10-01  2001-11-10   900,000
    ******  ********  End of report   ********

                                                                         Bottom
    F3=Exit      F12=Cancel       F19=Left      F20=Right      F21=No split
    Last column of report.
MA    A                    MW                                            03/032
    I902 - Session successfully started          A232 - HP LaserJet 4050 on IP_10.134.223.223
```

Figure 9.18: RUNQRY Command Output Using New Version of EMPPF

Now, we could use PDM's *Change using DFU* option (18) on the physical file to update
each record with the proper information for work phone.

Recompiling Programs and Queries That Use a Changed Physical File

Once you have created a new version of a physical file (in this case, EMPPF), you need to recompile any programs or query definitions that directly refer to the physical file. The system uses a safety feature called **level checking** to ensure that when a program or query opens a file, the file's current record format agrees with the version that was stored in the program or query when it was created. If the record format does not agree—and in the case of EMPPF it would not—the system issues a level-check error to call attention to the discrepancy. A level check is generated at the time a program or query tries to use the changed file and can be overridden by executing the **OVRDBF** (Override with Database File) command. To run the query EMPSALQ1 without recompiling and without a level check, for example, you would execute the command

```
OVRDBF  FILE(EMPPF) LVLCHK(*NO)
```

Although you can override level checks, it is best to recompile the query definition or program. When changes to a file have no effect on a related query or program, simply recompiling the query or program without change eliminates the level check. However, if the new file was created because of a need to add fields to the old file, you might want the program or query to use those new fields. This would require some change to the program or query and subsequent recompilation, thereby eliminating the level-check problem.

For example, in Chapter 7 we created a join Query for i5/OS query using the employee file EMPPF and the zip-code file ZIPPF. Now that we have changed EMPPF, the next time we try to run that query without using OVRDBF, a level check will result. The message would say *"Level for file EMPPF in CIS001 does not match query (I C)."* The system would expect a reply of either I to ignore the warning and try to continue, or C to cancel the request (to run the query). In this case, because the fields used in the join were not deleted or changed in the new file, entering I and running the query would produce correct output. But if we did not want to include the new fields in the query, and we wanted to avoid a level check in the future, we could simply take option 2 on the query from the Work with Queries screen and immediately exit (with the *Save definition* option set to Y). This action would cause the query to be recompiled, eliminating the level check.

Dealing with Based-On Logical Files

You might imagine that existing logical files built over the original EMPPF physical file will still function properly because none of their fields have been eliminated. To some extent, you would be right. However, because we renamed EMPFF to OLDEMPPF, those logical files' based-on pointers were changed to OLDEMPPF and still point to OLDEMPPF.

Remember that a logical file's based-on physical file is first identified in its PFILE or JFILE record-level keyword. When we renamed physical file EMPPF to OLDEMPPF, the pointers in all logical-file objects based on EMPPF were changed so that they reference the same file by its new name, OLDEMPPF. Even though we re-created file EMPPF, the logical-file references were not changed back again. Thus, if we wanted to delete file OLDEMPPF, even though we had all object authority to the file, we could not do so. The system will not let us delete any physical file that still has a logical file based on it. If the physical file was deleted, the logical file would be cut off from its data source—an unacceptable condition in the IBM i OS. Therefore, we must first change the logical-file pointers so they reference the new file before we can delete the old file. The source DDS for the logical files still names the original file (EMPPF) in the PFILE or JFILE keyword value. The easiest way to reconnect the logical files to the new EMPPF is to recompile them.

To be sure you understand the need to recompile the logical files, let us examine the DSPDBR command output for file OLDEMPPF. Figure 9.19 shows partial output from this command.

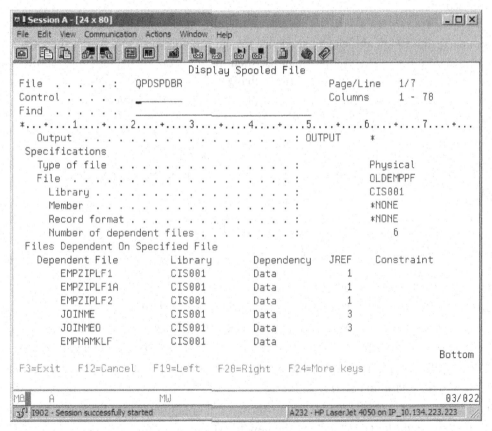

Figure 9.19: DSPDBR Command Output for File OLDEMPPF Before Recompiling Logical Files

As you can see, all the logical files originally based on EMPPF are now dependent on OLDEMPPF, so they all need to be recompiled to base them once again on EMPPF.

Those logical files naming the physical-file record format (EMPPFR) and not naming individual fields will automatically pick up the new field WORKPHONE when they are recompiled. This situation would cause a problem for any non-SQL application using the files (something we address shortly).

At the same time, if the logical file projected only certain fields to its record format by naming them individually, any new physical-file field would not be added to the logical file's record format automatically, thus keeping the same file-level ID and avoiding a level-check error when an application program or query opens the file. If you wanted to include a new field, you would need to edit the logical file's source code, adding a field-name entry that identifies the new field to the DDS before the recompile. The new field would change the record format of the logical file so that programs and queries using it would need to be recompiled.

In summary, those logical files whose record format remains unchanged after they are recompiled do not require programs that use them to be recompiled. But a logical file that, after being recompiled, will include new or changed fields from its based-on physical file will have a different record format; thus programs using this logical file need to be recompiled to avoid level checks.

Once we have recompiled the logical files, the DSPDBR command output for OLDEMPPF should show no remaining dependent logical files. At that point, we can delete file OLDEMPPF.

The following list summarizes the steps we have described for changing the record format of a physical file without losing existing data:

1. Rename the existing physical-file object. This step changes file references in all based-on logical-file objects. (EMPPF becomes OLDEMPPF.)
2. Add new fields (and change existing field lengths, if necessary) in the source DDS of the original physical file. (Source member EMPPF in QDDSSRC is changed.)
3. Compile the modified source member, creating a new (empty) file object. (New EMPPF now exists with no data.)
4. Use the CPYF command with record-format field mapping (*MAP) to copy data from the renamed file (OLDEMPPF) to the new file (EMPPF).
5. Change the DDS of based-on logical files where needed to recognize new fields; recompile logical files.

6. Recompile all programs and queries that use the physical file, and any programs and queries that use changed logical files.

As you can see, it is not difficult to modify an existing database file if you take proper precautions. (One such precaution for production files would be to create a duplicate object in a secure library before you do anything else.) Then, by using PDM options and the powerful CPYF command, you can save data with no danger by renaming the physical file and then copying the data into a new, changed file.

As you work through the lab at the end of this chapter, you gain experience and confidence with PDM and various CL commands.

Using CHGPF to Modify a Physical File

Current releases of IBM i support an enhanced version of the **CHGPF** (Change Physical File) command that performs many of the functions we discussed above for changing the record format of a file while keeping the data intact. Originally, the CHGPF command was used to change certain file information from the way it was set at compile time. Values that could (and still can) be changed include maximum number of members, access path maintenance, file size, length of time a program waits for a record, whether deleted record space is reused, and whether record-format level checking is done.

Some powerful new parameters have been added that now permit an existing file that contains data to be rebuilt with new fields in only two steps. Renaming the current physical file is unnecessary, so the first step using the CHGPF command is to change the existing source DDS, adding the new fields or changing existing field attributes if necessary. The CHGPF command restores data by field mapping, just as the CPYF command with FMTOPT(*MAP) does; so, of course, one field attribute you would *not* want to change is Field name.

After changing the source DDS, you are ready to run the CHGPF command. Figure 9.20 shows the first screen of the CHGPF command prompt with additional parameters.

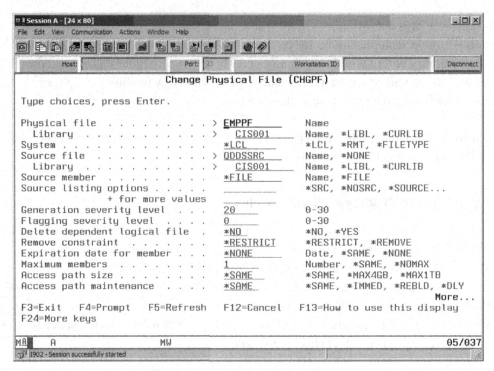

Figure 9.20: Change Physical File Command-Prompt Screen Showing Additional Parameters

The only required parameter is the Physical file name; but for our purposes, we must also specify the Source file parameter. The default value for this parameter is *NONE; by giving it another value, you are telling the CHGPF command not only that you are rebuilding the file, but also where to find the changed DDS to use as a blueprint.

In Figure 9.20, we are telling the CHGPF command to use the DDS in source file QDDSSRC in library CIS001. The Source member parameter defaults to *FILE; and as long as the member containing the source code has the same name as the physical file (this should normally be the case), there is no need to change it.

Using CHGPF has several advantages over the multistep process we described in previous sections; for example, there is no need

- To rename the old file
- To track down and recompile logical files just to redirect their based-on pointers
- To use the CPYF command—the CHGPF command builds its own temporary file and maps data back into the changed file
- To remove physical-file constraints from a renamed file and then add them back to the new file

In general, the use of CHGPF makes changing an existing physical file easier and less prone to error, especially if multiple logical files or physical-file constraints are based on the physical file. The system warns you if data could be lost in the process and gives you the option to cancel the command, or to ignore the warning and proceed. The default value of *NO on the Delete dependent logical file parameter automatically cancels the command if the new record format removes a field that is part of any based-on logical file's record format. Changing the value to *YES tells the command to delete any logical file that contains the removed field. In addition, the Remove constraint parameter, with its default value of ***RESTRICT**, automatically cancels the command if the new record format tries to eliminate a field that is the parent key for a foreign key field of a dependent physical file and the relationship is formalized by a database constraint. For example, if you wanted to make sure that all zip codes entered or changed in the employee file were actually contained in the zip-code file, you would use the following **ADDPFCST** (Add Physical File Constraint) command:

```
ADDPFCST   FILE(EMPPF)       +
           TYPE(*REFCST)     +
           KEY(ZIP)          +
           PRNFILE(ZIPPF)    +
           PRNKEY(ZIP)
```

Once the command is executed, DB2 enforces the rule that all EMPPF zip-code values must exist in ZIPPF.

Once this rule is established, DB2 does not let you remove the parent key field (ZIP) from the parent physical file's (ZIPPF's) record format with the CHGPF command unless the Remove constraint parameter of the CHGPF command is changed from its default value of *RESTRICT to *REMOVE. Doing so would permit removal of the referential constraint on file EMPPF that was established by the ADDPFCST command above, letting the CHGPF command be completed.

As you can see, the pumped-up CHGPF command is a powerful and convenient way to change a physical file's structure. And its built-in safeguards protect you against making certain mistakes.

Database File-Level Security

In earlier chapters, you learned how you could use logical files to restrict access to groups of records in a physical file through the Select and Omit DDS keywords. You also learned how, at the field level, projection lets you limit access by building a logical-file record format that includes only the fields users need to do their work. But what about the physical file itself? What authority do users have to it, and how can access to it be controlled?

Every object has at least two explicitly authorized users: the owner of the object, and everyone else not covered by another explicit authorization. "Everyone else" is given the special name ***PUBLIC**. The owner of an object has all authority to it—he can display or change the object's description, save and restore the object, rename it, copy it to another library, or delete it. If the object is an object—such as a physical file—that has a data component, the object owner can read the data, delete or add new records, and change existing records. Although most object types (e.g., *PGM, *QRYDFN) do not have a data component, there are others besides physical files that do. For example, a library's data component is the objects in the library; for an output queue, it is the spooled files in the output queue.

Figure 9.21 shows the **EDTOBJAUT** (Edit Object Authority) command output for file EMPPF in library CIS001. When you run this command, both the object name and type are required parameters.

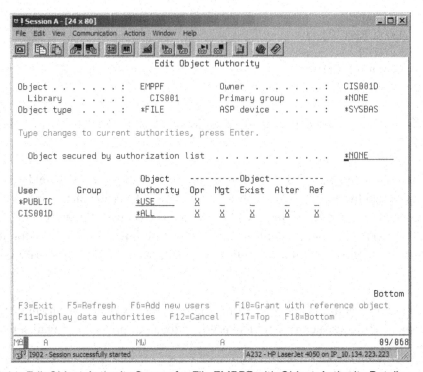

Figure 9.21: Edit Object Authority Screen for File EMPPF with Object-Authority Detail

Initially, the screen comes up with no detail displayed, but pressing F11 once displays object-authority detail, as you see in Figure 9.21. Pressing F11 again displays data-authority detail, as Figure 9.22 shows.

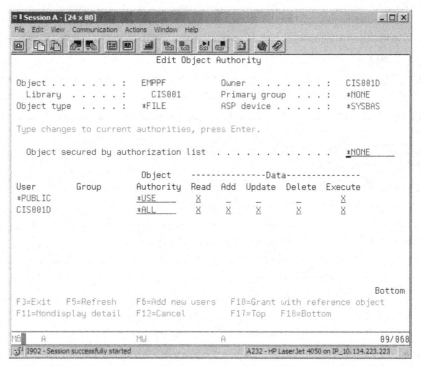

Figure 9.22: Edit Object Authority Screen for File EMPPF with Data-Authority Detail

Table 9.2 shows the detail object- and data-authority types and a brief statement of their usage.

Table 9.2: Object and Data Authority Types and Usage	
Object Authorities	**Usage**
Opr—Operational	Look at the object's description; do whatever the data authority permits
Mgt—Management	Move, Rename, and Create Duplicate Object; grant authority
Exist—Existence	Delete the object; perform SAVE and RESTORE operations
Alter—Alter	Add, Clear, Reorganize database-file members; change file structure (CHGPF)
Ref—Reference	Specify the object as parent file in adding a referential constraint (to a dependent file)
Data Authorities	**Usage**
Read	View the data (e.g., DSPFFD, RUNQRY) or read-only access from RPG, COBOL program
Add	Add records to a file, messages to a message queue
Update	Change records in a database file
Delete	Remove records from a file, spooled files from an output queue, objects from a library
Execute	Call a program

Because it is mildly irritating to toggle through several screens just to see or change the detail authorities for object and data, you should consider changing the User options parameter of the **CHGPRF** (Change Profile) command from *NONE to ***EXPERT**. This value condenses the detail-authority information into a single screen (Figure 9.23).

Note

From this point on, all authority-related screens in this text will be shown with the user-profile option set to *EXPERT.

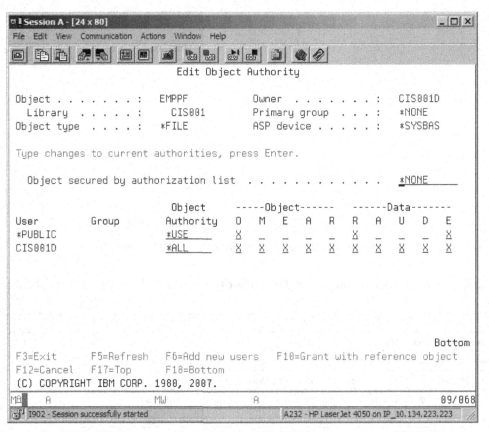

```
Session A - [24 x 80]                                          _ □ ×
File  Edit  View  Communication  Actions  Window  Help
 🗔 🖹 🖺 🖳 🖳 🖳 🖳 🖳 🖳 🖳 🖳 🖳 🖳 🗔 🖳 🖳
                       Edit Object Authority

Object . . . . . . . :   EMPPF          Owner  . . . . . . . :   CIS001D
  Library  . . . . . :    CIS001        Primary group  . . . :   *NONE
Object type  . . . . :   *FILE          ASP device . . . . . :   *SYSBAS

Type changes to current authorities, press Enter.

  Object secured by authorization list  . . . . . . . . . . .   *NONE

                       Object    -----Object------    ------Data-------
User          Group    Authority  O  M  E  A  R    R  A  U  D  E
*PUBLIC                *USE       X  _  _  _  _    X  _  _  _  X
CIS001D                *ALL       X  X  X  X  X    X  X  X  X  X




                                                              Bottom
F3=Exit      F5=Refresh   F6=Add new users   F10=Grant with reference object
F12=Cancel   F17=Top      F18=Bottom
(C) COPYRIGHT IBM CORP. 1980, 2007.
MA    A                  MW               A                      09/068
 🔊 I902 - Session successfully started         A232 - HP LaserJet 4050 on IP_10.134.223.223
```

*Figure 9.23: EDTOJBAUT Screen with User-Profile USROPT Parameter Set to *EXPERT*

As you can see, the owner, CIS001D, of object EMPPF has *ALL (all object) authority; but why does *PUBLIC have *USE authority? When an object is created, the authority parameter for the object, which determines public authority, is set to ***LIBCRTAUT** by default. This setting means that the system checks the create authority value of the library into which the object will go and uses the value found there. That value itself is normally set by default to the **QCRTAUT** system value. This system value specifies the default public authority given to an object when it is created into a library; this system value is shipped as *CHANGE. If this default value has not been changed, the object public authority will be set to *CHANGE on a newly created object. However, the system that was used to produce this book needed a tighter public authority; so the QCRTAUT system value on this system is set to *USE. Some tightly secured systems even have the system value set to *EXCLUDE. This explains why *PUBLIC is set to *USE in Figure 9.23.

After you create a library, you can use the **CHGLIB** (Change Library) command to change the Create authority parameter value. Of course, changing the value for an existing library has no effect on objects already created in it, but the change applies to newly created objects. For objects already in the library, you can use the **GRTOBJAUT** (Grant Object Authority) command to set an authority level for all or specified objects in the library. One execution of this command can affect the authorities of many objects.

For new objects, when they are created, you can specify an authority class such as *USE or *EXCLUDE instead of the *LIBCRTAUT default for each object's Object Authority parameter value. This setting overrides the Create authority, and in this way you can choose a particular public authority class for each object at the time you create it.

If the object already exists and you own it, you can change explicit authorities if you need to. Look again at Figure 9.23. Suppose you want to give user MEYERB change capability, give YOUSUFS use capability, and exclude everyone else. The **F6** function key lets you provide explicit authority to other user profiles not currently in the list. Pressing F6 from the Edit Object Authority screen for EMPPF takes you to the Add New Users screen you see in Figure 9.24. (Two new users have already been entered in the figure.)

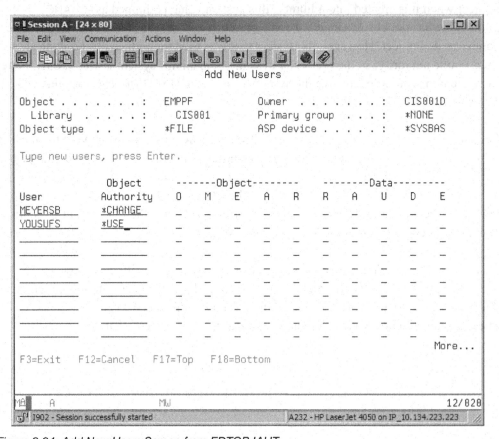

Figure 9.24: Add New Users Screen from EDTOBJAUT

On this screen, you can enter user-profile names and specify authority levels either by typing an X for each object and data authority you want to provide, or by using an authority-class special value such as *CHANGE.

Now, return to the Edit Object Authority screen and change *PUBLIC's authority to *EXCLUDE. We can do this simply by typing over the current value (*CHANGE) in the Object Authority column. When we press Enter to save the change, the resulting screen will look like the one in Figure 9.25.

```
I Session A - [24 x 80]                                              _ □ ×
File  Edit  View  Communication  Actions  Window  Help
 ▣  ▤  ▤  ▥  ▥  ▦  ▦  ▦  ▥  ▥  ▥  ▥  ▤  ▦  ◈
                       Edit Object Authority

Object . . . . . . . :   EMPPF        Owner . . . . . . . :   CIS001D
   Library . . . . . :   CIS001        Primary group . . . :   *NONE
Object type . . . . :   *FILE         ASP device . . . . . :   *SYSBAS

Type changes to current authorities, press Enter.

   Object secured by authorization list . . . . . . . . . . .   *NONE

                       Object   -----Object------   ------Data-------
User       Group       Authority  O  M  E  A  R    R  A  U  D  E
*PUBLIC                *EXCLUDE   _  _  _  _  _    _  _  _  _  _
CIS001D                *ALL       X  X  X  X  X    X  X  X  X  X
MEYERSB                *CHANGE    X  _  _  _  _    X  X  X  X  X
YOUSUFS                *USE       X  _  _  _  _    X  _  _  _  X



                                                             Bottom
F3=Exit      F5=Refresh    F6=Add new users   F10=Grant with reference object
F12=Cancel   F17=Top       F18=Bottom
Object authorities changed.
MA       A            MW                                      09/068
  I902 - Session successfully started    A232 - HP LaserJet 4050 on IP_10.134.223.223
```

Figure 9.25: Object Authorities Added and Changed for Object EMPPF

Figure 9.25 clearly shows the different authority levels for the four classes: *ALL, *CHANGE, *USE, and *EXCLUDE. Considering this information, we can make a couple of observations. First, given the ultimate power of ***ALL** object authority, you would have to be very careful about who owned objects in a production environment to avoid possible harm to critical data, programs, and so on. For enterprise database files especially, it should go without saying that indiscriminately granting *ALL authority to casual users is asking for trouble. At the other extreme, for a user who has ***EXCLUDE** authority, an object's very existence would be unknown; any attempt to display the object's description or work with it in a PDM list would be thwarted. At the least, object operational authority is required to perform any action on an object. So you could assign a user who needs to view but not change, add, or delete records in a file the class ***USE** authority, which would provide the minimal object operational and data-read authorities.

All levels of explicit authority provided to users of an object are still subordinate to that user's access to the library in which the object exists. For example, in Figure 9.25, users MEYERSB and YOUSUFS are given some degree of access to object EMPPF in library CIS001. Nevertheless, if the object authority for library CIS001 were defined as in Figure 9.26, any attempt by either user to access EMPPF would fail.

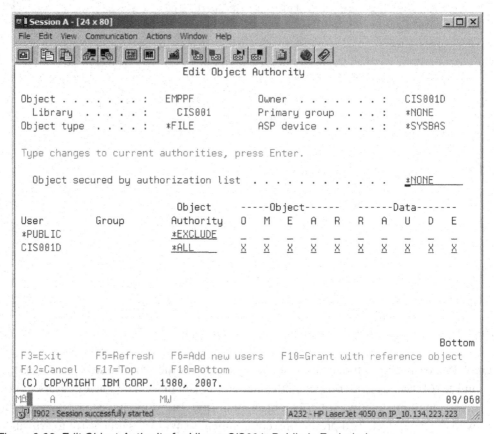

Figure 9.26: Edit Object Authority for Library CIS001, Public Is Excluded

This would be true as well for any other user not having the user-profile ***ALLOBJ** (all object) special authority. A user profile with *ALLOBJ special authority is extremely powerful (and potentially dangerous); in a production environment this authority should be granted only to the security officer. It overrides any explicit or public revocation of authority.

If neither MEYERSB nor YOUSUFS has *ALLOBJ authority, an attempt by either user to run the **WRKOBJPDM** (Work with Objects Using PDM) command on library CIS001, for example, would result in a message similar to that you see in Figure 9.27.

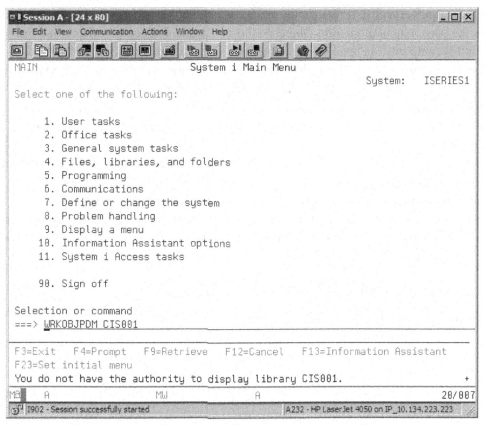

Figure 9.27: Main Menu Showing Failed Command Attempted by User MEYERSB or YOUSUFS and Error Message

For MEYERSB and YOUSUFS to use the data authority granted for object EMPPF, they would need at least object operational authority to library CIS001, which contains the physical file. You can provide the proper level of object authority in three ways (short of giving *ALLOBJ special authority). You can use F6 from the Edit Object Authority screen for the library to grant explicit authority to each user (you would do so in the same fashion as adding new users for a file or program in a library). Alternatively, you can use an authorization list or group profiles; when dealing with large numbers of users on today's systems, most system administrators use some combination of authorization lists and group profiles to control access to the system's objects.

Authorization Lists

An **authorization list** is an IBM i object that identifies a group of users and specifies individual authority levels for each user. Authorization lists are especially useful when a certain group of users needs authority to several different objects and/or libraries. Different users in the list can have different object- and data-authority levels. Then, instead of having to add individual **private authorities** for each of the needed objects, you can secure each object with the authorization list. (Private authorities are any other user-profile names that appear under the User column of the Edit Object Authority screen. The object owner's authority and *PUBLIC authority are not considered private.) If the group of users is subject to change (employees come and go), it is much easier to maintain one authorization list than the explicit private authorities for the tens or hundreds of objects secured by the authorization list. Although different users can be given different levels of authority on an authorization list, an individual's authority would be the same for all objects secured by that authorization list.

To create an authorization list, you use the **CRTAUTL** (Create Authorization List) command. The only required parameter is the name of the list. Once you create an authorization list, you can edit it using the **EDTAUTL** (Edit Authorization List) command. The Edit Authorization List screen is similar to the Edit Object Authority screen and lets you add users to the list using F6. If we use that function key to add MEYERSB and YOUSUFS to the list with minimal authority, the edited list would look like the one in Figure 9.29.

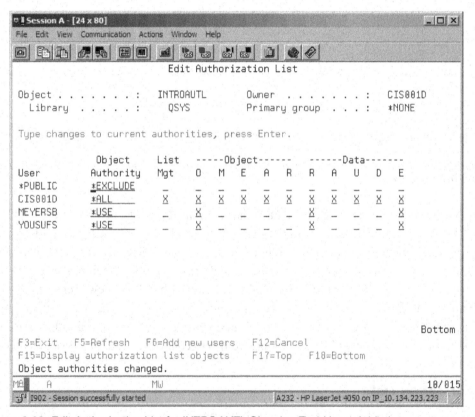

Figure 9.28: Edit Authorization List for INTROAUTL Showing Two Users Added

Our two user profiles have been given only *USE authority on this list. We intend to secure the library by setting *PUBLIC authority on the library itself to *EXCLUDE; the *USE authority level is adequate for them just to gain access to the library.

Notice that an authorization list also has public authority, and *PUBLIC authority is set
to *EXCLUDE on this list. However, to use the *PUBLIC authority assigned through the
authorization list and not the *PUBLIC authority granted for an object itself, you would need
to change the object's *PUBLIC authority to *AUTL.

Notice also that a new authority level, List Management (List Mgt), is shown. List-
management authority lets the owner of the list change the authority of list members or add
new members to the list. The owner of the list can grant list-management authority to other list
members. A user with list-management authority can add new members to the authorization
list, granting them authority up to but not exceeding the manager's own authority.

Once you have created an authorization list and added members to it, you need to secure
the necessary objects whose access the list will control. You do this by replacing the default
(*NONE) with the name of the authorization list in the Object secured by authorization list
entry field of the Edit Object Authority screen. Figure 9.29 shows the authorization list name
(INTROAUTL) entered for library CIS001.

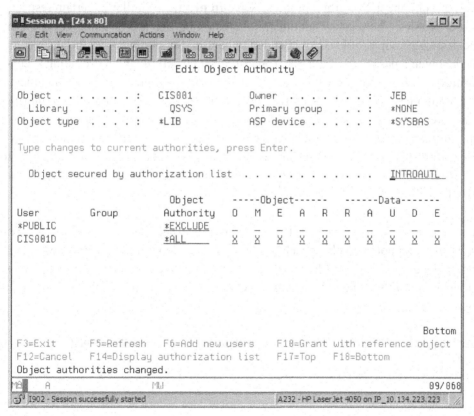

Figure 9.29: Edit Object Authority Showing Library CIS001 Secured by Authorization List

Now, when any authorization-list member attempts to access the library through PDM, that user will be presented with a list of all objects in the library from which he or she is not explicitly excluded.

Then, the specific object authorities come into play. Reviewing Figure 9.25, you can see that MEYERSB, for example, will be able to run a change DFU on EMPPF because he has been given *CHANGE object authority; but YOUSUFS will not have this option. He was given only *USE authority to EMPPF, which provides read-only access. He can display records using a temporary DFU (option 18); but any attempt to change records, add new records, or delete records will not be permitted. DFU will respond to such attempts by displaying the End Data Entry screen (a not-too-subtle hint) and the message *"You are not authorized to perform the requested operation."*

Group Profiles

The third way to provide access to a library, as well as to grant object authority to groups of users, is through the use of group profiles. A **group profile** is similar in certain respects to other user profiles. The security administrator creates a group profile and gives it a user-profile name. A group profile is not intended to be used for signing on to the system, so it should be given a password of *NONE. You also must be careful about providing special authorities—such as spool control or job control—to a group profile because members of the group inherit any special authorities in addition to their own individual authorities. After we create the group profile, we assign individual users to it by changing the Group profile parameter of each group member's user profile. (The security administrator must also perform this task.) Users with similar system needs can be assigned to the same group profile. There can be as many different group profiles as there are groups of users with distinct needs.

Once the membership of a group profile has been decided, the group profile can be given explicit private authority to objects and libraries, just like any other user profile. A group profile can be granted different levels of authority for different objects, and all members of the group are implicitly granted the same level of authority to a given object as the group profile specifies.

Figure 9.30 shows the group profile MSTR_IBMI added to the private authorities for physical file EMPPF.

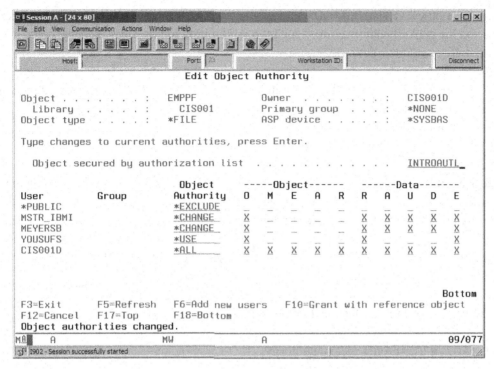

Figure 9.30: Group Profile MSTR_IBMI Granted *CHANGE Authority

The *CHANGE authority for group MSTR_IBMI means that any user in this group could make changes to file EMPPF (with the exceptions noted below). Of course, the group (or its individual members) also needs at least object operational authority to the library.

To appreciate the pros and cons of these different approaches, you should know that the system uses a hierarchy of authorization checking. At the top is a user with *ALLOBJ (All Object) special authority. This special authority grants a profile all access to all of the objects on the system and overrides any attempted restriction through authorization lists, group profiles, or explicit private object authority.

If the requestor's user profile does not have *ALLOBJ special authority, the system next checks to see whether explicit object authority exists. If the user's name is in the list of private authorities shown by the EDTOBJAUT command, the user will have whatever level of authority is specified there. Explicit object authority takes precedence over both authorization lists and group profiles. And this is true whether the explicit authority limits or extends authority specified by the authorization list or group profile. For example, if MEYERSB were a member of group profile MSTR_IBMI, he would normally share the *CHANGE authority to object EMPPF. But YOUSUFS's explicit authority limits his access to *USE or read-only, and the explicit authorization—even though limiting in this case—takes precedence over the group profile's authority.

If no explicit authorization has been specified for a user, the system checks the authorization list (if there is one) that is securing the object. If the user is found on the object's authorization list, the authority level granted there applies.

If the requesting user is not on the authorization list for the object (or if there is no authorization list), the system checks to see whether the user is part of a group profile that has been given specific authority to the object. If the user is a member of such a group, the authority granted to the group applies to the user.

Last, if none of the other cases has been true, the user receives the *PUBLIC authority (or lack of it) granted for that object.

Following is an abbreviated authority-determining hierarchy:

- *ALLOBJ user-profile special authority
- User-name-explicit object authority
- Authorization-list member authority
- Group-profile member authority
- *PUBLIC authority

Which object-authorization method or combination of methods is most appropriate depends on the circumstances of use for each object. A nonsensitive object to which most users require some degree of access can be handled by granting to *PUBLIC users *USE or *CHANGE authority for the object. When all users' access to an object (except the owner) can be handled by the *PUBLIC authority, so that no private authorities need to be granted, authority checking is the fastest and most efficiently performed.

Groups of users who generally need the same level of authority to a certain set of objects are best handled by creating a group profile and granting explicit object authority of the necessary degree to the group profile. Group profiles, unlike authorization lists, do not permit the granting of variable levels of authority to different group members; but exceptions to the group-granted authority level can be handled by specifying private object authority for individual group members when necessary. As we described above, such individual user authorization always overrides the group authority. In addition, an object can have several different groups, with different levels of authority among its explicitly authorized users. When one group will be the only profile needing special authority beyond *PUBLIC (and the owner), an efficient way to provide the authority is to make that group the **primary group** of the object. Each object can have one primary group associated with it. If the object already exists, this association can be made through the **CHGPGP** (Change Primary Group) command. The group profile so assigned must have a Group ID number. The security officer assigns this number when he or she creates the group profile, or the ID can be added later using the Group ID number parameter of the **CHGUSRPRF** (Change User Profile) command.

Once an object has been assigned a primary group, the primary group is granted authority to the object (using F6 from EDTOBJAUT). As long as no private authorizations are granted (that is, only the owner, the primary group, and *PUBLIC appear under the EDTOBJAUT User heading), authority checking for group members is very fast because primary group information is kept with the object itself, and there is no need for private authority lookups in the requesting user profile.

Authorization lists are most useful when objects generally restricted to public use require different levels of authority among a group of users. Unlike members of a group profile, different users in an authorization list can be granted varying levels of authority (e.g., *ALL, *CHANGE, *USE), and the user-specific authority applies to all objects secured by the authorization list. However, each object can be secured by only one authorization list. So if different groups of users need different degrees of authority within groups, some combination of authorization list, group profiles, and individual private authorities may be required. The problem is that such complicated schemes not only are hard to manage, but also tend to be slower in granting (or refusing) the necessary authority to the requestor.

As we discussed above, to override an individual's authorization-list authority level for a particular object, you can grant private object authorization for that object to that individual. This type of override can either restrict the authority granted by the authorization list or group profile, or provide a higher level of authority.

Object-level security is one place where adherence to the old saw "Keep it simple" really pays off. As we mentioned above, the best case is to make public authority adequate for all requests. If that is not possible, a primary group or authorization list is still easy to manage and efficient, especially when no private authorities are used. Try to avoid long lists of private authorities, especially if any of them have less authority than *PUBLIC because this increases the number of private authority lookups. Combining long private authority lists with group profiles and authorization lists is almost sure to result in performance problems.

There is much more to learn about object-level security and authorization than we can possibly cover in this text. At best, you now have a general idea of how individual users can be given certain levels of authority to different objects on the system. Owners of objects can grant, change, or revoke authority to their objects. However, for objects important to the enterprise, the system security officer and/or database administrator will decide which users will have what levels of authority, set up group profiles and authorization lists, and manage and maintain these items. The security offered by library and object authorization, together with selection and projection at the record and field levels, should ensure that authorized users have adequate access to data in which they have legitimate business interests, and no access to data they do not need.

For more information about IBM i security issues, there is, of course, the IBM information center; and we highly recommend the following books:

- IBM Redbook: *Security Guide for IBM i V6.1* (SG24-7680).
- *IBM i and i5/OS Security and Compliance: A Practical Guide,* by Carol Woodbury (29th Street Press, 2009).
- *Experts' Guide to OS/400 and i5/OS Security,* by Carol Woodbury and Patrick Botz (29th Street Press, 2004).
- The IBM manuals *AS/400 Tips and Tools for Securing Your AS/400* (SC41-5300) and *Security–Basic* (SC41-5301); although a bit dated, they contain a lot of information.

In Summary

A member of a source physical file functions as instructions or design specifications for creating an object—it is not the object itself. To change an existing file object, you must save the data first, and then change the source member and recompile it. Doing so creates a new file that is similar to the old file but is a separate object that initially has an empty data member. You can copy the saved data from the old file into the new file using record-format field mapping. One way to save the data is to rename the old file. Renaming the file causes pointers in based-on logical files to be changed to the new name. Once you have created the new file, you must recompile the based-on logical files. The DSPDBR command is useful for listing the logical files based on a physical file.

The CPYF command is a powerful utility for copying existing data to a new record format. The CHGPF command is a convenient way to add new fields to an existing physical file. Using CHGPF, you do not need to rename, copy data into the new file, or recompile based-on logical files. Programs and queries using files that have been changed and re-created usually need to be recompiled to avoid system level checks.

Objects can be secured by granting appropriate levels of authorization. After *ALLOBJ authority, explicit user authorization has the highest priority, followed by authorization lists, and then by group profiles. If a user is not included among any of these, the public authority to the object applies. For a user to implement *USE or *CHANGE authority to an object, he or she needs at least *USE authority to the library that contains the object.

In the lab for this chapter, you will use the CPYF command to restore the data component of a physical file whose record format had been changed. This is a useful technique for solving a common problem that arises when you need to add fields or change field attributes in an existing file. You will use the DSPDBR command to determine the dependent logical files of a physical file, and you will recompile logical files to reestablish PFILE and JFILE pointers. You will examine the inquiry message that results from a level check on a query whose compiled record format disagrees with the file object's current record format.

Finally, you will examine the effects of granting various levels of object and library authority to a user by signing on to an alternate session as that user. In the additional lab exercise, you demonstrate, for yourself, the relationship between library and object authorization.

Key Terms

ADDPFCST	EDTOBJAUT
*ALL	*EXCLUDE
*ALLOBJ	*EXPERT
authorization list	F6 function key
CHGLIB	field mapping
CHGPF	group profile
CHGPGP	GRTOBJAUT
CHGPRF	level checking
CHGUSRPRF	*LIBCRTAUT
CPYF	*MAP
CRTAUTL	*NOCHK
CRTDUPOBJ	OVRDBF
CRTPF	primary group
CRTSRCPF	private authorities
*DROP	*PUBLIC
DSPDBR	QCRTAUT
DSPFD	*RESTRICT
DSPFFD	RUNQRY
DSPPFM	*USE
EDTAUTL	WRKOBJPDM

Review Questions

1. Compare the CRTDUPOBJ and CPYF commands. Explain a situation in which you would need to use the CPYF command.

2. List and explain the additional capabilities of the CPYF command we discussed in this chapter.

3. What are the criteria for deciding whether two record formats are the same?

4. When you are copying data from one file to another, what happens to fields that do not exist in the From file but do exist in the To file?

5. Under what circumstances does a level check occur?

6. Explain what happens to logical files when you rename the "based-on" physical file.

7. What happens when you try to delete a physical file that has associated logical files?

8. How would you remedy the situation in question 7?

9. Explain the steps required to recompile a physical file and preserve the data.

10. Explain the OVRDBF command and give an example of its use.

11. How does the CHGPF CL command simplify adding fields to a physical file?

12. Explain the purpose of the ADDPFCST CL command.

13. Investigate the CHGPF command using the online extended Help. What is the purpose of the Access path maintenance (MAINT) parameter?

14. Under what circumstances would a program using a logical file, based on a physical file that has changed, *not* have to be recompiled?

15. List the advantages of using the CHGPF command over the six-step process we discussed in this chapter to change the format of a physical file.

16. What is the importance of the ADDPFCST command to enforcing the integrity of a DB2 database?

17. List and explain the types and usage of object and data authorities.

18. List and explain the ways that you can give authority to an object on the system.

19. Explain the difference between an authorization list and a group profile.

20. Explain the object-authority-determining system hierarchy.

21. How would you override an individual's authorization-list authority level for a particular object?

Lab 9

Introduction

Upon completion of this lab, you will be able to use various PDM options, including 3=Copy to create a duplicate object and 7=Rename. You can use these options and the CPYF command to make changes to the record format of an existing database file without losing the data already in the file. You will become aware of several important CPYF parameters and learn to move data from one file to another at the level of corresponding (mapped) same-named fields. You will also examine logical-file descriptions using the DSPFD command to see how renaming a physical file affects the logical files built over it.

In the lab, you will also use the CHGPF command to change a physical file whose source member you have already changed. You will observe the record format of the changed file and its relationship to its logical files.

Part 1

Goals   Use the CRTDUPOBJ command to copy a file.

Use the DSPDBR command to identify the logical files based on a physical file.

Rename objects using a PDM option.

Edit a DDS source member, adding a new field.

Compile a DDS source member and check for successful completion.

Use the DSPFD command to identify the physical file on which your logical file is based.

Start at   WRKOBJPDM, your library.

Procedure   Take Work with Objects Using PDM option 3, and create a backup of STUPF.

Using the DSPDBR command, determine dependent logical files of STUPF.

Using the DSPFD command on STULF1, verify its based-on file.

Rename file STUPF to OLDSTUPF.

Add a field to the source DDS of STUPF; recompile.

9.1.   After you sign on, run the WRKOBJPDM command. Make sure you are looking at the object list for your own current library.

When it becomes necessary to change the record format of an existing file, it is always a good idea to make a backup copy of the file in case the change does not go according to plan. Although copying a large file can be quite time consuming and can require significant system resources, it is nonetheless a necessary precaution. Even the most careful programmer is not entirely immune to a careless mistake. In this lab, you copy a file so that you have the experience of using the CRTDUPOBJ command.

You could use the CPYF command and prompt to copy your current physical file, STUPF, to a temporary backup file. But to simply clone an object without change, you can take the PDM Copy option on file STUPF and save some keystrokes.

Type the option number for Copy next to STUPF in the PDM list, and press F4 to prompt.

9.1.a.   What command does this option invoke?

This command is similar in function to the CPYF command, but it has fewer options. However, it works for object types other than files. You can use it to duplicate an object in the same library under a different name, or to copy (and optionally rename) an object into another library. This command is especially useful for cloning multiple-member source physical files (e.g., copying all members of QDDSSRC to another library). Notice that the first three parameter values are supplied from the PDM list screen information.

Now press F12 to return to the Work with Objects Using PDM screen.

You should still see the option number on the input field for STUPF. Press Enter to run the option.

9.2.   The Copy Objects screen (Figure 9.31) has two input fields, To library and New Name.

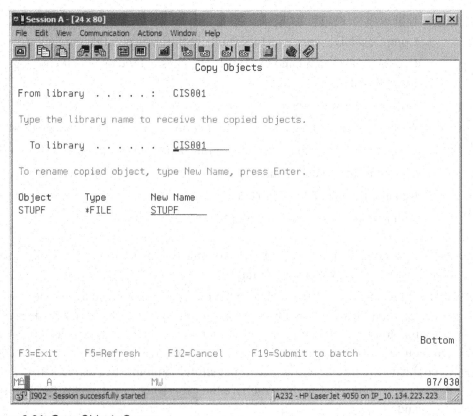

Figure 9.31: Copy Objects Screen

Notice that the current values provided for these fields are the original file's library and object names. Try running the option with those defaults (just press Enter).

9.2.a.   What message is displayed?

Usually, when a file is copied, it is placed in a different library with the original name, or it is placed in the same library but given a different name. With the names already supplied, you can change one or the other easily.

Move the cursor down and change the New Name to STUPFCPY; press Enter.

9.2.b.   What message is displayed when the command finishes execution?

9.3.   You have now made a copy of your original STUPF physical file. To verify that the data was copied to the new file, use the DSPPFM command to display the data in the file you just created. Prompt for parameters, or enter the file name as a positional parameter value. Then press Enter.

9.3.a.   Does the copied file appear to contain the same data as your original file? Press the function key to shift your view to the right, and examine the rest of the data.

The copied file is a safeguard in case of an accident. We will not do anything more with it now, but it would be wise for you to keep it until you are sure you have successfully completed this lab.

9.4.   We will now rename the original file object, STUPF, to OLDSTUPF. Renaming the file removes the entry for STUPF in your library; it will not be necessary to delete the original STUPF before you create a new file using the same name.

After changes are made to the DDS source code of member STUPF, it can be recompiled using its original name, which in effect changes the record format of STUPF. Renaming the *FILE object STUPF to OLDSTUPF changes the pointers of any related logical files (e.g., STULF1) to reference the renamed physical file. This change prevents the problem of unattached logical files that we mentioned in the text. If, for example, you chose to copy STUPF to STUPFCPY, and then simply delete the original STUPF, you would first have to delete any logical files built over STUPF. Only then could you delete the physical file STUPF.

Before renaming STUPF, though, we should first find out which logical files are dependent on it by executing the command

```
DSPDBR STUPF
```

Please do that now. The bottom of the first screen of Display Database Relations shows the number of dependent files, and they are listed on the second screen. You should have at least one dependent logical file, STULF1.

Let's also verify the based-on relationship from the logical file's side. We can do that by checking the Files accessed by logical file value of STULF1, stored in the logical file's description.

Take option 5 on logical file STULF1 from your Work with Objects Using PDM list screen. This option creates a temporary spooled file of the DSPFD command output. You could see the same information by executing the DSPFD command, with a parameter value to name the file, from a command line. From PDM, the list item on which the option is taken determines the parameter value.

Scan through the information. Check the Database File Attributes and the Access Path Descriptions values. Just before the Select/Omit Description is the list of Files accessed by logical file. For a simple logical file, we can expect this to be a short list of one. The screen should look like the one in Figure 9.32.

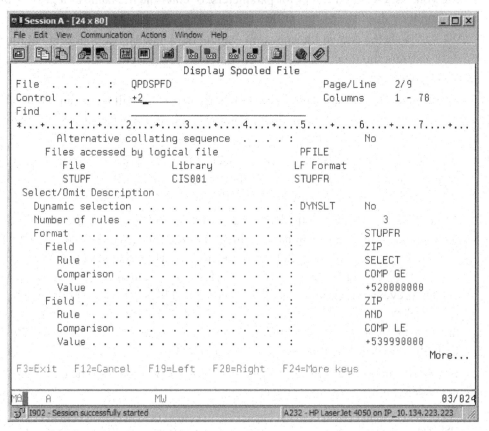

Figure 9.32: DSPFD Command Output for Logical File STULF1

9.4.a. Write the name of the based-on physical file on the answer sheet.

When you are finished with the display, press F12 to return to the PDM screen.

9.5. You will now rename the physical file. From the Work with Objects Using PDM screen for your library, take the option to rename on file STUPF. This should take you to a Rename Objects screen like the one in Figure 9.33.

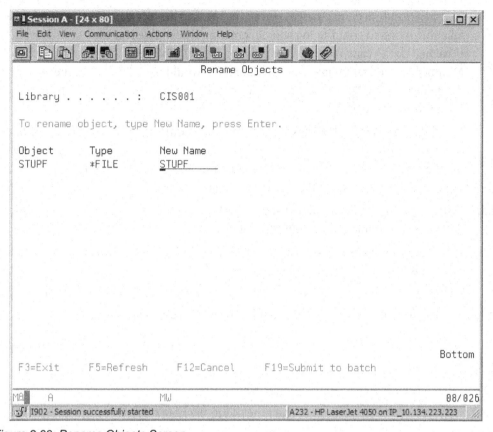

```
▣ I Session A - [24 x 80]                                          _ □ ×
 File   Edit  View  Communication  Actions  Window  Help
 [icons]
                         Rename Objects

  Library . . . . . . :    CIS001

  To rename object, type New Name, press Enter.

  Object      Type       New Name
  STUPF       *FILE      STUPF




                                                           Bottom
  F3=Exit     F5=Refresh     F12=Cancel     F19=Submit to batch

 MA   A                      MW                             08/026
 I902 - Session successfully started     A232 - HP LaserJet 4050 on IP_10.134.223.223
```

Figure 9.33: Rename Objects Screen

Give file STUPF a new name of OLDSTUPF, and then press Enter. You should be returned to the PDM screen. The message at the bottom of the screen should tell you that the rename was successful.

Now use the Display option once again to check the description of logical file STULF1. Specifically, notice the file named under Files accessed by logical file. As you can see, the name has been changed to OLDSTUPF, the renamed physical file accessed through logical file STULF1.

Now press Enter or F12 to return to the Work with Objects Using PDM screen.

9.6. Choose the Work with option for your source physical file, QDDSSRC.

From the Work with Members Using PDM screen, edit source member STUPF. Insert a field called ACTBAL (account balance) right after the FNAME field. (We would not normally put new fields in the middle of name fields, but doing so will help you easily see the data when we display the changed file's data member.) Specify field ACTBAL as a signed numeric (zoned-decimal) field with a length of 7 and two decimal places.

9.7. Exit SEU, and save the changes. From the Work with Members Using PDM screen, take the option to compile the source, creating a new physical file. At this point, if we had not already renamed the existing data-file object, a Confirm Compile of Member screen would have appeared, and we would have had to tell the system to delete the old STUPF, which it could do only if we had already deleted its based-on logical file (or files).

Use the DSPMSG (Display Messages) command (or the appropriate PDM option) to be sure the compile was successful. If it was not, edit the source member and use the Browse/Copy option to pull the spooled file into a split screen. Determine the error, make corrections to the source DDS, and recompile.

9.8. When the compile is completed successfully, you will have a new version of file STUPF in your library, with field ACTBAL added.

Now return to the Work with Objects Using PDM screen by pressing F12 from the Work with Members Using PDM screen.

9.8.a. Does the new file, STUPF, appear on the list screen? Why or why not?

Refresh the screen, and make sure that file STUPF is listed.

Part 2

Goals   Verify the success of the Part 1 file change.

Use CPYF to move data from the old to the new file.

Verify the success of the CPYF command.

Delete the backup file.

Recompile the logical file (or files).

Start at   WRKOBJPDM or any command line.

Procedure   DSPFFD STUPF, check fields.

Perform the copy:

```
CPYF  FROMFILE(OLDSTUPF)  +
TOFILE(STUPF)             +
MBROPT(*ADD)              +
FMTOPT(*MAP)
```

DLTF STUPFCPY.

CRTLF on each logical file currently pointing to OLDSTUPF.

DLTF OLDSTUPF.

9.9.   Run the DSPFFD command on STUPF from the command line (or take the appropriate
       PDM option), and verify the presence of the new field. The second page of the
       display should now look like the one in Figure 9.34.

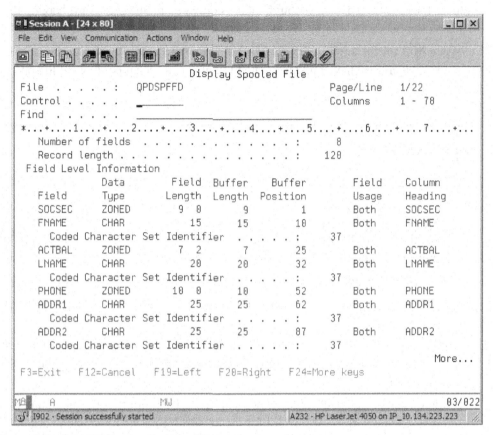

Figure 9.34: DSPFFD Output for New STUPF, Page 2

   9.9.a.   How many fields are now in physical file STUPF?

   9.9.b.   What is the total record length?

   Return to PDM and run the DSPPFM command on STUPF.

   9.9.c.   What does the message say?

9.10. We can now copy the data from the original file, OLDSTUPF, to the new version of
       STUPF. Of course, we could also use the copied file, STUPFCPY, as a data source in
       case anything happened to OLDSTUPF.

       The record format of the new STUPF is different from OLDSTUPF, so you need to
       copy corresponding fields of the From file to the To file for each copied record.

You could type the CPYF command on the command line and request command prompting, but using the Copy file PDM option on OLDSTUPF fills in some parameter values for you. Take option 15 on OLDSTUPF. Specify the newly compiled physical file, STUPF, as the To file. Although there is only one member to copy, leaving the From member default value of *ALL will be all right.

Type *ADD for the Replace or add records parameter. Leave the Create file parameter as *NO because we have already created the physical file and only want to copy the data.

Caution
Do not run the command yet!

Press the function key for Additional parameters and Roll Up (Page Down) until you see the Record format field mapping parameter. Use Help to find out what this parameter does and the meaning of the possible parameter values.

9.10.a. Define "Same record format" according to Help.

Find the parameter value that copies fields with the same name in the From file and the To file record formats.

9.10.b. If you use this value, how will fields in the To file (the new STUPF) that do not exist in the From file (the old renamed file) be handled (e.g., the ACTBAL field)?

Did you choose the *MAP value? If not, check the Help information again and make sure you end up with *MAP entered for the Record format field mapping parameter value. The CPYF command prompt screen should look like the one in Figure 9.35.

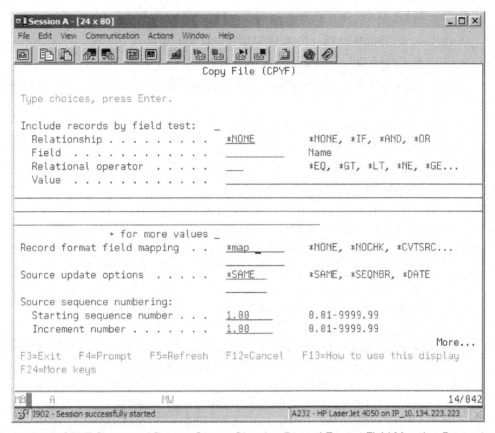

Figure 9.35: CPYF Command Prompt Screen Showing Record Format Field Mapping Parameter

9.10.c. If some fields in the old file (the From file) were not included in the new file and, thus, did not match any field names in the To file, which additional parameter value would you have to use?

When you are sure all values are correct, press Enter to run the CPYF command.

9.10.d. What message is displayed on the Work with Objects Using PDM screen?

9.11. Display the physical-file data member of STUPF to examine the changed physical file.

9.11.a. Locate the new field, ACTBAL. To what value has field ACTBAL been initialized?

Print a screen of the physical-file data and clip it to your answer sheet.

9.12. Return to the Work with Objects Using PDM screen. If the data was copied properly into the new version of file STUPF, you can now prepare to delete the other copies of the old file, STUPFCPY and OLDSTUPF.

First, take the PDM option to delete STUPFCPY. From the Delete screen, confirm by pressing Enter.

9.12.a. What message is displayed on the PDM screen?

9.13. Now take the Delete option for OLDSTUPF, and confirm.

    9.13.a. What message is displayed this time?

To find out why this message was displayed, move the cursor down to the message line and press Help.

You are not able to delete physical file OLDSTUPF because logical files are still pointing to that physical file.

Leave Help, erase the *Delete* option, and execute the CL command to display database relations on file OLDSTUPF.

9.14. The DSPDBR command lists all logical files currently dependent on a physical file. As we mentioned in the text, the system will not let you delete a physical file that has dependent logical files. When the rename command changed the name of STUPF to OLDSTUPF, it also changed the dependent logical files to point to the renamed file.

    9.14.a. Write on the answer sheet the names of logical files dependent on OLDSTUPF.

You need to delete these files before you can eliminate the OLDSTUPF file, and you need to change the logical files so that they will once again be based on the new version of STUPF. You can accomplish both goals by recompiling the logical files. The source DDS for the logical files will still refer to STUPF as the PFILE or JFILE parameter value. Even though the logical-file objects were changed by renaming the original STUPF to OLDSTUPF, this change had no effect on the source code originally used to create the logical files. Let's verify that by examining the source code of the first logical file in your list of dependent logical files (the list you developed in answer to question 9.14.a).

First, return to the Work with Objects Using PDM screen. Then take the Work with option on source physical file QDDSSRC.

9.15. From the Work with Members Using PDM screen, display the DDS source for the first logical file you listed in answer to question 9.14.a. Notice that its PFILE value is still STUPF, even though, as we saw in step 9.4, the rename operation changed the pointer in the logical-file object. This emphasizes the fact that, once created, a file object is a separate entity from the source DDS member used to create it. Changing the file object has no direct bearing on the DDS source member. To reestablish the based-on relationship between the logical file and the new, changed physical file with the original PFILE or JFILE name, you will simply recompile the logical file.

9.16. From the Work with Members Using PDM screen, take the compile option on the logical file. You should now see the Confirm Compile of Member screen (Figure 9.36).

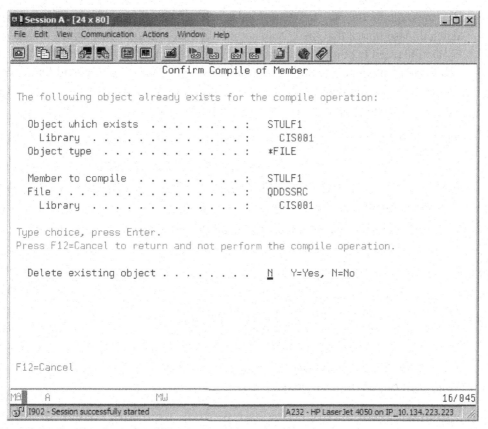

Figure 9.36: Confirm Compile of Member Screen

This is a very important screen, and whenever you see it, you should pay close attention to it. The system is warning you that an object already exists in your library with the same name and type as the new object you are trying to create. The implication is that if the existing object contains working code or data, the compile will wipe out that code or data. The existing file object is deleted as a result of the compile; so, for example, if you had a large data physical file and for some reason you recompiled the DDS source code to the same file name without saving the data, all the data in the file would be lost. It is important that you understand the implications for existing data files or programs when you create a new object. As a wise man once said, "This isn't Windows, and there isn't a Trash folder!" ☺

In this case, the source member you are compiling is a logical file. Because this file contains no data, and you are not changing the format of the logical file itself—you are only attempting to reestablish the based-on relationship to its physical file—it is safe to proceed. From the Confirm Compile of Member screen, change the Delete existing object value to Y, and then press Enter.

The message on the message line should indicate that your old logical file has been deleted. Also notice that there is an additional message to be displayed (indicated by the plus sign (+) on the right side of the message line). If you move the cursor down to the message line and press Page Down, you can see the second line of the message, which indicates that the compile was submitted as a batch job. The third message line tells you that the submitted job was sent to job queue QBATCH.

9.17. Display the message sent by the batch compile job to your message queue. Either take the user-defined PDM option, DM, or key in the DSPMSG command on a command line. Make sure the compile was completed successfully. Then press Enter or F12, and, from the Work with Members Using PDM screen, take the compile option on any other file dependent on OLDSTUPF.

When you have successfully recompiled all the dependent files on your list, return to the Work with Objects Using PDM screen.

9.18. Use the Display option on the first logical file on your list again, and check the Files accessed by logical file entry. The logical file should now point to physical file STUPF.

From the Work with Objects Using PDM screen, try again to delete file OLDSTUPF. You should be successful because OLDSTUPF should now have no logical files based on it. If the delete is not successful, use the DSPDBR command again to see which files are still based on file OLDSTUPF, and then recompile them. If all else fails, ask your instructor/mentor for help.

Part 3

Goals   Use DFU to update STUPF with new field data.

              Understand level check and how to respond.

Start at   WRKOBJPDM, your library.

Procedure Take PDM option 18 on STUPF.

              Change the ACTBAL field.

              Take PDM option 16 to run a query.

9.19. Now, take the PDM option on file STUPF to Change using DFU, and update the file using a temporary DFU program. Remember that Page Down (Roll Up) pages you through the file one record at a time. Also, when you make changes to a displayed record, temporary DFUs save the changes when you press Page Up/Page Down just as if you had pressed Enter on the updated record display.

Add values for field ACTBAL to each record, using a range of different values. Press Field exit after you type the numbers in field ACTBAL. Remember that the two low-order digits are cents, so if you enter 1234, for example, the number will be stored as 12.34.

9.20. Exit DFU, and return to the Work with Objects Using PDM screen. Take the Run option on query definition STUQRY1.

9.20.a. What screen is displayed?

9.20.b. The lowest line of the message information at the top of the screen should mention *"Level. . . ."* What does the whole line say?

Move the cursor up to that line. Press the F1 Help key.

You should now be looking at a display similar to the one in Figure 9.37.

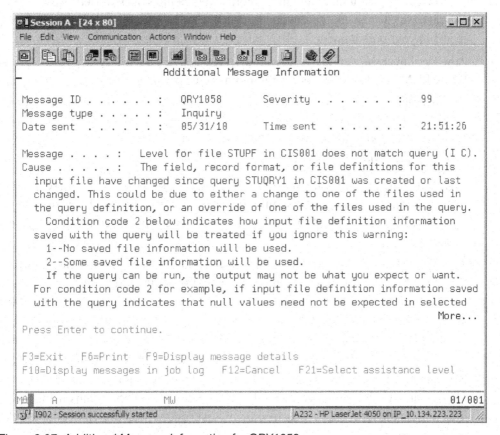

Figure 9.37: Additional Message Information for QRY1058

Read the Cause . . . and Recovery . . . sections of the message. Now look at the header information for this screen; notice that the message displayed here has both an ID and a message type. Because this is an INQUIRY type message, a response is required. To continue, you need to enter either C or I as indicated under Recovery. . . . But, first finish studying this screen.

What has occurred is a level check. The system is telling you that the file on which the query is based has been changed so that its record format no longer agrees with that stored in the query itself. Therefore, the query either may not run or may not include changes made to the record format of the file. The system is warning you that you may need to change and recompile the query for its results to be accurate, or even for it to run.

What happens if you try to run the query without change? Press Enter or F12 to return to the Display Program Messages screen. Use the Tab key to return the cursor to the reply line, and type I (ignore). Press Enter.

9.21. A message should have appeared briefly at the bottom of the screen indicating that the query was running and that records were being selected. Because no error message was displayed, it seems that the query ran successfully; but let's check the report in your output queue.

Page Up if necessary so that your output queue appears on your Work with Objects Using PDM list. Take the Work with option on the output queue.

At this point, several spooled files may be in your output queue. The query report should be the last spooled file in the queue. If you are not sure of this, press F11 to show the date and time the spooled file was created.

9.21.a. What is the file name of the query report?

Display that spooled file and make sure it is your query. The date and time in the upper-left corner of the header should indicate the current date and almost current time. In addition, the report should include the records you added recently via the logical file.

The report should have been run without error; but because you have not changed the query, the newly added account balance field is not included in the output. In essence, that is what the level check was warning you about. If, however, you had deleted fields that the report needed or had changed critical field attributes, you would not have been able to run the query without first changing and recompiling it.

Also, you should note that if a database file were accessed directly by high-level language (HLL) programs (e.g., COBOL or RPG) and you made changes to the file as you have done here, you would have to recompile the programs using that file—unless the level check was specifically overridden—before you could use the programs again.

Return to your Work with Output Queue screen, and delete all spooled files not required for this chapter.

Part 4

Goals   Use CHGPF to change an existing database file.

Use RUNQRY to verify a new field and default data value.

Start at   WRKOBJPDM, your library/QDDSSRC.

Procedure   Edit source member STUPF in QDDSSRC.

Add GENDER with a default value.

Use CHGPF to cause the file to be modified.

Observe the database relations on the changed file.

RUNQRY on the changed file.

9.22. From the Work with Objects Using PDM screen, take the Work with option on your DDS source physical file.

9.23. Edit member STUPF. Add a new field called GENDER after LNAME and before PHONE. Make it a one-character alphanumeric field. Use the DDS keyword DFT (default), and specify either M or F as the default value, depending on whether you think there are more males or females at your school or office. The finished screen should look like Figure 9.38.

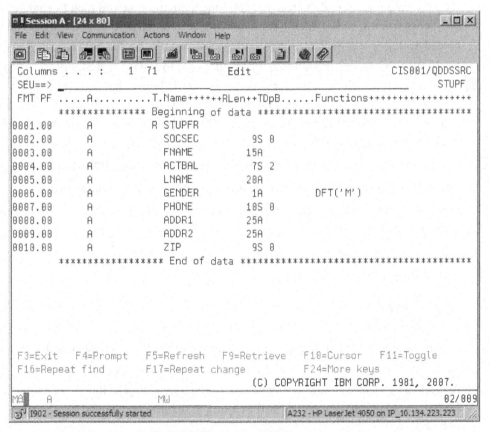

Figure 9.38: Adding a New Field, GENDER, to File STUPF

9.24. Stay in your edit session, and pull up the system command line by pressing F21. Type the command

DSPDBR STUPF

and verify that your student logical file (or files) are based on physical file STUPF. Press F12 to remove the System command line, and then exit SEU, saving your changed member.

9.25. From the command line on the Work with Members Using PDM screen, type the CHGPF command and prompt.

9.25.a. How many required parameters does the CHGPF command have?

Type STUPF for the file parameter and QDDSSRC in your library for the Source file parameter. Then press Enter.

9.26. By providing a Source file value, you tell the command that you plan to change the record format, so it displays some additional parameters that you may need to consider.

Notice that the Source member parameter defaults to *FILE, the assumption being that the member will have the same name as the file being changed. Notice also that the Delete dependent logical file value is set to *NO. This setting would stop the command if you were about to eliminate from the physical file any field needed by any based-on logical file.

Leaving all the default parameter values as they are, run the command.

9.26.a. What message appears on the message line of your screen?

9.27. Press F9 until you have retrieved the DSPDBR command to the command line, and then execute it.

9.27.a. Does STUPF still have the same logical files based on it?

9.28. Type the command

DSPFFD STUPF

on the command line, and verify that the new field GENDER is indeed in the record format of STUPF.

As you can see, the CHGPF command has added a new field to the STUPF record format and kept the logical files still pointing at the newly changed file. So now the only question is, how about the data?

9.29. Type the RUNQRY command on the command line, and prompt. Instead of naming an existing query, which—as we saw before—would not include newly added fields, we will ask Query for i5/OS to create a report "on the fly," using the current record format of STUPF. Doing this is possible only because STUPF is an externally described file.

Tab down to the Query file: File parameter, and type STUPF. Leave the other defaults alone, and run the command. You should see the newly added field GENDER in the report, as well as the ACTBAL field you added earlier in the lab. Notice that GENDER has the value assigned by the DFT keyword instead of the normal default of spaces.

As you have no doubt realized from this exercise, the CHGPF command provides a powerful and convenient way to modify an existing database file. It saves several steps compared to the rename/copy-file/recompile method we described in parts 1 and 2 of this lab, although it *is* important for you to understand all that is involved in a seemingly simple task such as adding a new field to a file. As the number of based-on logical files and constraints on the physical file increases, the convenience of CHGPF becomes more apparent. Like the CPYF command, CHGPF is a good command to get to know well.

Return to a command line or the Main menu, and sign off.

Additional Lab Exercise

You should attempt this exercise only after you have successfully completed the primary lab exercises for this chapter. In this exercise, you change authorities of your library and an object in your library, and you sign on as another student to see the effect these changes have on another user's ability to access your library and object.

> **Caution**
> You should check with your instructor before attempting this lab. Some system setup is required.

9.30. Sign on, and work with objects using PDM for your library. From the command line, prompt for the EDTOBJAUT command. This command requires two parameters, Object and Object type. Enter your library name and *LIB, respectively, for these parameters.

9.31. Initially, the screen displays no detail authority, but authorized users and the system-defined authority level granted to each are shown. To see detailed object authority, press F11 once. To see detailed data authority, press F11 again. Notice that you, the owner, have all object (*ALL) authority to your library.

9.31.a. What system-defined authority level is granted to the public?

For a library, data authority applies to the objects within the library. As you can see, *CHANGE authority to a library seems to allow any type of action to be taken on objects in the library that were not explicitly restricted. But let's examine that premise a little more carefully. (If your library is not *CHANGE public authority, make it *CHANGE for now.)

9.32. Return to the Work with Objects Using PDM screen for your library. Use PDM option *EA* (supplied by IBM) to edit the object authority of your source physical file, QDDSSRC.

9.32.a. What system-defined authority level is granted to the public for your source physical file?

(If the authority level is not *CHANGE, make it that for now.)

9.33. Now, start an alternate session. To do so on a PC keyboard, hold down Alt and press SysRq (System request), the Alt-er ego of Print Screen. Or if you are using 5250 emulation, look for a Sysreq pushbutton on your control panel. Otherwise, try holding down Shift and pressing Esc. (Still can't get it? Ask your instructor!)

When the broken line appears at the bottom of the display screen (turquoise on color monitors), press Enter. Alternatively, when you press Sysreq, a System Request window will pop up on your screen, and from there you can just press Enter. This should take you to the System Request screen (Figure 9.39).

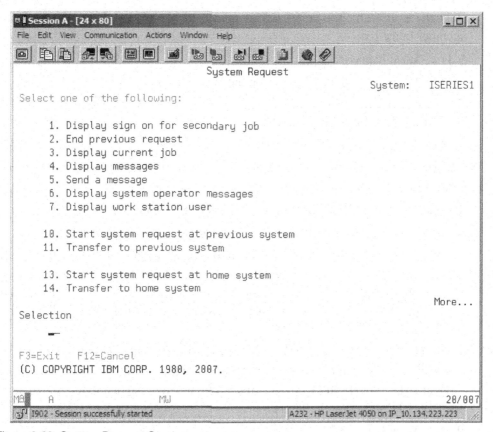

Figure 9.39: System Request Screen

The System Request screen provides several useful functions, including ending a program caught in a loop (option 2), sending a message to another user's message queue (option 5), and finding out who you currently are (option 7)—a need that can arise when you frequently switch back and forth between active sessions. Option 1 lets you start an alternate job or switch to an alternate job if one is already started. Take option 1 now to start another job.

9.34. You can sign on as yourself for a second session (if the system allows you multiple sessions . . . check with your instructor) if you need to alternate between different views of your empire. However, this time, from the sign-on screen, type INTROSTU as both User and Password, and then press Enter.

INTROSTU is a genuine student profile with the same class (*PGMR) and special authorities (*NONE) as yours. After you sign on as INTROSTU, go to the Work with Objects Using PDM screen, specifying your own library (not INTROSTU's). If your library had *CHANGE authority, INTROSTU should have no trouble bringing up a PDM list.

Take the Work with option on QDDSSRC, and then take the Edit option on the first member in the list.

9.34.a. What happened?

9.34.b. What message is displayed on the message line?

Try making a syntactically valid change to one of the records, and then press F3 to exit. From the Exit screen, with Change/create member set to Y, press Enter.

9.34.c. What happened?

Change the Change/create member value to N, and then return to the Work with Members Using PDM screen.

Based on this experience, complete the following sentence on the answer sheet:

9.34.d. "Just because I have *CHANGE authority to a source physical file. . . ."

> To change a member of the source physical file, you need more than *CHANGE authority; you also need object-management authority to the object (QDDSSRC). Because the system-defined *CHANGE authority does not provide this, you—as INTROSTU—are not able to change a member of the file.

9.35. From the Work with Members Using PDM screen, take the option to copy the member you just tried to change. Remember, you are INTROSTU, looking at another student's (i.e., your) source physical file. Copy the member, using the same name, to file QDDSSRC in library INTROSTU.

9.35.a. What happened?

Change the library of your Work with Members Using PDM screen to INTROSTU. (Now you are INTROSTU looking at INTROSTU's own QDDSSRC member list.)

9.35.b. Is the copied member there?

9.35.c. Can you change the copied member?

9.35.d. Can you delete the copied member?

If you have not done so, delete the copied member from INTROSTU/QDDSSRC.

9.35.e. On the answer sheet, write your conclusions about the limitations and capabilities of *CHANGE authority on source-file members.

9.36. Return to the Work with Objects Using PDM screen for your own library (not INTROSTU's). You should still be signed on as INTROSTU.

Take the PDM option to Change using DFU on the student physical file STUPF. Remember that you are INTROSTU trying to change another student's physical file.

9.36.a. What happened?

9.36.b. Are you able to change records in the physical file?

9.36.c. What conclusions do you draw regarding the power of *CHANGE authority for physical database files?

9.37. Exit DFU and, without signing off as INTROSTU, switch sessions back to your own user profile's alternate job. (Shortcut: Press Alt and SysRq to bring up the broken turquoise line, type 1—for Display sign on for alternative job—on the line, and press Enter. Or, if you have a Sysreq pushbutton, just push it and type 1 in the Window's input field.)

9.38. From your own job, use the EDTOBJAUT command (PDM option EA) on the STUPF physical file that INTROSTU just changed. Under Data authority for *PUBLIC users (press F11 twice to get to the data authorities), erase the X for Update, and press Enter to register the change.

9.38.a. What happened?

9.39. Now switch back to the alternate session for INTROSTU, and try the DFU program on STUPF again.

9.39.a. Does the DFU come up?

Try changing a record and pressing Enter on the change.

9.39.b. What happened?

9.40. Exit DFU, and (remembering that you are INTROSTU) back out to the Main menu, but don't sign off. Switch sessions back to your own job again. This time, from the Edit Object Authority screen for physical file STUPF, press F6. Add user INTROSTU, and give him or her *EXCLUDE authority. Note that you are just excluding INTROSTU from one physical-file object.

9.41. Switch sessions back to INTROSTU's job. Retrieve the WRKOBJPDM command to bring up the list of objects in your own (not INTROSTU's) library.

9.41.a. What happened to STUPF?

9.41.b. What is your conclusion, based on your response to 9.41.a?

9.42. As INTROSTU, return to the Main menu. Switch sessions, back to your own job. First, change the authority on STUPF to *ALL for INTROSTU. After that change is registered, return to a command line and retrieve the EDTOBJAUT command for your library. Run the command.

Change the public authority of your library to *EXCLUDE, and execute the command.

9.43. One last time, return to the alternate job for INTROSTU. From the Main menu, retrieve the WRKOBJPDM command for your library, and run it.

9.43.a. What happened?

Keep in mind that you have given INTROSTU *ALL authority to your STUPF file. As INTROSTU, enter the following command to invoke a temporary update DFU on (your own) STUPF:

UPDDTA your_lib/STUPF

9.43.b. What happened?

9.43.c. What conclusion can you draw regarding the relationship of library and
object authority?

At this point, you can sign off as INTROSTU and return to your own job. You can leave the public authority on your library set to *EXCLUDE. This value prevents unauthorized users from accessing your source files, programs, data files, and so on.

Hopefully, you concluded above that if you are *EXCLUDED from a library, you can't do anything with any object in the library, even if you have *ALL authority to that object. For object authorities to be used, you must have at least object operational authority to the library that contains the objects.

In this lab, you have seen how authority can be granted and revoked at different levels to give various users adequate access to the data they need without endangering files that need to be protected. Group profiles and authorization lists extend this ability to tailor authorities to suit the needs of most applications.

Although you need *SECADM (security administrator) special authority to create group profiles, you could create an authorization list and test its function by adding INTROSTU or one or two of your classmates to the list, and then securing your library and/or objects in your library using the authorization list. To check out the various authorization-list commands, try GO CMDAUTL.

Using IBM i Navigator

Overview

In the first nine chapters of this text, we used the traditional IBM i tools. In this chapter, we introduce one of the products associated with IBM's IBM i Access product. As a platform moves from the traditional 5250 interface to graphical user interfaces (GUIs), students should be knowledgeable in both the traditional tools and the GUI interfaces. In Chapter 10 we focus on the IBM i Navigator portion of IBM i Access for Windows, and in Chapter 14, we introduce IBM i Access for Web.

Topics we cover in this chapter include how to connect to the server and perform basic operations such as replying to messages and managing printer output printers and jobs. We also offer a short introduction to work management, including WRKACTJOB, job queues, output queues, and subsystems. Finally, we discuss using IBM i Navigator to work with databases (you can find a more in-depth discussion of using Navigator in Chapter 13 of this text, *Introduction to SQL*), and we introduce the file systems available in the IBM i OS.

Objectives

Students will be able to

- Create a connection to a Power System server running the IBM i OS
- Complete basic operations such as handling messages, printer output, printers, and jobs
- Understand work management, including handling active jobs, job queues, output queues, and subsystems
- Navigate databases, create schemas, and copy, delete, display, and edit tables
- Understand that the IBM i OS has multiple file systems
- Copy a Microsoft Word document from a PC to the integrated file system (IFS)

Introduction to IBM i Access

In this chapter, we will be working with IBM i Navigator, which is part of the IBM i Access family. This family of products allows users access to the system in a number ways; we have listed the products below and provided a short description of them.

- *IBM i Access for Windows*—This client application provides TCP/IP connection from a Windows client to an IBM i system; a part of this suite is IBM i Navigator.
- *IBM i Access for Linux*—This product enables a connection to an IBM i system using a Linux client.
- *IBM i Access for Web*—This product provides browser-based access to the system. It requires no software to be loaded on the client.
- *IBM i Navigator*—IBM released this product in V4R5 and enhanced it in V5R1 and V5R2; it allowed users to remotely monitor the system using an Internet phone, a PDA with a wireless modem, or a traditional Web browser. IBM i 7.1 does not support Navigator for i.

 Note

For more information about the IBM i Access product, see *http://www-03. ibm.com/systems/i/software/access/index.html*.

IBM released a new product named IBM Systems Director Navigator for i at V6R1 and greatly enhanced it in v7.1. This Web-based product consolidates IBM i management tasks and is IBM's strategic management tool for IBM i. It is important to note that most (eventually all) of the functionality available in the IBM i Navigator interface will be available in Systems Director Navigator. Many of the functions are beyond the scope of this text, and the SQL and database functionality had not been included at the time this book was being written. Therefore, we have elected to concentrate on IBM i Navigator for this edition of the book. For those who are interested, additional information about IBM Systems Director Navigator for i is available in the IBM Information Center. We recommend you take the time to investigate it.

IBM i Access for Windows has the components you see in Figure 10.1.

Figure 10.1: Components of IBM i Access for Windows

Depending on which software was installed on your computer, you might not have all components. You can see what portions of the product are installed by going to and pressing the Windows Start button; then select Programs, navigate to IBM i Access for Windows, and finally, right-click the IBM i Access for Windows icon, and select Open.

Discussing all of these components is beyond the scope of this book; however, the Information Center includes a section on using IBM i Access for Windows. For additional information, see Paul Tuohy's book, *The Programmer's Guide to iSeries Navigator* (MC Press, 2006), which covers many of these features in greater depth than this text.

In the center of Figure 10.1, you can see the IBM i Access for Windows Properties Shortcut icon. Double-clicking this icon brings up the properties window in Figure 10.2. This window has a number of tabs at the top. If you select the General tab, you can see the version of IBM i Access for Windows and the service level installed on your computer. Users often have problems with the software when the client software is not properly updated or does not match the operating system (OS) level on the server. One advantage of IBM moving the administration software to a Web interface using IBM Systems Director Navigator for i is that you do not need to be concerned with the software levels on the user's PC.

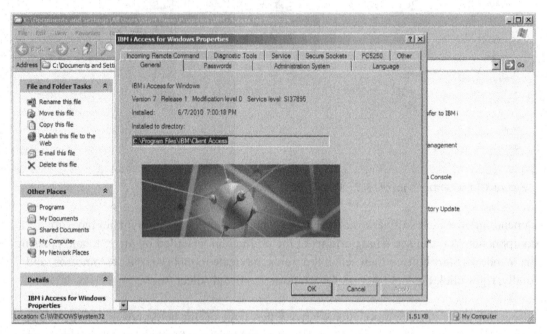

Figure 10.2: Properties of IBM i Access for Windows

Accessing Help

IBM i Navigator includes a comprehensive Help system. You access this system by clicking Help in the toolbar at the top of the main window or by pressing F1. This Help system is searchable, as Figure 10.3 shows. Additional help is always available online at the Information Center.

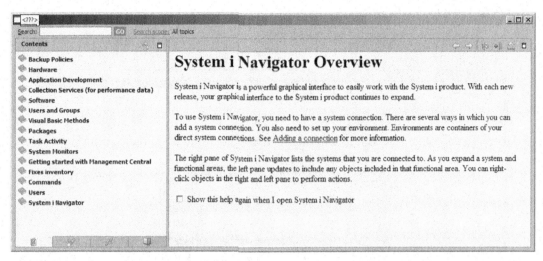

Figure 10.3: IBM i Navigator Help Window

Note

As you can see in Figure 10.3, you may encounter some screens or documentation that refer to the Navigator product by its former name, System i Navigator.

Creating a Connection to the System

In this section, we describe how to create a new connection to a system.

The first time you open IBM i Navigator for Windows, you see a window like the one in Figure 10.4. When you click Yes to create a new connection, you are presented with the window you see in Figure 10.5.

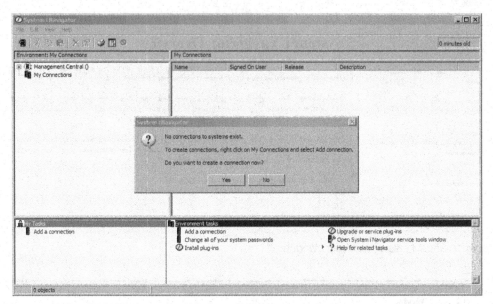

Figure 10.4: First IBM i Navigator for Windows Window

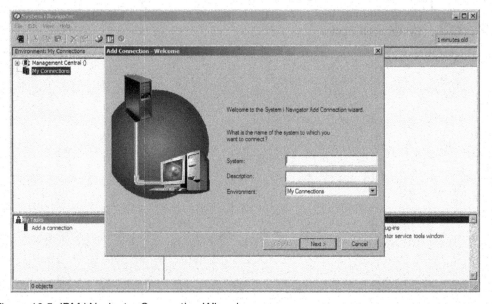

Figure 10.5: IBM i Navigator Connection Wizard

The window in Figure 10.5 prompts you for the system name and a description. The
default environment is My Connections. The system name can be a URL or an IP address,
depending on your environment.

Note
You will need to check with your instructor to find out the URL or IP address
for your system. Some systems also require Secure Sockets Layer (SSL) to be
installed and turned on for access to the server; your instructor can help with
these difficulties.

We suggest you get in the habit of entering an adequate description in the Description field;
doing this may not be important in school, but many environments include a number of
IBM i systems or partitions, and keeping the connections straight can be a challenge.

Key in your system's address and a description. Clicking Next then presents you with the
window in Figure 10.6.

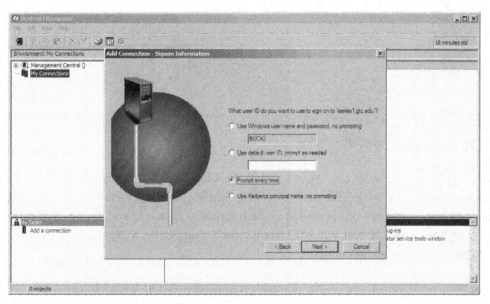

Figure 10.6: Prompt for User ID Window

This window prompts you to select one of four options. In most environments, you will
not be able to use the Windows user name and password or the default user ID prompt
because not many systems use the same name for the IBM i user ID and the Windows user
and password. The last option uses the Kerberos protocol for single sign-on; any discussion
of Kerberos is beyond the scope of this text. For our purposes, we will choose the third

option, Prompt every time. This choice causes IBM i Navigator to prompt for a user ID and password each time the connection is opened.

After you select Prompt every time and click Next, the window that appears on the left in Figure 10.7 is displayed. Clicking the Verify Connection button here brings up the Verify IBM i Connection window (shown on the right in the figure). this window displays messages about the status of IBM i Navigator's ability to connect to your system.

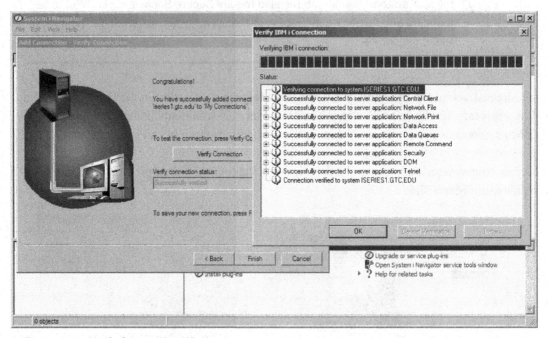

Figure 10.7: Verify Connection Window

A number of circumstances can cause errors in the Verify IBM i Connection window: The system might not have a specific server running; you might have entered the wrong URL or IP address; you might not be connected to the Internet or network; and, finally, you might require an SSL connection. If you have trouble connecting to the system, consult your instructor for additional instructions.

After the server-connections verification has completed properly, click OK in the Verifying IBM i Connection window. Then click Finish in the wizard window. This takes you to the main IBM i Navigator window, which you see in Figure 10.8.

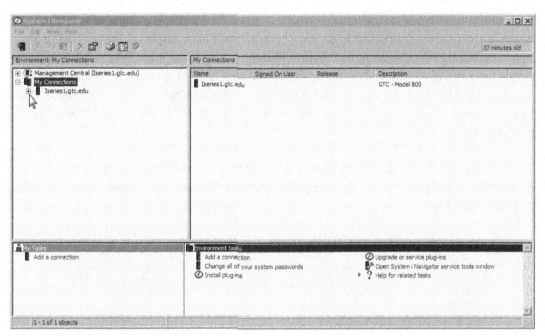

Figure 10.8: The Main IBM i Navigator Window

Take a minute to investigate the toolbar at the top of this window. The File section contains
a number of options; you can open additional windows, create additional connections, add
plug-ins to the product, and run diagnostics. The diagnostics are useful if you feel you have
a slow connection. Choosing this option actually checks the speed of your computer, the
speed of your network connection, and even the speed of your IBM i server.

Options included under the Edit section of the toolbar include standard Windows options
of Find, Cut, Copy, and Paste. The View section contains a number of options to customize
the view of IBM i Navigator. The Help section provides a link to the Help topics,
which constitute a comprehensive Help system for the product and include a link to the
Information Center. Check the About section of the Help to see which version of the product
is installed.

We will now look at the windows that the main IBM i Navigator window includes. In the
upper-left quadrant is a window that displays the Management Central and My Connections
icons. Management Central is a comprehensive system-management tool that enables
an administrator to manage multiple systems from one interface; we will not discuss
Management Central in this text. My Connections lists all your current system connections
and enables you to connect to them. The upper-right window of the Navigator display shows
you an expanded view of any selection you click on in the left window.

The bottom-right Navigator window is called the *TaskPad*; it displays a list of subtasks based on the function you select in the top-left window. For example, in Figure 10.8, we have selected the My Connections function; the subtasks shown in the TaskPad are related to this function. If you clicked on the actual connection Iseries1.gtc.edu, the subtasks in the TaskPad would change. By right-clicking subtasks in the TaskPad and selecting Add to My Tasks, you can customize the My Tasks window, which appears in the lower-left window of the Navigator display.

The first step in logging into the system is to expand the + sign to the left of our new connection, as the arrow in the preceding figure shows. You are then prompted for a User ID and Password (Figure 10.9).

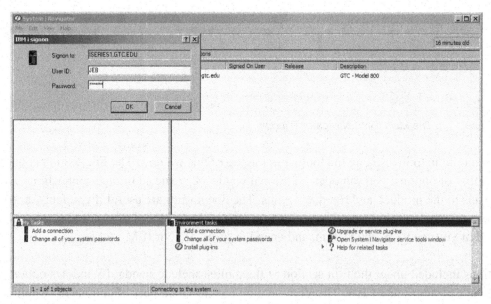

Figure 10.9: Main IBM i Navigator Windows Showing Prompt for User ID

After you enter your user ID and password and click OK, you see the window in Figure 10.10.

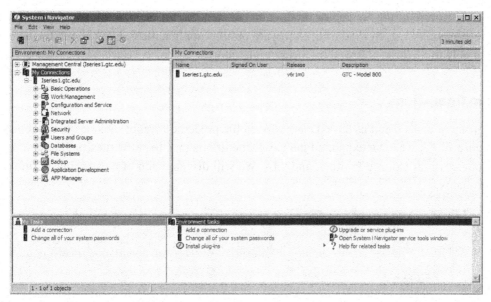

Figure 10.10: Main IBM i Navigator Windows Showing the Available Options for This User

The user for this example has many administrative rights on the system, which explains why so many tasks are available. Most users on the system will not have these options. For example, when we use the student ID used throughout this book (CIS001D) to connect to the system, many of the options shown in this figure are not available to us as a student user. Figure 10.11 shows the available tasks for student users.

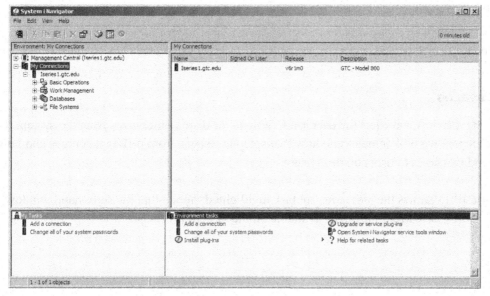

Figure 10.11: Main IBM i Navigator Windows Showing the Available Tasks for Our Student User

One great feature of the Navigator product is that the allowed functions for a user are stored on the system; and, even if all of the software options are installed on the client, the user has access only to the tasks allowed by the administrator.

Basic Operations

The group of tasks listed as Basic Operations in the preceding figure includes four subtasks. In Figure 10.12, we have expanded the Basic Operations task to show these subtasks: Messages, Printer Output, Printers, and Jobs. We will discuss each of these subtasks and their functionality.

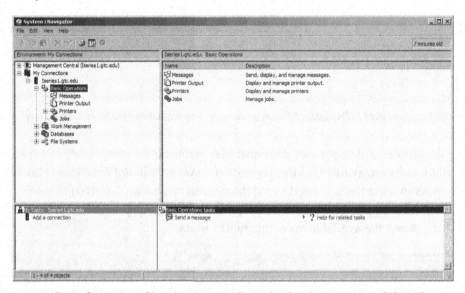

Figure 10.12: Basic Operations Showing Allowed Tasks for Our Student User CIS001D

Messages

The Messages subtask lets the user send, reply to, or display messages from the system. In this section, we will demonstrate how to display messages from different sources and how to send messages to users on the system.

Figure 10.13 shows the Messages subtask highlighted; notice that the right-hand window shows the four current messages available on the system for this user.

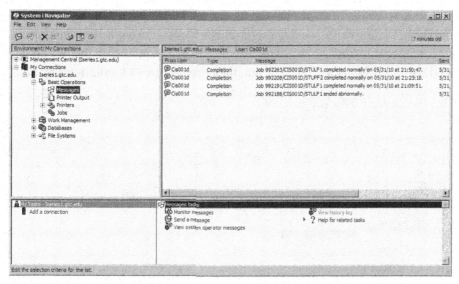

Figure 10.13: Messages Subtask Highlighted with Messages Available for This User

Each message shows the user who sent the message, the type of message, the message text, and a timestamp of when the message was sent. The messages you see are from a previous chapter, when we were compiling the logical files. Three of the jobs completed normally, which usually means that these logical files were created. The fourth job shows the status as "ended abnormally"; this means that its logical file was not created.

To see the details of this message, right-click the message, and then select Properties. Figure 10.14 shows the results.

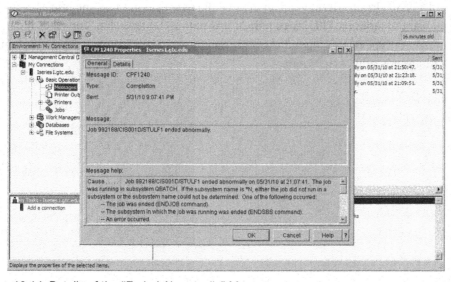

Figure 10.14: Details of the "Ended Abnormally" Message

Another important feature of IBM i Navigator is the capability to change which messages are displayed. In Figure 10.15, we have right-clicked Messages in the left window and then selected Customize this View and Include. You also might want to note that we could have highlighted Messages in the left window and then pressed the **F11 function key**.

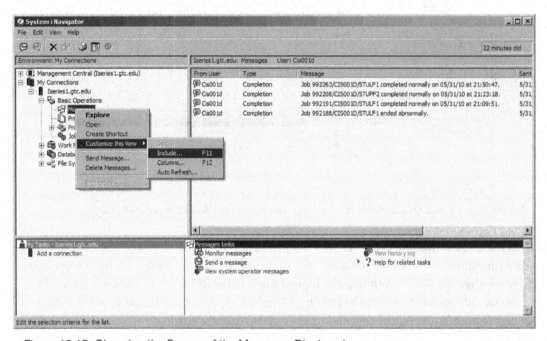

Figure 10.15: Changing the Source of the Messages Displayed

As a result of selecting Include or pressing F11 in Figure 10.15, the pop-up window in Figure 10.16 is displayed. Here, you can change the user or point to a specific message queue you want to monitor. The lower part of this pop-up window lets you filter the message by the severity or type of message; this option can be an important feature on a system that produces thousands of messages a day.

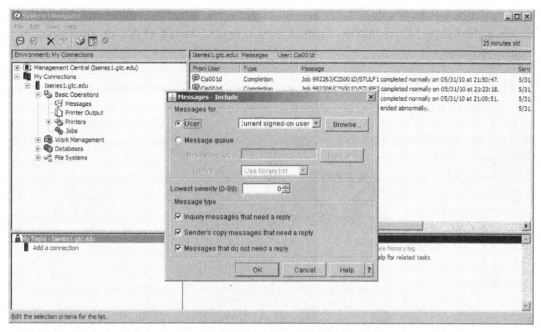

Figure 10.16: Changing the Source of the Messages Displayed, Continued

In Figure 10.17, we have changed the values to permit us to monitor the system operator **(QSYSOPR) message queue**. You can monitor any message queue to which you have access rights on the system.

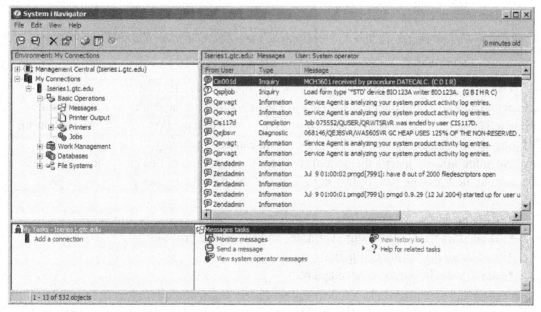

Figure 10.17: System Operator (QSYSOPR) Message Queue

By default, the system displays the newest messages at the top of the right-hand window shown in the figure. Notice that the highlighted message at the top of this example is an inquiry message.

Besides monitoring messages, you can answer messages; Figure 10.18 shows the results of right-clicking a message.

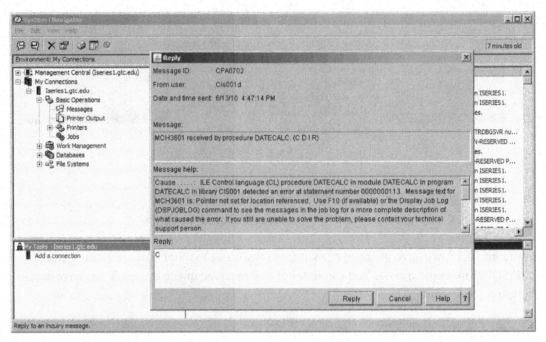

Figure 10.18: Replying to an "Inquiry" Message on the System Operator (QSYSOPR) Message Queue

This window provides the following information: the message ID (CPA0702 in this case), the actual message, and the message Help for the message. In the example, the message Help tells you that the message occurred in a CL program named DATECALC. At the bottom of the pop-up window is a Reply box, where you can key in a reply to the message. The system automatically inserts the default reply for the message; in this case, there is a C (for Cancel) in the Message box. Following is a list of the possible replies to this message:

- C—Cancel the CL procedure.
- D—Dump the CL procedure variables and cancel the procedure.
- I—Ignore the failing command.
- R—Try the failing command again.

You can accept the default reply by clicking Reply, or you can enter a different reply. For this example, we will click Reply and take the default reply to cancel the program.

Sending Messages

At times, you might want to send a message to a user, to all users on the system, or to a workstation; you can accomplish these operations by right-clicking Messages in the top-left Navigator window and selecting Send message. Doing so opens the window you see in Figure 10.19.

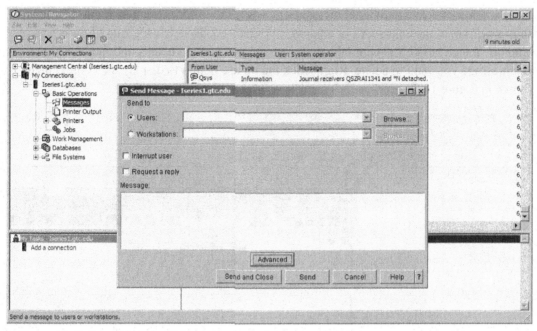

Figure 10.19: Send Message Window

Notice that you can send the message to a specific user or a specific workstation. Note also the Browse button in the top-right corner of the pop-up window; you can use this button to browse for a specific user. If you select the Workstations radio button, you are able to browse for a specific workstation.

In the middle of the pop-up window is an Interrupt user check box. Selecting this option sends a "break message" to the selected workstation or user. You should use this option sparingly because many users find it very unsettling. The second check box, Request a reply, asks the user to send a reply to your message.

You type your request message in the Message text box, in the lower part of the window in Figure 10.19. To control where the reply is sent and the coded character set identifier (CCSID) used for the message, you can click the Advanced button.

Deleting Messages

Finally, you can delete individual messages or select groups of messages. Figure 10.20 shows a group of messages for our student user CIS001D. To delete a group of messages, hold down the Shift key, click on the first message you want to delete, and then click on the last message you want to delete. Right-click the mouse button to display the context menu shown in Figure 10.20.

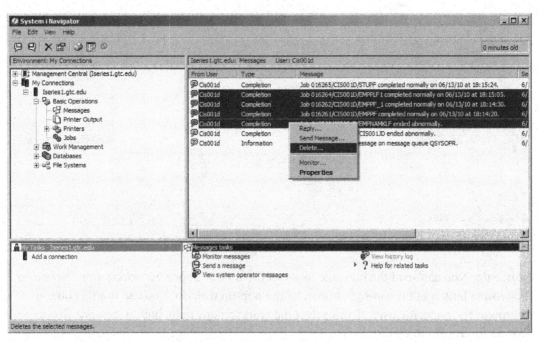

Figure 10.20: Delete a Group of Messages for User CIS001D

When you select Delete here, you will be asked to verify that you want to delete the selected messages. When you click the Delete button in the Confirm Delete pop-up window, the selected messages are deleted.

Printer Output

In Chapter 4 we covered the printing process in detail; in this chapter we will discuss how to manage spool files using IBM i Navigator (we will not go over the IBM i printing process again). Figure 10.21 shows the spool files for our student user CIS001D.

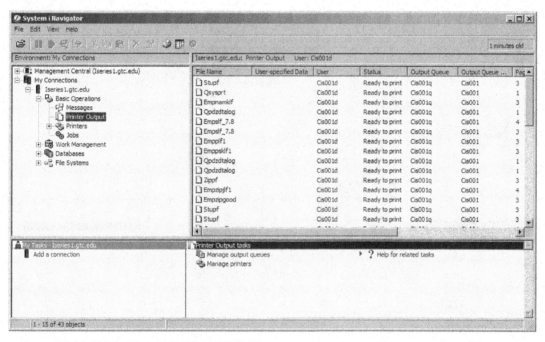

Figure 10.21: Printer Output for User CIS001D

When you click the Printer Output icon in the left window of this screen, you will see all the spool files for the logged-in user in the right window, including the details for those files. By sliding the slider to the right, you can see all the information you are used to seeing in a 5250 session. Many of the tasks that we demonstrated when we discussed messages are available when you work with spool files. Refer to Figure 10.15, where we right-clicked the Messages icon to control the displayed messages. In this case, right-click the Printer Output icon, select Customize this View, and Include. Figure 10.22 displays the resulting window, which you can use to manage the spool files.

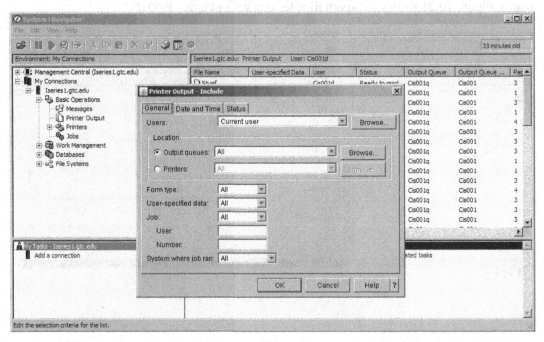

Figure 10.22: Printer Output – Include

Look at the options to control which spool files are displayed; you will immediately notice that you can control the display of files by user, output queue, or printer. Other options include Form type, User-specified data, or Job. Two additional tabs at the top of the window let you filter the displayed spool files by date and time (Date and Time tab) and by 12 different statuses (Status tab).

You can also view spool files using IBM i Navigator. Double-clicking a spool file opens the **AFP Workbench for Windows Viewer**. You will be required to enter your user name and password twice before the viewer opens. This requirement is not because of a problem with your PC or your system; it exists because the credentials from IBM i Navigator are not automatically passed to the AFP viewer. (IBM currently has no plans to change this interface; therefore, the duplication of effort is not a "problem"—it is a "feature." ☺)

Figure 10.23 shows a spool file after it has been opened in the AFP Viewer.

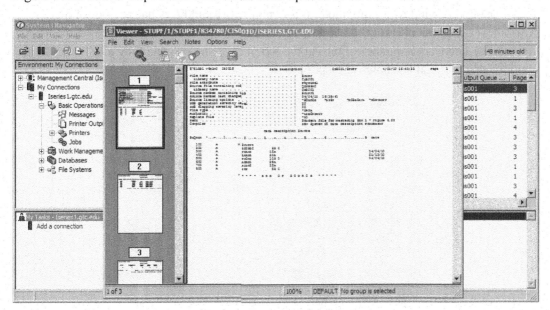

Figure 10.23: Spool File Opened in AFP Vewer

There are a number of advantages to using the AFP Viewer over displaying files in a 5250 session. These advantages let you

- Display a file using WYSIWIG (What You See Is What You Get) in the viewer and show how the file will be printed
- Search the file as with the WRKSPLF command, but with the option to designate a case-sensitive search
- Print the file on your PC printer
- Copy and paste multiple screens of data at one time
- Zoom in on the file using the toolbar

Note

Many users find it easier to drag and drop spool files onto their PC than to open the AFP viewer. Once the spool file is on your PC, it has been converted to a standard PC text file, which you can then easily open using Notepad or Word.

Right-clicking a spool file and selecting Properties displays the window you see in Figure 10.24. Using this window is equivalent to issuing the **CHGSPLFA** (Change Spool File Attributes) CL command, but the window is much easier to navigate than the command. As you can see, there are a number of tabs at the top of this window, and they allow the user to manipulate additional attributes of a spool file.

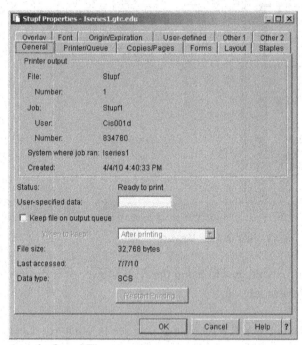

Figure 10.24: Properties of a Spool File

The most-used tabs in the window are Printer/Queue, Copies/Pages, and Forms. Using the Printer/Queue tab, you can easily move the spool file to a printer, change the output queue on which the spool file resides, or manage the current output queue. The Copies/Pages tab lets you change the total number of copies to print, start printing at a specific page, or end at a specific page. The Forms tab lets you specify a particular form, type a line on the page before you print it, or change the source drawer used for the printer.

Deleting spool files is very similar to deleting messages; you right-click the spool file or files that you want to delete and then click Delete. You will be asked to verify the delete, just as when you delete messages.

Printers

The Printers subtask allows you to stop, start, and hold printers and to work with spool files that are in spool queues assigned to these printers. The functionality provided in this subtask is similar to the capabilities you would have if you typed GO PRINTER in a 5250 session. You can filter the displayed printers in the same manner as we did with Messages and Spool Files.

Figure 10.25 shows the printers on the system used for this book; it is easy to see the status of all the printers on the system. The printer Bio114 is in the status of Held; Bio123a and Bio125 are started and Waiting for printer output. A number of other printers are Stopped or Unavailable.

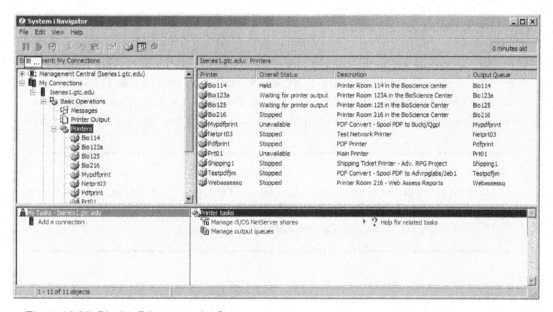

Figure 10.25: Display Printers on the System

To take specific action on a printer, right-click the printer, as Figure 10.26 shows.

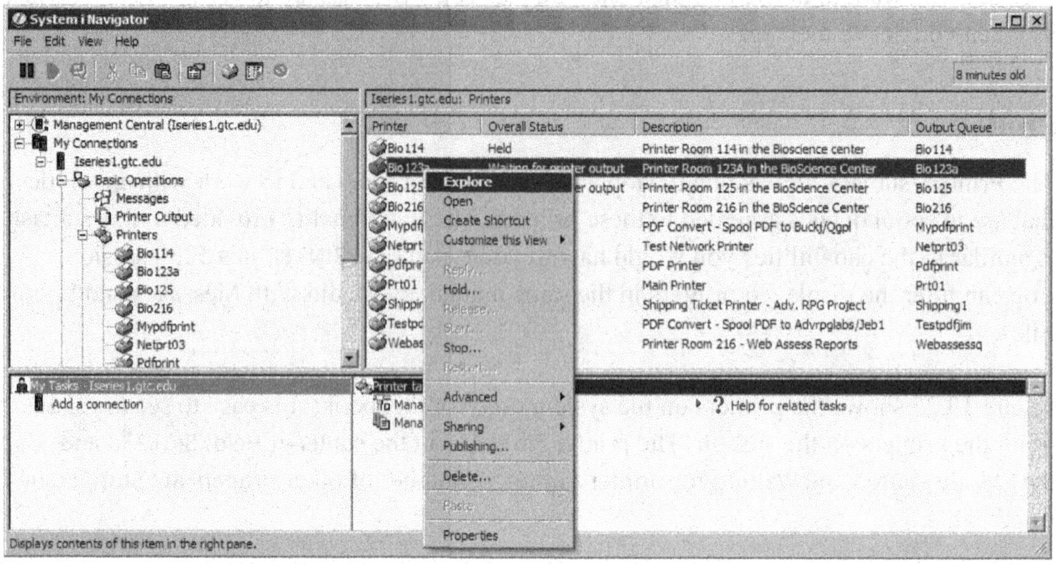

Figure 10.26: Right-Clicking a Printer

Notice that, as you can see in the context menu, you have the ability to Hold or Stop the printer. Other options—Reply, Release, Start, and Restart—are grayed out. These options are available only when the status of the printer permits them. Currently, we could Stop or Hold this printer; these options tell us that the printer is started and waiting for files to print.

> **Note**
> It is important to remember that you need to have the correct access rights to manipulate the status of a printer. Without the correct authority to the printer, you will receive a *"Not Authorized"* message.

We will now look at an example of working with spool files using IBM i Navigator. First, having right-clicked on the printer you are interested in, select Explore from the context menu; this option lets you look at the spool files currently assigned to that printer. In Figure 10.27, you can see that there is a spool file on the selected printer with a status of Ready to print. (Figure 10.26 shows that the printer is started and waiting for the files to print.)

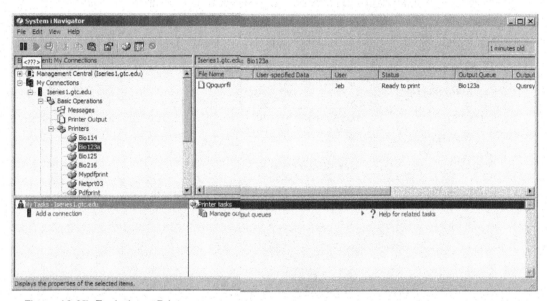

Figure 10.27: Exploring a Printer

We need to figure out why this spool file is not printing. The printer is started, there are no messages on the printer, and the spool file is in a status of waiting to print. Something else is keeping the file from printing. One of the first things to check is whether the form type on the printer is the same as the form type that the spool file requires.

Mastering IBM i

Right-clicking the spool file in the right-hand window of Figure 10.27 and selecting Properties opens the properties for the spool file. From there, selecting the Forms tab displays the window you see in Figure 10.28.

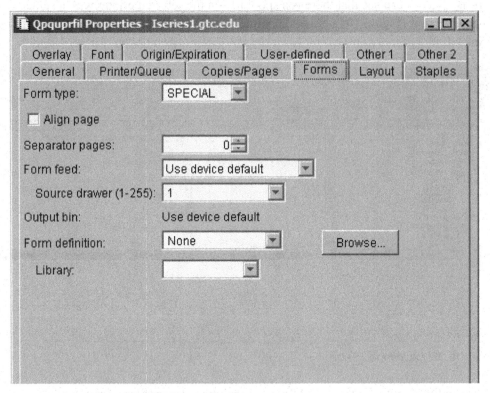

Figure 10.28: Form Properties of a Spool File

Notice that this spool file is set to a form type of SPECIAL. If you remember our earlier discussions of the spooling process, you will recall that it is not unusual for jobs to create spool files with different form types. The form type information is important. For example, your job might be to produce payroll checks; in that case, you would want to be sure that the check forms, and not blank paper, are in the printer before the spool file was printed.

Now, right-click the designated printer in the left-hand window of Figure 10.27 and select Properties to open the properties for printer Bio123a. Once this window is open, you see a number of tabs at the top of the window. When you select the Forms tab (Figure 10.29), you can see that the current form type on this printer is Std.

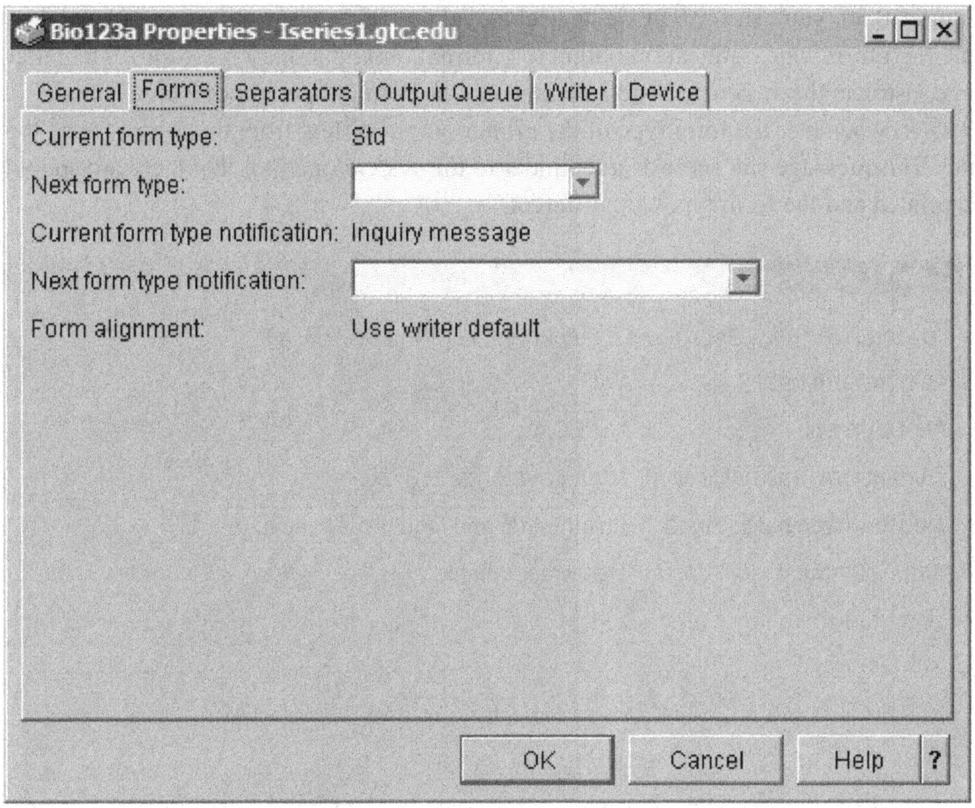

Figure 10.29: Form Properties of the Printer Bio123a

As long as the form types do not match between the spool file and the printer, the spool file will not print. The best way to resolve this problem is to change the printer to the form type SPECIAL. Changing the spool file form type to Std is also an option. However, if you have multiple spool files with a form type of SPECIAL, you would have to change each spool file, and on many systems this could be quite a task. Changing the printer's form type to match the spool file instead will enable you to print all spool files with the SPECIAL form type without further intervention.

In Figure 10.30, you can see that we have changed the printer's form type to SPECIAL and set the Next form type notification option to Information and inquiry messages. The latter change instructs the system to send a message to the system operator message queue (QSYSOPR) whenever the form type of the printer output differs from the form type of the printer. This message can serve as a reminder to the system operator that there are spool files to be printed and the form types are different.

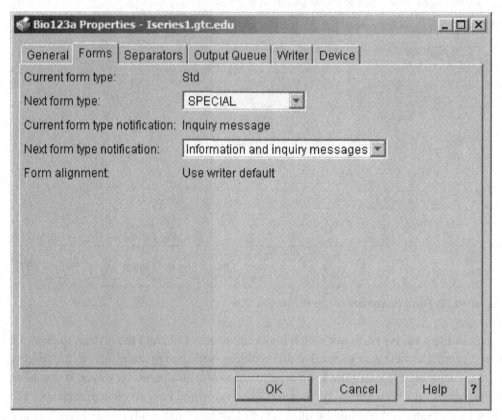

Figure 10.30: Form Properties of the Printer Bio123a—Changed to SPECIAL

The form type on the printer is changed as soon as you click OK. However, when you go back to look at the printer, a message is displayed. Right-clicking the printer lets you reply the message (10.31).

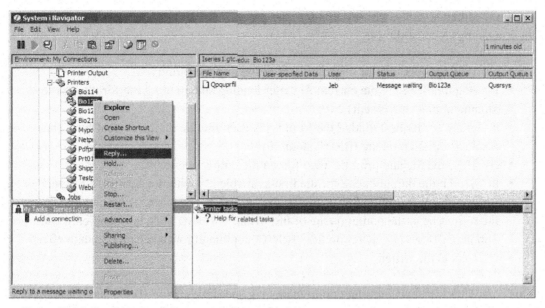

Figure 10.31: Replying to a Message on Printer Bio123a

Click Reply on the context menu to bring up the message window in Figure 10.32.

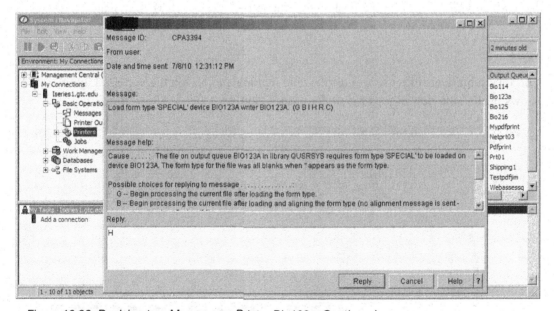

Figure 10.32: Replying to a Message on Printer Bio123a, Continued

There are numerous possible answers to the message in this example. This system defaults
to H, which lets you "hold" the file and print the next one in the queue. In this case, you can

input a G and click Reply, which will allow the spool file to print. The possible replies and their meanings are as follows:

- G—Begin processing the current file after loading the form type.
- B—Begin processing the current file after loading and aligning the form type (no alignment message is sent).
- I—Ignore the request to load the form type. Print the file on the current form type (same as option 0 on the IBM System/36).
- H—Hold the file and print the next file on the output queue.
- R—Search the output queue for the first available file with the correct form type. Reply value R is useful after using the CHGWTR (Change Writer) command to change the form type or the output queue of the writer. *FILEEND must be specified for the option (OPTION) parameter on the CHGWTR command for the change to take effect.
- C—Cancel the writer.

This completes our short introduction to managing spool files using IBM i Navigator. You will learn many additional features as you work with the product. One handy aspect of working with spool files in IBM i Navigator is that you can drag spool files onto a printer. You accomplish this when you are displaying spool files, by dragging a spool file from the right window to the list of printers shown in the left window of IBM i Navigator.

Jobs

The Jobs subtask enables users to display and manipulate jobs on the system. Figure 10.33 shows the default view of jobs for student user CIS001D.

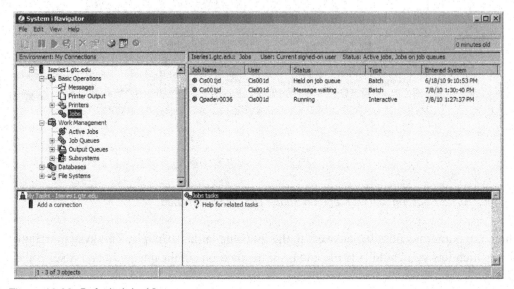

Figure 10.33: Default Jobs View

The default view shows the Job Name, User, Status, Type, and the date/time the job entered the system. Notice that there are three jobs shown for this user, and that all three have a different status. The first job is a batch job in a status of Held on job queue. The second job is also a batch job, with a status of Message waiting. Finally, the third job is an interactive job, and its status is Running. The third job tells us that this user is logged on to the system using an interactive job—in this case, a 5250 session.

You can change the default view to permit the user to see additional information about a job. To do so, you right-click the Jobs icon in the left window, select Customize this View, and then select Columns, as in Figure 10.34.

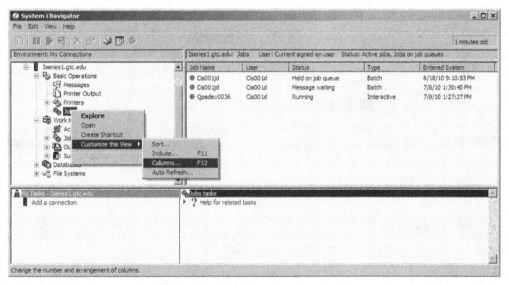

Figure 10.34: Changing the Column Information

Figure 10.35 shows the available columns that can be added to the display. In this case, we are adding the Total CPU Time to the display. Notice that Status is highlighted in the right column; if you clicked the Add After button and then clicked OK, the Total CPU Time value would be displayed after the status of the job. This information could be very important if the system is heavily loaded and you are looking for jobs that use large amounts of CPU.

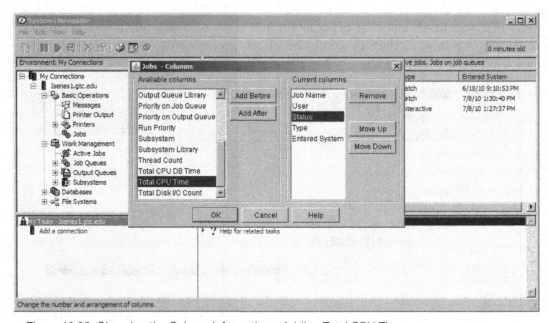

Figure 10.35: Changing the Column Information—Adding Total CPU Time

By default, IBM i Navigator displays the job information for the current signed-on user. This display changes to show information about any user on the system. Figure 10.36 shows the windows that are displayed after you right-click the Jobs icon, select Customize this View, and then select Include.

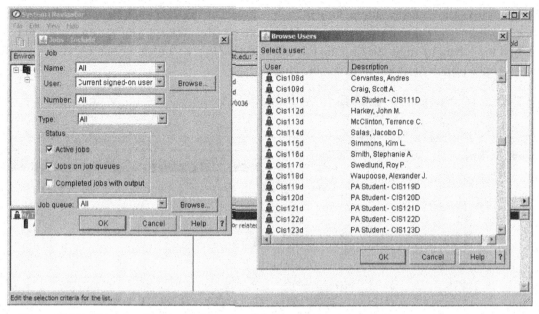

Figure 10.36: Changing the User Information Displayed

This window includes a number of options; you can filter by job name, user, number, job type, or job queue. There are also checkboxes to filter by Active jobs, Jobs on job queues, or Completed jobs with output. At this time, these options might not seem important; however, when you have a system that runs thousands of jobs at a time, it can be difficult to keep track of jobs without the ability to filter them.

Notice the Browse button beside the User drop-down box in Figure 10.36. Clicking Browse displays a pop-up window similar to the one you see on the right in this figure. In this window, you can scroll and find a specific user, which allows you to change the user displayed in a jobs window.

Figure 10.37 shows that right-clicking the job whose status is Held on job queue gives you the capability to release this job. You could also answer the message you see on the second job of the screen by right-clicking the job and selecting Reply—much the same as when you answered a printer message earlier in the chapter.

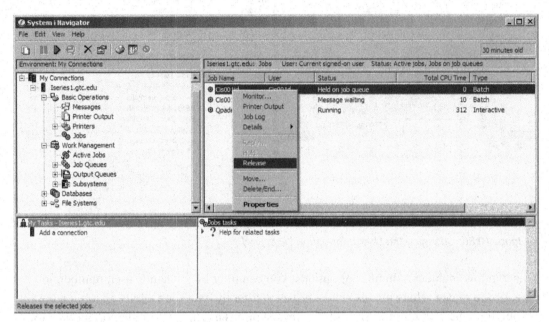

Figure 10.37: Managing Jobs for the Current User

Work Management

The IBM i OS's ability to manage many jobs is one of the most important considerations when companies decide to adopt this OS. The following discussion will give you insight into how to manage jobs on the system. A detailed discussion of work management is beyond the scope of this book. We will, however, discuss the subtasks under work management so that you have an understanding of how to control jobs on the system.

Active Jobs

One of the first steps in work management is to know what jobs are running on your system. The IBM i OS provides the **WRKACTJOB** (Work with Active Jobs) CL command, which enables you to work with all the active jobs on the system. Figure 10.38 shows the command after you prompt F4 and press F9 to display all parameters.

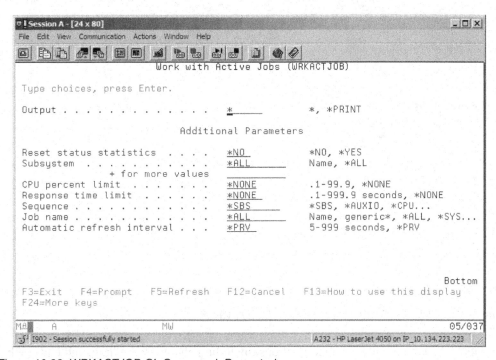

Figure 10.38: WRKACTJOB CL Command, Prompted

You have gained enough experience using the IBM i command line to obtain Help to explain the majority of the WRKACTJOB parameters. We do want to point out that you can filter the jobs shown by subsystem, CPU percent limit, or job name.

In Figure 10.39, we have taken the defaults for the WRKACTJOB command. Here, under the subsystem QBATCH, the job first shown is that in which our student user CIS001D had submitted a job (note the arrow) to batch. This job is waiting for a message to be answered.

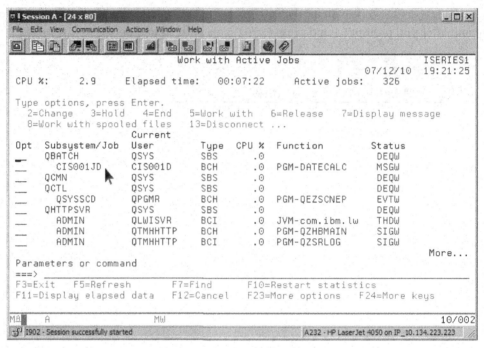

Figure 10.39: WRKACTJOB CL Command – Default Values

The WRKACTJOB command has many options, including changing, holding, and ending the jobs or associated subsystems. Notice that one option is 7=Display message. You could put a 7 on the job in QBATCH and answer the message from the screen. In the following discussion, we will show you how to do this in IBM i Navigator.

Caution

This discussion on work management shows you how to access and change jobs. It is important to understand that on an IBM i system you have many users accessing the system at the same time. Changing jobs or subsystems indiscriminately can negatively affect all the users on the system. It is your responsibility *not* to make changes that will affect other users. You also should know that the system logs these changes, and they could end up with the system administrator. You could then be having a deep discussion concerning your career. A word to the wise!

When you click on the Active Jobs subtasks under Work Management, you are presented with the screen in Figure 10.40. This is the same information that is displayed when you use the WRKACTJOB command. All of the functionality that users are used to seeing when they use the CL command in a 5250 session is included in IBM i Navigator. The figure shows the default columns. As with the printers, messages, and jobs we discussed previously, you can add columns to the display and easily sort that display by clicking on any of the column headings. Notice the arrow in the right window; this is the student job from our earlier discussion of the WRKACTJOB command, with a status of Message waiting.

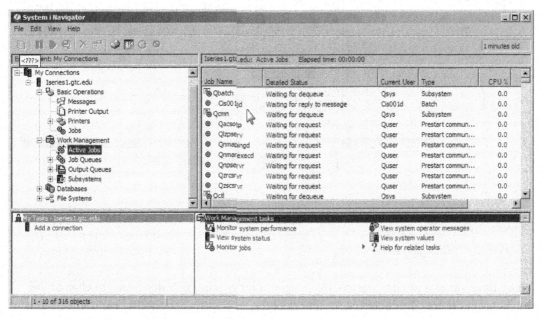

Figure 10.40: IBM i Navigator—Active Jobs

If you select the Details option offered in Figure 10.41, you are presented with a number of options. These options are very similar to taking option 5 on a job when you use the WRKACTJOB command to work with the job. You could also answer the message by right-clicking and then clicking Reply.

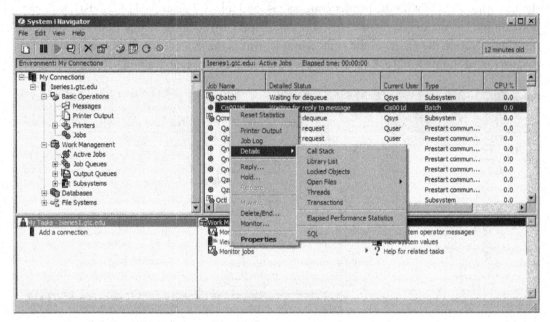

Figure 10.41: Changing a Job

Many times, after a job has started, the programmer or administrator needs to change the attributes of the job. To do this, you can select the Properties option after right-clicking the job (refer to Figure 10.41). Doing so presents the window you see in Figure 10.42.

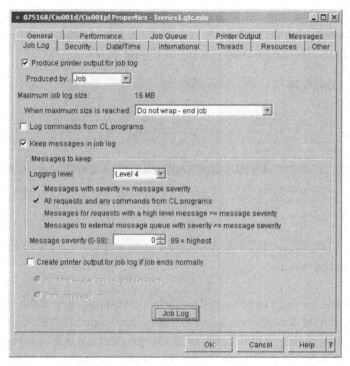

Figure 10.42: Changing Job Properties

When this window first opens, the General tab is displayed. This tab reports the Job name, User, Number, Type, Detailed status, time the job Entered system, Subsystem, and Job description name.

We have switched to the Job Log tab in Figure 10.42 to show some of the important options available when you deal with job logs. Here, you can change the **Logging level** and **Message severity** for the job. There are four logging levels, from 1, which logs the least information, to 4, where practically everything is logged. There are also 99 levels of message severity; the higher the message severity number, the more severe the error condition. If you are having problems with a job, you can use these two values to help solve (debug) the problem by writing additional information to the job's job log.

We need to emphasize the importance to you, as a new user to the IBM i system, of understanding messages on the system. If you click the Job Log button in Figure 10.42, you are presented with the Job Log screen you see in Figure 10.43.

Message ID	Message	Sent	Type	Severity
CPA0702	MCH3601 received by procedure DATECALC. (C D I R)	7/8/10 1:30:40 PM	Sender's copy	99
CPF9999	Function check. MCH3601 unmonitored by DATECALC at statement 0000000113, instruction ...	7/8/10 1:30:40 PM	Escape	40
MCH3601	Pointer not set for location referenced.	7/8/10 1:30:40 PM	Escape	40
	CALL PGM(CIS001/DATECALC)	7/8/10 1:30:40 PM	Current request	0
CPI1125	Job 075168/CIS001D/CIS001JD submitted.	7/8/10 1:30:40 PM	Information	0
CPF1124	Job 075168/CIS001D/CIS001JD started on 07/08/10 at 13:30:40 in subsystem QBATCH in Q...	7/8/10 1:30:40 PM	Information	0

Figure 10.43: Job Log Window

The messages in this job log are presented with the newest message at the top of the window. The fourth line down shows a call to a program named DATECALC in library CIS001. The message highlighted in black is an Escape message with a severity of 40. The preceding message is a function check, and it shows you the statement number that caused the problem in the program. This detail can be very helpful in finding why the program "**abended**" (an acronym for *ab*normal *end* of a job, a term that originated from an error message on the IBM System/360). The final message received in this group is the one that needs to be answered. Understand that you are looking at the job log and cannot answer messages at this level. Instead, you can answer the message with the appropriate response using the Active Jobs window and the Reply option (refer back to Figure 10.41).

Job Queues

Job queues are an important part of the IBM i OS work-management process. As you can see in Figure 10.44, when a user submits a job to the system, it goes into a job queue and is eventually processed by the subsystem to which the job queue is attached. The order in which the jobs are processed is dependent on the priority of the job when it is submitted.

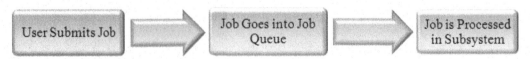

Figure 10.44: Job Processing Sequence

The Job Queues subtask lets you look at the job queues on the system. This subtask is broken down into Active Job Queues and All Job Queues. Clicking the Active Job Queues icon displays all job queues that are currently assigned to an active subsystem (Figure 10.45).

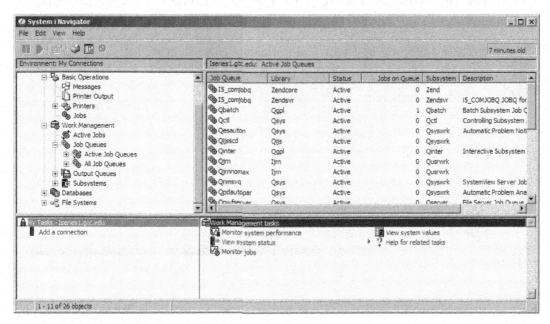

Figure 10.45: Active Job Queues Window

Right-clicking one of the job queues lets you look at the queue's Properties and choose from the Hold, Release, and Clear job-queue options.

Output Queues

The Output Queues subtask allows users to control any output queue to which they have access rights. The right window of Figure 10.46 shows a number of output queues on the system.

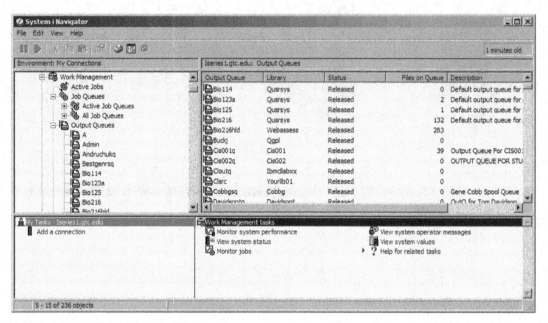

Figure 10.46: Output Queues Window

In this window, you can see the status of each output queue and how many files are on the queue. As with printers and messages, you can customize the columns shown. Right-clicking a specific queue lets you Hold, Release, or Clear the queue. Selecting Properties after right-clicking a specific queue, and then selecting the Writers tab, shows you the writer attached to the queue, as well as the writer's status.

Subsystems

IBM defines a subsystem as a "single, predefined operating environment to which the system coordinates workflow and resource usage." We discussed subsystems in Chapter 1 of this text. Looking at Figure 10.47, you can see we have expanded the Subsystems subtask as well as the Active Subsystems icon below it.

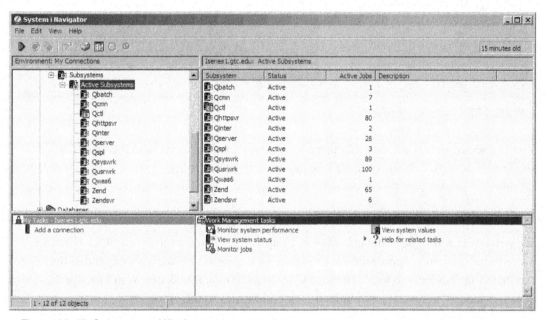

Figure 10.47: Subsystems Window

Many of the subsystems shown are used by the system and normally are not changed by programmers. Historically, the two subsystems that programmers most often deal with are **QBATCH** (the batch subsystem) and **QINTER** (the interactive subsystem). This tradition is rapidly changing as more and more applications are moved to the Web. The figure shows several other subsystems—the **QHTTPSVR** (Apache) **subsystem**, the **Zend** (Zend Core) **subsystem,** and the **Zendsvr** (Zend Server) **subsystem**—that are dedicated to Web applications and run Web servers. Today's programmers must be familiar with these technologies and be able to work in these Web environments.

When you expand the Active Subsystems icon in Figure 10.47, you can see, in the right window, which subsystems are active on the system. You also can see the status and the number of jobs that are active, as well as the description of the subsystems. You can add and remove columns from this display just as you could with the printers, output queues, or jobs subtasks. If you right-click one of the subsystems—for example, if you right-click the QBATCH subsystem and select Job Queues—you will be presented with a window similar to Figure 10.48.

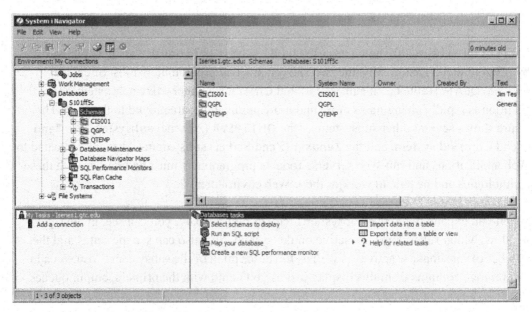

Figure 10.48: Job Queues Window

You can see from this window that three job queues are associated with the QBATCH subsystem. Right-click one of these job queues to Hold or Clear it.

Databases

We will cover additional database tasks in Chapter 13 when we introduce SQL. However, a short introduction is appropriate at this time. In Figure 10.49, we have expanded the Databases tasks icon, the local database icon (S191ff5c on this system), and finally the Schemas icon. The system automatically added libraries to the view.

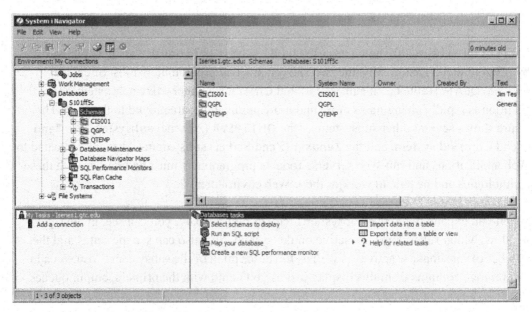

Figure 10.49: Databases Tasks Window

We will now look at our student library, CIS001. In Figure 10.50, we have expanded this library to see all the allowed subtasks. Using this window, you can create new tables (physical files), views (logical files), and many other SQL-related objects.

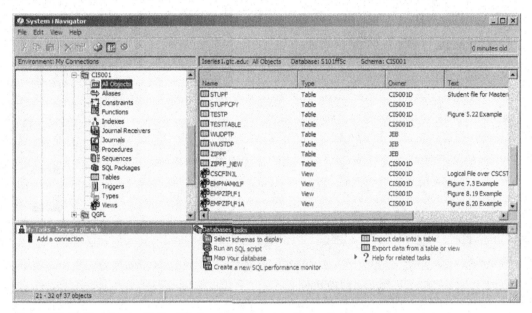

Figure 10.50: Databases Tasks Window, Expanded to Show Subtasks

Right-clicking the STUPF table (physical file) that we created in an earlier chapter displays the options you see in Figure 10.51.

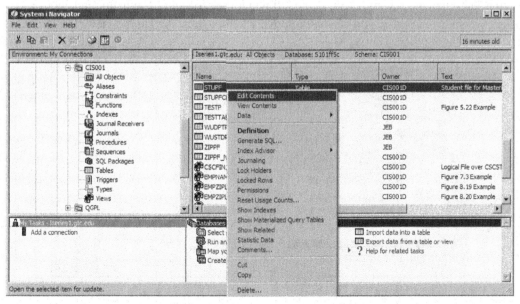

Figure 10.51: Databases Tasks Window, STUPF Physical File Options

Using IBM i Navigator, you can easily display or edit data in the file, as Figure 10.52 shows.

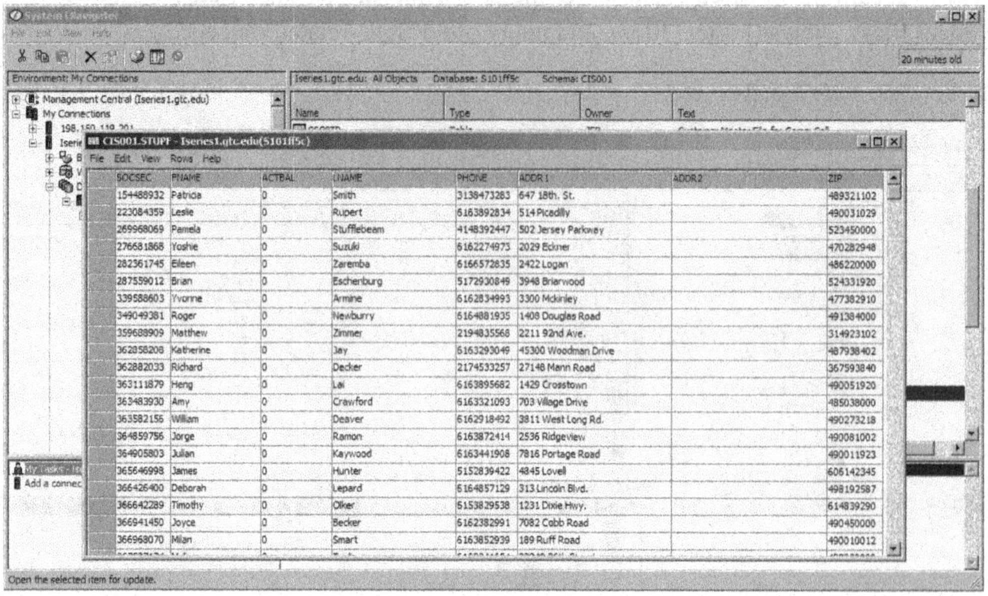

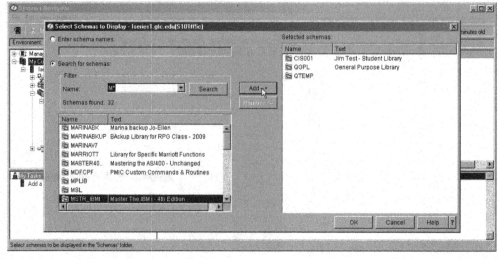

Figure 10.52: Edit Table Contents Window

Many other options are available using the context menu in Figure 10.51, including Cut, Copy, Delete, and Rename. Exercise caution when you use these options because, unlike Windows computers, the IBM i OS does not have a Recycle Bin.

If you right-click the Schemas icon in the left window of System i Navigator and choose Select Schemas to Display, you can add/remove schemas (libraries) in the view (Figure 10.53).

Figure 10.53: Add a Schema to Our View

Caution
We cannot emphasize enough that if you want to remove a library from your schema view, use the Remove from List option. *Do not* select the Delete option. Delete means *delete* (the library or schema), and *not* remove from the schema view. Trust us; we have had students find this out for themselves!

File Systems

The **integrated file system** (IFS) is similar to the personal computer and UNIX operating systems. The IFS is part of the IBM i OS and supports stream input/output and storage management. IBM added this IFS file system to the OS in V3R1, but IBM i users have largely ignored it until recent years. With the open-systems movement in the past few years, and products such as PHP and MySQL becoming more important to the IBM i community, these file systems are used more every day. Meanwhile, IBM continues to enhance the capabilities of the IFS with every release of the OS.

The IFS comprises 10 unique file systems; each file system has its own rules for interacting with data storage and its own set of logical structures. Figure 10.54 shows a graphical view of the IBM i file systems.

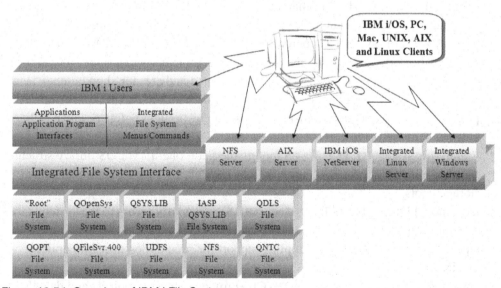

Figure 10.54: Overview of IBM i File Systems

The integrated file system has several key features; these features allow a seamless integration with many computer platforms. These features include

- Stream file support—Support is designed for efficient use in client/server applications. The system allows storage of information in **stream files** (strings of bytes that are accessed by their relative position in the file) as contiguous strings of data. For example, the strings of data might consist of the picture elements in a picture or text in a document.
- **Hierarchical directory structure**—Like branches of the tree, you can access objects by specifying the path through the directories to the object.
- **Common interface**—The IFS interface allows applications and users access to documents, database files, stream files, and other objects.
- Common view of stream files—The stream files can be stored locally on your system, on a remote Windows NT server, on another IBM i system, or on a remote local area network (**Network File System,** or NFS).

We will not deal with all of these file systems in detail in this text. However, it is important for you as a new IBM i user to understand that these file systems exist and to appreciate the power they give the IBM i system to integrate with many systems in today's IT environment. The following list summarizes the 10 supported file systems and includes a short description of each.

- Root (/) file system—Has the characteristics of the DOS and OS/2 OSs and takes advantage of stream file support; has a hierarchical directory structure.
- Open systems file system (**QOpenSys**)—Is compatible with UNIX-based standards and, like the Root file system, takes advantage of directory support and stream files.
- User-defined file systems (**UDFSs**)—Can be created and are stored on independent storage pools or an auxiliary storage pool. An **independent auxiliary storage pool** (IASP) is a collection of disk units that can be brought online or taken offline independently of the rest of the storage on the system.
- Library file system (**QSYS.LIB**) —Supports the traditional IBM i/OS library structure.
- Independent ASP QSYS.LIB—Supports IBM i/OS library structure on independent storage pools.
- Document library services file system (**QDLS**)—Supports access to the system's folder structure and access to documents and folders.
- Optical file system (**QOPT**)—Supplies support for stream files stored on optical media.
- IBM i/OS NetClient file system (**QNTC**)—Provides access to objects and data that are stored on Linux operating systems and integrated xSeries servers running Windows NT 4.0 or higher. The QNTC file system also provides access to data stored on remote

servers running Windows NT 4.0 or higher, Linux Samba 3.1, or supported versions of i5/OS NetServer.

- IBM i/OS file server file system (**QFileSvr.400**)—Is accessed through a hierarchical directory structure and provides access to file systems that reside on remote IBM i systems.
- Network File System (NFS)—Provides access to a remote network file server (NFS) and the data and objects stored on it.

The IFS Root file system stores

- PDF files, spreadsheets, and Word documents that users can access from mapped drives on their PC or copy/paste from and to their PC
- HTML, Java, JSP, PHP, and XHTML files for use in Web applications
- Data imported from or exported to other platforms
- Database files used with MySQL
- Program source files for which the ILE compilers RPG IV, ILE COBOL, C, and C++ allow you to specify an IFS directory instead of a source member

This list continues to grow as more UNIX and Web applications are ported to or installed on IBM i systems. A few years ago, IBM and Zend (*http://www.zend.com*) entered into an agreement to provide and support PHP software for the IBM i OS, which has been a boon to bringing IBM i systems to the Web.

It is not unusual for a user to be given a folder under the Root file system's /home folder, for storing documents. A properly secured IFS will limit the access of users to specific folders. In the following example, we will create a folder and copy a Word document to the new WordDoc folder within the CIS001D folder.

You can see in Figure 10.55 that we have expanded File Systems → Integrated File System → Root folders → home, right-clicked CIS001D, and selected New Folder.

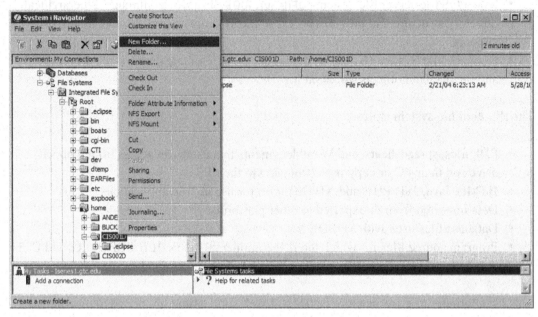

Figure 10.55: Creating a New Folder in the Root File System

In Figure 10.56, we have entered the value WordDoc for the name of the new folder, and we have left the default value for Audit objects created in folder to use the **QAUDJRN** system value. This value determines whether the IBM i OS creates an auditing entry in the system auditing journal when the object is used or changed. We have left the default value for Scan objects created in folder; this value determines whether the system scans the folder when exit programs are registered—for example, if the system is using antivirus software. Finally, we also have left the default for the Restrict rename and unlink option. If this option is checked, objects within the folder can be renamed and unlinked (deleted) if the user is the owner of the object or the owner of the folder, or if the user has all object (*ALLOBL) special authority.

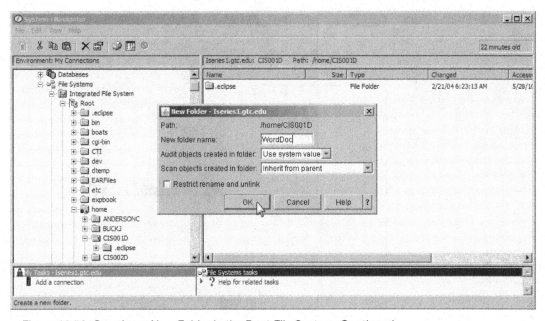

Figure 10.56: Creating a New Folder in the Root File System, Continued

When we click OK, a folder is created under the folder CIS001D. We can now "drag and drop" or "cut and paste" files/folders from the PC to our newly created folder, as Figure 10.57 shows.

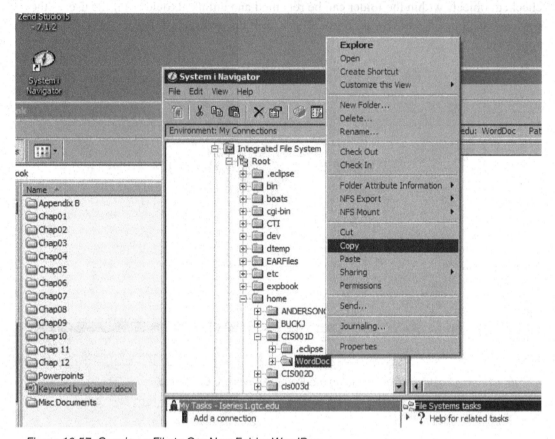

Figure 10.57: Copying a File to Our New Folder WordDoc

 Caution

As IT professionals, we often have access to data not available to other users. We should always be cognizant that we are responsible for the security and availability of the systems we work on and not modify the system in any way that could jeopardize that security.

In Summary

This chapter has provided a brief introduction to IBM i Access for Windows. We started with basic operations, which include how to display and reply to a message, as well as how to send a message to a user workstation.

Printer output is an important part of any system. You learned you how to look at printer output by user or by output queue, including how to use the AFP viewer to display a spool file. You saw how to display all the printers on the system and how to work with the spooled files assigned to those printers, as well as how to hold or cancel specific output.

Work management is important to the programmer, system user, and administrator. You learned about the WRKACTJOB CL command and how you can accomplish the same functions using IBM i Navigator. You were warned about changing jobs or subsystems without careful consideration because doing so could impact the overall performance of the system and affect your users. Job queues are a key part of work management, and we discussed the process that occurs when a user submits a job to a subsystem.

After a job has entered the system, you can use IBM i Navigator to manipulate its properties. You learned some of the options for changing an active job, and you saw how the message logging level and severity of the job can help you debug problems.

In previous chapters, you learned how to update physical files (tables) using DFU. In this chapter, we discussed using IBM i Navigator to display or update data in a file. Many of the options you are accustomed to using in Windows Explorer are available in IBM i Navigator, such as copying, deleting, or renaming files.

The integrated file system (IFS) is a significant part of the IBM i OS and is being used more as software such as PHP and MySQL becomes more prevalent on the system. Our discussion included the major features of the IFS and the names and descriptions of the 10 supported file systems.

In the upcoming lab, you will send and reply to a message from another user, submit a program to BATCH, display a message from the job, and cancel the job. You will create a new schema (library) and copy a physical file from another library. Finally, you will create a folder in the IFS and copy a Word document to the folder.

Key Terms

abended	logging level
AFP Workbench for Windows Viewer	message severity
CHGSPLFA	Network File System
common interface	QAUDJRN
F11 function key	QBATCH
hierarchical directory structure	QDLS
independent auxiliary storage pool	QFileSvr.400
integrated file system	QHTTPSVR subsystem

QINTER	stream files
QNTC	UDFSs
QOpenSys	WRKACTJOB
QOPT	WRKOBJ
QSYS.LIB	Zend subsystem
QSYSOPR message queue	Zendsvr subsystem
SBMJOB	

Review Questions

1. List the IBM i Access products, and give a short explanation of each.

2. When users have problems with the IBM i Navigator product, what should they check?

3. Why should you verify your connection to the system?

4. What is the difference between Management Central and My Connections?

5. What is the purpose of the TaskPad and My Tasks? Explain how they are related.

6. Why would you want to add subtasks to the My Tasks window?

7. List the subtasks under Basic Operations, and write a short description of each.

8. In the text, we discussed the message CPA0702; list the possible replies and their meanings.

9. Explain how you would send a message to a user on the system using IBM i Navigator.

10. List the ways you can filter the spool files that are shown when you display Printer Output using IBM i Navigator.

11. When filtering spooled files, you have the ability to filter on a number of statuses. List the statuses.

12. What are the advantages of displaying spool files using the AFP viewer?

13. What steps would you take to display a spool file on your PC using Notepad?

14. We discussed the options available to answer a message on a printer in this chapter; list and explain each option.

15. Why should you be careful when working with jobs on an IBM i system?

16. When you are changing a job, a number of logging options are available. List and explain these options.

17. Explain the work-management process that occurs when a job is submitted to the system.

18. When you display the Job Queues subtask on the system, there are two options. Name them and explain the differences between the two.

19. In the past few years, there has been additional interest in the IFS. Explain what has driven this interest.

20. List and explain the features of the IFS we discussed in this chapter.

21. List and explain the 10 file systems supported in the IBM i operating system.

22. List the uses we discussed in this chapter for the Root file system. List three additional uses not discussed in this chapter.

23. When you create a folder in the IFS, one option is Restrict rename and unlink. What is the significance of this option being checked?

24. Explain the difference between Remove from list and Delete when you are working with schemas.

Lab 10

Introduction

In this lab, you will become more familiar with the subtasks we discussed in this chapter. You should have created a connection to your system and successfully logged in. For Part 1, you will need to get a user ID from one of your classmates. In Part 2, you will submit a program to the QBATCH subsystem; this program will send a message that you will reply to. In Part 3, you will create a new schema and copy the physical file (table) STUPF to the new schema. In Part 4, you will copy a Word document to your personal folder in the Root file system.

After completing these exercises, you should feel more comfortable using the IBM i Navigator product. As we said in the text, you will be amazed at the capabilities provided you as you become more familiar with the product.

Part 1

Goals   Manage messages, including deleting messages and sending messages.

Start at   IBM i Navigator open and logged in.

Procedure Ask one of your fellow students for her user ID.

Send a message to your fellow student.

Wait for your fellow student to reply to your message.

Refresh your messages and see your fellow student's reply.

Note
You should try to complete this exercise with a fellow student. This is not a
requirement, because the message will remain on her message queue until
she answers it. However, completing the steps as a team will expedite the
exercise.

10.1. Ask one of your fellow students for her system user ID.

10.2. After your classmate has shared her ID, navigate to the Messages subtask.

Expand Basic Operations.

Right-click the Messages subtask.

From the context menu, click Send Message.

You should now see the window in Figure 10.58. Here, enter your fellow student's
user ID, check the Request a reply check box, and enter a short message to your
classmate.

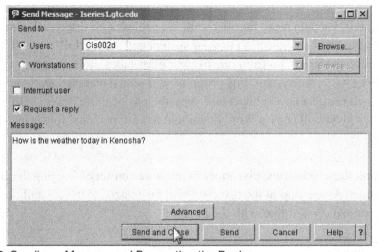

Figure 10.58: Sending a Message and Requesting the Reply

Click the Send and Close button.

Navigate back to your IBM i Navigator window, and display your messages.

10.2.a. Do you see your message displayed?

If you do not see your message . . .

10.2.b. How do you refresh the displayed messages?

10.3. Contact your fellow student, and see whether she received and replied to your message. Your message should appear in her message window as Figure 10.59 shows. Notice in this example that we sent a message from CIS001D to CIS002D.

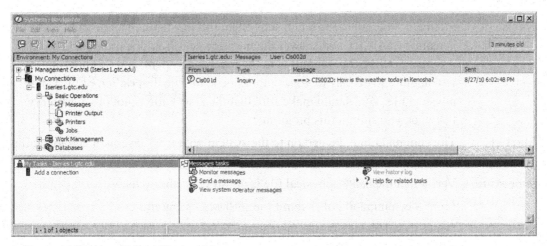

Figure 10.59: Your Fellow-Student Messages

10.3.a. Explain how your fellow student would answer your message.

10.4. After your fellow student has replied to your message, Display your messages. You will see her reply, as in Figure 10.60.

10.4.a. Do you have to refresh your messages to see her reply?

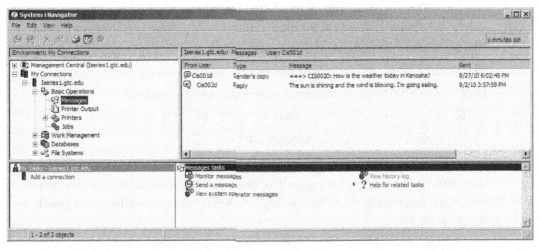

Figure 10.60: Displaying Your Message and a Reply

10.5. To complete this lab, you will need to delete your messages.

    10.5.a. How do you delete the messages from this lab exercise?

Part 2

Goals   Submit a program to the batch subsystem (on most systems, this subsystem is named QBATCH), and answer the message sent from the program. The CL program SENDMSG is submitted to the batch subsystem, and this program will attempt to display to your output queue the file description of the EMPPF physical file. You should make sure that the EMPPF file is not in your library list when you submit this program.

Start at   The command line, logged on to the system with a 5250 session and logged in to IBM i Navigator.

Procedure   Verify that the EMPPF physical file is not in your library list.

    From the command line, submit the SENDMSG program.

    Using IBM i Navigator, navigate to the Jobs subtask under Basic Operations.

    Find the SENDMSG program that you just submitted.

    Display the job log for the SENDMSG job.

    End the SENDMSG program.

10.6. Verify that the EMPPF physical file is *not* in your library list before you submit the program.

Use the **WRKOBJ** (Work with Objects) command to verify that EMPPF is not in your library list. **Note:** Use the online Help to familiarize yourself with the command.

    10.6.a. What is the purpose of this command?

    10.6.b. Why is the WRKOBJ command an easy way to look for objects?

    10.6.c. Write the WRKOBJ command to find the EMPPF file anywhere on the system.

At the 5250 command line, type WRKOBJ EMPPF, and then press Enter.

    10.6.d. Is the EMPPF file in your library list?

    10.6.e. In what library is the file located?

If the EMPPF file was in your library list, use one of the Change Library commands to remove this library from your library list. **Note:** We covered these commands in previous chapters.

    10.6.f. Which command did you use to remove the library?

    10.6.g. How will you put this library back in your library list at the end of this lab?

10.7. From the command line, submit to the batch subsystem the SENDMSG program located in the INTROCLASS library.

The command you will use for this action is the **SBMJOB** (Submit Job) command. After you key SBMJOB at the command line and press F4, your 5250 session should look similar to Figure 10.61.

> 10.7.a. Use the online Help to investigate the SBMJOB command. Give a short description of this command.

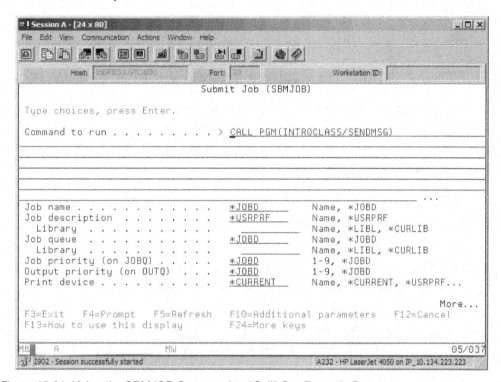

Figure 10.61: Using the SBMJOB Command to "Call" Our Example Program

Type CALL PGM(INTROCLASS/SENDMSG) into the SBMJOB screen as shown in Figure 10.61.

> 10.7.b. What happens if you press F4 after you key in the CALL statement as instructed?

When you press Enter, the SENDMSG program will be submitted to the batch subsystem.

> 10.7.c. How could you check to see the status of this program from the 5250 command line?

10.8. Using IBM i Navigator, navigate to the Jobs subtask under Basic Operations. You should see a window similar to Figure 10.62.

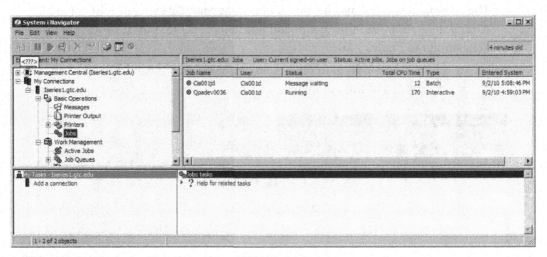

Figure 10.62: Displaying Your Jobs Using IBM i Navigator

10.9. Looking at the top-right window of the display shown in the figure, you can see two jobs that belong to student user CIS001D.

    10.9.a. How does your window differ from the one in Figure 10.62?

    10.9.b. In the example, you can see that the job at the top of the window has a message waiting. How would you answer this message?

    10.9.c. The second job in the example shows a type of Interactive. What does this tell you about the job?

10.10. After you submit your SENDMSG program, you should have a job with a message waiting.

    10.10.a. How can you find out what the message says?

    10.10.b. How can you display the job's job log?

    10.10.c. How would you answer the message waiting?

    10.10.d. Why should you display the job log before you answer the message?

10.11. Because this job cannot be "fixed" while it is running:

    10.11.a. What is the correct response to end this program?

    10.11.b. Before you submit the job again, what should you do to ensure it runs normally?

Note: For those of you who are interested, the source code for the CL program used in this exercise should be in the source physical file QCLLESRC in the library INTROCLASS.

Part 3

Goals Create a new schema, copy the STUPF table from the INTROCLASS library to the new schema, and add three records to the table.

Start at Logged into the system using IBM i Navigator.

Procedure Navigate to the Schemas icon.

Create a new schema.

Add the INTROCLASS schema to your IBM i Navigator view.

Copy STUPF to the scheme you just created.

Add three records to the STUPF table.

Note

To name the new schema in our example, we will append WRK to the CIS001 student library. Therefore, this example will show CIS001WRK. You should ask your instructor for the naming convention you should use.

10.12. Navigate to the Schemas icon under Databases in the left window of IBM i Navigator.

10.13. Right-click the Schemas icon and select New/Schema, as you see in Figure 10.63.

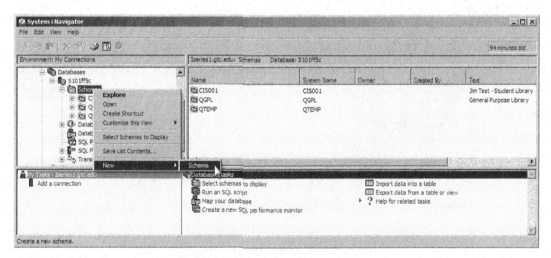

Figure 10.63: Creating a New Schema Using IBM i Navigator

10.14. Enter the name of the new schema (library) and add some text that describes the schema (Figure 10.64).

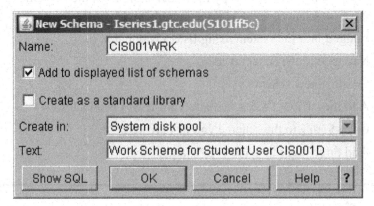

Figure 10.64: Creating a New Schema Using IBM i Navigator, Continued

Note: Be sure to check with your instructor for the proper naming convention of your new schema.

10.15. Add a schema named INTROCLASS to the list of displayed schemas.

10.16. Right-click the Schemas icon in the upper-left window, and choose Select Schemas to Display (Figure 10.65).

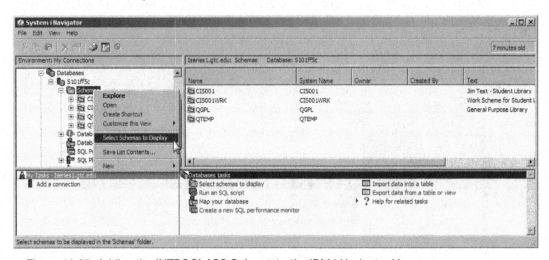

Figure 10.65: Adding the INTROCLASS Schema to the IBM i Navigator Vew

10.17. Enter the name of the schema to display (Figure 10.66), click Add, and then click OK.

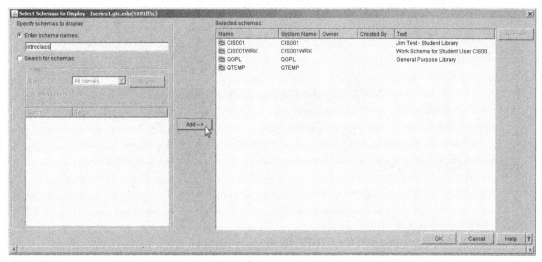

Figure 10.66: Adding the INTROCLASS Schema to the IBM i Navigator View, Continued

10.18. Expand the INTROCLASS schema, and navigate to the Tables icon.

10.19. Right-click the STUPF table, and select Copy (Figure 10.67).

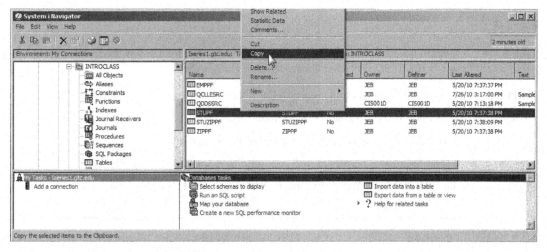

Figure 10.67: Copying the STUPF Table

10.20. Navigate back to the schema you just created. (For this example, we used CIS001WRK.)

10.21. Expand the schema, right-click the Tables icon, and then select Paste.

10.22. After the table has been copied, right-click the STUPF icon and select Edit; your window will be similar to what you see in Figure 10.68.

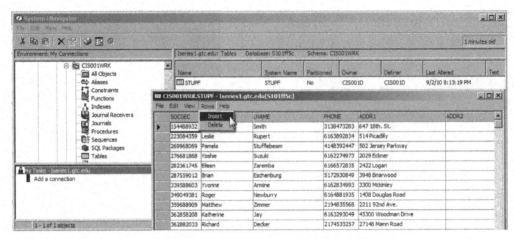

Figure 10.68: Adding Records to the STUPF Table

10.23. Insert three records in the table.

    10.23.a. How do you save records?

    10.23.b. What other options do you have when you are in Edit mode?

Part 4

Goals   Create a new folder under the Root file system, and copy a Word document to this folder.

Start at   Logged into the system using IBM i Navigator.

Procedure   Navigate to your personal folder on the system.

    Create a new folder under your personal folder.

    Open Windows Explorer and navigate to a folder on your PC.

    Drag and drop a Word document from your PC to your new folder on the IFS.

Caution

Check with your instructor before you attempt this lab, to make sure you have a folder under the Root file system. *You should also be aware that system administrators frown on you storing personal files on their system.*

10.24. Navigate to your personal folder. In our example, we use our student user ID; the folder is CIS001D.

10.25. Click the + sign next to the File Systems icon to expand the folder.

10.26. Click the + sign next to the Integrated File System icon to expand the folder.

10.27. Click the + signs next to the Root icon and the home icon to expand the folders.

10.28. Locate and right-click your personal folder, and then select New Folder from the pop-up window, as you see in Figure 10.69.

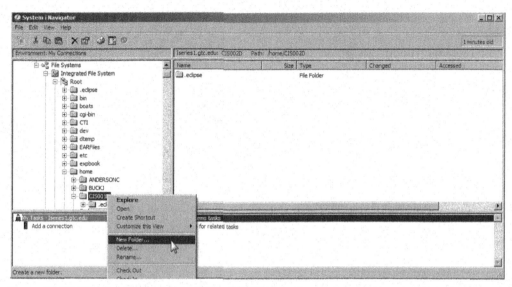

Figure 10.69: Creating a New Folder Using IBM i Navigator

10.29. Name the new folder Chap10Part04, as in Figure 10.70. Leave the defaults for the other options.

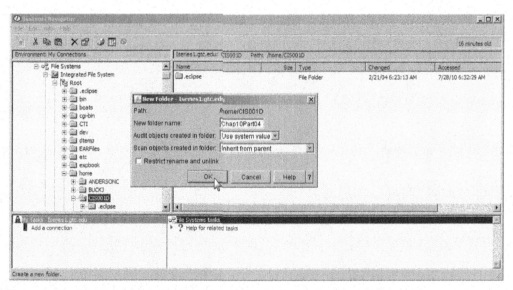

Figure 10.70: Creating a New Folder Using IBM i Navigator, Continued

You have now created your new folder in the system under the Root file system.

10.30. Next, you need to copy a Word document to this new folder. As you can see in Figure 10.71, we have opened Windows Explorer and dragged and dropped a document to our new folder.

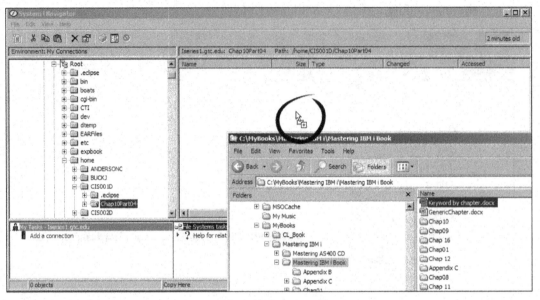

Figure 10.71: Copying a Document to a New Folder Using IBM i Navigator

Notice the accent we have included in Figure 10.71. The encircled arrow shows you where the document will be copied.

Using Remote System Explorer

Overview

In this chapter, we discuss Rational Developer for Power 8.0 (RDP 8.0), the graphical tool that will replace SEU, SDA, PDM, and CODE Designer. We start with a short discussion of how IBM's Rational toolset came about and continue with an introduction to its major component, Remote System Explorer (RSE), covering RSE's major features and use. First, you will learn how to connect to a Power system running the IBM i OS; then, you'll learn to navigate the system using RSE. In Chapter 6, you studied the CRTSRCPF command; in this chapter, you will use RSE to create a source physical file. After you copy a CL program from another library into your student library, you will then open and edit the member. You will make some changes to the member and then save, compile, debug, and run it.

Objectives

Students will be able to

- Create a connection using RSE
- Navigate their current library list
- Create a source physical file in their library
- Manipulate their library list
- Copy a source member from another library
- Edit, save, and compile the source member
- Set a service point
- Debug a program
- Set a monitor while debugging
- Set a breakpoint while debugging
- Submit a program to batch

History

During the mid-to late-1990s, a number of toolsets were becoming available that gave programmers a complete environment for developing code. As Java became more widespread, a number of these **Integrated Development Environments** (IDEs) were becoming popular, and a general-purpose tool, called Microsoft Visual Studio, was gaining widespread acceptance. At IBM, different developers (depending on the platform and/or language) were creating IBM's development tools. During this time, we also saw the emergence of application servers designed to decouple the presentation layer from the background (database access and OS tasks) layers. There were two schools of thought: one that focused on Microsoft's proprietary runtime environment, and the open-source community that was revolving around open-industry Java development.

IBM and Eclipse

IBM wanted a common platform for all its development tools and decided that the open-industry/source initiative made more sense than a proprietary toolset. Using a common platform for programming tasks allowed programmers to learn one development environment, and, by using plug-ins, they could easily develop code for different types of applications. In November 1998, the IBM software group began work on the development-tools platform that eventually became known as the Eclipse platform.

Part of this initiative was the need for third-party business partners to develop plug-ins. At first, business partners were reluctant to invest in this unproven platform. To increase exposure and accelerate adoption, IBM decided in November 2001 to adopt the open-source licensing and operating model. By 2003, the first major releases of Eclipse were being well received. However, industry analysts told IBM that the marketplace perceived Eclipse as an IBM-controlled effort. To change this perception, IBM helped create the Eclipse Foundation as a nonprofit organization supported by dues from member companies and with its own independently paid, professional staff. You can learn more about Eclipse at *http://www. eclipse.org*.

The IBM Rational Toolset

By 2004, IBM had committed to having its Rational Software Division use Eclipse as the core for all of its software development tools. This Rational suite of products covers a number of platforms and languages and includes software to develop Web sites using languages such as C/C++, Enterprise Generation Language (EGL), HTML, Java, JavaScript, and Java Server Pages (JSP). The Rational toolset also allows programmers to develop software using languages such as RPG ILE and COBOL.

In this chapter, we introduce **Remote System Explorer** (RSE), a set of tools for developing native IBM i applications using RPG, COBOL, CL, and DDS. If you are interested in more in-depth information about RSE than we present in this chapter, pick up *The Remote System Explorer* by Don Yantzi and Nazmin Haji (MC Press, 2008).

In this text, we use **Rational Developer for Power 8.0** (RDP 8.0), which at the time of this writing is the latest version of the toolset. Older versions include **WebSphere Development Studio Client for System i** (WDSc) and **IBM Rational Developer for System i** (RDi). The previous products used CODE Designer to develop print files and screens using DDS. RDP 7.6 was the first version to use the new screen designer, which we discuss in Chapter 12. With the release of RDP 7.6, we finally had one tool to accomplish all of the programming tasks today's RPG or COBOL programmers require.

Note

Before starting this chapter, you should have at least RDP 7.6 installed on your workstation. IBM makes this software available to colleges and students. Previous versions such as WDSc and RDi should allow you to complete the labs in this chapter. However, in Chapter 12, where we discuss the new screen designer, these older tools will cause you problems.

The RDP installation process is simple, and there are fewer hardware requirements than for previous versions. IBM recommends a minimum of a 1GHz processor and 1GB of RAM. The supported OSs range from Microsoft Windows XP Professional with Service Pack 2 to Windows 7 Professional Enterprise and Ultimate editions running in 32-bit mode.

Getting Started

When you start RDP, you will be prompted for the storage location of your workspace, as you can see in Figure 11.1.

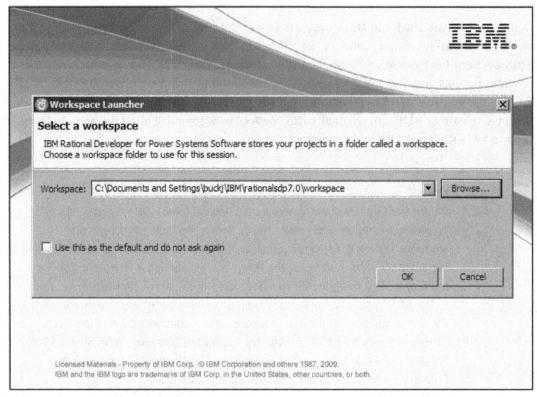

Figure 11.1: Selecting a Workspace Location

By default, RDP stores the default workspace under Documents and Settings. Most programmers create a folder under the root directory—for example, C:\RDPower\ workspace—that will simplify finding it. The workspace is just a Windows folder that stores local projects (e.g., Java, Web pages), your personal preferences, server connection information, and information concerning the state of the workbench. Following is some additional information about workspaces.

- Do not use a network drive for your workspace. The workspace is updated regularly, and for performance reasons it is important to keep it on a local drive. Many programmers use a USB drive to store their workspace, which allows them to take their projects and preferences from one workstation to another. This approach works well as long as the versions of the Rational product on the workstations are the same.
- Many programmers use multiple workspaces for different projects; one workspace for Java projects and another for RPG or COBOL projects is suggested. It is also a good

practice to properly name the workspaces to help you differentiate between them. For example, you might create a workspace called JavaWorkspace for your Java projects and another called RPGWorkspace for your RPG projects.

- We do not recommend selecting the check-box option to Use this as the default and do not ask again (refer to Figure 11.1) because when RDP starts without asking for a workspace, it confuses many users. However, you can reset this option under Preferences in the workbench.
- It is important to back up your workspace, especially for projects that store project information (e.g., Java programs, Web pages) locally in the workspace.

When you click OK in Figure 11.1, the Welcome page is displayed, as you see in Figure 11.2. We cannot overemphasize the value in taking the time to investigate this page. Once closed, this screen is available later by clicking Help and then Welcome in the toolbar at the top of the workbench. For some of you moving from the 5250 environment to the RDP graphical environment, the First Steps guidance is invaluable.

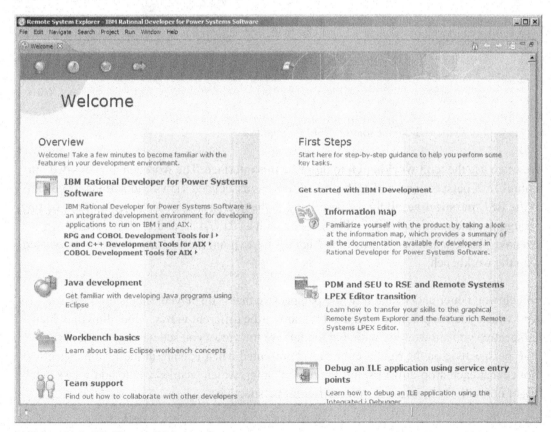

Figure 11.2: Workbench Welcome Page

To close the Welcome page, click the X on the tab in the upper-left corner of the window. Figure 11.3 shows the RSE perspective, which is the perspective you will use most often for coding RPG, COBOL, DDS, or CL.

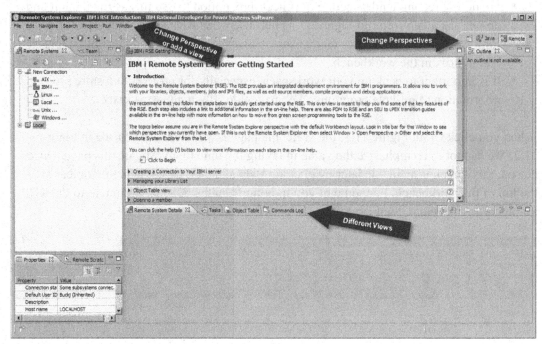

Figure 11.3: Remote System Explorer (RSE) Perspective

We often use the term **workbench** to describe this interface. The workbench is divided into a number of perspectives, and each perspective has associated views and actions. If you are in the **RSE perspective**, all the views related to the tasks associated with compiling, editing, debugging, and running traditional languages such as RPG, CL, and COBOL are shown. We have placed a number of arrows in Figure 11.3 to point out important actions associated with the workbench.

To help you better understand how the perspective that is displayed affects the views with which you are presented, Figure 11.4 shows the different views, depending on which perspective you are working with. On the left are the views you see when you are in the RSE perspective; on the right are the views presented when you are in the Java perspective. Notice that each drop-down list has the option Other, which enables you to add views that might normally be associated with a different perspective.

Remote System Explorer Perspective - Views   **Java Perspective - Views**

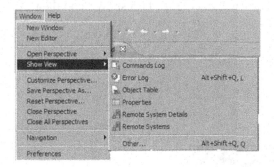
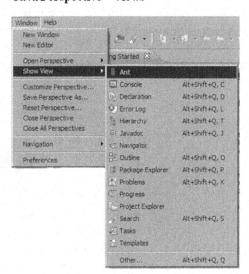

Figure 11.4: Comparison of Views

It seems to be a trait of us as programmers never to let well enough alone; IBM is aware of this and has been kind enough to let us reset a perspective to its default values. You accomplish this by clicking Window and then Reset Perspective on the toolbar at the top of the workbench. As we become more familiar with the workbench, many of us create a perspective with specific views and then save our custom perspective by clicking Save Perspective As and naming it. Also under Window, you can select **Preferences** and change many defaults for the workbench. Remember: These changes are specific to the workspace you are working in, and not to RDP.

Creating a Connection

Besides connecting to an IBM i system, you also can connect to a number of other OSs, including AIX, Linux, UNIX, and Windows. This capability supports IBM's goal of using one IDE to develop software on many platforms.

To create a connection to an IBM i Power System, you right-click the IBM i icon in the Remote Systems view on the left side of the workbench, as Figure 11.5 shows, and then select New Connection.

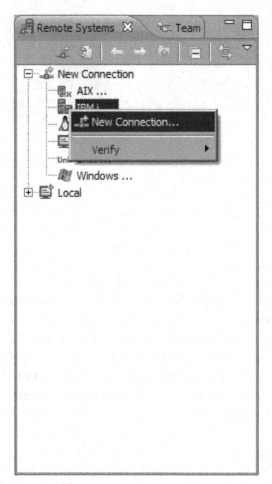

Figure 11.5: Remote Connections View

Figure 11.6 shows the first window of the connection wizard. You are first prompted for a **parent profile**; do not confuse this parent profile with your user ID on the system. The parent profile is used to identify you within a group of users sharing RSE configuration information, and it should be unique. The connection wizard creates this default profile based on the host name of your workstation.

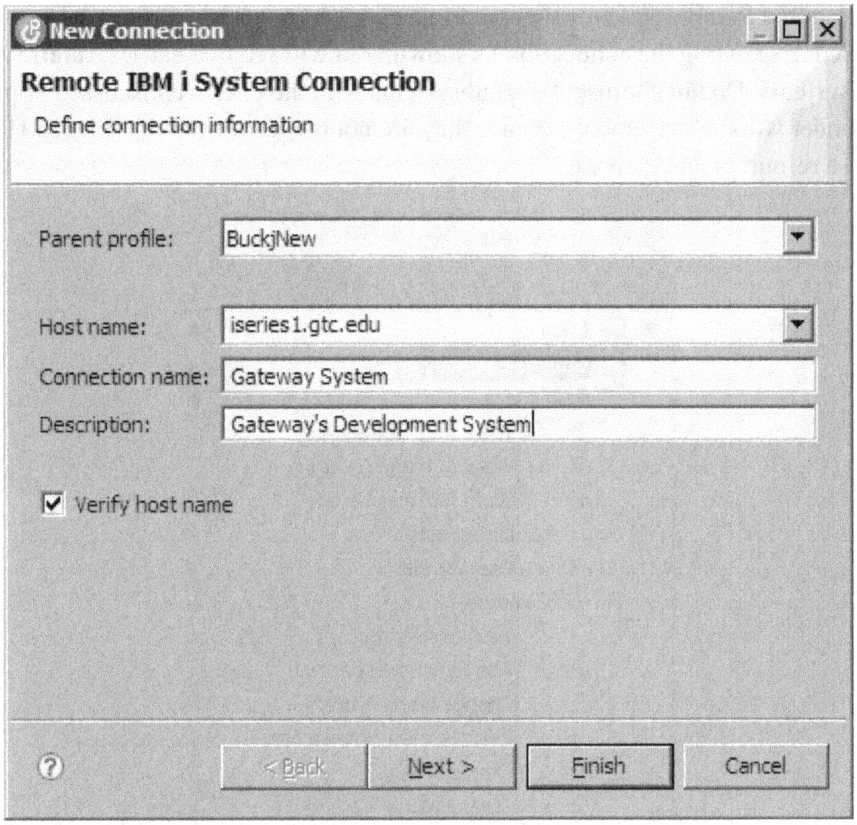

Figure 11.6: Connection Information Window

Under the **Host name** field, enter the URL or IP address of your server, as you did when you created a connection to your system in IBM i Navigator. The **Connection name** field can be anything you want; it will be displayed in your list of connections in RSE. The **connection Description** field is optional and is displayed only when you look at the properties of the connection. The **Verify host name** option is selected by default and verifies that a valid address is entered. If the address cannot be resolved, the wizard will give you an error message. If you click Next, you will be presented with an informational window explaining that normally run startup programs will not be executed, how to verify your connection, and how to check for the status of required PTFs for RSE. In this example, simply click Finish.

If you look at the Remote Systems view in Figure 11.7, you can see that the connection has been created. Expanding the connection as shown, you will see five entries, referred to as **RSE subsystems**. Do not confuse these subsystems with the ones we discussed in previous chapters under work management because they are not related. Following Figure 11.7 is a list of these resources and their uses.

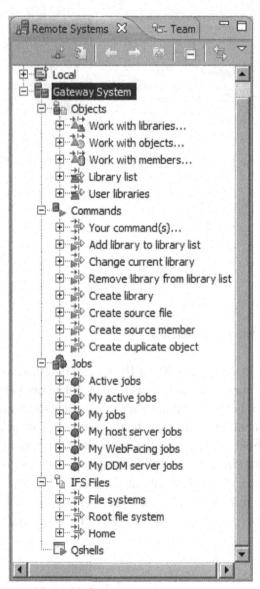

Figure 11.7: Remote Systems View with Connection

- Objects—Use this subsystem to access libraries, objects, and members. Perform actions, just as with commands WRKLIBPDM, WRKOBJPDM, and WRKMBRPDM, which we discussed in previous chapters.
- Commands—Use this subsystem to execute prepopulated commands, or to create your own, and to view the messages that result from executing these commands.
- Jobs—Use this subsystem much like the Jobs subtask in IBM i Navigator; think of it as a graphical WRKACTJOB command.
- IFS Files—This subsystem has the functionality of using the **WRKLNK** (Work with Object Links) CL command or of using the File Systems tasks in IBM i Navigator.
- Qshells—Use this subsystem to start or access active Qshells. It is comparable to the **STRQSH** (Start Qshell) CL command.

Expanding the Library list icon under Objects in the Remote Systems view, you will see a window prompting for your IBM i user ID, as in Figure 11.8. We recommend you do not select the Save user ID or Save password check-box options. Doing so would allow someone using your workstation to access the system (a security risk), and it can cause problems when you change your password. After you enter your user profile and password (in this example, we used our CIS001D student user ID) and click OK, the system will verify your profile credentials.

Figure 11.8: Remote Systems Connection Login Window

Library List: Add, Change, Remove Libraries

After your user ID and password have been validated, the Remote Systems view will be similar to the one in Figure 11.9.

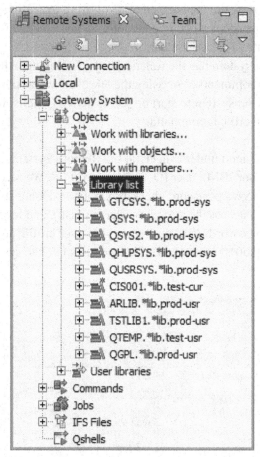

Figure 11.9: Library List in Remote Systems View

The library list displayed is based on system value settings, the current user profile, and the job description. RSE uses the same library list that users receive when they logon using a 5250 emulator session. However, if the user profile normally runs a startup program, this program is not executed with RSE.

Changing the Library List

A right click on the Library list icon presents the pop-up window you see in Figure 11.10. We list and explain the available options following the figure.

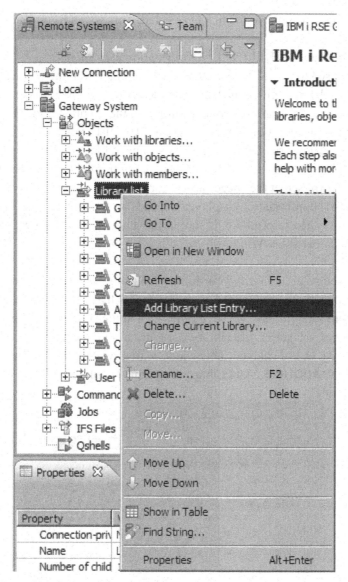

Figure 11.10: Library List Context Menu of Options

- Go Into—Navigates down one level.
- Go To—Navigates similarly to Windows Explorer (back, forward, and up one level).
- Open in New Window—Navigates similarly to Windows Explorer (Open or Explore).
- Refresh—Lets you refresh the details below the selected icon. This option is important because sometimes, when changes are made on the system, you need to refresh the view for these changes to appear.
- Add Library List Entry—Is the same as running the ADDLIBLE CL command.
- Change Current Library—Is the same as running the CHGCURLIB CL command.

- Rename—Lets you rename the object selected. This works for most objects on the system.
- Delete—Delete means DELETE! *Use this option with caution*!
- Move Up—Used to move the Library list icon up in the Remote Systems view.
- Move Down—Used to move the Library list icon down in the Remote Systems view.
- Show in Table—Opens an object table similar to the traditional PDM view. Many programmers who are used to the traditional PDM list like this view.
- Find String—Allows searches for specific strings in files. Take care not to search numerous libraries and source files because doing this can take some time. In general, you will be surprised at the speed of the search.
- Properties—The information displayed depends on the type of object selected. For Windows users, the information is similar to what you would expect when looking at an object's properties in Windows.

In this example, you want to modify your library list using RSE. You accomplish this just as you would in a 5250 session (using CL commands such as CHGCURLIB, CHGLIBL, and EDTLIBL). In the preceding figure, we have right-clicked the Library list icon in the Remote Systems view. When you select Add Library List Entry from the context menu, the pop-up window in Figure 11.11 is displayed. This window gives you all the options you are familiar with when using the **ADDLIBLE** (Add Library List Entry) command.

Figure 11.11: Add a Library to Your Library List

A great feature of RSE is that the CL command that will be submitted to the system is displayed in the lower portion of the window. This information often helps programmers new to the system or those who have used the traditional 5250 CL commands to make the transition to the new GUI interface.

In the example, we are adding the library INTROCLASS to our library list. The default position is at the beginning of the user library list, which starts immediately after the user's current library.

When you click OK, Figure 11.12 shows that the library INTROCLASS has been added to the library list. You just as easily could have changed the current library to INTROCLASS by selecting the Change Current Library option in Figure 11.10.

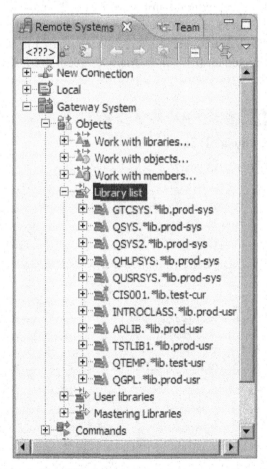

Figure 11.12: Add a Library to Your Library List

Note

We added the INTROCLASS library in our library list because, in the next few examples, we will be creating a source physical file in the CIS001 student library, and then we will copy a sample CL source member from the INTROCLASS library to the new source physical file.

Creating a Source Physical File

In this section, we will create a source physical file called QCLLESRC in the student library CIS001. Right clicking the CIS001 library and then selecting New, followed by Source Physical File displays the pop-up window in Figure 11.13. We have chosen to name the file QCLLESRC, and we have entered text to describe the file. The default system length of a source member is 92; RSE by default enters a record length of 112, the standard for ILE source members. If we created an ILE source file with a length of 92, we could truncate code in a member.

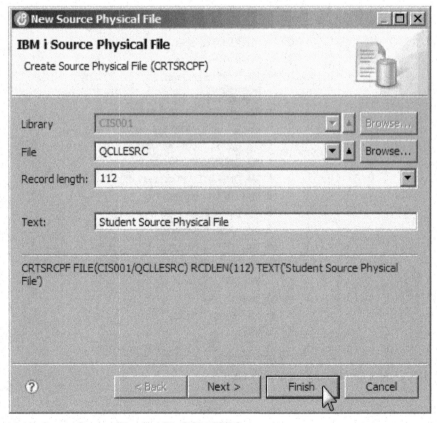

Figure 11.13: Create Source Physical FileQCLLESRC

Click Finish to have the QCLLESRC source physical file created in the CIS001 library.

Note

Many companies use naming conventions that include LE in the file name to distinguish ILE source files from the older, non–Integrated Language Environment files. For example, new ILE source members will be placed in a source physical file named QCLLESRC rather than QCLSRC.

Copying a Member

After clicking the + sign to the left of the INTROCLASS library to expand it and then expanding the QCLLESRC source physical file, you right-click the source member CHAP11EXP and select Copy to copy the member (just as you would in Windows Explorer), as Figure 11.14 shows.

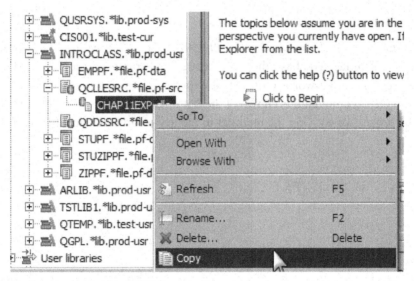

Figure 11.14: Copying a Member in RSE

Now you navigate to the student library, CIS001, and then to the newly created source physical file QCLLESRC. Finally, right-click the QCLLESRC source physical file and select Paste, as in Figure 11.15.

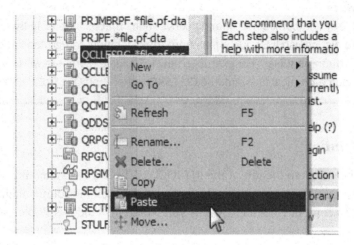

Figure 11.15: Pasting a Member in RSE

The window in Figure 11.16 shows that the **CPYSRCF** (Copy Source File) CL command is actually being submitted. You have the option to see All Parameters (equivalent to pressing F9 in a 5250 session) or Keywords (equivalent to pressing F11 in a 5250 session). Notice that the complete CL command is shown at the bottom of the window. Clicking OK will complete the process of copying the member to the new source physical file, QCLLESRC.

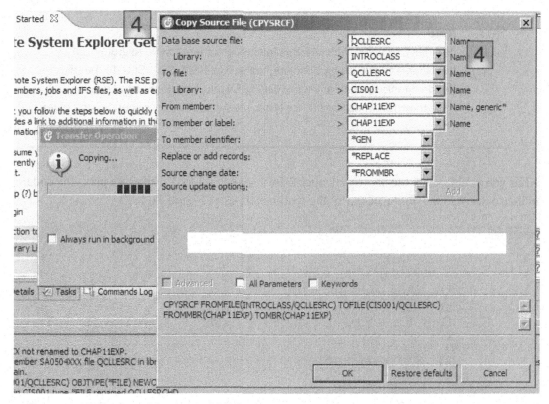

Figure 11.16: Pasting a Member in RSE,Continued

Opening and Editing a Member

Now that you have copied this simple CL program into your source physical file, you double-click the member to open it, just as you would in Windows. The member opens in the default editor. The **Remote Systems LPEX Editor** is RDP's source editor for RPG, CL, COBOL, DDS, and C/C++ members. This editor has all the features of older products such as PDM and SEU, plus many additional ones. Some of the more notable features include

- *Case-sensitive help*—Press F1 to display Help (RPG and COBOL only).
- *Prefix commands*—These include commands such as SEU's CC, D, C, and M.
- *Syntax checking*—This process runs automatically every time you exit an edited or inserted line.
- *Content assist*—Pressing Ctrl+space causes the editor to propose, display, and insert completion code (RPG and COBOL only).
- *Source prompting*—Pressing F4 causes the editor to assist filling in code (similar to pressing F4 in SEU).
- *Outline view*—This view displays a structured outline of the items defined in the file.
- *Conversion*—This function converts RPG code from fixed to free format.

Note

IBM has had some difficulty enticing its customer base to migrate from the older, and eventually obsolete, tools (e.g., PDM, SDA, SEU) to the new Rational tools. As with any tool, RDP/LPEX takes some effort to master; but once they have mastered these tools, most programmers abandon the older ones.

After you double-click the source member CHAP11EXP, the LPEX Editor displays the code in the source window in the center of the workbench, as in Figure 11.17.

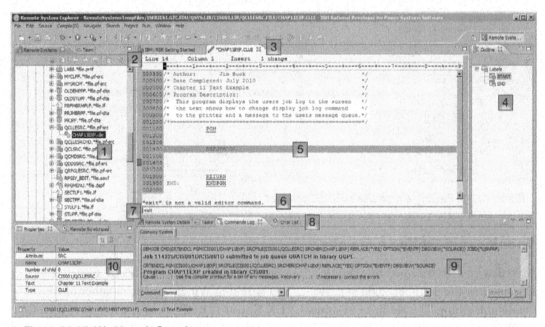

Figure 11.17: Workbench Overview

The figure shows the workbench environment used to code CL or RPG programs. Some of the important areas of this environment are identified:

1. ***Remote Systems (Explorer) view***—Used to navigate through libraries, objects, and source members. Also used to open, edit, or compile your code, or to run program objects.

2. ***Status line***—Shows the insertion mode (change or browse), number of changes since the last save, current line number, and column location.

3. ***Editor tabs***—Show all the members that are currently open. Notice that the active document is displayed in a different color.

   Note: In Figure 11.17, the current member is CHAP11EXP, and there is an asterisk by the name to show that there are pending changes to the member. A handy feature of the LPEX Editor is that it will expand to encompass the entire workbench when you double-click the current-member tab. This feature works well when you want just the editing window and not any of the other views.

4. ***Outline view***—Very useful in larger programs because it lists the variables, labels, and subroutines. Clicking any of the icons will cause the editor to change the current line to that area. *This feature of the Outline view might seem insignificant when you are writing small programs, but remember: Many programs are thousands of lines long and can be difficult to navigate.*

5. ***Current line***—Highlighted to show the current line being edited.

6. ***Editor message line***—Displays any messages from the editor.

7. ***Editor command line***—You can enter any valid editor command on this line.

   Note: We have intentionally entered an invalid command to demonstrate a message on the message line.

8. ***Error List view***—Lists any errors from your last compile or verify.

9. ***Commands Log view***—This view is similar to displaying the job log.

   Note: We have bolded two lines in this view; the first one shows that the compile was submitted to batch, and the second one shows that the compile was successful. Such information is very useful when you are compiling programs and want to see whether a compile was successful.

10. ***Properties view***—Shows the properties of the object that is highlighted in the RSE window.

Editing and Saving

In Chapter16, we discuss CL programming in greater depth; but for now, think of CL programs as a collection of CL commands that can be compiled into a program object. The current chapter's example includes a program that displays a person's job log to the screen. Before we make any changes, we need to explain a number of program statements to help you understand how the program works. The details of the program are displayed in Figure 11.18 and discussed following the figure.

```
/ *CHAP11EXP.CLLE  X
 Line 22       Column 1      Replace  4 changes
       +----+----1----+----2----+----3----+----4----+----5----+----6----+----7----+----8---
000500/* Chapter 11 Text Example                                      */
000600/* Program Description:                                         */
000700/*  This program displays the users job log to the screen       */
000800/*  the text shows how to change display job log command        */
000900/*  to the printer and a message to the users message queue.*/
001000/*========================================================*/
001100             PGM
001200
001201
001202
001300
001400 START:      DSPJOBLOG
001500
001600
001601
001800             RETURN
001900 END:        ENDPGM
002000
```

Figure 11.18: Sample CL Code

- Line 001100 is the **PGM** statement, which tells the compiler this is the start of the CL program.
- Line 001400 is the **DSPJOBLOG** statement, which tells the program to display the job log to the screen.
- Line 001800 is the **RETURN** statement, which tells the CL program to return to the caller program or to the operating system when it reaches that line.
- Line 001900 is the **ENDPGM** statement, which tells the compiler this is the end of the CL program. All CL commands must be coded between the PGM and ENDPGM statements.
- Line 001400's START: statement and line 001900's END: statement are two CL program **labels** used to help document the program.

We should note at this time that before CL had looping structures (DOFOR, DOUNTIL, and DOWHILE), labels were used in GOTO statements. For example, we could GOTO START to control a program's flow. Today, the coding of GOTOs is strongly discouraged.

In the example, we will change this CL program to accomplish the following tasks:

- Send the job log to a spool file.
- Display a message to the user's message queue when the program ends.
- Add a variable named &CURDAY to the program.
- Retrieve the day of the week from the **QDAYOFWEEK** system value.

When you use SEU at a 5250 command line, you can type in a CL command and press F4 to prompt the CL command. This functionality is incorporated into the LPEX Editor. Refer to line 001400 in Figure 11.17, and note that the current line has the DSPJOBLOG (Display Job Log) CL command. Pressing F4 causes the window in Figure 11.19 is displayed.

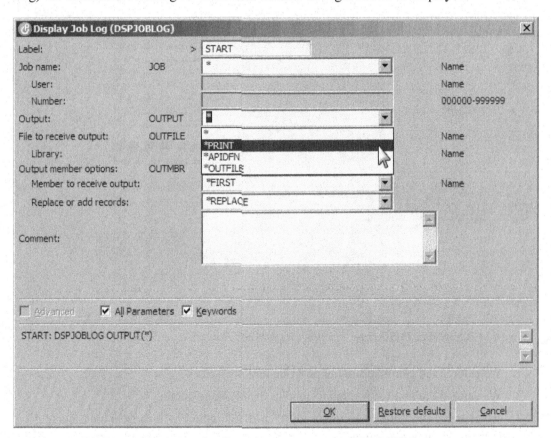

Figure 11.19: Window Displayed after Pressing F4 on the DSPJOBLOG Command

In this window, we have checked the All Parameters and Keywords checkboxes to display all the parameters and keywords for the command. We have also clicked the down arrow in the OUTPUT parameter and selected *PRINT. After we click OK, the editor will change the CL command to DSPJOBLOG OUTPUT (*PRINT). When the program is executed, this code change will cause the program to send the output of the command to the job's spool queue.

We also want to change the program to send a message to the caller's message queue when the program is complete. We will do this by inserting the **SNDPGMMSG** (Send Program Message) command. This versatile command can be used only in a CL program, but you can use message files as well as send text to message queues or users. Figure 11.20 demonstrates entering the command, with the detailed steps following the figure.

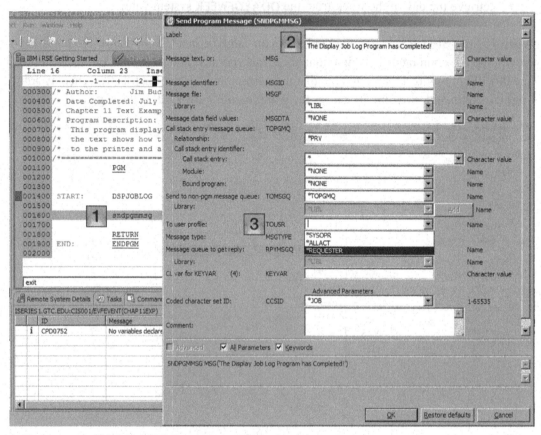

Figure 11.20: SNDPGMMSG Entered in the Program and Prompted

1. We entered the command in the program and pressed F4.
2. We entered the text we wanted to send to the message queue.
3. We changed the TOUSR parameter to *REQUESTER, which will cause a message to go to the user's message queue.

After we click OK, the resulting CL command is

SNDPGMMSG MSG ('The Display Job Log Program has Completed!') TOUSR (*REQUESTER)

We need to accomplish two additional tasks before we are done. First, we want to declare a character variable named &CURDAY. Second, we want to retrieve the "day of the week" from the QDAYOFWEEK system value and store it the &CURDAY variable.

To declare a variable in CL, you use the **DCL** (Declare CL Variable) command, just as we did with the SNDPGMMSG command. We can type DCL into our sample program and then press F4. In Figure 11.21, we have entered data into four parameters for this command; the details describing the parameters are shown following the figure.

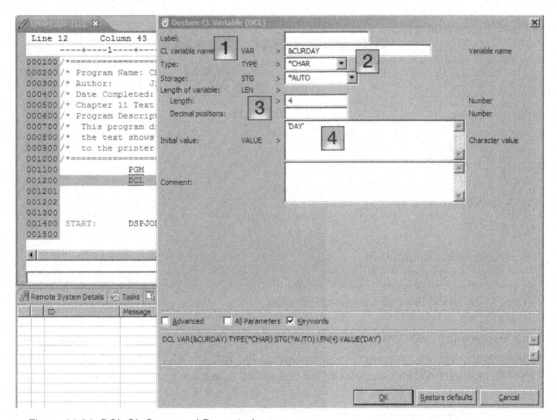

Figure 11.21: DCL CL Command Prompted

1. VAR—The name of the variable—in this case, &CURDAY; all variables in CL need to start with an ampersand (&).

2. TYPE—The type of variable. In this case, we are storing characters, so the type is *CHAR.

3. LEN—The length of the variable is four (*SUN, *MON, *TUE, and so on).

4. VALUE—This field is optional; if no value is specified, the variable will contain the default for the data type. We have set the value to 'DAY' to demonstrate the need to put apostrophes (') around a character field.

After we click OK, the code will look like this:

```
DCL      VAR(&CURDAY) TYPE(*CHAR) STG(*AUTO) LEN(4) VALUE('DAY')
```

We will use the **RTVSYSVAL** (Retrieve System Value) command to retrieve the QDAYOFWEEK system value and store the current value in the variable &CURDAY. We accomplish this in the same manner we did previously. Figure 11.22 shows that we have typed RTVSYSVAL into our program source and pressed F4.

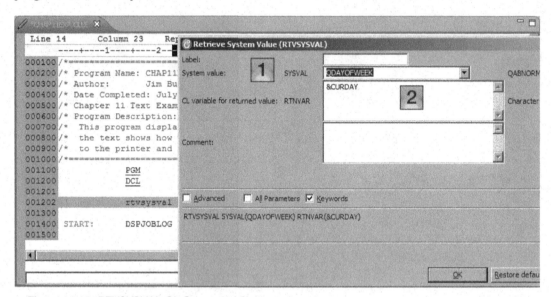

Figure 11.22: RTVSYSVAL CL Command Prompted

We prompted the RTVSYSVAL CL command and selected QDAYOFWEEK (number 1) to be returned to the SYSVAL parameter; then we entered the variable &CURDAY (number 2) in the RTNVAR parameter. When we click OK, the completed command is entered into the program:

```
RTVSYSVAL  SYSVAL (QDAYOFWEEK) RTNVAR (&CURDAY)
```

We have now satisfied the requirements for the program, and we need to save it. When you use SEU to enter your code, you actually change the member on the system. When you use the LPEX Editor, a copy of the member is transferred to your PC and the "save" process copies this member back to the system. We can save the sample member by clicking the Save icon on the toolbar at the top of the workbench (similar to Microsoft Word) and selecting File and then Save from the toolbar; as an alternative, we can use the keyboard shortcut Crtl + S.

Compiling

In the previous example, we used F4 prompting to enter the commands; doing so greatly reduces the possibility of syntax errors. As you become more familiar with CL programming, you may enter many of the commands without F4 prompting, and the chances of syntax errors increase. To avoid using system resources to compile a program, the LPEX Editor lets you syntax-check your program by clicking Source and then Syntax check all. This feature lets you check the syntax without compiling the program on the system.

After you have saved the member, there are two ways to compile it. From the toolbar at the top of the workbench, you can click Compile; then, based on the source member type, the workbench presents you with the type of compiles that are appropriate. You can also right-click the member in the RSE view and, from the drop-down box, select Compile. You will use the **CRTBNDCL** (Create Bound CL Program) command if you want an executable program, or **CRTCLMOD** (Create CL Module) if you want to create a module that will be bound together with another module to create an executable program. In the example, we have selected the CRTBNDCL option (Figure 11.23).

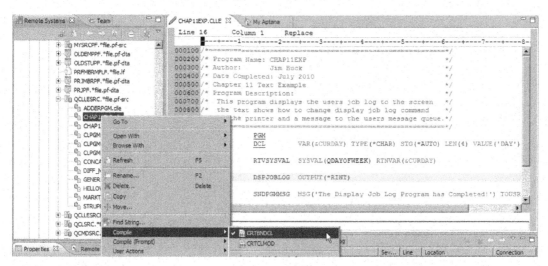

Figure 11.23: Compiling the Member from the RSE View

Figure 11.17 showed you the Commands Log view, which tracks all commands and the results of the command. In Figure 11.24, we show you the Error List view, which displays any errors that result from the compile attempt. Our sample program did not compile because we have one error with a severity level of 30.

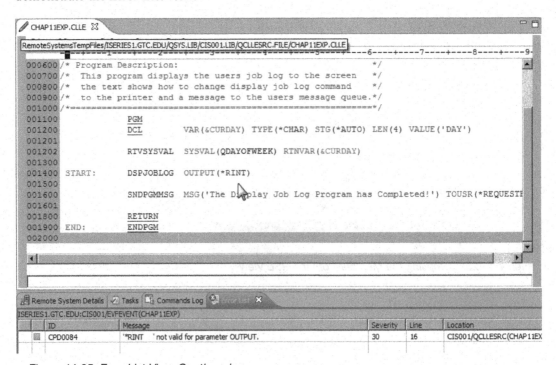

Figure 11.24: Error List View

As we mentioned, you will often key in commands without prompting as you become more familiar with the CL language, and this practice often leads to syntax errors. In Figure 11.25, we intentionally misspelled *PRINT (note the arrow) and compiled the CL member to demonstrate the Error List view.

Figure 11.25: Error List View, Continued

The error list shows the error, an error message describing the error, the message severity (30), and the location of the error. Notice that the error list shows the error occurring on line 16, while the actual line number is 14 (001400). That is because the Error List view lists the physical line number in the member, not the sequence line number. If we were to click this error message, our current line would be set to line 14, as Figure 11.26 shows. We have corrected the problem in this figure by changing the OUTPUT parameter value to *PRINT. Notice that there is now a check mark by the error message (in the lower-left corner of the screen) to signify that we have addressed this problem.

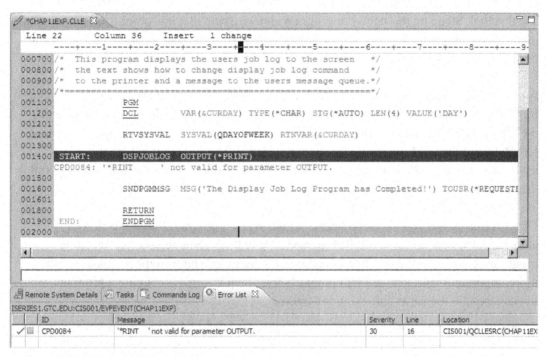

Figure 11.26: Error List View, Corrected

Now that we have addressed the error that the compiler previously found, we can save the member and recompile. If the program compiles, the Error List will show the message *"Events file contains no messages."* This message, which you see in Figure 11.27, signifies that the compiler found no syntax errors. However, it is always a good idea to check the Commands Log to ensure that the object was actually created.

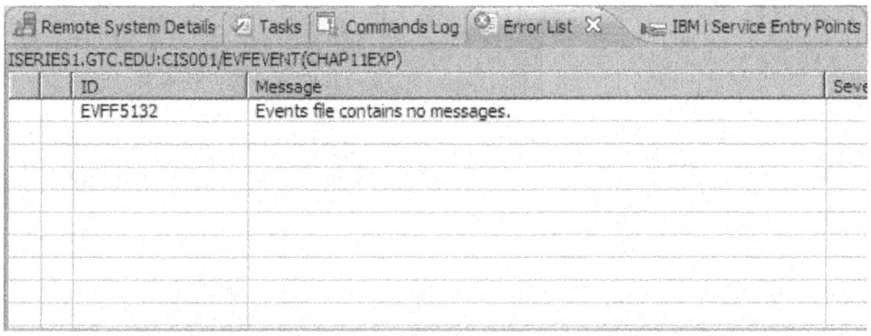

Figure 11.27: Error List View After Correcting Error and Recompiling

Debugging Overview

IBM's Integrated i Debugger is a debugging tool that is relatively easy to use and is indispensable to the programming professional. We have been amazed over the years at the reluctance of students to use a debugger, watching them spend hours "poking and hoping" before they finally give up. You can avoid this frustration by taking time to learn how to use this tool. Stepping through your program and verifying that it is processing a file in the manner you anticipate, and that the variables used in your program contain the values you think they do, can save you hours of frustration as a student/programmer.

A tremendous benefit of the Integrated i Debugger is that when you move from debugging RPG, COBOL, or CL programs to debugging Java or C/C++, you do not need to relearn the Debug interface. The client/server design of this tool lets you debug programs running remotely on your IBM i system while using a graphical tool on your workstation. You can set breakpoints and monitors, step line-by-line through a program while it is running, and examine or change variables.

Figure 11.28 shows you the Debug perspective. When a program is debugged, RDP automatically switches from the RSE perspective to the Debug perspective and stops program execution at the first line of code. In the figure, we have numbered some of the more important views that you will regularly use when you are debugging a program. We list and explain the views following the figure.

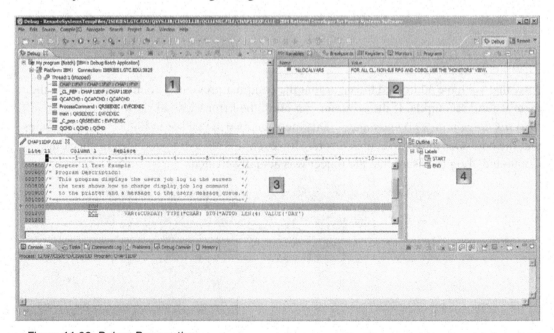

Figure 11.28: Debug Perspective

1. The **Debug view** allows you to manage debugging a program. This view shows you the stack and processes associated with the program you are debugging. A number of icons enable you to control the debugging process. Figure 11.29 shows these icons and explains their use.

Debug Controls		1 2 3 4 5 6 7 8 9
Nbr	**Name**	**Description**
1	Remove Launch	Remove terminated Launches from the debug view
2	Restart	Restart the program
3	Resume	Resume execution of suspended program
4	Suspend	Suspend execution of a running program
5	Terminate	End the Debug session this will not stop program execution.
6	Animated Stepping	Automatically step through the program. The default time between steps is 2000 ms.
7	Step into	If the current line is a procedure or program the debugger will start debugging the first line of the procedure or program.
8	Step Over	Execute the current line and stop at the nex executable line.
9	Step Return	Continue running until the call returns

Figure 11.29: Controlling the Debug Process

2. The views in this area are all related to monitoring the values of variables, registers, and monitors and to editing/disabling breakpoints. The three views most often used are the Variables, Monitor, and Breakpoints views. The **Variables view** lets you monitor variables if you are debugging RPG or COBOL ILE programs compiled at V5R3 or greater, and C/C++ programs. The **Monitors view** lets you monitor and modify variables, registers, or expressions. Finally, the **Breakpoints view** enables you to edit, disable, or remove breakpoints.

3. The **Source view** lets you watch your program source code as the program is being debugged. This capability is important because the program must be compiled with the appropriate debugging information. Oftentimes students and seasoned programmers compile a program from the 5250 session, try to debug it in RDP, and are confused because their source is not available. By default, RDP compiles programs to include this information; if you compile programs from PDM, however, you must change your compile options to include it.

4. The **Outline view** displays a structured outline of the current open program source. Using the Outline view, you can quickly navigate around your program or easily find where variables are used. (After having used SEU for many years, and spending countless hours/years moving back and forth trying to find variables or subroutines in RPG programs, we find this feature indispensable.)

Debugging a Program

In the next few pages, we give examples of the different ways that you can start the IBM i Debugger and set breakpoints and monitors. As with any tool, mastering this debugger will take some effort; but, as we stated previously, the time you will save will outweigh the time you take to familiarize yourself with it.

Service Entry Points

The most effective way to start a debugging session is to set an **SEP** (Service Entry Point). The capability to set an SEP was added to WDSc at Version 6.0, and it works with interactive, batch, Web, and Web services applications. When an SEP is set in a program and the program is executed by the same profile that set the SEP, the program is suspended and the debugger automatically connects to the job. When this occurs, RDP switches to the Debug perspective and you can then begin debugging the program.

We need to set the SEP on the program object that we want to debug. Figure 11.30 shows the process. Once the SEP is set on our sample program, CHAP11EXP, we can call or submit the program from the 5250 command line.

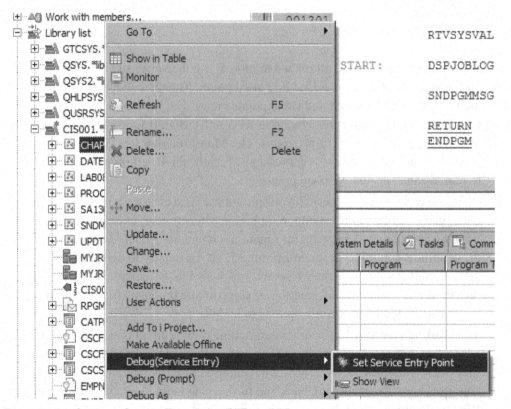

Figure 11.30: Setting a Service Entry Point (SEP) in RDP

A number of options are available from the IBM i Service Entry Points view you see in Figure 11.31. It is important to remember that if you recompile a program, you need to refresh the SEP; doing this is necessary because when you recompile a program, you create a new program object, and the SEP still references the old program object. You can remedy the situation by clicking Refresh, which will associate the SEP with the new program object. Another important thing to remember about SEPs is that they should be removed when you are finished debugging your program. The SEP is a system-wide attribute set on the program object, and every time the program is executed, the system will attempt to start a debug session.

Previously, we said that a debug session will be started whenever the program is executed by the user who created the SEP. However, you can modify an SEP and associate it with a different user. This feature is invaluable when you are trying to debug a program that another user is running. In Figure 11.31, we have right-clicked the SEP (IBM i Service Entry Points) tab and selected Modify.

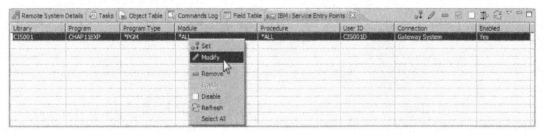

Figure 11.31: IBM i Service Entry Points View

With this action, the window in Figure 11.32 is displayed; here, we can change the user (note the arrow) to a different user and then click OK. When the user runs the application, the debug session will start, and we can debug the program as it runs.

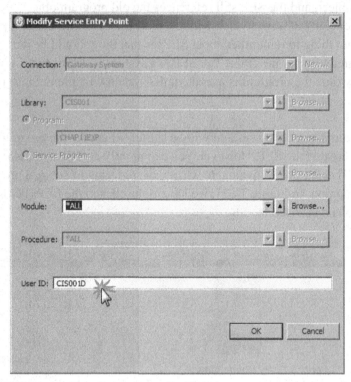

Figure 11.32: IBM i Service Entry Points View, Continued

"No-Prompt" Batch Debugging

You also can right-click a program object and, using a context menu, navigate to Debug As, and then select Batch, as in Figure 11.33. We refer to this approach as "no-prompt" debugging. Also on this context menu is a selection called Debug (Prompt). The resulting options are the same as on the Debug As menu, except that a launch configuration window appears that lets you manipulate the way a job is debugged. This option is especially important for programs that need parameters or different job attributes to run properly.

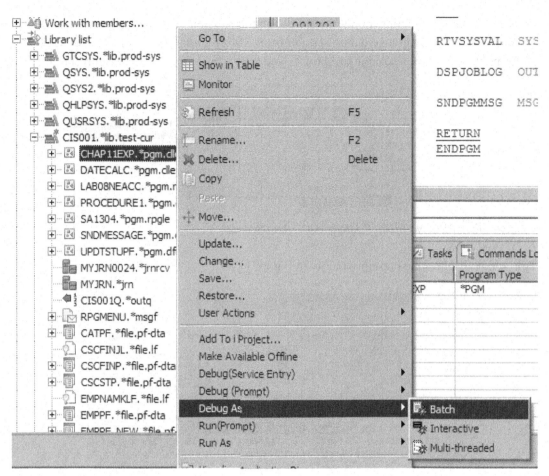

Figure 11.33: "No-Prompt" Batch Debugging

Interactive Debugging

There are two ways to start an interactive debugging session. In this example, we are using the CHAP11EXP program that we modified earlier in the chapter. This is a very simple CL program, but the debugging principles work the same for any type of interactive program.

The first method for starting an interactive debugging session requires the use of the RSE server. We start an interactive debug session from RSE by right-clicking the CHAP11EXP program object and then selecting Debug As and Interactive, as you see in Figure 11.34.

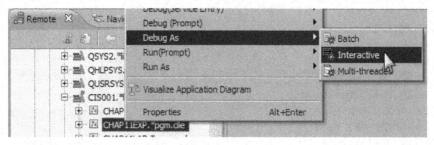

Figure 11.34: RSE "No-Prompt" Interactive Debug Session

This action displays the pop-up window in Figure 11.35.

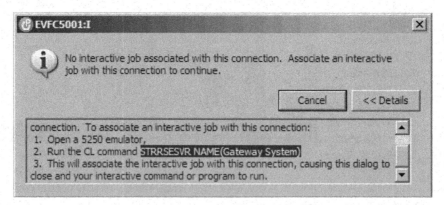

Figure 11.35: STRRSESVR Interactive Debug Session

Starting the debug session in this way requires us to associate the RSE connection with a 5250 interactive session. So we now need a 5250 session for that purpose. In Figure 11.36, we have opened a 5250 session, and we have copied and pasted (or keyed in to the 5250 session) the STRRSESVR NAME('Gateway System') command on the command line. Notice that we have also enclosed the connection name within apostrophes; there can be no spaces in the connection name otherwise.

Figure 11.36: Entering the STRRSESVR Command into a 5250 Session

After we press Enter, we see the screen in Figure 11.37. The session is now "locked" to the RSE connection and can be released only if we end the RSE connection or use the Release Interactive Job action for the RSE connection.

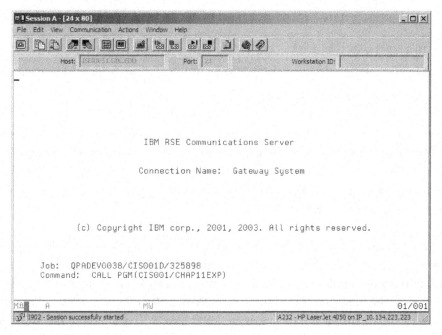

Figure 11.37: STRRSESVR Interactive Debug Session

As we step through the program in a debug session, the screen in Figure 11.37 will change. Debugging programs in this manner is painful, and many of us have never understood why IBM has not included an interactive session view in its Rational products.

The second way to start an interactive debug session is the most efficient and painless option. You first set an SEP, as we described earlier, and then you open a 5250 session and call the program, as Figure 11.38 shows.

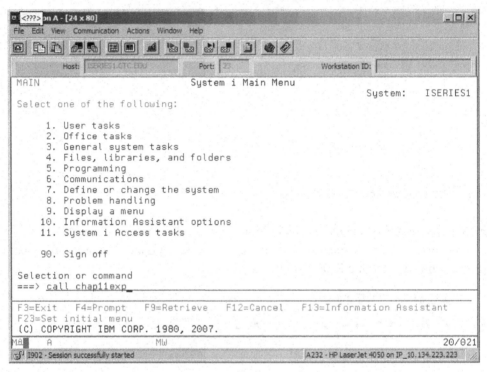

Figure 11.38: Starting an Interactive Debug Session

For example, if you have a program that displays a screen, you can enter data, and when you press Enter, control is returned to the program and the debug session. At that time, the data you entered is available to the debugger. If at some point during the debug process the program displays another screen, you again can enter data. After you press Enter, control once again is passed back to the debug session.

When we press Enter, the RDP workbench automatically switches to the Debug perspective and stops program execution at the first line of our CL program, as Figure 11.39 shows. If we look at the top-right corner of the workbench, we can see that the Variables view is active. We see the message *"FOR ALL CL, NON-ILE RPG AND COBOL USE THE 'MONITORS' VIEW"* displayed; this message tells us we will need to use the Monitors view to display any variables in the CL program.

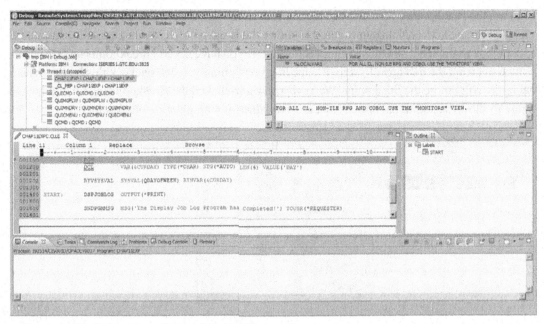

Figure 11.39: Debug Perspective at Start of Debug Session

Our first order of business is to set a breakpoint in our program (Figure 11.40). Breakpoints are important because we want the debugger to suspend the program at certain points during its execution. If we double-click the vertical rule (left of the program's source numbers— note the arrow), we can set a breakpoint. You also can set a breakpoint by right-clicking a line of code and selecting Add/Remove Breakpoint.

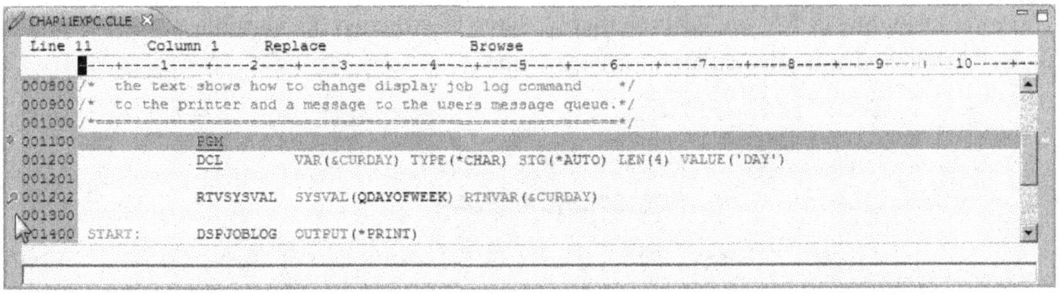

Figure 11.40: Setting a Breakpoint

Clicking the Breakpoints tab in the top-right corner of the workbench causes the Breakpoints view to become active. Notice in Figure 11.41 that the Breakpoints view displays our breakpoint, and the box to the left of the breakpoint is checked. If you have several breakpoints and decide you do not want the debugger to stop at a specific breakpoint, you can uncheck this box and the debugger will ignore the breakpoint. We have also right-clicked the Breakpoints view in this figure to show the additional options that are available for manipulating breakpoints.

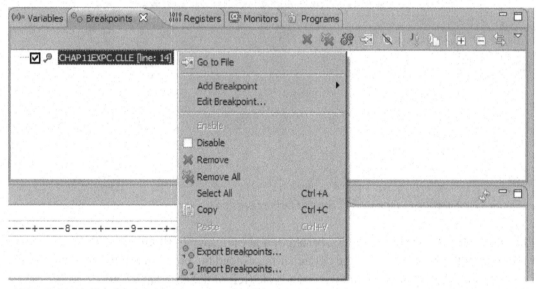

Figure 11.41: Breakpoints View

We also want to set a monitor so that we can watch the values in our variable &CURDAY. If you refer to Figure 11.42, you will see that we have highlighted the variable &CURDAY and then right-clicked and selected Monitor Expression.

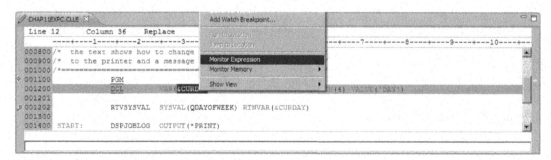

Figure 11.42: Debug Perspective at Start of Debug Session

In Figure 11.43, you can see that we now have a monitor for the &CURDAY variable. Earlier in the chapter, when we entered the DCL statement, we initialized the variable to the value DAY. The Monitors view shows us that when the program starts, the value DAY is stored in the &CURDAY variable.

We also have highlighted and right-clicked the &CURDAY monitor to show the additional options available. The Change Value option can be very useful when you are debugging a program because you can change the value of the variable as it is running.

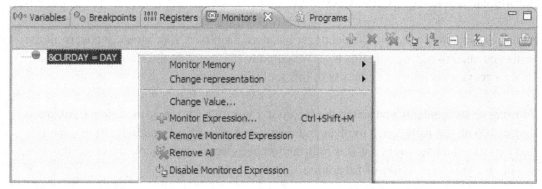

Figure 11.43: Monitors View at Start of a Debug Session

After setting the monitor, we need to step through the program and verify that our code works. In Figure 11.44, you can see that we are stepping through the program and that the current line being executed is line 001400. Note that the arrow in this figure shows we have been clicking the Step over icon to execute each line of the program. In the upper-right corner of the figure, you can see that the variable &CURDAY now has a value of *SAT. This value has changed from DAY because, as we stepped through the program, we executed line 001202 when we retrieved the day of the week using the RTVSYSVAL command, and then we stored it in our variable.

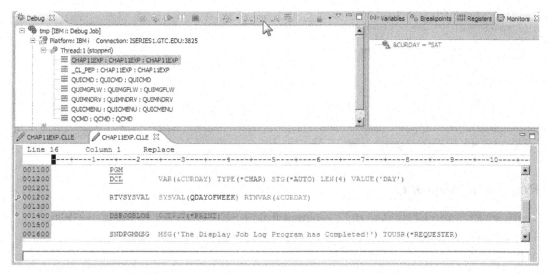

Figure 11.44: Stepping Through Our CL Program

Clicking Step over again will execute line 001400, which will cause the job log to be sent to the user's output queue. We could continue stepping through the lines of code in our program until the program ended normally, or we could click Terminate, which would cause the program to end.

Although this introduction to the debugger has used a simple CL program, it covers all the skills you need to begin using this tool. We emphasize again that the Help available from IBM to get you acclimated to the use of this tool is impressive.

To bring up the contents you see in the screen in Figure 11.45, we opened Help Contents under Help on the workbench toolbar, and then we searched for Debugging. It is important that you take the time to review this information because once you have mastered this tool, it will save you many hours of frustration.

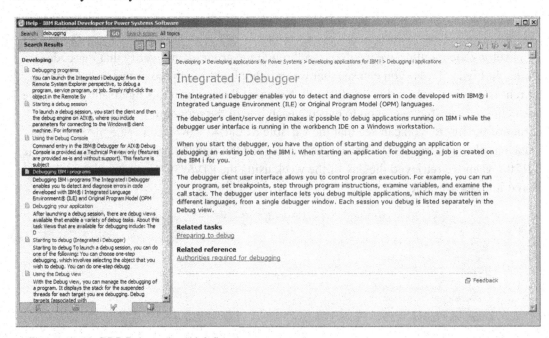

Figure 11.45: RDP Debugging "Help"

Running a Program

There are a number of ways to run a program from RSE, as the context menu in Figure 11.46 shows. Remember: As the callout in the figure highlights, you need to run the program object and *not* the source member.

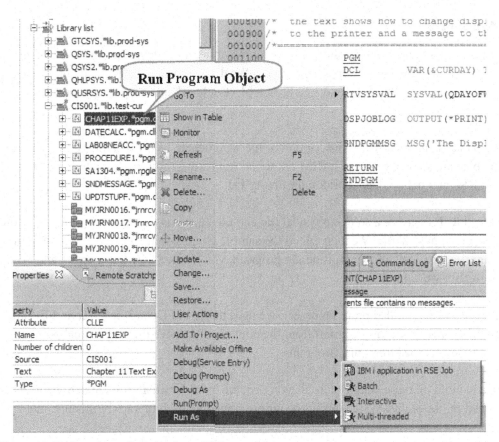

Figure 11.46: Running a Program from RSE

In most instances, you would run your program as either a batch or an interactive program. The option IBM i application in RSE Job allows you to run your program in the same job as the RSE communications server. This option is useful if you have made changes to your environment (for example, your library list) and you need your program to run in this environment. The Multi-threaded application option will create a job in the QUSRWRK subsystem, and it runs the program in that subsystem.

In Summary

We started this chapter with a short history lesson about how the Eclipse toolset became an important tool in the open-source community. We discussed why IBM decided to base the Rational toolset on the open-source Eclipse toolset rather than a proprietary toolset such as Microsoft's Visual Studio.

The chapter continued with a description of the workbench, its perspectives and views, and how to create a connection to an IBM i system. You learned how to navigate the system using RSE and manipulate your default library list.

We used RSE to create a source physical file and then copy an example CL program to our new source physical file. We then edited the sample CL program and added a number of features to the code. After compiling the program, you learned how to fix errors and verify the program we compiled.

Once we had a compiled program object, we used the IBM i Debugger to set an SEP, and then we called the sample program from the command line. We then set a breakpoint and a monitor and stepped through a program.

You can build on these simple steps as you become more familiar with the debugger. As we said before, the ability to step through your program and monitor variables is invaluable.

Key Terms

ADDLIBLE

Breakpoints view

Commands Log view

connection description

connection name

CPYSRCF

CRTBNDCL

CRTCLMOD

current line

DCL

Debug view

DSPJOBLOG

editor command line

editor message line

editor tabs

ENDPGM

Error List view

host name

IBM Rational Developer for System i

Integrated Development Environments

labels

Monitors view

Outline view

parent profile

PGM statement

Preferences

Properties view

QDAYOFWEEK

Rational Developer for Power 8.0

Remote System Explorer

Remote Systems LPEX Editor

Remote Systems view

RETURN
RTVSYSVAL
RSE perspective
RSE subsystems
SEP
SNDPGMMSG
Source view
status line

STRQSH
Variables view
Verify host name option
WebSphere Development Studio Client
    forSystem i
workbench
WRKLNK

Review Questions

1. Summarize the industry environment that led to IBM developing Eclipse, releasing Eclipse to the open-source community, and eventually developing today's Rational products.

2. When you are using Eclipse-based tools such as RDP, what is the function of the workspace?

3. Why is it important to back up your workspace?

4. What is a function of the Welcome page in RDP?

5. Explain the difference between a *perspective* and a *view* in RDP.

6. What is the importance of verifying the host name when you are using RDP to connect to a server?

7. List and describe the RSE "subsystems" we described in this chapter.

8. Why is it important to "Refresh" views?

9. What features available in SEU have been incorporated into the LPEX Editor?

10. Figure 11.17 displays a number of important areas; list and explain the purpose of these areas.

11. We used the SNDPGMMSG CL command in the CL program in this chapter. Research this command and list some additional features not discussed here.

12. Why is the Outline view an important tool for today's programmer?

13. Explain the difference between the CRTBNDCL and CRTCLMOD commands.

14. Explain the difference between the Variables and Monitors views.

15. Why is setting a Service Entry Point (SEP) the most effective way to start a debugging session?

16. Why do you need to refresh an SEP when you recompile a program?

17. Why is it important to remove an SEP when you have completed debugging a program?

18. What type of applications can be used with an SEP?

19. When you login to the IBM i server and expand the Library List icon, you are presented with a library list. How does the system assign you this library list?

20. What is the default record length for an ILE member when you create a source file in RSE? What is the default length when you use the CRTSRCPF command?

21. Why is it important not to create a source file with a record length less than 112?

Lab 11

Introduction

In the following lab, you will practice what we demonstrated in this chapter. In the first part, you will change your library list and then submit an RPG program to batch. In the second part, you will create the needed source files, copy a print file and RPG program to your library, and then compile them. In the third part, you will edit the RPG program, add more code, and then compile and submit the program to batch.

Before you begin this lab, you should have RDP installed on your PC and have created a connection to your system.

Part 1

Goals   Add the library INTROCLASS to your library list, and submit the CHAP11LAB program library to batch.

Start with   RDP open, connected to your IBM i system, and with the Remote System (Explorer) perspective displayed.

Procedure   Change your library list.

           Expand the library object.

           Submit the program object to batch.

11.1. Verify that you have opened RDP and are connected (logged in) to your IBM i server.

       On the left side of the workbench, you should see the Remote Systems view.

11.2. Expand the connection (in our example, Gateway System) and then the Objects icon by clicking the + sign on the left of the icon. Your RSE view should be similar to the one in Figure 11.47.

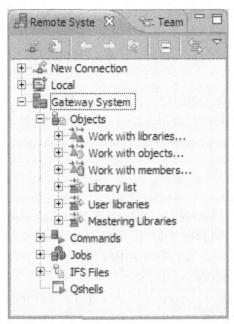

Figure 11.47: RSE View with Objects Expanded

11.3.   Expand the Library list icon by clicking + to the left of the icon.

    11.3.a.   What libraries are in your library list?

11.4.   Right clicking the Library list icon allows you to select Add Library List Entry, which will add a library to your library list.

11.5.   Key in INTROCLASS in the Additional Library parameter.

    11.5.a.   What command is executed when you click OK?

11.6.   After you click OK, expand the INTROCLASS icon.

11.7.   Navigate to the CHAP11LAB program object icon.

11.8.   Right-click the CHAP11LAB program object icon to display a context menu. Select Run As and then Batch, as in Figure 11.48.

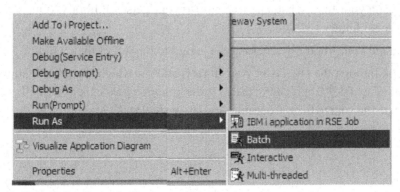

Figure 11.48: Submit the Example Program to Batch

11.8.a. How can you check to see whether the job was submitted in the workbench?

11.9. Open a 5250 session, and work with spooled files to see the output from the program.

11.9.a. What CL command did you use to work with your spool files?

11.9.b. Describe the report that the program developed.

11.10. Ask your instructor whether you should print the report on a printer.

Part 2

Goals　　Create the needed source physical files in your student library, and then copy an RPG file and print file (DDS) to the correct source files.

Start with　　RDP open, connected to your IBM i system, and with the Remote System (Explorer) perspective displayed.

Procedure　　Navigate to your personal library, expand your library, and verify that QDDSSRC and QRPGLESRC are not in your library.

If these two source files do not exist, create them in your library.

Navigate to the INTROCLASS library, and copy the DDS and RPGLE source members to the correct source files in your library.

Compile the DDS for the print file.

Compile the RPG source file.

Verify that both source files were compiled.

Submit the program object to the batch subsystem.

Verify that the program produced a report.

11.11. Verify that you have opened RDP and are connected (logged in) to the IBM i server.

11.12. Expand your library list, and navigate to your personal library. (Our student user's personal library is CIS001.)

11.13. Expand your library by clicking the + sign to the left of the icon.

11.14. Look through the objects in your library, and see whether you have source files named QDDSSRC and QRPGLESRC. If these source files exist, you will not have to create the source files. Continue this lab at step 11.22.

11.15. If the two source files mentioned in the previous step do not exist, right-click your library, and select New and then Source Physical File, as in Figure 11.49.

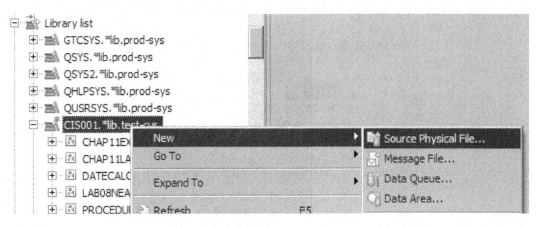

Figure 11.49: Create New Source Physical File

11.16. Enter QDDSSRC in the file parameter, and leave the Record Length parameter at the default value.

11.17. Enter a description of the source file in a Text parameter.

11.17.a. What did you enter for a description in the Text parameter?

11.18. Click Finish.

11.19. Enter QRPGLESRC in the file parameter, and leave the Record Length parameter at the default value.

11.19.a. What is the default value of the Record Length parameter?

11.20. Enter a description of the source file in a Text parameter.

11.20.a. What did you enter for a description in the Text parameter?

11.21. Click Finish.

You should now have the two source files you need to continue this lab.

11.21.a. What happens if you try to create another source file with the same name?

11.22. The next step is to verify that the library INTROCLASS is in your library list.

Note: If you just completed Part 1 of this lab, the library should still be in your library list. If you did not complete Part 1, or if you closed your connection and then logged back in to the system, the library is probably not in your library list.

11.23. Highlight the Library List icon, and press F5; doing this will cause the workbench to refresh the view. If the library INTROCLASS is not displayed, you will need to add it as you did in Part 1.

11.24. After you have verified that library INTROCLASS is in your library list, expand it by clicking the + sign beside the icon. In Figure 11.50, we have circled the three source physical files in the library.

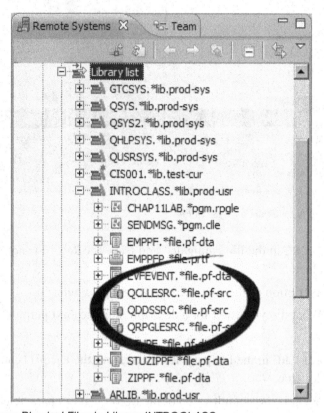

Figure 11.50: Source Physical Files in Library INTROCLASS

11.25. Expand the QDDSSRC source file, right-click the EMPPFLP print-file member, and then select Copy.

11.26. Navigate back to your personal library, right-click the QDDSSRC source file, and select Paste.

    11.26.a. What are you required to do before the Copy process is completed?

11.27. Navigate back to the library INTROCLASS, expand the QRPGLESRC source file, and highlight the member CHAP11LAB; then select Copy.

11.28. Navigate back to your personal library, right-click the QRPGLESRC source file, and select Paste.

    11.28.a. What are you required to do before the Copy process is completed?

    11.28.b. What happens if you try to Paste the source member a second time?

11.29. In the preceding steps, you copied the printer file DDS and the associated RPG source code to your library and placed them in the correct source files. Now look at the objects in your personal library, and see whether the physical file EMPPFL exists.

11.29.a. Does the physical file EMPPFL exist in your library?

Note: In this exercise, we want to demonstrate that you do not need to have the associated physical file EMPPFL in your library to create a print file and program object. Because the library INTROCLASS is in your library list and contains the file EMPPFL, we want to make sure we use this file to create the program and print-file objects.

We now want to create a print-file object by compiling the DDS named EMPPFLP, which is located in the source file QDDSSRC.

11.30. Navigate to the QDDSSRC source file in your personal library, and expand it.

11.31. Right-click the DDS member named EMPPFLP, and select Compile and then CRTPRTF, as Figure 11.51 shows.

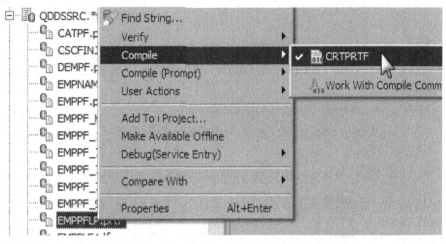

Figure 11.51: Compile the Print File

11.32. After you click CRTPRTF, RSE will submit the compile of the print file to batch.

11.32.a. From the workbench, how would you check to see whether the job was submitted to batch and the object was created?

11.33. After you have verified that the print file object was created, you need to compile the RPG program. The steps involved in doing this are the same as those you used to compile the print file.

Note: Before the RPG program will compile, the EMPPFL physical file must be in your library list, and the print file object must have been created. A very high-level explanation of this process is that when the system tries to compile the RPG source file, it looks first at the file descriptions at the top of the program and then in your library list for the described objects. If either the print file object or the physical file is missing, the RPG program will not be compiled.

11.34. After you have verified that the RPG compile was successful, as Figure 11.52 shows, sign on to a 5250 session and work with your spool files. Find the output from your compile, and display this print file.

11.34.a. Where did the compiler find the EMPPFL and EMPPFLP files? **Hint:** Find 'External name'.

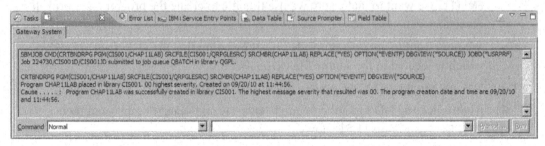

Figure 11.52: Commands Log View of Compile Process

11.35. You now need to submit the RPG program to batch.

11.36. Click and expand your personal library in the Remote Systems view, and then press F5.

11.36.a. What does the F5 command key do?

11.37. Right-click program object CHAP11LAB, and select Run As and then Batch, as in Figure 11.53.

11.37.a. How do you verify that the program was submitted and completed?

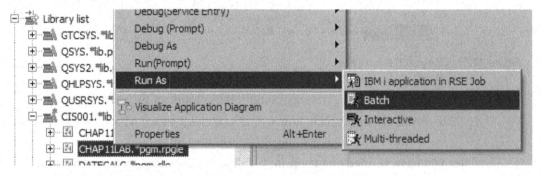

Figure 11.53: Submit a Program to Batch

11.38. Open a 5250 session and verify that a report was created in your output queue.

Part 3

Goals   Edit the CHAP11LAB RPG source file; add code, compile, and submit the program object to batch.

Start with   RDP open, connected to your IBM i system, and with the Remote System (Explorer) perspective displayed.

Procedure   Navigate to the QRPGLESRC source file in your personal library, and open the CHAP11LAB source member.

Use Content Assist and SEU commands to add the appropriate code to the RPG member.

Save and compile the member.

Submit the program object member to batch.

Review the program output in your output queue.

Note

We understand that this is not an RPG programming class. The example used for this exercise is a simple report program that is well documented (ask your instructor to explain it in detail). By the time you reach this section of the lab, you have seen the output from this program and understand that it lists all the records in the EMPPFL physical file.

The code we will add to this program will check an indicator's status, and if the indicator is ON, the program will write a new set of headings on the report. In Figure 11.54, we have circled the OFLIND keyword. This keyword specifies an overflow indicator; the programmer uses this keyword to eject to the next page of a report, usually by printing headings.

11.39. Expand your personal library, and navigate to the QRPGLESRC source file.

11.40. After you expand the QRPGLESRC source file, double-click the CHAP11LAB source member. Your workbench should be similar to the one you see in Figure 11.54.

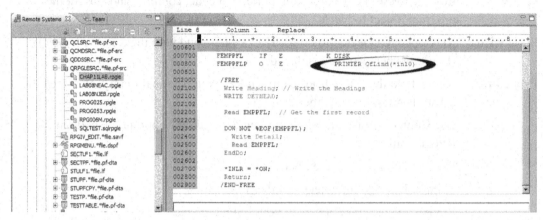

Figure 11.54: RPG Program Code

11.41. Position your cursor on line 002500, and key in i3, as you see in Figure 11.55 (note the arrow). Press Enter. Doing this will insert three lines in your source member. This action demonstrates that the LPEX Editor has many of the same functions as SEU and also gives you an area for inserting your code.

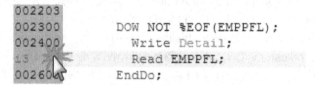

Figure 11.55: Insert Lines in RPG Program Code

11.42. You now need to insert an IF statement to check the status of the *in10 indicator. If you knew the syntax of an IF statement, you could key it in. Because you are new to RPG, you will use a handy feature of the LPEX Editor called Content Assist.

11.43. Move your cursor to column 8 on line 002502, type IF, and then press Ctrl+space. You can see an example of Content Assist in Figure 11.56.

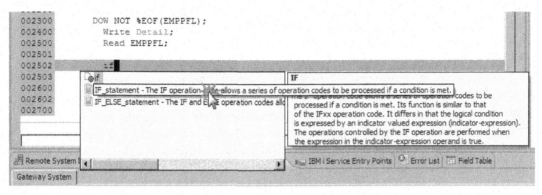

Figure 11.56: Using Content Assist

11.44. Once the Content Assist window is displayed, you can use your down arrow key to highlight IF_statement; then press Enter. Doing so will insert an IF statement template.

11.45. In Figure 11.57, we have changed the statement to check the status of the *in10 indicator.

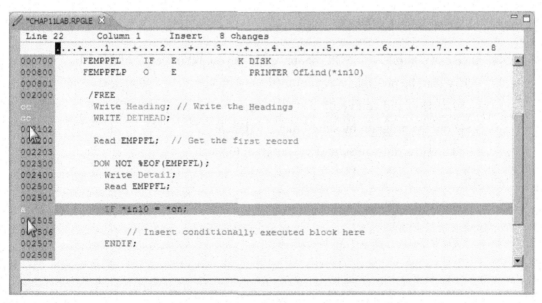

Figure 11.57: Adding Code and SEU Block Commands

11.46. We also used the SEU CC copy block command (note the arrow pointing to these statements at line 002102) to copy the two WRITE statements into the IF statement. (Note the arrow on line 002505 pointing to the a, which designates where to copy these two lines of code.) So theWRITE statements are executed when the IF statement is true.

11.47. The last line of code you need to insert will turn off the overflow indicator after you have written the two heading lines. Figure 11.58 shows the completed code.

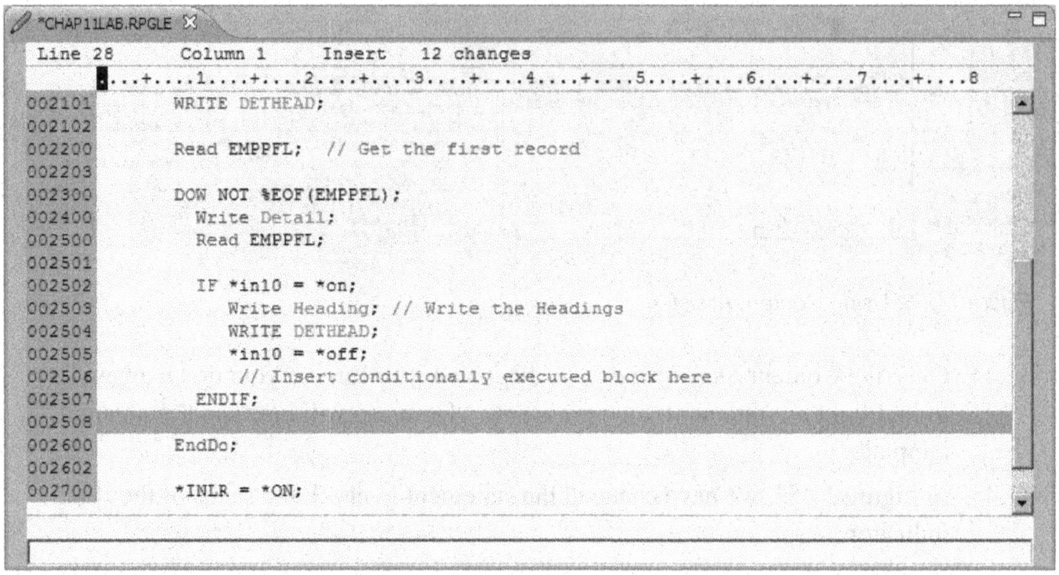

```
*CHAP11LAB.RPGLE ✕

 Line 28       Column 1      Insert    12 changes
      ▌...+....1....+....2....+....3....+....4....+....5....+....6....+....7....+....8
002101      WRITE DETHEAD;
002102
002200      Read EMPPFL;   // Get the first record
002203
002300      DOW NOT %EOF(EMPPFL);
002400        Write Detail;
002500        Read EMPPFL;
002501
002502        IF *in10 = *on;
002503          Write Heading; // Write the Headings
002504          WRITE DETHEAD;
002505          *in10 = *off;
002506          // Insert conditionally executed block here
002507        ENDIF;
002508
002600      EndDo;
002602
002700      *INLR = *ON;
```

Figure 11.58: Final Code for This Lab

11.48. Save and compile your RPG source code as you did in Part 2 of this lab.

11.49. Verify that the program was compiled.

11.49.a. How did you verify that the program was compiled?

11.50. Now run the program by submitting it to batch.

11.50.a. How did you submit the program to batch?

11.51. Signon to a 5250 session, and verify that the program produced a report and that it now prints the headings when the report reaches the end of the page, as in Figure 11.59.

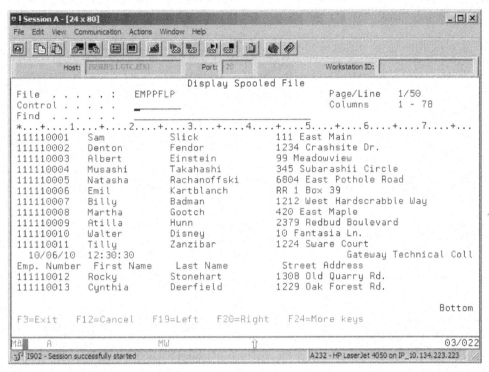

Figure 11.59: Final Output for This Lab

CHAPTER **12**

Using Screen Designer and Report Designer

Overview

In this chapter, we work with two related features of RDP, Screen Designer and Report Designer. These features allow today's programmer to maintain and develop 5250 screens and printed reports. And the functionality of Screen Designer and Report Designer is so similar that if you know how to use one, you will also be able to use the other.

We start by working with the print file that we used in the Chapter 11 lab. We add a record and a text constant to that print file. We then create a display screen, add two records and some text constants to this source member, and show how to add database fields to the display screen. We pull everything together in the lab portion by continuing to work on the print file and the display file and adding and formatting other fields. In the additional optional labs, we add a counter to the RPG report program and use an interactive RPG program to test our display screen.

Objectives

Students will be able to

- Articulate the development history of IBM's screen-designer and report-designer GUI tools
- Modify a print file using RDP and Report Designer
- Create a display file using RDP and Screen Designer
- Add records to a display or print file
- Add text constants to a display file
- Add database fields to a display screen
- Add "named" fields to a print file
- Modify properties of screen and report file elements

History

In recent years, many new applications developed for IBM i have Web interfaces. However, many applications in use today still use the 5250 interface. Some of the major reasons for this are that

- Companies have not had the resources to rewrite or reface the application
- The application does not lend itself well to a Web application
- Users are satisfied with the 5250 application as it is; as a result, the company has not expended the IT resources to modify it

Consequently, today's programmer needs the skills to modify and even write new applications using the 5250 interface. Over the years, IBM has provided the following three graphical design tools for developing 5250 applications:

- **Screen Design Aid** (SDA) was introduced for the System/34 and was part of the Application Development Toolset (ADTS). Although SDA is still in use in many shops, IBM has not enhanced it for a number of OS releases.
- **CODE Designer** is a feature of the IBM VisualAge RPG and CODE product.
- **Screen Designer** and **Report Designer** are part of the Rational Developer for Power (RDP) and were first introduced at Version 7.6 of the product.

Developing reports is an important part of every programmer's life. For many years, IBM's **Report Layout Utility** (RLU) was the standard. If you ask any programmer who has used RLU, he will usually shake his head and say, "It was better than nothing." The CODE Designer product included a built-in tool that allowed drag-and-drop report designing; however, since IBM has discontinued any development effort with this product, we will not discuss it here. IBM's new Screen Designer and Report Designer, which are part of RDP, are the focus of this chapter.

Getting Started

Print files and 5250 display files are both designed using DDS, and the process of developing them is similar. In Chapter 11, we copied and compiled a print file member called EMPPFLP; in this chapter, we will use this source member to demonstrate some of the features of the Report Designer.

In Figure 12.1, you can see that we have navigated to the QDDSSRC source physical file and right-clicked the member EMPPFLP. As this figure shows, we could open the source member with a number of editors. If we just wanted to edit the source code, we could open it in the Remote Systems LPEX Editor. The computer we used when writing this book also has the IBM VisualAge RPG and CODE product installed. Therefore, we could have opened the member with the CODE editor or CODE designer. In the following example, we will be using RDP's Report Designer.

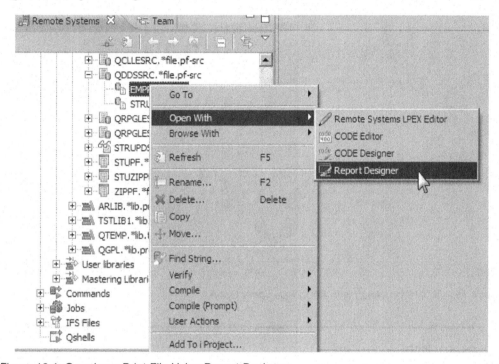

Figure 12.1: Opening a Print File Using Report Designer

Modifying a Print File

Once we have opened the EMPPFLP source file member, as in Figure 12.1, our workbench looks similar to Figure 12.2.

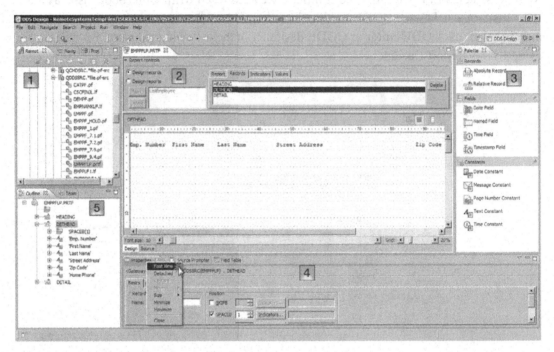

Figure 12.2: RDP Workbench with Report Designer Open

Note

The figures displayed throughout this chapter depend on RDP's current perspective being DDS Design. If you are comparing your workbench to the figures shown here, and you are not currently in the DDS Design perspective, your workbench will differ slightly.

The figure shows the workbench after the EMPPFLP source member has been opened in the **DDS Design perspective**. The numbers 1 through 5 highlight the views that often are used in the workbench when the Report Designer or Screen Designer is being used:

1. *Remote System Explorer (RSE)*—When you are using either the Report Designer or the Screen Designer, open your members and compile them from this view.

2. ***Report Designer area***—Used to design your report; it supports dragging and dropping of fields onto a report.

3. *Palette*—Contains elements that you can drag and drop onto the design surface.

4. *Additional views*—Contains the Field Table view, which displays fields from a database file; the Source Prompter view, which displays the DDS source code; and the Properties view, which displays the properties of a selected element.

5. *Outline view*—Clicking any element or record from this view will select it in the design view; this is an easy view from which to change properties.

You also should notice that we have right-clicked the tab at the top of the Properties view and selected **Fast View**. This feature, which we will discuss in more detail shortly, lets you "hide" a view and quickly restore it as needed.

To produce the screen in Figure 12.3, we double-clicked the EMPPFLP.PRTF tab at the top of the design view. Doing this expands the view to take up the complete workbench, giving us an excellent work area. At first, you might think that we will not be able to access the other views from here. Once again, to help you understand some of the features of this perspective, we have numbered specific areas and discuss them following the figure.

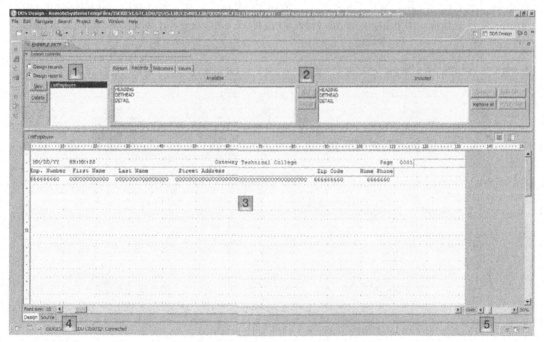

Figure 12.3: Expanded Design View

1. *Report controls*—This control area permits you to switch between the Design records and the Design reports options. Design records lets you work on a specific record; Design reports lets you work on all the records in the print file.

2. *Records view*—You can remove or add records to the design area from this view.

3. *Design area*—This is the work area for report design.
4. *Fast View bar*—Views that have been set to Fast View are located in this area.
5. *Minimized bar*—Views that have been minimized are located here.

Now that you have an overview of the workbench features, the best way to become familiar with the tool is to make some modifications to the print file. We saw the output of the CHAP11LAB program in Chapter 11. Now we will add another record to the print file, as well as a constant that displays End of Report. Then, in the lab at the end of the chapter, we will add a counter to the RPG program and modify this record to display the number of employees on the report.

Adding Records to a Print File

We have already opened the EMPPFLP print file; in Figure 12.4, we have double-clicked the Design view tab in the upper-left corner (of Figure 12.3) to return that portion of the screen to the default size. Now notice the upper-right corner of the workbench in Figure 12.4. We have right-clicked the tab at the top of the Palette view and selected the Minimize option. This action will minimize the view so that we can access it when the design area is maximized.

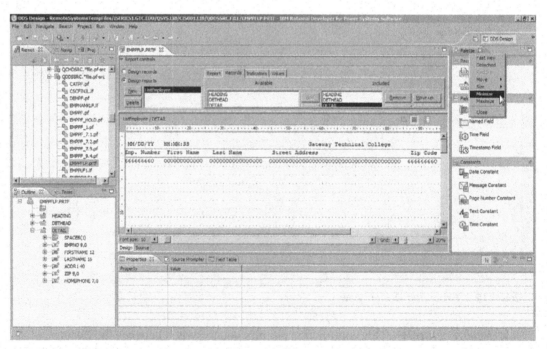

Figure 12.4: Minimizing the Palette

We should probably note at this time that the Palette actually has two forms. One form resides outside the editor, much like the views you are accustomed to using, and is available when you are in the DDS Design perspective. The second form is integrated. It is located inside the design editor and is available whenever you open a member in either the Report Designer or the Screen Designer.

Now that we have minimized the palette and maximized the design area, we can click on the minimized Palette icon to access it, as Figure 12.5 shows.

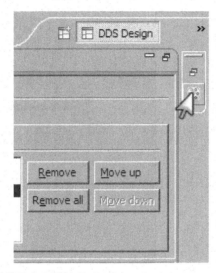

Figure 12.5: Accessing the Minimized Palette

Next, we want to add a record to the print file. Figure 12.6 shows that we have selected the Relative Record from the palette and are in the process of dropping it on the design view. We must take care to place the record in the area where we want the record located on the report.

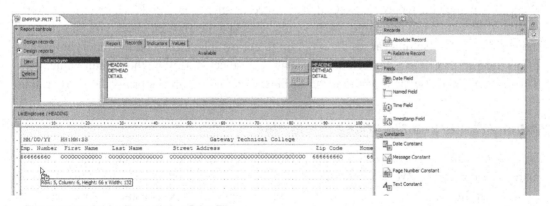

Figure 12.6: Add a Record to a Print File

Once we have added a record to the print file, we need to change some of the properties. In Figure 12.2, we demonstrated putting the Properties view in Fast View. This placed the icon for the Properties view in the lower-left corner of the workbench in the Fast View bar (see Figure 12.3). Whenever we want to change the properties of an element, we highlight the element and then click the Properties icon. The Properties view will expand, as you see in Figure 12.7. We can now change the record name, add "spaces" or skips" to the record, or add valid DDS keywords. A DDS keyword allows the print file or display file to perform a special function. Some keywords used in print files are SPACEA, SKIPB, EDTWRD, and COLOR.

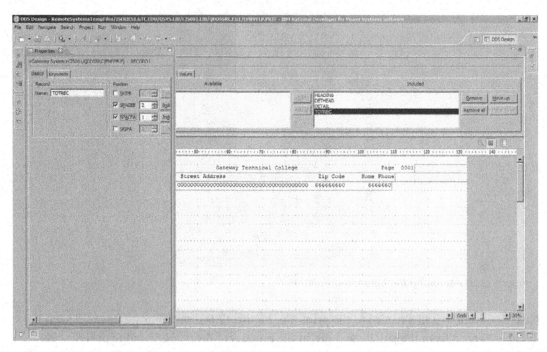

Figure 12.7: Modify the Properties of a Record

We have renamed the record TOTREC; if we wanted to refer to it in an RPG, CL, or COBOL program, we would use this name. We have also checked the **SPACEB** check box and changed the value to 2. This setting causes the program to put two blank lines on the report before it prints the line. The **SPACEA** check box also has been selected, leaving the default value of 1. This setting will cause the program to start printing on the line after it prints the TOTREC line.

Adding Fields and Modifying Properties

Now that we have placed a record in our print file, we need to add a text constant that will display End of Report. We accomplish this in much the same way as we placed a new record in our print file. Figure 12.8 shows dragging and dropping the text constant onto the TOTREC record.

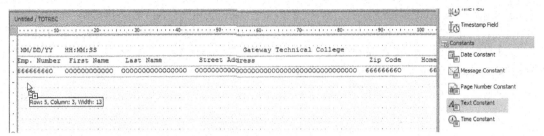

Figure 12.8: Add a Text Constant to a Record

Once we have placed the text constant on the printer design area, we click the Properties icon in the lower-left corner of the workbench. The workbench then displays the Properties view, as in Figure 12.9.

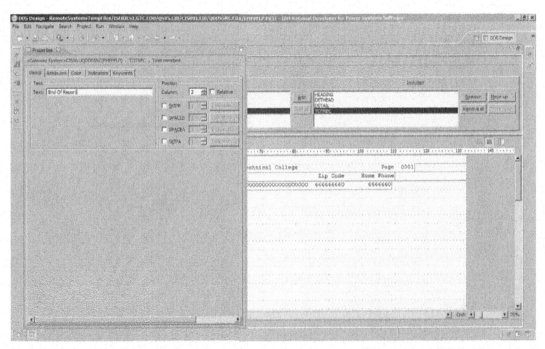

Figure 12.9: Modify Text Constant Properties

When we first place the text constant on the Design area, we can edit the text. Our goal here is to demonstrate that a number of properties can be manipulated by changing the text displayed in the Properties view. We change the text displayed using the Basics tab in the Properties view. A number of other tabs are available that let you change the attributes and color and add indicators or keywords. A discussion of these additional attributes is beyond the scope of this discussion; but as you develop your skills, they will become important.

Finally, we want to use the Properties view to add formatting to the HOMEPHONE number field. We will use a DDS **EDTWRD** (Edit Word) keyword to accomplish this for now. Think of edit words as a template that can be placed over a number. You cannot use an edit word on nonnumeric fields. The edit word we will use is '***-****'; it is demonstrated in Figure 12.10.

> **Note**
>
> Here and throughout the rest of this chapter, we show the * for display purposes only. When you enter the edit word, you should replace the * with spaces, as you see in Figure 12.10. Unlike when you use SEU, you *should not* enter the quotation marks in the example edit word.

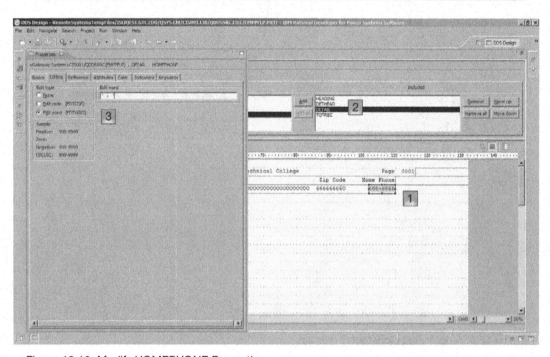

Figure 12.10: Modify HOMEPHONE Properties

Once again, the numbers in the figure highlight some screen areas:

1. As you add an edit word to a field, the edit is displayed in the Properties view's "sample" box and in the design area.
2. When you click a field, the *Report controls* area shows you the record in which the field is located.
3. You add an edit word by clicking the Editing tab in the Properties window.

Note

In the lab at the end of this chapter, this source member is referred to as EMPPFLP2. If you have been working through the chapter, you should save the print file EMPPFLP as EMPPFLP2.You will continue to modify this file so you can gain additional experience using the Report Designer.

For those who have not been working through the chapter, the file EMPPFLP2 is available in the QDDSSRC source file in the INTROCLASS library, as discussed in the lab.

Creating a Display Screen

As we stated previously, you create both print files and display screens using DDS, and the procedures for creating them are very similar. They both contain records that the program writes to, and the records contain fields that are displayed. The major difference between a screen and a print file is that with a screen, an interactive program receives data from a screen, uses this data in its processing, and then displays the results of the processing back to a screen. With a report, the report program receives data from a database file, processes that data and writes it to a print file, and then prints the data on a report.

In the next portion of this chapter, we guide you through the steps necessary to create a display screen. In the chapter lab, you create a screen that you will use later in a CL program you will write in Chapter 16.

Create the Display Screen Source Member

To create the display screen source member, we first navigate to the RSE view and right-click the QDDSSRC source file. Next, we select New, and then Member, as Figure 12.11 demonstrates.

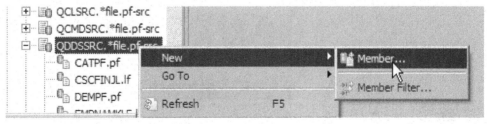

Figure 12.11: Create a Display File Source Member

We will name our sample screen CHAP12DSP, select DSPF from the slider window, and enter text to describe the display file we are creating (Figure 12.12). Adding text is not required, but doing so is important for documentation purposes.

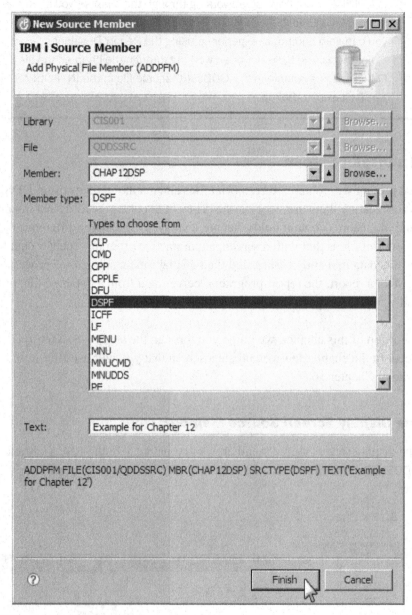

Figure 12.12: Create a Display File Source Member

When we click Finish, the new source member will open by default in the LPEX Editor. However, we do not want to edit this member in the LPEX Editor, so we click X in the top-right corner of the New Source Member window to close it.

When you create a new object, it is sometimes necessary to refresh the RSE view. You do this by highlighting the QDDSSRC file in RSE and pressing F5 to have RSE display the new source member. Right-click the member, and navigate to Open With and then Screen Designer, as you see in Figure 12.13. The workbench knows to open your source member with Screen Designer because you selected DSPF for the file type of this member.

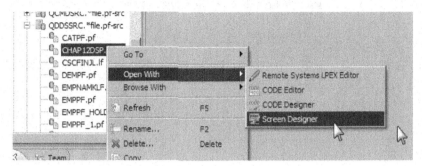

Figure 12.13: Opening CHAP12DSP in Screen Designer

Add a Record

Figure 12.14 shows our new member open in the Screen Designer. You should immediately notice how similar the workbench is to our previous example using Report Designer. The Palette view has very limited options because we have not added a record yet. Notice that Standard Record has been highlighted, and the arrow in the center of the design area shows that we are dragging a standard record onto the design area, which now looks like a 5250 screen.

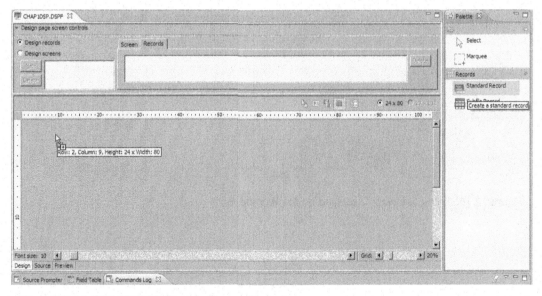

Figure 12.14: CHAP12DSP Open in Screen Designer

We now have a record placed on the screen design area, and the Palette view contains a number of elements that we can drag and drop onto our new record (Figure 12.15).

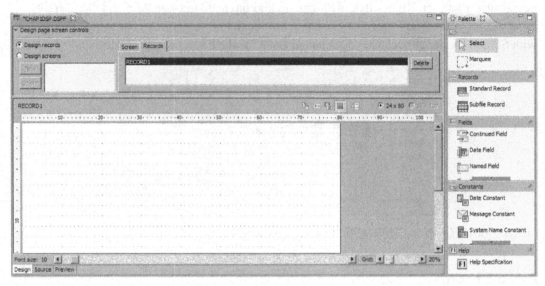

Figure 12.15: Screen Designer with One Record

We want to change the name RECORD1 to SCRN1. The Properties view icon is still in the bottom-left corner of our workbench, in the Fast View bar. After we click the icon, the workbench will look like Figure 12.16.

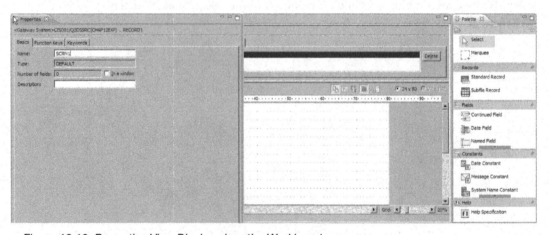

Figure 12.16: Properties View Displayed on the Workbench

We will repeat the above process so that our example will have two records because we are designing this display screen to work with an RPG program. The RPG program first displays SCRN1 to allow the user to enter an employee number. When the user presses Enter, the program reads the employee's database record and then displays information about the employee on SCRN2, as Figure 12.17 depicts.

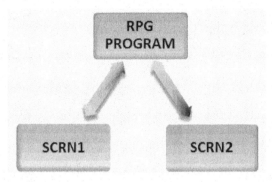

Figure 12.17: RPG Program Logic

Add Keywords to a File or Record

Previously, we used the EDTWRD keyword to format fields on a report. You will use **keywords** extensively in coding DDS for physical files, display files, and printer files. There are three levels of DDS keywords: file, record, and field. Some keywords can be used on multiple levels.

- *File-level keywords*—Keywords used at this level are available throughout the file. For example, the REF keyword is used to retrieve field descriptions for fields used in the source member.
- *Record-level keywords*—Keywords used at this level are available throughout the record. For example, the CAnn (CA01–CA24) keywords can be used at the file or record level. We will discuss this example in greater depth in the next few pages.
- *Field-level keywords*—Keywords used at this level are related only to the fields to which they are assigned. For example, the EDTWRD keyword is related only to the HOMEPHONE field we discussed previously. If we also wanted to edit the WORKPHONE, we would have to put an EDTWRD keyword on that field. Remember also that the EDTWRD keyword is valid only on numeric fields; if you try to use this keyword on any other type of field, it is ignored.

We will need to add several file-level keywords to our screen for it to function properly. The best way to access the file-level properties is to use the Outline view. In Figure 12.18, we have clicked the file-level icon for our display-screen source member.

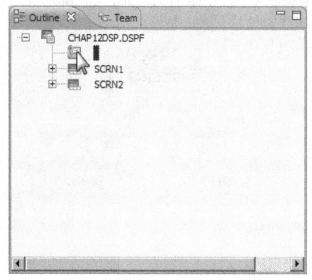

Figure 12.18: Outline View

We then click the Properties icon located in the Fast View bar at the bottom-left corner of our workbench to expand the Properties view for the source member and enable us to add keywords. Figure 12.19 shows the file-level properties for the source member.

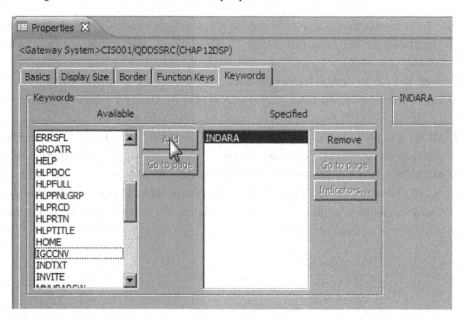

Figure 12.19: File-Level Properties View

Adding the INDARA Keyword

In Figure 12.19, we have selected the Keywords tab, navigated to the **INDARA** keyword, and clicked ADD. The INDARA keyword takes the data that results from the user pressing a function key and places it in a 99-bit data structure that the RPG program uses to decide which function key has been pressed. Think of the INDARA keyword as an interface between the display screen and the program.

Setting Up the Function Keys

We now need to enable the function keys that the program will need to use with the example screen. When using the program, the user can press F12 (exit a screen) or F3 (exit the program and return to the command line).

Figure 12.20 shows how we set up F3. The steps to accomplish this are

1. Select the Function Keys tab.
2. Click the box under F3.
3. Select the Command Attention radio button.
4. Check the Indicator check box, and change the associated value to 3.
5. Check the Description check box, and key in a description of the function key.

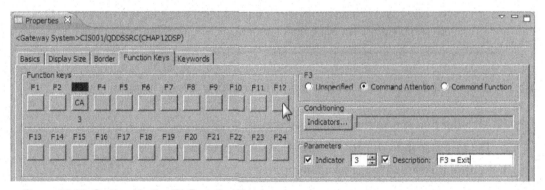

Figure 12.20: Setting Up the F3 Function Key

We perform the same steps for F12; Figure 12.21 shows the completed window.

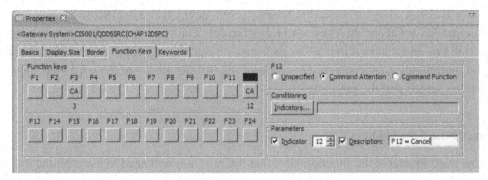

Figure 12.21: Setting Up the F12 Function Key

You must take care when assigning CAnn numbers because the same CAnn number cannot be used at both the file and record levels. For example, if you use CA03 at the file level, you cannot use it at the record level.

Note

You will not need to add or modify the function keys in the lab at the end of this chapter. The display file you will copy from the INTROCLASS library will already have these keys set for you. You will become more familiar with function keys when you take an RPG class. We have added them here so that our sample program will function properly.

Here is a short explanation of what happens when a user presses a function key:

1. All other function key indicators are set Off.
2. The response indicator for the specified CAnn is set On.
3. Control is returned to the program.

The program then uses a data structure and additional program logic to decide which key was pressed and how the program should react based on this key.

Because we have described the function keys at the file level, when a user presses either F3 or F12 while using the SCRN1 or SCRN2 screen, the program will be aware of which key was pressed and can make processing decisions based on the function key that was pressed.

Add Fields to the Record

Figure 12.22 shows our display file with the two records (SCRN1 and SCRN2), and we are in the process of dragging constants onto the screen design area. We have placed the date constant on the left side of the screen design area and the time constant on the right side of the screen design area. We are about to drop a text constant for the screen heading on the top center of the screen design area.

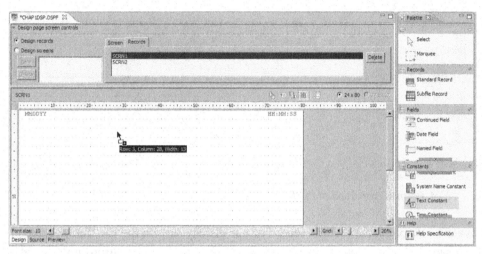

Figure 12.22: Placing Fields on the Screen Design Area

If we refer to the top-left corner of the screen design area in this figure, we see the constant MMDDYY. Figure 12.23 shows the "basic" properties of this constant, and we can change whether the date displayed is the job date (*JOB) or the system date (*SYS). The difference between the values of these two dates is this: If a job would start before midnight and continue into the next day, the **job date** (*JOB) would show the date the job started. If this value were set to the **system date** (*SYS), the variable would show the current system date.

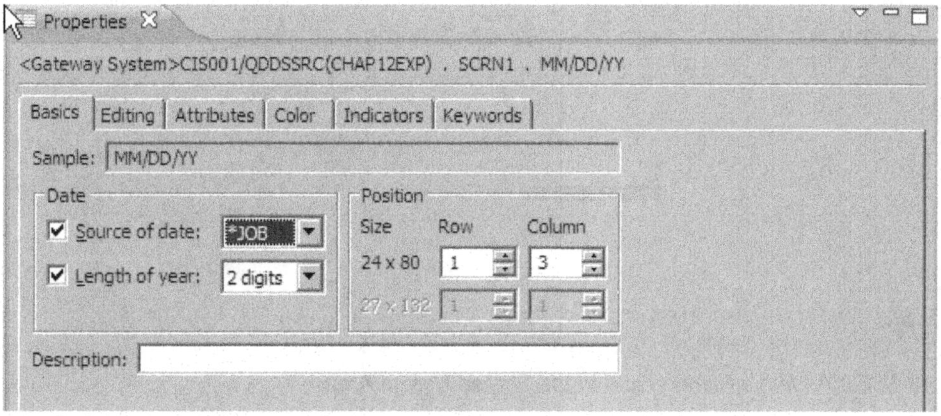

Figure 12.23: Date Properties of the MMDDYY Constant

In Figure 12.24, we have selected the Editing tab and entered the Edit word '**/**/**' to properly format the output of the date (see the note earlier in the chapter regarding the use of the *).

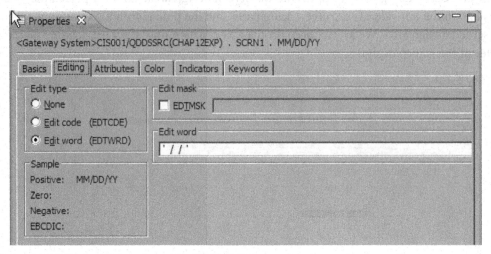

Figure 12.24: Format Properties of the MMDDYY Constant

We have almost completed the first record of our display screen; the last field we need to add is a Named Field, as you see in Figure 12.25. This field will be "**input only**," which means that it is not intended for displaying data but only for inputting data. We also have added several additional text constants to make the screen more informative to the user. (We maximized the screen design area in the figure by double-clicking the CHAP12DSP.DSPF tab at the top-left corner of the window.)

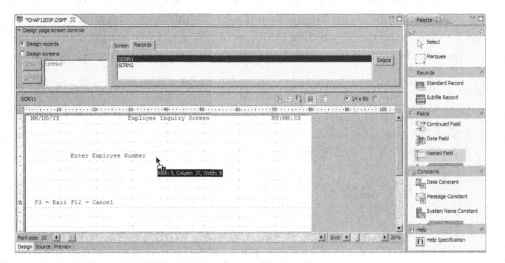

Figure 12.25: Adding a Named Field to the Screen Design Area

Note

When you are designing a report or a screen, you should always enter text constants that adequately describe the field and help the user understand the report or screen. We suggest using the proper case for all text constants. Avoid using "all caps" (all uppercase letters) in headings and prompts.

After placing our named field on the design area, we need to adjust some of the properties. Figure 12.26 shows these changes.

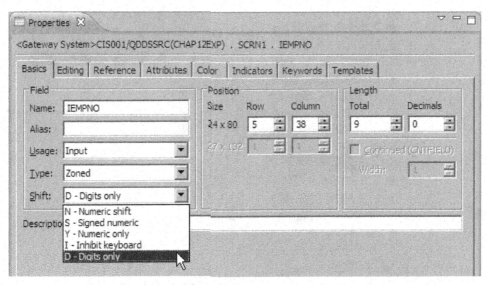

Figure 12.26: Changing Properties of Our Input-Only Named Field

As you see, we named our field IEMPNO, changed the Usage to Input, changed the Type to Zoned, and set the Shift option to allow only digits to be entered. We have also described the variable as nine digits long with no decimals. The input field should be in the same format as the database field you are going to read. In this case, the EMPNO field on the Employee master is numeric.

We have now completed our first record, and we need to work on the second record, SCRN2. After it reads the database, the RPG program will display the SCRN2 record, which displays the information about the employee.

Add Database Fields to a Record

Another feature of the workbench is the capability to display file information in a **table view**. You can display member information, fields and their descriptions, or the actual data. For our purposes, we will display the field descriptions so we can drag and drop the fields onto our screen design area. In Figure 12.27, we have navigated back to the INTROCLASS library, right-clicked the EMPPFL table, and selected Show in Table and then Fields.

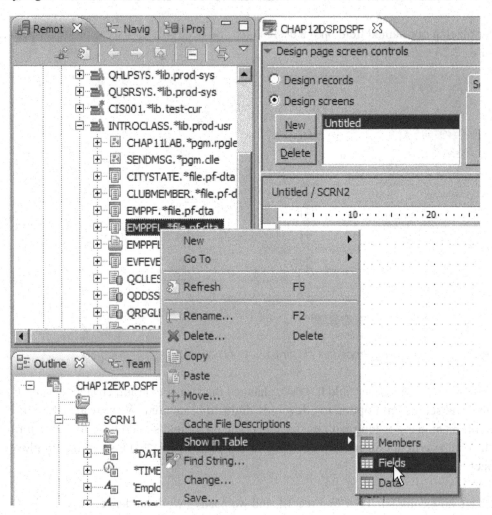

Figure 12.27: Displaying Database Fields and Field Table

Figure 12.28 shows the workbench after we have added the EMPPFL table. We have numbered some areas to highlight important points, which we go into following the figure.

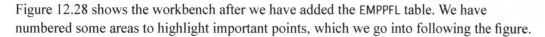
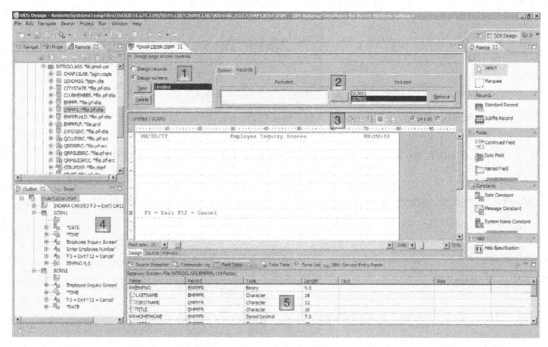

Figure 12.28: The Workbench Showing Additional Features

1. Switching from Design records to Design screens provides additional options when you are working with multiple records and screens that are not available when using Design records. For example, with the Design screens options, the report will be displayed showing all the records in the source member; this makes it easier to see what the final report will look like.

2. When using Design screens, you must move your records from Excluded to Included for them to be displayed when Design screens is selected.

3. If you are designing a screen, you can turn on Draw records transparent, which shows underlying screen records. From this area, you also can show the gridlines or set preferences.

4. Outline view lets you click an element, causing that element to be selected; it then moves the editor to the record where the element resides.

5. The Field Table shows the fields for the EMPPFL table.

The minimized Field Table icon is displayed in the bottom-right corner of the workbench, as Figure 12.29 shows (note the arrow).

Figure 12.29: The Workbench Showing Additional Features

We click the Field Table icon, which causes the table to be displayed as you see in Figure 12.30.

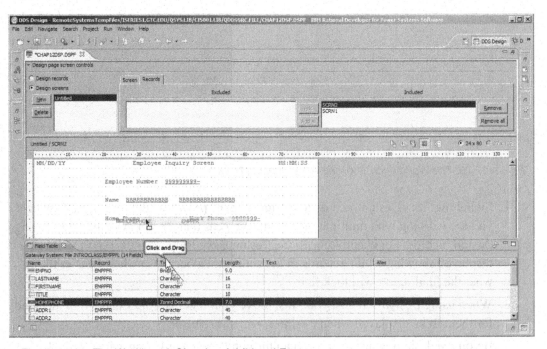

Figure 12.30: The Workbench Showing Additional Features

We then start dragging the required database fields onto the screen design area. The process is the same as placing constants on the screen design area. As you can see, we have dragged a number of the fields onto the design area. Figure 12.30 shows us dropping the HOMEPHONE field onto the design area.

Notice that we have also added text constants to make the screen more informative for the user. We have not shown the details for accomplishing this task because we demonstrated how to add text constants when we were working on the SCRN1 record.

We have added a number of database fields to the screen, so we now need to change the properties of some of those fields. The employee number field is displayed as 999999999, which is the default for numeric fields. The 9s represent an input/output field. The intent of the screen is just to display data, not to allow users to change anything. In Figure 12.31, we have highlighted the employee number field and selected the Properties icon from the lower-left corner of the workbench in the Fast View bar.

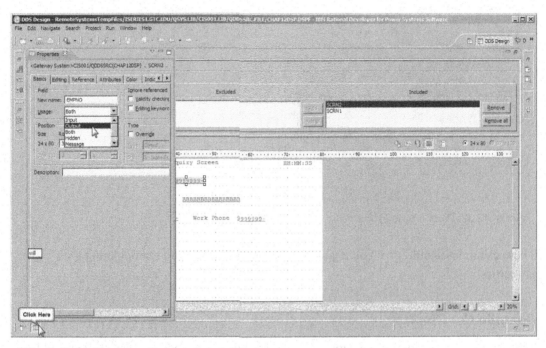

Figure 12.31: Employee Number Properties

Once the Properties view is displayed, we select the Usage parameter drop-down box and then select Output. To complete the record, we will need to change the properties of all the fields that we add to it to Output.

In Figure 12.32, we have selected the WORKPHONE database field and changed the usage to Output. We then clicked the Editing tab, selected the Edit word option, and added the edit word '***-****' (see the note earlier in the chapter regarding the use of the *).

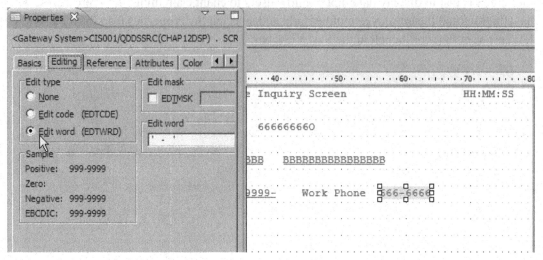

Figure 12.32: Work Phone Properties

These examples should give you a good start on adding fields and manipulating their properties.

Compile the Display

The CHAP12DSP example screen now has a completed SCRN1 input screen. We have added several fields and text constants to SCRN2 to make the screen functional. In the lab at the end of the chapter, you will add other fields so that the screen will display all the information from the employee file.

At this point, we have completed enough of the screen that we should compile the DDS into a display screen object. If you look at Figure 12.33, you can see an arrow labeled **Minimized Views**. Whenever you expand the design area to fill the workbench, any view groups that are on the workbench become "minimized groups" around the perimeter of the workbench. In this example, we have clicked the RSE minimized icon and then selected Compile and CRTDSPF from the context menu.

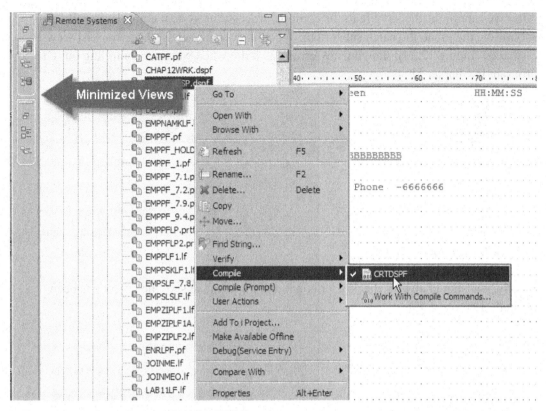

Figure 12.33: Compiling the CHAP12DSP Screen

Display screens and print files must be compiled into objects before they can be used. RDP knows which command to use to compile the source member by the member type that was chosen when the source member was created. In this example, we chose a type of **DSPF** (Display File) when we created the CHAP12DSP source member; so RDP has chosen the **CRTDSPF** (Create Display File) command. If we were compiling a printer file, which has a type of **PRTF** (Print File), RDP would have chosen the **CRTPRTF** (Create Print File) command.

After we submit the display file to the compile process, the system compiles the file by submitting the job to the batch subsystem. When the compile ends, the Error List view is displayed (Figure 12.34), showing any errors, as it did when we were compiling our CL program in Chapter 11.

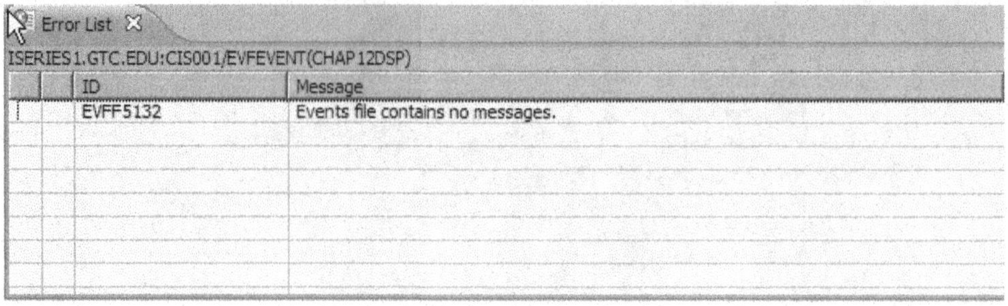

Figure 12.34: Error List View

Finally, you should always check your command log to make sure the object has been created (Figure 12.35).

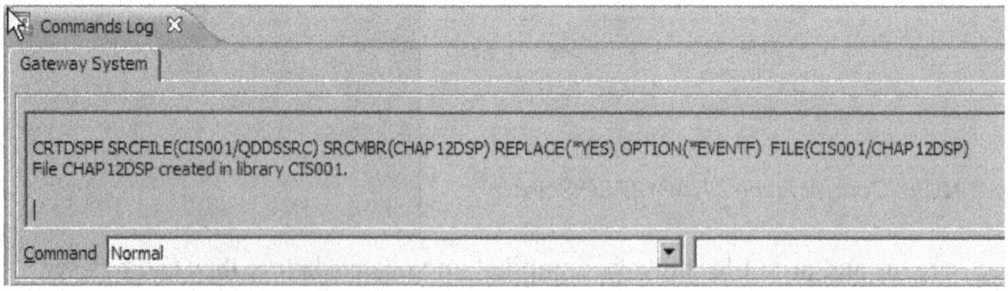

Figure 12.35: Commands Log Vew

In Summary

We started this chapter with a brief discussion of the history of IBM's Screen Designer and Report Designer tools. We explained why today's programmers still need to have the skills to develop 5250 display screens and reports. We then modified the EMPPFLP printer file by adding a record and a text constant.

We created the CHAP12DSP display file and added two records to the file. The first record (SCRN1) had an employee-number input field. As we developed the second record (SCRN2), we added a number of text constants and showed how to add database fields to this record. We discussed the logic of a simple interactive program. This step-by-step development of the CHAP12DSP sample display file also has added to your knowledge of the screen portion of this GUI development tool.

In the following labs, you will complete the print file and the display file. You also will add a counter to an RPG program and use the CHAP12DSP display file in a RPG program.

Key Terms

CODE Designer	minimized views
CRTDSPF	outline view
CRTPRTF	palette
DDS Design perspective	PRTF
design area	record-level keywords
DSPF	records view
EDTWRD	report controls
Fast View	Report Designer
Fast View bar	Report Designer area
field-level keywords	Report Layout Utility
file-level keywords	Screen Design Aid
INDARA keyword	Screen Designer
input only	SPACEA
job date	SPACEB
keywords	system date
minimized bar	table view

Review Questions

1. Describe the two palettes that are available in RDP.
2. Give an example of a property you could change on a numeric field. Why would you change this property?
3. What is the field type restriction when you are using the EDTWRD discussed in the text?
4. Explain the major difference in the functionality of print files and display files.
5. How do you refresh the RSE view?
6. How does RDP decide whether to open a member in the Screen Designer or the Report Designer?
7. When you first open a new member, the palette has a limited number of elements. Explain why this occurs.
8. Explain how the system date and job date can have different values while the program is running.
9. What file information can be displayed in the Table view?

10. How does RDP know which command to use to create an object from a print file or display-screen source file?

11. List and explain the different levels of keywords.

12. Describe the function of the INDARA keyword.

13. Why do you need to describe the function keys used in a display screen?

14. Describe what happens when the user presses a function key.

15. Investigate three additional DDS keywords not mentioned in the text. List and explain them.

16. When designing a display screen or printer file, what functionality does the Outline view provide?

17. What is the purpose of the Fast View bar?

18. Explain the functional difference between a field that is displayed using a number of 9s and one that is displayed with 3s. What does it mean when a field is displayed using 6s?

19. Explain how you could use the Table view in RDP when you are designing reports or screens.

Lab 12

Introduction

This lab will help you develop your Screen Designer and Report Designer skills. In Part 1, you will add a named field to display the total employees in the EMPPFL file. In Part 2, you will add text constants and database fields to the CHAP12DSP display screen we worked on in this chapter. In Part 3, you will create a display-screen menu that we will use in Chapter 16. This chapter also has two additional optional labs; in Lab 12-A, you will modify a report program to count the number of employees and write the TOTREC on the report. In Lab 12-B, you will copy, compile, and run an RPG program to test the CHAP12DSP display screen.

Note
The version of RDP that we used when writing this chapter sometimes did not show the Edit tab. You can resolve this issue by clicking the Reference tab.

Part 1

Goals	Modify a print file using Report Designer to show the total number of employees processed.
Start	With RDP open and connected to your server.
Procedure	Verify that the DDS Design perspective is the current perspective.
	Add the INTROCLASS library to your library list.
	Copy the EMPPFLP2 printer file to your personal library.
	Add a Total field to the report.
	Format the Zip Code and Home Phone fields.

12.1. In this portion of the lab, you need to copy the EMPPFLP2 printer-file source member from QDDSSRC in the INTROCLASS library to your personal library. You then open the member in the Report Designer, with DDS Design as the current perspective. **Note:** This is the member to which we added the TOTREC record and End of Report constant earlier in this chapter.

Navigate to the RSE perspective, and verify that the INTROCLASS library is in your library list. If it is not, add it as we have demonstrated previously.

Caution

It is important that the library where the data file exists is in your library list when you are working on a printer or screen source member because RDP receives field descriptions from the data file. Failure to follow this guideline will cause field lengths and other attributes to "disappear." You can fix this problem by adding the library where the physical file exists to your library list and then highlighting each field and selecting Properties.

DDS Design should be displayed in the top-right corner of the workbench, as in Figure 12.36. If this is not your current perspective, change it as shown.

Figure 12.36: Copy EMPPFLP2 Source Member

12.2.   Using the RSE view, navigate to the INTROCLASS library and expand it. Navigate to the QDDSSRC source member, right-click the EMPPFLP2 print-file source member, and select Copy, as you see in Figure 12.37. Then navigate to the QDDSSRC file in your personal library, right-click the file, and select Paste. Be sure to answer the *"Copy Source File (CPYSRCF)"* message by clicking OK.

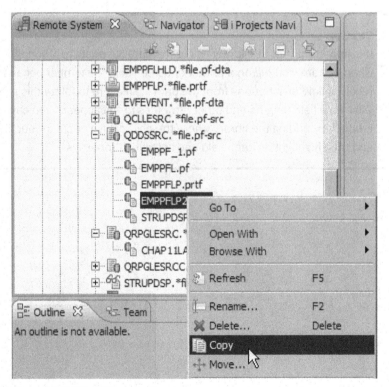

Figure 12.37: Copy EMPPFLP2 Source Member

12.3.   Right-click the EMPPFLP2 source-file member in the QDDSSRC source file in your personal library, and select Open With and then Report Designer. Your workbench should now look similar to Figure 12.38.

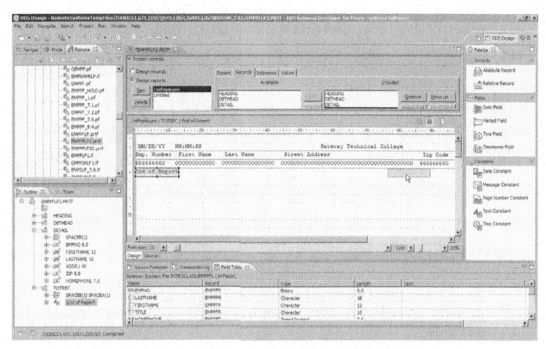

Figure 12.38: Workbench with the EMPPFLP2 Source Member Open

You should have noticed in Figure 12.38 that we are in the process of dragging the End of Report text constant to the right side of the report. We want to use the Properties view to change the text of this constant to Total Employees.

Expand the Properties view as Figure 12.39 shows, and, under the Basics tab, change the text.

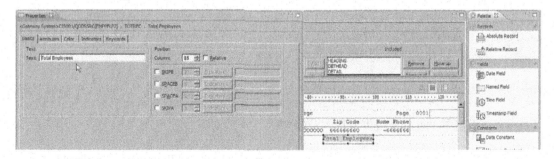

Figure 12.39: Using the Properties View to Change Text

12.4. In the optional Lab 12-A at the end of this chapter, you will add an accumulator to count the number of records processed in this report. We now need to add a named field to the TOTREC record to display this accumulator on our report. We will name this accumulator for the RPG program TOTEMPS. Figure 12.40 shows us in the process of dragging a named field onto the TOTREC record.

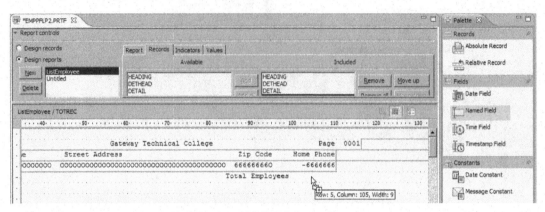

Figure 12.40: Adding a Named Field to the TOTREC Record

We have now placed the named field on the TOTREC record. We need to move the field to the right of the Total Employees text constant and change the field properties.

In Figure 12.41, we have moved the field, opened the Properties view, and renamed the field TOTEMPS. You need to edit the following properties:

- Change the field to Zoned Decimal.
- Change the field length to five with zero decimals.
- Set editing to EDTCODE using 1.

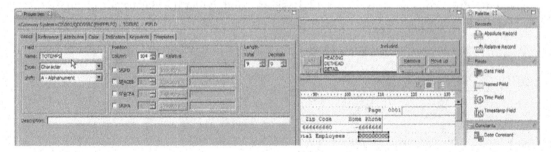

Figure 12.41: Changing the Named Field Properties

12.4.a. What happened to the tabs when you changed the Type to Decimal?

12.4.b. How did you enter the EDTCODE?

12.5.   Add the edit words (EDTWRDs) for the fields.

- Add the EDTWRD to the Zip Code field.
- Add the EDTWRD to the Home Phone field.

Your completed print file should like Figure 12.42.

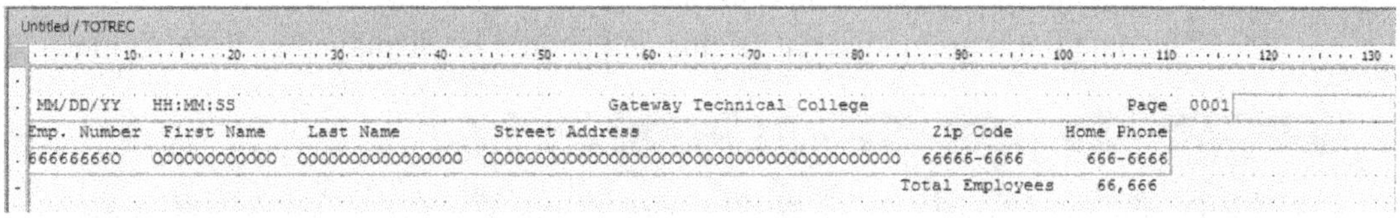

Figure 12.42: Completed Printer File

12.5.a.   Write the EDTWRD you used for the Zip Code field.

12.5.b.   Write the EDTWRD you used for the Home Phone field.

Compile the printer file as we described earlier in this chapter. Make sure that the print file is compiled.

12.5.c.   How did you check to make sure your print file was compiled?

You will use this print file for the additional lab (12-A) at the end of this chapter.

Part 2

Goals   Modify a screen using Screen Designer.

Start with   RDP open and connected to your server.

Procedure   Verify that the DDS Design perspective is the current perspective.

Verify the INTROCLASS library to your library list.

Copy the CHAP12DSP source member from the QDDSSRC file in the INTROCLASS library to the QDDSSRC file in your personal library.

Open the CHAP12DSP member in the Screen Designer.

Open the EMPPFL physical file in the Field Table view.

Add the required text constants to the design area.

Add and format the additional database fields.

Add the error message to be issued if the employee number is not found.

Compile the CHAP12DSP member, and verify that it was created.

12.6. In this chapter, we created the CHAP12DSP display file and in this section of the lab, we will add and format the database fields and text constants. Figure 12.43 shows the completed screen record. The requirements for the fields are as follows:

- The fields should be placed on the screen as shown in the figure.
- All text constants should be in blue and in proper case.
- All data fields should be "output only."
- The date fields are native date fields and should be displayed in *USA format.

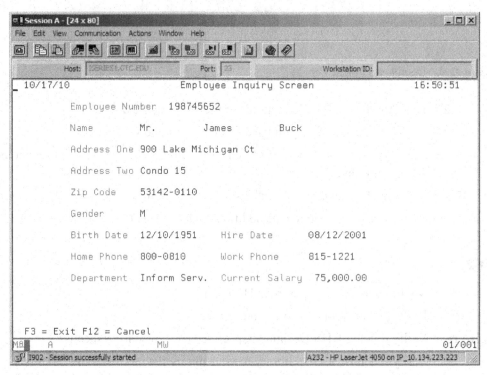

Figure 12.43: Completed SCRN2 Record in the CHAP12DSP Display File

12.7. Verify that the DDS Design perspective is the current perspective. If it is not, change to this perspective.

12.8. Verify that the INTROCLASS library is in your library list. If it is not, add it to your library list.

12.9. Copy the CHAP12DSP source member from the QDDSSRC file in the INTROCLASS library to the QDDSSRC file in your personal library.

Note

This member might already be in your library if you have worked through the chapter. If you receive the message that the member already exists, *do not* overwrite it.

12.10. Open the CHAP12DSP member in the Screen Designer.

12.11. Open the EMPPFL physical file located in the INTROCLASS library in the Field Table view.

12.12. Add the required text constants to the design area, as in Figure 12.43.

12.13. Add and format the additional database fields; be sure to make them "output only."

12.14. Make SCRN1 the active screen.

If the user enters an employee number that is not in the database, we need to display a message on SCRN1. Note the arrow in Figure 12.44.

```
MM/DD/YY                    Employee Inquiry Screen              HH:MM:SS




                   Enter Employee Number    333333333

















          Employee Number not found. Please enter a different Number

          F3 = Exit F12 = Cancel
```

Figure 12.44: Completed SCRN1 Record in the CHAP12DSP Display File

The CHAP12EXP RPG program sets ON indicator 90 if the read fails. You need to add a text constant with the following properties:

- The text should read, "Employee Number not found. Please enter a different Number."
- The text color should be Red.
- Display if the indicator 90 is set ON.

Click the Red radio button and then the Add button, as Figure 12.45 shows.

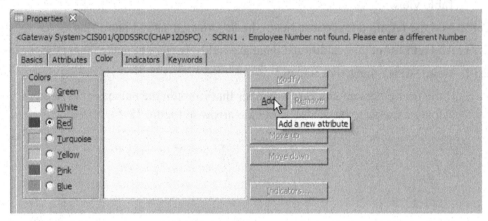

Figure 12.45: Color Properties of Text Constant Error Message

The Properties window will look like Figure 12.46; you now need to click the Indicators button to add an indicator to turn the text Red when the program turns on indicator 90.

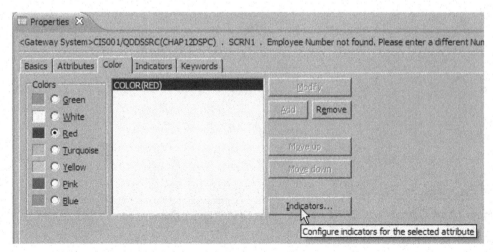

Figure 12.46: Color Properties of Text Constant Error Message, Continued

Key 90 into the box and click OK, as in Figure 12.47.

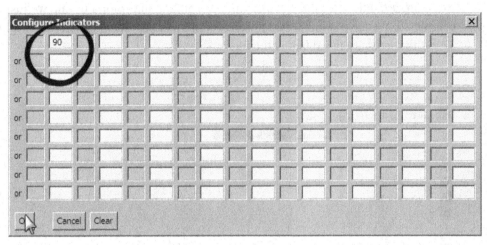

Figure 12.47: Adding a 90 Indicator to the Text Constant Error Message

Figure 12.48 shows the completed Color properties.

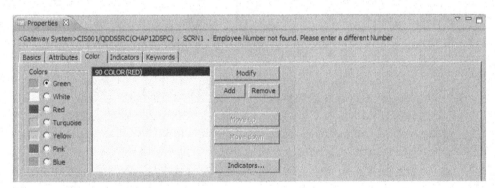

Figure 12.48: Color Properties of Text Constant Error Message

Click the Attributes tab to set the display attributes for the text constant field. Adding DSPATR(ND) for this field is similar to adding the color attribute we just completed. We have summarized this procedure and numbered the steps in Figure 12.49; the steps are listed below the figure.

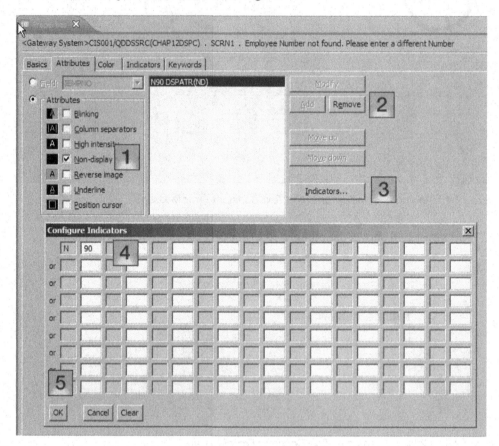

Figure 12.49: Nondisplay Properties of Text Constant Error Message

a. Select the Non-display check box.

b. Click Add.

c. Click Indicators.

d. Key in N and 90 as shown.

e. Click OK.

Close the Properties tab for this field.

Save the CHAP12DSP member.

12.15. Compile the CHAP12DSP member, and verify that the display file was created.

You will use this display file for the additional Lab 12-B at the end of this chapter.

Part 3

Goals   Create a screen using Screen Designer.

Start with   RDP open and connected to your server.

Procedure   Verify that the DDS Design perspective is the current perspective.

Create a new DSPF source member named STRUPDSP. **Note:** You will use this file in the Chapter 16 CL program you will write.

Add text constants to the member.

Add the named input field to the member.

Compile the member and verify that it was created.

In this portion of the lab, you will create a display file that will display four selections. The user will make a selection, and, based on the selection, the CL program will change the user's enviroment (library list) and execute some CL commands. You will write this program in Chapter 16.

12.16. Verify that the DDS Design perspective is the current perspective; if it is not, change to this perspective.

12.17. Create a new DSPF source member named STRUPDSP.

Add a "standard" record to the source member. The default name RECORD will work.

12.18. Add text constants to the member as Figure 12.50 shows. The text constants should be yellow and in proper case.

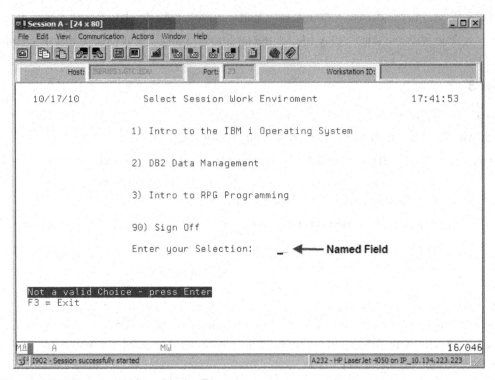

Figure 12.50: Completed Menu Display File

12.19. Add a named field called &CHOICE; the field should be "input only" as shown in Figure 12.50. You need to add this text constant with a color of Yellow and change the color to Red if indicator 40 is set ON.

Add the named constant with the text "Not a valid Choice - press Enter." This constant should be shown as a reverse image when indicator 40 is ON. The steps are the same as we demonstrated in Part 2 of this lab. Figure 12.51 shows the completed indicator window.

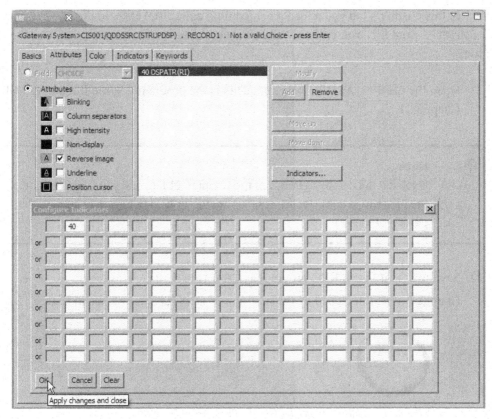

Figure 12.51: Properties for the Named Constant Field

12.20. Compile the member, and verify that it was created.

Optional Lab 12-A

Goals   Modify the CHAP11LAB RPG program.

Start with   RDP open and connected to your server.

Procedure   Open the CHAP11LAB RPG program, which is located in the QRPGLESRC source file in your personal library.

Save the CHAP11LAB RPG program as CHAP12LAB.

Add the records-processed counter.

Verify that your library contains the EMPPFLP2 print file object that you worked on in Part 1 of this chapter's lab.

Compile the CHAP12LAB RPG program.

Verify that the program compiled.

Run the program, and verify that the total number of records is displayed.

In Part 1 of this chapter's lab you added a named field called TOTEMPS to the TOTREC record of the EMPPFLP2 print file. You will now add an accumulator to the program that uses this print file.

12.21. Open the CHAP11LAB RPG program. This is the program you modified in the lab in Chapter 11.

Note

If you did not complete Part 3 of the Chapter 11 lab, or if you could not get the program to compile, ask your instructor for help before you continue this portion of the lab.

12.22. Save the CHAP11LAB RPG program as CHAP12LAB.

Change the print file used by the program to EMPPFLP2 as you see in Figure 12.52.

```
000600     //****************************************************************
000601
000700     FEMPPFL      IF   E           K DISK
000800     FEMPPFLP2    O    E             PRINTER OfLind(*in10)
000801
002000     /FREE
```

Figure 12.52: Change Print File Used in the CHAP12LAB RPG Program

12.23. Add the records-processed counter (Figures 12.53 and 12.54).

```
002100        Write Heading; // Write the Headings
002101        WRITE DETHEAD;
002102
002200        Read EMPPFL;  // Get the first record
002203
002300        DOW NOT %EOF(EMPPFL); // Read records until "End of File"
002400          Write Detail;      // Write a Detail line on the report
002500          Read EMPPFL;       // Read another record
002501
002502          IF *in10 = *on;    // Check for "End of Page"
002503            Write Heading;   // Write the Report Headings
002504            WRITE DETHEAD;   // Write the column Heading
002505            *in10 = *off;    // Turn the indicator off
002507          EndIf;
002600        EndDo;
002602
002700        *INLR = *ON;   // Turn ON he Last record indicator
002800        Return;        // Return to the caller (OS or program)
002900     /END-FREE
```

Figure 12.53: CHAP12LAB RPG Program, Continued

After you insert three blank lines using i3, as Figure 12.53 shows (following line 002507), you need to add a counter to the program to count the number of records processed. You will not need to identify the TotEmps variable in the program because it is described in the display file.

Key the following code into the program, as Figure 12.54 shows:

```
// Accumulate the records that are processed
TotEmps += 1;
```

```
002504              WRITE DETHEAD;   // Write the column Heading
002505                *in10 = *off;   // Turn the indicator off
002507            EndIf;
002508
002509            // Accumulate the records that are processed
002510            TotEmps += 1;
002512
002600        EndDo;
002602
002700            *INLR = *ON;     // Turn ON he Last record indicator
```

Figure 12.54: Add the Accumulator to the CHAP12LAB RPG Program

You also need to add a WRITE statement to write on the report the TOTREC record that we added to the report earlier in the chapter. To do so, key the following code in the program, as in Figure 12.55:

```
Write TOTREC;   // Write the record on the report
```

```
002509            // Accumulate the records that are processed
002510            TotEmps += 1;
002512
002600        EndDo;
002601
002602        Write TOTREC;   // Write the record on the report
002603
002700            *INLR = *ON;     // Turn ON the last record indicator
002800        Return;          // Return to the caller (OS or program
002900        /END-FREE
```

Figure 12.55: Add WRITE Statement for TOTREC Record

12.24. Verify that your library contains the EMPPFLP2 print file object that you worked on in Part 1 of this lab. **Note:** If you did not complete the lab, or if you had problems compiling the print file, ask for help from your instructor before you continue.

12.25. Compile the CHAP12LAB RPG program.

12.26. Verify that the program was compiled.

12.27. Run the program, and verify that the total number of records is displayed. Your spool file should look similar to the screen in Figure 12.56. Note the arrow highlighting the employee total.

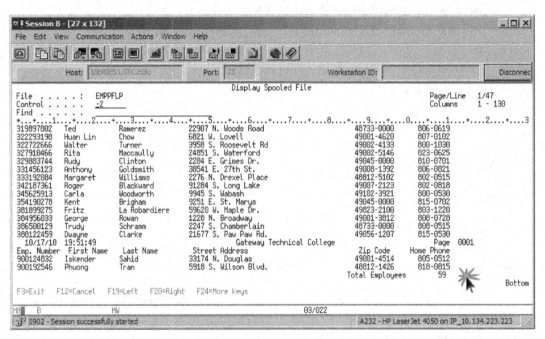

Figure 12.56: Printer Output from CHAP12LAB

Optional Lab 12-B

Goals   Copy the CHAP12EXP RPG program, compile the program, and run it from the 5250 command line.

Start with   RDP open and connected to your server.

Procedure   Copy the CHAP12EXP source member from the QRPGLESRC file in the INTROCLASS library to the QRPGLESRC file in your personal library.

Open the CHAP12EXP RPG program in your QRPGLESRC source file.

Verify that your library contains the CHAP12DSP display file object that you worked on in Part 2 of this chapter's lab.

Compile the CHAP12EXP RPG program.

Verify that the program was compiled.

Run the program, and verify that your display screen works.

Caution
If you did not complete Part 2 of this chapter's lab, or if you could not compile the CHAP12DSP display file, ask your instructor for assistance. You will not be able to complete this lab without this display file object.

12.28. Copy the CHAP12EXP program source code from the INTROCLASS library QRPGLESRC source file to your personal library QRPGLESRC source file.

This program was written to allow you to test your screen and to help you better understand how an interactive program works. You will not need to change any code in this program.

12.29. Open the CHAP12EXP RPG program.

12.29.a. Can you find where your display file is opened in this program?

12.29.b. How many WRITE statements are in this program?

Close the program. If RDP prompts you to save the program, reply No.

Compile the program from the RSE view.

12.30. Verify that the program was compiled.

12.30.a. How did you verify that the program was compiled?

Log in to a 5250 session.

Add the INTROCLASS library to your library list.

12.30.b. What command did you use to add this library to your library list?

Call the program from the command line by keying CALL CHAP12EXP.

Enter a valid employee number, and press Enter.

12.30.c. How can you find a valid employee number?

After the program displays the data from a valid employee number, press Enter. You will be returned to SCRN1.

Key in an invalid employee number, and press Enter.

12.30.d. What screen is displayed?

12.30.e. What is the error message?

Press F3 to exit the program and return to the command line.

Introduction to SQL

Overview

Structured Query Language (SQL) has become the mainstay for data manipulation on most platforms today. It is important for today's IBM i professional to understand the traditional DDS tools, but most new database systems are created and manipulated using SQL. The intent of this text is to expose the student to both the traditional tools and the latest tools and concepts. SQL is a complete database language with data-definition, data-manipulation, and data-control components.

Whole books are written about SQL—some quite large. In this chapter, we provide just a taste of SQL to give you a hint of its capabilities. SQL is a powerful language, and you should learn it well before you try to apply it to a production database. Our scope here is limited to that part of the Data Manipulation Language (**DML**) that lets you retrieve information from the database and change (update, insert, and delete) records in the database. Also included is a short introduction to Data Definition Language (**DDL**) Create statements, which let you create SQL objects, and DROP statements, which let you delete SQL objects.

Objectives

Students will be able to

- Use interactive SQL to describe a schema and a table
- Explain the difference between a schema and a library
- Understand the SQL terminology as it compares with traditional IBM DDL terminology
- Write SQL statements that list, insert, delete, or change data in an SQL table
- Describe and write various Join statements
- Use SQL scripts and SQL Assist to write and run SQL statements

A Short History of SQL

Andrew Richardson, Donald C. Messerly, and Raymond F. Boyce at IBM developed the precursor of today's SQL in the 1970s. This version, called SEQUEL, was developed to manipulate data stored in IBM's original database product, System R. System R, which IBM patented in 1985, was a research project that was the first to demonstrate that a relational database management system (RDBMS) could provide good transaction-processing performance. The American Institute of Standards and Technology standardized SQL in 1986 as SQL-86, and in 1987 the International Organization for Standardization (ISO) standardized SQL. Although the original SQL standard designated the official pronunciation of SQL as *"es queue el,"* many people still mispronounce the abbreviation as *"sequel."*

Introduction to SQL Terms

Before we continue, we will compare the terminology of SQL and the traditional DB2 system file-access methods. Table 13.1 lists the common terms for both methods of access.

Table 13.1: Comparison of SQL and System File-Access Terms	
SQL Term	**Traditional File-Access Term**
Schema—A number of related objects that a user can reference by name; consists of a library, a journal, a journal receiver, an SQL catalog, and, optionally, a data dictionary. A *schema* is often referred to as a *collection* or a *database*.	**Library**—A number of related objects that a user can reference by name.
Table—A set of columns and rows.	**Physical file**—A set of records.
Row—The horizontal part of a table that contains a serial set of columns.	**Record**—A set of related fields.
Column—The vertical part of a table of one data type.	**Field**—One of more bytes of related information of one data type.
View—A subset of columns and rows of one or more tables.	**Logical file**—A subset of fields or records of up to 32 physical files.
Index—A collection of data in the columns of a table, logically arranged in ascending or descending order.	**Index**—A type of logical file.
Package—An object that contains control structures for SQL.	**SQL package**—An object that contains control structures for SQL statements.
Catalog—A set of tables and views that contain information about tables, packages, views, indexes, and constraints.	(No similar object.)

Introduction to SQL

In the IBM i OS, we can use SQL on physical and logical files created by compiling DDS source code, as well as on SQL-created tables (physical files) and views (logical files). This is an important feature because many Power Systems using the IBM i OS contain DB2 databases that were not created with SQL. In today's programming environment, we need to use SQL's powerful query and update capability to access these databases.

SQL statements can exist in and be executed from several different environments on the system. In this chapter, we limit our discussion to what IBM calls *dynamic SQL* statements submitted to the interactive **Run SQL Scripts** interface, which is part of IBM i Navigator. In addition to interactive SQL, in which you type a statement on an SQL command line (similar to a CL command), you also can use SQL from within a C, COBOL, Java, or RPG program. The statements can be **static SQL**, in which the statements are hard coded but typically use host program variables for comparison values, or as **dynamic SQL**, in which the program prepares the SQL statement as a character string that is then passed to the IBM i DB2 database manager for execution. When used from within a program, SQL typically takes over all or much of the traditional file input/output (I/O) and data-access responsibilities from the program logic.

Interfaces Used to Enter SQL Commands

Previous versions of this text have used the traditional STRSQL interface within a 5250 session to enter, run, and display the results of SQL statements, as you see in Figure 13.1.

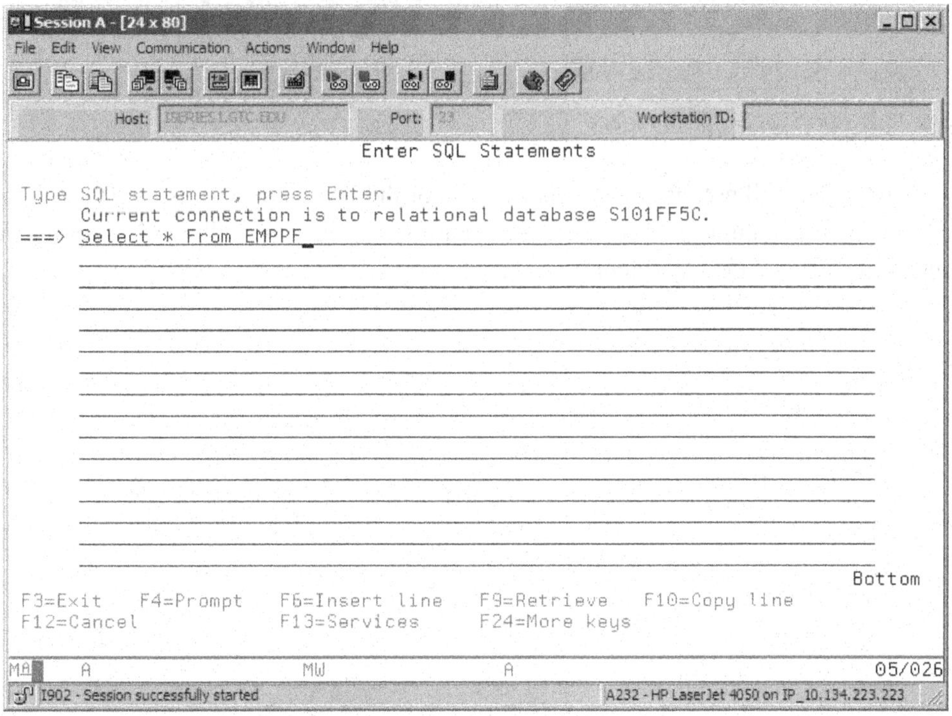

Figure 13.1: STRSQL Interface Using a 5250 Session

The goal of this book is to introduce the new tools IBM has released for today's IBM i programmer. Although the examples in this chapter will work with traditional tools such as the 5250 interactive STRSQL program, we will use the Run SQL Scripts interface, part of the IBM i Navigator product, in this chapter. Figure 13.2 shows this interface.

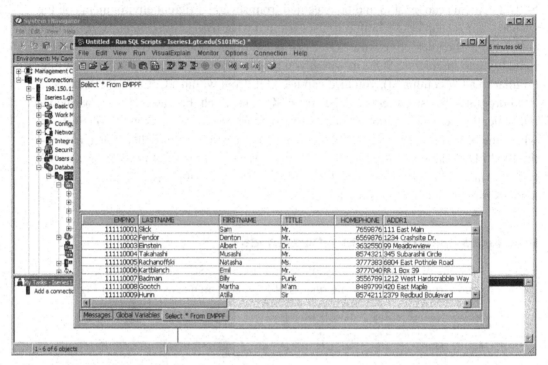

Figure 13.2: Run SQL Scripts Interface

In this chapter, we will not discuss all the features of the Run SQL Scripts interface. For our purposes here, you should consider the interface as an editor, which allows you to run and display the results of SQL statements.

An additional feature of this editor is the capability to run CL commands that do not require an interactive display. Figure 13.3 shows the CPYF CL command after it has been entered and executed. The messages from the command are also displayed in the lower pane. The complete command is

CL: CPYF INTROCLASS/EMPPF CIS001/EMPPF CRTFILE(*YES)

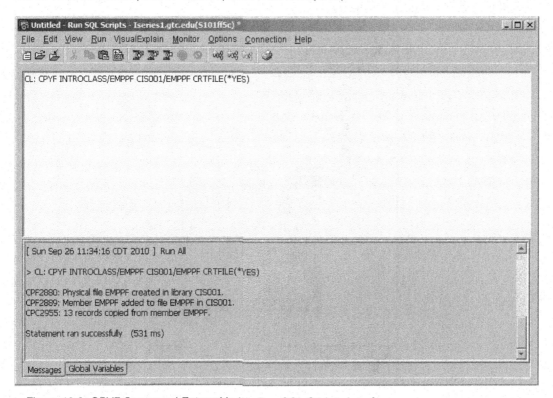

Figure 13.3: CPYF Command Entered in the Run SQL Scripts Interface

You can enter numerous commands in this window at the same time. All commands must end with a semicolon (;), and you must designate CL commands by starting them with CL:.

Starting the Run SQL Scripts Interface

In Chapter 10 we introduced IBM i Navigator, and you learned how to connect to the server. You also learned about a number of IBM i Navigator features, including a short introduction to the database tools. In this chapter, we have connected to our system and have expanded the Databases icon, right-clicked the local database icon (on this system, S191ff5c), and clicked Run SQL Scripts, as Figure 13.4 shows.

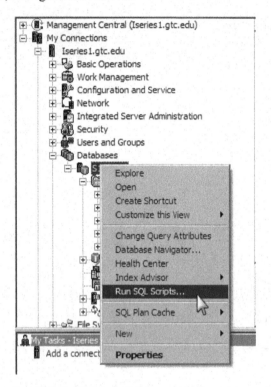

Figure 13.4: Starting the Run SQL Scripts Interface

Figure 13.5 shows the open Run SQL Scripts interface with the "input" and "output" panes. We use the upper, input pane (labeled 1) to create and edit SQL and CL commands. The lower, output pane (2) displays the results from running an SQL or CL command.

In the figure, we have selected Options from the toolbar at the top of the window and then Display Results in Separate Window. Selecting this option will open another window to display the results of an SQL command. After we have selected this option, the output pane will display any messages resulting from running a command.

If we had not selected this feature (note the arrow), we could have clicked the tabs at the bottom of the window to switch panes and see messages and results.

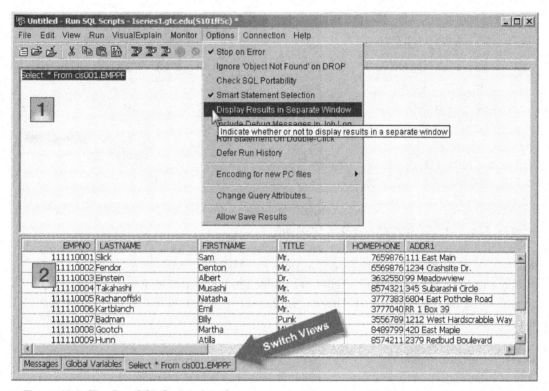

Figure 13.5: The Run SQL Scripts Interface

In Figure 13.6, we have run our simple SQL statement again. The results are displayed in a new window, and we now can see any messages that result from running the commands.

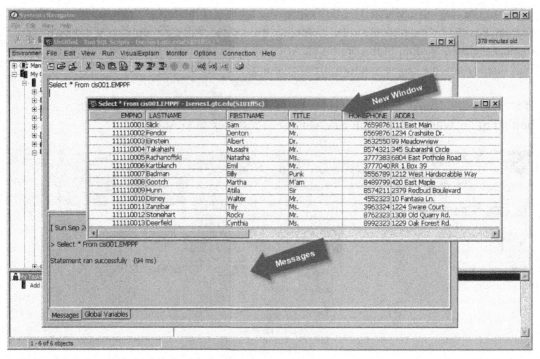

Figure 13.6: Run SQL Scripts Interface, Continued

Run SQL Scripts uses Java Database Connectivity (**JDBC**) to connect to the IBM i DB2 database to run commands. You might have noticed in the preceding figures that the SQL command we used was qualified. This means that we included the schema and table name, as follows:

Select * From cis001.EMPPF

We needed to qualify the table because when we started Run SQL Scripts, we were at the logical database level and not on a specific schema. We can change the default schema by clicking the Connection option from the toolbar at the top of the window and then selecting Use Temporary JDBC Settings, as in Figure 13.7.

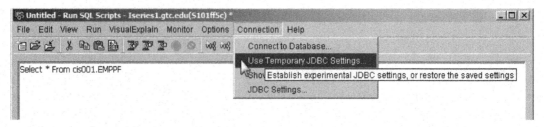

Figure 13.7: Change Connection Settings

Selecting the Use Temporary JDBC Settings option displays the window in Figure 13.8. Here, we have changed the Default SQL schema to our student library CIS001.

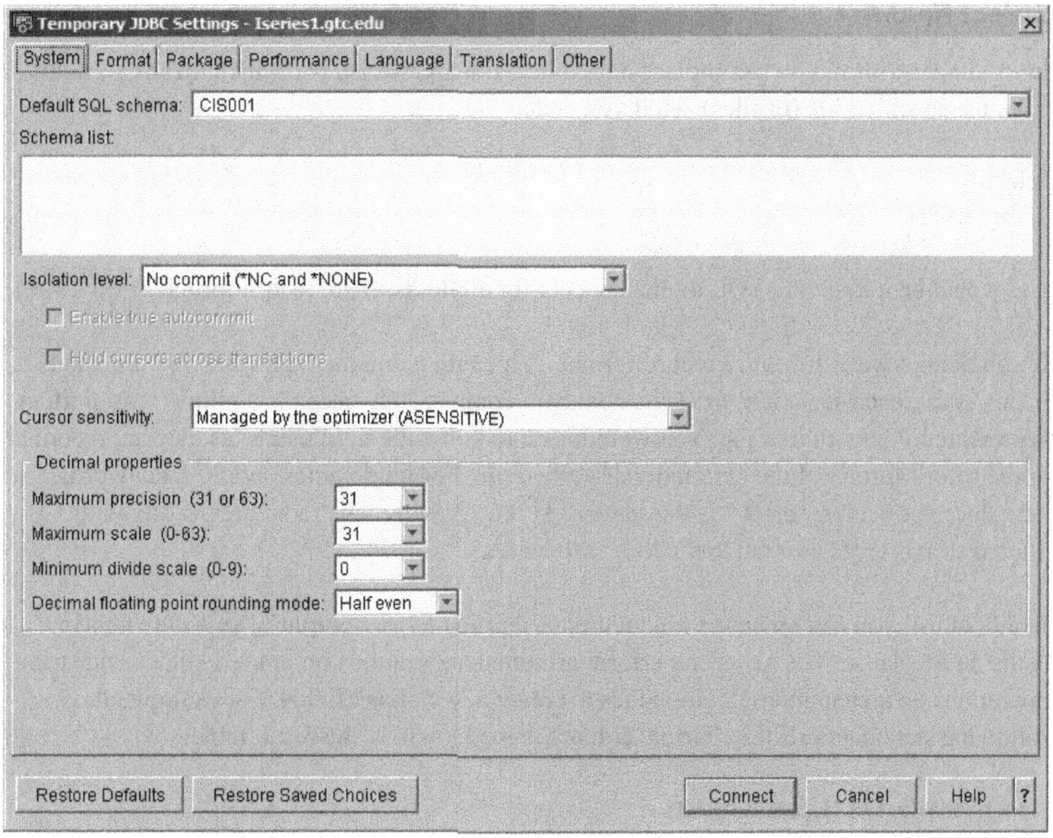

Figure 13.8: Change Connection Settings, Continued

A number of tabs at the top of the window let you change additional defaults. For this example, we will change the default schema and click Connect. This change will enable us to write unqualified SQL statements, such as

Select * From EMPPF

SQL Syntax

The basic form of an SQL statement to obtain information from a database table or tables is

Select *field-list*
 From *file-list*
 Where *conditional-expression*

We will look at each of the values (in italics) more carefully.

Select field-list

In its simplest form, you can replace a field list with an asterisk (*), which means all fields from the specified file (or files). So if you coded

```
Select *
 From EMPPF
```

you would be instructing SQL to display data for all fields in the record format of file EMPPF.

If you did not want the entire record format, you could name the fields that you did want, in any order, each separated from the next by a comma. SQL uses the comma (,) as an **item separator** for any kind of list. You would need to know the field names as they are recorded in the record format of the externally described file. For field names and SQL keywords, case does not matter: select * is the same as SELECT *. Only when you are dealing with quoted strings (e.g., 'Human Res') does case matter.

In a field list, you can rename a field temporarily (just for the output of that statement) using an **AS** clause. You also can perform arithmetic operations on numeric fields and string operations on alphanumeric field values to create new **"alias" fields**. For example, the following statement creates a virtual column named RAISE in the result table:

```
Select EMPNO, LASTNAME, SALARY,
 SALARY * .035 As RAISE
 From EMPPF
```

RAISE does not exist in the base table. It is calculated for each row of the result table as 3.5 percent of that employee's salary, by multiplying each record's current value of SALARY by the constant value .035. You can also use addition, subtraction, and division operators in this type of arithmetic expression.

Functions that work on the value of a field for each selected record are called **scalar functions**. You can use scalar functions, as well as constants and arithmetic or string operators, to create virtual columns. For example, to create a field called NAME, which consists of the first initial plus the last name, and display it along with employee number, you could code

Select Substring(FIRSTNAME,1,1) Concat '. ' Concat
  LASTNAME As NAME, EMPNO
  From EMPPF

Figure 13.9 displays the result of entering this SQL command in the input window and
selecting the Run icon (note the arrow).

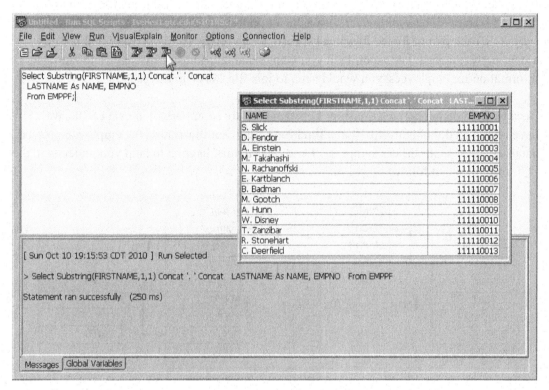

Figure 13.9: Display Output of Virtual Column NAME and EMPNO from File EMPPF

Instead of spelling out **Concat** (concatenation operation), an alternative is to specify the two
bar or pipe symbols (||). (Shift+Backslash provides the bar character on most keyboards.)
The **Substring** scalar function has three arguments, as in Query for i5/OS—source string,
starting position, and length—but you use commas to separate the arguments.

SQL has many scalar functions for numeric and alphanumeric fields, data-type conversion,
date and time operations, and trigonometric operations. You can find explanations of these
functions at the IBM Information Center, in IBM's *DB2 for i SQL Reference Version 6
Release 1,* or in *SQL for DB2,* by James Cooper and Paul Conte (29th Street Press, 2009).

From file-list

For a simple SQL query, file-list consists of one file name. All fields named in field-list must be contained in that file's record format—or be derived from it if they are alias fields. The preceding examples require that we name only EMPPF.

If you need data from two or more files, you must name each contributing file in the file list. The result will be a *join select*. Just as in a join logical file or a join query in Query for i5/OS, each pair of joined files must specify a join relationship to ensure that records are properly matched. For example, if you wanted name, address, city, state, and zip-code information for employees, you would need to join file EMPPF to file ZIPPF.

Because field names and relationships between files are so important in using SQL, we have reproduced, in Figure 13.10, the **Bachman diagram** illustrating the employee-project database we used in earlier examples. Please refer to this diagram to help you understand the SQL examples that follow.

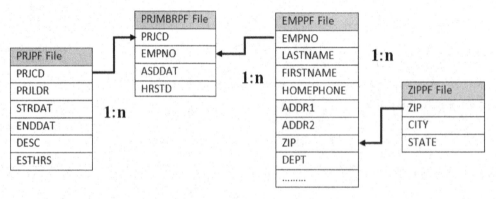

Figure 13.10: Bachman Diagram

The Run SQL Scripts interface has some additional features that we should mention. You can enter multiple SQL statements by separating them with a semicolon, adding comments as you see in Figure 13.11.

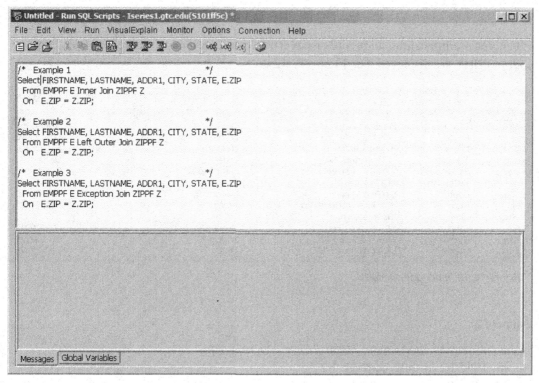

Figure 13.11: Run SQL Scripts Window with Multiple SQL Statements

If you are working and want to save your work to continue later, you can also save the contents of the input pane as an SQL script by selecting Save from the File drop-down menu in the top-left corner of the window.

If you later want to open the Run SQL Scripts interface without opening IBM i Navigator, you should save the SQL script. You can then double-click the script to open it. The Run SQL Scripts interface will open, and you will be prompted for a database connection, your user ID, and your password.

You can use the **From** clause to specify three types of Join operations: Inner Join (type 1), Left Outer Join (type 2), and Exception Join (type 3). The following three examples show the proper syntax and the results for each of these Join types.

Example 1

Select FIRSTNAME, LASTNAME, ADDR1, CITY, STATE, E.ZIP
  From EMPPF E Inner Join ZIPPF Z
  On   E.ZIP = Z.ZIP

When you use **Inner Join**, all records from EMPPF that have a matching record (same zip code) in ZIPPF are displayed (see Figure 13.12).

FIRSTNAME	LASTNAME	ADDR1	CITY	STATE	ZIP
Sam	Slick	111 East Main	Cedar Rapids	IA	524043367
Denton	Fendor	1234 Crashsite Dr.	Guthrie Center	IA	501153498
Albert	Einstein	99 Meadowview	Clarinda	IA	516321200
Musashi	Takahashi	345 Subarashii Circle	Cedar Rapids	IA	524066523
Natasha	Rachanoffski	6804 East Pothole Road	Cedar Rapids	IA	524021010
Emil	Kartblanch	RR 1 Box 39	Swisher	IA	523389910
Martha	Gootch	420 East Maple	Pleasantville	IA	502257810
Atilla	Hunn	2379 Redbud Boulevard	Anamosa	IA	522053421
Walter	Disney	10 Fantasia Ln.	Amana	IA	522032378
Tilly	Zanzibar	1224 Sware Court	Kalona	IA	522479012
Rocky	Stonehart	1308 Old Quarry Rd.	Amana	IA	522032378
Cynthia	Deerfield	1229 Oak Forest Rd.	Amana	IA	522032378

Figure 13.12: Inner Join Results

Example 2

Select FIRSTNAME, LASTNAME, ADDR1, CITY, STATE, E.ZIP
  From EMPPF E Left Outer Join ZIPPF Z
  On   E.ZIP = Z.ZIP

When you use **Left Outer Join**, all records from EMPPF will be displayed. If an employee record is unmatched in ZIPPF, default values are displayed for CITY and STATE (see Figure 13.13).

FIRSTNAME	LASTNAME	ADDR1	CITY	STATE	ZIP
Sam	Slick	111 East Main	Cedar Rapids	IA	524043367
Denton	Fendor	1234 Crashsite Dr.	Guthrie Center	IA	501153498
Albert	Einstein	99 Meadowview	Clarinda	IA	200
Musashi	Takahashi	345 Subarashii Circle	Cedar Rapids	IA	066523
Natasha	Rachanoffski	6804 East Pothole Road	Cedar Rapids	IA	524021010
Emil	Kartblanch	RR 1 Box 39	Swisher		523389910
Billy	Badman	1212 West Hardscrabble Way ...-		-	524566789
Martha	Gootch	420 East Maple	Pleasantville	IA	502257810
Atilla	Hunn	2379 Redbud Boulevard	Anamosa	IA	522053421
Walter	Disney	10 Fantasia Ln.	Amana	IA	522032378
Tilly	Zanzibar	1224 Sware Court	Kalona	IA	522479012
Rocky	Stonehart	1308 Old Quarry Rd.	Amana	IA	522032378
Cynthia	Deerfield	1229 Oak Forest Rd.	Amana	IA	522032378

Figure 13.13: Outer Join Results

Example 3

Select FIRSTNAME, LASTNAME, ADDR1, CITY, STATE, E.ZIP
  From EMPPF E Exception Join ZIPPF Z
  On   E.ZIP = Z.ZIP

When you use **Exception Join**, only EMPPF records that have no matching ZIPPF records are displayed (see Figure 13.14). Because the field list includes the CITY and STATE fields, they will take default values. (Understanding the mechanism of an Exception Join, we normally would not request fields from the right side file.)

FIRSTNAME	LASTNAME	ADDR1	CITY	STATE	ZIP
Billy	Badman	1212 West Hardscrabble Way ...-	-		524566789

Figure 13.14: Exception Join Results

Notice that as far as syntax is concerned, the only difference among the three statements is in the join specification keywords: Inner Join, Left Outer Join, and Exception Join.

The From clauses in the preceding examples assign abbreviated names—E and Z—to the EMPPF and ZIPPF files, respectively. These abbreviated names are called *correlation names*, and they can be used for qualification when fields with the same name are referenced in two or more files. The intended purpose of a **correlation name** is to correlate, or synchronize, record pointers between records of two files (or copies of the same file) in something called a correlated subquery, an example of which we will look at later. Although we could have used the full file name for qualification (e.g., EMPPF.ZIP), an abbreviated name is easier to deal with even if we are not using correlated subqueries.

If no qualification had been used, SQL would not have known which ZIP field was being referenced and would have displayed the message *"Column name ZIP is ambiguous."* The qualifier serves the same purpose as the JREF keyword required for nonunique field names in a join logical file and the file ID field of a Query for i5/OS join.

You can join more than two files in a single SELECT statement, and you can use more than one type of join. Suppose, for example, that you needed to list all employees with projects in the PRJMBRPF file, showing each project code to which an employee is assigned, and that you wanted to show the project leader and project description for each PRJMBRPF record. This information comes from the PRJPF file. To avoid listing employees with no projects, you would want an Inner Join between EMPPF and PRJMBRPF. However, if you suspected there might not yet be a PRJPF record created for a new project code already assigned in the

PRJMBRPF file, you would want to specify a Left Outer Join between PRJMBRPF and PRJPF. The SELECT statement to accomplish all that would be

```
Select E.EMPNO, LASTNAME, PM.PRJCD, PRJLDR, DESC
  From EMPPF E Inner Join PRJMBRPF PM
  On   E.EMPNO = PM.EMPNO
  Left Outer Join PRJPF P
  On   PM.PRJCD = P.PRJCD
```

Figure 13.15 shows the output from this Select statement.

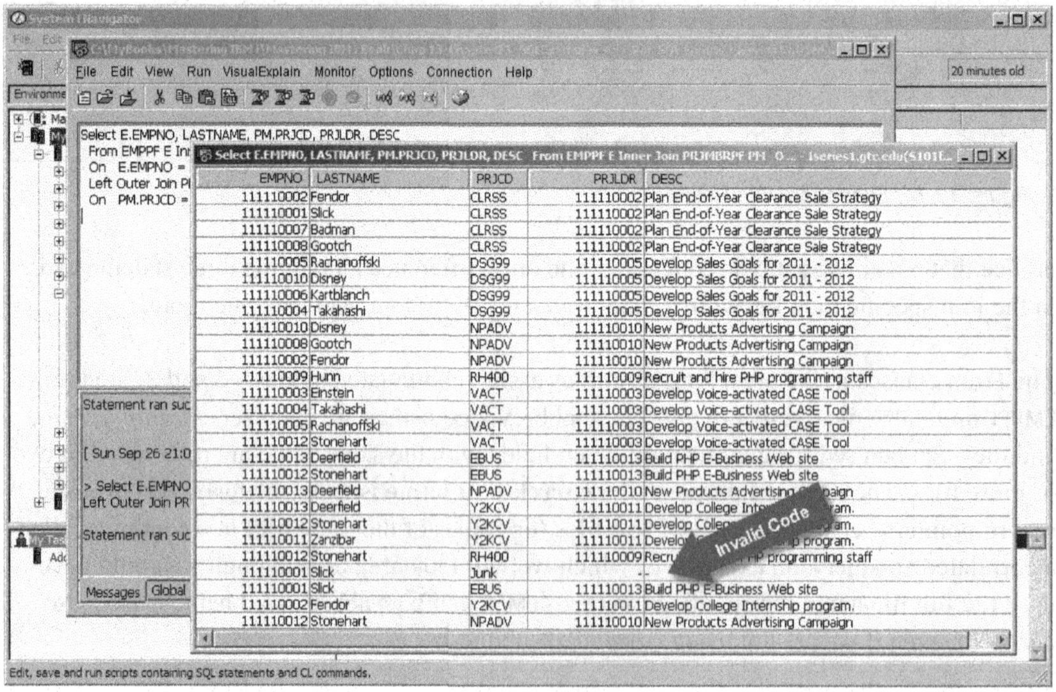

Figure 13.15: Join of Three Files (EMPPF, PRJMBRPF, and PRJPF)

Notice that the output shows a project Junk for employee Slick. This invalid project code was inserted into PRJMBRPF using Slick's employee number to test the join operation. Project Leader (PRJLDR) and Description (DESC) are empty for project Junk because no matching PRJPF record was found. This is exactly as we would expect with the Left Outer Join specified between those two files.

Note that in earlier versions of the IBM DB2 database, the keywords Inner Join, Left Outer Join, and Exception Join were not recognized in SQL, and the only type of true join permitted was the Inner Join. A Where clause was used to specify the join relationship, and the output would not have shown the Junk project record because it was unmatched in the project file. The code to accomplish an Inner Join, without the Join keyword, would be

```
Select  E.EMPNO, LASTNAME, PM.PRJCD, PRJLDR, DESC
  From  EMPPF E, PRJMBRPF PM, PRJPF P
  Where E.EMPNO = PM.EMPNO
  And   PM.PRJCD = P.PRJCD
```

Figure 13.16 displays the results of implementing this code.

EMPNO	LASTNAME	PRJCD	PRJLDR	DESC
111110002	Fendor	CLRSS	111110002	Plan End-of-Year Clearance Sale Strategy
111110001	Slick	CLRSS	111110002	Plan End-of-Year Clearance Sale Strategy
111110007	Badman	CLRSS	111110002	Plan End-of-Year Clearance Sale Strategy
111110008	Gootch	CLRSS	111110002	Plan End-of-Year Clearance Sale Strategy
111110005	Rachanoffski	DSG99	111110005	Develop Sales Goals for 2011 - 2012
111110010	Disney	DSG99	111110005	Develop Sales Goals for 2011 - 2012
111110006	Kartblanch	DSG99	111110005	Develop Sales Goals for 2011 - 2012
111110004	Takahashi	DSG99	111110005	Develop Sales Goals for 2011 - 2012
111110010	Disney	NPADV	111110010	New Products Advertising Campaign
111110008	Gootch	NPADV	111110010	New Products Advertising Campaign
111110002	Fendor	NPADV	111110010	New Products Advertising Campaign
111110009	Hunn	RH400	111110009	Recruit and hire PHP programming staff
111110003	Einstein	VACT	111110003	Develop Voice-activated CASE Tool
111110004	Takahashi	VACT	111110003	Develop Voice-activated CASE Tool
111110005	Rachanoffski	VACT	111110003	Develop Voice-activated CASE Tool
111110012	Stonehart	VACT	111110003	Develop Voice-activated CASE Tool
111110013	Deerfield	EBUS	111110013	Build PHP E-Business Web site
111110012	Stonehart	EBUS	111110013	Build PHP E-Business Web site
111110013	Deerfield	NPADV	111110010	New Products Advertising Campaign
111110013	Deerfield	Y2KCV	111110011	Develop College Internship program.
111110012	Stonehart	Y2KCV	111110011	Develop College Internship program.
111110011	Zanzibar	Y2KCV	111110011	Develop College Internship program.
111110012	Stonehart	RH400	111110009	Recruit and hire PHP programming staff
111110001	Slick	EBUS	111110013	Build PHP E-Business Web site
111110002	Fendor	Y2KCV	111110011	Develop College Internship program.
111110012	Stonehart	NPADV	111110010	New Products Advertising Campaign

Figure 13.16: Select Three Files Using a Where Clause

In this example, all the files needed to obtain the desired information are listed in the From file list, with their correlation names, if used. Following the file list, one join relationship for each pair of files is coded as a Where condition. It is imperative that one equality relational expression (E.EMPNO = PM.EMPNO) is provided to define the **equijoin relationship** (a join condition that uses the equal sign, =, as the comparison operator for each pair of files). This expression defines to SQL, by the line connecting the relationship-supporting fields of the related files, the relationship between two files documented in the Bachman diagram.

Although this syntax is still supported, you should avoid it. It is prone to errors because SQL does not check to make sure the join relationship is present. Running an SQL join select without one or more join relationships can result in a huge amount of totally useless output. Always name the join type using the On clause to specify the join relationship. If you forget an On, the syntax checker will catch it.

Where conditional-expression

You use the **Where** clause to limit the rows selected for the result table; it works in much the same manner as DDS Select/Omit entries used for logical files. In fact, anything you can do with Select/Omit you can certainly do with Where expressions; but the versatility and power of SQL's Where expression considerably exceeds DDS's Select/Omit.

Probably the most common Where expression is some kind of relational expression, in the general form

operand1 relational operator operand2

Operands can be field names, constants, string expressions, arithmetic expressions, scalar functions, and special registers, such as CURRENT_DATE.

Relational operators include =, >, <, >=, <=, and <> (not equal). You can combine multiple relational expressions into complex expressions by using the logical operators Not, And, and Or. Regardless of how complex a set of expressions may become, SQL always evaluates the expression to a single True or False result, which determines whether a row is selected for the result table (True) or rejected (False).

We will start with some simple examples of the Where clause. Assume that each of the following eight examples begins with

```
Select  *
 From  EMPPF
```

Example 1

List the employees who earn less than $25,000.

... Where SALARY < 25000

Notice that no editing symbols are used in the numeric constant; both $25,000 and 25,000 would be errors.

Example 2

List employees who earn less than $25,000 and are in the Sales Department.

```
... Where SALARY < 25000
    And DEPT = 'Sales'
```

The constant 'Sales' must be typed exactly as the value is stored in the database, and in the same case. Neither 'sales' nor 'SALES' would produce any results. Alphanumeric constants must be enclosed in apostrophes (').

Example 3

List all employees who have a zip code in the range of 514000000 to 523000000 (inclusive).

```
... Where ZIP >= 514000000
    And ZIP <= 523000000;
```

You cannot imply the subject (operand 1) in the second expression; that is, the expression

```
ZIP >= 514000000 And <= 523000000
```

would be an error. However, there is a simpler syntax for a range test such as this one. It uses the SQL Between keyword and would be written as

```
... Where ZIP Between 514000000 And 523000000
```

The expression treats the range values as inclusive,

Between Value1 And Value2

so the statement above is exactly equivalent to the And complex expression of Example 3.

Example 4

List all employees born between the months of January and March.

```
... Where Month(BIRTHDATE) Between 1 And 3
```

Here, we use the scalar **Month date function** to extract the month value from the date field BIRTHDATE. Other often-used date functions include **Year** and **Day**, which extract the four-digit year and the two-digit day of the month, respectively, from a date field or expression.

Example 5

List all employees born in the month of November, December, January, or February.

```
... Where Month(BIRTHDATE) = 11
    Or Month(BIRTHDATE) = 12
    Or Month(BIRTHDATE) = 1
    Or Month(BIRTHDATE) = 2
```

Here, we use several relational expressions, each connected to the next by Or. However, a far simpler approach is to use the In function. The **In** function reduces the need for multiple Or statements. One way to use an In function works just the same as a VALUES keyword in DDS. You code the values you want to test against as constants, separated by commas, and enclose the whole list in parentheses. So, for our example, we would code

```
... Where Month(BIRTHDATE) In (11,12,1,2)
```

Example 6

List all employees who live in Cedar Rapids, Iowa.

You know there are several zip codes for Cedar Rapids, but you are not sure what they are. Of course, you could look them up and code them in a static In function list, as above, but SQL can also look them up. SQL can create a list of Cedar Rapids zip codes for you from the data in file ZIPPF and then compare each employee's zip code against the list. To accomplish this, we simply code another Select statement as the In function list value:

```
... Where ZIP In
      (Select ZIP From ZIPPF
        Where CITY = 'Cedar Rapids')
```

When a Select statement is nested inside an outer Select statement's Where clause, it is referred to as a **subquery**.

If we wanted the results to include employees from several different cities, we could use an In function inside the subquery:

```
... Where ZIP In
      (Select ZIP From ZIPPF
         Where CITY In ('Clarinda',
                        'Kalona',
                        'Amana'))
```

Note the need for *two* closing right parentheses to balance the expression.

Example 7

List all employees who are not project leaders.

... Where EMPNO Not In
   (Select PRJLDR From PRJPF)

In this case, although EMPNO and PRJLDR are not the same field, they share the same domain because they are the Social Security numbers of employees. We instruct SQL to create a list of project leaders using the subquery, and then we ask for employees who are not in that list. Using the **Not** logical operator with a subquery produces the same result as an Exception Join:

Select E.*
  From EMPPF E Exception Join PRJPF
    On EMPNO = PRJLDR

By qualifying * to the correlation name E for EMPPF, we can avoid including all the fields from PRJPF in the output. If we had simply coded Select *, all fields from both files would have gone to the output, and all the PRJPF fields would have had default values. Figure 13.17 shows the output of this Select.

EMPNO	LASTNAME	FIRSTNAME	TITLE	HOMEPHONE	ADDR1
111110001	Slick	Sam	Mr.	7659876	111 East Main
111110004	Takahashi	Musashi	Mr.	8574321	345 Subarashii Circle
111110006	Kartblanch	Emil	Mr.	3777040	RR 1 Box 39
111110007	Badman	Billy	Punk	3556789	1212 West Hardscrabble Way
111110008	Gootch	Martha	M'am	8489799	420 East Maple
111110012	Stonehart	Rocky	Mr.	8762323	1308 Old Quarry Rd.

Figure 13.17: Select Using "E."*

Example 8

List all employees who have *Road* or *Rd* in their address.

... Where ADDR1 Like '%Road%'
  Or ADDR1 Like '%Rd%'

The **Like** logical operation provides a powerful technique for matching a search string against a substring of a field from each record. Two **wildcard** characters, the percent sign (%) and the underscore (_), can be used. The **% character** is replaced in the target string by any number of unknown characters, while the _ **character** is replaced by exactly one unknown character. For example, LIKE '%at' would return True results for *hat, Hat, cat, Rat,* or *Frat*, while LIKE '_at' would return True results for *hat, Hat, cat,* or *Rat*, but False results for *Frat*. Neither would return true results for *Fraternity*.

In the solution for Example 8, we checked the ADDR1 field but overlooked ADDR2. We could add ADDR2, checking to the Where clause with more Or operators:

```
... Where ADDR1 Like '%Road%'
    Or ADDR1 Like '%Rd%'
    Or ADDR2 Like '%Road%'
    Or ADDR2 Like '%Rd%'
```

Or we could combine ADDR1 and ADDR2 using concatenation:

```
... Where ADDR1 Concat ADDR2 Like '%Road%'
    Or ADDR1 Concat ADDR2 Like '%Rd%'
```

As an alternative, we could try putting it all into a single simple expression:

```
... Where ADDR1 Concat ADDR2 Like '%R%d%'
```

This method seems like a clever way to perform a fairly complex search with a single statement because the middle % could substitute for *oa* of *Road* or for the zero characters between the *R* and *d* of *Rd*. In addition, this expression would certainly pull out all addresses containing *Road* or *Rd*. However, it could also give us more than we bargained for. For example, Mr. Hunn lives at 2379 Redbud Boulevard. Figure 13.18 shows the SQL statement results of using the single expression.

EMPNO	LASTNAME	FIRSTNAME	TITLE	HOMEPHONE	ADDR1		ADDR2		ZIP
111110005	Rachanoffski	Natasha	Ms.	3777383	6804 East Pothole Road	...		...	524021010
111110006	Kartblanch	Emil	Mr.	3777040	RR 1 Box 39		Falcon Road	...	523389910
111110009	Hunn	Atilla	Sir	8574211	2379 Redbud Boulevard		Apt. B	...	522053421
111110012	Stonehart	Rocky	Mr.	8762323	1308 Old Quarry Rd.	...		...	522032378
111110013	Deerfield	Cynthia	Ms.	8992323	1229 Oak Forest Rd.	...		...	522032378

Figure 13.18: Select Using "Where ADDR1 Concat ADDR2 Like '%R%d%'"

Some Additional SQL Capabilities

If you tell SQL to retrieve rows that have the same column values, it will do that, duplicating those rows in the result table. For example, if you wanted to list the employee numbers of any employees assigned to any project, you might simply type

```
Select EMPNO
  From PRJMBRPF
```

But you would soon see that many numbers are repeated in the output—for example, if an employee were assigned to four projects, his or her employee number would appear four times in the output list. You also would notice that employee numbers appeared in no particular order, making it difficult to analyze the list. In fact, because this request uses a single file and requires no index search, the output is ordered by the relative record numbers of the physical file or in arrival sequence, even if the file itself is keyed.

SQL provides the **Distinct keyword** for eliminating duplicate rows of the result table. You can use the **Order By clause** at the end of any Select statement to sort the output by one or more sort fields.

Therefore, to correct the above statement, we could type

```
Select Distinct EMPNO
  From PRJMBRPF
  Order By EMPNO
```

Now we would have a sorted list of unique employee numbers. The Order By clause defaults to ascending order (abbreviated Asc), but you can specify descending sequence by using the abbreviation Desc.

Using Order By, we should be able to handle the following request: List all employees by last name, showing department and salary. The output should be sorted by department and then, within department, from highest to lowest salary.

```
Select DEPT, FIRSTNAME, LASTNAME, SALARY
  From EMPPF
  Order By DEPT, SALARY Desc
```

The output in Figure 13.19 shows how the data has been sorted by descending salary within department.

DEPT	FIRSTNAME	LASTNAME	SALARY
Human Res	Atilla	Hunn	135000.00
Marketing	Walter	Disney	168300.00
Marketing	Martha	Gootch	56100.00
MIS	Rocky	Stonehart	70609.00
MIS	Cynthia	Deerfield	70609.00
MIS	Tilly	Zanzibar	52717.00
Research	Albert	Einstein	299950.00
Research	Musashi	Takahashi	75000.00
Sales	Emil	Kartblanch	48250.00
Sales	Denton	Fendor	33150.00
Sales	Natasha	Rachanoffski	32000.00
Sales	Sam	Slick	28000.00
Sales	Billy	Badman	22500.00

Figure 13.19: EMPPF Data Ordered by DEPT, SALARY Descending

Notice that employees Stonehart and Deerfield are in the same department and have the same salary, but that Stonehart comes before Deerfield. This occurs because we did not request sorting by last name; and in the physical file, the Stonehart record has a lower relative record number and so comes first. We could easily fix this problem by adding a third Order By entry for LASTNAME.

Caution

A warning about the use of the Order By clause: It can cause a significant hit on system performance, especially when you are dealing with large files that lack appropriate indexes. Therefore, you should use the Order By clause with caution and only when required.

In addition to the large number of scalar functions available, SQL has some useful column functions. These **column functions** work on a set of field values as a whole—for example, all SALARY values in the result table—as opposed to scalar functions, which work on a field of each record. To see the difference, consider the following examples.

First, we will use a scalar function that returns a value for each row of the result table:

```
Select LASTNAME, SALARY, Decimal(SALARY * 1.035,7,0)
   As NEW_SALARY
 From EMPPF
```

The **Decimal scalar function** is useful to format a calculated value to a fixed precision (total digits) and scale (number of decimal digits). Its syntax is

Decimal (expression, precision, scale)

In addition, if the result were stored in a data file, its type would be packed decimal. For display purposes, the result is converted to readable numbers. The Decimal function works on the SALARY field of each record sent to the result table. With this function, the results of the preceding Select statement appear in Figure 13.20.

LASTNAME	SALARY	NEW_SALARY
Slick	28000.00	28980
Fendor	33150.00	34310
Einstein	299950.00	310448
Takahashi	75000.00	77625
Rachanoffski	32000.00	33120
Kartblanch	48250.00	49938
Badman	22500.00	23287
Gootch	56100.00	58063
Hunn	135000.00	139725
Disney	168300.00	174190
Zanzibar	52717.00	54562
Stonehart	70609.00	73080
Deerfield	70609.00	73080

Figure 13.20: Virtual Column NEW_SALARY Formatted to Integer Using the Decimal Function

Without the Decimal function, the results look like those in Figure 13.21—that is, the NEW_SALARY column would have five decimal places.

LASTNAME	SALARY	NEW_SALARY
Slick	28000.00	28980.00000
Fendor	33150.00	34310.25000
Einstein	299950.00	310448.25000
Takahashi	75000.00	77625.00000
Rachanoffski	32000.00	33120.00000
Kartblanch	48250.00	49938.75000
Badman	22500.00	23287.50000
Gootch	56100.00	58063.50000
Hunn	135000.00	139725.00000
Disney	168300.00	174190.50000
Zanzibar	52717.00	54562.09500
Stonehart	70609.00	73080.31500
Deerfield	70609.00	73080.31500

Figure 13.21: Virtual Column NEW_SALARY with Decimal Precision Calculated by SQL

SQL calculated the precision and scale of field NEW_SALARY based on the arithmetic expression. Looking at the difference in these two figures, you can see how the scalar Decimal function has affected each row of the result table individually. A scalar function is invoked and returns a value for each result row.

In contrast, a column function returns only one value. It manipulates the column data of each row by adding to an accumulator, comparing for minimum or maximum value, and so on. The final result of this row-by-row data manipulation is not available until all selected rows have been processed. The final value is the function applied to the entire set of column values. For example, you can use the **Sum column function** to total all salaries:

```
Select Sum(SALARY)
  From EMPPF
```

This statement instructs SQL to add the salary of each EMPPF record into an accumulator and to display the result after processing the last record. **Note**: This request is invalid (and nonsensical).

```
Select LASTNAME, Sum(SALARY)
  From EMPPF
```

Because LASTNAME has a value for each record, it *cannot* be paired with Sum(SALARY), which derives a single value for the entire result table.

However, suppose we want the total salary for each department. SQL provides the **Group By function** to group records by a common value of a field and then perform the Sum operation on each group. The statement would be

```
Select    DEPT, Sum(SALARY)
  From    EMPPF
  Group By DEPT
```

When you need a column function to act on a group of records, you must use a Group By clause to identify the grouping field or fields. The preceding statement instructs SQL to sort all EMPPF records by DEPT, then total the salary of the employees in each department, and then write one record for each department to the result table. It is important to understand that when you use Group By, the function works on the set of column values for each group; so one record per group is sent to the result table. Figure 13.22 shows the output from the statement.

Select DEPT, Sum(SALARY) From EMPPF Group By DEPT - 1...

DEPT	00002
Research	374950.00
MIS	193935.00
Human Res	135000.00
Marketing	224400.00
Sales	163900.00

Figure 13.22: Grouped Sum of Salary per Department

For example, say we want to list the last name, the employee number, the number of projects assigned, and the total hours spent on all projects for any employee who is working on two or fewer projects, or who has less than 50 total project hours to date. We also want to sort by last name.

This request calls for grouping project-member records by employee number and then selecting only those groups with no more than two projects or no more than 50 total hours. In addition, to get the last name, we need to join each group record with a matching record from the employee file, EMPPF, on employee number.

SQL provides a way to select or reject group records. The **Having clause** enables selection of group summary records in the same way that the Where clause enables selection of base table records. The syntax of the Having clause is

Having conditional-expression

Some constraints apply on the expression. Field names used in a Having expression must be specified in the Select field list. Function results can also be referenced in the Having expression and, except for Count(*), must also be identified in the Select field list. The **Count(*) expression** returns the number of rows in each group and can be referenced in a Having clause, even if it is not specified in the Select field list. You can also use subqueries in a Having clause.

We can produce the necessary Underutilized Employee Report with the following statement:

```
Select   LASTNAME, PM.EMPNO,
         Count(*) As NUM_OF_PROJECTS,
         Decimal(Sum(HRSTD),4,0) As TOTAL_HRS
 From    PRJMBRPF PM Inner Join EMPPF E
  On     PM.EMPNO = E.EMPNO
 Group By LASTNAME, PM.EMPNO
  Having Count(*) <= 2
     Or Decimal(Sum(HRSTD),4,0) <= 50
 Order By 1;
```

Assuming a referential constraint on PRJMBRPF, so that all employee-number values of any of its records must already exist in the parent file EMPPF, either an Inner Join or a Left Outer Join produces the same results using PRJMBRPF as the primary (left) file.

We must use both LASTNAME and EMPNO as the grouping fields. It is important to understand that only fields that will always have the same value for all records of a group can be used as grouping fields.

The Having clause limits the output to those group summary records whose count of projects is less than or equal to 2, or whose sum of all project hours is less than or equal to 50.

The Order By clause must also refer only to list items from the Select field list, but integer reference to the positional order of items of the Select field list is permitted. In the example, Order By 1 is equivalent to Order By LASTNAME. This feature is especially useful when the ordering column needs to be a function expression, to avoid having to rekey the expression. Figure 13.23 shows the output of the Underutilized Employee Report.

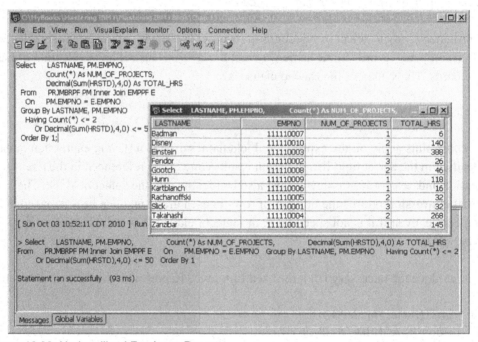

Figure 13.23: Underutilized Employee Report

Another example might help clarify when to use the Group By clause. For instance, let us say that we want to display the name and birth date of the oldest employee in the company.

Think of a date field as a numeric value with the high-order two digits being century, followed by year, month, and day. Therefore, the smaller the value of BIRTHDATE, the older the person. SQL's **Min function** returns the smallest value in a table or group. You might be tempted to try

```
Select FIRSTNAME, LASTNAME, Min(BIRTHDATE)
 From EMPPF
```

However, SQL would display the message *"Column FIRSTNAME or function specified in SELECT list not valid"* because you cannot combine column (field) names with a column function (Min) without using Group By. However, in this case, using Group By would be inappropriate because there are no groups of records in EMPPF with common values for the grouping columns FIRSTNAME and LASTNAME. What would result if you entered the following?

```
Select    FIRSTNAME, LASTNAME, Min(BIRTHDATE)
 From     EMPPF
 Group By FIRSTNAME, LASTNAME
```

SQL would create "groups" of records for each unique set of values for FIRSTNAME and LASTNAME, or, in our database, one group for each employee. And because the column function applies to each group, each employee's birth date would be the Min(BIRTHDATE) for the group (of one record). You would get a list of all employees' names and birth dates (see Figure 13.24). Of course, if you had two John Smith employees, you would get only one result row showing the elder Smith's birth date.

Select FIRSTNAME, LASTNAME, Min(BIRTHDATE) ...

FIRSTNAME	LASTNAME	00003
Albert	Einstein	1945-04-25
Rocky	Stonehart	1947-05-11
Billy	Badman	1975-07-18
Martha	Gootch	1948-02-21
Walter	Disney	1952-10-10
Natasha	Rachanoffski	1969-04-16
Tilly	Zanzibar	1947-05-11
Atilla	Hunn	1949-04-25
Sam	Slick	1966-06-06
Cynthia	Deerfield	1966-08-02
Musashi	Takahashi	1954-12-01
Denton	Fendor	1972-11-19
Emil	Kartblanch	1962-05-11

Figure 13.24: Group By FIRSTNAME, LASTNAME

How can we attach a name to a birth date and be sure that it is the minimum birth date? Use a subquery! If we move the Min function to a subquery, we can compare each employee's birth date against the Min(BIRTHDATE) value of the whole file and then select only the matching record.

```
Select  FIRSTNAME, LASTNAME, BIRTHDATE
 From  EMPPF
 Where BIRTHDATE = (Select Min(BIRTHDATE)
             From EMPPF)
```

Instead of a list, the subquery—(Select Min(BIRTHDATE) from EMPPF)—returns a single value, the oldest person's birth date, against which we are comparing each employee's BIRTHDATE, as in Figure 13.25. The Min and Max functions always return only a single value, even if several selected rows share the same minimum or maximum value. If a company's oldest employees were triplets born on the same day, Min(BIRTHDATE) would still return just one value—their common birthday.

FIRSTNAME	LASTNAME	BIRTHDATE
Albert	Einstein	1945-04-25

Figure 13.25: Where BIRTHDATE = (Select Min(BIRTHDATE) From EMPPF)

Now we might want to list the birth date of the oldest employee in each department. To satisfy this request, we can use DEPT as the single grouping field and write the Select statement as

```
Select    DEPT, Min(BIRTHDATE)
 From    EMPPF
 Group By DEPT
```

This Select statement would show each department and the birth date of its oldest employee (Figure 13.26). However, it would not tell us who the oldest employee is. When SQL requires you to name all Select list fields as grouping fields, there is no direct way to associate a department's oldest birth date with a name or number.

Select DEPT, Min(BIRTHDATE) From E...

DEPT	00002
Research	1945-04-25
MIS	1947-05-11
Human Res	1949-04-25
Marketing	1948-02-21
Sales	1962-05-11

Figure 13.26: Group By DEPT

The Select statement

```
Select    DEPT, LASTNAME, FIRSTNAME, Min(BIRTHDATE)
 From     EMPPF
 Group By DEPT, LASTNAME, FIRSTNAME
```

would take us right back to a list of all employees, as in Figure 13.27.

Select DEPT, LASTNAME, FIRSTNAME, Min(BIRTHDATE) From EMPPF Grou...

DEPT	LASTNAME	FIRSTNAME	00004
Human Res	Hunn	Atilla	1949-04-25
Sales	Badman	Billy	1975-07-18
MIS	Stonehart	Rocky	1947-05-11
Sales	Slick	Sam	1966-06-06
Research	Takahashi	Musashi	1954-12-01
Research	Einstein	Albert	1945-04-25
Sales	Fendor	Denton	1972-11-19
Sales	Kartblanch	Emil	1962-05-11
Sales	Rachanoffski	Natasha	1969-04-16
MIS	Deerfield	Cynthia	1966-08-02
Marketing	Gootch	Martha	1948-02-21
MIS	Zanzibar	Tilly	1947-05-11
Marketing	Disney	Walter	1952-10-10

Figure 13.27: Group By DEPT, LASTNAME, FIRSTNAME

However, leaving the name fields out of the Group By clause but keeping them in the Select list, as in

```
Select    DEPT, LASTNAME, FIRSTNAME, Min(BIRTHDATE)
  From    EMPPF
  Group By DEPT
```

would be a syntax violation.

There are two ways to include the oldest employee's name as well as birth date, and we will return to this problem a little later. But first we will look at another example of the use of the Having clause in a related request.

Say we want to list, for each department, the birth date of the oldest employee who is at least 50 years old. (If the oldest employee of the Sales department is only 48, you would not want a Sales department record in the output.) We could easily satisfy this request by using the Having clause to limit the group summary records to those that meet the age criteria, as follows:

```
Select    DEPT, Min(BIRTHDATE)
  From    EMPPF
  Group By DEPT
  Having  Year(Current_Date – Min(BIRTHDATE)) >= 50
```

In this example, we are extracting the year from the date-arithmetic expression Current_Date – Min(BIRTHDATE) and comparing it with 50 (see Figure 13.28). If you think of a date as a point on a time line, then, in SQL, any two points can be compared and their difference expressed in years, months, weeks, or days.

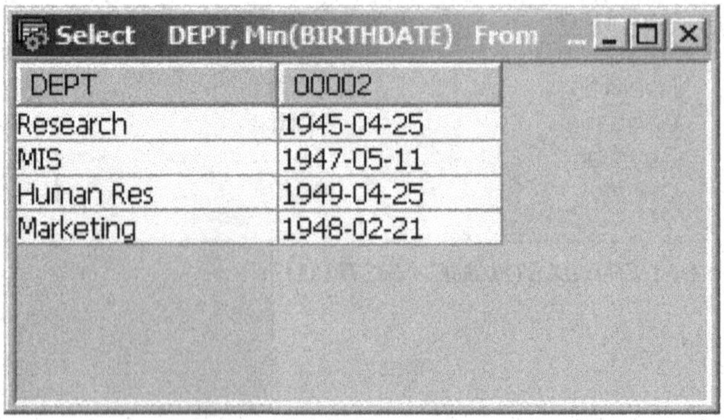

DEPT	00002
Research	1945-04-25
MIS	1947-05-11
Human Res	1949-04-25
Marketing	1948-02-21

Figure 13.28: Having Year(Current_Date - Min(BIRTHDATE)) >= 50

Another way to write the preceding Having clause is to use a **labeled duration**; that is, a date period expressed in one of the date units (e.g., years, months). Using labeled duration, our Having clause would be

Having Min(BIRTHDATE) + 50 years <= Current_Date

The + 50 years is the labeled duration. A labeled duration is always used to add or subtract some period of time to a known point of time, such as BIRTHDATE; and so it always starts with a plus or minus sign.

Returning to the question of how to include personal data with the birth date of each department's oldest employee, first visualize the output of the earlier statement, as Figure 13.29 shows.

```
Select    DEPT, Min(BIRTHDATE)
 From    EMPPF
 Group By DEPT
 Having Min(BIRTHDATE) + 50 years <= Current_Date
```

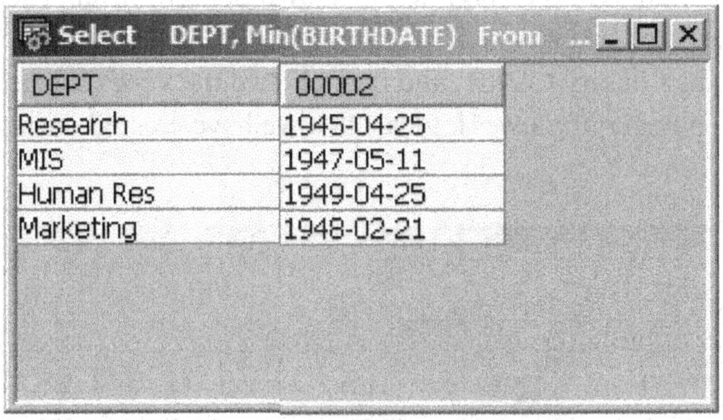

DEPT	00002
Research	1945-04-25
MIS	1947-05-11
Human Res	1949-04-25
Marketing	1948-02-21

Figure 13.29: Having Min(BIRTHDATE) + 50 years <= Current_Date

If we could find a way to store this data, we could join it to EMPPF records based on the values of DEPT and BIRTHDATE in EMPPF and then extract any other employee data we needed from the joined record. In fact, the data is already stored in file EMPPF; we just need to build a kind of logical file over EMPPF to get at the data.

SQL's version of a logical file is a **view**. Although a view is conceptually similar to a logical file, SQL's greater flexibility and ability to use functions and expressions make views far more powerful than logical files. For example, in a logical file there is no way to select group summary records based on the value returned by a column function, as we did in the previous example. Nevertheless, in SQL, creating such a view is easy; in fact, we already have most of the code for it. The only thing we need to do is prefix our earlier Select statement with a **Create View** statement and then name the virtual column created by the Min function. Here is the statement to create the view of department elders:

```
Create View  CIS001.DEPTELDER As
  Select    DEPT, Min(BIRTHDATE) As ELDERBDAY
    From    EMPPF
    Group By DEPT
    Having  Min(BIRTHDATE) + 50 Years <= Current_Date
```

We use the SQL Create statement to build base tables (physical files), views (logical files), indexes (access paths), and other SQL objects. The system object created by the Create View statement above will be a *FILE type object in library CIS001. It will be an externally described logical file, attribute LF, SQL type VIEW. We will include the Select statement used to define the record format, and to select the population of the view, in its file description; so we will have a permanent record of the criteria used in creating the view.

You can use the SQL Create command instead of the native CL commands CRTPF (Create Physical File) and CRTLF (Create Logical File) to build entire databases, but that is the topic of another class. Our purpose here is limited to showing how you can use a view to access certain data already stored in a physical file. In Figure 13.30, we have expanded databases, navigated to the student library CIS001, and then clicked the Views subtask (note the arrow). This figure shows a number of views (logical) that we have created during the process of writing this book.

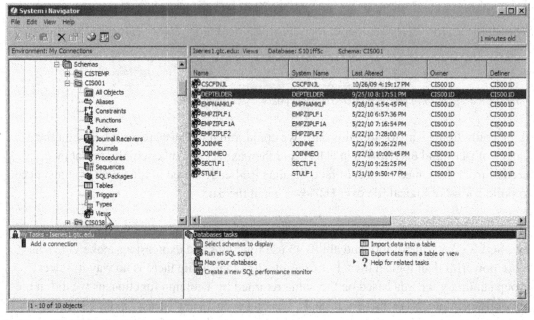

Figure 13.30: Using Navigator to Display Views

Now that we have created a view of departments and elder employees' birth dates, we can complete the original task by getting the employee-name data matched up with each row of the view. We can accomplish this by joining the view to its based-on physical file EMPPF using both department and birth date as join-relationship-supporting fields. By doing this, we can retrieve multiple same-age elders in the same department, if such a condition exists. Figure 13.31 shows the display output of the following statement:

```
Select DE.DEPT, FIRSTNAME, LASTNAME, ELDERBDAY
 From DEPTELDER DE Inner Join EMPPF E
  On DE.DEPT = E.DEPT
    And ELDERBDAY = BIRTHDATE
```

Select DE.DEPT, FIRSTNAME, LASTNAME, ELDERBDAY From DEPTELDER DE I...

DEPT	FIRSTNAME	LASTNAME	ELDERBDAY
Research	Albert	Einstein	1945-04-25
Marketing	Martha	Gootch	1948-02-21
Human Res	Atilla	Hunn	1949-04-25
MIS	Tilly	Zanzibar	1947-05-11
MIS	Rocky	Stonehart	1947-05-11

Figure 13.31: The Oldest Members of Each Department

Notice that the output includes the two oldest employees of MIS who have the same birth date, May 11, 1947.

If there were other reasons to keep the department elders view on hand, the preceding method of joining EMPPF to the view would be fine. However, a view is a persistent object, and if its only purpose is to provide the information in Figure 13.31, we can use another method, called a *correlated subquery*. This method requires neither the view nor the use of Group By and Having.

An **integer reference** implies running an inner select on a group of records that share a column value with (correlated to) the current row of the outer select. Because both the inner and outer selects reference the same file, we must, in effect, tell SQL to use separate copies of the file so that running the inner select doesn't change the current record pointer of the outer select. We specify the match condition using correlation names to qualify the fields. The code to create exactly the same output as you see in Figure 13.31 would look like this:

```
Select  DEPT, LASTNAME, FIRSTNAME, BIRTHDATE
 From  EMPPF  A
 Where BIRTHDATE <= Current_Date - 50 years
    and BIRTHDATE = (Select Min(BIRTHDATE)
```

```
            From EMPPF  B
            Where A.DEPT = B.DEPT)
   Order by DEPT
```

The outer select names an A copy of EMPPF, which will be read one record at a time in arrival sequence. As each record is read, it is examined to see whether its birth date is at least 50 years old. If so, the inner select is run to obtain the minimum birth date of the EMPPF B file records in the same department as the outer select's currently positioned record (Where A.DEPT = B.DEPT). When a match is made, the outer select record is placed in the result table. To agree with the grouped output of Figure 13.38, the result table is then ordered (sorted) by department. The power of a **correlated subquery** is its ability to compare column values from the inner (B) file against a column value of the current row of the outer (A) file. Note that the reference to DEPT in the outer select is unambiguously the A file, so there is no need for qualification.

File Maintenance Using SQL

We will now take a brief look at updating a database using SQL Insert, Update, and Delete statements. The SQL Insert statement lets you add individual rows to a table. The Update and Delete statements also work on individual rows, but they have the added capability to perform the operation on a set of rows. A row of the base table becomes a member of the set by testing True for a Where condition.

Each statement identifies a single file, which may be a physical file (**base table**) or an updatable logical file (**updatable view**). Some rules govern whether a view or logical file is updatable. It must not

- Identify more than one file in its From clause (no join logical files or views)
- Use the Distinct expression in its Select statement
- Use either the Group By or the Having clause in its outer Select statement
- Use a column function in its outer Select statement
- Use a correlated subquery on the same table identified in its From clause

The Insert Statement

The SQL **Insert statement** lets you add individual rows to a table. Insert can act directly on the base table or indirectly by inserting through a view or logical file within the limitations described above. The syntax of the SQL Insert statement is

```
Insert Into file-name
        (field-list)
    Values   (value-list)
```

Here is an example using file ZIPPF:

```
Insert Into ZIPPF
        (ZIP, CITY, STATE)
    Values   (531421444, 'Kenosha', 'WI')
```

In this Insert statement, because values were provided for all fields and in the same order as the record-format field order, the field list itself is optional. Therefore, the statement

```
Insert Into ZIPPF
    Values   (531421444, 'Kenosha', 'WI')
```

works just as well. The field list is required when you are not assigning values to all fields or when the values are not in the same order as the fields in the record format.

In either case, we must specify which field a certain value is assigned to by putting it in the same relative position in the value list as its corresponding field name in the field list (e.g., the first named field takes the first value). Any field not listed is not assigned a value in the newly inserted record and takes the default value (zeros or spaces, unless a different default value was assigned in the physical-file or base-table definition).

Numeric values may have a leading minus sign and a decimal point if the field allows for decimal precision. Alphanumeric values and date and time values must be enclosed in apostrophes. The Insert statement must not attempt to use values that are longer than the receiving field because doing so would cause significant digit truncation.

For example, the following statement would not work:

```
Insert Into ZIPPF
    Values   (531421444, 'WI', 'Kenosha')
```

SQL would return the error message *"Value for Column STATE too long."* Given the actual order of fields in the record—ZIP, CITY, STATE—this error message indicates that SQL could insert WI into the CITY field, but assuming the third value, Kenosha, should be assigned to the third field, STATE, it refused to do so because only the Ke part of the value would fit in this two-character field.

To add a new record to file PRJMBRPF, you could use the following Insert statement:

```
Insert Into PRJMBRPF
        (EMPNO, ASDDAT, PRJCD)
  Values   (111110012, '2010-08-01', 'NPADV')
```

Proper values are assigned to each listed field even though the fields are not in the same order as in the record format. The values correspond positionally with the fields in the field list. The date field is in *ISO format and enclosed in apostrophes. The hours-to-date field, HRSTD, is not listed and will be assigned the default value of zero in the new record.

The command-line Insert statement is a convenient way to add a record or two to a database file when you are working in an SQL session. But it is a slow and error-prone method of data-entry, and a custom program normally is used instead.

The Update Statement

SQL's **Update statement** lets you change records within a file, using constants and expressions to modify the values of named fields. The syntax for a **searched Update** with a Where clause is

```
Update   file-name
  Set   field-name = expression
  Where conditional-expression
```

It is important to remember that the Update statement can work on sets of records, not just single records. Whenever more than one record in the file tests True for the Where condition, all records testing True are updated according to the Set clause specification. For example, the statement

```
Update   CIS001.PRJMBRPF
  Set   HRSTD = HRSTD + 5
  Where  PRJCD = 'NPADV'
   And  EMPNO = 111110012
```

updates a single record in PRJMBRPF, incrementing the hours-to-date field by 5. How do we know only one record is updated? Because the Where condition tests for specific values of the two fields that together constitute the composite primary key for this file. When primary-key values are given to identify a record for update, only one record is updated. When the update is performed successfully, SQL displays the message *"1 rows were affected by the statement,"* as in Figure 13.32.

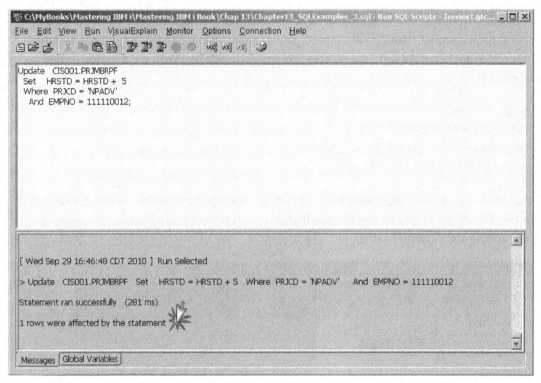

Figure 13.32: Result of Update Statement

The real power of the Update statement is its ability to change a set of records by executing one statement and selecting the set to be updated by evaluating the Where condition. The Where condition tests all records in the table or view, and all those testing True will be updated. For example, if you wanted to give a 6.5 percent raise to all MIS employees, you could do so easily by executing the following statement:

```
Update  EMPPF
  Set   SALARY = SALARY * 1.065
  Where DEPT = 'MIS'
```

This statement tests each record in the employee file for the condition DEPT = 'MIS' and applies the salary increase to all records that test True.

The Update statement's Set expression must reference only field names of the update table or view. It cannot identify an alias field derived from a scalar function, expression, or constant.

In an Update statement's Where clause, all listed column names must belong to the table or view being updated, unless a subquery is used to create a value or list of values used as a comparison operand. Thus, an attempt to give a 2 percent raise to the employees assigned to the New Products Advertising project (project code NPADV) with the following code would fail:

```
Update  EMPPF
  Set  SALARY = SALARY * 1.02
  Where EMPPF.EMPNO = PRJMBRPF.EMPNO
   And PRJMBRPF.PRJCD = 'NPADV'
```

The Where expression references non-EMPPF field names, so the Update statement would fail, as Figure 13.33 shows. Notice that PRJMBRPF.EMPNO is highlighted, which shows the reference to the PRJMBRPF table.

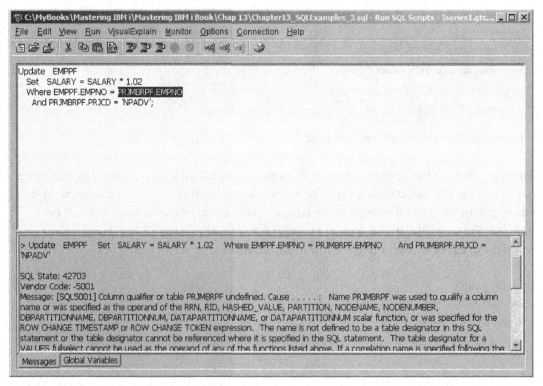

Figure 13.33: Update Statement Failure

We can accomplish the desired update, however, by using a subquery to create a list of employee numbers assigned to project NPADV. The modified Update statement would be

```
Update  EMPPF
  Set   SALARY = SALARY * 1.02
  Where EMPNO In
      (Select  EMPNO From PRJMBRPF
        Where PRJCD = 'NPADV')
```

This statement has no ambiguous column references and violates no update rules. Therefore, it updated five records in the EMPPF table. The messages pane in the Run SQL Scripts window verifies this, as you can see in Figure 13.34.

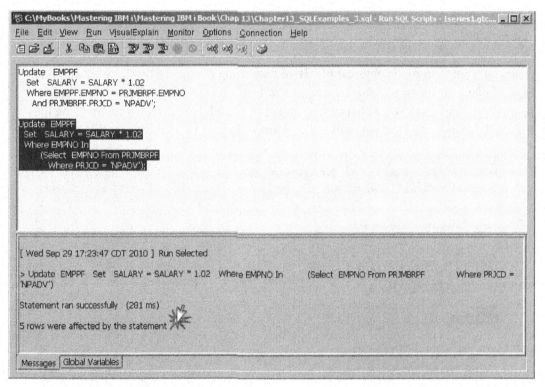

Figure 13.34: Update Statement Success

When the same update rule can be applied to multiple records in a file, SQL offers a convenient way to get the job done using a single statement. However, for updating one record at a time, it is not as easy to use as a custom-written file-maintenance application. For programmers, SQL can provide a quick way to change test data, but it is not a safe or efficient tool for nontechnical users.

The Delete Statement

The SQL **Delete statement** removes one or more records from a file, either directly from the base table (physical file) or through an updatable view. The syntax of the Delete statement is similar to that of the Update statement, but the Delete statement lacks a Set clause:

Delete
  From *file-name*
  Where *conditional expression*

As with the Update statement, multiple rows (or all rows) in a Delete statement can be deleted with a single statement. For example, the statement

Delete
  From EMPPF

clears all records from the physical file. If you are using the 5250 STRSQL command line, SQL displays the message *"You are about to alter (Delete or Update) all of the records in your file(s)"* and gives you a chance to change your mind. However, if you are using the Run SQL Scripts interface, you will *not* be warned. Figure 13.35 illustrates this point.

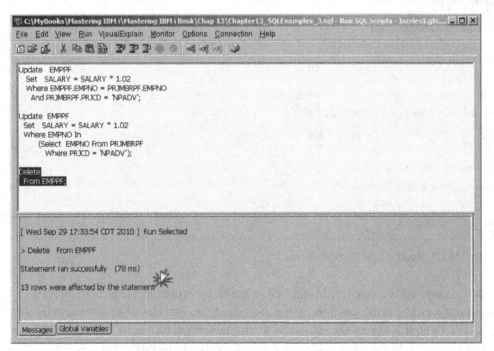

Figure 13.35: Delete Statement Results

The preceding Delete statement would have the same effect as the following **CLRPFM** (Clear Physical File Member) command.

CLRPFM EMPPF

This command removes all records from the member but does not actually delete the file. The SQL counterpart to the **DLTF** (Delete File) CL command is the SQL **Drop** statement.

The rules for forming the Where clause of a Delete statement are basically the same as those for an Update statement—any referenced field names must belong to the file named in the Delete From statement, with the exception of a field named in a subquery. For example, if you wanted to delete all employees who are older than 40 from the EMPPF file, you could do that using a labeled duration with the following statement:

Delete
 From EMPPF
 Where Current_Date > BIRTHDATE + 40 years

Figure 13.36 shows the result of this Delete statement. Like the Update statement, the SQL Delete statement is useful when you need to delete a set of records having some common characteristic.

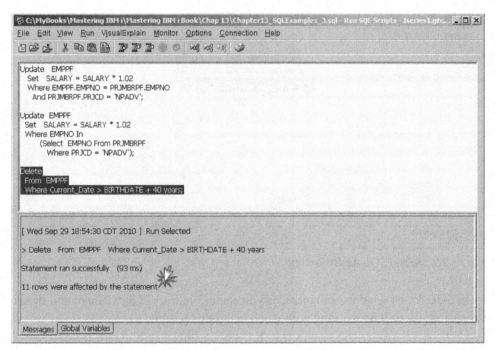

Figure 13.36: Delete Statement Results with Labeled Duration

Using SQL Assist/Prompt

An additional feature of the Run SQL Scripts interface is SQL Assist. This feature allows
the user to create fairly sophisticated SQL statements with little or no knowledge of SQL.
Although students should learn to write SQL statements without depending on a feature
such as SQL Assist, this is a great tool to help you as a new SQL programmer develop SQL
statements while you learn the syntax. This tool can also be an asset to the seasoned SQL
programmer who would like to develop templates for more sophisticated SQL statements
without having to key in the complete statements. We will guide you through a short
demonstration of how the SQL Assist tool works, and we encourage you to use it as a
learning aid.

With Run SQL Scripts open and connected to a database, you can press F4, or, from the
toolbar, click Edit, and then SQL Assist/Prompt CL, as in Figure 13.37.

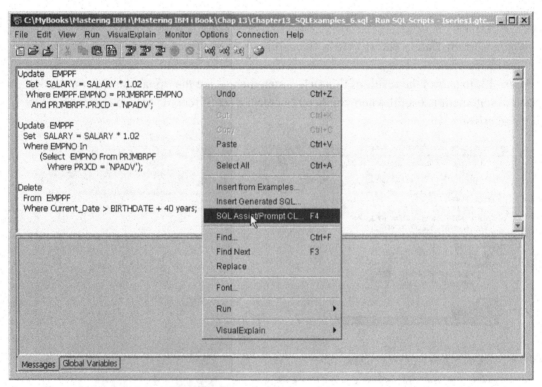

Figure 13.37: Starting SQL Assist/Prompt

The main SQL Assist window will open, as you see in Figure 13.38; we have numbered the
three areas that we will be working with when using this product.

Chapter 13 Introduction to SQL • 695

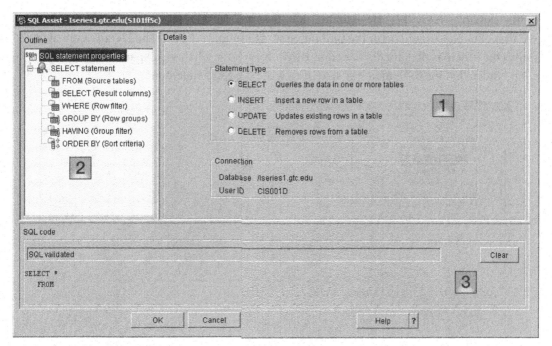

Figure 13.38: SQL Assist Main Window

An explanation of each area follows.

1. *Details*—After you select the type of statement you want to create, this area is where you fill in the options to create the SQL statement.

2. *Outline*—After you select the statement type from the Details view, you use this area to select additional functions for the selected SQL command.

3. *SQL code*—As you define the SQL statement, it is displayed in this area. You also have the option to Clear the statement.

In this example, we will create a simple SQL Select statement with a few designated fields. We first click the From icon in the outline view, as in Figure 13.39. The Details view then shows the schemas that are displayed in IBM i Navigator when we expand the Schemas icon. Notice that the SQL area has started to write the SQL statement.

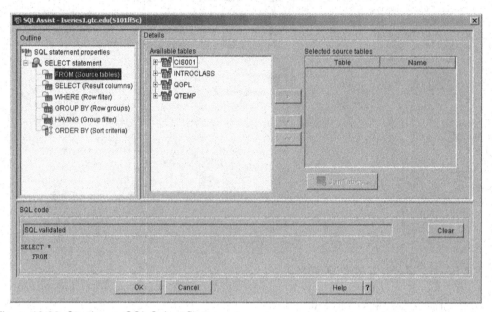

Figure 13.39: Starting an SQL Select Statement

We next expand the CIS001 student schema by clicking the + sign on the left of the icon. Then we navigate to and click the EMPPF table in the CIS001 schema. After we click the > button in the details area, we can see that this table has been selected for our Select statement, as Figure 13.40 shows.

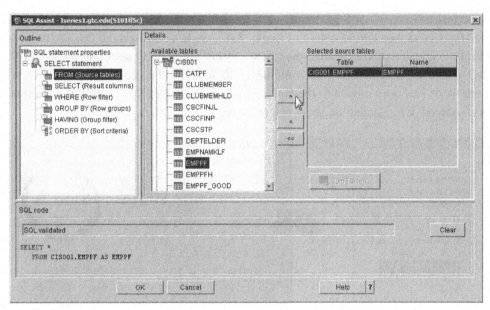

Figure 13.40: Selecting a Table

In Figure 13.41, you can see that we have clicked the SELECT icon and expanded the CIS001 .EMPPF table in the Details view. We could have individually selected the columns we wanted displayed by highlighting each one and clicking the > button. Instead we chose to hold down the Ctrl key and select all the fields we wanted to display; then we clicked >.

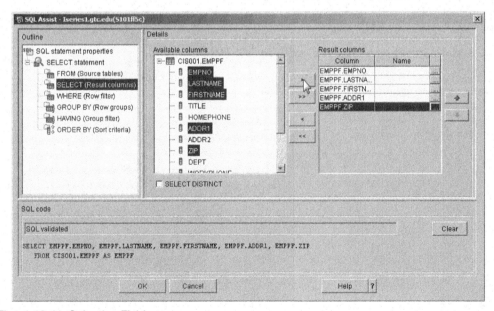

Figure 13.41: Selecting Fields

Our next task is to have our **SQL result set** (the results of an SQL Select statement) sorted by LASTNAME and then FIRSTNAME. In Figure 13.42, we have clicked the ORDER BY icon in the Outline view and then expanded the CIS001.EMPPF table. After selecting the fields we wanted to sort on, we clicked >. We could have changed the sort order from ASC to DESC after the fields had been moved to the *Sort columns* area. Notice that to limit the number of fields displayed, we selected the Show result columns only option.

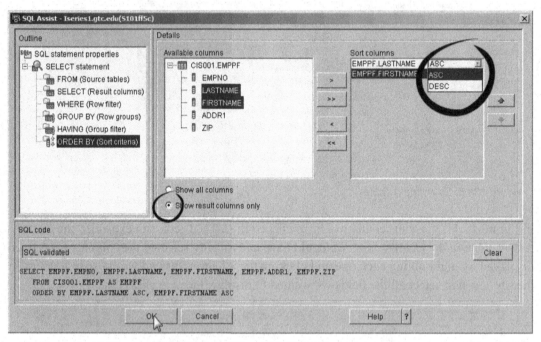

Figure 13.42: Sorting on LASTNAME and Then FIRSTNAME

We have completed our sample Select statement, and Figure 13.43 displays the results. We cannot run this SQL statement from SQL Assist. Instead, we would run it using the Run SQL Scripts interface, as in previous examples in this chapter.

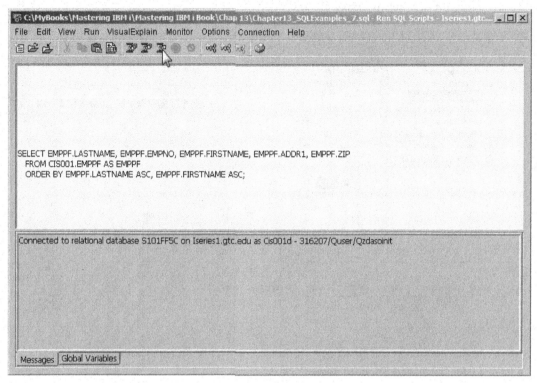

Figure 13.43: Completed Select Statement

Using SQL Assist, we can prompt our completed statement and add additional functionality. We will now prompt the Select statement we created, and then we will do an Inner Join with the ZIPPF table so that we can display the city and state columns in our SQL result set.

In Figure 13.43, we prompted the SQL Select statement that we created in the previous steps. We then expanded the CIS001 schema, navigated to the ZIPPF table, and added it to the *Selected source tables* window, as you can see in Figure 13.44. The Join Tables button is now available for use, and we have clicked it.

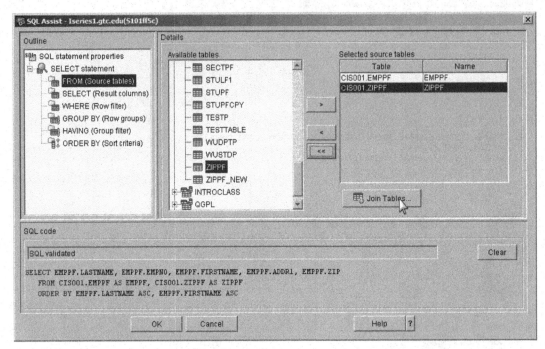

Figure 13.44: Completed Select Statement, Next Screen

We are presented with the information message in Figure 13.45. This is not an error message, but a message telling us that the ZIP column in the EMPPF table is not defined as a foreign key. A discussion of foreign keys is beyond the scope of this text. For now, we will need to manually link the ZIP column in the EMPPF table to the ZIP column in the ZIPPF table without the help of SQL Assist.

After we click OK, as in Figure 13.45, the Join Tables window in Figure 13.46 is displayed.

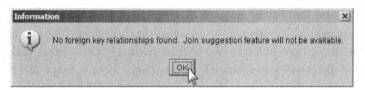

Figure 13.45: "OK" Verification Window

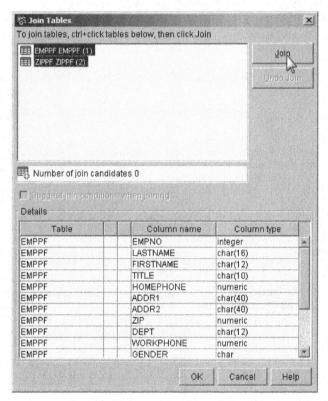

Figure 13.46: Add Tables to Join

This window let us tell SQL Assist which tables to join. We have highlighted the EMPPF and ZIPPF tables; if we were to use the scroll bar to look at the fields in the details window, we would see that all the fields in both tables are available. Next, we click Join.

After we click Join, the Join Tables window changes, as you can see in Figure 13.47. We can now describe the relationship between the columns that will create the join and then select the Join Type from the drop-down box. We will leave the choice as Inner Join because we want to include all the EMPPF records that have matching records in the ZIPPF table.

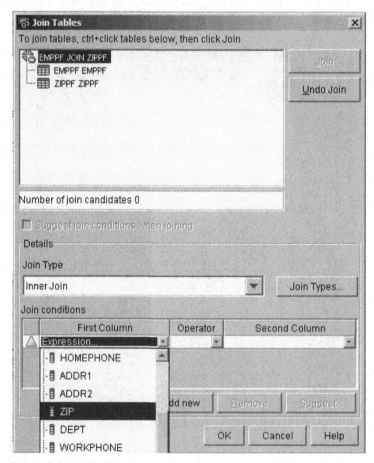

Figure 13.47: Select Criteria for the Inner Join

In the figure, we have selected the First Column drop-down box and navigated to the ZIP column for the EMPPF table. The next step is to select the Operator drop-down box, select the equal sign (=), and finally select the Second Column drop-down box, where we then select the ZIP column from the ZIPPF table. After that, we click OK to complete the join and close the window.

Now that we have completed our Inner Join, we need to add the CITY and STATE columns from the ZIPPF table to our SQL result set. Figure 13.48 shows the main window, in which we have selected the SELECT icon in the Outline view.

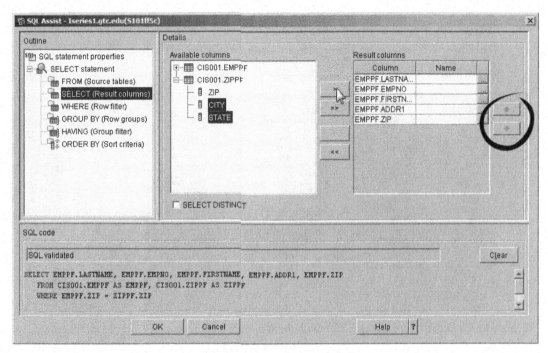

Figure 13.48: Add the CITY and STATE Fields to the SQL Statement.

In the figure, you can see the CIS001.ZIPPF table is shown in the *Available columns* window. We have expanded this table and selected the CITY and STATE columns. You can see that we are in the process of clicking > to add the columns to the *Result columns* view. Once all the columns we want to display have been added, we can adjust the order of the columns by selecting a column and moving it up or down in the *Result columns* view by using the up or down arrows (which are circled in the figure). Once we are satisfied with the order of the columns, we click OK.

This action returns us to the Run SQL Scripts main window, where we can run the SQL statement (Figure 13.49).

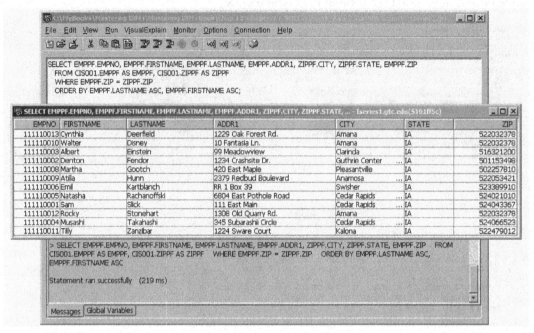

Figure 13.49: Output from Our SELECT Statement

This short introduction should demonstrate to you that SQL Assist can help you quickly create SQL statements.

In Summary

In this brief discussion of SQL, we have focused both on some useful techniques for getting information from a relational database and on the SQL file-maintenance statements Insert, Update, and Delete. Although this short tour is not a comprehensive introduction to SQL, it should help you understand the usefulness of the language, particularly the code-efficient capability it offers to query databases. It is no wonder that SQL has become the standard database language. When you use SQL within HLL programs, you can combine the power and ease of coding SQL data access with the screen- or report-formatting flexibility of the HLL to create programs that are faster to design, code, and test, and whose maintenance costs will be far less over time.

This chapter covers many of the SQL statements that are used in today's programming environment. In addition to covering the Select, Insert, and Delete statements, we discussed how to code different SQL join statements. We cannot overemphasize the importance of developing strong SQL skills. Students with this foundation, and the tools described in this chapter, should be able to enhance their skills to meet the demands of today's programming environment.

Key Terms

_ character
% character
"alias" fields
AS clause
Bachman diagram
base table
CLRPFM
column functions
Concat
correlated subquery
correlation name
Count(*) expression
Create Table statement
Create View statement
Day (date function)
DDL
Decimal scalar function
Delete statement
Distinct keyword
DLTF
DML
Drop statement
dynamic SQL
equijoin relationship
Exception Join
From clause
Group By function
Having clause
In function

Inner Join
Insert statement
integer reference
item separator
JDBC
labeled duration
Left Outer Join
Like logical operation
Min function
Month date function
Not logical operator
operands
Order By clause
relational operators
Run SQL Scripts
scalar functions
searched Update
SQL result set
static SQL
subquery
Substring
Sum column function
updatable view
Update statement
view
Where clause
wildcard
Year (date function)

Review Questions

1. Under what circumstances does case matter when you are writing SQL statements?
2. Why would you want to create an "alias" field?
3. What is the format of the Substring scalar function?
4. Research two additional SQL scalar functions not discussed in this chapter, and then list their use and format.
5. Explain how to open the Run SQL Scripts interface without opening IBM i Navigator.
6. How can incorrectly using the Where clause instead of using the correct join operation lead to incorrect results in your SQL query?
7. Explain the differences between the SQL joins we discussed in this chapter.
8. What is the purpose of the SQL Where clause?
9. What is wrong with this expression: Amount >= 514 And <= 523?
10. Give an example of using the Like logical operation.
11. Why would you use the Distinct keyword?
12. What is the purpose of the Group By clause?
13. A "view" in SQL is comparable to what file type in DB2 system file-access methods? What is a view's purpose?
14. Describe the concept of a correlated subquery.
15. List the rules that govern when a view or logical file is updatable using SQL.
16. Under what circumstances is the field list required when you use an SQL Insert statement?
17. What types of fields need to be enclosed in apostrophes when you use the SQL Insert statement?
18. When you use an Update statement with a Where clause, what "rule" should you observe unless you use a subquery?
19. What CL command is the equivalent of the SQL Drop statement?
20. Research the SQL Create command, and then explain what you can create with it.

Lab 13

Introduction

In this lab, we introduce some additional SQL topics and practice the SQL concepts introduced in this chapter. In Part 1, you will create a collection that you will use for the balance of the labs. In Part 2, you will copy the structure and data of two tables from the

INTROCLASS library to the schema you created in Part 1. In Part 3, you will manipulate the structure and data in these tables. In addition, in Part 3 you will practice the joins that we discussed in this chapter.

We will use two tables: CLUBMEMBER and CITYSTATE (see Figure 13.50). The relationship between these two tables is similar to the relationship between the EMPPF and ZIPPF tables we discussed earlier, whose relationship was shown by the Bachman diagram in Figure 13.10.

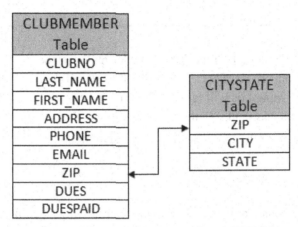

Figure 13.50: Bachman Diagram for CLUBMEMBER and CITYSTATE Tables

Notice in Figure 13.50 that there is no CITY or STATE field in the CLUBMEMBER table. A corresponding record should exist in the CITYSTATE table for every ZIP code in the CLUBMEMBER table.

Part 1

We briefly introduced the SQL Create command earlier in the chapter. This is a powerful command, used to create schemas, tables, indexes, and views. We can use the terms *schema*, *collection*, and *database* interchangeably in DB2. We use the generic term *database* in the SQL world.

Goals	Create a collection or database for use in this lab.
Start with	Run SQL Scripts open and connected to your personal library.
Procedure	Use the Create command to create an SQL database for use in this lab.
	Change your Default SQL Schema to the new schema using Temporary JDBC Settings.

Verify that you are connected to the IBM i server and that the default schema is your personal schema (library). We covered this topic in detail in the text of this chapter. In this portion of the lab, you will issue the SQL Create Database command.

Caution

In this example, we have appended SQL to our student library (CIS001) for continuity reasons. You should consult your instructor to verify your college's naming convention for this lab.

13.1. In the toolbar at the top of the Run SQL Scripts interface, select File and Save, and then name your SQL script Chap13Lab_CIS001D.sql. Use your System ID instead of CIS001D. Doing this will let you continue your work later; or, if you are to turn in the lab, you can send it to the instructor.

The basic form of the SQL Create Schema statement is

Create Schema *Schema_Name*

To create our schema, we would key in the following code in the Run SQL Scripts input window:

Create Schema CIS001SQL

Note: Remember to use your college's naming convention, *not* our example name.

13.1.a. Write the SQL command you used to create your schema.

After you have executed the SQL statement, you should receive a completion message similar to the following one:

[Sun Oct 03 16:23:53 CDT 2010] Run Selected

> create schema cis001sql

Statement ran successfully (3500 ms = 3.500 sec)

When you are creating an SQL script file, it is a good idea to document your code. Figure 13.51 demonstrates doing this. In addition, notice that there is a semicolon (;) at the end of the Create statement. It is important that you append a semicolon when you are entering multiple statements in an SQL script because the semicolon tells the interface where each SQL statement ends.

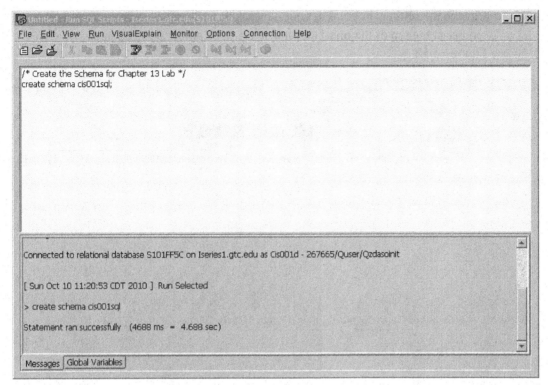

Figure 13.51: Documenting SQL Code in a Script File

If you were to view this schema with PDM or IBM i Navigator, you would see a number of files that the system has placed in the schema. A discussion of these files and their contents is beyond the scope of this text. You should understand that the system uses these files for SQL purposes. We recommend that you *do not attempt* to modify or delete any of these files.

13.2. Change the settings to point to your new schema. Click Connection from the toolbar at the top of the interface, and select Use Temporary JDBC Settings, as in Figure 13.52.

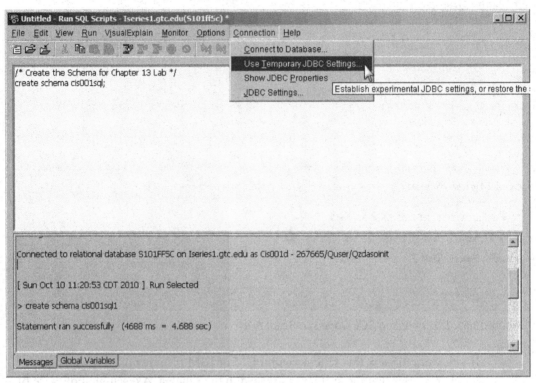

Figure 13.52: Change the Database Connection with Use Temporary JDBC Settings

13.3. Change the Default SQL schema parameter to use your new schema. Doing this will enable you to use unqualified SQL statements for the balance of the labs. We used our example student's new schema (CIS001SQL) for the example in Figure 13.53; you should use the schema you just created. Then click Connect.

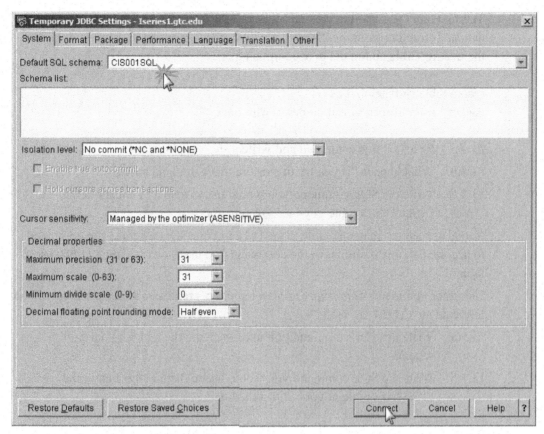

Figure 13.53: Change the Database Connection with "Use Temporary JDBC Settings," Continued

Save your SQL script file, and ask your instructor whether you should turn it in when you have completed the lab.

Part 2

Goals   Create work tables in your new schema using the data and structure from the tables in the INTROCLASS schema.

Start with   Run SQL Scripts open and connected to your system.

Procedure   Create the tables in your new work schema from the tables in the INTROCLASS schema.

In Part 1, you created a schema that you will use to store your tables for this lab. The next step is to create two work tables in your new personal schema. You will use two tables located in the INTROCLASS library.

13.4. The first table you want to create is called CLUBMEMBER. You will need to copy the data and structure from the INTROCLASS library using one SQL command. Here is the **Create Table** command to accomplish this:

```
create table clubmember as
(select * from introclass.clubmember) with data;
```

13.4.a. Research this command and write a short explanation.

13.4.b. What happens if you try to execute this command twice?

13.4.c. Write the SQL command you would use to display the data in the CLUBMEMBER table in your SQL schema.

13.5. You also need to create the table CITYSTATE in your SQL schema. The command to accomplish this is similar to the command you used to create the CLUBMEMBER table.

Using the command from step 13.4 as a template, create and execute the command to create the CITYSTATE table.

13.5.a. Write the SQL command you used to create the table in your SQL schema.

13.5.b. Write the SQL command you would use to display the data in the CITYSTATE table in your SQL schema.

Part 3

Goals   Manipulate the data in the CLUBMEMBER table you created in Part 2 of this lab.

Start with Run SQL Scripts open and connected to your personal schema.

Procedure   Use an SQL Insert statement to insert records into a table.

Use an SQL Update statement to update records in a table.

Use an SQL Delete statement to delete rows from a table.

Use SQL Join statements to query CLUBMEMBER and CITYSTATE tables.

Use the SQL Alter Table statement to drop two fields from your CLUBMEMBER table.

In previous sections of this lab, you created a new SQL schema and created tables from the INTROCLASS library. You will need to complete those sections of the lab before you attempt this lab.

13.6. Use the SQL Insert statement to insert three records into your CLUBMEMBER table. Insert *three* records from the table below. Make sure you use the proper case when you insert the records.

Field Name	Record One	Record Two	Record Three
ClubNo	60000	60001	60002
Last_Name	Buck	Anderson	Sonney
First_Name	Shannon	Sue	Thomas
Address	100 Sheridan Rd.	200 Lakeview Ave.	1200 Riverview
Phone	2629908769	9098765314	6547892341
Email	SJBuck@mail.com	Suzie@mailer.com	tsonney@acer.com
Zip	53142	53147	54603

Document your SQL commands as in Figure 13.51.

13.6.a. Write the SQL commands you used to complete this portion of the lab.

13.7. Use the SQL Insert statement to insert records into your CITYSTATE table. Insert records that match the city, state, and zip code for the new members that you inserted in step 13.6.

Field Name	Record One	Record Two	Record Three
Zip	53142	53147	54603
City	Kenosha	Lake Geneva	La Crosse
State	WI	WI	WI

Document your SQL commands as in Figure 13.51.

13.7.a. Write the SQL commands you used to complete this portion of the lab.

13.8. Use the SQL Update statement to update fields in your CLUBMEMBER table. Update the DUES field in the CLUBMEMBER table with a value of 250.00. The basic form of the SQL Update statement is

Update   *file-name*

   Set   *field-name = expression*

Document your SQL commands as in Figure 13.51.

13.8.a. Write the SQL command you used to complete this portion of the lab.

13.9. Update the DUESPAID field in the CLUBMEMBER table with a value of N.

Document your SQL commands as in Figure 13.51.

13.9.a. Write the SQL command you used to complete this portion of the lab.

13.10. Increase the dues by 5 percent for records in the CLUBMEMBER table with a zip code equal to or greater than 75457 and equal to or less than 91200. **Note:** This field is a character field.

Document your SQL command as in Figure 13.51.

13.10.a. Write the SQL command you used to complete this portion of the lab.

13.11. Delete rows from the CLUBMEMBER table with zip codes that contain the characters T4.

13.11.a. How many records were deleted from the table?

Document your SQL command as in Figure 13.51.

13.11.b. Write the SQL command you used to complete this portion of the lab.

13.12. Delete rows from the CITYSTATE table with zip codes that contain the characters T4.

13.12.a. How many records were deleted from the table?

Document your SQL command as in Figure 13.51.

13.12.b. Write the SQL command you used to complete this portion of the lab.

13.13. Use the following SQL command to check to see whether the CITY and STATE fields exist in the CLUBMEMBER table:

Select * from clubmember

If you see these two fields, use the following Alter Table SQL statement to remove the CITY and STATE columns from the table:

/* Alter Table */
alter table clubmember drop column city drop column state

Caution
Depending on how the system you are working on is configured, you might not be able to issue the preceding statement from the Run SQL Scripts interface. This is not a problem with the SQL command. It is the result of DB2 sending a warning message to the Run SQL Scripts interface and the interface being unable to reply to the message. You can run the command from the STRSQL command line. If you need help, ask your instructor for assistance.

13.14. Use an SQL Left Outer Join to query the CLUBMEMBER and CITYSTATE tables. Display the CLUBNO, FIRST_NAME, LAST_NAME, ADDRESS, and ZIP fields from the CLUBMEMBER table and the CITY and STATE fields from the CITYSTATE table.

13.14.a. How many records *did not* have city and state data displayed?

13.14.b. What was the CLUBNO for the record(s)?

Document your SQL command as in Figure 13.51.

13.14.c. Write the SQL command you used to complete this portion of the lab.

13.15. Use an SQL Inner Join to query CLUBMEMBER and CITYSTATE tables. Display the CLUBNO, FIRST_NAME, LAST_NAME, ADDRESS, and ZIP fields from the CLUBMEMBER table and the CITY and STATE fields from the CITYSTATE table.

13.15.a. Was the record from step 13.14.b displayed in your query?

13.15.b. If this record was not displayed, why not?

Document your SQL command as in Figure 13.51.

13.15.c. Write the SQL command you used to complete this portion of the lab.

13.16. Use an SQL Exception Join to query CLUBMEMBER and CITYSTATE tables. Display the CLUBNO, FIRST_NAME, LAST_NAME, ADDRESS, and ZIP fields from the CLUBMEMBER table and the CITY and STATE fields from the CITYSTATE table.

13.16.a. How many records were displayed?

13.16.b. Was the record from step 13.13.b displayed in your query?

13.16.c. If this record was displayed, why?

Document your SQL command as in Figure 13.51.

13.16.d. Write the SQL command you used to complete this portion of the lab.

Ask your instructor whether you should save and turn in the SQL script you used in this lab.

CHAPTER 14

Using IBM i Access for Web

Overview

IBM access for Web is a Web server–based product that enables users to access a Power System running the IBM i OS. In this chapter we discuss the portions of this product that students use most often. We will concentrate on the 5250 Access interface and the functionality provided with the product's database functions.

Objectives

Students will be able to

- Start and log on to the system using IBM i Access for Web
- Start a 5250 session
- Change the configuration of an active session
- Save an active 5250 session
- Use Tables actions to display, update, and find database records
- Use the Run SQL database function to write an SQL statement
- Use the SQL Wizard to create a query
- Save an SQL statement to My Requests
- Edit a saved request
- Work with spool files and create a PDF file
- Work with output queues, messages, and jobs
- Create a query that includes joining and sorting
- Create a query that requires the user to input data at runtime

Introduction to IBM i Access for Web

The IBM i Access for Web page in Figure 14.1 is the default page displayed to an administrator, not the page most users will be allowed to access. We show this Web page to give you an understanding of all the functions available when you use this product (see arrow). The functions listed following the figure are available to you as the administrator; we will discuss the functions available to the typical user as we work through the chapter.

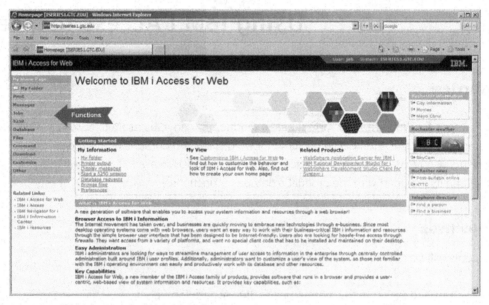

Figure 14.1: IBM i Access for Web Main Page

- *My Folder*—As a user, you have your own **personal folder**; you use this folder to store the results of operations when you use Access for Web. For example, if you create an SQL query, you can save the SQL output in your *My Folder*.
- *Print*—To control printer output and manage printers. Similar to the WRKSPLF CL command and the printer functions available from the Printer Menu (GO PRINTER).
- *Messages*—To manage messages (send, delete, or display) and message queues.
- *Jobs*—To list and manage users and server jobs.
- *5250*—To open a 5250 session, configure a session, or save a session.
- *Database*—To manipulate tables (insert, change, or delete rows), manage requests, and create SQL queries.
- *Command*—To run or save CL commands, list or use previously saved CL commands, or search for CL commands.
- *Download*—To download files from the **integrated file system (IFS)** that are available for distribution through Access for Web. You can use this option to store files for users.

- *Customize*—To set preferences for Access for Web, set policies for users (features a user or group has access to), and change system settings for Access for Web on the current server.
- *Other*—To change your password, display a summary of the connections (users) on the server, or set traces for different categories (Information, Diagnostic, Warning, Errors, or IBM Toolbox for Java).

You access IBM i Access for Web by keying the correct TCP host name in a browser. The general format is

http://*servername:port*/webaccess/iWAHome

where *servername* is the DNS name or IP address of your server and *port* is the port that the Apache server is configured to listen from for HTTP requests. In Figure 14.2, we have entered the correct TCP host name and are logging on to the system using our student ID CIS001D.

Figure 14.2: Access for Web Login Window

Note

To work through the text and complete the labs in this chapter, you will need to ask your instructor for the TCP host name for the server your college uses. The functions available to you may differ from the functions we discuss in this chapter. The available functions depend on how your school has customized the access for your user profile. In this chapter, we use the functions allowed at our college.

After our user ID and password have been verified, the Web page you see in Figure 14.3 is displayed. Notice that some of the functions on the **function menu** displayed in Figure 14.1 are not available to our student user. In the following sections, we will discuss each of the functions available to our student user.

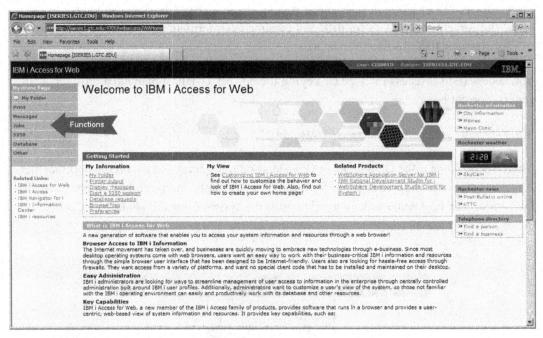

Figure 14.3: Access for Web CIS001D Main Page

5250 User Interface

The capability to access the system with a 5250 user interface without having to install any software on the user's PC can make the administration of a large number of PCs and users much easier. The fact that the company's computer support personnel do not have to update software on PCs can reduce the cost of users accessing the system. Also, in today's global IT environments, administrators can let new users in remote locations access the system simply by creating a user profile and sending the system's TCP host name link to the users.

Clicking the 5250 function in the function menu displays the Web page in Figure 14.4 and presents us with the three choices you see here.

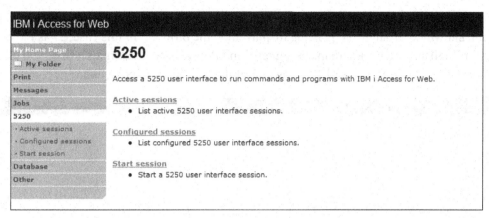

Figure 14.4: Access for Web 5250 User Interface Functions

A great feature of Access for Web is that IBM has included on the Web pages much of the documentation that a new user needs to use the product. As a result, we will not have to cover some topics in as much detail as we have in previous chapters. For this example, we will select the Start session option to proceed to the Start Session Web page, which lets us log in and start a new 5250 session, as you see in Figure 14.5.

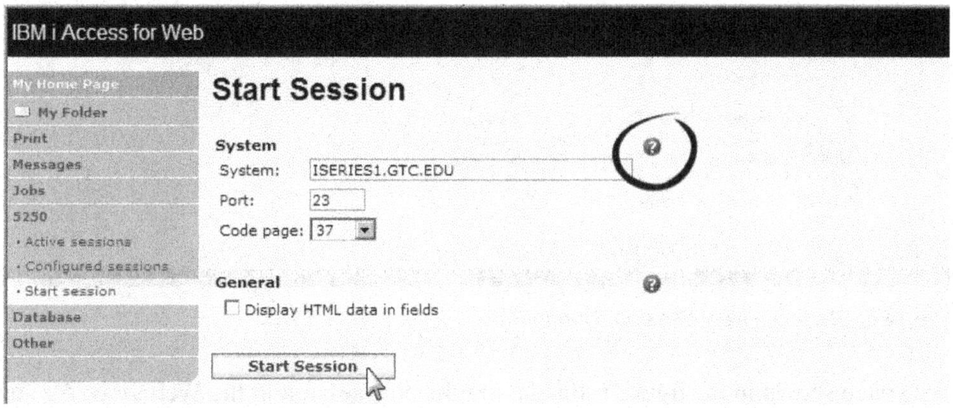

Figure 14.5: Starting a New Session

In the figure, we have highlighted (circled) a question mark (?). As you work with Access for Web, you will notice these question marks on many of the pages. Clicking a question mark opens a Web page with Help for that topic. This online Help allows the new user to quickly become acclimated to the new environment.

On the Start Session page, the **system parameter** (System field) defaults to the system that is running Access for Web. However, you can enter any TCP host name or IP address for a system running the IBM i OS, even if the system is not running Access for Web. The port you see entered in Figure 14.5 is the default Telnet port.

The Code page parameter facilitates data conversion between the EBCDIC **code page** on the system and whatever language is being displayed on the browser. In this case, 37 is the code page for English, Dutch, Brazilian Portuguese, and Portuguese. To start a session, you click the Start Session button. Figure 14.6 shows what the new session looks like.

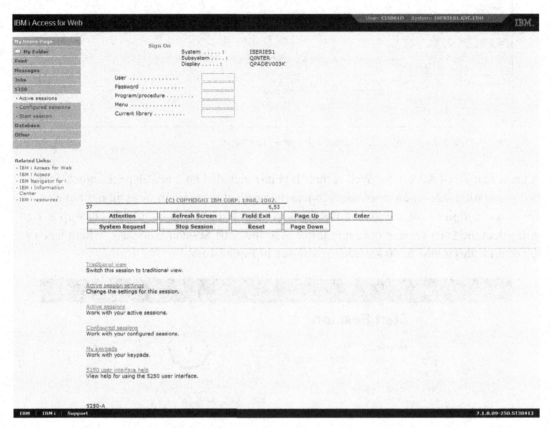

Figure 14.6: Starting a New Session, Continued

The Web page shown in the figure is displaying the new session in the Web view. As you can see, one option in the lower portion of the page is Traditional view. Clicking this Web link will change the 5250 display to look more like a traditional 5250 Telnet session.

The next Web link, Active session settings, lets you change many of the properties of the session; Figure 14.7 shows the Active Session Settings page.

Figure 14.7: Active Session Settings

As we stated previously, because of the large amount of online Help available to the user, we will not delve into all the options available. We do want to make note of some of the buttons at the bottom of the page, which we have listed here, with a short description:

- OK—Sets any changes made to the page for the life of the current session.
- Save—Saves the changes and takes you to another Web page, where you need to name the session.
- Cancel—Cancels any changes and returns you to the active-session Web page.
- Save As Defaults—Saves the changes so that any new sessions will have the changes incorporated in the active session.
- Load Defaults—Sets the page to the defaults saved previously.
- Load Shipped Defaults—Sets the active session to the defaults for Access for Web as it was shipped from IBM.

We will click Save. When we do so, Access for Web forwards us to the Web page where we can save our configuration settings. We name the session MySession and then again click Save (Figure 14.8).

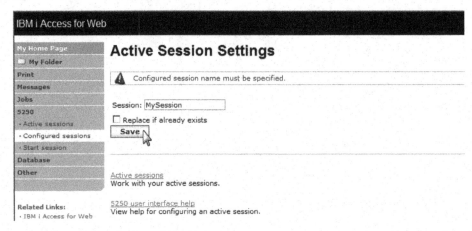

Figure 14.8: Save Active Session Settings

Depending on what changes we have made, or if we have connected to a different system, we might need a more descriptive name. For example, if we have connected to a different system, we would want to include the system name to help us remember what system the session connects to. We might name the session MySession_iSeries1.

We are now at the Web page that we can use to log in to a 5250 session (Figure 14.9). Notice the number of buttons at the bottom of the figure that we can click on. These buttons take the place of function keys or combined keystrokes in a 5250 Telnet session.

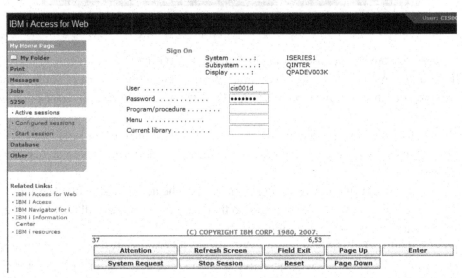

Figure 14.9: Login Screen

When you use the Access for Web 5250 user interface, you can access many of the features that you are familiar with in a 5250 Telnet session. For example, the function keys that you are familiar with in a standard 5250 Telnet session still function.

In Figure 14.10, we are now logged in and at the main menu. You should be aware that if we moved to another Web page, our session would seem to "disappear." Actually it does not close, but you do have to reconnect to it.

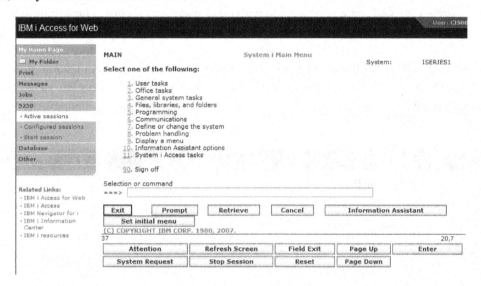

Figure 14.10: System Main Menu

For example, if you want to check your messages and so click the message function on the left side of the Web page, you will need to click 5250 and then Active sessions. You will then see the Active Sessions Web page, as in Figure 14.11.

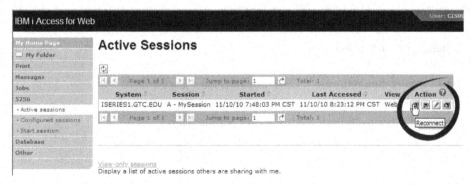

Figure 14.11: Active Sessions Web Page

Your session will need to be reconnected; in the figure, we have highlighted the icon you must click to go to your previous screen. The other three available icons here, with a short description of their functions, are

- *Stop*—Ends the connection to the server. If you are in the middle of the screen, all your data is lost.
- *Edit*—Lets you edit the configuration of the session.
- *Share*—Lets you share your session with other users and groups. These additional sessions are read-only, and no changes can be made or any commands executed.

Our discussion of the 5250 user interface would not be complete without mention of the Configured Sessions Web page you see in Figure 14.12. This page displays any saved sessions you have created; this information is stored on the server and is available from any PC.

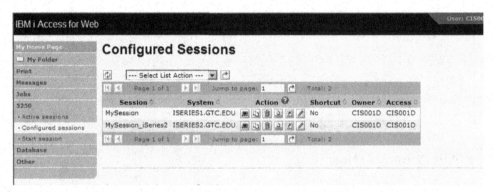

Figure 14.12: Configured Sessions Web Page

As we mentioned earlier, it is important that you give your sessions a meaningful name. Our student user has created two "saved" sessions that connect to two different systems. Note the number of icons to the right of the system name; from left to right, with a short description of each, these icons are as follows:

- *Start*—Starts the configured 5250 user interface session
- *Copy*—Creates a copy of a configured session
- *Delete*—Removes the selected session configuration

- *Rename*—Renames the selected session
- *Create shortcut*—Allows users or groups access to the configured session
- *Edit*—Changes session configuration settings

This short introduction to using the 5250 user interface covers its major features; you will find that the interface is easy to use and has many benefits. For example, one of our favorite features is that clicking on the number next to any item on a system menu is the same as keying in the number and pressing Enter.

Database Function

Chapter 13 gave you a foundation in using the SQL language. There, we introduced SQL and used the Run SQL Scripts interface. You can use the examples and labs we described in that chapter when you are using Access for Web's database functions, which you see in Figure 14.13. Therefore, rather than discuss SQL topics in the next few sections, we will concentrate on how to use this database tool.

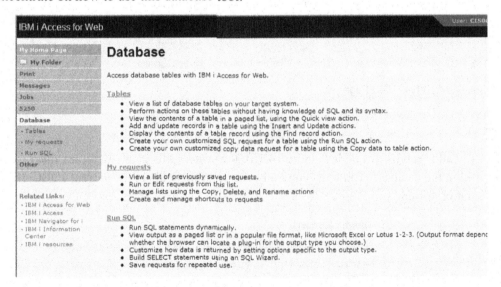

Figure 14.13: Database Function Web Page

Tables

When you click the Tables link, the Tables Web page in Figure 14.14 is displayed. In this example, the administrator has set the table filter to ***USRLIBL** for the CIS001D student user; because this user is not allowed to customize Access for Web, she has access only to tables in her library list. We have circled the actions available to the student user. The following sections introduce each action (from left to right) and provide a screen shot and short description.

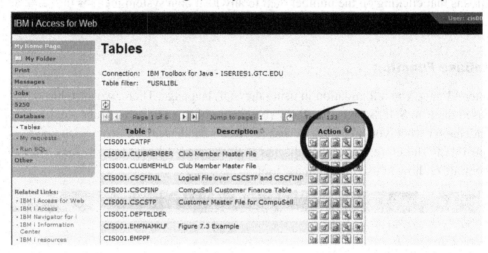

Figure 14.14: Tables Web Page

Insert

When you add records to a table (Figure 14.15), the system fills in any default values described in the database. You must enter any date or time fields in the current JDBC driver configuration format.

Insert Record

To insert a record, specify column values and click Insert Record.

Column	Type	Value	Description
EMPNO	INTEGER (10,0)	0	
LASTNAME	CHAR (16)		
FIRSTNAME	CHAR (12)		
TITLE	CHAR (10)	Mr.	
HOMEPHONE	NUMERIC (7,0)	0	
ADDR1	CHAR (40)		
ADDR2	CHAR (40)		
ZIP	NUMERIC (9,0)	0	
DEPT	CHAR (12)		
WORKPHONE	NUMERIC (7,0)	0	
GENDER	CHAR (1)		
BIRTHDATE	DATE (10)	CURRENT_DAT	
HIREDATE	DATE (10)	CURRENT_DAT	
SALARY	DECIMAL (8,2)	0	

Insert Record

Figure 14.15: Insert a Record

Update

Figure 14.16 displays the first page that results from the Update or delete records action, which lets you to select a record based on a value in any of the fields. In this example, we enter an M in the GENDER field and then click Select Records. **Note:** If you leave the values blank, all the records in the table are returned.

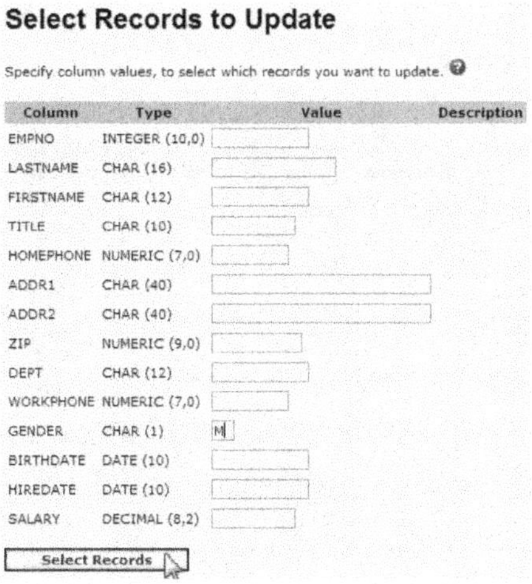

Select Records to Update

Specify column values, to select which records you want to update.

Column	Type	Value	Description
EMPNO	INTEGER (10,0)		
LASTNAME	CHAR (16)		
FIRSTNAME	CHAR (12)		
TITLE	CHAR (10)		
HOMEPHONE	NUMERIC (7,0)		
ADDR1	CHAR (40)		
ADDR2	CHAR (40)		
ZIP	NUMERIC (9,0)		
DEPT	CHAR (12)		
WORKPHONE	NUMERIC (7,0)		
GENDER	CHAR (1)	M	
BIRTHDATE	DATE (10)		
HIREDATE	DATE (10)		
SALARY	DECIMAL (8,2)		

Select Records

Figure 14.16: Select a Record

Figure 14.17 shows the records selected from the EMPPF table with the column GENDER = "M". The two actions available (Update and Delete) are circled.

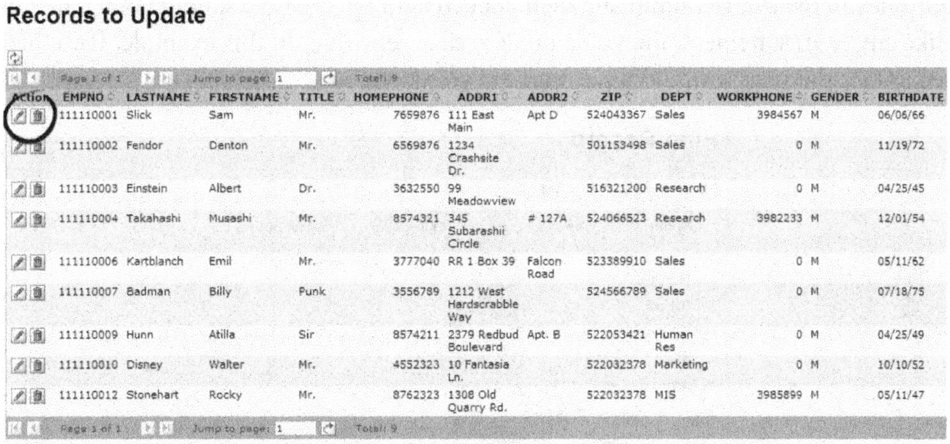

Records to Update

Page 1 of 1 Jump to page: 1 Total: 9

Action	EMPNO	LASTNAME	FIRSTNAME	TITLE	HOMEPHONE	ADDR1	ADDR2	ZIP	DEPT	WORKPHONE	GENDER	BIRTHDATE
	111110001	Slick	Sam	Mr.	7659876	111 East Main	Apt D	524043367	Sales	3984567	M	06/06/66
	111110002	Fendor	Denton	Mr.	6569876	1234 Crashsite Dr.		501153498	Sales	0	M	11/19/72
	111110003	Einstein	Albert	Dr.	3632550	99 Meadowview		516321200	Research	0	M	04/25/45
	111110004	Takahashi	Musashi	Mr.	8574321	345 Subarashii Circle	# 127A	524066523	Research	3982233	M	12/01/54
	111110006	Kartblanch	Emil	Mr.	3777040	RR 1 Box 39	Falcon Road	523389910	Sales	0	M	05/11/62
	111110007	Badman	Billy	Punk	3556789	1212 West Hardscrabble Way		524566789	Sales	0	M	07/18/75
	111110009	Hunn	Atilla	Sir	8574211	2379 Redbud Boulevard	Apt. B	522053421	Human Res	0	M	04/25/49
	111110010	Disney	Walter	Mr.	4552323	10 Fantasia Ln.		522032378	Marketing	0	M	10/10/52
	111110012	Stonehart	Rocky	Mr.	8762323	1308 Old Quarry Rd.		522032378	MIS	3985899	M	05/11/47

Page 1 of 1 Jump to page: 1 Total: 9

Figure 14.17: Update Returned Records

Quick View

The Quick View displays all the records in a table with no update or delete capabilities. This view is handy for quickly scanning data. However, if the table has many records, Quick View is not of much use because the data is not sorted, and you will become frustrated trying to find the record(s) you are looking for. It is much easier to use the Find Record action, which we discuss next.

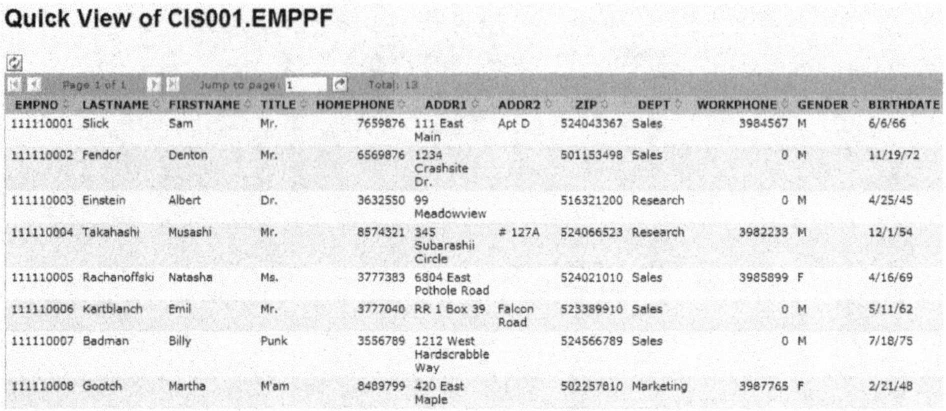

Quick View of CIS001.EMPPF

EMPNO	LASTNAME	FIRSTNAME	TITLE	HOMEPHONE	ADDR1	ADDR2	ZIP	DEPT	WORKPHONE	GENDER	BIRTHDATE
111110001	Slick	Sam	Mr.	7659876	111 East Main	Apt D	524043367	Sales	3984567	M	6/6/66
111110002	Fendor	Denton	Mr.	6569876	1234 Crashsite Dr.		501153498	Sales	0	M	11/19/72
111110003	Einstein	Albert	Dr.	3632550	99 Meadowview		516321200	Research	0	M	4/25/45
111110004	Takahashi	Musashi	Mr.	8574321	345 Subarashii Circle	# 127A	524066523	Research	3982233	M	12/1/54
111110005	Rachanoffski	Natasha	Ms.	3777383	6804 East Pothole Road		524021010	Sales	3985899	F	4/16/69
111110006	Kartblanch	Emil	Mr.	3777040	RR 1 Box 39	Falcon Road	523389910	Sales	0	M	5/11/62
111110007	Badman	Billy	Punk	3556789	1212 West Hardscrabble Way		524566789	Sales	0	M	7/18/75
111110008	Gootch	Martha	M'am	8489799	420 East Maple		502257810	Marketing	3987765	F	2/21/48

Figure 14.18: Update Returned Records Quick View

Find Record

The Find Record option displays the contents of a table record. In Figure 14.19, we have entered Sales in the DEPT column and then clicked Find Record. We should note at this time that, like any SQL statement, the value input is case sensitive. In this example, if we had entered SALES, the search would have returned no records.

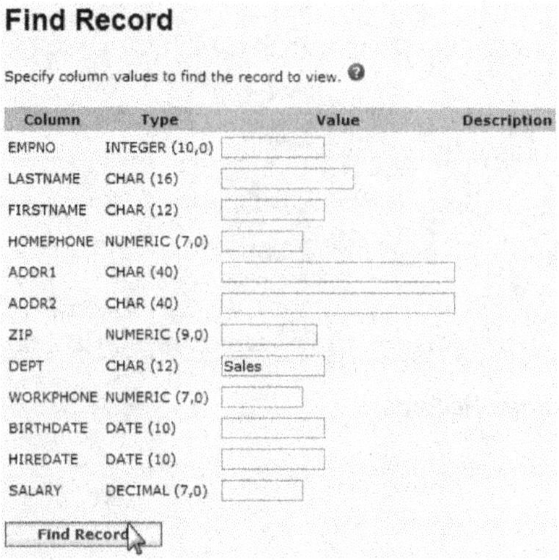

Find Record

Specify column values to find the record to view.

Column	Type	Value	Description
EMPNO	INTEGER (10,0)		
LASTNAME	CHAR (16)		
FIRSTNAME	CHAR (12)		
HOMEPHONE	NUMERIC (7,0)		
ADDR1	CHAR (40)		
ADDR2	CHAR (40)		
ZIP	NUMERIC (9,0)		
DEPT	CHAR (12)	Sales	
WORKPHONE	NUMERIC (7,0)		
BIRTHDATE	DATE (10)		
HIREDATE	DATE (10)		
SALARY	DECIMAL (7,0)		

Find Record

Figure 14.19: Find Record Option

Figure 14.20 shows the results of clicking Find Record. The only action available is to View the record. Clicking this action displays the Column name, Type, Value, and any description associated with a column.

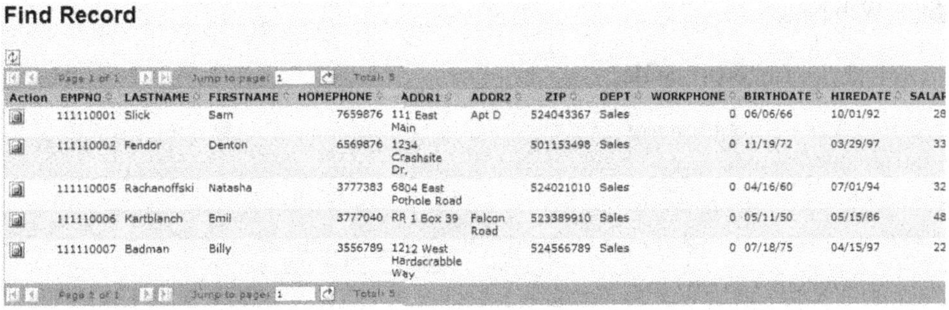

Figure 14.20: Find Record Results

Run SQL

The Run SQL option calls the Run SQL Web page with the SQL statement initialized to SELECT * from the selected table. As you can see in Figure 14.21, when you click this action, you are forwarded to the Run SQL Web page. The SQL Statement window is filled in with an SQL SELECT statement. In the next section, we discuss the Run SQL Web page in detail.

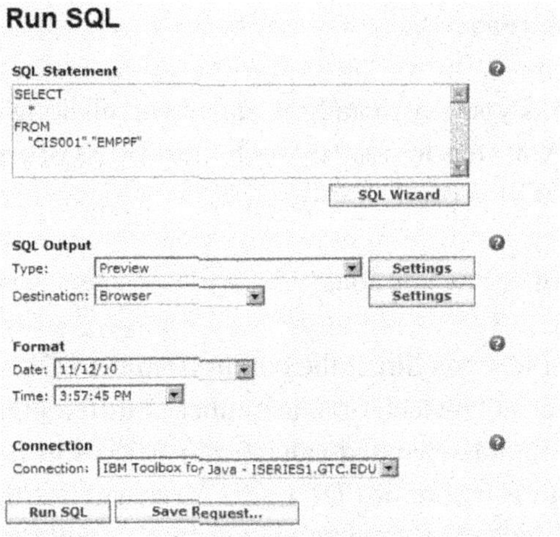

Figure 14.21: Run SQL Option

Run SQL Web Page

The Run SQL function allows the user to create SQL statements and then save the statements and/or save the results of the statements in a number of file formats. Figure 14.22 shows the Run SQL Web page.

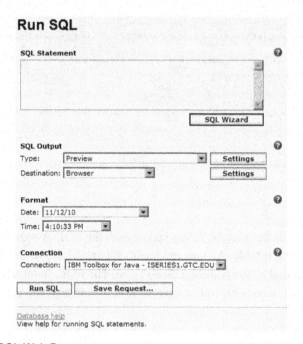

Figure 14.22: Run SQL Web Page

The *SQL Statement* box lets you key in an SQL statement; clicking the SQL Wizard button starts a wizard that takes you step-by-step through the process of creating an SQL statement. We will demonstrate the SQL Wizard shortly.

The *SQL Output* section offers two options:

- The Type parameter lets you direct the output from the SQL select statement to the Web page (if you select Preview) or to a number of different file types. The supported file types include comma-separated value (.csv), Microsoft Excel (.xls), and Adobe **Portable Document Format**, or PDF (.pdf). You can click the Settings button for additional options, depending on the type of file. You will gain experience with the settings in the lab at the end of the chapter.

- The Destination parameter dictates where the results of the SQL statement will go. The default value is Browser, which sends the results to the browser. You also have the option to send the output to the integrated file system or to your personal folder (we will discuss the personal folder toward the end of the chapter).

The *Format* section lets you change the format of dates and times in the columns returned by the SQL statement. The *Connection* section displays the connection type and the system to which you are connected. With the correct authority, you can connect to a system that is not running Access for Web, and you can use SQL statements to return data.

Figure 14.23 shows that we have keyed in an SQL statement that will return all the columns from the SQL schema that we created in Part 1 of the Chapter 13 lab. We also have selected the drop-down box and changed the output Type to Portable Document Format (.pdf).

Note

When using Run SQL, you must use SQL *dotted notation* to specify table names. For example, CIS001SQL.clubmember is a valid table name. The use of just the table name will result in an error.

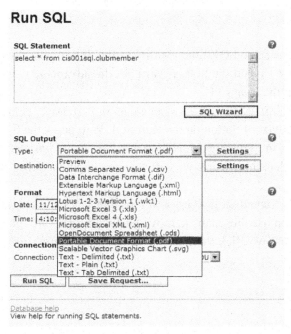

Figure 14.23: Run SQL Web Page, Continued

If we were to click the Run SQL button, Access for Web would run the SQL statement and produce a PDF file like the one in Figure 14.24. Although this report is sufficient for us to look at the data in the table, it would be useless to our users because the table is unsorted and the formatting is inappropriate. In the next section, we will use the SQL Wizard to create a usable report.

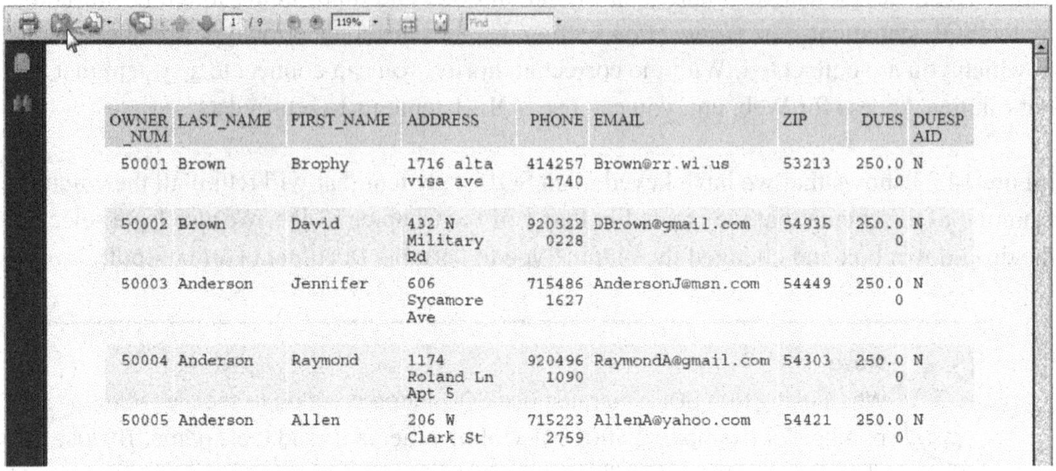

OWNER _NUM	LAST_NAME	FIRST_NAME	ADDRESS	PHONE	EMAIL	ZIP	DUES	DUESP AID
50001	Brown	Brophy	1716 alta visa ave	414257 1740	Brown@rr.wi.us	53213	250.0 0	N
50002	Brown	David	432 N Military Rd	920322 0228	DBrown@gmail.com	54935	250.0 0	N
50003	Anderson	Jennifer	606 Sycamore Ave	715486 1627	AndersonJ@msn.com	54449	250.0 0	N
50004	Anderson	Raymond	1174 Roland Ln Apt 5	920496 1090	RaymondA@gmail.com	54303	250.0 0	N
50005	Anderson	Allen	206 W Clark St	715223 2759	AllenA@yahoo.com	54421	250.0 0	N

Figure 14.24: Run SQL results PDF file

SQL Wizard

The SQL Wizard has the same SQL functionality as the SQL Assist/Prompt tool that we worked with in Chapter 13. But the SQL Wizard has the advantage that you do not have to install any software on the user's PC.

After we click the SQL Wizard button on the Run SQL Web page, the SQL Wizard Web page is displayed, as you see in Figure 14.25. Notice that the wizard has started to write our SQL statement; as we complete the wizard, we will see our statement being written.

Directly under the SQL statement is a series of tabs that you progress through as you use the wizard. You also can use these tabs to move back and forth through the wizard to make changes or skip sections. We click Next, as the arrow in the figure shows.

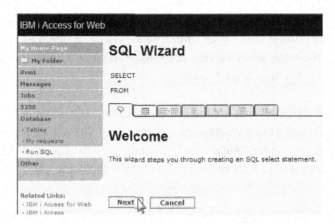

Figure 14.25: SQL Wizard Web Page

If we know the table and its location, the page in Figure 14.26 lets us enter the schema and table in **SQL dotted notation** (i.e., in the format Schema.table). In this example, we click Find, as shown in the figure, to have Access for Web guide us through the process of selecting the table.

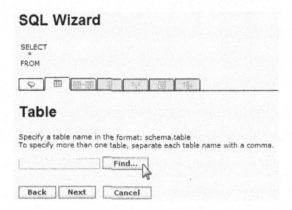

Figure 14.26: SQL Wizard—Table Web Page

Figure 14.27 shows the Find Table Web page presented by the wizard.

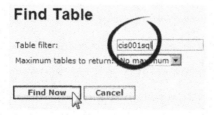

Figure 14.27: SQL Wizard—Find Table Web Page

The default for the Table Filter parameter is *USRLIBL; this value will display all the schemas and tables in the user portion of the user's library list. We have keyed in the schema (CIS001SQL) where the table for this example exists. You should remember the CLUBMEMBER table from Chapter 13. We then click Find Now.

Figure 14.28 reports the tables that are located in the CIS001SQL schema. We are going to create a report based on the CLUBMEMBER table, so we click CIS001SQL.CLUBMEMBER in the Tables list and then click OK. **Note:** The list of tables in this figure might differ from what is in your schema, but you should have the CLUBMEMBER and CITYSTATE tables from Chapter 13.

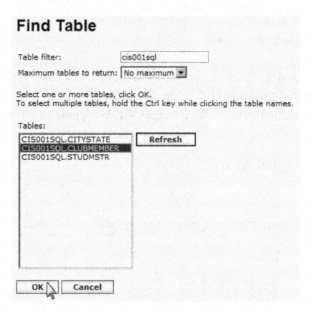

Figure 14.28: SQL Wizard—Find Table Web Page, Continued

The wizard now returns us to the Table Web page. In Figure 14.29, it shows us an updated SELECT statement and has moved to the second tab. To continue creating our SELECT statement, we click Next.

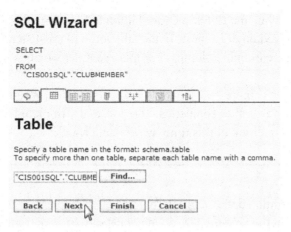

Figure 14.29: SQL Wizard—Table Web Page

We come now to the Columns Web page, where we choose the fields we want on our report. As you can see in Figure 14.30, we select the LAST_NAME, FIRST_NAME, EMAIL, and ZIP columns.

SQL Wizard

SELECT
*
FROM
"CIS001SQL"."CLUBMEMBER"

Columns

Select which columns to include. If no columns are selected, all columns ar

Column	Description	Heading
☐ OWNER_NUM	Member Number	Column name ▼
☑ LAST_NAME	Last Name	Column name ▼
☑ FIRST_NAME	First Name	Column name ▼
☐ ADDRESS	Address	Column name ▼
☐ PHONE	Phone	Column name ▼
☑ EMAIL	Email	Column name ▼
☑ ZIP	ZIp Code	Column name ▼
☐ DUES		Column name ▼
☐ DUESPAID		Column name ▼

To change the order in which columns are included, click Column Order.

Column Order

Back   Next   Finish   Cancel

Figure 14.30: SQL Wizard—Columns Web Page

At this point, we could click the Column Order button to rearrange the order of the columns that are displayed on our report. In the lab, you will create a report, and one of the requirements will be to rearrange columns. For this example, we click Next.

The Condition Web page (Figure 14.31) would allow us to add a Where clause to our report. In the lab, you will create a rather sophisticated report that will include a Where clause. We will bypass creating a condition at this time by selecting Next.

Note
The Condition option lets you "hard code" a condition or prompt the user for a value at the time the SQL statement is run. This sophistication enables you to create reports for which users can enter their own parameters when they run the SQL statement.

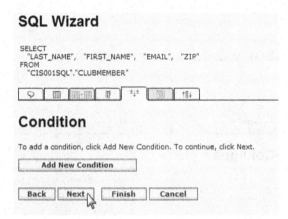

Figure 14.31: SQL Wizard—Condition Web Page

When we click Next, we are forwarded to the Sort Web page (Figure 14.32), which lets us set the Order By criteria for our SELECT statement. The figure shows that we have selected the LAST_NAME and FIRST_NAME columns for our sort. We should also point out that we can select whether the fields are sorted in Ascending or Descending order on this page. After we select the desired columns, we click Sort Order.

Figure 14.32: SQL Wizard—Sort Web Page

The Sort Order Web page displayed in Figure 14.33 is reminiscent of setting the sort order in Query for i5/OS, which we discussed in Chapter 7. The sort order happens to be the default for these two fields because of their order in the previous Web page.

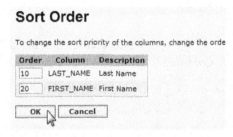

Figure 14.33: SQL Wizard—Change Sort Order Web Page

If we had multiple columns in the wrong order for our sort, we would enter numbers in ascending order based on the sort order we wanted. The Wizard would re-sequence the columns based on these numbers.

Once we are satisfied with the order, we click OK.

We have now completed our SQL statement using the SQL Wizard. The completed SQL statement is displayed (Figure 14.34). At this time we could click any of the tabs and make any needed changes to our statement. We are satisfied with our efforts, so we will click Finish.

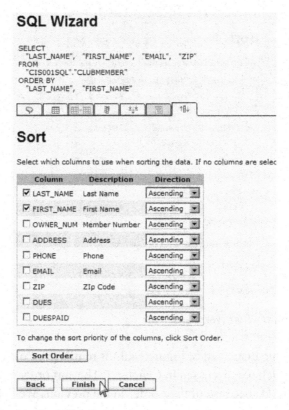

Figure 14.34: SQL Wizard—Sort Web Page

Figure 14.35 shows the "completion" Web page that verifies that the SQL statement creation was completed properly. We click Continue to complete the wizard.

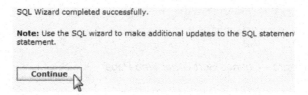

Figure 14.35: SQL Wizard—Completion Web Page

With that, we are returned to the Run SQL Web page (Figure 14.36). For now, we will not make any changes to the SQL Output section of the page. Instead, we will click the Run SQL button to see the results of our efforts, as shown in the figure.

Figure 14.36: Run SQL Web Page—Run SQL Statement

After we click Run SQL, Access for Web runs the SQL statement we created using the Wizard. Then it displays the SQL Output Web page you see in Figure 14.37.

Figure 14.37: Run SQL—Output Web Page

The results of the SQL statement are displayed here, and you can see that the fields are listed and the output is sorted in the correct order. To return to the Run SQL Web page, we would click the Back button on our browser. It is important to remember that if we were to click the Run SQL link on the left of the Web page, we would lose our SQL statement. In the next section, we will show how to save the SQL statement so that we can run or edit it later.

My Requests

The My Requests Web page lets you run and manage the SQL statements and reports you have created. Before saving our SQL statement, we will make two changes to the SQL Output section of the Web page. First, we will change the Type parameter to create a PDF file from the SQL statement output. Second, we will change the output destination to Personal Folder.

There are three options to direct the output of SQL statements; these options, with a short description of each, are

- Browser—This output destination can be used only when the Type is Preview. Control is not returned to the browser until the SQL statement has been completed.
- Integrated File System (IFS)—Output is stored in a folder in the IFS. A status message that contains completion information about the request is sent to the user's personal folder. Control is immediately returned to the browser because the SQL statement runs in the background.
- Personal folder—Output is stored in the user's Access for Web personal folder. Control is returned to the browser, and the SQL statement runs in the background.

As Figure 14.30 shows, after we have made the changes discussed above, we click Save Request.

Figure 14.38: Run SQL Web Page—Save Request

We are forwarded to the Save Request Web page (Figure 14.39), where we name the request and enter a description for future reference. Throughout this book, we have emphasized the importance of entering descriptions when you create an object (e.g., file, program, query); as in the past, doing so is equally important here. As you continue to create objects, including descriptions that reference the functions will save you time and frustration. After we enter a request name and description, we press Save Request.

Save Request

Request name:	ListClubMemberTable
Description:	Lists table by Lastname by Firstname

☐ Replace if already exists

Save Request

Figure 14.39: Save Request Web Page

Figure 14.40 shows the Save Request confirmation Web page and related options.

Figure 14.40: Save Request Web Page

We click the My requests link here, which forwards us to the My Requests Web page you see in Figure 14.41.

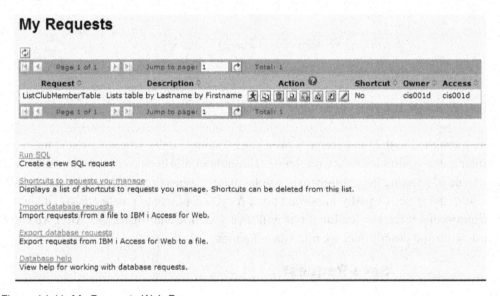

Figure 14.41: My Requests Web Page

The My Requests Web page displays a list of requests and several options, including a link to the Run SQL Web page. Some of these options are beyond the scope of this text, but the Access for Web Help text covers them in detail.

A number of actions are available for working with saved requests. These actions, as shown from left to right, are as follows:

- Run—Used to execute a saved SQL statement.
- Copy—Creates a copy of the SQL statement; any changes to the original SQL statement are not picked up by this copy.
- Delete—Deletes the saved request and any shortcuts created that are associated with the request.

- Rename—Renames a database request or shortcut. Renaming the shortcut does not affect the original saved request.
- Create automated task—Creates a Java archive (.jar) that can be used to run an Access for Web database request from another system. A discussion of this feature is beyond the scope of this text; however, you can find detailed information in the Access for Web Help system.
- Transfer—Transfers ownership of the saved request to or from a group profile. This transfer allows management of the request by multiple system profiles.
- Create shortcut—A shortcut allows the request to be shared with other users and groups on the system.
- Edit—Used to edit a saved request. Shortcuts cannot be edited.

Print

In Chapter 4, we discussed the IBM i OS printing process in detail. To avoid rehashing the content of that chapter, it suffices to say that all the options available from the 5250 command line also are available using Access for Web. The Print function includes options for working with printers and output queues. These options are well documented and allow the management of printers (e.g., starting, stopping) and output queues (e.g., holding, clearing).

We will now discuss some of the additional features available when you use Access for Web. In Figure 14.42, you can see that the Print Web page shows all the options for this function in the column on the left. We will click the Printer output link.

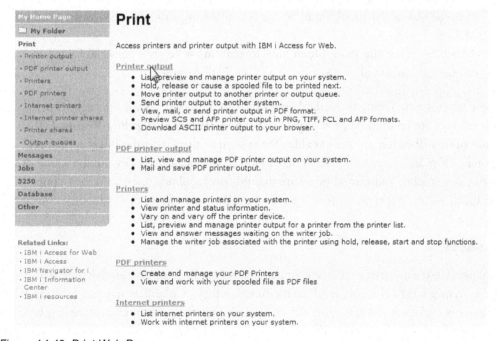

Figure 14.42: Print Web Page

The Printer Output Web page (Figure 14.43) is very similar to the WRKSPLF command screen. Some additional printer output options not available with WRKSPLF include the capability to convert spool files to various formats and to select when the spool files are displayed. The files are displayed as they will be printed.

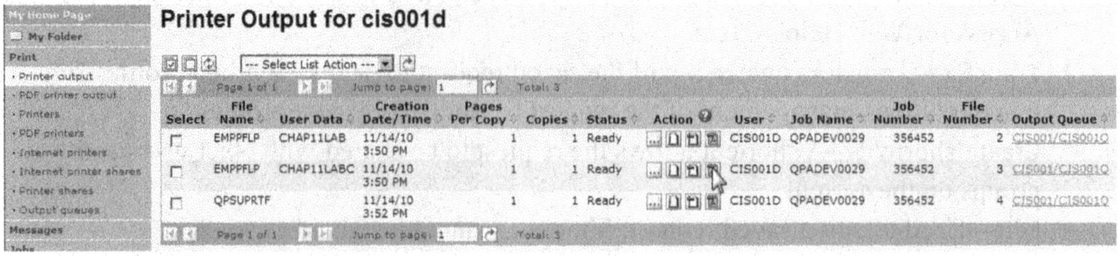

Figure 14.43: Printer Output Web Page

Following is a list of the actions available on this Web page (from left to right), including a short description of each:

- Work with—Work with management functions, which include moving spool files to another printer or output queue, moving to another system using the **SNDTCPSPLF** (Send TCP/IP Spooled File), changing attributes with the CHGSPLFA (Change Spool File Attributes) command, or copying spool file contents to a database using the **CPYSPLF** (Copy Spooled File) command.
- View—View the print file using the preferred format set under *Preferences*. On our system, the administrator has set this value to PDF.
- View As—View the spool file in one of the following formats: PNG, TIFF, PCL, or AFP.
- View PDF—View the spool file in PDF format; move to your personal folder or another out queue; allows saving to a PC in PDF format.

You use the other two options available in Figure 14.42 to work with *Internet printers*. These printers are configured on the system using the **Internet Printing Protocol** (IPP). The use of this IP-based protocol enables the system to print over the Internet hundreds or thousands of miles away. An in-depth discussion of IPP printing is beyond the scope of this text, but as a student you should be aware that this protocol provides for access control, authentication, and encryption, which allows the IBM i system to print globally if necessary.

Messages

In Chapter 10, we discussed message management (sending, receiving, deleting, and viewing) using IBM i Navigator. All of the functionality available when you're using IBM i Navigator is included in Access for Web. Although in Access the functions are displayed in a Web interface and arranged differently (see Figure 14.44), users should become acclimated quickly to managing messages. As a result, we feel there is no need for an in-depth discussion of message handling using Access for Web.

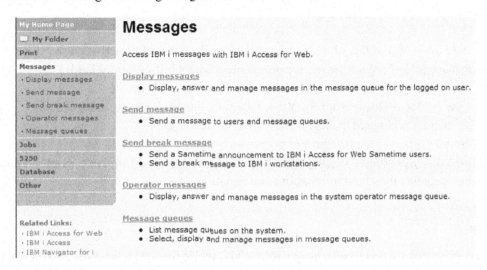

Figure 14.44: Messages Web Page

Jobs

Access for Web is not an administration tool, but a user's interface to the IBM i OS. As a result, it does not have the robust capability to manage jobs that using 5250 command-line CL commands or IBM i Navigator does. The Jobs function includes the basic actions users require to manage their jobs; as you see in Figure 14.45, it contains two areas:

- The *Jobs* section lists IBM i OS jobs (e.g., interactive, batch).
- The *Server jobs* section lists host server jobs running for the current user.

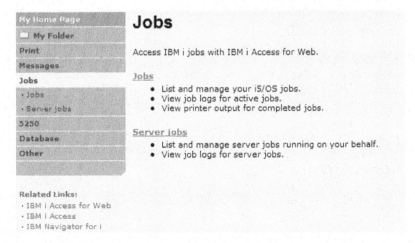

Figure 14.45: Jobs Web Page

The actions available for the Jobs and Server jobs sections are the same, with the exception of Printer output, which is not available for the Server jobs section. The available actions, with a short description of each, are

- Hold job—Makes the job inactive; available only if the job is active on the system
- Release job—Enables the job for processing if the job is currently held
- Delete/end job—Ends the job; available only if the job is active
- View job log—Displays information, including the job ID, type, date, text, and severity of all logged messages; available for active jobs
- Printer output—Displays printer output from a job
- View job properties—Displays job properties, including performance, printer output, message handling, and international information

Other

As a student user, two sections are available to you under the Other function, as you see in Figure 14.46. The *Change password* section lets you change your passwords just as if you had typed the **CHGPWD** (Change Password) CL command at a 5250 command line.

The *About* section displays information about Access for Web, including Product Information, Request Information, Web Properties, IBM i Toolbox for Java Properties, Connection Pool Settings, and System Properties. A detailed discussion of this section is beyond the scope of this book.

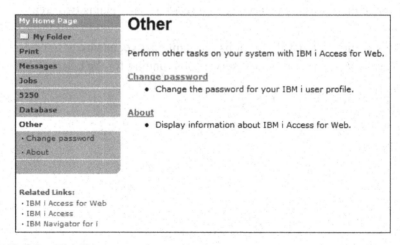

Figure 14.46: Other Web Page

In Summary

We began this chapter with an overview of the functions available to you when you use IBM i Access for Web. We then described how to use the 5250 user interface to access the system and how to modify the active 5250 session and then save the session for use later. Access for Web is a well-documented, easy-to-use interface to the system that can save companies IT expense through reduced user-training costs, less maintenance on user workstations, and lower administration costs.

We described the Tables function and gave examples of using the Insert, Update, Quick View, and Find Record actions. We also described the Run SQL function and the options available, including the SQL Wizard, which provides a step-by-step process that enables someone new to SQL to create fairly sophisticated query reports. The SQL Wizard function allows field selection, sorting, table joining, and even hardcoded or runtime use of conditions. The output from the Run SQL tool can be displayed in the browser or in a number of different file formats, including .csv, .html, .xls, .ods, and .pdf.

We continued our discussion about additional features available, including the print features. When working with printer files, the user is able to convert these files to a number of different file formats.

Key Terms

*USRLIBL	Internet Printing Protocol
CHGPWD	personal folder
code page	Portable Document Format
CPYSPLF	SNDTCPSPLF
function menu	SQL dotted notation
integrated file system (IFS)	system parameter

Review Questions

1. Compare the Access for Web functions available to the administrator and the typical user. Why should some of the functions not be available to the typical user? (Use the Access for Web Help system if necessary to complete your responses.)

2. How can using Access for Web simplify administration and reduce costs?

3. To open a 5250 session or to access data on another system, is it necessary for the remote system to be running Access for Web?

4. What is the function of the Code page parameter?

5. Explain the difference between the *Web view* and the *Traditional view* when you are using an Access for Web 5250 session.

6. List and explain five settings available in the Active Session Settings Web page. (Use the Access for Web Help system if necessary.)

7. Explain the difference between the Load Defaults and Load Shipped Defaults buttons on the Active Sessions Settings Web page.

8. Why is it important to use descriptive names when you are saving a 5250 session?

9. Explain how you "reconnect" to an active 5250 session after you move to another Web page.

10. When you share a 5250 session, what can other users do with your shared session?

11. List and explain the actions you have available when you are working with "saved" sessions.

12. List and explain the actions available to our student user in the Tables Web page.

13. When you are using the Find table action, what information is displayed when you click the View action?

14. List and explain the options available in the *SQL Output* section of the Run SQL Web page.

15. List three file types (not discussed in the text) to which the results of the SQL statement can be output.

16. After you run an SQL statement, why is it important to click the browser's Back button instead of clicking Run SQL from the function menu?

17. Three options are available to control the destination of output from an SQL statement. List and describe these options.

18. What is the purpose of Internet printers when you are using Access for Web?

19. List and describe the options available when you are working with jobs.

Lab 14

Introduction

The four labs in this chapter let you practice topics we covered in this chapter. In Part 1, you will start an active session, make changes to the session, and then save it as a configured session. In Part 2, you will use the Update action to add rows to the CLUBMEMBER and CITYSTATE tables. In Part 3, you will create a Join SQL statement using the CLUBMEMBER and

CITYSTATE tables and then save this SQL statement in My Requests. In Part 4, you will copy the request you saved in Part 3 and then add a zip code condition that will be prompted each time the request is run.

Note

You should have the CLUBMEMBER and CITYSTATE tables in your current library to complete this lab. You have learned several ways to copy tables from one area to another; now would be a good time to practice this skill. The current library of our student user is CIS001.

Part 1

Goals   Start a 5250 session, change the properties of the session, and save the session.

Start   Logged in to your system using IBM i Access for Web.

Procedure   Access the 5250 function.

Access the Start Session link.

Click the Start Session button.

Click the Active session settings link.

Change the parameters to Show active settings.

Change Traditional view and Web view session parameters.

Save the session as a configured session.

14.1.   Access the 5250 function by clicking the correct link.

14.2.   Click the Start Session link.

14.3.   Click the Start Session button.

14.4.   Click the Active session settings link.

14.5.   Change the Traditional view and Web view parameters to Show active settings. Doing this will show you an active session running.

14.6.   Change the parameter for the Traditional view so the function keys are not displayed.

Change the "traditional" background color to Yellow, and change the foreground colors White to Silver and Green to Black. Your completed session should look like the one in Figure 14.47.

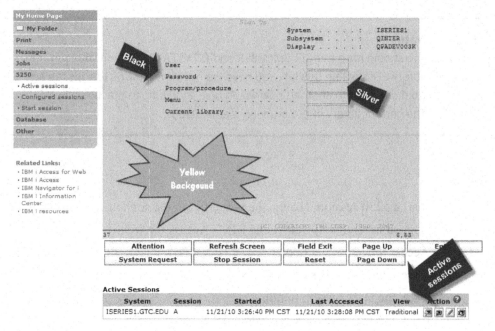

Figure 14.47: Changed Active Session

14.7.   Save the session as a configured session with the name Lab14Session.

Create a shortcut for this session using your instructor's user profile (System ID). To do so, click the Shortcut action, as Figure 14.48 demonstrates.

Figure 14.48: Create a Session Shortcut

After you click the Shortcut action, you are forwarded to the Create Shortcut Web page, where you can change the name of the shortcut or allow access to the shortcut by another user.

Add your instructor's system ID to the Access parameter, and then click Create Shortcut, as you see in Figure 14.49.

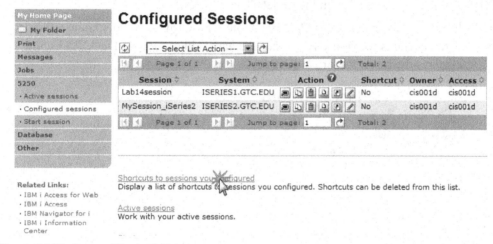

Figure 14.49: Name the Shortcut

You are returned to the Configured Sessions Web page (Figure 14.50); if you click the Shortcuts to sessions you configured link, you can see the shortcut you just created. Do not delete this shortcut; your instructor will use it to evaluate this lab.

Figure 14.50: Access Shortcut List

Part 2

Goals   Add records to the CLUBMEMBER and CITYSTATE tables.

Start   Logged in to your system using IBM i Access for Web.

Procedure   Access the Database function.

                Access the Tables section.

                Click the Insert action on the CLUBMEMBER table.

                Insert four rows in the CLUBMEMBER table.

                Insert the required zip code information in the CITYSTATE table.

14.8. Access the Database function.

14.9. Access the Tables section, and then locate the CLUBMEMBER table in your current library, as you see in Figure 14.51.

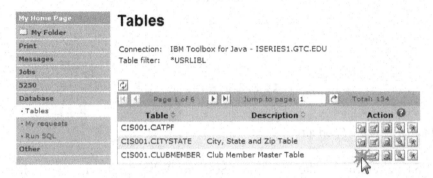

Figure 14.51: Tables Web Page

14.10. Click the Insert action on the CLUBMEMBER table.

14.11. Insert four rows in the CLUBMEMBER table. These rows should contain valid data with zip codes for your city. Do not use names like "Donald Duck."☺ Figure 14.52 displays the Insert Record Web page.

Figure 14.52: Insert Record Web Page

14.12. Locate the CITYSTATE table in your current library. Insert the required zip code information in the CITYSTATE table. Insert the necessary zip code entry in the table.

Use the table Find action to find the records you added to the table.

Ask your instructor whether you should do a print screen of the Find results.

Part 3

Goals   Create an SQL Join statement using the SQL Wizard. This join will allow you to display the CITY and STATE fields from the CITYSTATE table. Save the SQL statement as a saved request. Run the saved request.

Start   Logged in to your system using Access for Web.

Procedure   Access the Database function.

Access the Run SQL section.

Access the SQL Wizard.

Create an SQL statement joining the CLUBMEMBER and CITYSTATE tables.

Select the required fields to display.

Sort the joined tables.

Change the display options.

Save the SQL statement.

Display the My Requests Web page.

Run the saved request.

Display the output from My Folder.

14.13. To access the Database function, click the Database link on the left side of the Access for Web Web page.

14.14. To access the *Run SQL* section, click the Run SQL link on the Access for Web Database Web page.

To access the SQL Wizard, click the SQL Wizard button.

14.15. Now you will create an SQL statement joining the CLUBMEMBER and CITYSTATE tables.

On the first SQL Wizard screen, click Next. On the resulting Table Web page, click Find.

14.16. On the Find Table Web page, enter the schema you created in Part 1 of Lab 13. Then click Find Now, as in Figure 14.53.

Note
The screen examples for this chapter use our student schema CIS001SQL. You need to substitute your schema.

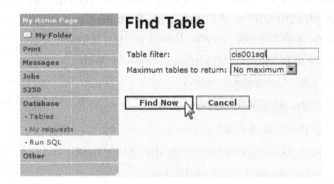

Figure 14.53: Find Tables in the CIS001SQL Schema

On the Find Table Web page, hold the Ctrl key as you click the CITYSTATE and CLUBMEMBER tables; doing this will select both tables. Click OK to go to the next Web page, as Figure 14.54 shows.

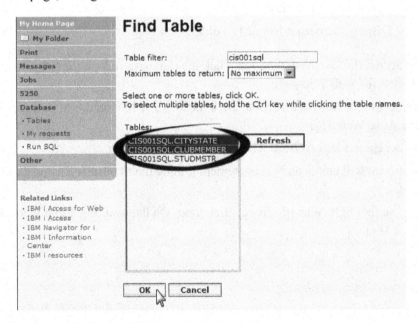

Figure 14.54: Select the Required Tables

No changes are required on this page (SQL Wizard). Notice in Figure 14.55 that the wizard has started to write the SQL statement required for joining the two tables. Click Next.

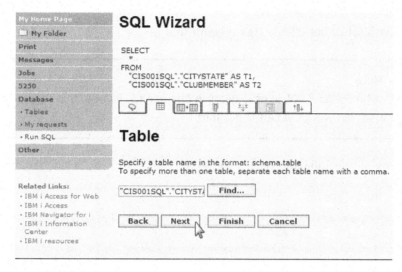

Figure 14.55: Click Next

On the resulting Join Web page, click Join Tables, as in Figure 14.56.

Figure 14.56: Click Join Tables

On the resulting Join Type Web page (see Figure 14.57, which shows a portion of this page), there are seven types of joins for you to select from. Notice that the join types are explained here; this documentation helps SQL novices to decide the type of join they want to use.

You will select the LEFT OUTER type for this lab.

Note

We discussed SQL joins in detail in Chapter 13. Refer to this chapter if you need to review the Left Outer Join.

After you select the join type, click Next.

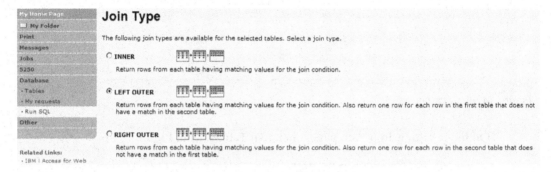

Figure 14.57: Select the Join Type

It is important that you select the correct table on the resulting Web page. The "first" table will be the "left" table in the completed SQL statement. Select the radio button to the left of the CLUBMEMBER table, as in Figure 14.58.

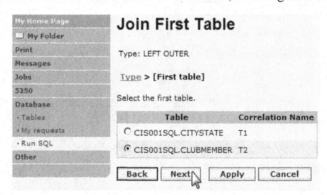

Figure 14.58: Select the "First" Table

The "second" table will be the CITYSTATE table, which contains the CITY and STATE information you want to display on your completed report. After you select the CITYSTATE table, click Next, as in Figure 14.59.

Figure 14.59: Select the "Second" Table

Next, you need to set a condition for the join. Click Add New Condition, as in Figure 14.60.

Figure 14.60: Add a Condition to Join the Two Tables

Figure 14.61 shows the columns in the CLUBMEMBER table. Select the radio button for the T2.ZIP column; then click Next.

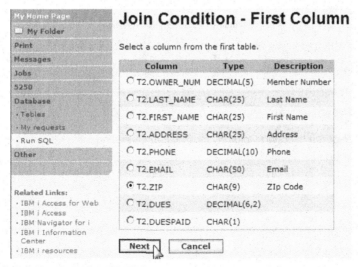

Figure 14.61: Select Zip Field CLUBMEMBER Table

The join requires that the zip code fields in both tables be equal. So select the Exactly equal to radio button; then click Next, as in Figure 14.62.

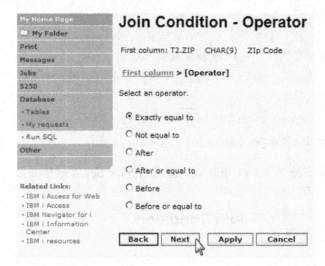

Figure 14.62: Select the Condition Operator

Figure 14.63 displays the columns from the CITYSTATE table. Select the radio button next to the T1.ZIP column. You have now completed the condition that needed to be set up to complete the join, so click Finish Edit.

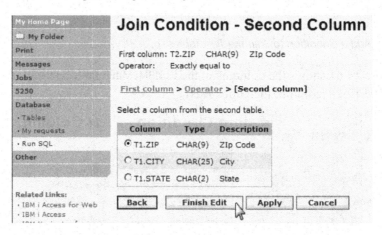

Figure 14.63: Select the "Second Column" for the Join Operation

The Join Condition Web page is now displayed (Figure 14.64), showing the completed join condition. If you needed to add another condition or join additional tables, you could add additional conditions at this time. Click Finish Edit.

Figure 14.64: Finish the Join Condition

The SQL Wizard Web page is now displayed (Figure 14.65), showing the updated SQL statement, including the join. Click Next to continue.

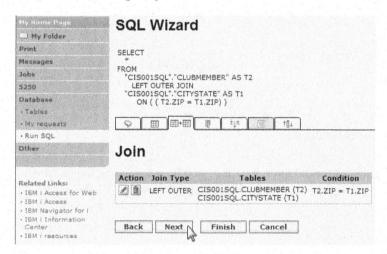

Figure 14.65: Completed Join

On the Columns Web page (Figure 14.66), select the fields to be displayed. You will need to change the order of the fields for this report. To do so, click Column Order.

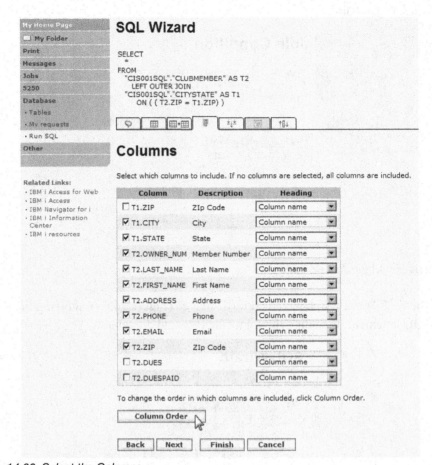

Figure 14.66: Select the Columns

In the text of this chapter, we discussed how to change the order of the fields. Change the column order as you see it in Figure 14.67. Press OK.

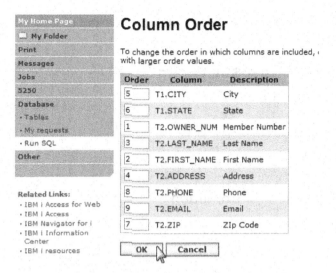

Figure 14.67: Select the Order in Which Columns Will Be Displayed

Figure 14.68 shows the columns in the correct order for the report. Click Next, as shown.

Figure 14.68: Select the Columns to Display

Figure 14.69 shows the resulting Condition Web page for this lab; once again, click Next.

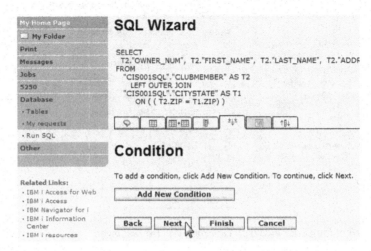

Figure 14.69: Click Next

14.17. Sort the joined tables (see Figure 14.70).

The report needs to be sorted by the LAST_NAME and then the FIRST_NAME fields. Click the check boxes to the left of the T2.LAST_NAME and the T2.FIRST_NAME columns. The fields are listed in the order you want them sorted. If you needed to change the sort order, you would click the Sort Order button.

Click Finish when you are done.

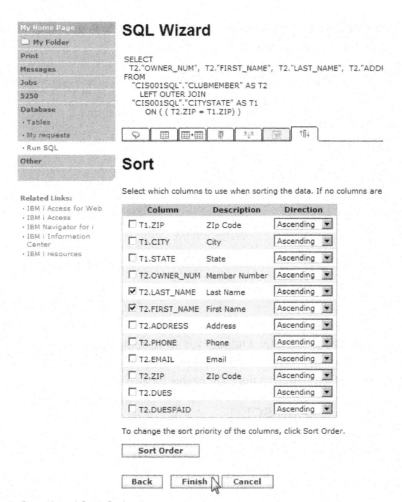

Figure 14.70: Completed Sort Order

The SQL Wizard completion Web page (Figure 14.71) is displayed. Click Continue here to return to the main Run SQL Web page.

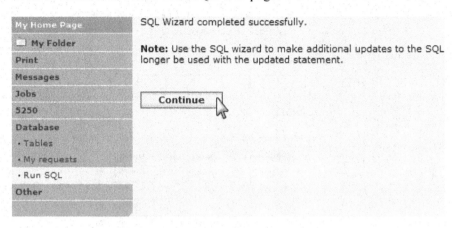

Figure 14.71: Wizard Completion Message

14.18. You will now change the display options (Figure 14.72). Two changes are in order here. First, change the SQL Output Type to Portable Document Format (.pdf); second, change the Destination to Personal folder. After making these changes, click the Settings button to the right of the Type parameter.

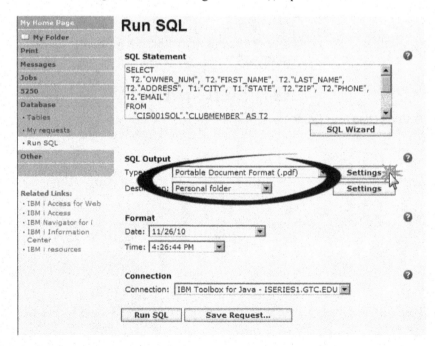

Figure 14.72: Change Display Options

The Portable Document Format Output Settings Web page is now displayed (Figure 14.73). Here, you configure settings specific to the PDF file that will be created when you run this request.

Make three changes to the PDF settings, as follows:

a. Change the Page Label text to display Date, time, page number.

b. Change the Table Header text to display Listing of CLUBMASTER table by Lastname By Firstname.

c. Change the Table Footer text to display Chapter 14 Lab Part 4 Join CLUBMASTER and CITYSTATE Tables.

After making these changes, click OK to return to the main Run SQL Web page in Figure 14.74.

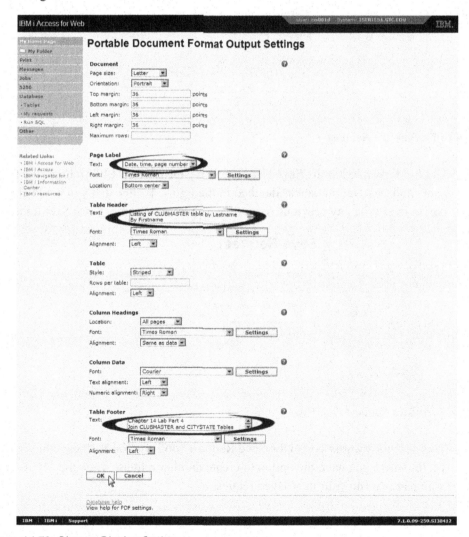

Figure 14.73: Change Display Options

You will now save the SQL statement as a request. To do so, click Save Request.

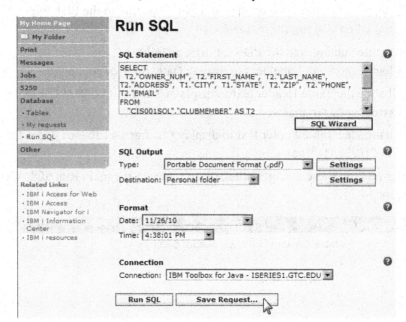

Figure 14.74: Save the Request

You are forwarded to the Save Request Web page (Figure 14.75). Enter the Request name and Description data as detailed in the figure. Notice that you could check the box to overwrite any previous requests with the same name. Click Save Request.

Figure 14.75: Save Request Web Page

This action forwards you to the Save Request confirmation Web page in Figure 14.76, where you have the option to create another request, view the My Requests Web page, or run your new saved request.

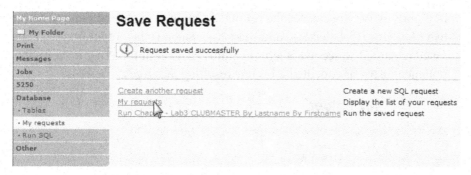

Figure 14.76: Save Request Confirmation Web Page

14.19. Click the My Requests link. The My Requests Web page is displayed and shows your newly created saved request (Figure 14.77).

14.20. Click the Run action, as the figure demonstrates.

Figure 14.77: My Requests Web Page

You are then forwarded to the Run SQL Request Web page (Figure 14.78); here, you are notified that the results of the request will be placed in your personal folder.

14.21. Click the My Folder link.

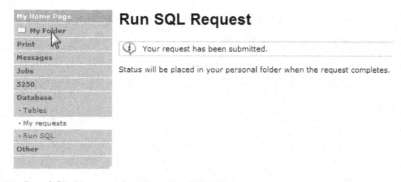

Figure 14.78: Run SQL Request Confirmation Web Page

In Figure 14.79, you can see the results of running your saved request. There are two files. One is labeled SQL output in PDF, which is the output from running your saved request. The second is labeled Status [SQL output in PDF]; it shows the SQL statement that was executed, plus any resulting messages.

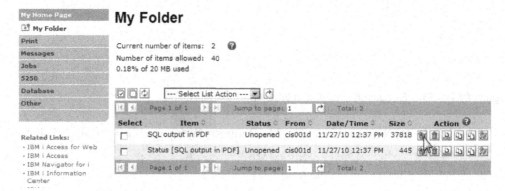

Figure 14.79: My Folder Web Page

We will not go into details regarding the actions available on this Web page; by now, you should be familiar enough with the product for our purposes.

Click the Open action, as Figure 14.79 shows (note the arrow).

Figure 14.80 displays the printer output from your saved request. The total report is nine pages long; and, as you can see, the heading and footer text you entered is displayed.

Listing of CLUBMASTER table by Lastname By Firstname

OWNER_NUM	FIRST_NAME	LAST_NAME	ADDRESS	CITY	STATE	ZIP	PHONE	EMAIL
16135	Mihaly	Anderson	3508 Hunters Glen Rd	Artois	CA	90702	2035541 28	Anderson@yahoo.com
16145	Ivan	Clark	4915 Schewn RD	Ventura	CA	90554	9254521548	Clark@hotmail.com

Pages deleted for display purposes

| 42059 | Daniel | Yamamoto | 3171 Williamsbu rg Rd. | Ann Arbor | MI | 48108 | 7349735555 | happysad10987@yah oo.com |
| 16152 | Thomas | Young | 3320 Tqurus Dr | Orange County | CA | 90255 | 2653595645 | Young@ca.rr.com |

Chapter 14 Lab Part 4
Join CLUBMASTER and CITYSTATE Tables

11/27/10 12:37:30 PM Page 9

Figure 14.80: PDF Printer Output Displayed

Part 4

Goals   Copy the request you created in Part 3 to a new request. Add a condition to the request that would allow the user to enter a zip code to create a report that shows club members in a specific zip code.

Start   Logged in to your system using Access for Web, and at the My Requests Web page.

Procedure   Copy your saved request from Part 3.

Edit your new request.

Add a new condition to the request.

Save the request.

Run the request.

Display the output.

14.22. Copy your saved request from Part 3 of the lab.

Click the Copy action, as Figure 14.81 shows.

Figure 14.81: Copy a Saved Request

Figure 14.82 displays the Copy Request Web page. Name the new request Chap14 - Lab4 CLUBMASTER By Lastname By Firstname.

Figure 14.82: Copy a Saved Request, Continued

Then click Copy Request, which forwards you to the My Requests Web page you see in Figure 14.83.

14.23. Now, you will edit your new request. Click the Edit action, as you see in Figure 14.83.

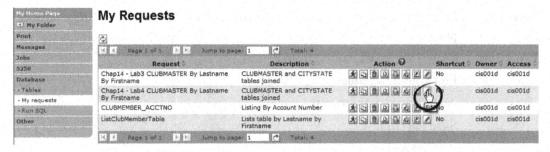

Figure 14.83: Edit a New Saved Request

14.24. You will now add a new condition to the request from the resulting Edit SQL Request Web page (Figure 14.84). Click SQL Wizard on this page.

Caution

Notice that the completed SQL statement that we created in an earlier lab is displayed. Any changes to this statement will result in the statement being "lost" to the wizard. If you decide you need to change the SQL statement, do so through the wizard and not by editing the SQL statement.

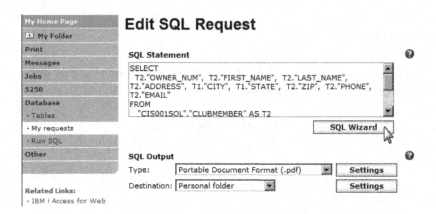

Figure 14.84: Start SQL Wizard

Click the Condition tab on the wizard's Welcome Web page, as you see in
Figure 14.85.

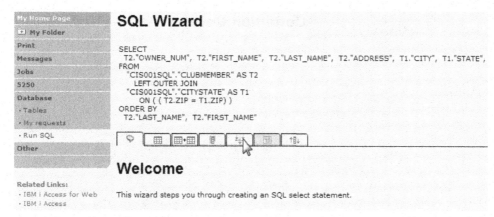

Figure 14.85: Click Condition Tab

From the resulting Condition Web page (Figure 14.86), click Add New Condition.

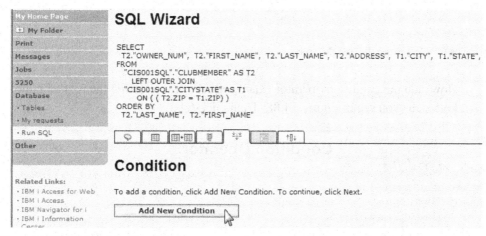

Figure 14.86: Click Add a Condition

In the Condition Column Web page that results, select the radio button to the left of the T2.ZIP column, and then click Next, as in Figure 14.87.

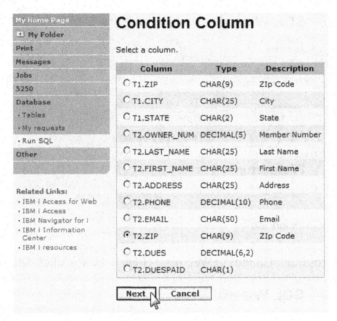

Figure 14.87: Select the T2.ZIP Column

Now, add the condition operator Exactly equal to by selecting the related radio button, as you see in Figure 14.88. Then click Next.

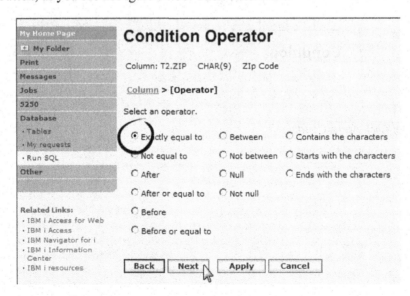

Figure 14.88: Select the Operator for the Condition

Two options are available when you are setting a condition value (see Figure 14.89). The first is to specify a hardcoded value; this option would not let users specify a value when they run the request. The second option allows users to enter a value when they run the request.

Select the radio button to the left of Prompt for condition value when request is run, and then click Next, as in Figure 14.89.

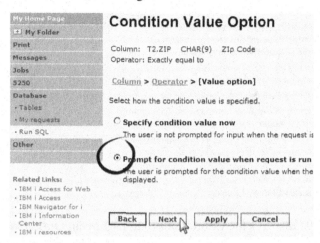

Figure 14.89: Prompt for a Condition at Runtime

Figure 14.90 displays the Condition Prompt – Option Web page. There are three options to select from, and these options are well documented. For our purposes, select the Enter value option, and then click Next.

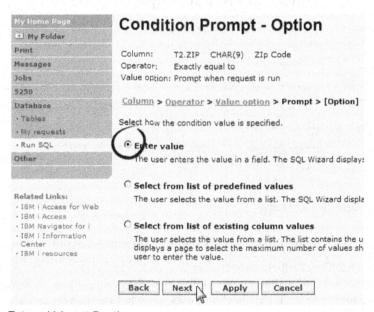

Figure 14.90: Enter a Value at Runtime

Figure 14.91 displays the Condition Prompt – Initial Value Web page. In this example, we have entered a valid zip code from our table. This value can be overwritten when the user runs the request.

Click Next.

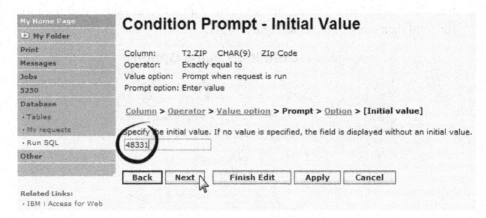

Figure 14.91: Enter a Zip Code

Figure 14.92 displays the Condition Prompt – Layout Option Web page. This Web page lets you display text to assist the user in deciding what value to enter, as well as a label that names the value.

On this Web page, select Text and label from the drop-down list. Then click Next. **Note:** The Next button is hidden in Figure 14.92.

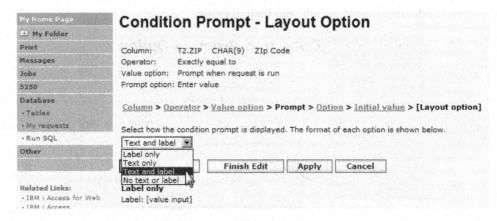

Figure 14.92: Select Text and Label

Figure 14.93 shows the resulting Condition Prompt – Layout Settings Web page. We have added some additional text to help the user decide what to enter for the prompt. Also notice that we have entered some HTML tags to highlight the text for the user, and we have checked the box to the left of Text contains HTML tags. Doing this will cause the text to be bolded when it is displayed.

Enter the following text:

Enter the Zip code you want to search for

Click Finish Edit.

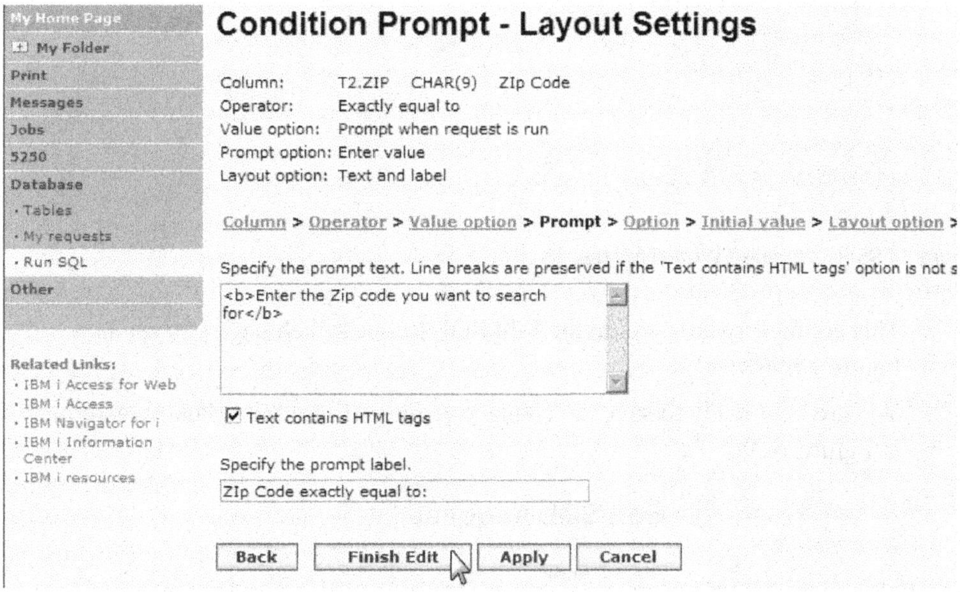

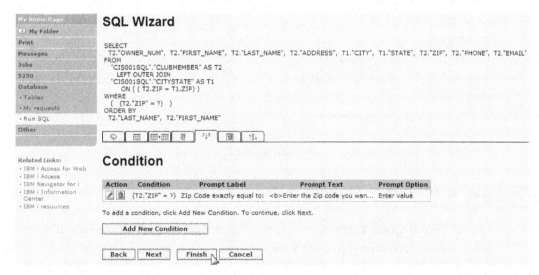

Figure 14.93: Add Text for User Prompting

You now have completed adding the condition to your new request.

Click Finish, as in Figure 14.94.

Figure 14.94: Completed Condition

In the resulting completion screen, click Continue, as you see in Figure 14.95.

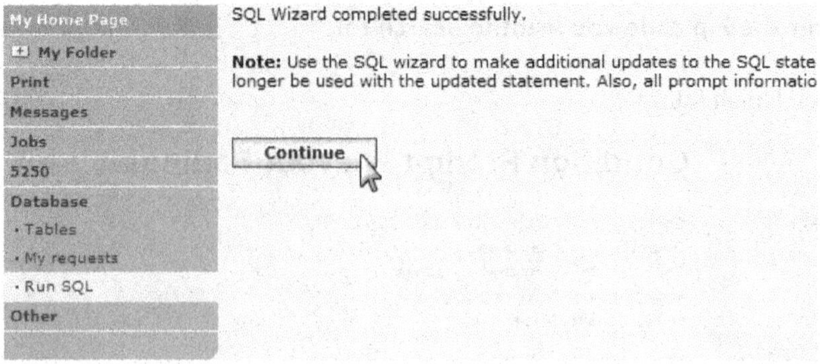

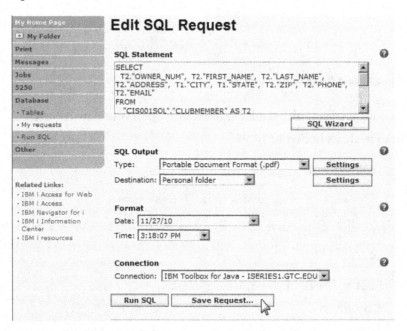

Figure 14.95: Completed Wizard Message

This action forwards you to the Edit SQL Request Web page you see in Figure 14.96.

14.25. You are now ready to save the changed request. To do this, click Save Request, as in Figure 14.96.

Figure 14.96: Save the Changed Request

On the Save Request Web page you see in Figure 14.97, check the Replace if already exists box, and then click Save Request.

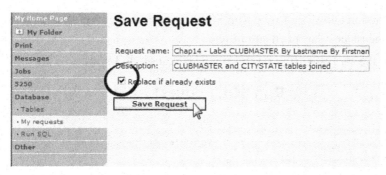

Figure 14.97: Save the Changed Request, Continued

14.26. Run the request.

> After you are forwarded to the Save Request completion Web page, you should click the Run the saved request link to submit your changed request, as the arrow in Figure 14.98 shows.

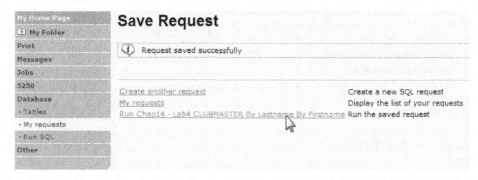

Figure 14.98: Run the Request from the Save Request Web Page

> The Run SQL Web page (Figure 14.99) now displays the text and the label that we created earlier in this lab. The user has the ability to override the default value we entered.

> Click OK.

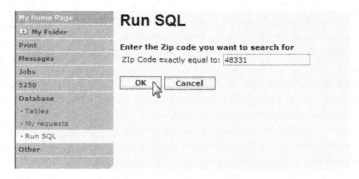

Figure 14.99: Submit the Request

This action takes you to the Run SQL Request verification Web page, which shows that the request has been submitted.

Click the My Folder link on this page, as you see in Figure 14.100.

Figure 14.100: Submit the Request

Taking this action will move you to the My Folder Web page in Figure 14.101.

14.27. You are now ready to display the output. Notice on the My Folder Web page that there are now four entries: the two original entries from an earlier lab and two "unopened" entries.

Click the Open action for these two unopened entries, as Figure 14.101 demonstrates.

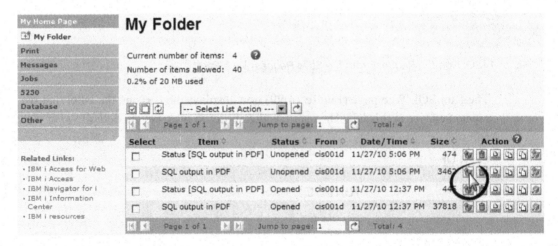

Figure 14.101: Open a Spool File Action

Figure 14.102 shows the output from your modified and saved request.

Listing of CLUBMASTER table by Lastname By Firstname

OWNER_NUM	FIRST_NAME	LAST_NAME	ADDRESS	CITY	STATE	ZIP	PHONE	EMAIL
42038	Elizabeth	Buchanan	35266 Glengary Cir	Farmington Hills	MI	48331	2485535555	BuchananMs10974@gmail.com
42015	Patrick	Franks	35267 Glengary Cir.	Farmington Hills	MI	48331	2485535555	luckoftheirish11279@hotmail.com
42081	Cinthia	Waldstein	38361 Fleetwood Dr.	Farmington Hills	MI	48331	2487885555	germanamerican71023@aol.com

Chapter 14 Lab Part 4
Join CLUBMASTER and CITYSTATE Tables

Figure 14.102: Spooled Output Displayed

After you have viewed the output from running the request, close the PDF file and return to the My Requests Web page, as you see in Figure 14.103.

Here, click the Create Shortcut action, as the demonstrates.

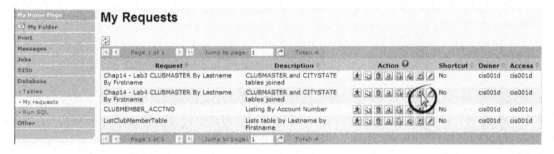

Figure 14.103: Create a Shortcut

This action forwards you to the Create Shortcut Web page (Figure 14.104), where you can add users to the shortcut to allow them to run the request.

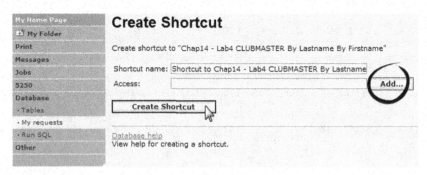

Figure 14.104: PDF Add a Shortcut

On this page, enter your instructor's system ID for the Access parameter, and then press Create Shortcut. Doing so will allow your instructor to verify that you have completed the labs for this chapter.

15

Introduction to DB2 Web Query for i

Overview

In this chapter, we introduce DB2 Web Query for i, the replacement for Query for i5/OS. This powerful new product includes all of the features and functionalities missing in the dated Query for i5/OS tool, such as a graphical interface, industry-standard SQL access methods, the capability to query Oracle and Microsoft SQL Server databases, and modern output formats such as HTML, PDF, XML, and Microsoft Excel.

To demonstrate the features of DB2 Web Query for i, we will create a profit margin inventory report and a profit margin chart, and then we will import these reports into a compound document. In the labs at the end of the chapter, you will enhance the profit margin report and chart. You will also create a new profit margin yearly chart and report and then create a compound document that incorporates the report and chart. Finally, you will use a Query/400 object that you created in the Additional Lab in Chapter 8 to produce a report using DB2 Web Query.

The intent of this chapter is not to make you a master of the DB2 Web Query for i tool. But this short introduction should demonstrate the power of the product's InfoAssist interface and be exciting to you, today's IBM i programming student.

Objectives

Students will be able to

- Create a report using InfoAssist
- Create a chart using InfoAssist
- Create a compound document using InfoAssist
- Create a synonym to access database tables
- Add calculations to a report and chart

Continued

- Format columns in a report
- Insert a line break and subtotals in a report
- Create a filter for a report
- Create a table join for a report or chart
- Create a report based on a Query/400 object

DB2 Web Query for i

In Chapter 7, we discussed the Query for i5/OS product, which has been available to IBM i users since the AS/400 system was released in June 1988. This optional licensed program was originally called **Query/400**, and it is still in use in many IBM i shops worldwide today. As you learned in Chapter 7, the Query for i5/OS product is easy to learn and creates usable reports.

Over time, IBM realized that thousands (millions?) of these queries had been created over the years and were still being used regularly in business. As companies moved to a new query tool, they would need not only that new tool but also a way to reuse these original query objects.

IBM and Information Builders, Inc., entered into a product alliance in 2007. The result of this alliance was a new product called **DB2 Web Query for i** (referred to as DB2 Web Query from here on). This new product includes all of the features and functionalities missing in the dated Query for i5/OS tool, such as a graphical interface, industry-standard SQL access methods, the capability to query Oracle and Microsoft (MS) SQL Server databases, and modern output formats such as HTML, Adobe Portable Document Format (PDF), XML, and Microsoft Excel.

And although we do not discuss it in this chapter, there is an optional product called the DB2 Web Query Developer Workbench Client that is used for advanced development. This PC integrated development environment (IDE) is discussed in the *Getting Started with DB2 Web Query for i* IBM Redbook (SG24-7214).

At the time we are writing this textbook, the DB2 Web Query product is available to customers who have a license for the older Query for i5/OS product and are current on their software maintenance agreements. This availability should help organizations investigate the new features of, and also migrate their older query objects to, DB2 Web Query.

Note

The Redbook *Getting Started with DB2 Web Query for i* is a great resource. We recommend downloading it and, if possible, working through the tutorials available. A database comes with this Redbook, and you should ask your instructor whether this database is loaded on your system.

Query for i5/OS Limitations

We introduced Query for i5/OS in this text because so many of these queries are in use today that it is important for you as a student to understand the use of this product. Even though Query for i5/OS has served us well for many years, companies should move to the new DB2 Web Query product for a number of reasons. Following are the major Query for i5/OS limitations, with a short explanation of each.

- Available only with the 5250 interface—Industries are moving to graphical interfaces because the 5250 interface is not appealing to today's user.
- Limited output capabilities—Query for i5/OS will not generate reports in any of the graphical formats such as HTML, PDF, XML, or Excel.
- Lack of support for foreign (non-DB2) databases—Query for i5/OS is limited to using locally defined DB2 databases. Today's companies usually have data stored in multiple database formats, including Oracle and MS SQL Server. Using Query for i5/OS would require companies to import that data into DB2 or to use different reporting tools.
- Limited reporting capabilities—Once a query is developed in Query for i5/OS, and a different view of the data is needed, the query must be changed or a new query created. Creating reports that allow the user to easily manipulate the view of the data is impossible.
- Proprietary non-SQL interface—SQL has become the industry standard for manipulating databases. As a result, IBM will not expend the resources to maintain a proprietary database-reporting tool.
- Does not use the SQL Query Engine (**SQE**)—When V5R2 of the operating system was released, a new query engine named SQE was also released and was intended to replace the Classic Query Engine (**CQE**). This new query engine has new features that will not be incorporated into CQE. IBM will continue to support the older query engine but will not enhance it in the future. Although a discussion of these features is beyond the scope of this text, we recommend the IBM Redbook *Preparing for Tuning the SQL Query Engine on DB2 for i5/OS* (SG24-6598) for those students who are interested.

DB2 Web Query Features

As IBM continues to move IBM i interfaces to Web-based environments, the introduction of DB2 Web Query has given the platform an excellent reporting tool. Following are the features that make DB2 Web Query the ad hoc reporting tool for IBM i.

- *Web-based interface*—Today's users want a Web interface, and this type of interface also makes management easier because no software needs to be installed on the user's PC.
- *Migration of Query/400 objects*—The capability to use Query/400 objects allows the company to migrate reports, and thereby lower migration costs.
- *InfoAssist development tool*—The release of this tool combines the features of the Report Assistant, Graph Assistant, and Power Painter tools.
- *Numerous report output formats*—Formats include Excel 2000 and 2007, HTML, Microsoft PowerPoint, PDF, and new technology formats such as Active PDF and Active Flash.
- *Native to IBM i*—Server-side components run natively on the IBM i OS, which simplifies administration, security, maintenance, and backups.
- *Data adapters*—This feature enables reports to be generated from numerous database formats:
  - DB2 CLI—The recommended adapter for use with single-member DB2 files and DDS- or SQL-generated tables; uses SQE, so it will have the latest DB2 enhancements
  - DB2 Heritage—Interfaces with multiple-member or multiple-record-format DB2 files, and generates OPNQRYF commands
  - Query/400—Creates metadata for existing Query/400 reports; submits a RUNQRY command and uses CQE
  - MS SQL Server—Allows use of data from MS SQL Server 2000 or later, and even allows joining of data between DB2 and SQL Server
  - JD Edwards for Oracle—Provides access to data stored in Oracle databases, letting users of this enterprise resource planning (ERP) system seamlessly integrate and develop reports and charts

Domains

DB2 Web Query uses domains to organize, secure, and classify reports. In the examples we use in this chapter, the CIS001D student user will store and develop reports in a domain named Programming Students. Under this domain are subfolders for each programming student. DB2 Web Query does not control the authority to these lower-level student folders. (Figure 15.5 shows the organization of the domains on the system we used to develop this book; you will need to ask your instructor to explain to you how domains are organized on your system.)

Users

DB2 Web Query has three types of users: 1) The administrator can create domains and subfolders for use by developers and basic users. 2) Developers can create, modify, and run reports within specified domains. 3) A basic user is allowed to run reports only in the specified domain. We should note that the OS security overrides any security implemented by DB2 Web Query. Therefore, a user also must have access rights to any objects (tables, views, stored procedures) used in the report. DB2 Web Query users must be specifically defined in DB2 Web Query before they are allowed any access.

Metadata

DB2 Web Query uses metadata to access DB2 tables on your system. Think of **metadata** as a catalog of your database objects (tables, views, and so on). This catalog tells DB2 Web Query where the database objects reside and how they are related. Before you can start creating reports or charts, you need to create this metadata, which is also referred to as a **synonym**. In the next few pages, we will guide you step-by-step through the process of creating a synonym for the tables we use in this chapter.

Getting Started with DB2 Web Query

After we enter the correct URL to access DB2 Web Query on the system, we are presented with a Web page like the one you see in Figure 15.1. We enter the student system ID and password and then click Logon.

Note

The general URL for accessing DB2 Web Query is http://*myserver*:11331/ webquery, where *myserver* is the URL for your server. You should check with your instructor to find out the correct URL for your college.

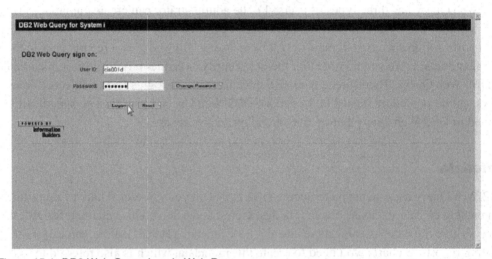

Figure 15.1: DB2 Web Query Log-in Web Page

Figure 15.2 shows, in the background, the main Web page for DB2 Web Query. There are a number of domains on this system. In this chapter, we will use the Programming Students domain. Although partly covered by another window in the figure, this domain has a folder for individual students. We will use the folder for the CIS001D student profile to store the reports and charts developed in this chapter.

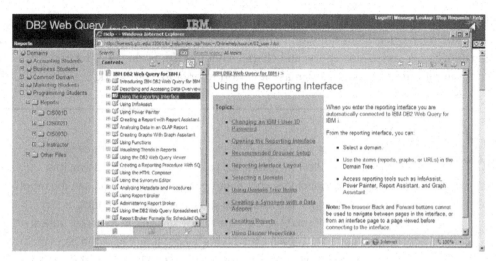

Figure 15.2: DB2 Web Query Help

DB2 Web Query Help

Before we continue, we should make note of the online Help that is available when you use DB2 Web Query. Clicking the Help link in the top-right corner of the main page (note the arrow in Figure 15.2) will open the Web page you see in the foreground of Figure 15.2. The information contained in this online Help is invaluable; it is divided into categories and includes screen prints and links to guide the user through the online Help. Take a few minutes to explore this resource.

In Figure 15.3, we have right-clicked our student folder CIS001D and selected the New Folder option.

Figure 15.3: DB2 Web Query Main Web Page

In the next few figures, we will be creating one folder named Reports and one named Graphs. DB2 Web Query does not require these lower-level folders, but using them gives us the capability to organize our reports and charts. Although doing this may seem unnecessary for our examples, it is a good idea to make an effort to organize our work.

Caution

We recommend that you have InfoAssist (which we will introduce you to shortly) open and follow the examples presented in the text; doing this includes creating the folders under your profile folder. You will use the report and chart we develop in the text when you work through the labs at the end of the chapter. If you take the time to investigate the toolbars, panes, ribbons, and options, you will gain a better understanding of the product.

If the synonyms already exist that we are creating here, you should use the existing ones rather than re-create them. Prefixing your reports using the naming conventions described by your instructor is also very important. *Failure to follow these naming conventions could cause problems for other users on the system.*

After we select New Folder in Figure 15.3, the pop-up Web page in Figure 15.4 is displayed. We have entered the value Reports for the Folder Name parameter and clicked Save.

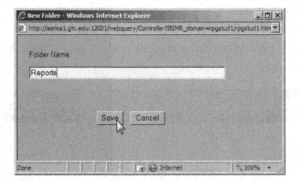

Figure 15.4: Creating the Reports Folder

In Figure 15.5, we have circled two of the lower-level folders that we created for use in this chapter. Later, we will create additional folders for storing compound documents and imported Query/400 objects.

We now need to define the metadata that we will use to access our DB2 tables for this chapter. In Figure 15.6, we have right-clicked our student folder CIS001D and, on the context menu, have selected the Metadata option.

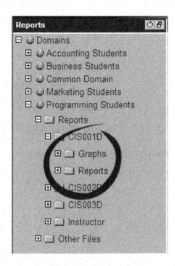

Figure 15.5: Reports and Graphs Folders

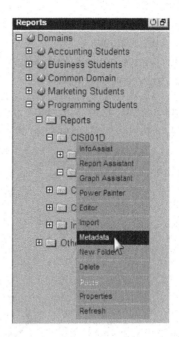

Figure 15.6: Creating Metadata

Figure 15.7 shows the pop-up Web page you use to create synonyms in DB2 Web Query. We have expanded the Configured and the DB2 cli icons, right-clicked the *LOCAL icon, and selected the Create Synonym option.

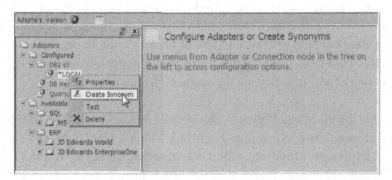

Figure 15.7: Creating Metadata, Continued

The panel on the right of the pop-up Web page changes, as you see in Figure 15.8. Several options are available in the Restrict object type to drop-down list. The following restrictions can be applied:

- External SQL scripts
- Stored procedures
- Tables, views, and other objects
- Table log records

For this demonstration, we will leave the default setting, Tables, Views and Other Objects. This option essentially lets you view any database object in a specific library (schema).

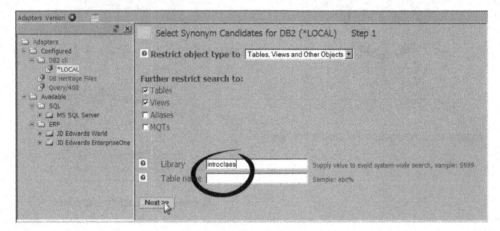

Figure 15.8: Creating Metadata, Step 1 Window

We could further restrict the objects presented (limit the number and type of objects returned) by selecting one or more of the check boxes under the Further restrict search to option. In Chapter 13, we discussed tables and views. At this time, we need to define aliases and MQTs. An **alias** lets SQL reference a table or view by another name, and a materialized query table (**MQT**) is a table that contains the results of a previously run SQL statement. An in-depth discussion of MQTs is beyond the scope of this text.

We have keyed in the introclass library in the Library parameter and then clicked Next. The panel on the Web page changes again, as Figure 15.9 shows. Here, we select the With foreign keys check box to properly "link" any tables that have foreign keys. We enter the value CHP15_ for the optional Prefix parameter, which will help us distinguish tables included in our synonym from others on the system that might have the same name and be located in different libraries. We then select the tables that we want to include in our synonym for this chapter. Finally, we click Create synonym.

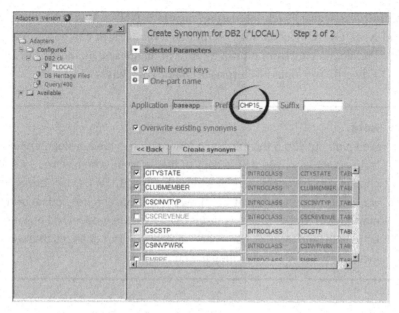

Figure 15.9: Creating Metadata, Step 2 Window

Once again, the Web page changes, as you see in Figure 15.10, to show us that our new synonym was successfully created with the tables we selected.

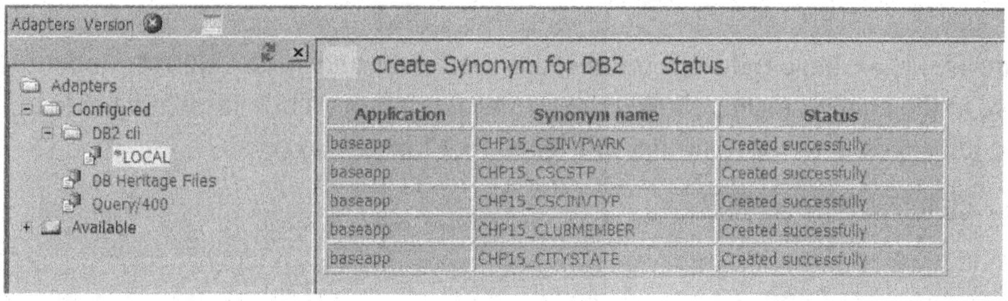

Figure 15.10: Creating Metadata, Web Page Showing Success

Lower on the Web page in Figure 15.10 is a Back button (not shown in the figure) that would have allowed us to create additional synonyms, but we chose to close the page.

Introducing InfoAssist

InfoAssist was released with DB2 Web Query, Version 1 Release 1 Modification 2 (Version 1.1.2). InfoAssist actually combines many of the functions of DB2 Web Query's Report Assistant, Graph Assistant, and Power Painter into one tool. Combining these three tools into InfoAssist makes the development process much easier. For example, you can create a report in InfoAssist and easily convert it to a chart; then you can open a document and import the report and chart into this document.

IBM refers to InfoAssist as a "Rich Internet application" (**RIA**). It is built on Asynchronous JavaScript and XML (**AJAX**) technology. With this tool, the user can develop very complex reports, charts, and documents from multiple types of databases, including DB2, MS SQL Server, and JD Edwards World and Enterprise (Oracle) databases.

Note

We found out about the InfoAssist feature late in the development of this text and actually used a beta copy of the software when we were writing this chapter. The introduction of this tool into the DB2 Web Query environment was important enough that we threw the original chapter outline away and started over. By the time this text is available, the product will no longer be in beta, and there will be enhancements and/or changes that were not available when we were writing the chapter.

Getting Started with InfoAssist

We start this section by opening InfoAssist and describing the features of the InfoAssist application window. We then create a profit margin inventory report over an inventory table and develop a chart. We complete the chapter by importing these reports into a compound document.

In Figure 15.11, we have right-clicked the Reports folder under the CIS001D student folder and then, in the context menu, clicked the InfoAssist option. While InfoAssist is loading the required resources, a window similar to Figure 15.12 is displayed.

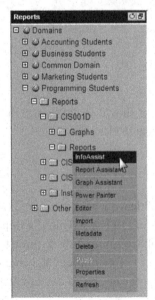

Figure 15.12: InfoAssist Loading Resources

Figure 15.11: Starting InfoAssist

After InfoAssist has started, the **splash screen** is displayed (Figure 15.13). A number of options are available on this Web page. We list and describe those options—first those available in the Getting Started column and then those in the Help column—following the figure.

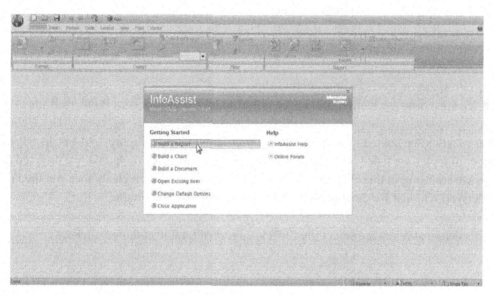

Figure 15.13: InfoAssist Splash Screen

The Getting Started column offers six options:

- Build a Report—Starts InfoAssist in the Interactive view and prompts for a data source, to allow the user to design a report
- Build a Chart—Starts InfoAssist in the Interactive view and prompts for a data source, to allow the user to design a chart
- Build a Document—Starts InfoAssist in the Document view, letting the user create **compound documents** that can include additional text, images, reports, and charts
- Open Existing Item—Opens a dialog box that lets the user open a previously designed report or chart
- Change Default Options—Opens the Preferences window, where the user can make changes to the following items:
  - Startup Options—Turns the splash screen on/off and sets whether InfoAssist starts in Report, Chart, or Document mode
  - Layout—Changes page size and orientation
  - View—Sets the Design view mode, Preview Data method (actual source data or sample records), Record limit, Data pane view, Query pane view, and Output Target (explained later in this chapter)

- ○ Format—Lets the user select Report, Chart document, or output type (e.g., HTML, PDF)
- ○ Environment and Styling—Sets application and document themes (a number of predefined themes are available, or users may use their own)
- Close Application—Exits InfoAssist

The Help column offers two options:

- InfoAssist Help—Is built on online Help
- Online Forum—Opens a link to the Information Builders' Focal Point Web site

When we click the Build a Report option, the pop-up window in Figure 15.14 is displayed. A number of tables are listed in this window. When we created our metadata, we prefixed the tables we are using in this chapter with Chp15_. Therefore, we can easily pick out the tables for the synonym that we created from other tables with the same name.

For this demonstration, we select the CHP15_CSINVPWRK table and then click OK.

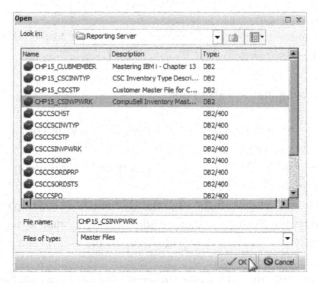

Figure 15.14: Select CHP15_CSINVPWRK Table

InfoAssist Application Window Features

Selecting the designated table in Figure 15.14 displays the **InfoAssist application window** you see in Figure 15.15. To help you understand the features in this window, we have labeled the important areas in the figure and include a description of each feature immediately following the figure.

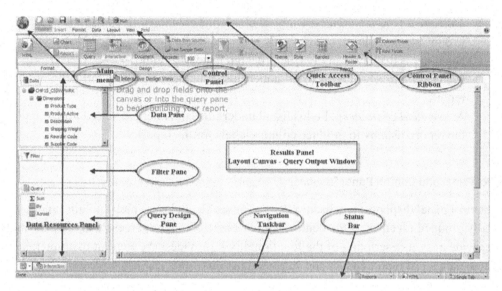

Figure 15.15: InfoAssist Application Window Components

Application Main Menu

The InfoAssist Main menu, accessed via the globe-shaped icon in the upper-left corner of the InfoAssist application window, is similar to the Office button in a Microsoft Office 2007 application. The Main menu button provides file options for New, Open, Save, Save as, Run, Run Deferred, or Close. The user also has the capability to edit Options (user preferences). A list of recently used files is also displayed.

Data Resources Panel

The Data Resources panel comprises three panes:

- *Data Pane*—Lists the fields for the table you have selected for the report. This pane lets you drag and drop fields to the layout canvas or Query pane for display or sorting.
- *Filter Pane*—Displays the results of creating a filter. You can drag and drop fields onto this pane, or you can right-click a field in the Data pane and select the Filter option. This selection causes a wizard to open, letting you create a filter.
- *Query Design Pane*—Functions as the main design pane for developing a query. The number and type of containers available on this pane change depending on the type of document you are creating. Three containers are available when you are developing a report:

- *Measure Σ field container*—Right-clicking this container gives you the capability to Sum (default), Print, or List fields specified under this container. **Note:** The container is displayed in the Query design pane as Σ Sum.
- By *field container*—Fields listed under this container are sorted vertically on the report.
- Across *field container*—Fields listed under this container are sorted horizontally on the report, usually to produce column labels for the report.

Control Panel and Control Panel Ribbons

The control panel displays the tabs, or *ribbons*, described below, which contain functions logically grouped together on the control panel ribbon. We show screenshots of each ribbon and provide a short description of the functionality it provides. We suggest that you take the time to create a test report and try the various functions—the best way to learn is to do!

- **Home Ribbon**—The Home ribbon, shown in Figure 15.16, contains the most-used functions from the Format, Design, Filter, and Report tabs:
  - *Format group*—Changes the output type to the various formats (e.g., Excel, HTML, PDF)
  - *Design group*—Switches between different development views or changes the number of records returned when you are developing the report
  - *Filter group*—Adds filters to the report (a field must be selected for this group to be available)
  - *Report group*—Contains options to change the theme and the style, and to add headers, footers, and totals to the report

Figure 15.16: Home Ribbon

- **Insert Ribbon**—The Insert ribbon (Figure 15.17) is not available in the Interactive or Query design views. In the Document view, you as the developer can add images, charts, reports, existing reports, and text to the current document.

Figure 15.17: Insert Ribbon

- *Format Ribbon*—The Format ribbon offers different options depending on whether you are developing a report or a chart. The output type (e.g., Active Report, HTML, PDF) and destination (switches between Chart and Report) options remain the same. We explain the differences between these ribbons below.

  The **Format ribbon (reports)** display, which you can see in Figure 15.18, contains the following navigation and features options:
  - ○ *Navigation*—Includes options that affect output navigation and display:
    - ▪ *Table of Contents*—Creates the list of contents for a report; freezes generated output with column titles that remain visible as the user scrolls through the report
    - ▪ *Pages on Demand*—Outputs one page at a time and gives the user the option to access additional pages
  - ○ *Features*—Includes options for specialized report processing:
    - ▪ *Title Popup*—Allows mouse hovers to display additional text
    - ▪ *Accordion*—Displays each vertical sort field for expandable views of data
    - ▪ *Repeat Sort Values*—Displays all the sort field data instead of blanks after the first value is displayed

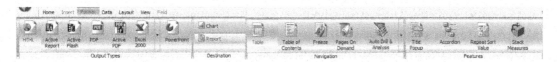

Figure 15.18: Format Ribbon—Reports

The **Format Ribbon (charts)** display, which you can see in Figure 15.19, contains the following navigation and features options:
- ○ *Chart Types*—Includes a variety of chart types
- ○ *Features*—Includes options for 3D effects, Rotate chart, Reference lines, Annotate, and Grid lines
- ○ *Labels*—Lets you manipulate Axes and Legend labels

Figure 15.19: Format Ribbon—Charts

- **Data Ribbon**—The Data ribbon (Figure 15.20) contains options to create Detail (defined) and Summary (computed) fields, Join files, and Advanced filters.
  - *Calculation group*—Creates virtual calculation fields:
    - *Detail (Define) field*—Value is calculated for each record that is processed.
    - *Summary (Compute) field*—Value is calculated after all the sorting is processed.
  - *Join group*—Creates SQL joins.
  - *Filter group*—Creates filters (SQL WHERE clause) that can be hardcoded or prompted when the report is run.
  - *Data Source group*—Adds or changes a data source. This option is available only in the Document view. You can add a data source to a document to develop additional reports within the document.

Figure 15.20: Data Ribbon

- **Layout Ribbon**—The Layout ribbon (Figure 15.21) contains the Page Setup and Report group options that control general report settings:
  - *Page Setup group*—Allows you as the developer to set margins; change page orientation, paper size, units (inches, centimeters, or points); and turn page numbering on/off.
  - *Report group*—Allows you as the developer to add cell padding and turn on Autofit Column (the column's width is reduced to the size of the largest data item). The Auto Overflow option expands the report area to show all data. If the data component extends beyond the bottom margin of the current page, the component is displayed on the next page.

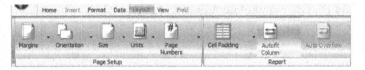

Figure 15.21: Layout Ribbon

- **View Ribbon**—The View Ribbon (Figure 15.22) provides access to viewing options for reports and charts.
  - *Design group*—Allows you as the developer to switch between the Query, Interactive, and Document design views
  - *Show/Hide group*—Allows you as the developer to show or hide the resources (Data, Filter, and Query panes); when in the Document view, can enable the Ruler and Grid displays

○ *Data Panel group*—Controls the way the fields are displayed in the data resources panel using the three listed options:

- *Logical view*—Displays the fields by data type
- *List view*—Displays the fields with additional information about the field (e.g., title, alias, format) by data type
- *Structured view*—Lists the fields as they are arranged in the actual file

All of these views offer options to display the actual field name, title, or description. The List view also has options to display the file reference, alias, and format.

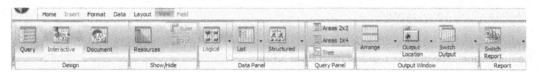

Figure 15.22: View Ribbon

- **Field Ribbon**—The Field ribbon (Figure 15.23) is available when you select a data source field in the layout canvas or the Query design pane. The options available on this tab depend on the data type of the field that is selected:
  ○ *Filter group*—Allows you as the developer to add a filter (WHERE clause) based on the selected field option, including Exclude, Include, and Prompt.
  ○ *Sort group*—Allows sorting (ascending or descending) on the selected field. Selecting Rank will insert a rank column that is based on the value in the field.
  ○ *Break group*—Is available with a sorted field. Includes Page Break, Line Break, Subtotal (numeric fields), Sub Header, Sub Footer, and **Recompute** (similar to a subtotal but calculated only for the current sort break) options.
  ○ *Style group*—Controls the font and formatting characteristics for the data field or title.
  ○ *Format group*—Enables field formatting based on the type of field functions, including formatting with commas, date formatting, adding floating and nonfloating currency, and formatting with percent signs.
  ○ *Specific group*—Allows aggregation (Sum, Average, Count, Minimum, Maximum), traffic lights (field color changes based on value), and data bars on the selected field.
    - *Visibility group*—Lets a selected field be made invisible. **Note:** A field by default is visible.
    - *Links group*—Allows a hyperlink or drill-down **procedure** (chart or report) to be added to a field. Drill-down procedures are not covered in this chapter, but a drill-down link would cause another procedure to be called when the field is clicked.

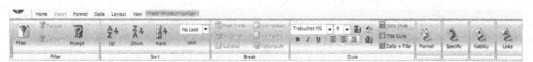

Figure 15.23: Field Ribbon

- ***Series Ribbon***—The Series ribbon (Figure 15.24) is available only when you are working with charts. This ribbon lets you as the developer change chart properties and options, including working with a specific series, changing the chart type, and adding trend lines or markers.

Figure 15.24: Series Ribbon

Results Panel, Navigation Taskbar, and Status Bar

The Results panel, located in the main area of the InfoAssist application window (which you saw back in Figure 15.15), is a multifunction panel that displays the output window (results from running a query), layout canvas (preview displayed as the report is designed), or Query design pane.

At the bottom of the InfoAssist application window, a navigation taskbar provides access to all the active windows and the editor that created these reports. The status bar, also at the bottom of the application window, provides the capability to display the status of the last action on the left, the name of the current report, the current output format (e.g., Excel, HTML, PDF), and the output target. The Output Target button controls how new output is displayed; options include

- *Single Tab* (the default)—Creates a new output window when the report is first run, and then refreshes this window each time the report is run
- *New Tab*—Creates a new window the first time the report is run and a new tabbed window each time the report is run
- *Single Window*—Creates a new window when the report is first run, and then updates this window each time the window is opened
- *New Window*—Creates a new window when the report is first run, and then creates a new window each time the report is run

---

Note

As we demonstrate building a report in this chapter, we will design the report using features that we ourselves found useful. You should be aware that, as with most modern applications, there are numerous ways to accomplish a task. For example, when we designate a field as a sort field, we find it easiest to right-click the field in the Data pane and select the Sort option. This task also can be accomplished by dragging the field onto the By icon in the Query design pane.

Creating the Profit Margin Inventory Report

Now that you have an understanding of the InfoAssist application window features and ribbons, we can begin developing the profit margin inventory report. We have listed the requirements for a profit margin inventory report for a fictitious company called Compusell Corporation (CSC), which sells computer equipment and office supplies.

- The report is sorted first by product type and then by part number.
- The fields displayed will be Product Type, Part Number, Part Number Description, Quantity On Hand, Shipping Cost, and Average Cost.
- Detail (defined) fields named Inventory Cost and Profit Margin are displayed on the report.
  - The Inventory Cost (InvCost) field is calculated by adding the shipping and average costs.
  - The Profit Margin (ProfitMargin) field is calculated by subtracting the inventory cost from the selling price.
- The report will have a line break when the Product Type changes.
- The columns will be subtotaled at each Product Type break, and there will be column totals at the end of the report.

The first step is to add these sort fields in the order required for this sort. Figure 15.25 shows that we have right-clicked the Product Type field in the Data pane and have selected the Sort option. These actions place the Product Type field in the Query pane under the By icon and also place the field on the layout canvas.

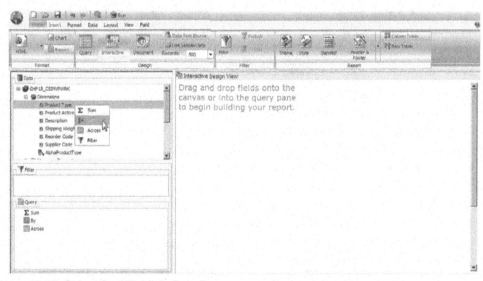

Figure 15.25: Select Sort Fields in Data Pane

We then proceed to do the same with the second sort field, Product Number. You can see the results of these actions in Figure 15.26.

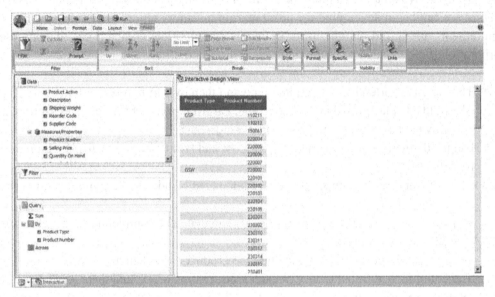

Figure 15.26: Select Sort Fields in Data Pane, Continued

The next step is to change the Σ Sum field container (the default) to Print, as Figure 15.27 shows. This action changes the report from a summary report to a detail report.

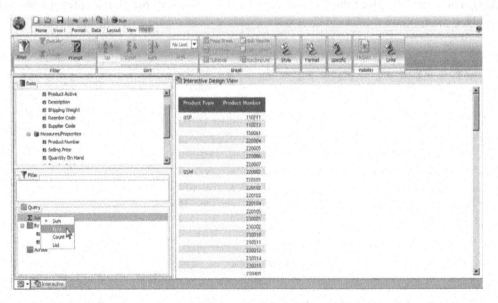

Figure 15.27: Changing from a Summary Report to a Detail Report Using the Query Pane

Next, we need to add the fields to the report. We accomplish this by right-clicking the field in the Data pane and selecting Print, as in Figure 15.28. As we stated earlier, a number of ways exist to accomplish these tasks. We also could have dragged the fields onto the layout canvas or dropped them onto the Print icon in the Query pane.

Note

We suggest you try different methods of placing fields; as you gain experience, you will develop your own methodology for developing reports.

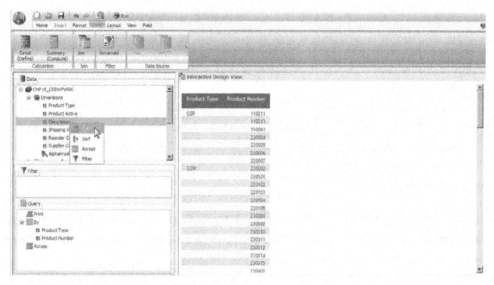

Figure 15.28: Adding Fields to the Report

The fields required for the report include those under the Print and By icons, as follows:

- Under the Print icon, the fields should be placed in the following order:
  1. Description
  2. Quantity On Hand
  3. Selling Price
  4. Shipping Cost
  5. Average Cost

- Under the By icon, the fields should be placed in the following order:
  1. Product Type
  2. Product Number

As Figure 15.29 shows, we have placed all of our data fields on the report. Because of the length of some of the titles, we decided to shorten them to consolidate the report. Again, we right-click the field in the Query pane, and then we select Change Title.

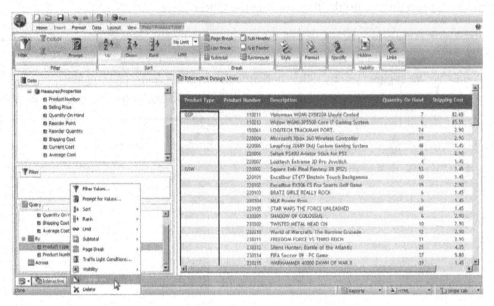

Figure 15.29: Changing Field Titles

The pop-up window in Figure 15.30 is displayed. Because this is an internal report, users will understand that Type will stand for Product Type. We have entered this value and then selected OK.

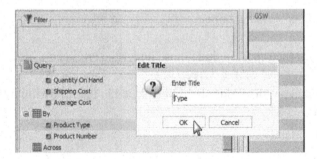

Figure 15.30: Changing Field Titles

Figure 15.31 shows our report after we have shortened a number of the column titles. Also in this figure, we have clicked the Data option on the control panel, and the Data ribbon is displayed. We have clicked the Detail (Define) button in the Calculation group.

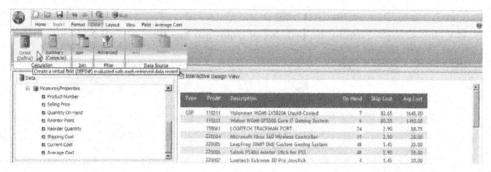

Figure 15.31: Creating a Detail Field

Clicking the Detail button displays the **Field creator dialog box** you see in Figure 15.32. Using this dialog box, we will create our defined field InvCost.

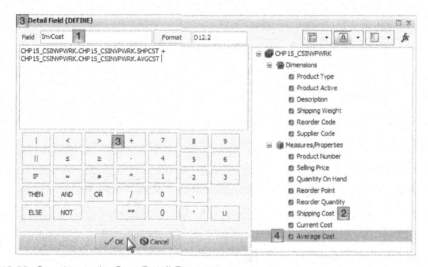

Figure 15.32: Creating an InvCost Detail Field, Continued

Here are the steps that are necessary to create the field in Figure 15.32:

1. Name the field InvCost.
2. Double-click the Shipping Cost field.
3. Click the + button.
4. Double-click the Average Cost field.
5. Click OK (note the arrow).

We then navigate to the new InvCost field in the Data pane, as you see in Figure 15.33. This figure also shows that we are in the process of dragging this field onto the layout canvas.

Figure 15.33: Adding the InvCost Defined Field to the Report

The final calculated field that we need to define for the report is the ProfitMargin field. Figure 15.34 demonstrates creating this field; we have listed the steps following the figure.

Figure 15.34: Creating a ProfitMargin Detail Field

1. Name the field ProfitMargin.
2. Double-click the Selling Price field.
3. Click the - button.
4. Double-click the InvCost field.
5. Click OK (note the arrow).

Notice that we have used the InvCost field in our new calculation. The ability to use a previously calculated field is a handy feature of DB2 Web Query. Now that we have created the field, we will add it to our report, as we have shown previously. We will also change the headings on the columns to make the report more readable.

The last changes we need to make to satisfy the requirements for the Profit Margin Inventory report are to change the report so that DB2 Web Query inserts a line break and subtotals when the Product Type changes, and to add column totals at the end of the report. In Figure 15.35, we have clicked Product Type in the Query pane, which switched us to the Field – Product Type ribbon. We then clicked the Line Break and Subtotal options, which we have circled in this figure. You should notice that the line break and the subtotals are displayed on the layout canvas.

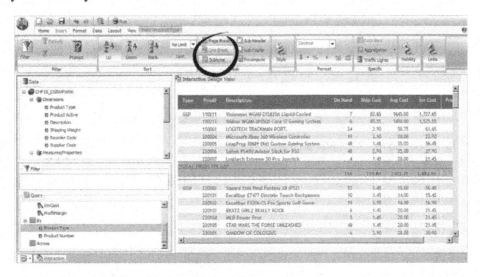

Figure 15.35: Inserting a Line Break and Subtotals

Finally, Figure 15.36 shows that we have clicked Home in the control panel and then the Column Totals icon in the Report group.

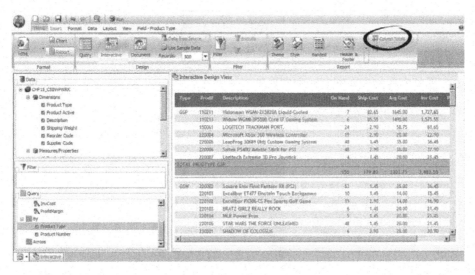

Figure 15.36: Inserting Column Totals

We have now satisfied the requirements for the Profit Margin Inventory report. We have clicked the Main Menu button (globe-shaped icon) in the upper-left corner of the InfoAssist application window, and the application main menu is displayed, as you see in Figure 15.37.

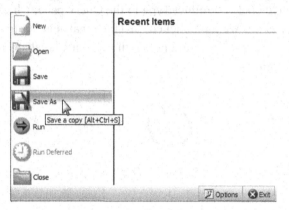

Figure 15.37: Saving the Profit Margin Inventory Report

We then click Save As, name our report CIS001d_List CSINVPWRK Inventory Table, and select OK, as Figure 15.38 shows.

 Caution
Be sure to name your report using the correct naming conventions your instructor has provided. Failure to follow these naming conventions will cause problems for you and other users on the system. We will save the report as CIS001d_ List CSINVPWRK Inventory Table, using our student user profile as we have throughout this text.

Figure 15.38: Saving the Profit Margin Inventory Report, Continued

The status bar, located on the lower-right side of the InfoAssist application window, lets you switch between reports (if you have more than one open); you also can change the output type (currently set to HTML in our example), and you can change the way the output is displayed using the Output Target button. In Figure 15.39, we have selected New Window, which will cause the report to be opened in a new browser window when it is run.

Figure 15.39: Running the Profit Margin Inventory Report

After we run the report, Figure 15.40 shows the new inventory report, including line breaks, subtotals, and column totals.

PC	340347	Compaq 500B VS675UT Microtower Bus PC	30	17.40	355.55	372.95	103.04
*TOTAL PRODTYPE PC			130	77.50	3596.05	3,668.55	1,784.17
PRS	310001	Epson DURABrite Ultra ink cartridge	25	5.80	9.75	15.55	-.60
	310002	Canon CLI-221M Magenta Ink Tank	13	4.35	9.45	13.80	.70
	310003	HP 920 CH635AN Magenta Officejet	12	2.90	4.20	7.10	-.60
	310004	Epson T096120 UltraChrome K3 Photo Black	38	2.90	8.25	11.15	1.35
	310005	Brother LC-41C Cyan Ink Cartridge	45	5.80	13.25	19.05	-4.10
	310006	Canon BCI-6R Red Ink Tank Cartridge	72	11.60	8.95	20.55	-7.60
	340337	HP Q2612A 12A Black Print Cartridge	150	2.90	42.00	44.90	35.09
	340338	Brother TN110M 3 Pack	75	2.90	110.00	112.90	52.09
	340339	HP 05A CE505A Black Toner Cart - 3-Pack	100	2.90	200.50	203.40	36.59
	340340	HP LaserJet P3015DN Mono Laser Printer	35	2.90	415.25	418.15	121.84
*TOTAL PRODTYPE PRS			565	44.95	821.60	866.55	234.76
PRT	130101	HP P1102w CE657A LaserJet Pro	15	20.30	99.00	119.30	29.70
	130103	HP Photosmart Premium All-in-One C309	6	29.00	179.50	208.50	66.50
	130201	Epson Artisan 800 Color Inkjet Printer	4	21.75	175.00	196.75	72.25
	132209	HP Deskjet D1660 Inkjet Printer	72	29.00	276.00	305.00	116.00
	132210	HP LaserJet Pro P1606DN Laser Printer	6	58.00	865.00	923.00	72.00
	132211	HP Color LaserJet CP1215 Laser Printer	24	59.45	440.00	499.45	31.55
	150010	Microsoft - Wireless Laser Desktop 4000	4	1.45	31.50	32.95	16.05
*TOTAL PRODTYPE PRT			131	218.95	2066.00	2,284.95	404.05
PSP	112240	Ultra M923 ATX Black Full Tower	100	47.85	40.00	87.85	-2.85
	114432	Western Digital WD1002FAEX Caviar Black	10	2.90	22.00	24.90	45.10
	320013	Western Digital Caviar SE 250GB Hard Dri	40	4.35	36.50	40.85	16.10
	330010	Sabrent 3.5" USB 2.0 to IDE/PATA Externa	130	1.45	9.50	10.95	3.55
	330021	SanDisk 2GB Memory Stick Pro Duo	34	1.45	9.75	11.20	3.80
	330022	Transcend 1GB Micro SD Card	56	2.90	6.00	8.90	.60
	330023	Wintec 3FMUSDCK4GB-R FileMate Micro SDHC	81	5.80	9.75	15.55	-1.05
*TOTAL PRODTYPE PSP			451	66.70	133.50	200.20	65.25
TOTAL			3300	2030.00	35217.93	37,247.93	14,706.61

Figure 15.40: Running the Profit Margin Inventory Report, Continued

Creating a Profit Margin Chart

In this section, we will use InfoAssist to create a pie chart based on the CSINVPWRK table. This pie chart will show the company's profit margin for different product types based on the current sales, shipping costs, and average cost. The formula is

(SELLPR – (AVGCST + SHPCST)) / SELLPR * 100

The result of this formula will be a percent of the profit margin for a specific line item (Part Number). We will discuss shortly exactly how the chart will interpret this data to present the chart.

First we navigate to the CIS001D student GRAPHS folder. We right-click the folder and select InfoAssist, as Figure 15.41 demonstrates.

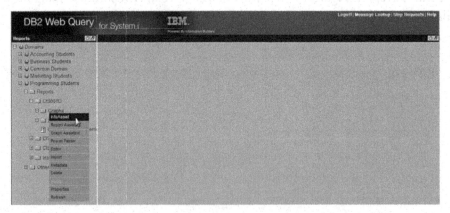

Figure 15.41: Starting InfoAssist

After DB2 Web Query opens, the splash screen in Figure 15.42 appears; here, we select Build a Chart.

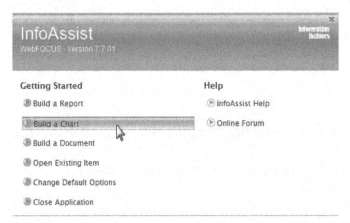

Figure 15.42: Select Build a Chart

DB2 Web Query displays the Open window (Figure 15.43). Here, we select the CHP15_
CSINVPWRK table, and then we click OK.

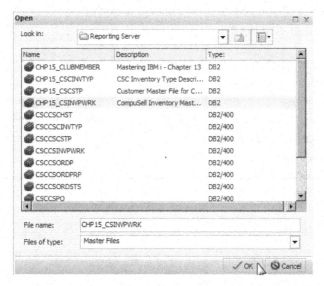

Figure 15.43: Select the CHP15_CSINVPWRK Table

Figure 15.44 shows the application window in the Chart mode. We have selected the Format
tab and the Pie chart type (circled in the figure). The chart will be based on the total profit
margins for a specific product type. Therefore, we are dragging the Product Type field onto
the Slices icon in the Query pane. This action will sort the records in the table by product
type, and each product type will be a "slice" of the chart.

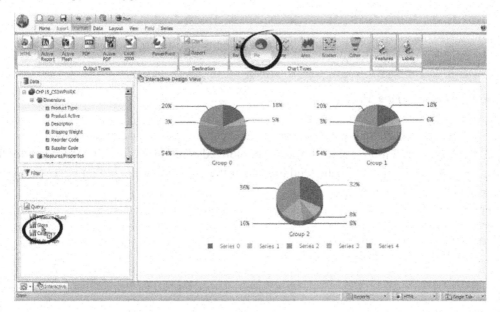

Figure 15.44: InfoAssist Application Window, Chart

Before we go any further, we should save the chart. Figure 15.45 shows that we have clicked the Save icon on the quick-access toolbar (located at the top left of the application window), and the Save window is displayed. We have named the chart CIS001D_ProfitMargin_Chart and are in the process of clicking OK.

Note
You will use this chart in the lab at the end of the chapter; but now would be a good time to check with your instructor regarding the naming conventions used at your college. When saving your chart, you should name the chart according to those conventions.

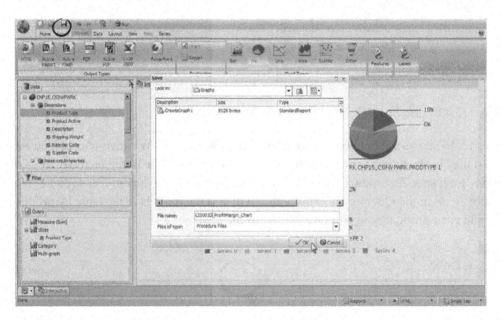

Figure 15.45: Saving the Chart

After we save the chart, the next step is to create a calculated field that we will call ProfitMarginPercent. Figure 15.46 shows the completed calculation for this field. To enter the calculation, we click the field name and then enter the calculation, including the right and left parentheses as required.

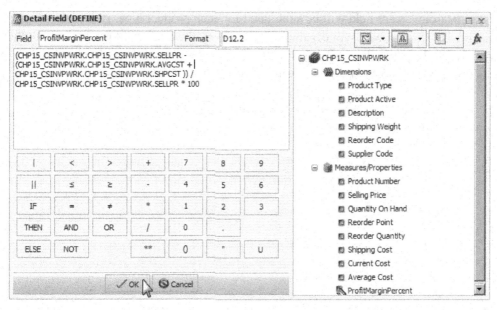

Figure 15.46: Create the ProfitMarginPercent Detail (Define) Field

 Caution

When you have completed entering your calculation, it should look exactly like the one shown below. If you misplace or fail to enter parentheses in the correct place, your chart will not be displayed properly.

```
(CHP15_CSINVPWRK.CHP15_CSINVPWRK.SELLPR -
(CHP15_CSINVPWRK.CHP15_CSINVPWRK.AVGCST +
 CHP15_CSINVPWRK.CHP15_CSINVPWRK.SHPCST)) /
 CHP15_CSINVPWRK.CHP15_CSINVPWRK.SELLPR * 100
```

The ProfitMarginPercent field will be subtotaled for each product type. Before the chart is displayed, DB2 Web Query will divide the subtotals by the total profit margins for all the product types. Then the chart will display the percentage of the total profit margins for each product type. Figure 15.47 shows the data for the chart.

Product Type	ProfitMarginPercent	Charted
GSP	214.55	7%
GSW	366.85	13%
HDD	113.33	4%
HEN	205.78	7%
LPC	149.49	5%
MON	153.84	5%
NET	259.14	9%
OFS	147.56	5%
OSW	868.26	30%
PC	122.26	4%
PRS	29.52	1%
PRT	144.46	5%
PSP	138.24	5%
	2,913.28	100%

Figure 15.47: Data Used in the Chart

Figure 15.48 shows that we placed the ProfitMarginPercent field under the Measure (Sum) icon in the Query pane. Once we accomplish this, the chart is displayed on the layout canvas.

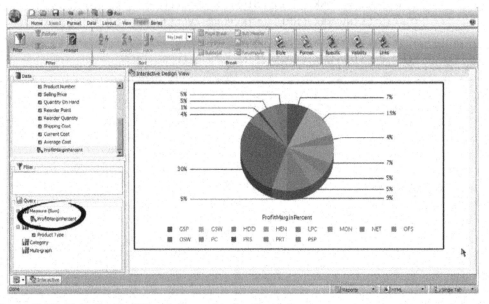

Figure 15.48: Place the ProfitMarginPercent in the Query Pane

Enhancing Charts

The profit margin chart is very informative and gives us a good idea of the profit margins for different product types. However, we need to know the product type codes to be able to decipher the chart.

A common mistake we might make when we are creating charts is not giving users all the information they need to read the chart. To avoid this error, we need to enhance our chart to include the Type Description field instead of the Product Type code. The Type Description field is stored in an associated table named CHP15_CSCINVTYP.

In Figure 15.49, we have selected the Data option on the control panel, and the Data ribbon is displayed. We will create a join to the CHP15_CSCINVTYP table by clicking the Join button in the Join group.

Figure 15.49: Data Ribbon

After we click Join, the Join window is displayed. We click Add New in this window, as Figure 15.50 shows.

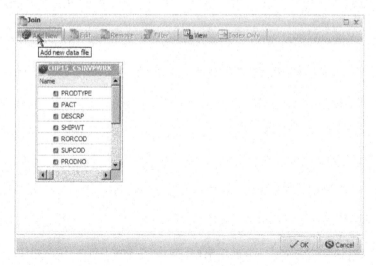

Figure 15.50: Join Window

The window in Figure 15.51 lets us select the table CHP15_CSCINVTYP. This table is keyed by the product type and contains the Type Description field we need for the chart. We have selected this table and clicked OK, as shown.

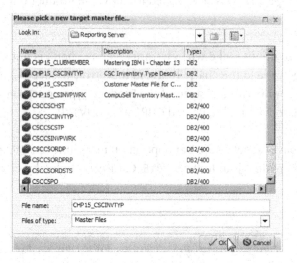

Figure 15.51: Select table Window

Figure 15.52 shows that the table CHP15_CSCINVTYP has been imported into our chart. DB2 Web Query is "smart" enough to understand that these two files are related, and it displays the relationship between the PRODTYPE field in the CHP15_CSCINVTYP table and the PRODTYPE field in the CHP15_CSINVPWRK table. To complete the join, we click OK.

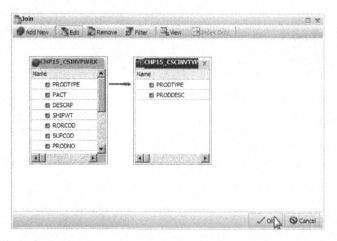

Figure 15.52: Join Window Showing Joined Tables

After we complete the join, we need to add the Type Description field to the chart. Figure 15.53 shows the four-step process, which we describe following the figure.

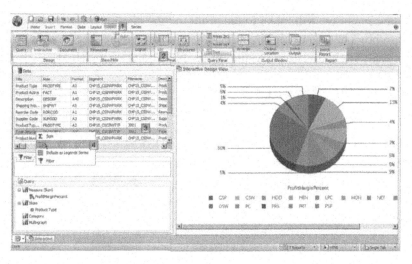

Figure 15.53: Adding Type Description to the Category Axis

1. Select View on the control panel to display the View ribbon.
2. Select the List option on the View ribbon. Doing this will change the view in the Data pane to show us the details of the fields in the chart.
3. Notice that under the Filename column in the Data pane, the two fields from the CHP15_ CSCINVTYP table are shown as J001. J001 is the description for the join we just created.
4. Right-click the PRODDESC field in the Data pane, and then select Include as Category Axis.

Figure 15.54 shows the results of these four steps. Notice that the PRODTYPE field has been replaced with the Type Description field (PRODDESC) under the Slices icon, and these descriptions are now displayed on the layout canvas.

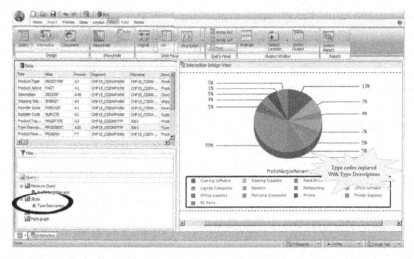

Figure 15.54: Adding Type Description to the Category Axis, Continued

The final enhancement we will make to the profit margin chart is to expand the slice for the Office Software product type to highlight it. This product type has the highest profit margin, and we want to highlight this field's value for people who view the chart.

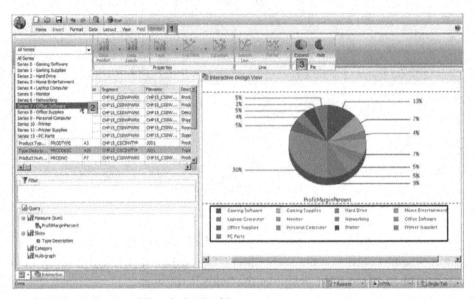

Figure 15.55: Expanding the Office Software Slice

Figure 15.55 shows the steps we took to produce the completed profit margin chart, shown in Figure 15.56.

1. Select Series on the control panel to display the Series ribbon.
2. Click the Down arrow in the Select option and select Series 7 – Office Software. This action will limit any changes to a specific series on the chart.
3. Click Expand in the Pie group to expand the Series 7 – Office Software slice.

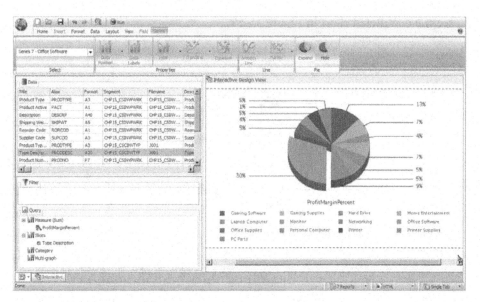

Figure 15.56: Completed Profit Margin Chart

Before we run the chart, we want to use the **Output Target** button to change the output target from Single Tab to New Window. When we run the chart, it will be displayed in a new Web page.

We should also note that the Output Format button lets you change the output type from HTML to any of the valid output types supported. The Reports button lets you switch between whatever reports or charts you currently have open in InfoAssist.

After we make the change you see in Figure 15.57, we run the chart by clicking Run on the quick-access toolbar, as Figure 15.58 shows.

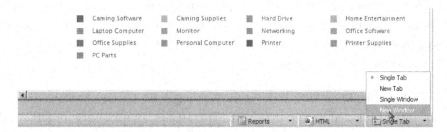

Figure 15.57: Change Output Target to the New Window

Figure 15.58: Run the Chart

You can see the completed chart in Figure 15.59.

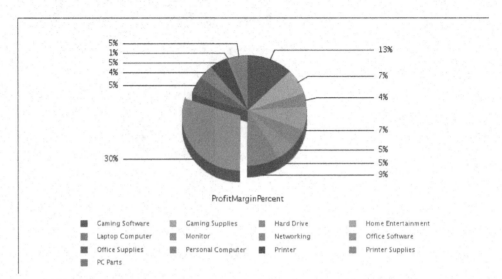

Figure 15.59: Completed Profit Margin Chart

We should save the chart before we continue with the next section on building a compound document. So we click Save on the quick-access toolbar, as in Figure 15.60.

Figure 15.60: Save the Profit Margin Chart

Creating a Compound Document

We have now created a report that shows the profit margin for the current inventory, and we have created a profit-margin percentage chart that shows profit-margin percentages by product type based on the current inventory. In this section, we will combine the chart and report into one compound document.

Figure 15.61 shows the Main DB2 Web Query Web page. We have right-clicked the student folder CIS001D and selected New Folder. **Note:** This step is not necessary for DB2 Web Query, but by now you understand the need to organize your work. ☺

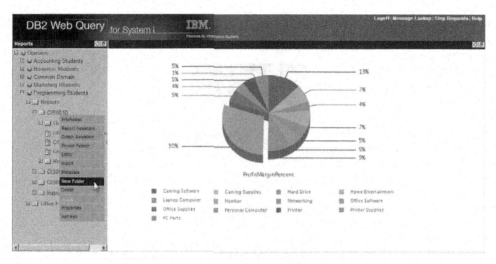

Figure 15.61: Create a Folder for Compound Documents

Figure 15.61 shows the window that lets us name our new folder; we have named the folder Documents and then clicked Save.

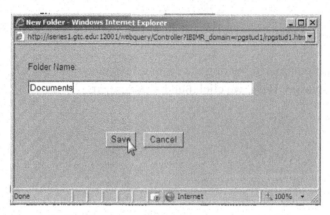

Figure 15.62: Name the New Folder—Documents

Next, we right-click the new folder Documents, and then we click the InfoAssist option to start InfoAssist, as Figure 15.63 shows.

Figure 15.63: Start InfoAssist

Once InfoAssist has completed loading the required resources, the splash screen you see in Figure 15.64 is displayed. Here, we click Build a Document.

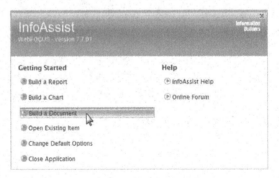

Figure 15.64: Select Build a Document from the Splash Screen

As Figure 15.65 shows, the Open window is displayed; the default selection for Files of type: is Master Files. Notice that this default shows the tables available in our development environment.

Our goal is to use the procedures (reports and charts) we have previously designed. As you see in Figure 15.65, we have changed Files of Type from Master Files to Procedure Files.

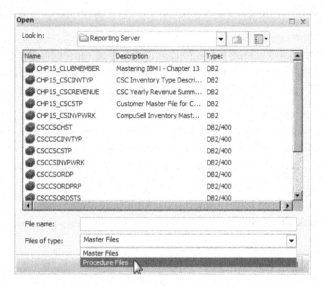

Figure 15.65: Select Procedure Files from the Open Window

DB2 Web Query, by default, looks for the procedures in the folder where the document was created. We just created a new folder named Documents, and it does not contain the procedures we need. So we will need to navigate to the folder where the necessary procedures are located. We click the Up One Level icon, as you see in Figure 15.66.

Figure 15.66: Navigate to the CIS001D Charts Folder

When we click Up One Level, DB2 Web Query takes us to the Domains level. From here, we need to navigate to the CIS001D student folder and then the Graphs folder.

Caution

The navigation steps in the following graphics represent the system that we used to develop this text. Your system is probably configured differently. You will need to work with your instructor to understand how your system is set up and follow the procedure the instructor gives you for storing and accessing your procedures. If you refer to Figure 15.63, you should be able to understand the navigation sequence that follows.

The CIS001D student folder is part of the Programming Students domain you see in Figure 15.67; we double-click this domain.

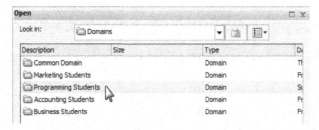

Figure 15.67: Navigate to the CIS001D Graphs Folder, Step 1

Next, we double-click the Standard Reports folder you see in Figure 15.68.

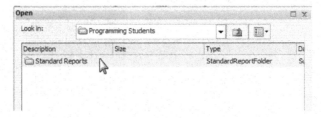

Figure 15.68: Navigate to the CIS001D Graphs Folder, Step 2

We then double-click the CIS001D student folder, as Figure 15.69 shows.

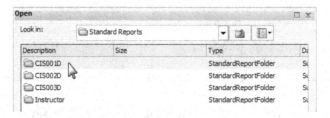

Figure 15.69: Navigate to the CIS001D Graphs Folder, Step 3

The chart we are going to insert into our document is located within the Graphs folder, so we double-click this folder, as Figure 15.70 shows.

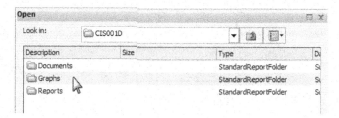

Figure 15.70: Navigate to the CIS001D Graphs Folder, Step 4

Finally, in the Graphs folder, we highlight the CIS001D_ProfitMargin_Chart that we created earlier in this chapter and click OK, as you see in Figure 15.71.

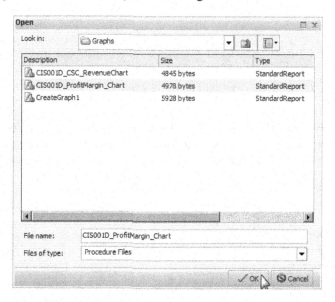

Figure 15.71: Select the CIS001D_ProfitMargin_Chart Chart

This action inserts the chart in the upper-left corner of our new document, as in Figure 15.72.

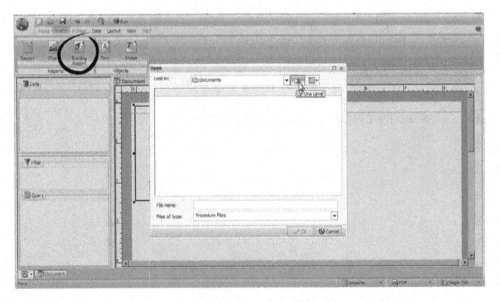

Figure 15.72: CIS001D_ProfitMargin_Chart Chart Inserted

We now need to insert the report that we created earlier in the chapter. The navigation process will be similar to the process we have just demonstrated. After we click Existing Report on the Insert ribbon, the Open window is displayed, as you see in Figure 15.73. We then click the Up One Level icon next to the arrow in this figure.

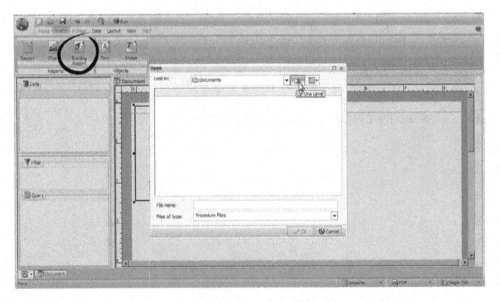

Figure 15.73: Navigate to the List CSINVPWRK Inventory Table Report

Next, we navigate to the Reports folder that contains the List CSINVPWRK Inventory Table report; then we highlight this report and click OK, as in Figure 15.74. This action inserts the List CSINVPWRK Inventory Table report into the new document.

Figure 15.74: Insert the List CSINVPWRK Inventory Table Existing Report

Figure 15.75 shows that we are moving the report down the document to make room for the chart to display (note the arrows). Moving objects around in a document is similar to moving objects around in a Windows application (click and drag). As a result, we will not describe this process in detail.

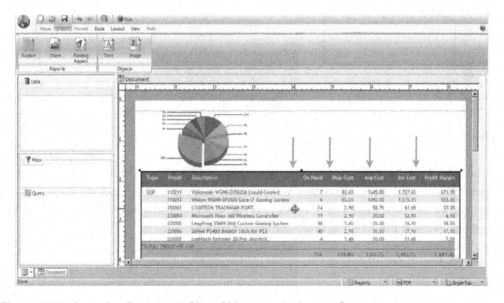

Figure 15.75: Arranging Report and Chart Objects on the Layout Canvas

We have moved the chart and the report down so that we have room to add a report heading to the document. In Figure 15.76, we click Text in the Objects group.

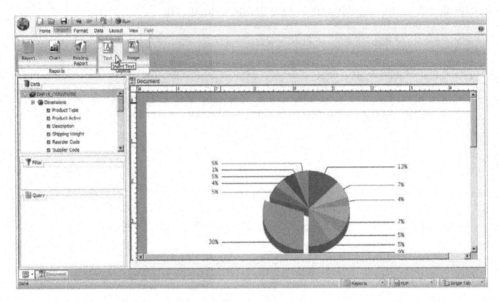

Figure 15.76: Insert a Text Box into the Document

When we click Text, a text box is inserted in the upper-left corner of the layout panel, as you can see in Figure 15.77.

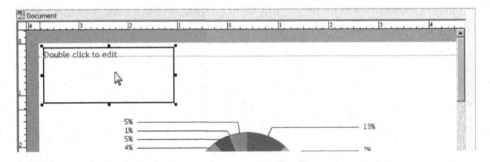

Figure 15.77: Insert a Text Box into the Document, Continued

In Figure 15.78, we have inserted text in the text box and centered the text box on the page. We then right-clicked the text box, and we are in the process of changing the text size to 24. Notice that we can take a number of other options, including additional font-change options and options to insert the date, the time, and page numbers.

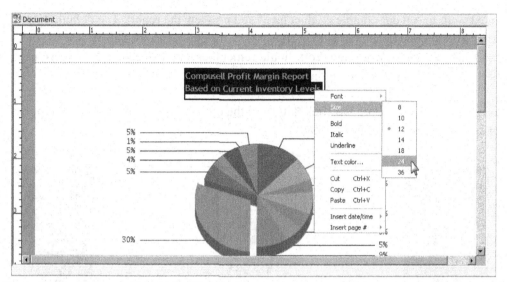

Figure 15.78: Adding and Modifying Text Heading

We have completed developing our report, and now we want to save it. We click Save on the quick-access toolbar, and the window in Figure 15.79 appears. In our example, we save the document as CIS001D_Compound_ProfitMargin_Document. We click OK, as you see in the figure, to complete the save operation.

Figure 15.79: Saving Completed CIS001D_Compound_ProfitMargin_Document File

Caution
Remember to use the naming convention that your instructor has given you.
We have used the student ID CIS001D to prefix the example.

We next want to run our completed document and preview the report. The default output type for a compound document is PDF; this is fine for our purposes, but we want to output the document in a new Web page. You should remember that to accomplish this, we need to click the Output Target button on the status bar and select New Window.

To run the completed report, we click Run from the quick-access toolbar, and the report is displayed as you see it in Figure 15.80.

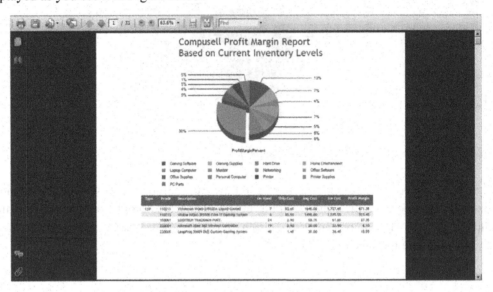

Figure 15.80: Output of CIS001D_Compound_ProfitMargin_Document File

Summary

We started this chapter with a brief history of query reporting on IBM i and a short discussion covering the limitations of Query/400. While Query/400 has served the system well for many years, the limitations, including its 5250 interface, limited output capabilities, lack of foreign database support, difficulties modifying reports, the proprietary non-SQL interface, and use of the dated Classic Query Engine (CQE) has caused today's businesses to look for a new query-reporting tool. To this end, IBM and Information Builders entered into an alliance in 2007, which resulted in a new query-reporting tool called DB2 Web Query for i. This new tool addresses the limitations of the Query/400 product.

We went on to discuss the latest version of DB2 Web Query (Version 1.1.2), which now includes InfoAssist. InfoAssist combines the features previously in the Graph Assistant, Report Assistant, and Power Painter portions of DB2 Web Query. InfoAssist's interface is based on a ribbon concept, where particular functions are grouped logically. We described working concepts such as metadata, Detail (Define) and Summary (Compute) fields, and how the functions are distributed on the different ribbons.

The majority of this chapter has been a step-by-step tutorial. We started by creating the needed metadata to access the tables on our system, and then we continued by creating a profit margin report and profit margin chart. Finally, we imported the profit margin report and profit margin chart into a compound document.

In the labs at the end of the chapter, you will modify the profit margin report to display the product description rather than the product type. You will include a filter to permit the user to select specific product types to limit the output of the report. Next, you will create a yearly profit margin report and chart, which you will then convert into a compound document. Finally, you will use a Query/400 object that we created in Chapter 13 to develop a report in DB2 Web Query.

Key Terms

AJAX	Insert ribbon
alias	Layout ribbon
compound documents	metadata
CQE	MQT
Data ribbon	Output Target button
DB2 Web Query for i	procedure
EDIT	PTOA
Field creator dialog box	Query/400
Field ribbon	recompute
Format ribbon	RIA
Format ribbon (charts)	Series ribbon
Format ribbon (reports)	splash screen
Home ribbon	SQE
InfoAssist	synonym
InfoAssist application window	View ribbon

Review Questions

1. List the limitations of Query for i5/OS.
2. List the features available in DB2 Web Query that are not available with the Query for i5/OS tool.
3. List and explain the data adapters that are available with DB2 Web Query.
4. What are domains used for in DB2 Web Query?
5. Explain the terms *metadata* and *synonym*.
6. What is the purpose of the status bar?
7. What are the options available on the Output Target button?

8. Why is it important to use tools that use SQE instead of CQE?

9. What is an MQT?

10. Research AJAX technology on the Internet. What are the benefits of this technology? Explain how it makes a Web application more robust.

11. Explain the purpose of a Detail (Define) field and of the Summary (Compute) field. How do they differ in functionality?

12. List and explain the options on the InfoAssist splash screen.

13. Why is it a good idea to use Prefix parameters when you are creating synonyms?

14. Explain the difference between a report and a document.

15. List the three types of users in DB2 Web Query. What are the capabilities of each user type?

16. Explain the functionality of the Data pane, the Filter pane, and the Query pane.

17. What is the function of the Output Target button? List and explain the options available.

18. Explain why it is important that a company have a tool that allows the company to migrate Query for i5/OS reports.

19. List the steps involved in creating a table join using DB2 Web Query.

Lab 15

Introduction

In the following labs, you will enhance the report we created in the chapter text. You will then create a yearly profit margin report, profit margin chart, and compound document for the Compusell Corporation. You will create a report based on the CLUBMEMBER and CITYSTATE tables. One of the advantages of using DB2 Web Query is the capability it provides for you to use query objects developed with Query for i5/OS and import these objects into DB2 Web Query. In Chapter 8, we created a Query for i5/OS over the logical file SECTLF1. We will import this *QRYDFN query object and develop a report similar to the report that we developed in Chapter 8.

Caution

Before you attempt to complete the following lab, you should have worked through the exercises in the chapter text and saved the report, chart, and compound document. We will use the chapter text "procedure" names to reference the procedures in this lab. If the naming conventions at your college differ, you will need to substitute those names as you work through this lab.

Part 1

Goals   Enhance the CSC profit margin report.

Start with Logged into DB2 Web Query and with the CIS001d_List CSINVPWRK Inventory Table report open in InfoAssist.

Procedure   Add a join using the table CHP15_CSCINVTYP to the report.

Change the visibility of the Product Type to Hide.

Add the Product Description to the By icon.

Add a Product Type filter to the report.

Add Selling Price to the report.

Format Selling Price and Average Cost fields.

Save the report using the naming format requested by your instructor.

Run the modified CSC profit margin report.

Figure 15.81 shows the report we developed in this chapter that you will enhance in the following lab.

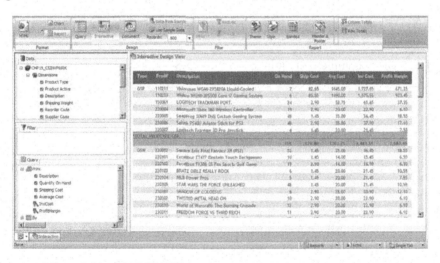

Figure 15.81: CIS001d_List CSINVPWRK Inventory Table Report

15.1.   Click the Data option on the control panel to change to the Data ribbon. Once the Data ribbon is displayed, click Join in the Join group, as in Figure 15.82, to add a join to the report, using the table CHP_CSCINVTYP.

Figure 15.82: Add a Join to the Report

The Join window will be displayed; click Add New, which will display the "Please pick a new target master file . . ." window. In this window, select the CHP15_ CSCINVTYP file that we created a synonym for in the text of this chapter.

Click OK to complete the file selection.

Figure 15.83: Add the CHP15_CSCINVTYP Table to the Report

Click OK to complete the join, as Figure 15.84 shows.

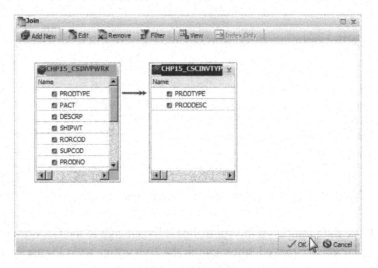

Figure 15.84: Complete the Join of the CHP15_CSINVPWRK and CHP15_CSCINVTYP Tables

After the join has been completed, the fields from the recently joined table will be displayed in the Data pane in the data resources panel, as you see circled in Figure 15.85.

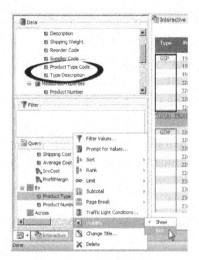

Figure 15.85: Complete the Join of the CHP15_CSINVPWRK

15.2.   You now need to change the visibility of the Product Type field in the report to Hide. You accomplish this by right-clicking the Product Type field in the Query pane, selecting Visibility, and then selecting Hide, as the figure shows.

   15.2.a.   What changes occurred in your report? Does the report still show subtotals?

15.3.   The next step is to add the product description to the By icon by dragging the Type Description field onto the icon. Figure 15.86 shows the process of dragging this field from the Data pane to the Query pane and placing it on the Product Number field under the By icon.

Figure 15.86: Add the Type Description Field to the By Icon

15.3.a. What does your report look like after you have placed the Type Description field in the Data pane?

15.3.b. What happens to your report if you delete the Product Type field from the Data pane? **Note:** If you decide to try this . . . be sure to put it back! ☺

15.3.c. Why should you place the Type Description field on the Product Number rather than directly on the By icon?

15.4. To give the user the capability to filter the report, you will add a Product Type filter to the report. To accomplish this, drag the Product Type field from the Data pane onto the Filter pane, as Figure 15.87 demonstrates.

Figure 15.87: Add a Product Type Filter to the Filter Pane

This action displays the window for creating a filter (see Figure 15.88). Click Prompt and select the Prompt using Data Values (Dynamic) option. Selecting this option will give the user a list of Product Type values directly from the database when the report is run. The user can then select one or more values at run time, which will limit the number of product types returned.

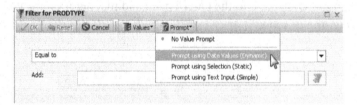

Figure 15.88: Add a Product Type Filter to the Filter Pane

The window changes, as you see in Figure 15.89. Here, you will change the prompt to read Select the Product Type(s) to be displayed:, click Allow Multiple Values for Prompt, and finally, click OK.

Figure 15.89: Add a Product Type Filter to the Filter Pane

Now, just for fun (☺), run the report. You should see a Web page like the one in Figure 15.90.

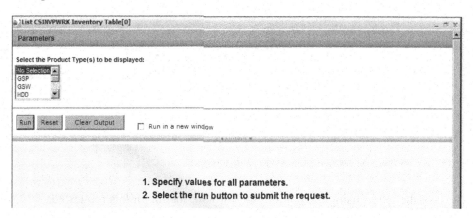

Figure 15.90: Select One or More Product Types and Submit the Report

15.4.a. How would you select more than one product type before you run the report? **Hint:** How do you select multiple values in Windows?

15.4.b. After you select one or more values and run the report, how has your report changed?

15.5. Add Selling Price to the report. Add the Selling Price field between the quantity On Hand and the shipping cost (Ship Cost) fields. The report format should look like the example in Figure 15.91.

Type Description	Prod#	Description	On Hand	Selling Price	Ship Cost	Avg Cost
Gaming Supplies	110211	Visionman WGMI-2X5820A Liquid-Cooled	7	2399.00	82.65	1645.00
	110213	Widow WGMI-3P5500 Core i7 Gaming System	6	2499.00	85.55	1490.00
	150061	LOGITECH TRACKMAN PORT.	24	99.00	2.90	58.75
	220004	Microsoft Xbox 360 Wireless Controller	19	29.00	2.90	20.00
	220005	LeapFrog 30689 Didj Custom Gaming System	48	55.00	1.45	35.00
	220006	Saitek PS40U Aviator Stick for PS3	48	55.00	2.90	35.00
	220007	Logitech Extreme 3D Pro Joystick	4	29.00	1.45	20.00

Figure 15.91: Selling Price Field Displayed on the Report

15.5.a. How did you place the Selling Price field on the report?

15.5.b. Why did you choose this method?

Format the Selling Price and Average Cost fields to include a comma separator. Select the field you want to format, which should change the ribbon to the Field ribbon for that field. Click the Format group, and then click the correct button.

The report should look like the one in Figure 15.92.

Type Description	Prod#	Description	On Hand	Selling Price	Ship Cost	Avg Cost
Gaming Supplies	110211	Visionman WGMI-2X5820A Liquid-Cooled		2,399.00	82.65	1,645.00
	110213	Widow WGMI-3P5500 Core i7 Gaming System		2,499.00	85.55	1,490.00
	150061	LOGITECH TRACKMAN PORT.	24			38.75
	220004	Microsoft Xbox 360 Wireless Controller	19	29.00	2.90	20.00
	220005	LeapFrog 30689 Didj Custom Gaming System	48	55.00	1.45	35.00
	220006	Saitek P540U Aviator Stick for PS3	48	55.00	2.90	35.00
	220007	Logitech Extreme 3D Pro Joystick	4	29.00	1.45	20.00
*TOTAL PRODTYPE GSP			156	5,165.00	179.80	3,303.75

Figure 15.92: Fields Displayed with Commas on the Report

15.6. Save the report using the naming format your instructor has requested.

Note

We have mentioned numerous times in this chapter the importance of saving your reports using the correct naming convention. We will save the report as CIS001D_ List CSINVPWRK Inventory Table.

15.7. Run the modified CIS001D_ List CSINVPWRK Inventory Table. If your instructor requires it, print the report and hand it in.

15.8. Close the CIS001D_ List CSINVPWRK Inventory Table.

15.9. Figure 15.93 shows the main DB2 Web Query window. After you click the completed report, notice that it is displayed.

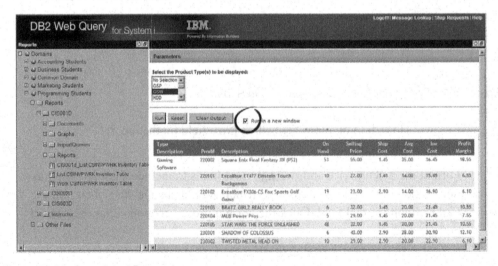

Figure 15.93: Completed Report

15.9.a.   What happens if you select a product type—for example, GSW, check the Run in new window check box, and then click Run?

Part 2

Goals   Create a CSC yearly profit margin report and chart.

Start with   Logged into DB2 Web Query.

Procedure   Right-click your student folder and select Metadata.

Create a synonym over the CSCREVENUE table.

Right-click your Reports folder and open InfoAssist.

Create a new report.

Create two defined fields and place the fields on the report.

Save the report.

Right-click your Graphs folder and open InfoAssist.

Convert the report to a bar chart.

Save the bar chart.

Format the legends.

Convert the bar chart to a compound document.

Save the compound document.

Import the report into the new compound document.

Format the compound document.

Save and run the compound report.

Caution
Depending on how your system is configured, you likely will not be required to create the metadata in steps 15.10 and 15.11 of this lab. You should consult with your instructor to find out whether this metadata exists. If you are adventurous, you might follow steps 15.10 and 15.11 to see whether the metadata has been created. **Hint:** You can see the metadata that has been created by creating a new report or chart and looking for the synonym CHP15_CSCREVENUE.

15.10. Right-click your student folder and select Metadata, as Figure 15.94 shows.

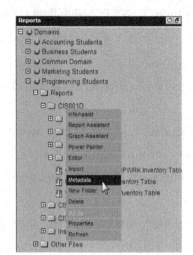

Figure 15.94: Create Metadata for the CSCREVENUE Table

15.11. Create a synonym over the CSCREVENUE table.

There are four steps in this process, which we discussed in the chapter. The quick review (see Figure 15.95) is

1. Right-click the *LOCAL icon and select Create Synonym. This action will repaint the window on the right side of the Web page.

2. Uncheck the Views check box (not required).

3. Enter the library INTROCLASS and the table name CSCREVENUE.

4. Click Next.

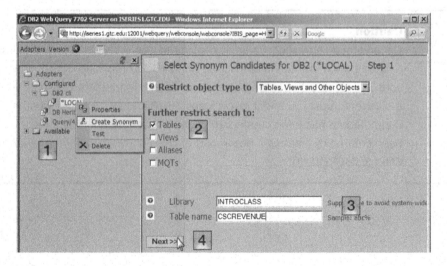

Figure 15.95: Create Metadata for the CSCREVENUE Table, Step 1 Window

The Web page is repainted, as Figure 15.96 shows; the four steps to completing this portion are

1. Check the With foreign keys check box.

2. Add the standard prefix CHP15_ for this chapter.

3. Check the check box next to the CSCREVENUE table.

4. Click Create synonym.

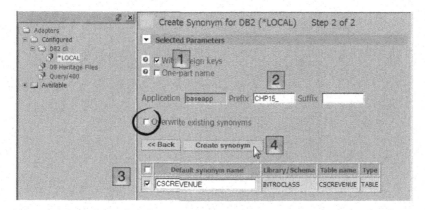

Figure 15.96: Create Metadata for the CSCREVENUE Table, Step 2 Window

You have completed the creation of a synonym for the CSCREVENUE table.

15.12. From the main DB2 Web Query Web page, right-click your Reports folder, and open InfoAssist.

15.13. From the InfoAssist splash screen, select Build a Report.

This action will display the Open window. Select CHP15_CSCREVENUE, and then click OK, as you see in Figure 15.97.

Figure 15.97: Select the CSCREVENUE Table

The data resources panel for your new report should look like the one in Figure 15.98.

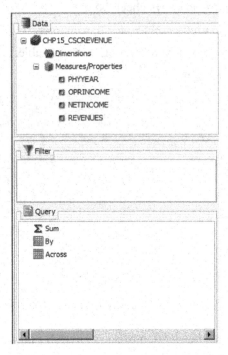

Figure 15.98: Data Resources Panel Showing the CSCREVENUE Table

This report will require two Detail (Define) fields, the Operating Profit Margin and Net Profit Margin fields. Create the required fields. The formulas for these two fields are, respectively:

OperatingProfitMargin = (OPRINCOME / REVENUES) *100

and

NetProfitMargin = (NETINCOME / REVENUES) * 100

Figure 15.99 displays the completed Operating Profit Margin Detail (Define) field.

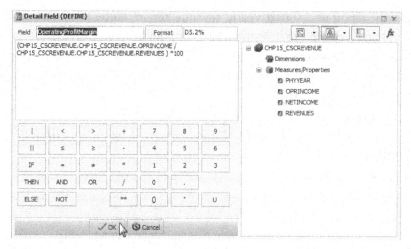

Figure 15.99: Completed Operating Profit Margin Detail (Define) Field

Click OK to complete the field.

Note

You might wonder why you need to multiply by a 100 in these formulas. Formatting a result as a percent just adds a percent sign to the result field. This is different than in some other development environments.

You now need to create a Net Profit Margin field.

Sort the report by year, and then add the fields you see in Figure 15.100.

Format the fields as in the completed report in the figure. This task includes changing the headings and formatting the dollar fields properly.

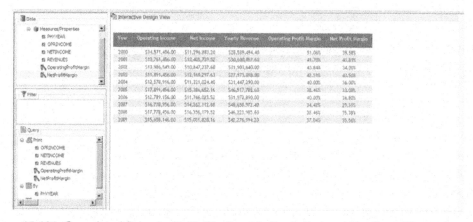

Figure 15.100: Completed Report with Fields Properly Formatted and Headings Changed

15.14. Save the report as CIS001d_Yearly Revenue Report. **Note:** Remember to follow the naming conventions your instructor has provided.

15.15. Convert the report to a chart. After you save your report, go to the Home ribbon and click Chart in the Format group. Doing this converts the report to a chart like you see in Figure 15.101.

The chart requires only the OperatingProfitMargin and NetProfitMargin fields. So delete the OPRINCOME, NETINCOME, and REVENUES fields from the Query pane. (**Note:** We have circled these fields in Figure 15.101.)

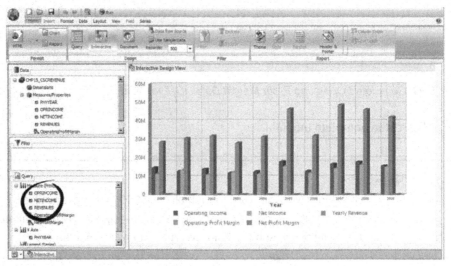

Figure 15.101: Converted Report to Chart

15.16. Save the chart as CIS001d_Yearly Revenue Chart in your Graphs folder, as Figure 15.102 shows.

Figure 15.102: Save the CIS001d_Yearly Revenue Chart

15.17. Now you will format the *x*- and *y*-axis legends. Highlight the percent fields on the *y*-axis, and then right-click and select Percent with two decimals, as you see in Figure 15.103.

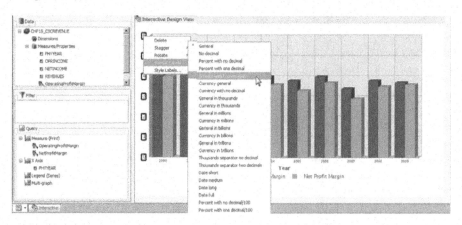

Figure 15.103: Format the Charts Legend

Change the Year on the *x*-axis to display PHYYEAR (Physical Year).

Save the completed chart, displayed in Figure 15.104.

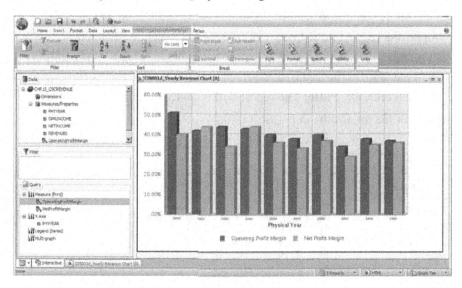

Figure 15.104: Completed CIS001d_Yearly Revenue Chart

15.18. Next, you will convert the CIS001d_Yearly Revenue Chart to a compound document. To do this, you need to navigate to the Home ribbon and click Document in the Design group.

Figure 15.105 shows the chart converted to a compound document.

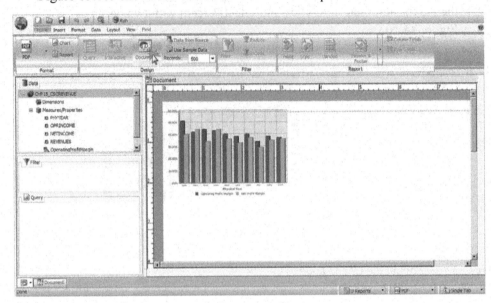

Figure 15.105: Converted CIS001d_Yearly Revenue Chart

15.19. Save the compound document as CIS001d_Yearly Revenue Document.

15.20. Import the report into the new CIS001d_Yearly Revenue Document.

To do this, go to the Insert ribbon and click Existing Report in the Reports group. Then navigate to the CIS001d_Yearly Revenue Report in the Reports folder, select it, and then click OK. **Note:** The report will be placed on top of your chart.

You can see the results in Figure 15.106.

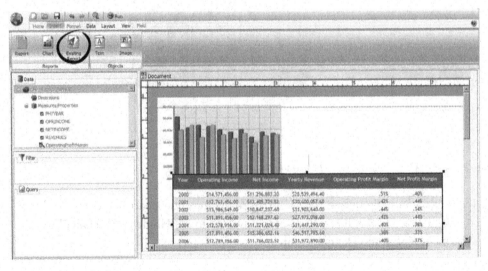

Figure 15.106: CIS001d_Yearly Revenue Document

15.21. Format the compound document so that it is formatted as you see in Figure 15.107.

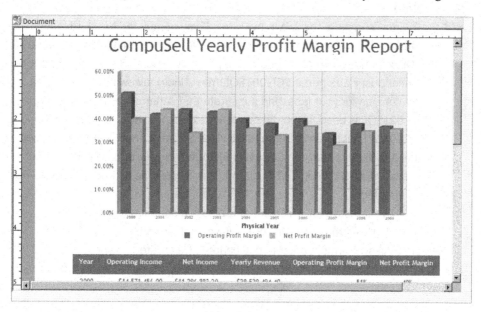

Figure 15.107: Final Formatting of the CIS001d_Yearly Revenue Document

15.22. Save and Run the compound report.

Part 3

Goals	Create a report using the CLUBMEMBER and CITYSTATE tables.
Start	Logged into DB2 Web Query.
Procedure	Right-click your Reports folder and open InfoAssist.
	Create a new report.
	Create or use the CLUBMEMBER and CITYSTATE synonyms.
	Create a join for the CLUBMEMBER and CITYSTATE tables.
	Format the telephone number.
	Save the report using the naming format your instructor has requested.
	Sort the report by State, Last Name, and First Name.
	Add required columns to the report.
	Run the club member report.

Note

You may complete this lab in two ways: If you completed the third lab in Chapter 13, you should have CLUBMEMBER and CITYSTATE tables in the SQL schema you created for that chapter. In Chapter 13, the schema for our student user was named CIS001SQL. You should review how you named the schema for your labs, and substitute that schema name whenever CIS001SQL is used. If you did not complete the lab, the CLUBMEMBER and CITYSTATE tables exist in the INTROCLASS library. The differences between these tables are that the CLUBMEMBER table in your SQL schema will not contain the CITY and STATE columns, and certain fields in the table will not be updated.

Ask your instructor which set of tables you should use to complete this lab. Using the tables in your SQL schema will allow you to practice creating synonyms. Earlier in this chapter, we created a synonym for the CLUBMEMBER and CITYSTATE tables that exist in the INTROCLASS library.

15.23. Right-click your Reports folder and open InfoAssist.

15.24. Create a new report using the InfoAssist splash screen.

15.25. Select the synonym for the CLUBMEMBER table. Check that there also is a synonym for the CITYSTATE table. These tables should be synonyms named CHP15_CLUBMEMBER and CHP15_CITYSTATE if you are using the tables located in the INTROCLASS library (Figure 15.108).

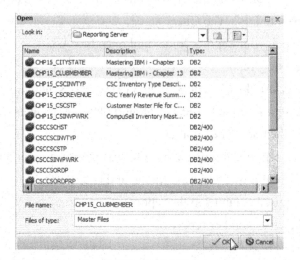

Figure 15.108: Select the Synonym for CLUBMEMBER Table

 Caution

If you are using the CLUBMEMBER and the CITYSTATE tables from your SQL schema, you should work with your instructor regarding the naming conventions for creating your own synonym.

15.26. Create a join using the Data ribbon, as the steps in Figure 15.109 demonstrate:

1. Click Join in the Join group on the Data ribbon.

2. Notice that the join was not created properly; it was created using the CITY fields. This error occurred because the tables did not have the foreign keys set up for the tables. You need to edit the join by clicking Edit.

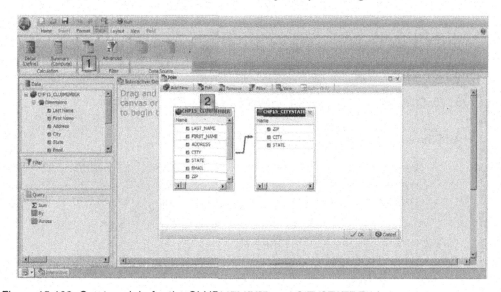

Figure 15.109: Create a Join for the CLUBMEMBER and CITYSTATE Tables

This action displays the Edit Join window you see in Figure 15.110. Name the join by entering TableJoin in the description text box. Remove CITY from each of the boxes, as you see in the figure.

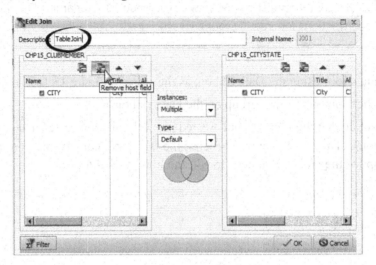

Figure 15.110: Change the Join for the CLUBMEMBER and CITYSTATE Table

Add the correct fields to the join, as in Figure 15.111.

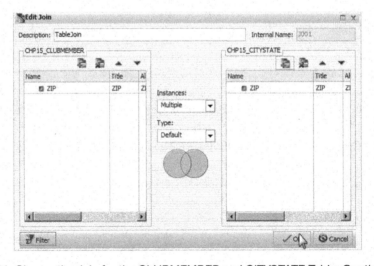

Figure 15.111: Change the Join for the CLUBMEMBER and CITYSTATE Table, Continued

Figure 15.112 shows the Join fields set up properly. Click OK, as shown, to complete the join operation.

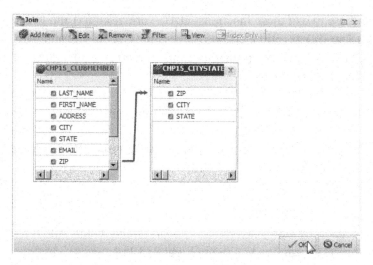

Figure 15.112: Completed Join for the CLUBMEMBER and CITYSTATE Table

15.27. Format the phone number field (AlphaPhone) by creating a Detail (Define) field. In previous examples in this chapter, we used these types of fields to do math calculations. We also can use Detail (Define) fields with a number of built-in functions. An in-depth discussion of these built-in functions is beyond the scope of this book, but you need to know that they exist. These functions are similar to functions you have used in other development environments. Figure 15.113 shows a partial list of the available functions. Notice in the top-right side of the figure that we have clicked the Function icon.

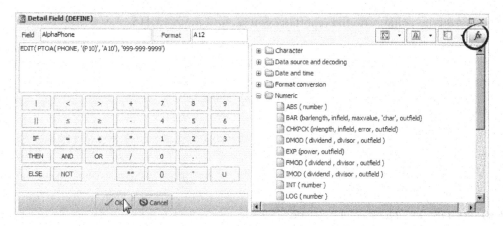

Figure 15.113: Format the Phone Number Field

You will use two of these functions: **EDIT** (Format Alpha) and **PTOA** (Packed to Alpha). The EDIT function lets you place a mask on an alphanumeric field. The PTOA function converts a packed-decimal field to an alphanumeric field. The code for accomplishing this is

EDIT (PTOA (PHONE , '(P10)' , 'A12') , '999-999-9999')

You also need to change the format of the **AlphaPhone** field to A12 as Figure 15.113 shows.

15.28. Save the report as CIS001D_Club Member Report, or use the naming format your instructor has established.

15.29. Sort the report by State, Last Name, and First Name fields. Add the fields to the By icon in the Data pane, as you see in Figure 15.114.

Figure 15.114: Sort the Fields in the Report, Step 1

15.30. Add the columns to the report, as you see in Figure 15.115.

Figure 15.115: Sort the Fields in the Report, Step 2

Your completed report should look like the one in Figure 15.116.

Tables we used for this example are from the INTROCLASS library. The club member Arndt does not have a corresponding zip code in the CITYSTATE field (1), and the Dues Paid field (2) was a field we updated in Chapter 13's lab.

Figure 15.116: Completed Report Format

15.31. Save the report.

15.32. Run the club member report, and ask your instructor how to hand it in.

Part 4

Goals   Create a report based on the Query for i5/OS object you created in the Additional Lab Exercise for Chapter 8.

Start with   Logged into DB2 Web Query.

Procedure   Create a folder named ImportQueries.

            Right-click your Reports folder and open InfoAssist.

            Select Build a Report from the DB2 Web Query splash screen.

            Use the synonym QRY15_SECTJQRY if it exists.

            If necessary, create the synonym.

            Save the report using the naming format your instructor has requested.

            Add fields to the report as in the original query.

            Format the Social Security and Phone Number fields.

            Save the report.

            Run the student report.

Note

To complete this lab, you must have completed the Additional Lab Exercise in Chapter 8. It is a good idea for you to review the Additional Lab Exercise to better understand the goal of this lab.

15.33. As you have done in previous labs, create a new folder named ImportQueries.

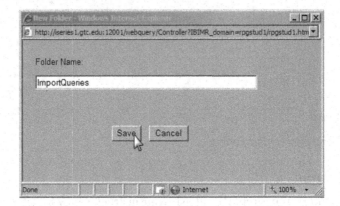

Figure 15.117: Create a New Folder Under Your Student Folder

15.34. Right-click your Reports folder and open InfoAssist, as Figure 15.118 shows.

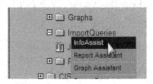

Figure 15.118: Start InfoAssist

15.35. Select Build a Report from the DB2 Web Query splash screen (Figure 15.119).

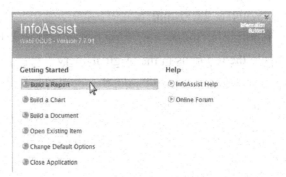

Figure 15.119: Select Build a Report from the Splash Screen

15.36. Open the QRY15_SECTJQRY synonym.

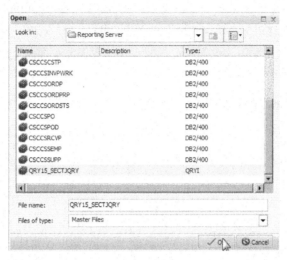

Figure 15.120: Open the QRY15_SECTJQRY Synonym

If the QRY15_SECTJQRY synonym exists, you can skip the next step.

15.37. If the synonym does not exist, ask your instructor if you should create it. If you need to create it, the basic procedure is the same as when we created synonyms earlier in this chapter. There is one important difference: When you create the synonym, you need to right-click the **Query/400** icon, as Figure 15.121 shows.

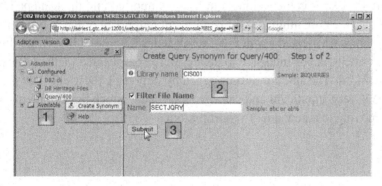

Figure 15.121: Create the QRY15_SECTJQRY Synonym

The three steps to create the synonym are

1. Right-click the Query/400 icon, and select Create Synonym.

2. Enter the values from Chapter 8 for the Library name and Name parameters.
   Note: Figure 15.121 shows the CIS001 library. You should use your personal library, and SECTJQRY is the name of the query from the Chapter 8 lab.

3. Click Submit.

15.38. Save the report using the naming format your instructor has requested. **Note:** We named the report using the same conventions we used in this chapter: CIS001D_ Imported Query SECTJQRY Report, as you can see in Figure 15.122.

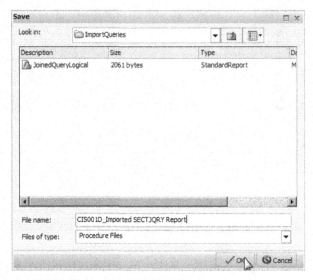

Figure 15.122: Save the CIS001D_Imported SECTJQRY Report

15.39. Add fields to your report as in the original query.

Figure 15.123 shows the Query for i5/OS report from Chapter 8. Notice that the CHI field created in the original query was imported into the Data pane as a data field. This feature might seem insignificant, but many of the queries created over the years were created as "defined result fields." Some of these calculations, besides being labor-intensive to create, were complicated mathematical expressions. The amount of time saved by importing these calculated fields as data fields is very significant and can save a company much development expense when it is moving to a new query-reporting tool.

```
                                        Current Student Enrollment by Section Number
                                        QUERY NAME . . . . . SECTJQRY
                                        LIBRARY NAME . . . . CIS001
                                        FILE        LIBRARY      MEMBER        FORMAT
                                        SECTLF1     CIS001       SECTLF1       JREC1
                                        DATE . . . . . . . . 01/06/11
                                        TIME . . . . . . . . 15:09:59
                                                  Final Lab Chapter 8
01/06/11  15:09:59                      Current Student Enrollment by Section Number                          PAGE    1
          Sect   Catalog  Catalog Name               Lect  Lab   CHI   Social       Last         First       Phone
          Nbr    Nbr                                 Hrs   Hrs         Security     Name         Name        Nbr
          14050  DG138U   Introduction to IBM i Con   2     2    3.00  367-55-9012  Eschenburg   Brian       517-293-0849
                                                                       366-42-6400  Lepard       Deborah     616-485-7129
                                                                       349-04-9381  Newburry     Roger       616-488-1935
                                                                       223-08-4359  Rupert       Leslie      616-389-2834
                                                                       154-48-8932  Smith        Patricia    313-847-3283

Section Number Total 14050
COUNT          5
          14051  DG132U   DB2 Database Management     3     2    3.50  269-96-8069  Stufflebeam  Pamela      414-839-2447
                                                                       276-68-1868  Suzuki       Yoshie      616-227-4973
                                                                       369-92-0174  Whitte       Andrea      616-498-5925
Section Number Total 14051
COUNT          3
          14052  PC230T   Abnormal Psychology         3     0    1.50  339-58-8603  Armine       Yvonne      616-283-4993
                                                                       365-64-6998  Hunter       James       515-283-9422
                                                                       367-58-7174  Taplin       Malissa     616-224-1654
                                                                       282-36-1745  Zaremba      Eileen      616-657-2835
                                                                       359-68-8909  Zimmer       Matthew     219-483-5568
Section Number Total 14052
COUNT          5
          14053  AR220T   Advanced Wheel-throwing T   0     6    6.00  900-10-8702  Al-Sharif    Amhad       616-366-8198
                                                                       368-94-0073  Beebe        Dennis      616-388-2511
Section Number Total 14053
COUNT          2
Total Students Enrolled
COUNT          15
* * *  E N D  O F  R E P O R T  * * *
```

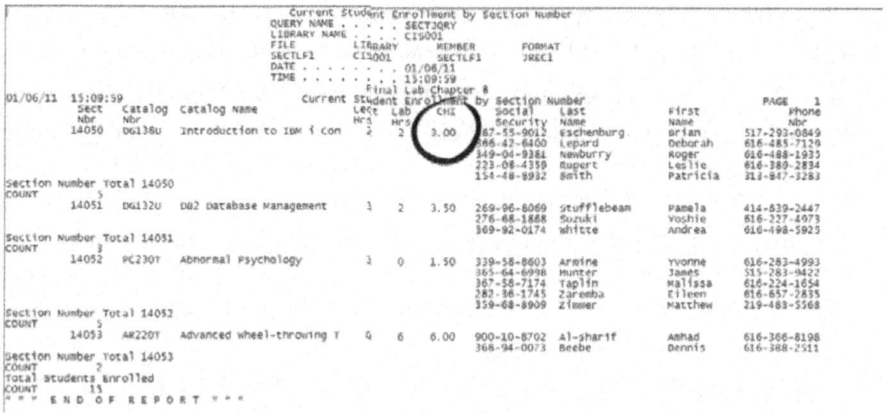

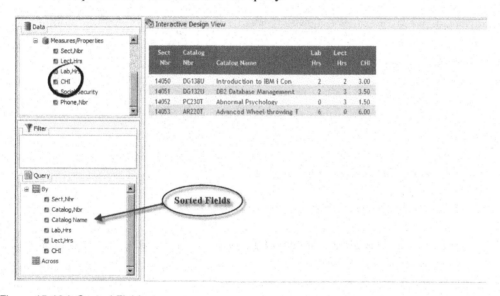

Figure 15.123: Query Report from the Additional Lab from Chapter 8

Add the fields you see in Figure 15.124 to the Query pane. Notice the field CHI that was imported as a data field into the query.

Figure 15.124: Sorted Fields

15.40. Format the Social Security and Phone Number fields with dashes. You will need to create two Detail (Define) alphanumeric fields to format these numbers.

Following are the code examples for the two fields, respectively. Figure 15.124 shows the completed AlphaPhone field. You will need to create an additional field called AlphaSSN.

AlphaPhone = EDIT (PTOA (PHONE , '(P10)' , 'A12') , '999-999-9999')

and

AlphaSSN = EDIT (PTOA (SOCSEC , '(P9)' , 'A11') , '999-99-9999')

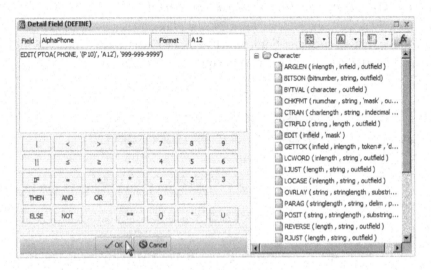

Figure 15.125: AlphaPhone Example

Add the AlphaPhone and AlphaSSN fields to the report, as Figure 15.126 shows.

Click the Section Number field, which will change the current ribbon to the Field ribbon, and then click Line Break in the Break group.

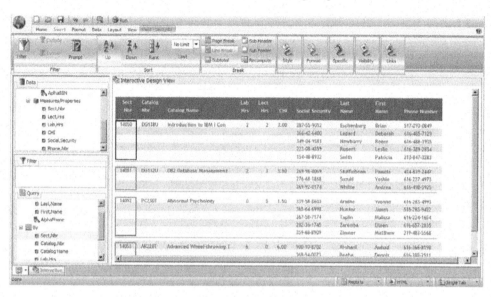

Figure 15.126: Completed CIS001D_Imported Query SECTJQRY Report

15.41. Save the report.

Run the student report.

CHAPTER 16

Getting Started with CL Programming

Overview

The Control Language (CL) of the IBM i OS is the programmers' and operators' tool for access to OS functions. Although you have used individual CL statements in all the preceding labs, in this chapter you will see how you can combine a number of related statements to create a separate program object.

We first review CL use and syntax, and then we present an overview of CL programs and their format. Next we look at the function of several specific commands used in CL programs to handle variable declaration and manipulation, file input/output (I/O), selection, iteration, and message sending. Some of these commands are used only within CL programs. They are provided to add structure, control, and flexibility to CL programs and are not used individually from a command line.

This chapter is intended as only a basic introduction to CL programming, to get you started on a couple of simple programs and to give you an idea of the capabilities. If you are a student with IBM i programming aspirations, you will want to take a CL programming class, if available, and certainly obtain a copy of a good CL programming textbook to work through, such as *Control Language Programming for IBM i* (MC Press, 2011).

Objectives

Students will be able to

- Describe common uses of CL programs
- Explain several advantages of using CL programs
- Specify the steps for creating a CL program
- Describe the parts of a CL program

Continued

- Articulate the functionality of the DCLF (Declare File) and DCL (Declare) commands
- Articulate the use of the different versions of the IF command
- Articulate the use of the DOWHILE, DOUNTIL, and DOFOR constructs
- Code the SELECT command
- Code the DOWHILE command
- Demonstrate selection and iteration control in a CL program
- Describe how a CL program can use an *OUTFILE for a display command
- Code, compile, and execute a CL program to use a display file
- Code, compile, and execute a CL program to create and access a data file

CL Review

As you have seen through the use of various CL commands in previous chapters, IBM i OS Control Language (CL) provides a single, consistent, and flexible interface to many different system functions. Individual CL commands are provided to certain classes of users and restricted from others based on their needs. This selective distribution is accomplished by assigning users to a user-profile class and further restricting use through command object authority and authorization lists. To summarize, CL

- Uses a single, consistent syntax
- Can be entered from the command line
- Can be placed in CL programs and often is included in batch jobs

You may remember from Chapter 2, or from your use of CL, that a CL command name usually consists of a verb that identifies the action, a noun that specifies the object of the action, and, optionally, a modifier that limits or narrows the range of the command. Figure 16.1 summarizes CL command notation.

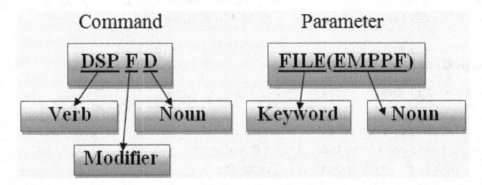

Figure 16.1: CL Syntax Notation

Recall also from Chapter 2 that CL commands can use two different types of notation to specify their parameter values

The following examples show the use of keyword notation:

DSPFD FILE(CATPF) TYPE(*ALL) OUTPUT(*PRINT)

Or, because the default value of the TYPE parameter is *ALL:

DSPFD FILE(CATPF) OUTPUT(*PRINT)

Or, because we are using keyword notation, even

DSPFD OUTPUT(*PRINT) FILE(CATPF)

The next example, and those that follow it, use positional notation:

DSPFD CATPF *ALL *PRINT

Or, because the second parameter value is the default:

DSPFD CATPF *N *PRINT

But not

DSPFD CATPF *PRINT

And certainly not

DSPFD *PRINT CATPF

The operating system helps with the preparation and use of CL commands by providing

- Prompting support for all commands
- Default values for most parameters
- Validity checking to ensure correct entry
- Selective authorization by user, user class, and group profile
- Extensive online Help for explanations of commands and parameters

CL Program Uses

There are many reasons to write CL programs, but most fall into one of the following three categories:

- *User interface*—CL programs can help give nontechnical users an interactive interface that is simple and easy to use. Such an interface lets users request application functions and control application flow, while it insulates them from command-line access. With such an interface, users do not require knowledge of CL or OS functions. And they can work with greater efficiency and less chance of error.
- *Operations*—Although many system-maintenance and housekeeping functions are built into IBM i, any system always requires specific operational procedures. When you can write these regularly needed operational procedures in CL programs, you can then test and store them in an efficient form that requires only a single command or menu choice for consistent, error-free execution. Applications might range from procedures that select records from database files to be input, to batch report programs, to procedures that selectively save objects or libraries to back up media at a certain time every night. For example, at the beginning of each semester, we use CL programs to create user profiles and class authorization lists, and to clean up output queues. At the end of the semester, we use other CL programs to remove authorization-list entries and to delete objects, libraries, and user profiles.
- *Job attributes*—Technical users and programmers may need to work in one of several different job environments, depending on immediate needs. These different environments may require changes to job attributes—for example, the composition or ordering of library-list entries, selection of output queue and/or message queue, or change of run or print priorities. In addition, users might need a special work screen (e.g., Work with Objects Using PDM for a specified library) after they sign on to the system. You can use a CL program as the initial program to automatically tailor the environment after sign-on. This initial program can execute appropriate CL commands based on the user choice from a menu-like display screen. Along the same lines, CL programs often manage **flow control**—the sequencing, setup procedures, and error handling of related high-level language (HLL) programs—in a multijob, multistep application process.

Advantages of CL Programs

Additional advantages of CL programs include the following:

- Using CL programs is faster and more accurate than keying in the commands individually.

- Some CL commands are available only from within a CL program. These include selection and iteration commands (e.g., IF-THEN, SELECT, DOWHILE, DOUNTIL), error-testing commands (e.g., MONMSG), and file-processing commands (e.g., SNDRCVF). In addition, CL programs let you declare and work with variables and retrieve values (e.g., system values, job attributes, object descriptions) that will be used as variables in a program.
- You can test and debug CL programs just as you can HLL programs. Once checked out, CL programs always provide consistent, error-free execution because the sequence of commands and the logic become part of the actual program. If factors outside the program require the program to be changed, you can modify and recompile the source CL program.
- CL programs can pass parameters to programs they call, and they receive parameters from other programs. The capability to pass parameters and for parameters to be passed makes CL programs very flexible and lets a single CL program meet the needs of different applications.
- CL programs can be bound with other Integrated Language Environment (**ILE**) HLL programs into a single, runable program object.

Creating CL Programs

A CL program is an object of type *PGM with an attribute of CLLE, and it exists as an independent entity. CL programs created before IBM released the ILE used a source member type of **CLP**. These programs are referred to as original program model (**OPM**) programs, and they do not support the features of the ILE model. All new CL programs should be created as ILE programs, with a type of **CLLE**. Previous versions of this text described OPM CL programs, but the current edition will work only with the ILE programming model.

Creating an ILE program comprises two steps. The first step is compiling the **source code** into a module, and the second step is binding the module into a program object. The three commands that we use to create CL objects, with a description of each, are

- **CRTCLPGM** (Create CL Program)—Creates OPM programs. There is no binding of OPM programs.
- **CRTCLMOD** (Create CL Module)—Creates a *MODULE object that must be bound into a *PGM object. Objects with a type of *MODULE cannot be CALLed.
- **CRTBNDCL** (Create Bound CL Program)—Combines the compiling and binding of CL source members into a program object (type *PGM).

Using RDP to Enter CL Source

We use Rational Developer for Power (RDP) to enter CL programs as source members of source physical file QCLLESRC. You learned about RDP and worked with a simple CL program in Chapter 11. You might want to review portions of that chapter before you start the lab for the current chapter.

We will create our program in the same manner we have created other members using Remote System Explorer (RSE). In our example, we will right-click the QCLLESRC source file in the student library CIS001. Figure 16.2 shows the RSE window correctly filled out for a new member called STRUPPGM, which will be a program to control the display file STRUPDSP, which you created in Lab 12.

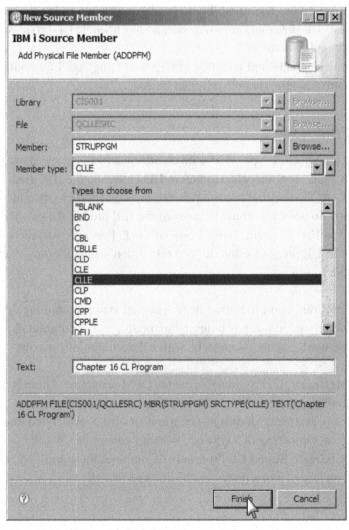

Figure 16.2: Create a New CL Program Using RSE

Note

Previous editions of this text used Source Entry Utility (SEU) to demonstrate entering CL commands into a CL program. We will be using RDP to demonstrate these commands, and we will be writing our programs as ILE programs.

Each CL command has its own unique prompt screen. Just type I (for Insert) in the source code editor, and then, on the blank line, type the command name (e.g., PGM). Press F4 if you need prompting; doing this takes you to the command-prompt screen for the command, where you can fill out the parameter values you need, as Figure 16.3 shows.

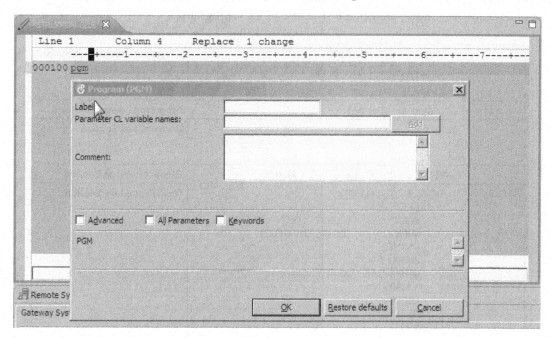

Figure 16.3: Prompting a CL Command Using RSE

You will notice that all commands have a **Label parameter** as the first parameter in the list. This parameter lets you attach a tag or label to any command in older versions of CL. These labels were used as an object of a **GOTO** command for iteration purposes. Current versions of CL have iteration commands such as DOUNTIL and DOWHILE, so labels are used for documentation purposes and, occasionally, to handle error conditions. Using the GOTO command is strongly discouraged for iteration, but you should be aware that there are many CL programs in use that still use labels for this purpose.

When you have finished with the command-prompt screen, clicking OK adds the command (in keyword notation) to your CL program. Pressing Enter inserts another line for you. In addition, if the command and its parameters will not fit on a single line, RDP inserts the continuation character (+) after a parameter and continues the command on the next line.

You will soon see exactly how this facility works, but first let us examine the general structure of a CL program.

CL Program Structure

Depending on their function, CL programs can take many different forms. Although the body of a program allows nearly limitless possibilities, a few general rules and guidelines apply. Figure 16.4 shows the general structure of a CL program.

	`/* Program ID - STRUPPGM        */`
	`/* Programmer - Jim Buck         */`
	`/* Example program for Mastering IBM i */`
		Program Information Section

	`PGM (&Parm1 &Parm2)`	**Program Linkage Section**

	`DCLF`
	`DCL`
	`DCL`
		Declarations Section

	`MONMSG (CPF0000) EXEC(GOTO ERROR)`	**Global Message Section**

`START:`	`DOUNTIL    (COND)`
	`    SELECT`
	`        WHEN      (COND)  THEN (STMT1)`
	`        WHEN      (COND) THEN(DO)`
	`          STMT2`
	`        ENDDO`
	`        OTHERWISE  DO /*  Comment  */`
	`          STMT3`
	`        ENDDO`
	`    ENDSELECT`
	`    ENDDO`
	`    /*  Comment  */`
	`    If (COND) STMT4`
	`      ELSE STMT5`
	`    RETURN`
		Main Procedure Section

`ERROR:`	`DMPCLPGM          /* Dump CL program */`
	`SNDPGMMSG MSG('Error occurred in PGM')`
	`RETURN`
		Error Procedure Section

`END:`	`ENDPGM`	**End Program**

Figure 16.4: General Structure of a CL Program

The **Program Information Section** is not formalized in a CL program and must be entered using comments. Comments are any text on a line bracketed by a beginning /* and an ending */. The **program ID** should at least identify the program by name, briefly state the program's purpose or function, and identify the program's author.

The **PGM statement** must be the first statement in the CL program. This statement also must list all CL variable names used to reference parameters passed to the program. These **parameters** are data elements passed to the program to enable the program code to behave differently based on the data received. For example, you might pass a date parameter to a program, and the program logic will then make decisions based on the value of that data (note the &Parm1 and &Parm2 in Figure 16.4). When the program receives no parameters, the PGM statement is optional, but it is usually used anyway. When parameters are passed, the position of the parameter-list variables in the called program must match the calling program's parameter list. Each variable in the PGM parameter list of the called program must be identical in size and type to the calling program's corresponding parameter.

For example, if an RPG program called a CL program and passed it a five-digit, packed-decimal section number, the CL program's PGM statement would look like this:

```
PGM  PARM(&SectNo)
```

Variable &SectNo would be defined as

```
DCL  &SectNo *DEC (5,0)
```

The **Global Message Section** of the program is used for overall MONMSG statements to handle unexpected errors in the program. In Figure 16.4, the MONMSG traps CPF0000, which is a special message identifier that looks for any message beginning with CPF. This program-level error trapping should always include a branch to a generic error routine. This is an example of one of the few occasions on which you should use a GOTO statement.

The **Declarations Section** may include DCLF and DCL statements. These statements, when present, must immediately follow the PGM statement and precede any other statements in the program.

The **DCLF** statement, if present, declares files to be accessed by the CL program. You can use up to five DCLF statements in a CL program. These files can be display files or database files. If you use more than one DCLF statement, each statement must include an open file identifier, as shown here:

```
DCLF  EMPPF OPNID(EMPPF)
```

You use **DCL** statements to declare variables needed by the CL program. **Variables** serve the same purposes in a CL program that they do in an HLL program—as counters, accumulators, indicators, or character strings. You can declare any number of variables in a single CL program.

The **Main Procedure Section** of the program follows. **Sequence operations** are implemented simply by one CL command following another. Practically any CL commands can be executed in any required order, but there are certain restrictions. For example, you cannot include commands that require an interactive environment in a program that will be run in batch. Selection logic is implemented using IF-THEN-ELSE or SELECT structures. When multiple statements must be executed for a certain selection result, the statements must be blocked within a DO-ENDDO group structure.

The **Error Procedure Section** is where any error processing is handled. It is important that some type of error processing be included in a CL program because it allows the programmer or operations personnel to track what occurred and to resolve any problems. We often use CL programs for many large batch-processing jobs; therefore, the error-processing routines are often very sophisticated.

The **ENDPGM** statement, which is optional, marks the end of the CL program. When the program encounters this command, control returns to the calling program (or interactive job).

The best way to understand how the parts of a CL program work together is to design, code, and test one. That is what we will do now.

Designing the Start-Up Program

The function of our sample program, which we will call STRUPPGM, is to set up a working environment based on a user's selection and then take the user to a departure point within that environment. Upon exiting from one environment, the user should be able to enter another environment, sign off the system, or return to the calling program.

The program will display a screen that lists the possible work environments and lets the user input a selection. This screen already exists as your Lab 12 display file STRUPDSP (Figure 12.50), which lets the user request and establish a certain work environment immediately upon signing on to the system. The display file allows the following choices:

- 1) Intro to the IBM i Operating System
- 2) DB2 Data Management
- 3) Intro to RPG Programming
- 90) Sign Off

You could also use function key F3, which ends the program. Of course, the display file and program could allow for many more choices, but for our purposes these three choices, plus sign-off, will suffice.

We make certain assumptions about each work environment:

- Each user will have a separate test library, and the user's current library will be set to this test library upon entry into the environment.
- Each user will have a separate output queue, which will contain the spooled files created while the user is working in the environment.
- There will be a class library (INTROCLASS) to which a user in that environment will have at least object operational authority.

An initial structure chart for such a program would look like Figure 16.5.

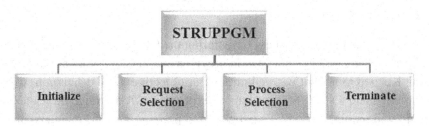

Figure 16.5: CL Sample Program Structure

Examining the process steps for each of these modules might produce the following tentative list:

1. *Initialize*
   - Declare the display file.
   - Declare a character variable for the message text.
2. *Request Selection*
   - Send (write) the display file to the display device.
   - Receive (read) the selection (CHOICE) entered by the user.
3. *Process Selection*
   - Evaluate CHOICE, and, if valid:
     ○ Change the library list.
     ○ Change the job (output queue).
     ○ Start Work with Objects Using PDM.
   - If invalid:
     ○ Turn on an option indicator.
     ○ Send (write) the display file to show the error.

4. *Terminate*

- End the program and transfer to the initial menu, or
- End the program (and the job) by signing off.

CL programs can have subroutines and procedures similar to RPG and COBOL. We will not discuss these concepts in depth in this chapter. You should understand the terms and have a general concept of their use. A **subroutine** is a named block of code with an identifiable beginning and end that is invoked for a specific purpose from other portions of the CL program. **Procedures** are similar to subroutines in that they are named blocks of code that perform a specific function, but the source is not included in the CL program. The procedure is compiled separately and bound together when the executable program object is created. Today's CL programmer has many of the same tools that are available in HLL languages such as RPG and COBOL.

Entering the Program

In this section, we examine the process for entering the CL program. As we go along, we will explain statements we have not used in previous chapters, but only as needed for the task at hand. Keep in mind that we are limiting our objectives (and discussion) to what is needed to compile and test a few very simple CL programs. A thorough understanding of CL programming will require a good CL textbook (and perhaps the IBM manuals) and many hours of designing, coding, and testing different types of applications.

Figure 16.6 shows the program ID and PGM statement for program STRUPPGM.

```
/ *STRUPPGM.CLLE  ☒
  Line 18        Column 24     Replace
     ----+----1----+----2--▊-+----3----+----4----+----5----+----6----+----7-
000101 /**********************************************************************/
000102 /*Program information Section                                        */
000103 /*   Display options list using display file STRUPDSP, input choice */
000104 /*     and then process selection, setting up work environment.      */
000105 /*     Signoff is allowed; F3 transfers to Initial Menu.             */
000106 /*                                                                   */
000107 /*     Parameters: none                                             */
000108 /*     DSPF variables:  &CHOICE  *CHAR 2  I/O  selection field        */
000109 /*                      &IN40    *LGL    O    option ind for error    */
000110 /*                      &IN03    *LGL    I    response ind for exit   */
000111 /*                                                                   */
000112 /*   Author: Jim Buck                          Modified: 10-10-2010  */
000113 /**********************************************************************/
000114          PGM             /* Program Linkage Section - NO Parms       */
000115 /**********************************************************************/
000116 /*  Declarations Section                                             */
000117 /**********************************************************************/
000118          DCLF    █
```

Figure 16.6: Program ID As Comments

The program ID consists of comments—each line begins with /* and ends with */. Because no parameters are being passed to the program, there is no parameter list and, technically, a PGM statement is not required.

Declaring a File

The DCLF (Declare File) command lets a CL program interact with a file—either a display file or a database file. As we have noted, a maximum of five DCLF commands are permitted in a program. Notice in Figure 16.6 that a new line has been inserted after line 17, and that we have keyed in the DCLF command to declare the display file. Prompting after we type the DCLF command takes us to a command-prompt screen for the command.

Figure 16.7 shows the DCLF command-prompt screen with the required File parameter name, STRUPDSP, typed in.

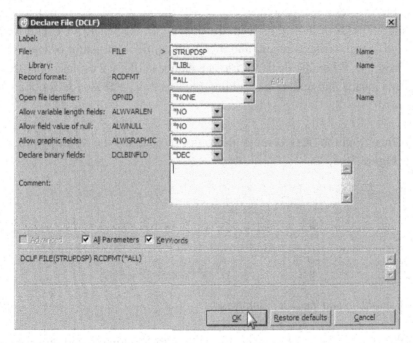

Figure 16.7: DCLF Command Prompt Screen

The first parameter, Label, which appears with all commands prompted from within a CL program, lets us attach a programmer-defined name to any command in the program. We do not need a label on the DCLF command because it is a declarative and not part of the body of the program.

The **Record format parameter**, which defaults to *ALL, lets us specify a particular record format. Our file has just one format, RECORD1, so the default value of *ALL will be fine.

When we compile a program that contains a declared file, all input and output fields that are named in the file become available to the CL program as variables. The program does not explicitly declare the variables, but it can reference them using the same name as that defined in the file (an ampersand, or &, must precede all CL variable names). Indicators defined in the display file—both response indicators associated with command attention/ function keys and option indicators used to condition display attributes, fields, and so on— are also available to the program. Each indicator will be referenced as a logical variable, whose name will start with &IN. For example, indicator 03, defined for command attention key CA03 in display file STRUPDSP, will be referenced as &IN03 in the CL program. The file named in the DCLF statement must exist at the time the program is compiled so that its fields and indicators can be included in the compiled program.

When a file is declared in a program, the file can be accessed using other CL commands that allow input/output operations to the file. A display file can use the **SNDF** (Send File) command, which writes a record to the display file; the **RCVF** (Receive File) command, which reads input fields or indicators from the display; or the **SNDRCVF** (Send/Receive File) command, which writes a record and then waits until an indicator or input data is sent back to the program. When the declared file is a database file, we can use only the RCVF command. This means that updating or adding records to a database file is not an option for a CL program.

We pressed Enter from the DCLF command-prompt screen, and the resulting program code is displayed in Figure 16.8.

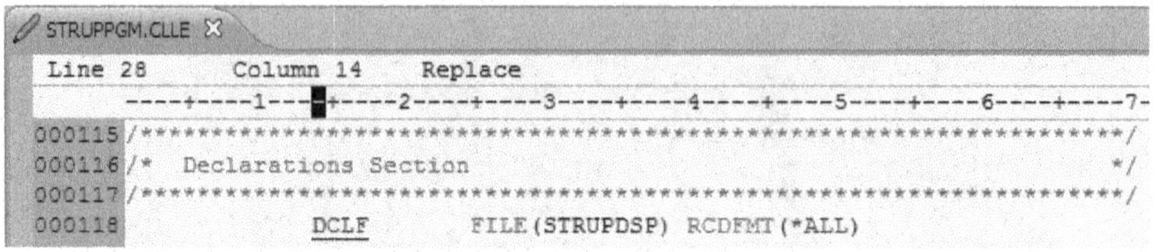

Figure 16.8: After Entering the DCLF Command

Notice that the DCLF command has been shifted over to column 14, and the parameter, in keyword notation, has been entered beginning in column 25. This is the standard indentation, but you can change it by inserting or deleting spaces on any line. Changing indentation may improve the readability of a nested IF statement, for example.

Declaring Variables

You use the DCL (Declare) command in a CL program to explicitly declare variables. All variable names begin with the & character. As we mentioned earlier, it is not necessary to declare variables made available through a file. Five types of CL variables exist. Those variable types, together with a short description of each, are

- *Decimal (*DEC)*—Numeric, packed-decimal variables.
- *Character (*CHAR)*—Character or string variables.
- *Logical (*LGL)*—Indicators that function as switches (on or off, true or false). **Note:** Logical variables can have only the value '1' for On/true or '0' for Off/false.
- *Integer (*INT) and (*UINT)*—Signed and unsigned integer variables.
- *Pointer (*PTR)*—Contains a memory address.

Figure 16.9 lists these variables types, showing default and maximum lengths as well as the default values. At the bottom of the figure are some examples.

DCL (Declare CL Variable)		
DCL VAR(&NAME) TYPE( ) LEN( ) VALUE( )		
TYPE( )	**LEN( )**	**VALUE( )**
*DEC	Default:	(15 5)	Default: (0)
	Maximum:	(15 9)	
*CHAR	Default:	(32)	Default: ( )
	Maximum:	(32,767)	
*LGL	1		Default: ('0')
*INT	Default:	4 bytes	Default: (0)
	Maximum:	4 bytes	
*UINT	Default:	4 bytes	Default: (0)
	Maximum:	4 bytes	
*PTR	Length cannot be specified; pointers have a length of 16.		
Note: *INT & *UINT can be only 2 bytes or 4 bytes.		
Examples		
1. DCL &CODES *CHAR 5 ABCD 2. DCL &AMT *DEC (5 2) 123.45 3. DCL &ON *LGL VALUE('1') 4. DCL &INT *INT 2 VALUE(34) 5. DCL &CHR *CHAR LEN(10) VALUE('Rainbow') 6. DCL &PTR *PTR ADDRESS(&CHR)		

Figure 16.9: CL Variable Types and Attributes

When a variable is declared, only its name and type are required. However, it is a good idea to explicitly include the length. If you do not declare the variable's length and value, the length will default as you see in Figure 16.9. Character variables default to a length of 32 and a value of spaces. Logical variables can only have a length of 1, so there is no need to declare a LEN attribute for a logical variable.

We use variables in CL programs much the same as we use them in HLL programs—to reference data items, or as indicators, counters, accumulators, and as working-storage items for data manipulation, intermediate arithmetic results, or type conversion, substring, or concatenation operations.

We have added two additional variables—&MyName and &EndPgm—that we will use in our CL program, as Figure 16.10 shows. Notice that these variables are in mixed case, which makes them easy to distinguish from CL commands. If you prompt for the DCL command, RDP always returns the command and the associated variables using keyword notation, and the variable will be in uppercase type.

```
000115/*********************************************************************/
000116/*   Declarations Section                                          */
000117/*********************************************************************/
000118          DCLF      FILE(STRUPDSP) RCDFMT(*ALL)
000119          DCL       &MyName *CHAR 15  'Jim Buck -'
000120          DCL       &EndPgm *LGL  VALUE('0') /* Off */
000122/*********************************************************************/
000123/* Global Message Segment                                          */
000124/*********************************************************************/
000125          MONMSG    MSGID(CPF0000) EXEC(GOTO ERROR)
000126/*********************************************************************/
000127/*   Main Procedure Segment                                        */
000128/*********************************************************************/
```

Figure 16.10: Additional Variables Used

Figure 16.10 also contains the **Global Message Segment** for our program, which includes a MONMSG command and a GOTO ERROR command. The **MONMSG** (Monitor Message) command checks for predefined errors; if an error occurs, whatever command was entered in the **EXEC parameter** will be processed. For example, if an untrapped command prefix (CPF) error occurs in the CL program, the GOTO command will cause the program to branch to the ERROR label and execute any CL commands in that section of the program. Following is an example of code that catches two errors, and the program branches to an error routine:

```
MONMSG  MSGID(CPF0001 CPF1999) EXEC(GOTO ERROR)
```

Changing the Value of a Variable

When you must set a variable to a value other than its initial value, or must increment it by some arithmetic expression, you need the **CHGVAR** (Change Variable) command. Figure 16.11 summarizes the CHGVAR command and provides examples of its use.

CHGVAR (Change Variable)
CHGVAR VAR(CL variable) VALUE(expression)

The current value of the CL variable is replaced by an expression.
• The expression may be
  ◦ a constant;
  ◦ another variable; or
  ◦ an arithmetic or logical expression.
• CHGVAR can convert data between decimal and character variables.

Examples
1. CHGVAR &AMT 2 2. CHGVAR &NAME 'ZZ TOP' 3. CHGVAR &CODE Z 4. CHGVAR &CNTR (&CNTR + 1) 5. CHGVAR &IN05 (&A > &B *OR &IN1O) 6. CHGVAR &IN03 (&CHOICE = QUIT) 7. CHGVAR &AMT ((&PRICE * &QTY) — &DISCOUNT)

Figure 16.11: CHGVAR Summary

The CHGVAR command has two required parameters. The first is the VAR (Variable) parameter, which names the variable to be changed. The second is the VALUE parameter, which specifies the new value that the variable will assume. The value can be expressed as a constant, another variable, or an arithmetic or logical expression. When you use an expression as the value, you must enclose it in parentheses.

You can use the CHGVAR command to convert from decimal to character types or, with caution, from character to decimal. A common reason for this type of conversion is to be able to display, as part of a message, a decimal variable value used as a counter or an accumulator.

Suppose, for example, that the variable &CNTR, shown in example 4 in Figure 16.11, had been used to count the objects deleted from a certain library. If you wanted to display that information as a message to the interactive job calling the program, you would first need to convert the information to a character type. If &CNTR were declared as a four-digit integer, you could declare a new variable as follows:

DCL &ACNTR *CHAR 4

And after the count was completed, you could convert the numeric &CNTR to a character variable by coding

CHGVAR &ACNTR &CNTR

This command would place the character equivalent of the packed-decimal value in &CNTR into the character variable &ACNTR. You could then concatenate the value to a message and send it to a message queue or job, using a command such as

```
SNDPGMMSG MSG(&ACNTR *BCAT 'objects have been deleted')
```

Control Structures

To implement a selection in CL programs, we use the IF or the SELECT statement. We achieve iteration, or looping, using the DOFOR, DOUNTIL, or DOWHILE statement, which we will discuss shortly.

If/Else Structures

The syntax of a simple IF statement is

IF *(condition)* THEN*(command)*

The *condition* can be a simple relational or logical expression, a negated expression using the logical operator *NOT, or a combined expression using the logical operators *AND and *OR. The keyword THEN is optional; if you use it, you must enclose the *command* value in parentheses. Although the syntax lets you execute only a single command for true or false results, you can group any number of commands within a **DO-ENDDO block structure**, and because DO is counted as a single command, this arrangement satisfies the syntax.

Table 16.1 lists the relational operators used with a CL IF command and their functions.

Table 16.1: Relational Operators Summary	
Operator	Function
< or *LT	Less than
> or *GT	Greater than
= or *EQ	Equal to
>= or *GE	Greater than or equal to
<= or *LE	Less than or equal to
< or *NL	Not less than
> or *NG	Not greater than
= or *NE	Not equal to

The alphanumeric versions of the relational operators (*EQ, *NL, and so on), as well as the logical operators *NOT, *AND, and *OR, must be separated from their operands by one or more spaces. For example, (&A *EQ &B) will compile, but (&A*EQ&B) will not. However, variables do not follow this rule; (&A=&B) is fine.

Testing logical variables does not require a relational operator, although you can use a relational expression if you like. For example, the statement

IF (&IN40 = '1')

is equivalent to

IF &IN40

and

IF (&IN40 = '0')

is equivalent to

IF (*NOT &IN40)

In the preceding examples, it is important to remember that a single logical variable (e.g., &IN40) is implicitly either true or false ('1' or '0') at any time—it does not require evaluation. Any other type of conditional expression, even *NOT &IN40, requires evaluation and must be enclosed in parentheses.

You would use the **ELSE** command in an IF statement to code a command to be executed for true results and a different command to be executed for false results. The ELSE command must always be paired with a preceding IF. CL has no ENDIF command, but because the IF command executes only one command (and a DO group is terminated by ENDDO), determination of scope should not be a problem. In the following notation, *commandn* means one command, but if that command were **DO**, you could include several CL commands in the DO-ENDDO block.

A linear nested IF takes the following general form:

```
IF          (condition1)   command1
ELSE IF         (condition2)   command2
  .
  .
  .

ELSE        commandn
```

A nonlinear nested IF takes the form

```
IF          (condition1) +
   IF          (condition2) +
      IF     (condition3) command1
      ELSE   command2
   ELSE       command3
ELSE          command4
```

and is justified by the fact that there are commands to be executed for false results of *condition1* and *condition2*. Without commands for false results of these conditions, a simpler alternative could be written

```
IF    (condition1 *AND condition2 *AND condition3) +
command1
ELSE   command2
```

The + characters you see in the examples above are **continuation characters**. When one command does not fit on a single line (or if you choose to break a command across lines), you must indicate that the command is continued on the next line. The + causes the command to be continued from the first nonspace character on the next line. If you break the command at the end of one parameter, be sure to leave at least one space between the rightmost character of the parameter and the +, or a syntax error will result.

For a nonlinear nested IF, the second IF command is actually the **THEN**(*command*) parameter value of the first IF command and syntactically part of it. Therefore, if you code it on a separate line, as is shown above, a continuation character is required at the end of the preceding line.

Instead of using continuation characters, as in the preceding example, we could have written the nested IF as

```
IF  (condition1) IF (condition2) IF (condition3) command1
ELSE command2
ELSE command3
ELSE command4
```

(assuming the first IF statement could ever fit on one line). In general, the earlier example is regarded as being easier to read and interpret.

Figure 16.12 summarizes the different forms of IF commands.

Simple IF:				
IF	(&A= &B)		CALL	PGMX

Negated IF:				
IF	(*NOT(&A	&B))	CALL	PGMX

Combined IF:	
IF	(&A=&B *AND &C = &D) CALL PGMX

Nested linear IF:				
IF	(&A = &B)		CALL	PGMX
ELSE IF	(GC = &D)		CALL	PGMY
ELSE	CALL	PGMZ		

Nested nonlinear IF:			
IF	(&A = &B) +		
IF	(= &D)	CALL	PGMX
ELSE	CALL	PGMY	
ELSE	CALL	PGMZ	

Figure 16.12: IF Command Variations

Selection Structure

The use of IF structures allows you as the programmer to make very complicated decisions within a program. These structures can become very difficult to set up and hard for other programmers to decipher. CL has a SELECT structure that can simplify the decision process.

The commands used to produce this case-logic, and a short description of them, are

- **SELECT and ENDSELECT**—Delineate the start and end of the block of commands
- **WHEN**—Evaluates the condition
- **OTHERWISE**—Names the command that should be executed if none of the WHEN conditions are satisfied

The Select group structure takes the following form:

```
SELECT
WHEN      COND(condition) THEN(CL-command)
OTHERWISE  CMD(CL-command)
ENDSELECT
```

When the Select structure is processed, only one WHEN command will be executed in the structure, and the OTHERWISE command will be executed only if none of the WHEN conditions is executed. The following code uses SELECT/WHEN/OTHERWISE to call different programs, depending upon different sales levels:

```
SELECT
   WHEN     (&PayRate *LE 15) /* Do nothing */
   WHEN     (&PayRate *LE 25) CALL PAYPGM1
   WHEN     (&PayRate *LE 50) CALL PAYPGM2
   OTHERWISE  CALL PAYPGM3
ENDSELECT
```

In this example, for &PayRate values of 0 to 15, nothing will happen; the rest of the lines in the SELECT group will be skipped. The comment on this line is documentary, but the "empty" command, without a comment, would have been allowed. For &PayRate in the 16 to 25 range, PAYPGM1 would be called. For &PayRate in the 26 to 50 range, PAYPGM2 would be called. For &sales above 51, PAYPGM3 would be called.

You also could use the DO command to execute blocks of commands, as the following example illustrates:

```
SELECT
  WHEN (&cost *LT 0)  /* Do nothing */
  WHEN (&cost *EQ 0) DO
    CHGVAR &status 'Y'
    CALL STATPGM
    DLTF TRANSFILE
    ENDDO
  OTHERWISE CALL CURPGM2
ENDSELECT
```

Iteration Structures

Iteration (loop control) has been greatly expanded in recent versions of CL. Programmers no longer need to GOTO a label to perform iterations in CL. The CL language now has the functionality to handle sophisticated iteration using the following commands:

- DOWHILE—A loop based on a conditional test
- DOUNTIL—A loop based on a conditional test; ensures the commands within the loop structure are executed at least once
- DOFOR—A loop for a specific number of iterations

DOWHILE Command

The **DOWHILE** command establishes a loop based upon a conditional test. All the commands between the DOWHILE command and its corresponding ENDDO command are repeated as long as the condition specified in the COND parameter remains true. The DOWHILE loop takes the form

```
DOWHILE COND(condition)
 . . . (group of CL commands)
ENDDO
```

The value for the COND parameter may be a logical expression or a logical variable (*LGL).

In the following example, the code inside the loop will be executed repeatedly as long as the &flag variable remains on. In this case, after the loop is completed, &int would have a value of 101, and &flag would be off ('0'). The program would then continue with the command following the ENDDO.

```
DCL &flag *LGL  VALUE('1')  /* On */
DCL &int  *INT

. . .
DOWHILE &flag
  CHGVAR &int (&int + 1)
  IF (&int *GT 100) CHGVAR &flag '0'
ENDDO
```

DOUNTIL Command

Like DOWHILE, the **DOUNTIL** command establishes a loop based upon a conditional test. All the commands between the DOUNTIL command and its corresponding ENDDO command are executed at least once and then are repeated until the condition specified in the COND parameter remains true. The DOUNTIL loop takes the form

```
DOUNTIL COND(condition)
 . . . (group of CL commands)
ENDDO
```

The value for the COND parameter may be a logical expression or a logical variable (*LGL).

In the following example, the code inside the loop will be executed once and will continue processing until the &flag variable is turned on. In this case, after the loop is completed, &int

would have a value of 101, and &flag would be on ('1'). The program would then continue with the command following the ENDDO.

```
DCL &flag *LGL  VALUE('0')  /* Off */
DCL &int  *INT
. . .
DOUNTIL &flag
  CHGVAR &int (&int + 1)
  IF (&int *GT 100) CHGVAR &flag '1'
ENDDO
```

DOFOR Command

As an alternative, CL offers the **DOFOR** command to establish a **count-controlled loop**. Unlike the conditional commands DOWHILE and DOUNTIL, the DOFOR command automatically increments a counter variable to ensure that the repetition occurs the desired number of times. The DOFOR command takes the form

```
DOFOR VAR(counter-variable)       +
    FROM(start-value) TO(end-value) +
    BY(increment-value)
```

The required **VAR parameter** identifies the counter variable; it must be an integer (type *INT or *UINT). The required FROM parameter sets the initial value for the counter; it can be an integer literal, a variable, or an expression. The initial value is assigned to the counter only once, prior to processing the loop the first time. The TO parameter sets the maximum value for the counter; this parameter is required and can be an integer literal, a variable, or an expression. The BY parameter is optional; it is an integer literal that sets the automatic increment value for the loop; the default value is 1.

DOFOR initially sets the counter variable to the FROM value and then tests it against the TO value. If the TO value is not exceeded, the loop will be executed. After each iteration of the loop, DOFOR adds the BY value to the counter variable and again tests it against the TO value; once the TO value is exceeded, control falls to the lines following the ENDDO.

In the following example, the code inside the loop will be executed 100 times. Before each repetition, the &int variable will be incremented by 1 and will be tested against the maximum value. If the value of &int is less than or equal to the TO value, the loop will be executed; if the value of &int exceeds the TO value, control will fall to the line following the ENDDO. In this case, after the loop is completed, &int will have a value of 101, and &flag

will be off ('0'). The &flag variable never gets turned on because the loop executes only 100
times; 101 repetitions would be required to turn it on.

```
DCL &flag *LGL  VALUE('0')  /* OFF */
DCL &int  *UINT
. . .
DOFOR &int FROM(1) TO(100)
 IF (&int *GT 100) CHGVAR &flag '1'
ENDDO
```

Early Exits

Two additional commands let you as the programmer to leave a loop early.

- The **ITERATE** command causes the remainder of the commands in a loop not to be
  executed and the next repetition to be executed; the **LEAVE** command terminates
  the loop.

In the code sample that follows, the LEAVE and ITERATE commands are included within a
DOUNTIL loop to explicitly control the processing path. Depending upon the value of the
&mode variable, the loop will call PGMA, PGMB, PGMC, PGMD, and/or PGME. When those
programs end, the loop will be repeated, and the DOUNTIL condition will be tested again.
After PGMA is called, if the value of &mode is 'EXIT', control will fall to the line following
the final ENDDO. In either case, the subsequent lines in the loop will not be processed during
that iteration.

```
DCL &mode *CHAR 6
. . .
DOUNTIL (&mode *EQ 'EXIT')
 CALL PGMA
 IF &mode = 'EXIT'   LEAVE
 IF &mode = 'ADD'    DO
  CALL PGMB
  ITERATE
  ENDDO
 IF &mode = 'CHANGE' DO
  CALL PGMC
  ITERATE
  ENDDO
 IF &mode = 'DELETE' DO
  CALL PGMD
  ITERATE
```

```
   ENDDO
   CALL PGME
   CHGVAR &mode ' '
ENDDO
```

File I/O in CL Programs

CL programs can access two types of files: display files (e.g., STRUPDSP, which you created in Chapter 12) and database files, both physical and logical. However, a single CL program can declare up to five files, and these files must exist at the time the CL program is compiled. When the program is compiled, data fields from the file are made available to the program as variables.

Besides the DCLF statement that identifies the file to the CL program, three other commands are commonly used to process files. You can use two of these commands—SNDF and SNDRCVF—only with display files. These commands write records to the display file, causing the display to appear on the workstation display screen. CL programs cannot directly write to a database file, so these commands are restricted to files of attribute DSPF. You can use the third command, RCVF, with both display files and database files. Figure 16.13 illustrates the actions of the SNDF and RCVF (or SNDRCVF) commands.

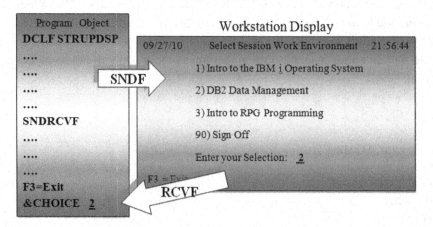

Figure 16.13: SNDF and RCVF Command Functions

The following subsections include a brief description of each of these commands.

SNDF (Send File)

As we noted earlier, the **SNDF** (Send File) command writes a record to a display device. The Display device parameter defaults to the value associated with the display file. The Record format parameter defaults to the record format named in the display file, if there is only one. If the display file has more than one record format, the Record format parameter must name the record to be sent. In many cases, including our sample program, it is not necessary to change any parameters, and you can simply code the command as SNDF.

When this command is executed, all constants defined for the record, as well as the current values of all output data fields, are written to the workstation display. If option indicators are defined for the record, they also will be output, using their current values. By setting these indicators before executing the SNDF command, the programmer controls the appearance of the display.

Although CL has no command to write a record to a database file in a manner similar to the SNDF command, CL programs can execute commands that add to or replace data records in existing files. These are typically some form of DSP*xxx* commands (e.g., **DSPOBJD**, or Display Object Description), and they let the output they generate be sent to an output file. You will use such a command in the lab for this chapter. At that time, we provide more detail about how these commands work.

RCVF (Receive File)

Again to review, the RCVF (Receive File) command is the opposite of SNDF: When used with a display file, RCVF reads any input fields defined in the record into the program variables. Also, if RCVF was triggered by a user pressing a function key, the result indicator (e.g., &IN03 for CA03) defined for that function key will be set On in the program. Figure 16.14 shows a command-prompt screen for a RCVF command.

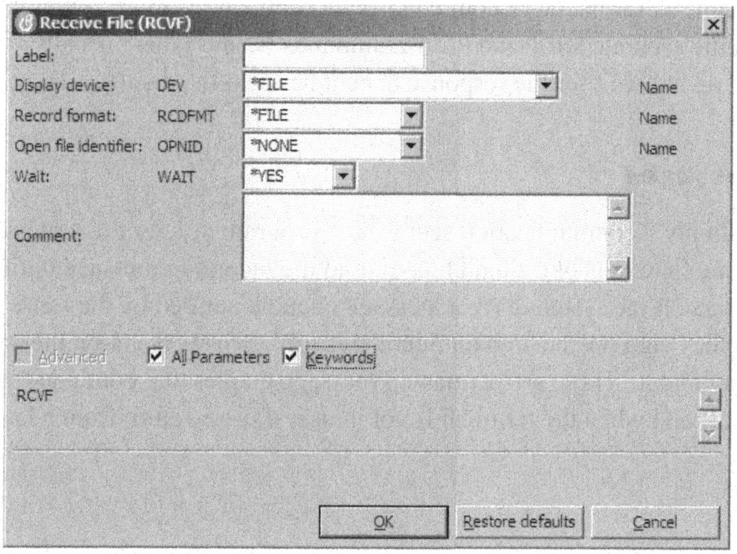

Figure 16.14: Receive File (RCVF) Command-Prompt Screen

The RCVF command has the same Display device and Record format parameters as the SNDF command. These parameters have the same default values and are used in a similar way. If the display file has more than one record format, you must name the record to be read. An additional parameter, Wait, tells the program what to do when it gets to the RCVF command. Usually, the program goes into a wait state until the request to receive the record is fulfilled. This happens when a user replies to a prompt or finishes typing in a data field and presses Enter (or an enabled function key, such as F3 or F12). This action triggers the input operation to the program, which lets the program logic continue. The default value for the Wait parameter is *YES; and unless you want the program to continue with some process not dependent on the data coming from the screen, you would use the default.

You can use the RCVF command with a database file. When the file named in the DCLF command is a physical or logical file, the RCVF command reads the next record sequentially from the file. As we mentioned earlier, CL has no command to write a record to a database file, and the RCVF command is limited to sequential access. This limitation means that if the physical or logical file uses a keyed-sequence access path, the records will be retrieved in order of their key-field values; otherwise, they will be retrieved in arrival sequence.

SNDRCVF (Send/Receive File)

The SNDRCVF (Send/Receive File) command combines the functions of the two previously described commands. It sends (writes) a record to the workstation display with all output fields and option indicators set to current values. Then it waits for the user's action (e.g., pressing Enter or F3) and receives (reads) the record from the display file, passing all input fields and response indicators into the program variables. The parameters, defaults, and usage are the same as for the RCVF command. This command is more commonly used in CL programs than the separate SNDF and RCVF commands because there usually is nothing for the program to do but wait for the response once it has sent the display-file record.

Sending Messages

A message is simply a communication sent from a program or a user to a message queue. A message queue functions like a mail box to hold the incoming message until it can be handled. All users on the system have a message queue identified by the same name as their user ID; when they sign on and start an interactive job, their workstation message queue also becomes available. These are permanent message queues that continue to exist after the users sign off and when the terminal is not in use; if users return from a later session to examine these message queues, they will still be there, and the old messages will still be available (unless they were deleted).

In addition to these message queues, every running program has a program message queue that is created when the program starts and that is deleted when the program ends. Furthermore, every job has an external message queue that is created when the job starts and that is available during the life of the job. An external message queue often is used to display an inquiry message (one that requires a reply) when a CL or HLL program experiences a severe runtime error during testing.

Several types of messages exist, but we mention only two here: the **informational message** and the **inquiry message**. Informational messages are just that—they inform the recipient of some condition or convey the results of a process. They are not usually used for error messages, and they do not require a response. In contrast, inquiry messages request a response, and they often are used to display error messages that require a reply.

You can use several types of commands to send messages; these commands follow, with a description of each.

- **SNDMSG** (Send Message)—You can use the SNDMSG command interactively or from within a CL program. SNDMSG works only with messages whose text is included within the MSG (Message text) parameter of the command. SNDMSG can deliver the message to a named message queue or to a user.
- **SNDBRKMSG** (Send Break Message)—The SNDBRKMSG command delivers messages only to a workstation message queue. If the workstation is active at the time of delivery, the command interrupts the job and displays the message. If the message is an inquiry message, you can specify a message queue for the response. As with the SNDMSG command, you can use the SNDBRKMSG command interactively or from a CL program, and the message text is part of the command.
- **SNDPGMMSG** (Send Program Message)—You can use the SNDPGMMSG command only from within a CL program. You can define the message text within the MSG parameter, or you can use a predefined message that exists in a message file and that has a unique message identifier. The SNDPGMMSG command can deliver its message to any type of message queue, including program and external message queues. For messages that require a response, you can designate a reply message queue. This command is especially useful when a running program needs to send a message back to the program that called it.

Message handling is a very rich feature of the IBM i OS, and it involves a degree of complexity entirely beyond this text. Nevertheless, you can refer to Figure 16.15 to see some common uses of these commands.

```
STRUPPGM.CLLE    DIFF_MSGS.CLLE
Line 46      Column 11    Insert
----+----1----+----2----+----3----+----4----+----5----+----6----+----7-
002100 /****************************************************************/
002101 /* Global Message Segment                                       */
002102 /****************************************************************/
002200            MONMSG     MSGID(CPF0000) EXEC(GOTO ERROR)
002400 /****************************************************************/
002401 /*   Main Procedure Segment                                     */
002402 /****************************************************************/
002500 START:
002501            SNDMSG     MSG('Hello from DIFF_MSGS to user CIS001D') +
002503                         TOUSR(CIS001D)
002504
002505            SNDMSG     MSG('Hello from DIFF_MSGS to MSGq QPADEV0038') +
002506                         TOMSGQ(QPADEV0038)
002507
002508            SNDBRKMSG  MSG('Hello from SNDBRKMSG to QPADEV0038') +
002509                         TOMSGQ(QPADEV0038)
002510
002600            SNDPGMMSG  MSG('Hello to *PRV program from SNDPGMMSG') +
002601                         TOPGMQ(*PRV)
002700
002701            SNDPGMMSG  MSG('Hello to *External MSGq from SNDPGMMSG') +
002702                         TOPGMQ(*EXT)
002800
002900            RETURN
003000 /****************************************************************/
003001 /*  Error Procedure Section                                     */
```

Figure 16.15: Sample Program to Illustrate Different Ways to Send Messages

The first command in this program, on line 2501, sends a message to the message queue for user profile CIS001D. Other possibilities for the TOUSR (To user profile) parameter are *SYSOPR, the system operator's message queue; *ALLACT, all currently active (signed-on) user profiles' message queues; and *REQUESTER, the user profile currently running this interactive job.

The second command, on line 2505, shows the alternative parameter to TOUSR—namely, TOMSGQ (To message queue). With this parameter, you identify by name the exact message queue to which you want the message delivered. We have chosen the message queue of the workstation to which we are currently signed on, but we could specify any other permanent message queue to which we had access.

The SNDBRKMSG command, on line 2508, delivers the message to the workstation message queue QPADEV0038 and interrupts the interactive job. If an operator needed to notify all users of an impending shutdown or of some emergency situation, the special value *ALLWS (instead of QPADEV0038) would broadcast the message to all workstations.

The first SNDPGMMSG command, on line 2600, sends the message text to the previous program's message queue by default—that is, the TOPGMQ (To program message queue) parameter uses the default value of *PRV. The previous program is the one calling this program; but if this program were run from a command line, the message would be displayed at that screen when the program finished.

The last SNDPGMMSG command is on line 2701. This command specifies *EXT, the external job message queue, as the recipient of the message.

If we ran this compiled program, after we first cleared both the CIS001D and QPADEV0038 message queues, the sequence of events would be as follows: First (if we have audio on), we would hear two beeps as the messages from the first two SNDMSG commands were delivered to the two empty message queues. The two beeps really sound like one long beep because the commands are executed one after another. After an instant, we would hear another beep as the break message was delivered and the job interrupted (break messages always beep as they interrupt an active job). The CL program is still running when the SNDBRKMSG command is executed, so we would see its message first. Figure 16.16 shows the first display after the program is called (note the arrow we used to highlight the message).

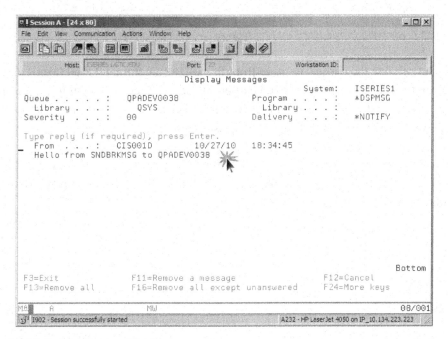

Figure 16.16: Break Message Display

The screen displays the break-message text and the program is interrupted, waiting for us to acknowledge the message. We do not need to reply; we can simply press F12 or Enter.

But, knowing that an earlier message was sent to the same workstation message queue, we can first Page Up to see whether that message was delivered. Pressing Page Up changes the display to that in Figure 16.17 (again, note the arrow highlighting the message).

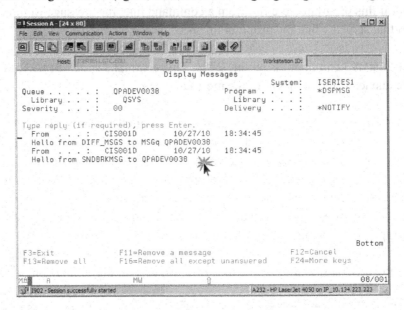

Figure 16.17: Showing Previously Sent Message As Well As Break Message

Now we can see that the earlier message from the SNDMSG command did make it to the queue. Even though the message arrived earlier, the SNDMSG command didn't interrupt the job, so we did not see its message first. The SNDBRKMSG command shows only its own message, even if other earlier messages still exist in the message queue.

When we press Enter from this display, the Main menu appears for an instant, but then we move on to the message delivered to the external job message queue. Figure 16.18 shows this display.

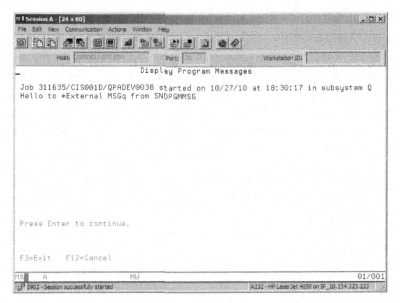

Figure 16.18: Display Program Messages Sent to *EXT

When we press Enter from the external message display, we return to the Work with Members Using PDM screen from which the program was called. Because this is the previous level to the called program, the defaulted SNDPGMMSG command message appears here. You can see the message displayed on the message line of the screen in Figure 16.19 (once again, note the arrow highlighting the message).

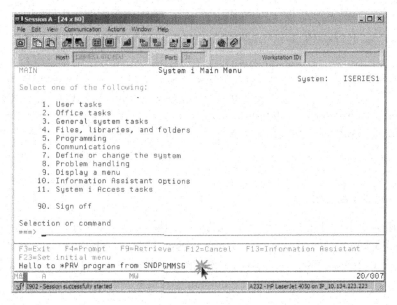

Figure 16.19: Message Delivered to *PRV Program

At this point, we can see that the message-waiting indicator is turned on, so running the DSPMSG (Display Messages) command will show us the waiting message. Because the messages sent to the workstation have not been cleared, we will first see the previously sent messages, just as we did in Figure 16.17. Whenever messages remain in our workstation message queue, execution of the DSPMSG command with no parameters first takes us to that queue. Pressing Enter from the workstation message-queue display brings up the message sent to user CIS001D's message queue. Figure 16.20 shows that display, with the arrow again highlighting the message.

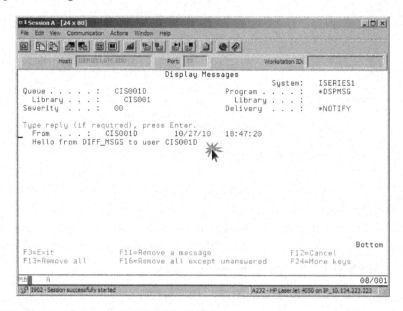

Figure 16.20: Display Messages for User CIS001D

As you can see from this example, a program can send a message to a user or another program in several ways. In fact, there are many more possibilities that we have not looked at here because their discussion belongs in a CL programming class. However, this overview should give you enough information to help you start sending messages from your CL programs.

Using Concatenation

Concatenation is the joining of two character variables or constants. In CL programs, programmers often use concatenation to form messages by combining several character variables and string constants to be assigned to a single variable, or to be used as a single message-text value. In fact, we often use concatenation when a CL program needs to communicate with its user, or to send a message to a message queue. For those reasons, we briefly introduce concatenation here.

Three different concatenation operations are available in CL programs: *CAT, *TCAT, and *BCAT. The following example illustrates their differences. First, we will assume two character variables declared as follows:

```
DCL     &VAR1   *CHAR 10 'LAKE'
DCL     &VAR2   *CHAR 10 'MICHIGAN'
```

When we include an explicit length in the declaration of a character variable, the string constant value is left aligned, and the remaining bytes are replaced with spaces. So the actual contents of &VAR1, for example, would be the four characters LAKE, followed by six spaces. Note that because the values LAKE and MICHIGAN consist solely of alphabetic characters, it is technically not necessary to enclose them in apostrophes ('); but using apostrophes to delimit quoted strings is a good habit to acquire.

The ***CAT operation** joins the full length of the first variable or string to the second variable or string. So the command

```
SNDPGMMSG  MSG(&VAR1 *CAT &VAR2 *CAT 'IS FUN')
```

would produce the message

```
LAKE    MICHIGAN  IS FUN
```

The ***TCAT operation** truncates any spaces to the right of the rightmost, nonspace character in the first variable. Then it joins what is left of the first variable to the second variable or string. In our example, this means that the five rightmost spaces of &VAR1 and &VAR2 would be truncated. The command

```
SNDPGMMSG  MSG(&VAR1 *TCAT &VAR2 *TCAT 'IS FUN')
```

would produce the message

```
LAKEMICHIGANIS FUN
```

The ***BCAT operation** is similar to *TCAT except that it leaves (or inserts) a single space after the last (rightmost) character of the first variable. In effect, this inserts a single space between the nonspace characters of the first variable and the variable or string to which it is joined. The use of *BCAT produces the proper formatting of our sample message. The command

SNDPGMMSG MSG(&VAR1 *BCAT &VAR2 *BCAT 'IS FUN')

would produce the message

LAKE MICHIGAN IS FUN

Finishing the Start-Up Program

You have now seen some CL commands that you have not used before, but which you need in order to make our sample program work. Before we can finish the program, we need to decide exactly what we want the program to do when the user has made a certain choice. For example, if the user enters choice 1 to set up the Intro to IBM i environment, which CL commands must we execute? For any class environment, we would want to

1. Use the DOWHILE command loop until the user exits the program or logs off the system.
2. Change the library list to make the user's library for that class current, and to place the class library first in the user part of the library list. Other libraries the user owns should probably follow the class library in the library list.
3. Change the current job so the user's output queue will display a message (30 or fewer characters) that identifies the user, and so that the class will be printed at the bottom of each page of printed output.
4. Send the user directly to the Work with Objects Using PDM screen, which shows all objects in the user's current library (selected above).
5. Check for an invalid entry using the OTHERWISE command. Turn on the &IN40 indicator, and execute the SNDRCVF command to redisplay the STRUPDSP screen.

Having decided the specific actions to be completed for any selection made, we can complete the source code for the start-up program. Figures 16.21 through 16.23 show the complete source code for the program that will use the display file STRUPDSP, which we created in Chapter 12.

```
 STRUPPGM.CLLE      DIFF_MSGS.CLLE
  Line 35      Column 96    Insert
    ----+----1----+----2----+----3----+----4----+----5----+----6----+----7----+----8----+----9----+
000101 /*****************************************************************/
000102 /*Program information Section                                    */
000103 /*    Display options list using display file STRUPDSP, input choice */
000104 /*    and then process selection, setting up work environment.   */
000105 /*    Signoff is allowed; F3 transfers to Initial Menu.          */
000106 /*                                                               */
000107 /*    Parameters: none                                           */
000108 /*    DSPF variables: &CHOICE *CHAR 2 I/O  selection field        */
000109 /*                    &IN40  *LGL    O    option ind for error   */
000110 /*                    &IN03  *LGL    I    response ind for exit  */
000111 /*                                                               */
000112 /*    Author: Jim Buck                        Modified: 10-10-2010 */
000113 /*****************************************************************/
000114              PGM           /* Program Linkage Section - NO Parms */
000115 /*****************************************************************/
000116 /*  Declarations Section                                         */
000117 /*****************************************************************/
000118              DCLF          FILE(STRUPDSP) RCDFMT(*ALL)
000119              DCL           &MyName *CHAR 15  'Jim Buck -'
000120              DCL           &EndPgm *LGL  VALUE('0') /* Off */
000121 /*****************************************************************/
000122 /* Global Message Segment                                        */
000123 /*****************************************************************/
000124 /*****************************************************************/
000125              MONMSG        MSGID(CPF0000) EXEC(GOTO ERROR)
000126 /*****************************************************************/
000127 /*  Main Procedure Segment                                       */
000128 /*****************************************************************/
000129              DOUNTIL       (&EndPgm = '1')
```

Figure 16.21: CL Source Code for Program STRUPPGM—Part 1 of 3

Let us step through the lines of the source program to see how it corresponds to the structure charts we presented earlier in Figures 16.4 and 16.5 and review how we have used the commands we have discussed in this chapter.

Lines 101–113

These lines are all comment lines, intended to provide program identification and documentation.

Line 114

The PGM statement is optional here, but it is usually included.

Lines 115–117

This section of comment lines highlights the declarative section of the program.

Line 118

This line declares the display file. The DCLF statement causes all variables and indicators of display file STRUPDSP to be available as program variables at compile time.

Line 119

This line declares the character variable &MyName, which is used as part of the print text for printed output. Lines 17 and 18 correspond to the Initialize module of the structure chart (Figure 16.5).

Line 120

This line declares a character variable, which is turned on when the user presses F3 to end the program.

Lines 122–124

These comment lines delineate program sections.

Line 125

This line has the MONMSG statement, which checks for an untrapped CPF error. If there is an error, it causes the program to branch to the ERROR label.

Lines 126–128

These comment lines delineate program sections.

```
000128  /****************************************************************/
000129              DOUNTIL      (&EndPgm = '1')
000130              CHGVAR       &CHOICE ' '
000131              SNDRCVF
000132
000133              SELECT
000134  /* User Pressed the F3 Function Key */
000135              WHEN         (&IN03)  THEN(CHGVAR VAR(&ENDPGM) VALUE('1'))
000136              WHEN         (&Choice = '1') THEN(DO) /* User Choose Selection 1   */
000137                  CHGLIBL      (CIS001 ALLUSER QTEMP QGPL) INTROCLASS
000138                  CHGJOB       OUTQ(CIS001/CIS001Q) PRTTXT(&MYNAME *BCAT 'Intro IBM i')
000139                  SNDPGMMSG    MSG('Intro IBM i!') TOUSR(*REQUESTER)
000140                  WRKOBJPDM    LIB(*CURLIB)
000141              ENDDO
000142              WHEN         (&Choice = '2') DO /* User Choose Selection 2  - DB2 */
000143                  CHGLIBL      (CIS001 ALLUSER QTEMP QGPL) INTRODB2
000144                  CHGJOB       OUTQ(CIS001/CIS001Q) PRTTXT(&MYNAME *BCAT 'Intro DB2')
000145                  SNDPGMMSG    MSG('Intro DB2!') TOUSR(*REQUESTER)
000146                  WRKOBJPDM    LIB(*CURLIB)
000147              ENDDO
000148              WHEN         (&Choice = '3') DO /* User Choose Selection 3 - RPG IV */
000149                  CHGLIBL      (CIS001 ALLUSER QTEMP QGPL) RPGCLASS
000150                  CHGJOB       OUTQ(CIS001/CIS001Q) PRTTXT(&MYNAME *BCAT 'RPG IV')
000151                  SNDPGMMSG    MSG('RPG IV!') TOUSR(*REQUESTER)
000152                  WRKOBJPDM    LIB(*CURLIB)
000153              ENDDO
000154              WHEN         (&Choice = '90') SIGNOFF /* User Choose Selection 90  */
000155              OTHERWISE    DO /* User Entered Something besides 1, 2 or 90  */
000156                  CHGVAR       &IN40 '1' /* Turn on error option indicator */
000157                  SNDRCVF
000158                  CHGVAR       &IN40 '0' /* Don't forget to turn off the error indicator */
000159              ENDDO
000160              ENDSELECT
000161
000162          ENDDO
```

Figure 16.22: CL Source Code for Program STRUPPGM—Part 2 of 3

Line 129

This line contains the DOUNTIL command and signifies the "top" of the program's loop. This loop continues until the variable &EndPgm is set to On.

Line 130

This line initializes variable &Choice to spaces before sending it out with the display file. Because we need to do this each time a new selection is made, this line is tagged with the command label REQUEST:.

Line 131

This line writes the display-file record and waits for the user's response. Lines 130 and 131 together initialize the workstation display and correspond to the Request Selection module of the structure chart (Figure 16.5).

Line 133

This line contains the SELECT command that starts the SELECT/OTHERWISE structure that evaluates the &Choice variable and then takes the appropriate action.

Line 134

This line contains a comment statement for the following WHEN command.

Line 135

This line contains the first WHEN command; the On status for &IN03 would occur if the user had pressed F3. The CHGVAR command will change the value of the &EndPgm variable to '1'. None of the following WHEN or OTHERWISE commands will be evaluated, and the loop will end the next time around. **Note:** The &EndPgm variable is a logical-type variable, and setting its value to '1' is equivalent to turning it On.

Lines 136–140

1. WHEN &Choice = '1' (user input on STRUPDSP display screen), the DO command starts the execution of the following block of commands:
   a. The CHGLIBL command changes the library list and makes the INTROCLASS library the current library.
   b. The CHGJOB command does not change the user's output queue but uses the PRTTXT parameter to cause the user's name and *Intro IBM i* to be printed on the bottom of every page of printed output.
   c. The SNDPGMMSG command sends a message to the user's message queue.
   d. The WRKOBJPDM command displays all the objects in the user's current library.

Line 141

This line contains the ENDDO command, which is associated with the DO command on line 136.

Lines 142–146

1. WHEN &Choice = '2' (user input on STRUPDSP display screen), the DO command starts the execution of the following block of commands:

    a. The CHGLIBL command changes the library list and makes the INTRODB2 library the current library.

    b. The CHGJOB command does not change the user's output queue but uses the PRTTXT parameter to cause the user's name and *Intro DB2* to be printed on the bottom of every page of printed output.

    c. The SNDPGMMSG command sends a message to the user's message queue.

    d. The WRKOBJPDM command displays all the objects in the user's current library.

Line 147

This line contains the ENDDO command, which is associated with the DO command on line 142.

Lines 148–152

1. WHEN &Choice = '3' (user input on STRUPDSP display screen), the DO command starts the execution of the following block of commands:

    a. The CHGLIBL command changes the library list and makes the RPGCLASS library the current library.

    b. The CHGJOB command does not change the user's output queue but uses the PRTTXT parameter to cause the user's name and *RPG IV* to be printed on the bottom of every page of printed output.

    c. The SNDPGMMSG command sends a message to the user's message queue.

    d. The WRKOBJPDM command displays all the objects in the user's current library.

Line 153

This line contains the ENDDO command, which is associated with the DO command on line 148.

Line 154

This line contains the WHEN statement, which evaluates the &Choice variable; if the variable is equal to '90', the SIGNOFF command is executed.

Lines 155–158

1. If the selection criteria for the previous WHEN command is not satisfied, the OTHERWISE command is executed, and the DO command starts the execution of the following block of commands:

    a. The CHGVAR command turns on the &IN40 indicator. This in turn causes the display screen to display the error message.

    b. The SNDRCVF command redisplays the STRUPDSP display screen.

    c. The CHGVAR command turns Off the &IN40 indicator. The program is going to go to the top of the loop (Line 129) and begin checking what the user input is, so the indicator should not be on.

Line 159
This line contains the ENDDO command, which is associated with the DO command on line 155.

Line 160
This line contains the ENDSELECT command, which closes the SELECT group that was started with the SELECT command on line 134.

```
000161
000162            ENDDO
000163 /*********************************************************/
000164 /*   Error Procedure Section                            */
000165 /*********************************************************/
000166 ERROR:     DMPCLPGM    /* Dump CL program */
000167            SNDPGMMSG  MSG('Error occurred in PGM') TOUSR(*SYSOPR)
000168            RETURN
000169 /*********************************************************/
000170 /*   End Program Section                                */
000171 /*********************************************************/
000172 END:
000173            ENDPGM
000174
```

Figure 16.23: CL Source Code for Program STRUPPGM—Part 3 of 3

Lines 161–162
This ENDDO is associated with the DOWHILE on line 129, sometimes referred to as the bottom of the loop. The next line of code to be executed is line 129.

Lines 163–165
These comment lines delineate program sections.

Lines 166–168
This block of code includes the ERROR: label. Any processing that needs to be completed before ending the program and returning to the calling program or the command line should be placed here. In this case, the SNDPGMMSG command is executed to send a message that there was a problem, and then the RETURN command is executed, returning to the command line or the calling program.

Lines 169–171
These comment lines delineate program sections.

Line 172

The END: label shows the end of the program section.

Line 173

The ENDPGM statement tells the compiler that nothing follows, and it marks the physical end of the CL program.

Creating a CL Program

We discussed creating objects in RDP in Chapter 11, so we will not cover this topic further here. Figure 16.24 shows us right-clicking the source member and selecting CRTBNDCL.

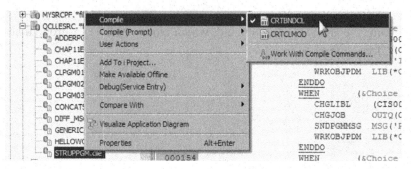

Figure 16.24: Creating a CL Program in RSE Using CRTBNDCL

When the CRTBNDCL command is executed, the results are displayed in the Commands Log view. When the message *"Program STRUPPGM created in the library CIS001"* is displayed (Figure 16.25), a new object of type *PGM is created in your library.

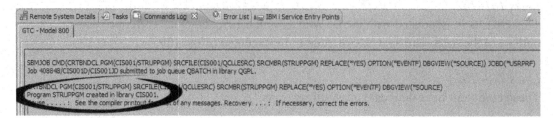

Figure 16.25: Verify That the Program Object Was Created

In Summary

A CL program is an object compiled from a number of related CL commands, which together perform some specific function. You can use CL programs to provide an interface between users and programs, or to provide a communications-and-control switch among multiple HLL programs. You also can use CL programs to standardize common operational procedures and to set up and manage different work environments.

CL programs usually have a number of sections, including a program ID section, declaratives, and a body. The declaratives begin with a PGM statement, and the body ends with an ENDPGM statement. We have actually broken the program into a number of additional sections to help you as a student learn to write structured and well-documented programs.

A single program can declare up to five files, but any number of variables. The five types of variables allowed are character (*CHAR), packed decimal (*DEC), logical (*LGL), integer (*INT and *UINT), and pointer (*PTR). When a file is declared, all fields and indicators defined in it become available to the program as variables, without explicit declaration.

Certain CL commands are allowed only within a program. Some of these commands have to do with the provision of selection or iteration: IF-ELSE, DO-ENDDO, SELECT, and the looping constructs (DOWHILE, DOUNTIL, and DOFOR). Others require the availability of variables to store returned values (e.g., RTVSYSVAL) or provide for the manipulation of variables (e.g., CHGVAR); or they require the program environment for their operation (e.g., MONMSG, SNDPGMMSG). CL programs can write to display files (SNDF), read from display files (RCVF), or do both (SNDRCVF). But only the RCVF command can read sequentially from database files.

Programmers often use concatenation to compose messages that include values of variables. You can use Send Message commands to send such messages to users, workstations, programs, or job message queues.

There are three CL commands to create a CL object from a source member: the CRTCLPGM command, used to create OPM program objects; the CRTBNDCL command, used to compile and bind an executable program object; and the CRTCLMOD command, used to create a nonexecutable module.

In the following lab, you will first create a start-up program to permit selection of a work environment and execution of the appropriate commands to change the library list and job attributes. An additional lab assignment will have you create a program to calculate the total storage used by objects within a specified library. Last, to help you understand the distinction between interactive and batch jobs, you will create a program to send a message and then time out. As part of this exercise, we demonstrate the difference between running this program as an interactive job and in batch mode.

Key Terms

*BCAT operation	GOTO
CALL	ILE
*CAT operation	informational message
CHGJOB	inquiry message
CHGLIBL	ITERATE
CHGPRF	Label parameter
CHGVAR	LEAVE
CLLE	Main Procedure Segment
CLP	MONMSG
CLRMSGQ	OPM
concatenation	OTHERWISE
continuation characters	parameters
count-controlled loop	PGM statement
CRTBNDCL	procedures
CRTCLMOD	program ID
CRTCLPGM	Program Information Section
DCL	RCVF
DCLF	Record format parameter
Declarations Section	SELECT
DO	sequence operations
DO-ENDDO block structure	SNDBRKMSG
DOFOR	SNDF
DOUNTIL	SNDMSG
DOWHILE	SNDPGMMSG
DSPFFD	SNDRCVF
DSPOBJD	source code
ELSE	subroutine
ENDPGM	*TCAT operation
ENDSELECT	THEN
Error Procedure Section	VAR parameter
EXEC parameter	variables
flow control	WHEN
Global Message Segment	

Review Questions

1. List the uses of CL programs. Can you think of additional uses?
2. List the advantages of using CL programs. Can you think of additional advantages?
3. List and describe the three commands that are used to create CL objects.

4. List the sections of a CL program, and describe the functionality of these sections.

5. Explain the differences between a subroutine and a procedure.

6. How many DCLF commands can be used in a CL program?

7. Why is it *not* necessary to explicitly declare variables when using a declared file in a CL program?

8. What command would the CL programmer use to receive data from a database file?

9. List and describe the variables types available in CL.

10. Why would a CL programmer used mixed-case font when coding variables in CL?

11. Describe the CHGVAR command. What types of expressions are allowed with this command?

12. Explain the rules for using continuation characters.

13. List and describe the different concatenation commands.

14. Write the required CL commands to initialize your first, middle, and last name. These variables should be 20 characters in length. Then write the SNDPGMMSG command to concatenate these variables together (removing any extraneous spaces) and send a message to the system operator message queue. **Note:** Ask your instructor if you also should do this with a CL program.

15. Investigate the PRTTXT parameter of the CHGJOB command and describe it.

16. Describe the iteration structures supported in CL.

17. Describe the SELECT/WHEN/OTHERWISE construct. Give an example of how you might find this useful.

18. Describe the DO-ENDDO block structure. Why is it useful to the CL programmer?

19. Why is the use of the GOTO command discouraged? When is it permissible to use this command?

20. What are the early exit commands in CL? Explain how the two commands differ.

Lab 16

Introduction

In this lab exercise, you enter the CL source code for program STRUPPGM, which we covered in the chapter. After a clean compile, you test the program to see how it works with display file STRUPDSP, and to make sure the program is responding properly to any choice value entered. To demonstrate the ease of changing display files, you then make a minor change to your STRUPDSP file and recompile it. Because the change you make will not affect the record format of the display file, you can test the modified display file without changing and recompiling the program.

The additional lab exercise will prove a little more challenging. In it, you design and enter the source code for a program to calculate the sum of storage space used by all objects in your library. In the process, you encounter—and fix—a compile error caused by a type mismatch. Then you experience a runtime error that causes the program to end abnormally. You use diagnostic information supplied by the error message to change the program, recompile the program, and then successfully execute the program.

Last, you write a short program and demonstrate the difference between a program running interactively and the same program submitted as a batch job.

Part 1

Goals   Enter source code for CL program STRUPPGM.

Compile the program.

Change and recompile the display-file source using RSE.

Change your user profile's Initial program parameter.

Start with   RDP open, connected to your IBM i system, and with the Remote System Explorer Perspective displayed.

Procedure   Create the QCLLESRC source file (if it does not already exist).

Create a CL source member in your QCLLESRC file, or copy the GENERIC_CL source member to your QCLLESRC file.

Enter source code using the LPEX Editor in RDP.

Compile and test the program.

Change the STRUPDSP DDS source member using RDP's Screen Designer.

Compile the changed display file and test it.

CHGUSRPRF Initial program parameter to STRUPPGM.

16.1. Create a source physical file for CL programs if you have not already done so. Right-click your library and select New Source Physical file. The source file name will be QCLLESRC, and the record length should be 112. Give the source file an appropriate description.

16.2. Right-click the QCLLESRC source file, and then create a new member called STRUPPGM, of type CLLE, with text such as "Start-Up Program for display file STRUPDSP."

Note

A CL member called GENERIC_CL was part of the instructor materials for this text. Ask your instructor whether you are to use this source member, and, if so, where it is located on your system.

16.3.   Enter the program commands.

To enter the program, it is usually easier to type only the command itself and then press F4 to prompt for parameters when necessary. Remember that when you use command prompting, the parameters you type will be entered in keyword notation.

Caution

In the body of the program, change all library and output-queue references to name your own libraries and output queues. These must exist before you try to test the program. Check with your instructor for names of common user libraries (e.g., ALLUSER) that you need to add to your user library list.

Enter the entire program shown at the end of this chapter. Whenever a name reference is used (e.g., Author: Jim Buck), change it to your own name. Use the SEU Copy line command to duplicate lines or blocks of code, and then make necessary changes using type-over, Delete, and Insert.

After you have entered the program, save the source member.

Caution

Before you can compile the program, the referenced file, STRUPDSP, must exist. If you were unable to successfully complete Part 3 of Lab 12, during which you would have created the display file, and if a copy of the display file is not available to you, you cannot continue with this lab.

16.4.   Compile the source program. Check your Commands Log and Error List to determine whether the compile was successful. Make the necessary changes to the source member, and then recompile.

16.5. At this point, assuming that you have clean compiles of the display file and the CL program, you should be ready to test the program. Remember, the libraries and output queues referred to in the program must exist before you can test the program. If you have not done so already, create any libraries and output queues referred to in the **CHGLIBL** (Change Library List) and **CHGJOB** (Change Job) commands in your program. If the class libraries do not exist, or if you are not authorized to use them, remove them from the CHGLIBL library lists in your program, or ask your instructor to grant you authority to them.

From the 5250 command line, type CALL STRUPPGM. When your display appears, enter the various options to test all functions.

16.6. If your program is working successfully now, use the **CHGPRF** (Change Profile) command with prompting to change your user profile so that it will execute your STRUPPGM program as the initial program to call. After you make this change, sign off, and then sign on again. Your program should be run, and you should see your display file. If the program is not found, or it if terminates abnormally, you can bypass the user-profile initial program by entering *NONE for *Program/procedure* from the sign-on screen. Doing this lets you get back on the system to locate and fix the error.

Part 2

In this portion of the lab, you gain familiarity with additional CL commands by first writing a CL program to accumulate the storage used by all objects in the student library and then displaying the total at the workstation as a program message.

Goals   Enter source code for CL program ADDERPGM.

               Compile the program.

Start with   RDP open, connected to your IBM i system, and with the Remote System Explorer Perspective displayed.

               The program uses the following CL commands:

- DCL—Declare (defines a program variable)
- DCLF—Declare File (defines a file to be accessed by the program)
- DSPOBJD—Display Object Description
- RCVF—Receive File (reads records from the file)
- MONMSG—Monitor Message
- CHGVAR—Change Variable (changes the value assigned to a variable)

- GOTO—Go To (a specified label)
- SNDPGMMSG—Send Program Message (sends a message to another program, message queue, or user)

Procedure   Sign on to the system.

Display *ALL objects in your library to an output file.

Name the output file to DSPODOUTF.

Return to RDP.

Create a new source physical file.

Enter the program's source code.

Save, compile, and verify that the compile was successful.

Change the SNDPGMMSG parameter.

Save, recompile, and verify the success of the compile.

Review the program logic.

Save, recompile, and verify.

Run the program from the 5250 command line.

16.7.   Sign on to your system using a 5250 session.

Many display-type (DSP*xxx*) commands allow the option of directing the output to a file instead of to a display device or printer. You first will create the file that the CL program will work with by running the **DSPOBJD** (Display Object Description) command interactively. Enter the command on the command line, and then prompt for parameters.

16.8.   Display *ALL objects in your own library. Use object type *ALL. Be sure to specify only your own library by name and not the default, *LIBL.

The Output parameter will be *OUTFILE. Press Enter.

16.9.   Because you have indicated your intention to send the output to a file, the command prompter requires you to name the output file. Name the file DSPODOUTF; the library parameter should be *CURLIB. Notice the output member options. The output will be placed in the first member, and it will replace any existing output if the DSPOBJD command is rerun specifying the same file to receive output. In other words, each time the command is run with the output file specified, the results of each run will replace the results of the previous run when the default parameter values are used.

After you type the file name, be sure the prompt screen looks like the one in Figure 16.26 (using your own library name, of course). Then press Enter.

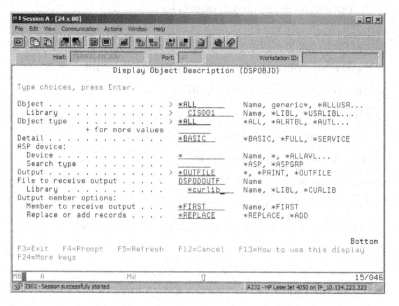

Figure 16.26: DSPOBJD Command Prompt Screen

16.9.a.   After the command is run, what is displayed on the message line at the bottom of your screen?

Refresh the PDM screen, and find the file you just created.

16.9.b.   What is its type and attribute?

16.9.c.   What text has been provided for this file?

When an output file is created from a DSPOBJD command, the system creates an externally described file to assign field names to each of the object-description attributes that the command references. For example, there will be a named field for the object name, another for the object type, and another for the text description. Each object that is accessed by the DSPOBJD command will create one record in the output file. Each record will describe one object and will store field values that are attributes of that object in the corresponding record-format fields.

To find out what the field names are, run the **DSPFFD** (Display File Field Description) command on DSPODOUTF. As you examine the field-level information of the DSPFFD output, keep in mind that the field text that describes the field applies to the name, data type, and length attributes listed *above* it, not below it.

Find the field name, data type, and field length of the Object size field, and write them in below, as well as on your answer sheet.

16.9.d. Name of field _____

16.9.e. Type (character or packed) _____

16.9.f. Size of field _____

16.10. Return to RDP, and click the QCLLESRC source file in RSE.

16.11. Using RSE, right-click the QCLLESRC source file to create a new CLLE source member named ADDERPGM. Be sure to make the member type CLLE and the record length 112, and type "Calculate sum of object size" for text.

Note

It would be helpful if you would review the STRUPPGM source as you key in the code for this assignment. The overall program statements are similar in structure.

Keep in mind the order of statements in a CL program:

a. Program Information Section (*/* programmer ID and program function */*)

b. Program Linkage Section, including the PGM statement

c. Declarations Section

d. Global Message Segment

e. Main Procedure Segment (selection, flow-control, and executable CL commands)

f. Error Procedure Section

g. End Program Statement

16.12. Use the LPEX prompting facility to enter your source CL program. Enter a Program Information Section to identify the program and its author. After that, for each statement, enter only the command and then prompt for parameters.

Note

As we pointed out previously, prompting a command will return your variables in upper case. You will need to change the case to mixed case to follow the naming conventions we discussed in this chapter.

The order of code entry should be as follows:

a. Enter the Program Linkage Section, including the PGM statement.

b. Declare the output file you created in steps 16.8 and 16.9.

c. Declare a variable to accumulate the sum of storage used by the objects in your library. Remember that all CL program variables (including field names from files) begin with the ampersand (&) character. Make the accumulator variable one byte longer than (with zero decimal positions), and of the same type as, the field from step 16.9.

d. Declare a variable named &EndPgm, as shown below. This logical variable will be used to end the DOUNTIL loop that we will code shortly.

```
DCL     &EndPgm *LGL  VALUE('0') /* Off */
```

e. Enter the Global Message Segment and the MONMSG code.

f. Enter the Main Procedure Segment.

g. Code a DSPOBJD command using the same parameters you used in steps 16.8 and 16.9. Be sure to specify objects in your library only!

h. Code a DOUTIL using the example shown in the STRUPPGM listing at the end of this chapter.

i. Code a RCVF command. It needs no parameter.

j. Enter the MONMSG command, as shown below. This will set the &EndPgm variable to '1' and end the loop.

```
MONMSG    MSGID(CPF0864) EXEC(CHGVAR VAR(&EndPgm) VALUE('1'))
```

k. Code a CHGVAR command to add the size of each object into the accumulator variable. The form of this statement will be

```
CHGVAR VAR(&Accum) VAL(&Accum + &Size)
```

But you must substitute, for *&Accum*, the name of the accumulator variable declared in your program, and, for *&Size*, the Object size field name from the DSPODOUTF file! (See your answer to question 16.9.e above.)

l. Code an ENDDO command. This ends the DOUNTIL command you coded earlier.

m. Code a SNDPGMMSG command. The message text will consist of a character-string literal (enclosed in apostrophes) concatenated to the accumulator. You can perform the concatenation by using the *BCAT function:

```
'Total storage used is' *BCAT &Accum
```

You want the function to include the value of the total storage accumulator in the message sent to your terminal:

SNDPGMMSG MSG('Total storage used is' *BCAT &Accum)

n. Code an ENDPGM statement.

Tip
If at this point the program seems a little fishy to you, that's a good sign! We have again intentionally allowed a couple of errors into our program to provide some debugging practice. They will soon be apparent.

16.13. Save the program and compile it. Check the Commands Log and the Error List view.

16.13.a. What does the message say in the Error List view?

If the program doesn't compile: Click the message in the Error List view, which will move you to the line of code that caused the error.

To correct the error, move the cursor up to the Declarations Section and declare another variable similar to the accumulator, but with a different name and character type. Then insert a CHGVAR command just before the SNDPGMMSG command to convert the numeric accumulator to character data type. The CHGVAR command should resemble the following command:

CHGVAR VAR(*&CHARVAR*) VAL(*&DECVAR*)

where *&CHARVAR* is the variable to be changed (to receive the converted value) and *&DECVAR* is the accumulator variable whose packed-decimal value will be converted.

Remember that the CHGVAR command works from right to left; in other words, the value of the right-side parameter replaces the previous value of the receiver variable (the left-side parameter).

16.14. Change the SNDPGMMSG command to use the character variable.

16.15. Save and recompile the program. Verify normal completion.

16.16. Execute the CL program using the **CALL** command.

16.17. Review your program logic:
- Declare variables and file.
- Execute the DSPOBJD command to place current data in the file.

- Begin a DOUNTIL.
- Read a record (one object description) from the file.
- Add the object size to the accumulator variable.
- Close the DOUNTIL with an end; loop to read another record.
- At end-of-file, change the numeric accumulator to character.
- Send a program message.
- End the program.

16.18. Exit and save; then recompile. Check for normal completion.

16.19. Now run the program (CALL) from the 5250 command line. Your message should be displayed at the bottom of the screen. If it is not, determine the reason the program failed, correct the error, and try again!

Next, we will code and run a program to demonstrate how submitting a job to the batch subsystem affects the interactive job.

Part 3

Goals Create a new source member in your QCLLESRC file.

Enter the source code for the MARKTIME program.

Start with RDP open, connected to your IBM i system, and with the Remote System Explorer Perspective displayed.

Procedure Enter source code for CL program MARKTIME.

Compile the program.

Clear your message queue.

Call the MARKTIME program from the command line.

Display your messages.

Clear your message queue.

Run the WRKACTJB command.

Submit the MARKTIME program to BATCH.

Display your message queue.

16.20. Create a new member in your QCLLESRC source file using RDP named MARKTIME.

16.21. Using the complete program listing located at the end of this chapter, key in the CL program.

Make appropriate changes to the comments, as Figure 16.27 shows.

```
000800 /*   Author:  Jim Buck                       Modified: 11-10-2010  */
000900 /***************************************************************/
001000            PGM          /* Program Linkage Section - NO Parms    */
001100 /***************************************************************/
001200 /***************************************************************/
001300 /*  Declarations Section                                       */
001400 /***************************************************************/
001500            DCL          VAR(&SYSDATE) TYPE(*CHAR) LEN(6)
001600            DCL          VAR(&SYSTIME) TYPE(*CHAR) LEN(6)
001700
001800 /***************************************************************/
001900 /*  Global Message Segment                                     */
002000 /***************************************************************/
002100            MONMSG       MSGID(CPF0000) EXEC(GOTO ERROR)
002200 /***************************************************************/
002300 /*  Main Procedure Segment                                     */
002400 /***************************************************************/
002500            RTVSYSVAL    SYSVAL(QDATE) RTNVAR(&SYSDATE)
002600            RTVSYSVAL    SYSVAL(QTIME) RTNVAR(&SYSTIME)
002700            SNDMSG       MSG('The program started on' *BCAT &SYSDATE *BCAT +
002800                           'at' *BCAT &SYSTIME) TOUSR(CIS001D)
002900            RCVMSG       WAIT(60)
003000            RETURN
003100
003200 /***************************************************************/
```

Figure 16.27: MARKTIME Source Code

For the SNDMSG command, remember that the whole message must be enclosed in parentheses, and the constant parts must be enclosed in apostrophes. Be sure to specify your own user ID for the TOUSR parameter value.

The RCVMSG command on line 2900 of the source code is usually used to retrieve the text and attributes of a message being sent to a specified message queue; it lets a CL program intercept and respond to messages. In that case, variables are included as parameter values to store message fields. When no message queue is specified, the current program's message queue becomes the default. When the WAIT parameter is used, the program will wait the specified number of seconds until a message becomes available. Because the previous SNDMSG command went to a user message queue, no message is expected in the program message queue; the program will wait the full 60 seconds and then go on. In effect, the RCVMSG command, as it is used here, halts processing for the specified amount of time.

16.22. After the program has been compiled successfully, clear the messages in your message queue. Do this either by using the DSPMSG command or by using the **CLRMSGQ** (Clear Message Queue) command. If you use the CLRMSGQ command, key it on the command line, prompt for parameters, and give it your message-queue name (user ID). Let the Library parameter default to *LIBL.

16.23. Run the program interactively using the CALL command.

16.23.a. Why does your terminal beep right away, but your keyboard remains locked, as Figure 16.28 shows?

Figure 16.28: Screen Inhibited

16.24. When the program has been executed, look at your message queue. The program should have sent a message to it. Using the Print key, print the message in your message queue.

16.25. Clear your message queue again.

16.26. From the command line, key in the WRKACTJOB (Work with Active Jobs) command, press F4, and then press F9.

Enter QBATCH for the Subsystem parameter (see Figure 16.29). Press Enter.

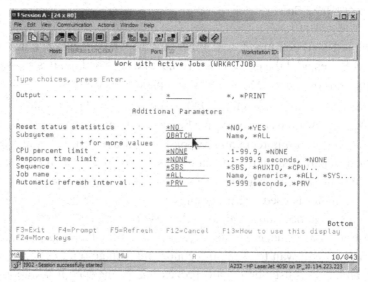

Figure 16.29: WRKACTJOB Command

16.26.a. How many jobs are running in QBATCH at this time?

16.27. Key the SBMJOB (Submit Job) command on the command line, and then prompt for parameters. For the command to run, type CALL MARKTIME. Do not put apostrophes around the command. Leave the other parameters at their default values, and execute the command by pressing Enter.

From the Work with Active Jobs screen, press Refresh and watch for your job to appear in the QBATCH subsystem.

16.27.a. Why does your terminal free up right away although the job is still running?

Continue refreshing the screen until your job disappears from the QBATCH subsystem.

16.28. Now examine your message queue again. You should see two messages associated with the submitted job.

16.28.a. Where did each message come from?

Congratulations! You have completed the last lab in this text! ☺

Lab 16 Source Listings

Note

Remember that we have used our student profile (CIS001D) and library (CIS001) in these code samples. You should replace these values with your own profile and library. If you have questions, consult your instructor.

STRUPPGM Source Code

```
/**********************************************************************/
/*Program Information Section                                      */
/*   Display options list using display file STRUPDSP, input choice  */
/*     and then process selection, setting up work environment.      */
/*     Signoff is allowed; F3 transfers to Initial Menu.             */
/*                                                                   */
/*     Parameters: none                                             */
/*     DSPF variables:  &CHOICE *CHAR 2  I/O  selection field       */
/*                      &IN40  *LGL    O    option ind for error   */
/*                      &IN03  *LGL    I    response ind for exit  */
/*                                                                   */
/*   Author: Jim Buck                    Modified: 10-10-2010       */
/**********************************************************************/
           PGM          /* Program Linkage Section - NO Parms       */
/**********************************************************************/
/* Declarations Section                                            */
/**********************************************************************/
           DCLF      FILE(STRUPDSP) RCDFMT(*ALL)
           DCL       &MyName *CHAR 15  'Jim Buck -'
           DCL       &EndPgm *LGL VALUE('0') /* Off */
/**********************************************************************/
/* Global Message Segment                                          */
/**********************************************************************/
           MONMSG    MSGID(CPF0000) EXEC(GOTO ERROR)
```

```
/***********************************************************************/
/*   Main Procedure Segment                                          */
/***********************************************************************/
          DOUNTIL    (&EndPgm = '1')
            CHGVAR     &CHOICE ' '
            SNDRCVF

          SELECT
          /* User Pressed the F3 Function Key  */
            WHEN      (&IN03) THEN(CHGVAR VAR(&EndPgm) VALUE('1'))
            WHEN      (&Choice = '1') THEN(DO) /* User Chose Selection 1  */
              CHGLIBL    (CIS001 ALLUSER QTEMP QGPL) INTROCLASS
              CHGJOB     OUTQ(CIS001/CIS001Q) PRTTXT(&MyName *BCAT 'Intro IBM i')
              SNDPGMMSG  MSG('Intro IBM i!') TOUSR(*REQUESTER)
              WRKOBJPDM  LIB(*CURLIB)
            ENDDO
            WHEN      (&Choice = '2') DO /* User Chose Selection 2  - DB2 */
              CHGLIBL    (CIS001 ALLUSER QTEMP QGPL) INTRODB2
              CHGJOB     OUTQ(CIS001/CIS001Q) PRTTXT(&MyName *BCAT 'Intro DB2')
              SNDPGMMSG  MSG('Intro DB2!') TOUSR(*REQUESTER)
              WRKOBJPDM  LIB(*CURLIB)
            ENDDO
            WHEN      (&Choice = '3') DO /* User Chose Selection 3 - RPG IV */
              CHGLIBL    (CIS001 ALLUSER QTEMP QGPL) RPGCLASS
              CHGJOB     OUTQ(CIS001/CIS001Q) PRTTXT(&MyName *BCAT 'RPG IV')
              SNDPGMMSG  MSG('RPG IV!') TOUSR(*REQUESTER)
              WRKOBJPDM  LIB(*CURLIB)
            ENDDO
            WHEN      (&Choice = '90') SIGNOFF /* User Chose Selection 90  */
            OTHERWISE  DO /* User Entered Something besides 1, 2 or 90  */
              CHGVAR     &IN40 '1' /* Turn on error option indicator */
              SNDRCVF
              CHGVAR     &IN40 '0' /* Don't forget to turn off the error indicator */
            ENDDO
          ENDSELECT


          ENDDO
/***********************************************************************/
/*  Error Procedure Section                                          */
/***********************************************************************/
  ERROR:    DMPCLPGM   /* Dump CL program */
            SNDPGMMSG  MSG('Error occurred in PGM') TOUSR(*SYSOPR)
            RETURN
/***********************************************************************/
/*  End Program Section                                              */
/***********************************************************************/
  END:
            ENDPGM
```

MARKTIME Source Code

```
/********************************************************************/
/*Program Information Section                                     */
/*   This program retrieves the system time and date. It then sends  */
/*   a message after waiting 60 seconds.                          */
/*                                                                */
/*   Program: MARKTIME                                            */
/*   Parameters: none                                             */
/*   Author: Jim Buck                    Modified: 11-10-2010     */
/********************************************************************/
          PGM           /* Program Linkage Section - NO Parms      */
/********************************************************************/
/********************************************************************/
/* Declarations Section                                           */
/********************************************************************/
          DCL      VAR(&SysDate) TYPE(*CHAR) LEN(6)
          DCL      VAR(&SysTime) TYPE(*CHAR) LEN(6)


/********************************************************************/
/* Global Message Segment                                         */
/********************************************************************/
          MONMSG    MSGID(CPF0000) EXEC(GOTO ERROR)
/********************************************************************/
/* Main Procedure Segment                                         */
/********************************************************************/
          RTVSYSVAL SYSVAL(QDATE) RTNVAR(&SysDate)
          RTVSYSVAL SYSVAL(QTIME) RTNVAR(&SysTime)
          SNDMSG    MSG('The program started on' *BCAT &SysDate *BCAT +
                      'at' *BCAT &SysTime) TOUSR(CIS001D)
          RCVMSG    WAIT(60)
          RETURN


/********************************************************************/
/* Error Procedure Section                                        */
/********************************************************************/
ERROR:    DMPCLPGM   /* Dump CL program */
          SNDPGMMSG MSG('Error occurred in MARKTIME PGM') +
                      TOUSR(*SYSOPR)


/********************************************************************/
/* End Program Section                                            */
/********************************************************************/
END:      ENDPGM
```

Index

Profile Commands (CMDPRF) menu, 58
program ID, in CL, 871
Program Information Section, in CL, 870–871
program structure, CL, 870–872, 873
program-described files, 167, 202
programming, 168. *See also* CL programming
Programming Development Manager (PDM), 6, 202, 172–183, 204–212, 308, 545, 564
  Compile option in, 221–224
  databases and, 165, 413
  logical files and, 351–353, 397–404
  SEU and, 215, 216–217
  Start PDM (STRPDM) and, 172, 173–174, 216
  Work with Libraries Using PDM (WRKLIBPDM) and, 174–178
  Work with Members Using PDM (WRKMBRPDM) in, 182–187, 216–217, 221, 236, 238–245, 351–352, 415, 466–470
  Work with Objects Using PDM (WRKOBJPDM), 172, 179–182, 224–229, 319–325, 423–424, 446
programming languages, 7
programs, licensed. *See* Licensed programs
programs run from RSE, 586–587
projection, in logical/join logical files, 347–351, 361–362
prompt entry/command prompt screens, 14–17, 38–41
prompt screens for CL commands, 869–870
Properties view, in Screen Designer/Report Designer, 607
PUBLIC authorization, 440

Q

Q, in commands, 46
QASTLVL system value to set level of Help, 146
QAUDJRN, 527
QBATCH, 3, 521, 522, 536–538
QCRTAUT, 443
QCTL, 3
QDAYOFWEEK system value, 567
QDDSSRC, 202
QHLPSYS, 62
QHTTPSVR, 521
QINTER, 3, 521
QRPGLE, 63
Qshells subsystem
  RSE and, 555

Start Qshell (STRQSH), 555
QSPL subsystem, printing and, 129–130
QSYS, 62
QSYS2, 62
QSYSLIB, 62
qualified names, 87–88
Query, 249–326
Query for i5/OS, 249–326. *See also* DB2 Web Query for i
  access path and, 367
  breaks, control breaks, defining report breaks in, 274–277
  column heading width adjustment in, 281, 312
  control breaks in, 250, 380–382
  converting data to DB2 Web Query for i formats, 855–861
  creating a query in, 307–318
  DDS and, 250
  date and time fields in, 269–270
  Define Query screen in, 309–311
  defining a query in, 254–270
  derived columns in, 284–287
  difference operation in, 299–300
  edit word creation in, 265–268
  editing options in, 262–268
  erasing old values in, 282
  executing query programs in, 250–251
  exiting, 289–290, 318
  F5 function key in, 250
  F11 function key in, 302
  F13 function key in, 250
  F14 function key in, 290
  F20 function key in, 258
  features of, 250
  field editing in, 263–264
  field selection and sequencing in, 277–279
  fields in, 250
  file selection in, Select File and, 255–257, 310
  finishing the report in, 287–289
  group indication in, 380–382
  Help for, 287
  join logical files, 358, 363–382, 390
  join query creation, 294–300
  joining files in, 291–293, 325–325. *See also* Joins
  joins in, specifying relationship in, 300–305
  layout of reports in, 250
  limitations of, vs. DB2 Web Query for i, 785
  numeric fields in, 261–262, 269–270, 313–315

  output type selection in, 317
  preview query layout in, 258–259, 267, 279
  previewing reports in, 250
  printer selection in, 323–325
  Query Utilities Menu (QUERY) in, 251–252
  recompiling programs/queries that use changed physical files, 434
  record selection in, 321–322
  records in, 250
  refining the query in, 270–290
  report breaks in, 250
  report column formatting in, 260–270, 280–283
  result fields in, 284–287
  Run Query (RUNQRY) in, 251, 320–321, 432–433
  sorting records in, 250, 271–273
  Specify Report Column Formatting screen in, 260–270, 280–283, 311–312, 314–316
  split screen in, 364–364
  SQL and, 250
  Start Query (STRQRY) and, 251–252
  summary functions in, 283–284
  thousands separator formatting in, 262
  Work with Objects Using PDM (WRKOBJPDM) in, 318, 319–325
  Work with Queries (WRKQRY) in, 252–253
Query Utilities Menu (QUERY), 251–252
Query/400, 784, 786
queue, job, 4
queues. *See also* Printers and printing
  Clear Output Queue (CLROUTQ) and, 56, 98–100, 104, 119, 146, 162, 163
  designating, 157
  output, 99
  output, user profile and, 8
  Work with Output Queue (WRKOUTQ) in, 104, 133–140, 150, 159–160, 237–241
QUSRLIBL, 63
QUSRSYS, 62
Q*xxx* libraries, 62

R

random access retrieval, 329
RANGE keyword in select/omit operations, 340–341, 390
Rational Developer for Power (RDP), 2, 6, 172, 545, 547, 604

modifying a print file in, 606–608
modifying print file properties in, 610, 633–637
opening a print file using, 605
Palette in, 607, 608, 609
Properties view in, 607
Records view in, 607–608
RSE view in, 606
Report controls in, 607
Report Designer area in, 606
RPG program compilation in, 648–649
RPG program modification in, 645–648
screen modification in, 637–643
Source Prompter view in, 607
table view in, 624
views in, 606–607
Workbench in, 606
screen header, 11
screen modified using Screen Designer/ Report Designer, 637–643
SDA, in commands, 46
secondary files, in joins, 294
security, 84. *See also* Authorities, authorization lists; User profiles
authorizations lists for, 447–450
databases and, file-level, 440–454
group profiles and, 450–454
security system values (*SEC), 6
SELECT, in CL, 883–884
Select field-list, in SQL, 660–661
Select statement, in SQL, 696, 699, 700
selection (restriction) and select/ omit operation, logical files and, 338–341, 345, 361–362
Selection line, 11
Send File (SNDF), 876, 888–889
Send Break Message (SNDBRKMSG) in, 891–896
Send Message (SNDMSG), 891–896
Send Program Message (SNDPGMMSG), 568, 891–896
Send TCP/IP Spooled File (SNDTCPSPLF), 746
Send/Receive File (SNDRCVF), 876, 890
SEQUEL, 652
sequence operations, in CL, 872
sequential record retrieval, 328–329
service entry points (SEPs), 576–578
SEU, in commands, 46
severity levels, messages, 517–518
sign-on, 8–10, 27–29
simple logical file. *See* Logical files, simple
simple object name, 86–87

single-level storage, 84
sorting
DB2 Web Query for i and, 803–804
IBM i Access for Web and, 765
Query for i5/OS and, 250, 271–273
SQL and, 698
Source Entry Utility (SEU), 6, 46, 202, 204–220, 236, 545, 564
cleared edit work screen in, 186
Copy command in, 217–220
databases and, 165, 172
Delete command in, 217
edit session in, 215
edit work screen in, 185–187, 209
exiting, 201–202
field insertion using, 200
file description compiled with, 220–224
format to use in, 186
Help for, 187–188, 187, 188, 190, 218
Insert command in, 217
line commands for, 188–190, 217–220
logical files and, 351, 394–397
member creation using, 183–187
Move command in, 218
PDM and, 215, 216–217
Start SEU (STRSEU) and, 183, 208, 214–215
target designator for Copy and Move commands in, 218–220
source language, 414
source physical file, 181, 213, 414–416
Create Source Physical File (CRTSRCPF) and, 213
creating, 205–207, 560–561, 592–596
RSE and, 560–561, 592–596
Source Prompter view, Screen Designer/Report Designer and, 607
Source view, debugging, 575
Specify File Selection Screen, 363–364
spool-control special authority, 136
spooled files, 101–105, 107–111, 127–163, 150, 152–163. *See also* Printers and printing
AFP Workbench for Windows Viewer in, 498–499
Change Printer Output screen for, 148
Change Printer Output screen in, 154–155
Change Spooled File Attributes (CHGSPLFA) in, 132, 141–146, 158
changing, 132–146

Clear Output Queue (CLROUTQ) in, 146, 162, 163
function keys in, 136–137
IBM i Navigator and, 497–508
messages about, 138
output queue designation for, 157
printer files and, 127–129
printer writer in, 129–131, 150
printing process and, 128–129
properties of/actions in, 500–501, 503–508
Send TCP/IP Spooled File (SNDTCPSPLF) in, 746
spool-control special authority in, 136
Work with All Printers screen in, 137, 162
Work With All Spooled Files screen in, 142, 157, 159
Work with Output Queue (WRKOUTQ) in, 133–140, 150, 159–160
Work with Printer Output screen for, 147, 152–155
Work with Printers screen in, 137, 161
Work with Spooled Files (WRKSPLF) in, 139–140, 150, 156–159
working with, 159–162
SQL, 7, 165, 170–171, 194, 414, 651–715, 785
alias fields in, 660
Alter Table statement in, 712–715
Assist/Prompt use in, 694–704
base tables in, 686
Classic Query Engine (CQE) and, 785
column functions in, 674
comments in, 663
concatenation in, 661
connection setting in, 658–659
CL commands in, 655
correlated subquery in, 685, 686
correlation names in, 665
Count expression in, 677–678
Create statement in, 684, 707–711
Data Definition Language (DDL) and, 651
Data Manipulation Language (DML) and, 651
dates, date functions in, 669
Decimal scalar function in, 675–676
Delete statement in, 692–693, 712–715
direct access storage device (DASD) and, 171